Bridging Microeconomics and Macroeconomics and the Effects on Economic Development and Growth

Pantelis C. Kostis
National and Kapodistrian University of Athens, Greece

IGI Global
PUBLISHER of TIMELY KNOWLEDGE

A volume in the Advances in Finance, Accounting, and Economics (AFAE) Book Series

Published in the United States of America by
IGI Global
Business Science Reference (an imprint of IGI Global)
701 E. Chocolate Avenue
Hershey PA, USA 17033
Tel: 717-533-8845
Fax: 717-533-8661
E-mail: cust@igi-global.com
Web site: http://www.igi-global.com

Library of Congress Cataloging-in-Publication Data

Names: Kostis, Pantelis C., editor.
Title: Bridging microeconomics and macroeconomics and the effects on economic development and growth / Pantelis C. Kostis, editor.
Description: Hershey, PA : Business Science Reference, [2021] | Includes bibliographical references and index. | Summary: "This book contains research on bridging the inconsistencies between microeconomics and macroeconomics and their effects on economic development and growth"-- Provided by publisher.
Identifiers: LCCN 2020012036 (print) | LCCN 2020012037 (ebook) | ISBN 9781799849339 (hardcover) | ISBN 9781799856641 (paperback) | ISBN 9781799849346 (ebook)
Subjects: LCSH: Economic development. | Microeconomics. | Macroeconomics.
Classification: LCC HD82 .B6964 2021 (print) | LCC HD82 (ebook) | DDC 338.9--dc23
LC record available at https://lccn.loc.gov/2020012036
LC ebook record available at https://lccn.loc.gov/2020012037

This book is published in the IGI Global book series Advances in Finance, Accounting, and Economics (AFAE) (ISSN: 2327-5677; eISSN: 2327-5685)

British Cataloguing in Publication Data
A Cataloguing in Publication record for this book is available from the British Library.

All work contributed to this book is new, previously-unpublished material. The views expressed in this book are those of the authors, but not necessarily of the publisher.

For electronic access to this publication, please contact: eresources@igi-global.com.

Advances in Finance, Accounting, and Economics (AFAE) Book Series

Ahmed Driouchi
Al Akhawayn University, Morocco

ISSN:2327-5677
EISSN:2327-5685

Mission

In our changing economic and business environment, it is important to consider the financial changes occurring internationally as well as within individual organizations and business environments. Understanding these changes as well as the factors that influence them is crucial in preparing for our financial future and ensuring economic sustainability and growth.

The **Advances in Finance, Accounting, and Economics (AFAE)** book series aims to publish comprehensive and informative titles in all areas of economics and economic theory, finance, and accounting to assist in advancing the available knowledge and providing for further research development in these dynamic fields.

Coverage

- Public Finance
- Development Economics
- Corporate Finance
- Finance
- Health Economics
- Economics of Innovation and Knowledge
- Stock Market
- Economics of Intellectual Property Rights
- Wages and Employment
- E-Accounting

IGI Global is currently accepting manuscripts for publication within this series. To submit a proposal for a volume in this series, please contact our Acquisition Editors at Acquisitions@igi-global.com or visit: http://www.igi-global.com/publish/.

The Advances in Finance, Accounting, and Economics (AFAE) Book Series (ISSN 2327-5677) is published by IGI Global, 701 E. Chocolate Avenue, Hershey, PA 17033-1240, USA, www.igi-global.com. This series is composed of titles available for purchase individually; each title is edited to be contextually exclusive from any other title within the series. For pricing and ordering information please visit http://www.igi-global.com/book-series/advances-finance-accounting-economics/73685. Postmaster: Send all address changes to above address.

Titles in this Series

For a list of additional titles in this series, please visit:
http://www.igi-global.com/book-series/advances-finance-accounting-economics/73685

Theory of Shocks and Self-Development Laws of Economic Systems Emerging Research and Opportunities
Olga Ivanovna Pilipenko (The Russian Presidential Academy of National Economy and Public Administration, Russia) Zoya Andreevna Pilipenko (Bank of Russia, Russia) and Andrey Igorevich Pilipenko (The Russian Presidential Academy of National Economy and Public Administration, Russia)
Business Science Reference • © 2021 • 250pp • H/C (ISBN: 9781799843092) • US $165.00

Handbook of Research on Emerging Theories, Models, and Applications of Financial Econometrics
Burcu Adıgüzel Mercangöz (Istanbul University, Turkey)
Business Science Reference • © 2020 • 300pp • H/C (ISBN: 9781799831969) • US $275.00

Circular Economy and Re-Commerce in the Fashion Industry
Archana Shrivastava (Jaypee Business School, JIIT, Noida, India) Geetika Jain (FMS, Amity University, Noida, India) and Justin Paul (University of Puerto Rico, Puerto Rico)
Business Science Reference • © 2020 • 204pp • H/C (ISBN: 9781799827283) • US $195.00

Mapping, Managing, and Crafting Sustainable Business Strategies for the Circular Economy
Susana Serrano Rodrigues (Polytechnic Institute of Leiria, Portugal) Paulo Jorge Almeida (Polytechnic Institute of Leiria, Portugal) and Nuno Miguel Castaheira Almeida (Polytechnic Institute of Leiria, Portugal)
Business Science Reference • © 2020 • 401pp • H/C (ISBN: 9781522598855) • US $195.00

Applied Econometric Analysis Emerging Research and Opportunities
Brian W. Sloboda (University of Phoenix, USA) and Yaya Sissoko (Indiana University of Pennsylvania, USA)
Business Science Reference • © 2020 • 264pp • H/C (ISBN: 9781799810933) • US $195.00

Handbook of Research on Accounting and Financial Studies
Luís Farinha (University of Beira Interior, Portugal) Ana Baltazar Cruz (School of Management, Polytechnic Institute of Castelo Branco, Portugal) and João Renato Sebastião (Polytechnic Institute of Castelo Branco, Portugal)
Business Science Reference • © 2020 • 487pp • H/C (ISBN: 9781799821366) • US $295.00

Emerging Tools and Strategies for Financial Management
Begoña Álvarez-García (Universidade da Coruña, Spain) and José-Pablo Abeal-Vázquez (Universidade da Coruña, Spain)
Business Science Reference • © 2020 • 357pp • H/C (ISBN: 9781799824404) • US $225.00

IGI Global
PUBLISHER of TIMELY KNOWLEDGE

701 East Chocolate Avenue, Hershey, PA 17033, USA
Tel: 717-533-8845 x100 • Fax: 717-533-8661
E-Mail: cust@igi-global.com • www.igi-global.com

Editorial Advisory Board

Table of Contents

Detailed Table of Contents

The necessity of searching for deeper roots plays a significant role in the evolution of the economic development and growth. This issue arises from the complex globalized world, the understanding of which requires an in-depth analysis. This issue is born again in the aftermath of the Great Depression of 2008, which highlighted the inability of economics to address it. The need to turn to the deeper roots is reinforced by the individual empowerment and the increasing need to understand economic and social phenomena. Thus, the relationship between economic theory and reality is under new foundations. The cultural and institutional background stand out as the deep roots affecting the way economies operate and raise questions of effectiveness in implementing economic policy when applied in the same way across all economies. For these two factors to be taken into account in economics, a more general and integrated view of economic development and growth is required. It is an attempt at an evolutionary perspective of economic science that illuminates the meso- and meta-economics approach.

In recent years, the concept of "institutions" has become central in scientific and political discourse. This reflects an increasing awareness of the role of institutions in the functioning of economies and in economic development more generally. Many of the catchphrases articulated within new institutional economics such as "institutions," "organisations," "transaction costs," "property rights," and "contracts" have become very common in orthodox economics discourse. This development is intellectually stimulating and interesting because it raises some fundamental issues with regard to the role and functioning of institutions. These concepts are seated on Smith's idea of the "harmony of interests." However, Smith sees power as dominant in the formation of institutional framework. This chapter aims to provide a Smithian critique based on the notion of power, arguing that the formation of institutions and institutional framework cannot be considered apart from the intrinsic power relations which are vested in society.

This chapter discusses the problems associated to an inadequate theory of economic policy. It begins by presenting the mainstream and heterodox approaches to policy. It contends that, according to the mainstream, policy must guarantee efficiency or, at the very least, consider it a key constraint, whereas according to heterodox economists, it may have a broader variety of goals. The latter's open system perspective implies that changes in the structure of the economy eventually feedback both on how people conceive of the economy and social welfare and on how the economy itself functions. The relevance of this issue, which is understated, emerges from the subsequent discussion of how neoliberal policies have changed the structure of the economy, the way people conceive of the economy, and even their voting behavior.

The authors add the monetary insights of Hyman Minsky to the 'real' Kalecki-Levy equation. The latter is embedded in the economics of Keynes and the former is expanded in the spirit of Minsky. They present their structural connections in a four-quadrant diagram as well as within a stock-flow-consistent model. The motivation arises from history and the revitalisation of the real bills doctrine. Accordingly, they make the case for the productive monetary emissions of a central bank acting in concert with the community of commercial banks. They define money as the emission of credit in the 'first moment' of the circuit. It is simultaneously the wage bill. Workers will consume basics and are free to prefer liquidity in the form of bank deposits. The latter they label cash or currency and a firewall separates it from money. The objective is the increase in output and employment called upon by the milieu in all countries of the world in which the 'dark forces' of uncertainty and pessimism have taken over. The policy stance is embellished by the introduction of central bank digital money.

Panel data analysis aims to overcome the weaknesses of its alternatives: country-by-country analysis is usually based on short samples, there is a significant country-specific distortion in the data, and it leads to biased estimates, and the cross-section analysis neglects the time dimension. In last two decades, tests for non-stationary panels sparked a large body of literature both on tests theory and on various empirical studies in multiple areas of micro- and macroeconomic research. The most popular studies include topics such as growth, finance, exchange rates, fiscal matters, and international trade, but also popular are studies in tourism, energy, resource demand and supply, IT and technology spreading, politics, inflation, international trade and current accounts, stock markets, etc.

Economic reforms include comprehensive and radical changes in the functioning of the economic system and its main rules. There is no clear and generally accepted classification of economic reforms in the literature. In this study, economic reforms are analyzed by classifying them as first-generation reforms and second-generation reforms. First-generation reforms are made in macroeconomics for the purposes of eliminating macroeconomic imbalances, ensuring stability, controlling inflation, ensuring fiscal and monetary discipline, reducing public debt. Second-generation reforms are microeconomic reforms, which include strengthening the infrastructure of the market economy, increasing efficiency, enhancing the competitive power, and strengthening the institutional infrastructure that creates competitive markets. The aim of this study is to examine the theoretical framework of first-generation and second-generation reforms in line with macroeconomic and microeconomic expectations and to explain and discuss the main areas of second-generation reforms.

The aim of the chapter is to introduce money as the necessary link between micro and macro levels. The author starts with a critical appraisal of the neoclassical monetary theory paradigm. The opening argument is that it is not possible to separate the relative prices and price level formation. The interdependence between the price of money and the prices of all the other goods leads to the conclusion of the gross complementarity of money what violates the gross substitutability principle. Further, it is argued that the function of money as medium of exchange in a decentralized monetary economy is only possible under cyclic sequencing of bilateral exchanges. The latter means that new macroeconomic constraint is added to the conventional micro equilibrium requirements. The macro constraint makes possible to derive the individual utility functions from macro variables such as the income velocity of money and the price level. The macro constraint allows also for optimal solutions under the second-best conditions.

This chapter reviews traditional and contemporary concepts of income taxation and their effects on economic development and growth. The author focuses on discussion issues related to the contemporary concepts of income taxation. The author also considers modern functions of personal income taxes relating to environmental protection and income inequality mitigation. Additionally, the author studies the potential of personal income taxation to apply as an instrument for maintaining sustainable economic development and social stability. This chapter analyzes the effects of progressive and proportional personal income taxation on economic development and growth. It presents a technological model of inspections and audits with the aim of improving the tax and social security control of individuals.

run (providing liquidity to different sectors) and considers the possibilities for a long-term recovery. A comparative perspective is particularly suitable for the Balkan countries with great institutional diversity of the monetary regimes. In particular, the two members of the EU, Bulgaria and Romania, have been following different principles of monetary regimes for decades (Currency Board versus discretionary Monetary Policy). Both Bulgaria and Romania follow closely the ECB monetary policy. Serbia, which is outside the EU, is not affected by the constraints of European integration and actually has its independent monetary policy (although the Euro is also an important external anchor).

Foreword

This volume assembles a range of papers that tackle diverse topics related to the economy and society within the classificatory scheme of "micro" and "macro". All sciences deal at their very heart with the nature of the "one" (micro) and the way "many" of them relate to each other (macro). Economics is no exception and most broadly construed economics may be seen as the study of the agent (micro) and of many agents as they interact in a commodity space (macro). This archetypical view may serve as a scaffold for all strands of theorizing, and it is – as this volume documents – an invitation for pluralism.

There are various ways of constructing economic theory based on the micro-macro scaffold. A useful construction device is given by the notion that all economic operations are based on knowledge. Simple as it may be, it allows us to distinguish between two levels of economic analysis: the level of knowledge for economic operations and the level of economic operations based on knowledge. The two levels are but two sides of a single theoretical coin, and to know the coin we must investigate both sides. Knowledge resides in the behavioral disposition of all agents conducting operations and it is embodied in all commodities or factorials that are distinct by their qualitative attribution. Ongoing economic operations such as production, consumption, and transaction are conducted on an extant knowledge base.

Today, there is much demand for pluralism calling for an ending of the dominance of mainstream economics, and requesting that heterodox strands be more prominently on the agenda of economics. While the critique is unison, the recognition of what the mainstream doctrine actually stands for depends crucially on what the own heterodox posture is. In the framework chosen, the criterion for distinguishing between major genres of theories refers to the way a theory deals with the two levels mentioned. The principal watershed is between economic theories that deal with knowledge and economic theories that do not. Clearly, neoclassical economics does not deal with knowledge. It deals with the operant level only, treating the knowledge of agents as behavioral law and knowledge embodied in technology, institutions, heuristics, and related variables as ceteris paribus clause. Yet, it appears that also theories that we associate unhesitatingly with heterodox economics often conduct their analysis under the assumption of given knowledge as well. In this case, the difference between orthodox and heterodox economics shows up at the operant level only.

Much of contemporary theorizing in economics occurs at the operant level: the behavioral disposition of agents is kept constant and the commodity space is being composed of "quantils" (commodity = quantity times price). This enables the construction of macro based on micro by employing procedures of aggregation. While there are arguably major differences between neoclassical and Keynesian or Post-Keynesian economics, the major concern here is generally not with the structure and evolutionary dynamic of an economy stated in terms of heterogeneous agents and of heterogeneous commodities. Yet, quantification captures a constituent aspect of economic reality. The abstraction from knowledge and quality allows for formulating economic theories based on algebra and computation and for adopting quantitative methods of measurement and statistical inference. Several papers discuss topics of micro and macro along these lines. They address issues such as aggregation procedures from micro to macro and back, the role of money as a link between micro and macro, the Minsky-Levy-Kalecki heterodoxy, and policy topics related to employment, labor productivity growth, taxation, trade, as well as economic growth.

Exploring the structure and evolutionary dynamic of an economy, the procedure of micro-macro aggregation has limited explanatory power. Instead, explanatory principles are required that allow us to explore how micro behavior emerges into a complex macro structure that evolves in time. The theoretical architecture must be enriched by an intermediate level– call it meso - that enables us to strive for the envisaged results. The architecture of the knowledge level is one of micro-meso-macro. Meso in this architecture represents a structural component and a process component. A knowledge "bit" such as a technology, institution, or behavioral heuristic is a component of a "deep" structure of the economy, and economic evolution occurs if at least one of the structural components changes restructuring the system. Various papers of the volume advance their arguments against this background, and the papers by Kafka, Ramazzotti, and Kiryakova-Dineva et al. allow explicitly for a micro-meso-macro framework demonstrating its usefulness when exploring various dimensions of the economy and society.

Kurt Dopfer
University of St. Gallen, Switzerland

Preface

At the eve of the recent global financial crisis, but also under the pressure caused by the Covid-19 pandemic, it is particularly interesting to find out which are the theoretical constructs or economic models that can be used to analyze today's reality. Both were proven unable to provide interpretations of what really lead to the crisis and what has to be done from now on. Indeed, the outburst of the recent crisis was just one more evidence of their failure. During the last decades, the mainstream microeconomic and macroeconomic analysis was proven to be insufficient for exploring the dynamic and complex interactions among humans, institutions, and nature in our real economy. On the one side microeconomics is filled with black-box models that fail to study the actual contractual relations between firms and markets, while on the other side macroeconomics -over the last decades- were proven useless because they mistook the beauty of theoretical models for truth. Thus, questions have arisen about using new theoretical and empirical structures that would better describe our economic systems.

This book aims to analyze the hypotheses that govern the relationships of aggregate structures (macroeconomic analysis) that may are compatible with the assumptions that govern the behavior of the individuals, households, and firms (micro analysis), and vice versa, in trying to achieve sustainable economic development and growth. Moreover, modern evolutionary growth thinking is used in trying to bridge the inconsistencies between microeconomics and macroeconomics and confront their failures in order to better describe the economic reality.

The book is aimed toward students, academics, and policymakers who are interested in modern evolutionary growth thinking and on how microeconomics and macroeconomics are connected in trying to achieve sustainable economic development and growth. It is also aimed at libraries and researchers in the topics of modern evolutionary economics. The book can be used as supplementary material in post-graduate courses on microfoundations of macroeconomics, economic growth and development and evolutionary economics. The secondary market for this book is general readership. The analysis is expected to include all knowledge required even for non-familiar with the issues raised.

The book consists of 14 chapters, which are presented below. Each contributes separately and significantly in the topic under investigation.

In Chapter 1, Kafka (in this Edited Volume) presents a great analysis on how to better connect economic theory and economic reality. As she suggests, the complex globalized world, the understanding of which requires an in-depth analysis, as well as the aftermath of the Great Depression of 2008, which highlighted the inability of economics to address it, but also other factors such as the individual empowerment and the increasing need to understand economic and social phenomena, lead to the need of searching for the deeper roots of economic development and growth. Under those circumstances, the relationship between economic theory and reality is under new foundations, and economic policy effectiveness is under dispute. Kafka points out that the solution to this problem is to look into the deeper causes of economic development and growth, and sees cultural and institutional background as the deep roots affecting the way economies operate and raise questions of effectiveness in implementing economic policy when applied in the same way across all economies (one-size-fits-all policies). For these two factors to be taken into account in economics, a more general and integrated view of economic development and growth and methodological pluralism is required. The theoretical architecture to do so is an evolutionary perspective of economic science underlined by the development of mesoeconomics and metaeconomics that provide a connection between the micro and the macro analysis, highlighting the role of culture and institutions.

In Chapter 2, Manioudis and Meramveliotakis (in this Edited Volume) provide a Smithian critique based on the notion of power, arguing that the formation of institutions and institutional framework cannot be considered apart from the intrinsic power relations which are vested in the society. They attempt to offer a definitional context of the notions, concepts and ideas found in New Institutional Economics. Then, Manioudis and Meramveliotakis pinpoint the neoclassical micro foundations whereas new institutionalists are mostly rested on. Based on these neoclassical micro foundations, New Institutional Economics try to erect the macro theory of economic growth and development. The common parlance within New Institutional Economics is that both the growth and the development are determined by the existed institutional framework. Thus, institutional emergence is a pivotal issue for the economic growth and subsequently an analysis of institutional emergence should be included in theory of development and growth. They conclude that the inability of neoclassical economics to predict and prevent the financial crisis of 2008 explicitly questions the validity of mainstream economic theory in analysing and prescribing for our economy. The financial meltdown and the depression that followed reveal the constitutional role of institutions, as the rules of the game. New institutional economics highlight the importance of institutional framework in promoting economic growth and development.

In Chapter 3, Ramazzotti (in this Edited Volume) concentrates on the role of institutions as well. He distinguishes the mainstream's reliance on prices, and on the institutions that complement them, from the heterodox emphasis on institutions as a prerequisite for any economy, suggesting that different views of economic policy depend less on technicalities than on the overall outlook of the economy. Closed systems approaches focus on market performance, either as a goal or as a constraint. Open systems ones stress the interdependence between the economy and society, thereby acknowledging that policy may involve a broader variety both of goals, ranging from growth to freedom and happiness, and of constraints, whether allocative, social or cultural. The open system perspective implies that changes in the structure of the economy eventually feedback both on how people conceive of the economy and social welfare and on how the economy itself functions. This explains why, although most people suffered the detrimental consequences of neoliberal policies, they still support them. Ramazzotti concludes that alternative policy perspectives are possible that focus on the quality of life and institutional change rather than on prices-measured aggregates alone.

In Chapter 4, Correa (in this Edited Volume) attempts to integrate the monetary insights of Minsky with the 'real' Levy-Kalecki equation. The former connects more intimately with Keynes of the Treatise, the latter with Keynes of the General Theory. Correa presents the Keynes-Minsky-Levy-Kalecki in a four-quadrant diagram as well as within a stock-flow-consistent model. Quadrants 1 and 4 determine the points of effective demand as well as involuntary unemployment. Quadrant 3 gives equilibrium in the market for capital goods along with the MEC curve in quadrant 4. The novel feature in the case of the last two quadrants is that the private sector is paralyzed by 'the dark forces of ignorance and uncertainty' and so is unable to work out the calculations of profitability. It is the government in the form of the public sector that constructs the demand and the supply curves. Government in the form of Keynes' public works can be traced through quadrants 1 and 4.

In Chapter 5, Marinov (in this Edited Volume) presents a useful analysis regarding the use of panel non-stationarity methods in micro and macro-economic analyses. Panel non-stationarity tests emerged since the early 1990s, and in the recent years they became some of the primary instruments to study various micro- and macroeconomic issues. The main reason for their popularity is that these instruments help to overcome the problems resulting from the possible integrated nature of many economic variables. Panel methods are most valuable in cases where data is scarce, resulting in short series, i.e. in macroeconomic studies. Marinov presents a small part of the vast literature. Further areas of intensive research with panel data are tourism, resource demand and supply, IT and technology spreading, politics, inflation, international trade and current accounts, stock markets etc.

In Chapter 6, Kar (in this Edited Volume) analyzes economic reforms by classifying them as first-generation reforms and second-generation reforms. First-generation reforms are made in macroeconomics for the purposes of eliminating macroeconomic imbalances, ensuring stability, controlling inflation, ensuring fiscal and monetary discipline, reducing public debt. Second generation reforms are microeconomic reforms, which include strengthening the infrastructure of the market economy, increasing efficiency, enhancing the competitive power, and strengthening the institutional infrastructure that creates competitive markets. Kar tries to examine the theoretical framework of first-generation and second-generation reforms in line with macroeconomic and microeconomic expectations and to explain and discuss the main areas of second-generation reforms. He concludes that there is considerable assessment of the inadequacy of first-generation reforms and the need for second-generation reforms. Economic reforms are a long process with stages and both generations of reforms are indispensable and irreplaceable parts of this long process. It is impossible for first-generation reforms carried out without second-generation reforms to yield long-term and permanent results alone, and it is pointless to attempt second-generation reforms without first-generation reforms.

In Chapter 7, Ganchev (in this Edited Volume) introduces money as the necessary link between micro and macro level. Ganchev starts with a critical appraisal of the neoclassical monetary theory paradigm. The opening argument is that it is not possible to separate the relative prices and price level formation. The interdependence between the price of money and the prices of all the other goods leads to the conclusion of the gross complementarity of money what violates the gross substitutability principle. Further, it is argued that the function of money as medium of exchange in a decentralized monetary economy is only possible under cyclic sequencing of bilateral exchanges. New macroeconomic constraint is added to the conventional equilibrium requirements. This makes possible the derivation of the individual utility functions from macro variables such as the income velocity of money and the price level. Money allows also for optimal solutions under second best conditions. Ganchev also obtains a concept of decentralized economic system, subject to uncertainty and instability. In such a system the macroeconomic parameters affect the micro behavior and add uncertainty, on the one hand, but on the other, macro-economic regulation is both desirable and feasible.

In Chapter 8, Nikolova (in this Edited Volume) reviews traditional and contemporary concepts of income taxation and its effects on economic development and growth. Nikolova focuses on discussion issues related to the contemporary concepts of income taxation. Moreover, she considers modern functions of personal income taxes relating to environmental protection and income inequality mitigation. Additionally, Nikolova studies the potential of personal income taxation to apply as an instrument for maintaining sustainable economic development and social stability. This chapter analyzes the effects of progressive and proportional personal income taxation on economic development and growth. It presents a technological model of inspections and audits with the aim of improving the tax and social security control of individuals.

In Chapter 9, Visic (in this Edited Volume) provides a broader perspective on economic repercussions of robotization covering both microeconomic and macroeconomic aspects as well as other closely related sociological aspects. This broad perspective is needed for researchers, policy makers as well as managers while contemplating changes as stirring as robotization. Further, the chapter deals with the issue of education of future economists in the context of robotization. However, it is not about educating them about robots; it is about preparing them to be able to anticipate technological, economic and sociological changes so they can make rational decisions for themselves and for society as well. In that sense it emphasizes the need to make future economists more flexible, observant and consequently more efficient, regardless of their position on labor market. They should be able to perceive microeconomic and macroeconomic implications of their professional decisions, hopefully having both economic and noneconomic benefits in focus. In that sense this chapter serves as an alarm since existent (economic) lag between countries may become even bigger if it is not addresses in a timely manner.

In Chapter 10, Mlinaric, Josic and Thompson (in this Edited Volume) analyse the impact of economic diplomacy on bilateral trade flows in Croatia in the period from 1992 to 2017. The diplomatic representation can be observed as a micro factor and trade as a macro factor. The issue of diplomacy representatives as a micro factor that connects micro and macro analysis is not well analyzed in the relevant literature which is the most important contribution of this chapter. The hypothesis empirically tested states that diplomatic representation has had a positive and significant effect on bilateral trade flows (imports and exports) of Croatia. The results of the analysis have shown that the diplomatic representation via embassies and consulates is a relevant trade and trade-enhancing factor.

In Chapter 11, Kiryakova-Dineva, Kyurova and Chankova (in this Edited Volume) argue that the economic processes in the field of organizing events should not be conceived merely as resulting from macro- and micro-level relationships but rather as resulting from relationships on mesoeconomic level (where a large number of unresolved and unexplored issues still exist), discussed by the authors in terms of the black box relationships on the mesoeconomic level. The main aim of this study is to investigate a specific mega event so as to trace out and analyze the roles of the operators at the three levels of social-economic activity, and finally to identify the specific roles of the operators functioning at the mesoeconomic level. Making up a small part of scientific investigation in interdisciplinary research, the chapter proposes further perspectives for a proper application of mesoeconomics when discussing issues bridging micro-economics and macro-economics.

In Chapter 12, Sanchez (in this Edited Volume) uses a nonparametric, international production-frontier approach with a focus on euro area growth accounting. Sanchez uncovers that, for the period since 1980, euro area efficiency scores lie much below the world production frontier (gap mostly in the range of 10% to 20%), suggesting the need for structural reform efforts to enhance resource use. Moreover, the use of human capital series points to a significant effect on euro area labour productivity, while entailing a considerable reduction in the estimates of technological progress. This finding could be explained by the inappropriateness of technology, also in light of the evidence also reported here about non-neutral technological progress. Moreover, the analysis does noy detect considerable changes in cross-country distributions of labour productivity both before and after 1995.

In Chapter 13, Arachovas and Manioudis (in this Edited Volume) analyse the impact of the three (3) Memoranda of Understanding signed between the Greek governments and the troika, i.e. European Commission, ECB and IMF representations. Arachovas and Manioudis present a series of key macroeconomic and microeconomic figures and will argue that despite the fiscal consolidation, which came at an extremely high social and economic cost, Greek economy still has a lot challenges to tackle and serious impediments to overcome. The authors also shed some new light on whether Memoranda actually helped Greece to recover or used a whole country as a «guinea-pig» and as an example of compliance, allowing the final reader to decide.

In Chapter 14, Sahling, Nenovsly and Chobanov (in this Edited Volume) analyse to what extent the type of monetary regime in three Balkans countries (Bulgaria, Romania and Serbia) determines the scope and nature of reactions to the pandemic crisis in the short run (providing liquidity to different sectors) and consider the possibilities for a long-term recovery. They state that a comparative perspective is particularly suitable for the Balkan countries with great institutional diversity of the monetary regimes. In particular, the two members of the EU, Bulgaria and Romania, have been following different principles of monetary regimes for decades (Currency Board versus discretionary Monetary Policy). Both Bulgaria and Romania follow closely the ECB monetary policy. Serbia, which is outside the EU, is not affected by the constraints of European integration and actually has its independent monetary policy (although the Euro is also an important external anchor).

From the analysis provided in the present book, it seems that in order to bridge microeconomics and macroeconomics governments and policymakers have to focus on those factors that lie between the two subfields of the economic science. The connection of the two subfields lies towards a series of factors, analyzed in the several chapters, such as the cultural background, the institutional setting, the money, the monetary regimes, the diplomatic representation, the structural reforms, the taxation, or even in robotization. These are fields that lie within what is called mesoeconomics, which is defined as the rules of the economies that govern the relationship between the micro and the macro analysis. Mesoeconomics studies the institutional aspects of the economy that are not captured by microeconomics or macroeconomics. Governments and policymakers have to focus in such factors in order to better depict reality and through suitable economic policies to move their economies on a sustainable economic development and growth path.

Pantelis C. Kostis
National and Kapodistrian University of Athens, Greece

Acknowledgment

I would like to thank all the authors that contributed with their chapters in the development of this book. Their scientific contribution is very significant as they enhanced the importance of bridging microeconomics and macroeconomics and the effects on economic development and growth.

Moreover, I would like to thank Professor Kurt Dopfer, a distinguished academic for his work on evolutionary economics and mesoeconomics, for writing the forward of this book as well as for his valuable comments and his kind words. I am really honored for that.

Finally, I would like to thank from the bottom of my heart my Professor and my mentor Panagiotis E. Petrakis for our long-term cooperation, who patiently showed me the light and the beauty of scientific research. His contribution to my thinking and my course up to now are decisive for the development of this book and this is why I dedicate this work entirely to him; "*I am indebted to my father for living, but to my teacher for living well*" (Great Alexander for his teacher Aristotle)!

Chapter 1
Economic Theory and Economic Reality:
A Continuously Dialectic Relationship

Kyriaki I. Kafka
Department of Economics, National and Kapodistrian University of Athens, Greece

ABSTRACT

The necessity of searching for deeper roots plays a significant role in the evolution of the economic development and growth. This issue arises from the complex globalized world, the understanding of which requires an in-depth analysis. This issue is born again in the aftermath of the Great Depression of 2008, which highlighted the inability of economics to address it. The need to turn to the deeper roots is reinforced by the individual empowerment and the increasing need to understand economic and social phenomena. Thus, the relationship between economic theory and reality is under new foundations. The cultural and institutional background stand out as the deep roots affecting the way economies operate and raise questions of effectiveness in implementing economic policy when applied in the same way across all economies. For these two factors to be taken into account in economics, a more general and integrated view of economic development and growth is required. It is an attempt at an evolutionary perspective of economic science that illuminates the meso- and meta-economics approach.

INTRODUCTION

An integrated concept of economic development and growth is directly related to the comprehensive concept of human action. One of the challenges of economic science is approaching the multidimensional reality, as expressed by the action of Homo Holisticus. This definition, which is consistent with an evolutionary view of economics, more clearly approaches the real nature of the individual as it includes his biological, social (political) and economic origins. In other words, it is a combination of Homo Sapiens (a creature whose characteristics are based on genetic change and the principles of Darwinian evolution), Homo Economicus (an intelligent but one-dimensional being based on individual liberation and pursuing personal well-being) and Homo Socialis (which incorporates the cultural and institutional

DOI: 10.4018/978-1-7998-4933-9.ch001

dimension of the individual as part of the society to which he belongs, expressing elements of altruism and cooperation). This is the "heart" of the reflection and the general perspective of the present chapter.

The structure of the chapter is the following. Section 2 presents the connection of economic theory and economic reality under the new conditions that prevail in our complex economic systems. Section 3 presents institutions and culture as the deep roots of economic development and growth, and Section 4 the role of special conditions of economies and societies for economic policy making. Lastly, Section 5 presents the new theoretical architecture that is needed in order to better connect economic theory and reality.

THE CONNECTION OF ECONOMIC THEORY WITH REALITY UNDER NEW CONDITIONS

The theoretical thinking of the individual is correct to be developed beyond methodological, theoretical dogmatisms based on the real issues he is called upon to solve on the basis of the human intellect. Thus, developments in the real economic world activate correspondingly theoretical searches. Under conditions of complexity, however, the relationship between theory and reality is laid on new foundations.

The main fathers of classical political economy (Smith, Ricardo, Malthus, Mill, Marx) initially embraced the concept of political economy. It is a comprehensive conception of economics as a social science involving references to human nature but also to the general evolution of social phenomena. However, these works of the main fathers of science were criticized as more philosophical theorems (Papadogiannis 2012).

The later era was marked by the remarkable successes in the positive sciences. Thus, the belief was created that everything could be captured and predicted with equations, even the behavior of the individual. In this light, the core of economic theory was thought to be expressed in simple mathematical terms. The perspective of economics, which was moving away from the original character of the political economy, had now changed. The Marginal Revolution of the 1870s referred to the end of the prevailing classical political view of value theory (Hodgson 2001).

In the late 19th century, Marshal, Warlas, Edgeworth, Jevons, and Pareto attempted to rebuild economics to the standards of classical physics, emphasizing the laws of the market. However, this neglected complexity of the economic systems and led to a great simplification of economic theory, as it has ignored parameters such as uncertainty, expectations, society, politics, etc. As a result, the Neoclassicals perceived the economy as a simplified system in which individuals have predetermined relationships and homogenized behavior. Under this way of thinking, the economic phenomena have moved away from social phenomena. Menger's debate with Schmoller (Methodenstreit) was critical for the dominance of methodological individualism and homo economicus (Hodgson 2001).

The neoclassical model, however, cannot be universally accepted as it does not correspond to reality - at least in most cases - which is characterized by the complexity of economic systems. This is the point of concern regarding the fundamental differentiation of the general equilibrium model and the approach of the economy as a complex system.

The issues analyzed above highlight the deeper problems associated with the foundations of economic theory but also with the view that economies are complex systems that cannot be adequately described through a simple theoretical conception.

The characterization of the complexity of economies is based on the fact that economies are characterized by components that are constantly interacting. Complex systems describe how the interactions of the various components of the system shape the relationship of individuals and societies to their economic and social environment and how they shape individual and collective behaviors (Simon 1969).

The world in which we live is characterized as non-ergodic. Individuals live and make decisions under conditions of uncertainty, with limits to knowledge and prediction, always based on representations and images of the past (Petrakis 2018). These conditions hinder the ability to develop perfect strategies. For this reason, the main driving force that determines the evolution of purchasing systems and their change is collective knowledge, which in this sense, is the main evolutionary force. Therefore, the characterization of "disordered cognitive development" could be attributed to complexity, where individuals are constantly changing their behaviors and beliefs (Petrakis and Kafka 2018). The complexity of economic phenomena requires humans to be the focus of the analysis and to have an interconnection with other sciences such as biology, psychology, etc. (Hayek 1945).

To interpret reality more efficiently, the evolutionary view (Nelson and Winter 1974, 1982) takes into account the notion of cultural background as to how various behaviors, preferences, practices, and routines between individuals and businesses are transmitted over time following -among other factors- technological developments. The pioneer of the evolutionary economic view Veblen (1899) centered the individual at the heart of economic thought, arguing that the cultural background makes individuals complex entities characterized by behaviors and habits based on their instincts.

In his analysis, Veblen draws on Smith's (1776) view of the "invisible hand" and the view that the economy moves toward equilibrium while noting the "difference in spiritual attitude or point of view" while paralleling the concept of economic taxonomy with the idea of classification related to animal or plant species. He essentially rejects the equilibrium as defined by classical economists, saying that this equilibrium can be a description of reality but does not contain any evidence as to what process of change led to it. In addition, Veblen's view of Darwin explains future social and economic developments as the result of collective change observed in societies, economies, and institutions, and not as a result of individual changes.

Complex systems are characterized by adaptability (Allen 1990, Beinhocker 2006) and, at the same time, by self-organization. So the relationships that develop within a complex system that reflects the modern globalized world cannot be justified by the assumption that participants in the economic system develop behaviors of a representative person. In contrast, systems are made up of heterogeneous individuals, and individuals form completely different behaviors that respond differently to similar situations they face.

Particularly critical is the role of time, combined with the complexity of economic systems. The issue of time is one of the most severe criticisms of neoclassical economics (Smolin 2009, 2013) as the economy is taken into account as a simple system, where the concept of time is absent (Arthur 2013). In any dynamic model, there is a parameter that changes; in complex economic systems, this parameter is time (Harris 2003). With the introduction of time, there are developments that have not happened before in the past, a fact that leads to new structures, new institutions, and therefore, to new economic developments that determine the future.

Complex economic systems are characterized by another critical parameter, which is that the mental capacity of individuals is limited, and they are not able to process all the information available. This, combined with the fact that individuals are characterized by bounded rationality (Simon 1947) and informational limitations (Kirman 2016), leads economic operators to rely on normative rules rather than making decisions in a rational way, as the neoclassical view assumes. Behavioral Economics seeks to bridge the discrepancies between theory and practice regarding how economic actors behave and the existence of incomplete information, incorporating elements from the science of psychology and assuming that investors do not make the right decisions.

The arrival of the 21st century in the economic field marked by the global financial crisis of 2008 has revived the serious question of the relationship between theory and reality. The most severe issue was the general failure of the market system to operate effectively, something that could not be understood by economics (Krugman 2009). Part of this failure has been attributed by various experts to the fact that economic theory and economic policy use specific analytical tools. However, as Eichengreen (2009) argues, this is a problem that exists mostly due to the selective reading of the theory made by economic scientists and not so much to the weakness of the economic science itself.

The outbreak of the Great Depression of 2008, therefore, called into question the scientific content of Orthodox economic thought (Argitis 2019). The reason is that the Orthodox economic thought, influenced by the sterile Neoclassical view, has failed to escape the usual and unrealistic approaches to the structure and operation of real economies. The generalizations of the Orthodox economic view did not take into account the historical development, the institutions, and the cultural background of the individuals.

It is worth noting that complexity is not a concept that characterizes only the modern world. When the pioneers of economics - from 1720 to 1930 - quoted in their works the economic reality, static at first and then dynamic, it was nor simple neither approachable. What has changed, however, is the perception of the world that is now clearer, the movement and access to the amount of information, the ability of economists to analyze and compose knowledge and concepts, and the growing demand for understanding economic and social phenomena.

The role of the individual in the context of a changing environment, as it is shaped by the complex and globalized world, is considered particularly important. Thus, individuals - over the last few decades - have strengthened their ability to gain strength, skills, and abilities. This "mechanism" was developed so that they can make decisions and meet their present and future goals, within the changing conditions of globalization and complexity. The concept of empowerment initially refers to a process of changing the individual in which the individual improves and takes control of his decisions by changing his role in society. It then deals with a process of empowerment in which he gains the confidence to make decisions (Fride 2006). It is a two-way process that takes place between the individual and his environment. The result of this process is the creation of skills based on insight and ability, that is, on essential characteristics that may relate to political consciousness, the ability to work with others, the ability to deal with difficulties, and the effort to influence the environment (Keiffer 1984).

THE DEEP ROOTS OF DEVELOPMENT AND GROWTH

Given the need to approach the economic reality under the conditions described above, highlighting the importance of the deeper roots of economic development and growth is more than necessary.

Thus, identifying the deeper roots of economic growth and development answers a timeless question that concerns economics and is as follows: Why in some societies GDP per capita is higher than in some other societies? Decades ago, exogenous growth models emphasized on the accumulation of capital and the determination of technological progress exogenously. In contrast, endogenous growth models focused on the accumulation of human capital, investment, and knowledge as critical factors in economic growth.

However, the above approaches fail to fully explain the process of economic development and growth. For example, in Solow's Neoclassical view, the unexplained part of economic growth is what is called "Solow residual" (Solow 1957). It is the part of the growth that cannot be explained by the contribution of capital and labor and, among other things, can be attributed to factors such as the cultural and institutional background (Petrakis and Kostis 2013). Thus one can suspect that the current economic development and growth are the result of the existence of a series of mechanisms that affect the wealth of nations. More modern approaches place the institutional framework at the center of the discussion regarding the differences in wealth between countries (Tabellini 2010, De Jong 2011, Acemoglu and Robinson 2012, Alesina and Giuliano 2015). The institutional framework may concern informal or formal institutions. Thus, individuals have a reserve of information and data, due to the existence of the cultural and institutional background of the societies in which they live (Petrakis and Kostis 2014). These two types of settings are deeply rooted in the subconscious and the environment of individuals. They are responsible for shaping human behavior and dealing with different aspects of their daily lives. Their formation is essentially based on the historical and cultural heritage of each nation.

Thus, the deep roots of economic development and growth could be traced back to three levels (Spolaore and Wacziarg 2013): a) the geographical factors and how these factors are linked to the institutional structures of economies and societies, b) the biological factors and gene transmission, and c) the set of values, stereotypes, and human behavior. The second and third of these factors are the two ways in which human behavior is transmitted from person to person and from generation to generation, and both together express the cultural background of societies, as explained by dual inheritance theory. The persistence of these deep roots and historical legacy can set obstacles or promote economic development.

Geographical Factors and their Connection with Institutional Structures

Initially, it is widely accepted that geographical factors are directly related to economic development. For example, there has been a high correlation between per capita income and climatic conditions or temperature (Kamarck 1976, Masters and McMillan 2001, IPCC 2014), the onset of disease and epidemics (Bloom and Sachs 1998, Jack and Lewis 2009), natural resources (Sachs and Warner 2001, Eliasson et al. 2004). However, while one can easily understand that geography directly affects productivity, the indirect mechanism is not easily discernible.

Acemoglu et al. (2002), trying to identify the direction of causality between GDP per capita and geography, claim that the institutional framework interacts with economic development. They see institutions as either inhibiting or beneficial to the process of economic development (Acemoglu et al. 2004; Acemoglu and Robinson 2012). Thus, some institutions are strengthening investments in areas with low population density and low urbanization. In contrast, extractive institutions appear in regions where unfavorable geographical conditions prevail. Acemoglu et al. (2001) highlighted the biogeographical channels by which Europeans implemented institutions that promote productivity in low mortality regions and institutions that do not promote productivity in regions characterized by high mortality. Besides, Acemoglu and Robinson (2012) argue that formal institutions are the deepest cause of economic growth. These institutions are taken into account as holistic structures that include the cultural background of societies as well as the dimensions that make it up (trust, degree of cooperation, etc.). These dimensions are recorded as a result of the institutions. Engerman and Sokoloff (1997) hypothesized that significant differences between geographical areas in terms of observed inequalities in wealth, human capital accumulation, and concentration of political power were due to social beliefs and the institutional infrastructure of societies.

In conclusion, the quality of institutions is beneficial to the process of the economic evolution of societies. At the same time, the broader characteristics of the population may be responsible for the trend in the economic performance of their states. Thus, because institutions are a hallmark of a population and significantly affect the economic success or failure of populations, this is why they are attributed to one of the deepest roots of economic development and growth (Spolaore and Wacziarg 2013).

The Cultural Background of Societies

Population characteristics are integrated and projected through human behavior. By identifying the factors that shape human behavior, one can understand the different performance of economies due to other factors besides the widely used sources of growth (capital, technology, etc.).

The cultural background is a profound cause of economic development and growth that can provide explanations for how human behavior affects economic outcomes. Culture is for the society the same as the memory for individuals (Kluckhohn 1954). It includes whatever was functional at some point in the team's history and deserves to be passed on to future generations (Triandis 2009). Hong (2009) considers the cultural background as a set of "interconnected knowledge networks," which consist of: a) learned thought processes, b) constructions of beliefs, behaviors, and values, and c) inferior theories about the relations between the parties of the physical and social world (Chiu and Hong 2007). In a similar sense, Oyserman and Sorensen (2009) use the term Triandis (1996) to refer to "cultural syndromes" to define sets of interconnected features, which overlap and contrast, and which periodically come to the surface or disappear based on the circumstances. The cultural background, therefore, incorporates all beliefs, values, stereotypes, and rules, characterizing the members of a society and differentiating it from other societies.

From 1950 and then, the Neoclassical Model was the dominant expression of economic theory. At the same time, however, a new school of thought emerged known as Institutionalism, which focused on the role of institutions in the economy, with Veblen, Commons, and Mitchell as its prominent representatives. Later, the New Institutional Economics emerged, which included two distinct thinkers: North and Williamson, who were honored for their contributions with the Nobel Prize. They opposed the Neoclassical Model in search of a more coherent framework for studying economics while relying on history and cultural values. Veblen (1899) focused on the complex entity characterized by instinctive behavior and habits, opposed neoclassical economics because they took the behavior of economic actors for granted. Hence, they were not interested in the broader conditions that affect and shape it. For Veblen (1899), individual behavior is the result of an evolutionary process with psychological and biological aspects. Besides, it is human behavior that shapes institutions, which in turn affects economic activity. Thus, while until then, economic activity was analyzed given values and beliefs, Veblen's (1899) contribution differentiated values and beliefs between individuals. As a result, the concept of cultural background is now distinct, is used as an interpretive variable, and can be considered within economic theory but not as part of it. Thus, on the one hand, economic science lost its integrity, and on the other hand, the cultural background was now a whole distinct field of research (Petrakis 2017, Petrakis 2018).

The question arises as to how human behavior could be transmitted. This can happen through two main mechanisms (Petrakis 2017): a) cultural transmission and b) genetic information transmitted from one generation to the next. These two mechanisms are the mechanism of the evolution of human behavior.

Concerning cultural transmission, cultural characteristics can be transmitted from one generation to the next through social learning (Bandura 1963, 1971). Social Learning Theory focuses on modeling human behavior by observing people's attitudes and emotional responses.

At the same time, however, human behavior is incorporated into genes and is thus passed on to future generations. Genetic transmission is based on Darwin's theory, through the hypothesis of natural selection. It has its molecular basis in DNA as through it the human species biologically transmit specific characteristics to future generations (Spolaore and Wacziarg 2013).

However, these two mechanisms of human transmission should not necessarily be examined separately. From the 1960s to the early 1980s, dual inheritance theory emerged, also known as gene and cultural background evolution or as a biocultural evolution (Boyd and Richerson 1985, 2005, Houkes 2012). Proponents of the dual heritage theory argue that both the evolution of the cultural background and the genetic evolution together have contributed to the development of societies, human action, and the establishment of institutions (Boyd and Richerson 1985). Genes and the cultural background are constantly interacting in a feedback process, where changes in genes can lead to changes in the cultural background, which can then affect the genetic selection, and vice versa. Thus this theory provides answers to whether human behavior is a simultaneous result of genetic and cultural evolution. These changes, however, take time, so the importance of historical heritage in economic performance through productivity should not be overlooked.

"ONE SIZE DOES NOT FIT ALL" AND ECONOMIC DEVELOPMENT AND GROWTH: THE ROLE OF SPECIAL CONDITIONS OF ECONOMIES AND SOCIETIES

Since the outbreak of the 2008 crisis, the role of economic development and growth theories has been in the spotlight. However, the failure to predict and correct the crisis calls into question the traditional view of economics so far.

Thinking about theories of development and growth has always revolved around aggregate and centralized actions that refer to overall changes in economies (Rodrik 2007a). Examples are actions such as the Washington Consensus (Williamson 1990). For most economic policymakers, actions such as trade liberalization, privatization, taxation, and health and education-related policies are seen as universal for all countries (Wu 2017). However, there are significant disagreements over centralized approaches (Hirschman 1963, 1967).

So it seems that these centralized approaches to economic policy cannot work in all economies in the same way. Characteristically, Gerschenkron (1962) states that during their economic development, many European countries, instead of choosing the easy solution of copying the English model, followed different paths in their efforts to modernize based on their particular institutional background, their political, financial and social resources and their degree of effort towards industrialization (Alacevich 2016). Influenced by Gerschenkron, Hirschman (1963, 1967) states that any country that could undertake comprehensive programs would fail to be underdeveloped. But under this reasoning, why are there underdeveloped countries? The answer to this question is that not all economies can implement all economic programs or all economic policies equally effectively.

Thus, even the best-designed policies depend to no small extent on the conditions prevailing in each economy because only in this way can the advantages of each economy be exploited and overcome any local barriers to economic policy. The different problems facing economies require different methods that lead to economic growth. That is why it cannot be ensured that successful policies in one economy can be transferred to other economies and continue to be successful.

Rodrik (2007b) argues that the general problem is that economies do not take advantage of periods of economic growth to strengthen their institutional background. Besides, achieving economic growth requires reaching the right goals, not reaching all goals making one effort. As he characteristically states, what is needed is selective and well-targeted reforms and not laundry lists (Rodrik 2007b). An approach to the "laundry list" (Rodrik 2007b) is left to the following assumptions: a) every reform is good, b) the more areas are reformed, the better, and c) the greater the depth of reform the better.

Sachs (2005), citing the term "clinical economics," highlighted the need for a different policy approach between different economies, and made a relevant analogy to medical science.

Rodrik (2007b) - and a little later Hausmann et al. (2008) - in his book "One Economics Many Recipes" concludes that although the economic science is unique, there is no single recipe that leads to economic growth. What is needed is the development of some growth diagnostics to identify possible oppositions to the process of economic development and growth. The methodology he proposes resembles a decision tree. Starting from the base of the tree, the researcher should move to the various branches to identify issues that can be addressed through economic policy, and then economic policy should focus on addressing these limitations. Even if two countries have a common problem to solve, the different conditions that prevail in each country - other distortions, informal institutions (cultural background) - indicate the need for different solutions to the problem.

Shapley and Roth, who won the 2012 Nobel Prize for matching markets, are contributing to the discussion on the role of the cultural background in differentiating between economies and the need for a different economic policy approach.

Also, the United Nations, highlighting the role of the cultural background for sustainable development (United Cities and Local Governments 2015), state that many of the gaps and inefficiencies associated with the implementation of development policies are due to a lack of attention to local specifics and cultural values and dimensions that characterize every society and economy and are critical to the sustainability of development.

Apart from the cultural background, the role of the existing institutional structures is also significant. In an analysis of whether the size of the state should be common to all economies, Beckmann et al. (2014) highlight the existence of a positive effect of government operation on economic growth, but in the form of U as it depends on the quality of institutional structures and the general institutional infrastructure.

Especially after the outbreak of the 2008 economic crisis, many economists have expressed doubts about how to implement economic policies and the use of models (Krugman 2013, Mirowki 2013, Madrick 2014). A typical example is the implementation of supply-side policies in the heavily indebted countries of the Eurozone after the Great Depression of 2008. This is the implementation of a specific policy implemented in many Eurozone economies regardless of the particular conditions that may characterize each economy ("one-size-fits-all "policies). These policies were essentially aimed at changing the institutional framework of these countries to a more excellent functioning so that it could create conditions for sustainable growth by eliminating the weaknesses of the problematic productive models of indebted countries. However, in the case of the Eurozone, the implementation of a "one-size-fits-all" policy by the European Central Bank in combination with the absence of political and economic institutions within the European Union has only negative consequences for the European edifice, making it particularly vulnerable (Eichengreen 1991).

Garganas (2007) concludes one-size monetary policy does not fit all in Eurozone. He concludes by citing the different institutional backgrounds of the Union's economies that lead to varying effects of the various asymmetric exogenous disorders in each economy, and the different cultural backgrounds and different languages that lead to a small shift in the labor force between countries of the Union.

Besides, Wynne and Koech (2012) also criticized whether the Eurozone is an excellent monetary area and whether a single monetary policy in all economies is effective or not, concluding that it would be more effective for any economy to determine the appropriate size of interest rates based on the conditions prevailing in it (institutional and macroeconomic environment). The fact that the member states of the Eurozone are characterized by different macroeconomic, institutional, and cultural conditions is something that makes it impossible to effectively implement economic policies in the same way in all economies.

In general, the large asymmetries, imbalances, and discrepancies observed in the Eurozone, especially between the countries of the nucleus and the region (Kafka 2013, Kostis and Kafka 2020), prove that the implementation of policies to deal with situations of crisis and re-balancing should not be standard. The effectiveness of the institutional changes sought to tackle the crisis in the eurozone countries has been limited by the asynchronous change of institutions and cultural background (Kafka et al. 2020). The basic component of the cultural background in the process of changing the productive model was ignored, with the result that the new institutions were not synchronized with the established behaviors which did not change and were not prepared to accept the institutional changes (Petrakis et al. 2013).

Of course, policy differentiation is not the cure for all problems and carries risks. Such risks are related to the fact that attention is paid each time to the treatment of a single or even a few issues, can lead to the analyst's refusal to think that perhaps these problems are closely linked and interact with other issues that could possibly be addressed at the same time. In this regard, Wu (2017) concludes that there should be prudence in the use of tailored economic policies to the measures of each economy. The reason is that customized economic policies are usually concrete and have probably not been used in the past to have experience in how to implement them.

In conclusion, economic policymakers should be strategic, flexible, and not centralized (Rodrik 2007a, Wang 2015), although they should differentiate economic policy exercise on a case-by-case basis, with prudence. They should focus on addressing a smaller number of issues, but more effectively, taking into account social and economic entanglements in economic development and growth, rather than solving all issues at once.

CONNECTING THEORY AND REALITY THROUGH THE DEEPER ROOTS OF DEVELOPMENT AND GROWTH

In the modern world where complexity prevails, the empowerment of the individual, and the need for a deep understanding of economic and social phenomena, new approaches are needed in terms of economic development and growth. This is particularly necessary as a result of the inability of economic science to deal with the destabilizing events of the economy during the 21st century. More specifically, these approaches play a particularly important role in how theory and economic policy are interconnected and seek to reduce the gap between theory and reality, as they lead to a more detailed and efficient approach to the real complex world. At the heart of these approaches are the deeper roots of economic growth and development.

Looking for ways to incorporate these deeper roots into theoretical economic thought and economic policy, a new theoretical architecture is needed. An integrated view of economic growth and development is necessary. Such a perspective allows scientific subfields to communicate and interconnect. However, it also allows economics to get linked to related social sciences - since the institutional and cultural backgrounds are borrowed from other social sciences - in order to approach reality. This view is also necessary for the formulation of comprehensive and effective policies for economic development and growth in the sense that these policies will not conflict with the cultural and/or institutional background that acts as a deterrent to them. This chapter, therefore, adopts a conception of economics within an integrated framework of change that is based on the principles of understanding human action and taking into account the institutional framework 'as factors that affect economic outcomes. At the same time, a methodological framework is required to facilitate this multidimensional analysis. This is called methodological pluralism (Petrakis 2017).

This theoretical architecture, which takes into account the critical role of the institutional and cultural background and allows scientific sub-fields to communicate, lies in the mesoeconomic and metaeconomic approach (section 5.3). These two approaches, based on institutions (formal and informal), are developed in order to link the relationship between microeconomic and macroeconomic analysis and to cure their failures.

Figure 1 composes the perspective adopted, as analyzed above.

Figure 1. An overview of the relationship between theory and reality: The role of deeper roots

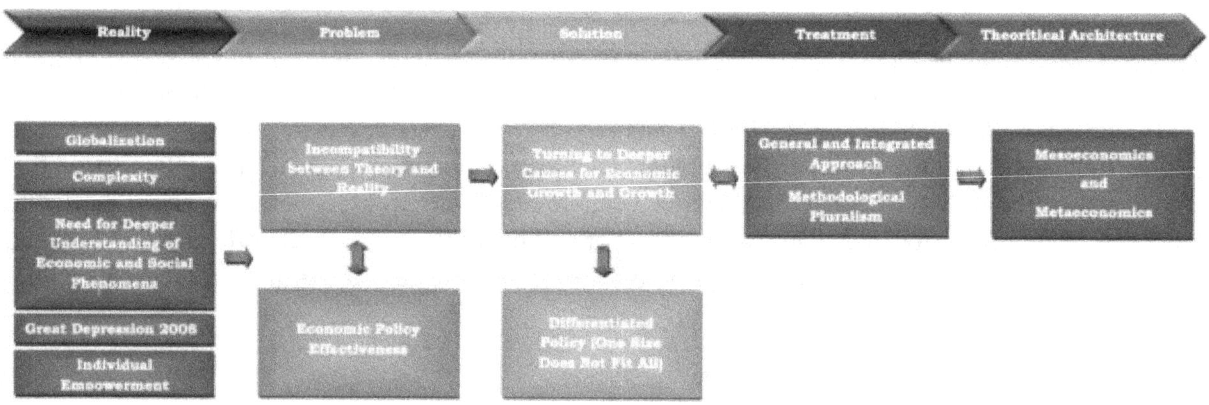

This view is in favor of an evolutionary view of economics.

It gets into the notion that individuals live in a world that is changing dynamically in the context of a rapidly evolving universe is therefore not considered static and unchanging (Hunt 2014, Purica 2015). Thus, evolutionary economic thinking sees economies as dynamic, ever-changing, chaotic, and complex systems, and not as systems in equilibrium (Foster 2004, Foster and Pyka 2014).

In addition, it is understood that nowadays and in the future, individuals will not be able to adequately understand economic phenomena unless they recognize the highly critical role of knowledge (Hayek 1945). According to Dopfer (2013) there is a dual approach to economic thinking about the role of knowledge. On the one hand, it is the level of knowledge required for economic action, and on the other hand, it is economic action under a given knowledge stock. Evolutionary economics deals with the first approach and the dominant neoclassical economics with the second (Dopfer 2013).

Besides, this chapter adopts the idea that today's reality is the evolutionary result of a path dependence that shapes economic, institutional, and cultural outcomes that cover the economic, social, political, and cultural environment of reality. The assumption of evolutionary change (as opposed to the timeless depiction of reality) highlights the birth and existence of a series of determinants that are embedded in today's economic reality.

At the same time, the view is adopted that the behavior of the individual is considered a consequence of natural human behavior (Petrakis 2018). Traditional economic theories generally consider individuals as entirely rational beings. However, the evolutionary economic view differs, rejecting the hypothesis of rational choice and identifying various complex psychological factors as key factors influencing economic outcomes. Based on this perspective, people's behavior and preferences are the results of gradual evolution during their lives. In this gradual evolution, the role of the cultural and institutional background is particularly critical as they are the means of transmitting information from the past of any society (Hodgson 1988, Knight 1997, Streit et al. 1997).

Finally, the approach is adopted that when economies face a financial crisis, a vision based on evolutionary economics is required and relates to the "micro-, meso-, macro-" analysis of Dopfer et al. (2004).

The Need for a General and Complete Economic Development and Growth

The global financial crisis of 2008 highlighted that when conditions of recession, crisis, and exogenous or endogenous shock are observed and even when these conditions are diffused between the various economies, the need for overall views becomes both temporal and interdisciplinary (Petrakis 2017).

This overall view of growth and development allows the sub-fields of economics to communicate and interconnect with each other as well as to communicate with related social sciences. Thus, a new approach is needed to be able to understand the world in which we live. This is an approach that requires the use of sciences such as psychology, anthropology, sociology, history, physics, biology, mathematics, computer science, and other sciences that study complex adaptive systems (Beinhocker 2007). This is why these adjacent sciences are considered necessary to be included in the justification of issues related to economic growth and development. Petrakis (2017) notes that economics -but also other social sciences- in the great moments of their evolution relied on concepts borrowed from different scientific fields. Typical are examples of expectations, animal instincts, etc.

From the above, the need for multilevel and diverse interdisciplinary research is considered particularly important, which contributes to the need for a general and integrated understanding of economic development and growth (Petrakis 2017). This perspective seeks to approach the multidimensional modern economic world in the most representative way.

Of course, it should be noted that such an approach may create problems related to the complexity of the issues under investigation. As a result, there are no clear indications of causal relationships between the various parameters. Thus, a general and integrated approach to economic development and growth requires careful management based on that there should be respect for the complex dimension of the issues under study and the ability to isolate the dominant causes that lead to the complex system. Scientists who are in favor of such an approach are facing great challenges as they can hardly accumulate the necessary knowledge and information to achieve an objectively excellent composition that follows a general and integrated approach to economic development and growth.

In this context, economists prefer to approach reality and interpret it with a "rich" portfolio of theoretical views. A pluralistic approach supports this view. In addition, it detaches the researcher from "the methodological consequences of a positivist mantle and the search for the predictive capacity of the theories used" (Petrakis 2018). Thus, the researcher must be able to clarify the problem for analysis, well document the theoretical background of the problem, and ultimately analyze the relationship between theory and reality.

The Need for Methodological Pluralism

Researchers who are interested in methodological issues and do not consider that the issues have been resolved by attaching to a specific conception (for instance, to the Neoclassical conception) should be able to defend the methodological standards that follow and the reasons that chose it (Hausman 1989).

Of course, from this point of view, the question arises as to the degree of methodological pluralism that needs to be pursued in order to finally capture the multidimensional reality and the implementation of effective economic policy (Petrakis 2018) satisfactorily. The degree of methodological pluralism lies in two main approaches: a) that of monists who argue that researchers should follow a single methodological approach and b) that of pluralists (such as Feyerabend 1975, Kuhn 1977, Laudan 1984) who argue that researchers should use a variety of methodological approaches to argue against the idea of a single methodology of monists, for the benefit of pluralism of methodological rules governing the evaluation of theory. The main feature of these methodological rules is that they can be differentiated and evolved over time and in accordance with the development of the scientific practices followed, but also they can be differentiated within the various sub-disciplines of the economic science as the interpretation of each rule also depends on the psychosynthesis and the knowledge of each scientist.

Pluralism-eclecticism allows for an in-depth focus on the methodologies used by researchers, utilizing whatever tools scientists have to offer that seems well-crafted and appropriate for this purpose (Hausman 1981). The pluralistic approach, on the part of economists, allows the communication of scientific sub-disciplines as well as the acceptance of the introduction of concepts from adjacent sciences. In this sense, the adoption of a pluralistic approach catalyzes the fragmentation and sterilization of the science in order to develop a more effective approach that will lead to better policy outcomes. These results may differ spatially and temporally between economies as they allow the deep roots of development and growth to be recognized in each economy (Spolaore and Wacziarg 2013).

A pluralistic methodological approach removes the researcher from attachment to the Neoclassical model, which despite its internal consistency, cannot adequately capture economic reality while at the same time being characterized by partial temporal (short-term analysis) and partial spatial (some developed economies) application. Of course, as mentioned above, the Neoclassical model - as well as newer versions - is an important starting point for economists and, at the same time, a valuable analytical tool and a criterion for reporting internal consistency for the formation of alternative scientific perspectives (Petrakis 2017).

The above-described pluralistic (alternatively extended eclectic) approach leads to the need for a theory of economic development and growth that "fits the facts." This fact is directly related to the exercise of economic policy as what is essential is the development of effective theories that can describe how reality changes under specific economic policy proposals (Petrakis 2018). Thus, any economic policy should be evaluated in the context of complex economic and social interactions. In this way, it is possible to identify the prospects and effectiveness of an economic policy.

Bridging Microeconomics with Macroeconomic Analysis: Mesoeconomics and Metoeconomics

The main distinction between economics is the distinction between microeconomic and macroeconomic analysis. The sum of the microeconomic data leads to the macroeconomic analysis, and the division of the macroeconomic analysis leads to the individual microeconomic data. In this sense, economics is based on simplifications concerning generalizations of mathematical logic, and thus one could argue that economics is based on the concept of algebraicism (Dopfer et al. 2004).

However, the question that arises is whether the hypotheses that govern the relations of general and aggregate quantities (macroeconomic analysis) are compatible with the hypotheses that govern the behavior of individual elements, ie. the behaviors of units such as individuals, households, business (microeconomic analysis), and vice versa.

It is not certain that the interconnection of the part with the aggregate is valid. This is the paradoxical "fallacy of composition" (Samuelson and Nordhaus 1992).

Aggregate models are more useful because they are characterized by the generality that would be lacking if we focused on a specific form of micro-foundations (Wren-Lewis 2012). Determining the degree of aggregation that is necessary at macroeconomic models requires additional unrealistic assumptions (Scarth 1988). The issue is for aggregate models to contain critical issues arising from various micro-foundations (Bergh and van den Gowdy 2003). However, this interface is not easy.

As a result, all of the above discussion has led to much criticism on economics because it pays close attention to microeconomics and macroeconomics. Attempts are being made in this direction to introduce new ideologies into the economy that better reflect the reality of our complex world (Sheng and Geng 2012).

According to Sheng and Geng (2012), Nobel Laureate Ronald H. Coase stressed that microeconomic analysis consists of many unexplored "black boxes" so that it cannot provide sufficient explanations and effectively study the relationship between firms and markets.

Besides, according to Solow (2010), modern macroeconomics has not only failed to solve economic and financial problems, but has been "predestined" to fail. The construction of the DSGE models, which were the main approach for macroeconomics before and after the crisis of 2008 and, more generally, models based on the representative agent, did not pass the test of good forecasting. Also, Paul Krugman (2009) argued that macroeconomics over the past three decades has proved inadequate because economists have failed to identify the errors of macroeconomic analysis, mistakenly believing that "beautifully structured" theoretical models can depict reality.

Argitis (2019) concludes that there is a need to revise the macroeconomic theory and policy approach through an approach that includes the critical role of institutions, developing a framework of analysis that is necessary for the development of a culturally holistic and evolutionary macroeconomic view.

Thus, the modern microeconomic and macroeconomic models are not sufficient to investigate the dynamic and complex interactions between people, institutions, and the nature of the real complex economy (Sheng and Geng 2012). This led to the search for new solutions.

The interconnection of micro- and macro-analyzes was made possible through the analysis of the mesoeconomics (Ng 1986, Dopfer et al. 2004) and the metaeconomics (Schumacher 1973). These are efforts to highlight the importance of the structures under which microeconomics and macroeconomic analysis operate. Dopfer et al. (2004), introduce the concept of mesoeconomics as an attempt to better approach the fundamental issues of coordination and change in economics, adopting the approach that economic development is a process of knowledge development, in the sense implied by Popper (1945) and explained to economists by Hayek (1937, 1945) and Loasby (1991, 1999). The core of a complex economic system lies in what is dealt with in the mesoeconomics, that is, the rules that are expressed in a number of institutions, both formal and informal (Foster 2011).

The focus of mesoeconomics is the institutional background under which economies operate, something that neither the microeconomic nor the macroeconomic approach analyzes. This inattention of microeconomic and macroeconomic analysis to the role of institutions regarding the economic activity of humans, firms, and economies, has its roots in the sterile environment of the Neoclassical approach, where there exist assumptions about perfect competition, complete information, and zero transaction costs. Thus, Dopfer et al. (2004), following an evolutionary economic approach, introduce the theory of Micro-, Meso-, Macro-economics as they believe that "an economic system consists of a population of rules, structures of rules and procedures concerning rules" (Dopfer et al. 2004, pp. 263). They define mesoeconomics as the study of the formal and informal institutional background, which includes economic, social, and political institutions, which essentially determine the rules of operation of the economies. They argue that mesoeconomics is the natural link between microeconomic and macroeconomic analysis, since the rules of microeconomic analysis, together with the institutions, essentially lead to macroeconomic results (Sheng and Geng 2012). Also, Dopfer (2012) introduces the mesoeconomics in the context of Schumpeter's analysis, arguing that entrepreneurs are driven to innovation (at a micro level), which a number of other entrepreneurs imitate (meso level), and this leads to creative destruction and therefore in equilirium in a new situation (macro level). Based on this logic, economic development occurs at deep levels during the transition from one general rule to another, causing changes at a more superficial level as new rules are adopted, destroying an old equilibrium and creating a new one.

Metaeconomics go even deeper than mesoeconomics, in the sense that they take into account even more profound features of economies that affect their operation with a focus on the role of human behavior. Schumacher (1973), in his work "Small is beautiful," defines metaeconomics as the humanization of economics. He notes that informal human and social institutions are complex structures whose governance is a dynamic process and requires systematic analysis. For this reason, metaeconomics include data from moral philosophy, psychology, anthropology, and sociology, which go beyond the goal of rationality and maximizing profit. Thus, in metaeconomics, economies are seen as complex, interactive, and holistic systems (Sheng and Geng 2012). In this way, the metaeconomics is called upon to provide answers as to why economies differ from each other in terms of their level of competitiveness and sustainability and on how and why institutional structures are evolving. In order to highlight the principles that determine how people behave and act economically, an analytical framework based on evolutionary economics is needed to treat the real economy as a complex system that constantly interacts with other systems. Metaeconomics began to emerge relatively recently since official statistics and measurements were not until recently able to take into account quality characteristics (Easterlin's paradox (Easterlin 1974)) related to the behavior of economic actors.

Sheng and Geng (2012) define this whole framework of "micro- meso- macro- economics" as "systemnomics" in the sense that it is a more comprehensive way to analyze economies as human economies characterized by complex interactions between the various subsystems (living systems, natural systems).

FUTURE RESEARCH DIRECTIONS

Future research could, through empirical analysis, record the extent to which the cultural background affects economic growth and the investigation of the negative cultural backlash of Norris and Inglehart (2019). In addition, in terms of the role of the institutional background, its impact on economic growth could be studied, as well as on variables that are a proxy for growth such as innovation. This empirical investigation could contribute to the issues of whether the institutional background differentiates economies from each other as well as the discussion of one-size-fits-all policies. Finally, future research could examine empirically whether the institutional and cultural backgrounds function in a complementary or substitute way in terms of their role in economic development. This issue is particularly important because most economies are characterized by stagnant growth patterns, which arise due to the presence of peculiar characteristics related to the institutional and cultural background (weak cultural and / or institutional background). In order to return to excellent growth patterns, economies will need to pursue policies that change the institutional environment and change the cultural background at the same time.

CONCLUSION

The present analysis focuses on the deeper causes that are necessary for the development and growth of economies. The need to look for these deeper causes stems from the complexity of the economic world, the empowerment of individuals' intellectual capacity, and the need for a deeper understanding of socio-economic phenomena, especially in the wake of the 2008 crisis. Thus it becomes clear that there are problems in the compatibility of theory with reality.

This chapter aims to highlight two such factors: the role of the cultural background and the role of the institutional background in economic development and growth. Thus, it is sought to analyze how these factors affect economic growth and development but also whether these factors are converging or not and how this process affects the product produced. In fact, the role of these two deeper causes of economic growth and development is so important that they significantly shape the way economies operate and raise issues of inefficiency in implementing economic policy when applied in the same way in all economies (one size does not fits all). A prime example is the fiscal adjustment programs of the Eurozone economies, where it has become clear that the same economic policy program can have completely different results when applied to economies and societies characterized by different conditions. In addition, these two factors hinder or promote the process of sustainable economic growth and development. The incompatible evolution of these two factors is caused by the excellent magnification model and ultimately leads to stagnant magnification patterns.

In order for these two factors to be taken into account in economics, as they are concepts derived from related social sciences, a more general and integrated view of economic development as well as the maintenance of a methodological pluralism is required (Petrakis 2017).

In this endeavor - which is compatible with an evolutionary view of economics - a new theoretical architecture emerges. This architecture refers to the meso-economic and meta-economic approach that allows analysis to focus on institutional and cultural background issues in order to bridge the inconsistencies between microeconomic and macroeconomic analysis and to heal the general view of economics about the complex real world by reflecting economic reality in a much more efficient way. Only through such a theoretical architecture can other factors be taken into account that are responsible for the effectiveness or not of the applied economic policies.

REFERENCES

Acemoglu, D., Johnson, S., & Robinson, J. A. (2002). Reversal of Fortune: Geography and Institutions in the Making of the Modern World Income Distribution. *The Quarterly Journal of Economics*, *117*(4), 1231–1294. doi:10.1162/003355302320935025

Acemoglu, D., Johnson, S. H., & Robinson, J. A. (2001). The Colonial Origins of Comparative Development: An Empirical Investigation. *The American Economic Review*, *91*(5), 1369–1401. doi:10.1257/aer.91.5.1369

Acemoglu, D., Johnson, S. H., Robinson, J. A., & Yared, P. (2004). *Income and De- mocracy.* Working paper, Massachusetts Institute of technology.

Acemoglu, D., & Robinson, J. A. (2012). Why Nations Fail: The Origins of Power, Prosperity and Poverty. New York: Crown.

Alacevich, M. (2016). Albert O. Hirschman and the Rise and Decline of Development Economics. Research in the History of Economic Thought and Methodology, 34, 13-39. doi:10.1108/S0743-41542016000034B001

Alesina, A., & Giuliano, P. (2015). Culture and Institutions. *Journal of Economic Literature*, *53*(4), 898–944. doi:10.1257/jel.53.4.898

Allen, P. M. (1990). Why the Future is Not what it was. *Futures*, *22*(6), 554–570. doi:10.1016/0016-3287(90)90127-4

Argitis, G. (2019). Evolutionary Financial Macroeconomics. Routledge.

Arthur, W. B. (2013). *Complexity and the economy: a different framework for economic thought.* SFI Working Paper: 2013-04-012, 2013-04-012.

Bandura, A. (1963). Behavior theory and indemnificatory learning. *The American Journal of Orthopsychiatry*, *33*, 591–601. doi:10.1111/j.1939-0025.1963.tb01007.x PMID:13966305

Bandura, A. (1971). Behavior therapy from a social learning perspective. *Proceedings of the XIXth International Congress of Psychology*.

Beckmann, J., Endrich, M., & Schweickert, R. (2014). *Government activity and economic growth: One size fits all?* Kiel Working Papers 1903, Kiel Institute for the World Economy (IfW).

Beinhocker, E. D. (2006). *The Origin of Wealth: Evolution, Complexity, and the Radical Remaking of Economics*. Harvard Business School Press.

Beinhocker, E. D. (2007). *The Origin of Wealth: The Radical Remaking of Economics and What It Means for Business and Society*. Harvard Business Review Press.

Bergh, J., & van den Gowdy, J. (2003). The microfoundations of macroeconomics: An evolutionary perspective. *Cambridge Journal of Economics*, *27*(1), 65–84. doi:10.1093/cje/27.1.65

Bloom, E. D., Sachs, J. D., Collier, P., & Udry, C. (1998). Geography, Demography, and Economic Growth in Africa. *Brookings Papers on Economic Activity*, *2*(2), 207–273. doi:10.2307/2534695 PMID:12295931

Boyd, R., & Richerson, P. J. (1985). *Culture and the Evolutionary Process*. University of Chicago Press.

Boyd, R., & Richerson, P. J. (2005). *The Origin and Evolution of Cultures*. Oxford University Press.

Chiu, C.-y., & Hong, Y-y. (2007). Social psychology of culture. New York: Psychology Press.

De Jong, E. (2011). Culture, institutions and economic growth. *Journal of Institutional Economics*, *7*(4), 523–527. doi:10.1017/S1744137411000117

Dopfer, K. (2012). The origins of meso economics. *Journal of Evolutionary Economics*, *22*(1), 133–160. doi:10.100700191-011-0218-4

Dopfer, K. (2013). *Evolutionary Economics*. Papers on Economics and Evolution, Max Planck Institute of Economics, No. 1308.

Dopfer, K., Foster, J., & Potts, J. (2004). Micro-meso-macro. *Journal of Evolutionary Economics*, *14*(3), 263–279. doi:10.100700191-004-0193-0

Douglas, M. (1987). *How institutions think*. Routledge & Kegan Paul.

Easterlin. (1974). *Nations and Households in Economic Growth: Essays in Honor of Moses Abramovitz*. New York: Academic Press, Inc.

Eichengreen, B. (1991). *Is Europe an optimum currency area?* NBER Working Paper Series, no. 3579.

Eichengreen, B. (2009, May). The Last Temptation of Risk. *The National Interest*.

Eliasson, L., & Turnovsky, S. J. (2004). Renewable Resources in an Endogenously Growing Economy: Balanced Growth and Transitional Dynamics. *Journal of Environmental Economics and Management*, *48*(3), 1018–1049. doi:10.1016/j.jeem.2003.12.004

Engerman, S. L., & Sokoloff, K. L. (1997). Factor Endowments, Institu-tions, and Differential Paths of Growth AmongNew World Economies: A View from Economic Historians of the United States. In How Latin America Fell Behind. Stanford University Press.

Fayerabend, K. P. (1975). *Against Method: Outline of an Anarchistic Theory of Knowledge*. New Left Books.

Foster, J. (Ed.). (2004). *Applied Evolutionary Economics and Complex Systems*. Edward Elgar Publishing. doi:10.4337/9781845421564

Foster, J. (2011). Evolutionary Macroeconomics: A Research Agenda. In Catching Up, Spillovers and Innovation Networks in a Schumpeterian Perspective. DOI doi:10.1007/978-3-642-15886-5_2

Foster, J., & Pyka, A. (2014). *Introduction: co-evolution and complex adaptive systems in evolutionary economics*. Jour -014-0339-7.

Fride. (2006). *The Individual as an agent of change: The Empowerment Process*. Development "In Perspective".

Garganas, N. C. (2007). Does one size fit all? Monetary policy and integration in the euro area. Address by Mr Nicholas C Garganas, Governor of the Bank of Greece, at a visit to the Central Bank of Chile, Santiago, Chile.

Gerschenkron, A. (1962). *Economic backwardness in historical perspective*. The Belknap Press of Harvard University Press.

Harris, D. J. (2003). *Joan Robinson on History versus Equilibrium*. J. *Robinson Centennial Conference*, Burlington, VT.

Hausman, M. D. (1981). *Capital, Profits and Prices: An Essay in the Philosophy of Economics*. Columbia University Press. doi:10.7312/haus90554

Hausman, M. D. (1989). Economic Methodology in a Nutshell. *The Journal of Economic Perspectives*, *3*(2), 115–127. doi:10.1257/jep.3.2.115

Hausmann, R., Rodrik, D., & Velasco, A. (2008). Growth Diagnostics. In J. Stiglitz & N. Serra (Eds.), The Washington Consensus Reconsidered: Towards a New Global Governance. New York: Oxford University Press.

Hayek, F. (1945). The use of knowledge in society. *The American Economic Review*, *35*(4), 519–530.

Hayek, F. A. (1937). Economics and knowledge. *Economica*, 4.

Hayek, F. A. (1945). The use of knowledge in society. *The American Economic Review*, *35*(4), 519–530.

Hirschman, A. O. (1963). *Journeys toward Progress*. Twentieth Century Fund.

Hirschman, A. O. (1967). *Development projects observed*. The Brookings Institution Press.

Hodgson, G. M. (1988). *Economics and institutions, A manifesto for a modern institutional economics*. Polity Press. doi:10.9783/9781512816952

Hodgson, G. M. (2001). *How Economics Forgot History: The Problem of Historical Specificity in Social Science*. Routledge. doi:10.4324/9780203519813

Hong, Y. (2009). A dynamic constructivist approach to culture: Moving from describing culture to explaining culture. In *Understanding Culture: Theory, research and application*. Psychology Press.

Houkes, W. (2012). Population thinking and natural selection in dual-inheritance theory. *Biology & Philosophy*, *27*(3), 401–417. doi:10.100710539-012-9307-5 PMID:22523438

Hunt, T. (2014). Evolutionary thinking. "A conversation with Carter Phipps about the role of evolutionary thinking in modern culture. *Commun Integr Biol.*, *7*(6). doi:10.4161/19420889.2014.993267

IPCC. (2014). *Climate Change 2014: Impacts, Adaptation, and Vulnerability. Contribution of Working Group II to the Fifth Assessment Report of the Intergovernmental Panel on Climate Change*. Cambridge University Press.

Jack, W., & Lewis, M. (2009). Health investments and economic growth: Macroeconomic evidence and microeconomic foundations. In M. Spence & M. Lewis (Eds.), *Health and Growth*. Commission on Growth and Development.

Kafka, K. I. (2013). *Competitiveness and success index of the economies in the Eurozone* (Master's dissertation). Department of Economics, National and Kapodistrian University of Athens.

Kafka, K. I., Kostis, P. C., & Petrakis, P. E. (2020). Why Coevolution of Culture and Institutions Matters for Economic Development and Growth? In Perspectives on Economic Development - Public Policy, Culture, and Economic Development. Intech Open Publications.

Kamarck, M. A. (1976). *The Tropics and Economic Development*. Johns Hopkins University Press.

Keiffer, C. (1984). Citizen empowerment: A developmental perspective. *Prevention in Human Services, 3*(16), 9–35. doi:10.1300/J293v03n02_03 PMID:10266759

Kirman, A. (2016). Complexity and Economic Policy: A Paradigm Shift or a Change in Perspective? A Review Essay on David Colander and Roland Kupers's Complexity and the Art of Public Policy. *Journal of Economic Literature, 54*(2), 534–572.

Kluckhohn, C. (1954). Culture and behaviour. In G. Lindzey (Ed.), *Handbook of social psychology* (Vol. 2, pp. 821–876). Addison-Wesley.

Knight, J. (1997). Social institutions and human cognition: Thinking about old questions in new ways. *Journal of Institutional and Theoretical Economics, 153*(4), 693–699.

Kostis, P. C., & Kafka, K. I. (2020). *Economic Success in Eurozone: The Widening Imbalances During the Crisis*. 4th International Conference of Development and Economy ICODECON, Kalamata, Greece.

Krugman, P. (2009, Sept. 2). How Did Economists Get It So Wrong? *The New York Times Magazine*.

Krugman, P. (2013). How Did Economists Get It So Wrong? *New York Times*.

Kuhn, S. T. (1977). *The Essential Tension: Selected Studies in Scientific Tradition and Change*. University of Chicago Press. doi:10.7208/chicago/9780226217239.001.0001

Laudan, L. (1984). *Science and Values: The Aims of Science and Their Role in Scientific Debate*. University of California Press.

Loasby, B. (1991). *Equilibrium and evolution: an exploration of connecting principles in economics*. Manchester University Press.

Loasby, B. (1999). *Knowledge, institutions and evolution in economics*. Routledge.

Loasby, B. J. (2001). Cognition, Imagination and Institutions in Demand Creation. *Journal of Evolutionary Economics, 11*(1), 7–21. doi:10.1007/PL00003857

Madrick, J. (2014). *Seven Bad Ideas: How Mainstream Economists Have Damaged America and the World*. Vintage.

Masters, W. A., & McMillan, M. S. (2001). Climate and Scale in Economic Growth. *Journal of Economic Growth, 6*(3), 167–186. doi:10.1023/A:1011398431524

Mirowki, P. (2013). *Never Let a Serious Crisis Go to Waste: How Neoliberalism Survived the Financial Meltdown*. Dean Baker, Central for Economic and Policy Research.

Nelson, R.R., & Winter, S.G. (1974). Neoclassical vs. Evolutionary Theories of Economic Growth: Critique and Prospectus. *Economic Journal, 84*(336), 886 –905.

Nelson, R. R., & Winter, S. G. (1982). *An Evolutionary Theory of Economic Change*. Harvard University Press.

Oyserman, D., & Sorensen, N. (2009). Understanding cultural syndrome effects on what and how we think: A situated cognition model. In Understanding Culture: Theory, research and application. Psychology Press.

Papadogiannis, G. (2012). *The rise and fall of Homo Economicus. The myth of the rational man and the chaotic reality*. Papadopoulos Publications.

Petrakis, P. E. (2017). *Economic Development and Growth. General and Integrated Approach*. Quaestor Publications.

Petrakis, P. E., Kostis, P.C., Kafka, K.I., & Valsamis, D.G. (2018). General Economic Growth and Development. Ropi Publications.

Petrakis, P. E., & Kafka, K. I. (2018). Sustainable Entrepreneurial Activity Within Complex Economic Systems. In Entrepreneurial Complexity. Taylor & Francis Group.

Petrakis, P. E., & Kostis, P. C. (2013). Economic Growth and Cultural Change. *Journal of Socio-Economics, 47*(C), 147–157. doi:10.1016/j.socec.2013.02.011

Petrakis, P. E., & Kostis, P. C. (2014). Medium Term Effects of Culture, Transactions and Institutions on Opportunity Entrepreneurship. *Journal of Innovation and Entrepreneurship, 3*(1), 11. doi:10.118613731-014-0011-3

Petrakis, P. E., Kostis, P. C., & Valsamis, D. G. (2013). *European Economics and Politics in the Midst of the Crisis, From the Outbreak of the Crisis to the Fragmented European Federation*. Springer.

Popper, K. (1945). *The open society and its enemies* (Vol. 1). Routledge.

Purica, I. (2015). Evolution of Financial Crises. *Nonlinear Dynamics of Financial Crises*.

Rodrik, D. (2007a). World Too Complex For One-Size-Fits-All Models. *Post-Autistic Economics Review, 44*.

Rodrik, D. (2007b). *One Economics, Many Recipes*. Princeton University Press. doi:10.1515/9781400829354

Sachs, J. (2005). *The End of Poverty: Economic Possibilities for Our Time*. Penguin.

Sachs, J. D., & Warner, A. M. (2001). The Curse of Natural Resources. *European Economic Review, 45*(4–6), 827–838. doi:10.1016/S0014-2921(01)00125-8

Samuelson, P. A., & Nordhaus, W. D. (1992). *Economics*. McGraw-Hill.

Scarth, W. M. (1988). *Macroeconomics*. Harcourt Brace Jovanovich.

Schumacher, E. F. (1973). Small is beautiful. *Abacus*.

Sheng, A., & Geng, X. (2012). *The new economics: Meso and Meta*. World Economic Forum.

Simon, H. A. (1947). *Administrative Behavior: A Study of Decision-Making Processes in Administrative Organizations*. Simon and Schuster, Free Press.

Simon, H. A. (1969). *The Sciences of the Artificial*. MIT Press.

Smith, A. (1981). *An Inquiry into the Nature and Causes of the Wealth of Nations, Liberty Fund* (R. H. Campbell & A. S. Skinner, Eds.). (Original work published 1776)

Smolin, L. (2009, Feb.). Time and Symmetry in Models of Economic Markets. Mss.

Smolin, L. (2013). *Time Reborn*. Houghton, Mifflin, Harcourt.

Solow, R. (1957). Technical change and the aggregate production function. *Review of Economics and Statistics, 39*(3), 312–320. doi:10.2307/1926047

Solow, R. (2010, July 20). *Building a Science of Economics for the Real World*. House Committee on Science and Technology.

Spolaore, E., & Wacziarg, R. (2013). How Deep Are the Roots of Economic Development? *Journal of Economic Literature, 51*(2), 325–369. doi:10.1257/jel.51.2.325

Streit, M., Mummert, U., & Kiwit, D. (1997). Views and comments on cognition, rationality, and institutions. Editorial preface. *Journal of Institutional and Theoretical Economics, 153*(4), 688–692.

Tabellini, G. (2010). Culture and Institutions: Economic Development in the Regions of Europe. *Journal of the European Economic Association, 8*(4), 677–716. doi:10.1111/j.1542-4774.2010.tb00537.x

Triandis, H. C. (1996). The psychological measurement of cultural syndromes. *The American Psychologist, 51*(4), 407–415. doi:10.1037/0003-066X.51.4.407

Triandis, H. C. (2009). Ecological determinants of cultural variation. In Understanding Culture: Theory, research, and application. Psychology Press.

United Cities and Local Governments. (2015). *Culture In The Sustainable Development Goals: A Guide For Local Action*. Academic Press.

van den Bergh Jeroen, C. J. M., & Gowdy, J. M. (2003). The microfoundations of macroeconomics: an evolutionary perspective. Cambridge Journal of Economics, 27(1), 65-84.

Veblen, T. (1899). *The Theory of the Leisure Class: An Economic Study of Institutions, Penguin twentieth-century classics*. Penguin Books.

Wang, S. (2015). One size does not fit all: The need for flexibility in policy responses to slow growth. *China Finance and Economic Review, 3*(1), 5. doi:10.118640589-015-0020-9

Williamson, J. (1990). What Washington means by policy reform. In Latin American Adjustment: How Much Has Happened? Institute for International Economics.

Wren-Lewis, S. (2012, Aug. 30). Arguments for ending the microfoundations hegemony. *Mainly Macro*.

Wu, H. (2017). One Size Does Not Fit All: The Rise of Tailor-Made Economic Policies, Kennedy. *The School Review*.

Wynne, M.A., & Koech, J. (2012). One-Size-Fits-All Monetary Policy: Europe and the U.S. *Economc Lette*.

ADDITIONAL READING

Acemoglu, D., & Jackson, M. O. (2017). Social Norms and the Enforcement of Laws. *Journal of the European Economic Association, 15*(2), 245–295.

Aghion, P., & Howitt, P. (1998). *Endogenous Growth Theory*. MIT Press.

Allen, P. M. (2014, April). Evolution: Complexity, uncertainty and innovation. *Journal of Evolutionary Economics, 24*(2), 265–289. doi:10.100700191-014-0340-1

Allport, G. W. (1937). *Personality*. Constable.

Arthur, W. B. (1999). Complexity and the Economy. *Science, 284*(5411), 107–109. doi:10.1126cience.284.5411.107 PMID:10103172

Banerjee, A. V. (1992). A Simple Model of Herd Behavior. *The Quarterly Journal of Economics, 107*(3), 797–817. doi:10.2307/2118364

Becker, G. S. (1976). *The Economic Approach to Human Behaviour*. University of Chicago Press. doi:10.7208/chicago/9780226217062.001.0001

Becker, G. S. (2000). A Comment on the Conference on Cost-Benefit Analysis. *The Journal of Legal Studies, University of Chicago Press, 29*(2), 1149–1152. doi:10.1086/468107

Boyd, R., & Richerson, P. J. (1988). The evolution of reciprocity in sizable groups. *Journal of Theoretical Biology, 132*(3), 337–356. doi:10.1016/S0022-5193(88)80219-4 PMID:3226132

Caldwell, B. (2002). Wieser, Hayek and Equilibrium Theory. *Journal des Économisteset des ÉtudesHumaines, 12*(1), 47–66.

Casson, M. C., Giusta, D. M., & Kambhampati, U. S. (2010). Formal and Informal Institutions and Development, Elsevier. *World Development, 38*(2), 137–141. doi:10.1016/j.worlddev.2009.10.008

Cavalli-Sforza, L. L., & Feldman, M. (1981). *Cultural Transmission and Evolution*. Princeton University Press.

Chamley, C. P. (2004). *Rational Herds: Economic Models of Social Learning*. Cambridge University Press.

Chiao, J. Y., & Ambady, N. (2007). Cultural neuroscience: Parsing universality and diversity across levels of analysis. In S. Kitayama & D. Cohen (Eds.), *Handbook of Cultural Psychology* (pp. 237–254). Guilford Press.

Davidson, P. (1996). Reality and economic theory. *Journal of Post Keynesian Economics*, *18*(4), 479–508. doi:10.1080/01603477.1996.11490083

Davidson, P. (2002). *Financial markets money and the real world*. Elgar. doi:10.4337/9781843765585

Dequech, D. (2000). Fundamental uncertainty and ambiguity. *Eastern Economic Journal*, *26*(1), 41–60.

Dequech, D. (2006). The new institutional economics and the theory of behavior under uncertainty. *Journal of Economic Behavior & Organization*, *72*(1), 70–78. doi:10.1016/j.jebo.2009.05.001

Diamond, J. M. (1997). *Guns, Germs, and Steel: The Fates of Human Societies*. W.W. Norton.

Douglas, M. (1987). *How institutions think*. Routledge & Kegan Paul.

Durham, W. H. (1991). *Coevolution: Genes, Culture, and Human Diversity*. Stanford University Press.

Ekelund, J. R., & Hébert, R. F. (2014). *A history of economic theory & method*. Waveland Press.

European Commission. (2011). *Empowering people, driving change*. Social Innovation in the European Union, Bureau of European Policy Advisers.

Fischer, S. (1993). The Role of Macroeconomic Factors in Growth. *Mon. Econ.*, *32*(3), 485–512. doi:10.1016/0304-3932(93)90027-D

Fontana, M. (2010). Can Neoclassical Economics handle Complexity? The Fallacy of the Oil Spot Dynamic. *Journal of Economic Behavior & Organization*, *76*(3), 584–596. doi:10.1016/j.jebo.2010.08.010

Frankel, J., & Romer, D. (1999). Does trade cause growth? *The American Economic Review*, *89*(3), 379–399. doi:10.1257/aer.89.3.379

Gale, D., & Shapley, L. S. (1962). College Admissions and the Stability of Marriage. *The American Mathematical Monthly*, *69*(1), 9–15. doi:10.1080/00029890.1962.11989827

Gallup, J., & Sachs, J. (2001). The economic burden of malaria. *The American Journal of Tropical Medicine and Hygiene*, *64*(1), 85–96. doi:10.4269/ajtmh.2001.64.85 PMID:11425181

Gallup, J., Sachs, J., & Mellinger, D. (1999). Geography and economic development. *International Regional Science Review*, *22*(2), 179–232. doi:10.1177/016001799761012334

Geanakoplos, J., & Polemarchakis, H. (1986). Existence, regularity and constrained suboptimality of competitive allocations when the asset market is incomplete, Cambridge University Press. In H. W. R. Starr & D. Starret (Eds.), *Uncertainty, Information and Communication: Essays in Honour of K.J. Arrow* (Vol. III, pp. 65–95). doi:10.1017/CBO9780511983566.007

Gorodnichenko, Y., & Roland, G. (2015). *Culture, institutions and democratization.Tech-nical report*. National Bureau of Economic Research. doi:10.3386/w21117

Greif, A. (1994). Cultural Beliefs and the Organization of Society: A Historical and Theoretical Reflection on Collectivist and Individualistic Societies. *Journal of Political Economy*, *102*(5), 912–950. doi:10.1086/261959

Grossman, G., & Helpman, E. (1990). Trade, Innovation, and Growth. *The American Economic Review, 80*, 86–91.

Guiso, L., Sapienza, P., & Zingales, L. (2006). Does Culture affect Economic Outcomes? *The Journal of Economic Perspectives, 20*(2), 23–48. doi:10.1257/jep.20.2.23

Henrich, J., & McElreath, R. (2007). Dual-inheritance theory: the evolution of human cultural capacities and cultural evolution. In *Oxford Handbook of Evolutionary Psychology, Series*. Oxford Library of Psychology. doi:10.1093/oxfordhb/9780198568308.013.0038

Hirschman, A. O. (1958/1963). *The strategy of economic development*. Yale University Press.

Hirschman, A. O. (1961). Ideologies of economic development in Latin America. In A. O. Hirschman (Ed.), *Latin American issues: Essays and comments* (p. 342). Twentieth Century Fund.

Hoeffler, S., Ariely, D., & West, P. (2006). Path dependent preferences: The role of early experience and biased searching preference development. *Organizational Behavior and Human Decision Processes, 101*(2), 215–229. doi:10.1016/j.obhdp.2006.04.002

Hofstede, G. (1980). *Culture's Consequences: International differences in Work-related Values*. Sage Publications.

Hofstede, G., Hofstede, J. G., & Minkov, M. (2010). *Cultures and organizations-intercultural cooperation and its importance for survival* (3rd ed.). McGraw Hill.

House, R. J., Hanges, P. J., Javidan, M., Dorfman, P. W., & Gupta, V. (2004). *Culture, Leadership and Organisations – The GLOBE study of 62 societies*. Sage Publications.

Inglehart, R. (1988). The Renaissance of Political Culture. *The American Political Science Review, 82*(4), 1028–1034. doi:10.2307/1961756

Kongsamut, P., Sergio, R., & Xie, D. (1997) Beyond Balanced Growth, NBER Working Paper W6159.

Kostis, P. C., Kafka, K. I., & Petrakis, P. E. (2018). Cultural Change and Innovation Performance. *Journal of Business Research, 88*(July), 306–313. doi:10.1016/j.jbusres.2017.12.010

Levine, R., Loayza, N., & Thorsten, B. (2000). Financial Intermediation and Growth: Causality and Causes. *Journal of Monetary Economics, 46*(1), 31–77. doi:10.1016/S0304-3932(00)00017-9

Loasby, B. J. (2001). Cognition, Imagination and Institutions in Demand Creation. *Journal of Evolutionary Economics, 11*(1), 7–21. doi:10.1007/PL00003857

Lucas, R. Jr. (1988). On the Mechanics of Economic Development. *Journal of Monetary Economics, 22*(1), 3–42. doi:10.1016/0304-3932(88)90168-7

Myrdal, G. (1968). *Asian Drama: An Inquiry into the Poverty of Nations*. Twentieth Century Fund.

Norris, P., & Inglehart, R. (2019). *Cultural Backlash: Trump, Brexit, and Authoritarian Populism*. Cambridge University Press., doi:10.1017/9781108595841

North, D. C. (1990). *Institutions, institutional change and economic performance*. Cambridge University Press. doi:10.1017/CBO9780511808678

Pareto, V. (1895). La Leggedella Domanda. *GiornaleDegliEconomisti, 10*(6), 59–68.

Pinderhughes, E. (1983). Empowerment for our clients and for ourselves. Social Casework. *The Journal of Contemporary Social Work, 64*(6), 331–338.

Polanyi, K. (1975). *The Great Transformation*. Rinehart. (Original work published 1944)

Popper, K. (1945). *The open society and its enemies* (Vol. 1). Routledge.

Rodrik, D. (2015). *Economics Rules: The Rights and Wrongs of the Dismal Science*. W.W. Norton and Company.

Rogers, A. R. (1988). Does Biology Constrain Culture? *American Anthropologist, 90*(4), 819–831. doi:10.1525/aa.1988.90.4.02a00030

Romer, P. (1990). Endogenous Technological Change. *Journal of Political Economy, 98*(5, Part 2), 71–102. doi:10.1086/261725

Roth, A. E. (2013). In 100 Years. In I. Palacios-Huerta (Ed.), *In 100 Years: Leading Economists Predict the Future* (pp. 109–119). MIT Press.

Sachs, J. D., & Malaney, P. (2002). The Economic and Social Burden or Malaria. *Nature, 415*(6872), 680–685. doi:10.1038/415680a PMID:11832956

Sachs, J. D., Mellinger, A. D., & Gallup, J. L. (2001). The Geography of Poverty and Wealth. *Scientific American*, (March), 71–74. PMID:11234509

Sankey, H. (2012). Scepticism, relativism and the argument from the criterion. *Studies in History and Philosophy of Science, 43*(1), 182–190. doi:10.1016/j.shpsa.2011.12.026 PMID:22326087

Schumpeter, J. A. (1921). *The Theory of Economic Development*. Harvard University Press.

Schumpeter, J. A. (1939). *Business Cycles, A Theoretical, Historical and Statistical Analysis of capitalist Process*. McGraw- Hill.

Smolin, L. (2009). *"Time and Symmetry in Models of Economic Markets," Mss., Feb. Smolin L. (2013) Time Reborn*. Houghton, Mifflin, Harcourt.

Stern, N. (2007). *The Economics of Climate Change.The Stern Review*. Cambridge University Press. doi:10.1017/CBO9780511817434

Van den Bergh Jeroen, C. J. M., & Gowdy, G. M. (2009). A Group Selection Perspective on Economic Behavior, Institutions and Organizations. *Journal of Economic Behavior and Organization, Elsevier, 72*(1), 1–20. doi:10.1016/j.jebo.2009.04.017

Way, B. M., & Lieberman, M. D. (2010). Is there a genetic contribution to cultural differences? Collectivism, individualism, and genetic markers of social sensitivity. *Social Cognitive and Affective Neuroscience, 5*(2-3), 203–211. doi:10.1093can/nsq059 PMID:20592043

Williamson, C. R., & Mathers, R. L. (2011). Economic Freedom, Culture, and Growth. *Public Choice, 148*(3-4), 313–335. doi:10.100711127-010-9656-z

Yew-Kwang, Ng. (1986). *Mesoeconomics: A Micro - Macro Analysis*. St. Martin's Press.

KEY TERMS AND DEFINITIONS

Cultural Background: Cultural background incorporates all beliefs, values, stereotypes, and rules, characterizing the members of a society and differentiating it from other societies.

Institutions: Institutions are the rules of a society and economy. The basic categorization is political, economic, and social institutions.

Mesoeconomics: Mesoeconomics is the natural link between microeconomic and macroeconomic analysis, since the rules of microeconomic analysis, together with the institutions, essentially lead to macroeconomic results.

Metaeconomics: Metaeconomics take into account even more profound features of economies that affect their operation with a focus on the role of human behavior. Metaeconomics is the humanization of economics. They include data from moral philosophy, psychology, anthropology, and sociology, which go beyond the goal of rationality and maximizing profit.

Chapter 2
New Institutional Economics and Economic Development:
A Smithian Critique

Manolis Manioudis
University of Crete, Greece & Institute of Commerce and Entrepreneurship (IN.EM.Y. of ESEE), Greece

Giorgos Meramveliotakis
Neapolis University Pafos, Greece

ABSTRACT

In recent years, the concept of "institutions" has become central in scientific and political discourse. This reflects an increasing awareness of the role of institutions in the functioning of economies and in economic development more generally. Many of the catchphrases articulated within new institutional economics such as "institutions," "organisations," "transaction costs," "property rights," and "contracts" have become very common in orthodox economics discourse. This development is intellectually stimulating and interesting because it raises some fundamental issues with regard to the role and functioning of institutions. These concepts are seated on Smith's idea of the "harmony of interests." However, Smith sees power as dominant in the formation of institutional framework. This chapter aims to provide a Smithian critique based on the notion of power, arguing that the formation of institutions and institutional framework cannot be considered apart from the intrinsic power relations which are vested in society.

INTRODUCTION

In recent years the concept of "institutions" has become central in scientific and political discourse. This reflects an increasing awareness of the role of institutions in the functioning of (market and non-market) economies and in economic development more generally. For instance, the International Monetary Fund (IMF) puts great emphasis on reforming corporate governance and financial institutions as a response to

DOI: 10.4018/978-1-7998-4933-9.ch002

economic crises. Accordingly, the poor economic performance of developing countries is conventionally explained in terms of the lack of a clearly defined and secure institutional framework. This is because, according to the mainstream idea, in the absence of an appropriate guarantee for the fruits of their sacrifices, people would not take the initiative to invest, whatever the policies regarding macroeconomic balances, trade and industrial regulations may be. This emphasis on institutions raises the need for a scientific theorisation of the issues involved, while also bringing to the fore some fundamental questions with regard to the origin and nature of different institutions, and to their desirability or otherwise, thus also raising the question of institutional change. Within economics, new institutional economics, the trend in economics that deals with the origin and evolution of (mainly capitalist) institutions within the mainstream tradition, has become well established. Many of the catchphrases articulated within new institutional economics such as "institutions", "organisations", "transaction costs", "property rights" and "contracts", have become very common in orthodox economics discourse. This development is intellectually stimulating and interesting because it raises some fundamental issues with regard to the role and functioning of institutions.

In November 2009, Oliver Williamson was awarded the Nobel prize in economics.1 This follows the award to Ronald Coase in 1991 and to Douglass North in 1993. Between them, Coase, Williamson and North, are the founders and most important representatives of new institutional economics. This third Nobel prize is symbolic of the continuing vitality of the new institutionalist research program within, and around the borders of, mainstream economics as well as the occasional idiosyncrasy of the Nobel awards.

New institutional economics conceives society as a network of voluntary contractual relations and analyses the economy in particular in terms of contractual agreements among atomised individuals. In particular, the emergence and evolution of institutions and institutional framework are elucidated on the grounds of the deliberate and voluntary personal decisions taken by individuals. Hence, institutional formation is explained in terms of voluntary contractual agreements based on the transaction costs minimisation principle. Subsequently, economic development and growth become an issue of individual's action to choose these institutions that generates efficiency. Within New institutional Economics, economic development and growth depend on the choice made by individuals to implement the favourable institutional framework. Based on the neoclassical microfoundations, new institutionalists construct and erect their macro-institutional theory for analysing economic development and growth. However, in such a context where social institutions emerge as a result of a transaction cost minimisation process at the individual level, the question of power and conflict simply does not arise.

Under these theoretical givens, the underlying assumption is that society embodies a fundamental level of "harmony of interests" that always eventually leads to beneficial "mutual agreements" between the contracted parties leading to new institutional formations. Although the idea of "harmony of interests" can be traced back to Smith's (1986 [1776]) work, and implies that if people understand their own individual interests correctly they will see that they are not incompatible with those of others, however Smith, himself, explicitly posits the notion of power as the main explanandum in the formation of institutions and institutional framework. Our aim is to provide a Smithian critique based on the notion of power, arguing that the formation of institutions and institutional framework cannot be considered apart from the intrinsic power relations which are vested in society. Thus, the issues of power and power relations must become sine qua non conditions for a comprehensive analysis of institutional arrangements.

Thus, in what follows we firstly attempt to offer a definitional context of the notions, concepts and ideas found in New Institutional Economics. Then, we pinpoint the neoclassical micro foundations whereas new institutionalists are mostly rested on. Based on these neoclassical micro foundations,

New Institutional Economics try to erect the macro theory of economic growth and development. The common parlance within New Institutional Economics is that both the growth and the development are determined by the existed institutional framework. Thus, institutional emergence is a pivotal issue for the economic growth and subsequently an analysis of institutional emergence should be included in theory of development and growth.

BACKGROUND

Definitions and Concepts

New institutional economics as a body of theory emerged in the 1970's and 1980's, although its roots lie further back in time. It could be argued that New Institutional Economics should be considered as an umbrella concept for a research programme with some quite distinct theoretical approaches. This includes: property rights theory (Armen Alchain, Harold Demserz, Yoram Barzel, Daron Acemoglou), transaction cost economics (Ronald Coase, Oliver Williamson), institutional economic history (Douglass North), common law (Richard Posner) and game theoretical approaches to institutions (Andrew Schotter, Jack Hirshleifer). It should be stressed that New Institutional Economics is often labeled as "Neo-Institutional Economic". According to Eggertsson (1990) the difference is defined as one of adherence or non-adherence to the full rationality concept of neoclassical economics, where New Institutional Economics subscribes to the full rationality concept and Neo-Institutionalism does not. Since we will return to this issue, we make explicit that in the definition of New Institutional Economics used here, both of the schools of thought Eggertsson describes and separates are included.

The origins of the New Institutional Economics can be traced back to Coases' (1937) analysis of the ontology of the firm. Coase, the originator of transaction cost theory, posits a fundamental question: why do firms and other no-market organisations exist in the first place? Although neoclassical economics emphatically stresses the role of the market and the price mechanism, the role of demand (households) and the role of supply (firms), the origins of the latter has never being a case of interest within the theoretical model of neoclassical economics. The answer to the question posed by Coase, which is the stepping stone for transaction cost economics within New Institutional Economics is that the firm exists since there is a cost of using the price mechanism. The "discovery" of transaction costs is Coase's enduring legacy to New Institutional Economics.

The term "new institutional economics" was coined by Oliver Williamson (1975) in his ambitious attempt to provide a grand theory of the evolution of economic institutions of capitalism. Williamson (1975; 1985) aims to analyse and explain both the origins of the factory system (i.e. capitalist firm) and the evolution of modern corporation (the so-called M-form and the U-form of organisation) in terms of transaction cost minimisation, incentive problems and the efficiency principle.

Within New Institutional Economics, Douglass North provides the most coherent and analytical conceptual definitional context of the fundamental terms used. To the most general level, the very existence of institutions is justified on the grounds of the minimisation of uncertainty and of shaping the human interaction. According to North (1990, 3-4) "institutions are the rules of the game in society or, more formally, are the humanly devised constraints that shape human interaction … in the jargon of the economist, institutions define and limit the set of choices of individuals. Institutional constraints include both what individuals are prohibited from doing and sometimes, under what conditions some individuals are permitted to undertake certain activities", otherwise, "in the absence of constraints we exist in a Hobbesian jungle and civilization is impossible" (p. 203).

Then, North (1990, 4-5), proceeds to provide a clear demarcation between the notions of institutions and organisations. The former constitutes the "rules of the game" while the latter are "the players of the game". Hence, for North it is exactly the interaction between the institutions and organisations that shapes and directs the institutional evolution of an economy. Thus, for North the institutional framework represents the "constitutive rules" of the game where various organisations interact. Institutions are broader in scope and have wider sets of institutional arrangements than those of organisations. Institutions should be seen as the field or the social environment in which organisations function. The latter are best seen as nested within and shaped by wider institutional arrangements.

Regarding the institutions themselves, North makes a further distinction between the formal and informal institutions. The former constitutes the society's material basis (property rights, law and the state), while the latter are cognitive characteristics that considerable form and shape the everyday life (habits, culture, incentives, etc.). An additional demarcation is between "hard" and "soft" institutions. The former include the formal rules backed by formal law of the political system, while the latter are informal rules, norms practices, conventions backed informal social sanctions. According to North the most significant institutional factors are often informal.

The bottom line is institutions are humanly devised constraints that shape the behaviour of individuals. They provide the social framework within which individuals organise themselves for purposeful activities. Institutions mediate between the socio-economic structure, socio-political culture and individuals. Thus, politics is constructed in form of institutional structure, since institutions are the vehicles through which the practice of politics are transmitted.

New Institutional Economics study institutions in relation to individual behaviour, at the micro level and then proceeds to the analysis of the societal structure at the macro level. In what follows, we firstly outline the neoclassical microfoundations of New Institutional Economics and then we analyse how these microfoundations are untilised by new institutionalists at the macro level for the analysis of economic development and growth.

The Neoclassical Microfoundations of New Institutional Economics.

New institutional economics does not break fundamentally from neoclassical economics. To the contrary, new institutional economics is a research program which is developed within and around the dominant neoclassical paradigm. In this vein, institutions are considered to be the creation of rational individuals, who decides on the basis of calculation of cost-benefits associated with alternatives. As such, the argument goes, institutions provide the incentive structure which affect the cost-benefit (i.e. the relative prices) and hence shape behaviour and decisions of the rational individuals.

More specifically, according to North (1995, 19), the new institutionalist approach "begins with the scarcity and hence competition postulate, it views economics as a theory of choice subject to constraints, it employs price theory as an essential part of the analysis of institutions and it sees changes in relative prices as a major force inducing change in institutions".2 These are the basic ingredients of the marginalist choice–theoretic approach and the static equilibrium theory of price (Coase 1988). As Richter (2005, 171) aptly exemplifies "the foundation stones of the NIE [New Institutional Economics] are the same as those of neoclassical economics: methodological individualism and individual rational choice given a set of constraints".

Using the Lacatosian (1970) terminology of "hard core" and "protective belt" as the essential parts of research programs,3 new institutional economics retains the "hard core" of neoclassical economics i.e. maximising behaviour, market equilibrium, and stable preferences. On the other hand, there is a modification in the "protective belt" in the form of information and transaction costs making property rights indispensable for the analysis of economic organisations.

However, as already indicated, new institutional economics does not attempt to overturn or replace neoclassical theory, but, rather, serves as "complementary to … conventional analysis" (Williamson 1975, 1). This means that new institutional economics builds on, modifies and extends neoclassical theory to permit it to come to grips and deal with institutions heretofore beyond its scope. In this vein, new institutional economics adds institutions as a critical constraint and analyses the role of transaction costs in the emergence and development of institutions and property rights. In this direction, new institutionalists take a step away from neoclassical economics by modifying the instrumental rationality assumption of neoclassical theory through the adoption of Simon's (1961 [1947]) concept of bounded rationality and Williamson's (1975; 1985) concept of opportunism. This is how Williamson (1975, 7) delineates the principal differences between neoclassical theory and his approach: "I expressly introduce the notion of opportunism and am interested in the ways that opportunistic behavior is influenced by economic organization and … I emphasize that it is not uncertainty or small numbers, individually and together, that occasion market failure but it is rather the joining of these factors with bounded rationality on the one hand and opportunism on the other that gives rise to exchange difficulties".

Thus, Furubotn and Richter (1998, 435-436) conclude that the new institutional economics is an amalgam of a critique of standard neoclassical economics based on the absence of transactions costs, and an apparent move towards greater realism through a move towards a more empirically relevant model. This is achieved primarily by mellowing the concept of a fully rational "economic man", acting with full knowledge and certainty, into a concept of a "boundedly rational" individual acting upon limited knowledge. As Simon (1991, 27) remarks, "the new institutional economics is wholly compatible with and conservative of neoclassical theory".

In this vein, Coase (1937) and Williamson (1985) analyse the origins of the capitalist firm as the result of mutual agreements between entrepreneurs and labourers aiming at minimising transaction costs. Similarly, Demsetz (1967) and Alchian and Demsetz (1973) argue that the emergence of private property is a result of a voluntary agreement between the members of the community. North and Thomas (1971; 1973) and Barzel (1997), on the other hand, explain the rise of serfdom in Western Europe and analyse the feudal relations between tenants and landlords respectively on the basis of voluntary individual contractual agreements. The common element in all these accounts is the perception of the establishment and evolution of institutional rules as the result of the common will and action of separate individuals.

New Institutional Economics and Economic Development

Based on the neoclassical microfoundations, new institutionalists construct and erect their macro-institutional theory for analysing economic development and growth. This is how methodologically New Institutional Economics attempt to bridge the gap between the micro and macro level of analysis, by providing a theoretical basis for explaining how and why economic systems and institutions evolve and change over time. In this context, institutions and organisations have a decisive explanatory value in the account of the historical evolution of economies and societies. In other words, new institutionalists stress the importance of the institutional setting within which economic activity takes place.

The broader claims of New Institutional Economics rests on the view that economic development and growth depends upon the existence of a favorable institutional environment, while the latter is the one that facilitates economic growth. Particularly, within New Institutional Economics development is seen as merely the summation of economic growth plus the institutional framework.

In New Institutional Economics the main focus in explaining economic growth or decline is turned towards the question of how well the state performs its functions and on the fact that not all property rights can be defined in contract. If property rights are well-defined (by the law), easily enforced (by the state) and easily measurable (in a contract) then there is a minimisation of market exchanges cost and subsequently the gains from trade will be realised. This refers to the micro-level of analysis, where the transition to the macro-level is achieved through a merely aggregation of the constitutive parts. Thus, as the argument goes, the key to the economic growth is therefore to make these "costs of exchange" as low as possible. The society's development and growth, in terms of trade and distribution, is dependent upon its specific property rights structure.

Applied the aforementioned rationale into economic history, new institutionalists argue that economic development is positively strongly correlated with the existence and function of private property rights, since societies which are primarily based on communal property were backward ones or societies based on planned economy were underdeveloped.

In the 1973 book, North & Thomas specify the essential prerequisites for economic growth in the establishment of "efficient property rights". According to authors, the rise of the Western World, i.e. the transition from feudalism to capitalism, can only be grounded in a thorough analysis of the institutionalised property rights. The historical evolution of the economic systems, slavery, feaudalism, capitalism, is a considered to be a journey towards to the most "efficient property rights". Furthermore, North and Thomas (1973) claim to trace the reasons for the divergent paths of growth in Europe in the success or failure to transform the economy into a basis for an efficient and prosperous society of well-defined property rights and a well-functioning state.

In his earlier work, North (1990) re-state the aforementioned rationale, albeit in a slightly different fashion. He argues that the reason why human beings create and establish institutions is to reduce the uncertainty, to minimise transaction costs in order to capture the full benefits of trade. And it is exactly these institutions, which minimise the transaction costs (i.e. "efficient institutions"), that are the locomotives of economic growth. On the other hand, the lack of them or the presence of "inefficient institutions" are the keys to explain the economic decline and stagnation.

Also important in North's theoretical development is a theory of the state since the latter is the institution that is "responsible for the efficiency of the property rights structure, which causes growth or stagnation or economic decline" (1981, 17). Thus, state play s significant role in institutionalised "efficient property rights", that are considered to be the key determinants of economic growth and development. Given the aforementioned, the absence of economic growth now can be easily explained in terms of policy. In North's (1994, 361) own words "it is polity that defines and enforces property rights and in consequence it is not surprising that efficient markets are so exceptional".

But then immediately an important question arises. What prevents individuals in an underdeveloped society, to change the "rules of the game" and to establish more "efficient" institutions? Here, North (1990) utilises the notion of path dependence (i.e. history matters) in order to explain the developmental divergence commonly observed between different societies. In a nutshell, North argues that some societies are underdeveloped because of their historical peculiarities. Actually, North provides a rather cliché story of how past knowledge, culture and ideology influences the present. In this context, the informal constraints and the mental models inherent in individuals and societies are the main reasons for "path dependence". Thus, "culture", "ideology", "custom", "knowledge" are served as the main explanatory variables not only to explain divergences in economic development but mainly to analyse why some societies are stuck to an "inefficient path".

However North's theory of "path dependence" cannot sufficiently explain cases where although there are not significant differences in culture, custom and history one, however, can observe considerable divergence in development. For instance, the difference between the North and South Korea, which despite a similar culture developed extremely differently.

Acemoglu and Robinson (2012) argue, similar to North, that the most important factor for a nation's prosperity is its institutional structure. The two authors strive to provide a coherent and valid answer to the fundament economic question why some countries are rich while others are poor. The answer that most convention economic growth theories provide to this question is that rich countries are the countries that adopt growth enhancing economic policies. However this answer in fact does not explain why some countries adopt such policies while others do not.

From the outset, Acemoglu and Robinson (2012) declare that they are going to analyse what are the political constraints that prevent the market forces for being used for economic growth. Particularly is the divergent paths of institutions that produce the divergence in development. In this vein, in the one extreme the authors place the so-called extractive institutions, i.e. institutions that they are designed to extract from the many for the benefit of the few. Extractive are those institutions that forced people to work on behalf of the elite at low wages and enable the elite to capture all of the spoils of the economic activity. These extractive institutions do not exist in a social vacuum, but they are supported by extractive political institutions. These, in turn, are institutions that concentrate power on the behalf of the elites without any sort of checks and enable them to use repression to get their way.

At the other extreme, the authors place the so-called inclusive institutions. Rather than extract, these institutions are trying to include more people under their umbrella. In particular, inclusive institutions provide secured property rights, allow free trade and create a market economy where a broad cross-section of society could participate on fairly level playing field. Moreover, this kind of institutions introduce a justice system, thus enable individuals to write contracts. Those are the hallmarks of inclusive economic institutions, however similar to extractive institutions, inclusive do not exist in a social vacuum. They have to be supported, in order to be credible, by the so-called inclusive political institutions. So, there is polar opposite of the extractive political institutions, inclusive political institutions create a more equal distribution of power, sometimes refer to as pluralism (i.e. political power being widely distributed), and they do not let anybody have complete, absolute control of the political power that rests with the state. At some level, the pluralism that inclusive political institutions embed is the right opposite of the idea of absolutism, i.e. political power in concentrated on one or on few individuals (e.g. kings and monarchs).

For the authors the most essential characteristics of inclusive institutions is that they create incentives for individuals to invest, to increase productivity, to innovate, to trade and generate economic growth. Thus, inclusive institutions are for the authors pretty much the only way to generate sustained economic growth. The latter is only accomplished when there is a societal transition from extractive institutions to inclusive institutions. So the question that arises is why some societies remain within extractive institutions, while others broke away from extractive institutions towards inclusive institutions? The answer is dependent on the way that each different society resolves the inherited social conflict. If conflict gets resolved in favor of those who already have power the extractive economic and political institutions will get strengthened, but when it does get resolved in favor of those revolting or protesting against those extractive institutions, there will be some movements away from these institutions. As this conflict occurs and is resolved in different ways, societies will embark on a path of change. How exactly this conflict will be resolved will push these societies in different directions.

Although, Acemoglu and Robinson (2012) enrich the theory of New Institutional Economics, by using the notions of power and conflict, they use them as universal, reified, and transhistorical concepts. Moreover, they do not offer any explanation of the sources of political power, how this power come into existence in the first place.

So, it could be fairly argued that what is omitted from the accounts of the new institutionalists, is that institutions are often imposed rather than chosen. Thus, the emergence and establishment of institutions is determined by the inherited power of classes or groups subject to the institution. Subsequently, any institutional theory of development requires to take into account the structural power relations and the balance of power existed in any given society. This leads us to the basic questions, problems and conceptions of the classical political economy and in particular Adam Smith

Institutions and Power: A Smithian Perspective

Each social formation (i.e. feudalism, capitalism etc.) comprises a level of systemic power and forms a certain nexus of power relations between classes, groups and individuals. In this perspective, social relations embody power relations expressed as a structure of domination and subordination that is never static but always subject to contestation and struggle. Thus, if power is an intrinsic fact of social life built in the very way in which production, the first act of social existence is carried out, then the exercise of power should be part and parcel of the process of establishing institutions and institutional framework. History is replete with examples of the process whereby the form of institutions and property rights are altered through the exercise of power. The enclosure movement of the sixteenth and seventeenth centuries in the European, and especially English, landscape constitutes a prominent example.

For Adam Smith the notion of power, which is embedded in social relations, serves as the main explanadum for the emergence and evolution of institutional settings and of the institutional framework. More specifically Smith discerns four types of power; wealth power, monopoly power, employer power and political power that form the social relations in capitalism. Thus for Smith power is an integral component of social formation, hence the pursuit and exercise of power by individuals, organisations, classes and governments should be conceived as an essential part in the analysis of institutions.

Smith arrays a variety of historical instances in which the established institutional framework was favourable to some specific groups of people (merchants, manufacturers and craftsmen), but not to common people. For instance, the famous institution of apprenticeship in his times, which had firstly been the product of a bye-law of many individual corporations, became later the "general and publick law of all trades carried on in market towns" (Smith [1776] 1976, 137). For Smith, this labour institution was enacted to endorse corporations' sole aim: "to keep the market always under stocked" (p. 141).

Generally, Smith had the heretic view that: "whenever the law has attempted to regulate the wages of workmen, it has always been rather to lower them than to raise them" (p. 152) and, more explicitly, "it is everywhere much easier for a wealthy merchant to obtain the privilege of trading in a town corporate, than for a poor artificer to obtain that of working in it" (p. 152). Smith believes that when the legislature attempts to regulate the differences between masters and their workmen, "its counselors are always the masters" (p. 157). Smith elaborates historical evidence to 'denude' these counsels. As an example, the famous bounty on foreign corn in 1688 was a typical example of such interdependence. His comment is of intense historical interest: *the country gentlemen, who then composed a still greater part than they do at present, had felt that the money price of corn was failing [...] But the government of King William was not fully settled. It was in no condition to refuse anything to the country gentlemen, from whom it was at that very time soliciting the first establishment of the annual land tax (p. 215).*

Essentially, therefore, Smith's understanding shows that the institutional (legal) framework of any form of societal organisation is decisively determined by the existed power relations. For him, the distribution of property in any society, determines its institutions and the type of political administration. Besides, according to Smith (p. 710), "The acquisition of valuable and extensive property [...] necessarily requires the establishment of civil government", since "where there is no property, or at least none that exceeds the value of two or three days labour, civil government is not so necessary". According to Smith, the inequality of fortune, which followed the domestication of animals during the pastoral stage of economic development, altered the relations of both power and dependence. This variance is crystallised in the formation of institutions which follow the unequal distribution of property. As such property, power and institutions are linearly interrelated. Smith associates the inequality of fortune with the rise of regular government: *The appropriation of herds and flocks which introduced an inequality of fortune was that which first gave rise to regular government. Till there be property there can be no government, the very end of which is to secure wealth and defend the rich from the poor (Smith [1762-1763] 1978, 404).*

Apart from this one-sided influence, Smith seems to believe that economic advancement is clearly connected with institutional transformation. He elaborates the dialectical relation between the function of economic forces and the type of political administration. For instance, he notes that, "In the end of the fifteenth and beginning of the sixteenth century, the greater part of Europe was approaching towards a more settled form of government than it had enjoyed for several ages before. The increase of security would naturally increase industry and improvement" (Smith [1776] 1996, 199). Smith associates the 'security' of economic transactions with material advancement. He believes that security is directly influenced by the state of economic development and observes that the evident insecurity in Turkey, Indostan, and most other governments of Asia, is related to the violence of feudal government (p. 285).4 Smith ([1766] 1978, 414) sketches out this scheme early in his Lectures where he notes that: *A Turkish bashaw or other inferior officer is decisive judge of everything, and is as absolute in his own jurisdiction as the signior. Life and fortune are altogether precarious, when they thus depend on the caprice of the lowest magistrate. A more miserable and oppressive government cannot be imagined.*

For instance, in feudal times, the frequency of treasure-trove, elevates the evident conditions of insecurity ([1776] 1996, 908). Smith uses political history in order to illustrate this view. According to him: *In the disorderly state of England under the Plantagenets, who governed it from about the middle of the twelfth, till towards the end of the fifteenth century, one district might be in plenty, while another at no great distance, by having its crop destroyed either by some accidents of the seasons, or by the incursion of some neighboring baron, might be suffering all the horrors of the famine (p. 204).*

In contrast, under the vigorous administration of the Tudors, who governed England during the latter part of the fifteenth and through the whole of the sixteenth century, when the economic improvement of England was forging ahead, no baron nor lord was powerful enough to rupture the public security (p. 204).

Evidently, for Smith, the material progress of a given societal organisation influences its political administration and its institutional framework. However, a deeper reading of this analysis suffices to show that in many (historical) instances institutional backwardness hinders the course of economic development. For Smith, a tolerable security is the crucial pre-condition for every man "to employ whatever stock he can command in procuring either present enjoyment or future profit" (p. 285). Historically, England's relatively rapid rate of growth is related to the general sense of safety enjoyed by her inhabitants. His reference is illustrious of this sense: "The security which the laws in Great Britain give to every man that he shall enjoy the fruits of his own labour, is alone sufficient to make any country flourish [...] and this security was perfected by the revolution" (p. 540). It is indicative that in his discussion concerning feudalism, he notices that anarchy and insecurity of property made the European economy go back to the age of agriculture and this regression was the origin of both poverty and barbarism.

Many authors have challenged the pure material character of Smith's theory of institutions (see inter alia: Kim 2009; 2012, Haakonssen 1981; 1982). These authors insist that institutions are crucial in determining economic progress since they ensure safety and liberty and indemnify 'the natural progress of things'. They observe that there are many instances where an institutional change is prior to any variation in the economic structure. However, despite this interesting view, a closer scrutiny of Smith's theory of institutions is sufficient to show that economic advancement and progress are the primal causes of institutional change. This view is astonishingly manifested in the early stages of economic development since "among savage and barbarous nations the natural progress of law and government is still slower than the natural progress of arts, after law and government have been so far established" (Smith [1776] 1976, 565). Despite the fact that political (institutional) changes may affect the form of economic advancement, the rule works primarily in the opposite direction since the economic element is regarded as the 'hard core' of societal organisation. Evidently, this analytical confusion owes its persistence in Smith's intrinsic (epistemic) contradiction, first pointed out by Marx: that of 'the esoteric and the exoteric part of his work' which is connected with Smith's a theoretical understanding of empirical reality (Marx [1863] 1951, 166). Substantially, changes in the superstructure (political administration) are more transparent than those in the economic structure. Such an empirical ascertainment impelled Smith to present many economic variations as affected by political administration. However, the core of his analysis is that the economic structure of social reality is the cornerstone of every other turn in the superstructure level. Smith's analysis (on this methodological issue) was much more explicit in his early works. For instance, in his Lectures Rhetoric and Belles Letters, he declares that: *Opulence and Commerce commonly precede the improvement of arts and refinement of every sort [...] Wherever the inhabitants of a city are rich and opulent, where they enjoy the necessaries and conveniences of life in ease and security, there the arts will be cultivated, and refinement of manners a never-failing attendant (Smith 1985, 137).*

In this Smithian work, the increasingly important and complex nature of property relations provides the key to the emergence of institutions – such as justice – which are dedicated to protect the property of the rich from the rapacious poor. Substantially, for Smith, as for most Scottish authors, laws and legal institutions are an inherent part of the economic structures of a given society and have to be understood as a structural element of societal analysis. It is indicative that in his early Lectures Smith ([1766] 1978, 405) notes that: *The appropriation of herds and flocks, which introduced an inequality of fortune, was that which gave rise to regular government. Till there be property there can be no government, the very end of which is to secure wealth, and to defend the rich from the poor.5*

Luban (2012, 276) illustrates the material character of Smith's analysis by noting that he "was an adherent of the 'four stages' theory of historical development, in which changes in the prevalent mode of subsistence (from hunting to pastoral to agricultural to commercial societies) correspond to changes in sociopolitical organisation". This motif was common among Scottish scholars and differentiates their approach to that of New Institutional Economics.

FUTURE RESEARCH DIRECTIONS

Future research may use the analysis of the classical political economy to delineate the role of institutions in promoting economic development. Furthermore, New Institutional Economics should be critically assessed through the notion of the relations of power in order to identify the course of economic development and growth. A new research program should access how relations of power (ideological, economic, political etc.) influence the course of societal transactions.

CONCLUSION

The inability of neoclassical economics to predict and prevent the financial crisis of 2008 explicitly questions the validity of mainstream economic theory in analysing and prescribing for our economy. The financial meltdown and the depression that followed reveal the constitutional role of institutions, as the rules of the game. New institutional economics highlight the importance of institutional framework in promoting economic growth and development. In this vein, the emergence and evolution of institutions are explained exclusively in terms of cost and efficiency considerations (i.e. minimisation of transaction costs). As such, the new institutional theory provides an analytical framework that fails to incorporate in a comprehensive manner any reference to social relations, power and conflict. Economic development and growth are merely analysed in terms of favorable institutional framework, which is emerged by individuals' reaction to transaction cost minimisation. According to Smith (alongside with other classical political economists, including John Stuart Mill and Karl Marx) institutions involve and represent social relations. The latter reflect the conflictual and antagonistic interests either at the individual level or between social groups and classes. Granted this, Smith moves on to reveal and analyse the underlying power relations that are intrinsic in any institutional formation. Thus, rather being explained in terms of cost and efficiency considerations, the emergence and evolution of institutions are explained via the systemic power relations which are vested in society. Thus, any theoretical attempt to analyse economic growth and development should take into account the underlined power relations and structural conflict existed in any given society. This chapter synopsises and criticises the main tenets of new institutional economics by contrasting Smith's views with regard to how institutions are come to existence and subsequently determine economic growth. As such, a return to the basic questions, problems and conceptions of the classical political economy of the Scottish Enlightenment and in particular Adam Smith may lead us to a better understanding of institutional emergence and evolution.

REFERENCES

Acemoglu, D., & Robinson, J. (2012). *Why Nations Fail: The Origins of Power, Prosperity, and Poverty*. Crown Publishers.

Alchian, A., & Demsetz, H. (1972). Production, Information Costs and Economic Organization. *The American Economic Review*, *62*(5), 777–795.

Alchian, A., & Demsetz, H. (1973). The Property Right Paradigm. *The Journal of Economic History*, *33*(1), 16–27. doi:10.1017/S0022050700076403

Barzel, Y. (1997). *Economic Analysis of Property Rights*. Cambridge University Press. doi:10.1017/CBO9780511609398

Carey, H. (1868). *The Harmony of Interests: Agricultural, Manufacturing and Commercial*. Industrial Publisher.

Coase, R. (1937). The Nature of the Firm. *Economica*, *4*(4), 86–405.

Coase, R. (1988). *The Firm, the Market and the Law*. University of Chicago Press.

Demsetz, H. (1967). Toward a Theory of Property Rights. *The American Economic Review*, *57*(2), 347–359.

Eggertsson, T. (1990). *Economic Behaviour and Institutions*. Cambridge University Press. doi:10.1017/CBO9780511609404

Furubotn, E., & Richter, R. (1998). *Institutions and Economic Theory: The Contribution of the New Institutional Economics*. The University of Michigan Press.

Haakonssen, K. (1981). *The Science of a Legislator: The Natural Jurisprudence of David Hume and Adam Smith*. Cambridge University Press. doi:10.1017/CBO9780511628276

Haakonssen, K. (1982). What might properly be called natural jurisprudence? In R. Campbell & A. Skinner (Eds.), *The Origin and Nature of the Scottish Enlightment* (pp. 205–225). John Donald.

Harris & Lewis. (Eds.). (1995). The New Institutional Economics and Third World Development. London: Routledge.

Kim, K. (2009). Adam Smith's theory of economic history and economic development. *European Journal of the History of Economic Thought*, *16*(1), 41–64. doi:10.1080/09672560802707407

Kim, K. (2012). Adam Smith's 'History of Astronomy' and view of science. *Cambridge Journal of Economics*, *36*(1), 799–820. doi:10.1093/cje/bes001

Lakatos, I. (1970). Falsification and the methodology of scientific research programmes. In Criticism and the Growth of Knowledge. Cambridge: Cambridge University Press.

Luban, D. (2012). Adam Smith on Vanity, Domination, and History. *Modern Intellectual History*, *9*(2), 275–302. doi:10.1017/S1479244312000042

Marx, K. (1951). *Theories of Surplus Value*. Lawrence and Wishart. (Original work published 1863)

Marx, K. (1990). *Capital* (Vol. I). Penguin. (Original work published 1867)

Meramveliotakis, G. (2020). The Issue of Efficiency and the Role of State in New Institutional Economics: A Critical Perspective. *New Political Economy*.

North, D. (1981). *Structure and Change in Economic History*. W. W. Norton & Company, Inc.; doi:10.1080/13563467.2020.1721450

North, D. (1990). *Institutions, Institutional Change and Economic Performance*. Cambridge University Press. doi:10.1017/CBO9780511808678

North, D. (1994). Economic Performance Through Time. *The American Economic Review*, *84*(3), 359–368.

North, D. (1995). *The New Institutional Economics and Third World Development.* doi:10.4324/9780203444290.pt1

North, D. (2005). *Understanding the Process of Economic Change.* Princeton University Press. doi:10.1515/9781400829484

North, D., & Thomas, R. (1971). The Rise and Fall of the Manorial System: A Theoretical Model. *The Journal of Economic History, 31*(4), 777–803. doi:10.1017/S0022050700074623

North, D., & Thomas, R. (1973). *The Rise of the Western World-A New Economic History.* Cambridge University Press. doi:10.1017/CBO9780511819438

Richter, R. (2005). The New Institutional Economics: Its Start, its Meaning, its Prospects. *European Business Organization Law Review, 6*(2), 161–200. doi:10.1017/S1566752905001618

Simon, H. (1961). Administrative Behaviour. New York: Macmillan.

Simon, H. (1991). Organizations and Markets. *The Journal of Economic Perspectives, 5*(2), 25–44. doi:10.1257/jep.5.2.25

Smith, A. (1976). *An Inquiry into the Nature and Causes of the Wealth of Nations* (R. H. Campbell & A. S. Skinner, Eds.). Clarendon Press. (Original work published 1776)

Smith, A. (1978a). *Lectures on Jurisprudence (A)* (R. L. Meek, D. D. Raphael, & P. G. Stein, Eds.). Oxford University Press. (Original work published 1762-1763)

Smith, A. (1978b). *Lectures on Jurisprudence (B)* (R. L. Meek, D. D. Raphael, & P. G. Stein, Eds.). Oxford University Press. (Original work published 1766)

Smith, A. (1985). *Lectures on Rhetoric and Belles Lettres* (J. C. Bryce, Ed.). Liberty Fund.

Williamson, O. (1975). *Markets and Hierarchies: Analysis and Antitrust Implications.* Free Press.

Williamson, O. (1985). *The Economic Institutions of Capitalism.* Free Press.

ADDITIONAL READING

Elliott, J. E. (2000). Adam Smith's Conceptualisation of Power, Market and Politics. *Review of Social Economy, 58*(4), 429–454. doi:10.1080/00346760050204292

Hodgson, G. (2004). *The Evolution of Institutional Economics: Agency, Structure and Darwinism in American Institutionalism.* Routledge. doi:10.4324/9780203300350

Hodgson, G. (2006). What are Institutions. *Journal of Economic Issues, XL*(1), 1–25. doi:10.1080/00213624.2006.11506879

Marglin, S. (1974). What Do Bosses Do? The Origins and Functions of Hierarchy in Capitalist Production. *The Review of Radical Political Economics, 6*(2), 60–112. doi:10.1177/048661347400600206

Menard, C., & Shirley, M. (2008). *Handbook of New Institutional Economics*. Springer. doi:10.1007/978-3-540-69305-5

Milonakis, D., & Manioudis, M. (2020). Adam Smith's Wealth of Nations and the economic past: Setting the scene for economic history? *European Journal of the History of Economic Thought*.(forthcoming)

KEY TERMS AND DEFINITIONS

Institutions: Formal and informal devices that structure the everyday human interactions, the "rules of the game."

Natural Progress of Things: The course of societal and economic development which is promoted through liberty and market.

Organisations: A group of individuals bound by some common purpose, the "players of the game."

Power: The capacity to direct the actions of others or to influence the course of events.

Transaction Cost: In a broad sense, the cost that it is associated with the emergence and evolution of institutions and organisations. In a micro context, the cost of writing, enforcing and monitoring contracts.

ENDNOTES

1 Alongside Elinor Ostrom, a political scientist.

2 From the central behavioural postulate of individualistic rational maximisation, new institutional economics constructs an (ahistorical) framework centred on the importance of relative prices. These are the main economic incentives to which individuals respond, and it is this rational response to prices that gives the approach its predictive potential. As North (1990, 84) puts it "institutions change and fundamental changes in relative prices are the most important source of that change". It should be noted, however, that in addition to the role of relative prices, North (1981; 1990) recognises the importance of ideology, culture and norms as crucial factors in the explanation of institutions. This suggests a form of eclecticism and allows North to avoid an overreliance on the rationality postulate of the neoclassical school. For a critique of North's analysis see Meramveliotakis (2020).

3 According to Lacatos (1970) a research program is an ensemble consisting of a hard core and a protective belt. The hard core is composed of the fundamental presuppositions of the program. It defines the program and its elements are treated as irrefutable by the program's practitioners. Hence, to participate in the program is to accept and be guided by the program's hard core.

4 Smith ([1762-1763] 1978, 25) notes in his early *Lectures* that "At this day in Turky and the Moguls dominions every man almost has a treasure, and one of the last things he communicates to his heirs is the place where his treasure is to be found".

5 For instance Smith believes that the general usage of metals, as coins, had been an institution that emerged due to the economic advancement of western societies. More specifically he notes that "In the progress of industry, commercial nations have found it convenient to coin several different metals into money" (Smith [1776] 1976, 53).

Chapter 3
Institutions and Economic Policy

Paolo Ramazzotti
Università di Macerata, Italy

ABSTRACT

This chapter discusses the problems associated to an inadequate theory of economic policy. It begins by presenting the mainstream and heterodox approaches to policy. It contends that, according to the mainstream, policy must guarantee efficiency or, at the very least, consider it a key constraint, whereas according to heterodox economists, it may have a broader variety of goals. The latter's open system perspective implies that changes in the structure of the economy eventually feedback both on how people conceive of the economy and social welfare and on how the economy itself functions. The relevance of this issue, which is understated, emerges from the subsequent discussion of how neoliberal policies have changed the structure of the economy, the way people conceive of the economy, and even their voting behavior.

INTRODUCTION

In late 2008, Queen Elisabeth II asked economists at the London School of Economics an embarrassing question: why nobody saw the financial crisis coming. The question was embarrassing from two points of view. First, it pointed out that many leading economists actually failed to understand what was going on at the time. Second, although the Queen presumably was unaware that some economists actually saw the crisis coming (e.g. Keen 1995; Minsky 1984), her question prompted another question: why did most economists disregard what their colleagues were foreseeing?

Both questions should have led to a reassessment of the (neoliberal) theories and practices that had dominated most economies during the previous decades. Counterintuitively, this did not happen. Albeit with a few exceptions – the most authoritative is Posner (2009) - most economists and policymakers did not question their views of the economy. Indeed, the situation was aptly depicted as "the strange non-death of neoliberalism" (Crouch 2011).

This situation raises various issues. Was the crisis an accident - a "black swan" - that policymakers and their economic consultants could hardly foresee, or was it determined by wrong policies? If policies were wrong, was it because of the theories that supported them? Considering the dramatic consequences

DOI: 10.4018/978-1-7998-4933-9.ch003

the crisis led to, why did policymakers not change their economic consultants and why did voters in democratic countries not oust the policymakers that allowed the crisis to occur? Why were alternative perspectives on economic policy not convincing?

The aim of this chapter is to deal with these issues by contending that a major problem is the mechanistic and linear view that most economists have of economic policy. It does not expect to provide a full-fledged answer to all of the above questions. It nevertheless intends to frame them in what is likely to be a more fruitful way. Rather than dealing with specific models, it focuses on the assumptions and general theoretical frameworks that lie in the back of the minds of economists and that they, often unwittingly, tend to take for granted. In other terms, it focuses less on what they look at than on the "lenses" they use to look.

The standard approach to economic policy that emerges from most economics textbooks is that its aim is to deal with the shortcomings of the economy. Policymakers must understand what these shortcomings are and act upon them in order to achieve the best possible economic performance. The role of economic theory is to help them achieve this task. The problem they must face, however, is that different strands of economic thought provide distinct outlooks both on those shortcomings and on the effectiveness of public action. Most discussions about policy focus on which theory provides the best account for extant problems. It is generally understood, however, that once this issue is clear, it is possible to devise the appropriate measures.

The above approach to policy is based on a range of extremely restrictive assumptions, which, at the very least, need to be made explicit. They have to do with how the coordination of economic activities occurs. More specifically, mainstream economics – which, from the perspective of this chapter, includes the different strands of neoclassical economics along with Austrian economics – emphasizes the coordinating function of relative prices. Although it generally acknowledges that institutions must complement prices, the latter are what ultimately characterizes an economy. Policy must either allow prices to work properly or make up for their shortcomings.

Heterodox approaches provide a different outlook. Schools of thought, such as, amongst others, Original Institutional Economics, Post Keynesianism and Marxism share the view that, while prices are important, they can operate only as part of an institutional setup that is a prerequisite for their existence. Contrary to the mainstream, prices are not the means to assess economic performance.

The difference between the mainstream and heterodox approaches to economics may appear subtle but it has important implications for a proper understanding of the scope for policy, that is, its goals and its means. In particular, it allows for a reassessment of the notion of development. It suggests that the constraints to economic change vary significantly, depending on whether they are associated to markets or to historically determined institutions.

The chapter is structured as follows. The next two sections discuss the role of policy in the light of the mainstream and heterodox approaches respectively. According to the first one, policy may be required when either prices do not function properly - and private agents are unable to provide an alternative - or when social issues, such as equity, are in order. As for the heterodox approach, it claims that what appear to be mere imperfections in the mainstream's price mechanism actually reflect interdependences among economic actors and between the economy and society. The coordination of these interdependences implies the existence of institutions that structure both the economy and society. Prices function only subject to this structuration. Policy is one of the means to establish institutions.

The aim of these two sections, therefore, is to explain what policy can do according to these two approaches. The discussion contends that the distinctive difference between them is that the mainstream views the economy as a closed system, whereas the heterodox schools of thought stress the interdependence between the economy and the society it is embedded in, that is, they conceive of the economy as an open system. Thus, while the mainstream claims that policy must guarantee efficiency or, at the very least, consider it a key constraint, heterodoxy acknowledges that policy may have to do with a broader variety of goals – ranging from growth to freedom and happiness - and constraints, whether allocative, social or cultural.

The distinctive difference here outlined leads to the section on "Economic policy and open systems". The point of departure is the standard theory of economic policy laid out by Tinbergen (1967), with its assumptions about economic theory and the social welfare function. What this section contends is that policy does not involve a linear process, whereby policymakers are supposed to enact policy and, as a result, affect economic performance. An open systems perspective implies that changes in the structure of the economy eventually feed back both on how people conceive of the economy and social welfare and on how the economy itself functions.

The final section, on policy and neoliberalism, has a twofold function. First, it discusses the theoretical peculiarity of neoliberalism. It explains how neoliberalism aims to organize the economy so that it is consistent with mainstream tenets, but follows heterodox approaches in its belief that no economy can exist independently of the preliminary structuring function of institutions. Second, it refers to the practical effects of neoliberal policies in order to underscore the relevance of the conceptual issues outlined in the previous sections. In particular, it shows how neoliberal policies have changed the structure of the economy, the way people conceive of the economy and even their voting behavior.

The concluding remarks return to the questions raised at the beginning of this introduction by stressing that what is at issue is less a matter of economic techniques than one of overall outlook of the economy in its relation with society.

PRICES, INSTITUTIONS AND POLICY: THE MAINSTREAM APPROACH

The mainstream approach to the economy is based on neoclassical theory. It is a very broad approach and it is not possible, here, to discuss all of its facets. It includes general equilibrium as well as partial equilibrium theorists and scholars who stress the intrinsic virtues of a market economy. It also includes scholars who acknowledge the market's shortcomings. The aim of this chapter is to point out the basic features of this approach rather than single out possible inconsistencies.

The main characteristic of neoclassical theory is that it focuses on a market economy where, given a set of conditions, economic agents choose according to the information they receive from prices. Prices reflect the scarcity of resources and the preferences of consumers. As far as prices correctly provide this information, individual choices are mutually consistent and conducive to the highest possible welfare.

The (Walrasian) general equilibrium approach is the one that most clearly points out how prices coordinate the economy. Given preferences, technology, endowments and the conditions for rational choice, prices are the means that allow agents to decide how to use available resources in order to maximize their objectives. In so far as the economy meets a range of requirements, it is possible to achieve a Pareto-optimal general equilibrium, i.e. a situation where no agent can be better off other than at the expense of another agent.

Partial equilibrium analyses do not focus on all the conditions for a consistent coordination. The "other things equal" assumption allows the scholar to avoid these issues. It is, nevertheless, the case that the allocative efficiency of a market economy requires that the "other things equal" do not prejudge general equilibrium. Should this condition not hold, the very existence of a partial equilibrium would be questionable.

As mentioned above, there are strands of thought within the mainstream that focus on the shortcomings of a market economy. Typically, these shortcomings go under the heading of "market failures". They traditionally include externalities, public goods, non-competitive market structures associated to economies of scale, information asymmetries. All of these circumstances preclude prices from providing the information required to use resources in the most efficient way. While there is no doubt that these "failures" exist, the issue is how to deal with them.

The general solution to this inefficiency problem is the introduction of a complementary coordinating instance: institutions, that is, rules[1]. There are two extreme types of institutions. The first one is provided by policymakers. A typical example is the Pigou Tax. The government assesses the divergence between private costs and social costs and levies a tax equal to that divergence. The second type of institution is a solution that private agents devise: the example, in this case, is firms (Coase 1988a). Given the existence of transaction costs, which make it costly to access goods on the market, private agents substitute organizations for market transactions.

The relevance of the distinction between these institutions lies in their exogenous (public) rather than endogenous (private) nature. It does not imply, however, that they are substitutes for one another. Indeed, there are intermediate situations where both public and private agents must act. A solution to an externality, for instance, may consist in allowing private actors to bargain according to their preferences but only once the government has assigned property rights. What is important is that these institutions are supposed to address economic agents towards an efficient resource allocation or, at least, make up for allocative inefficiency[2].

An issue that does not involve a market failure but is nevertheless important for social welfare is distribution. It has a twofold dimension. First, undesired poverty has a moral aspect. Most people are concerned that people live in grievous and inhuman conditions. They believe that a community should address this issue in one way or another (Rawls 2005). This "interference" with the allocative function of prices contrasts, however, with the second dimension, whereby distribution is the necessary outcome of price-based resource allocation. The implication is that, unless very restrictive assumptions – those that underlie the Second Theorem of Welfare Economics – hold, any action to redistribute income affects efficiency. This need not preclude some type of redistributive action, provided policymakers acknowledge the existence of an efficiency-equity trade-off (Okun 1975).

A trade-off depends on preliminary endowments, which are often assumed to depend on exogenous circumstances, so that there would seem to be no reason to judge whether they are just or not. It is, however, impossible to assume away a problem that is morally relevant for many people. The question, therefore, is whether a policy is conceivable that acts on endowments. In other terms, can government carry out such a policy and is it economically viable?

As far as the first issue is concerned, the mainstream views government as a non-market agent, which acts exogenously on the economy. Thus, a priori, there is no technical reason that prevents it from enacting a redistribution of endowments. Viability in turn is a more complicated matter. If we reason in comparative analytical terms, a Pareto optimal outcome is possible with any endowment. Since the set of relative prices associated to each endowment is different from that of other endowments, the two outcomes – the one before redistribution and the one after it - are not comparable. In so far as agents react to relative prices alone – this is the standard textbook assumption - they will be indifferent relative to the chosen one. A more realistic view is that agents do not rely on prices alone and that static comparative analysis is inappropriate to assess the endowment change. Under such circumstances it is likely that agents will realize that a different endowment makes them better or worse off and that they will react. This approach is reasonable but, precisely because it assumes that agents contrast, rather than adapt to, the economic setup, it involves an altogether different analytical procedure, which is discussed below

The mainstream approach leads to the following outline of economic policy. It is exogenous: it consists of actions taken by a non-market agent. Its rationale is to deal with an inadequate coordination of the economy. Inadequacy may relate to the inability of prices to provide the information that agents need to make their choices. It may also have to do with issues, such as equity, that transcend the efficient allocation of resources. Policy may have to deal with institutions that preclude the proper functioning of relative prices. It may also involve the introduction of institutions that allow relative prices to operate better. In all cases, policy is subject to the requirements of a coordination of the economy based on relative prices.

Whether policy is necessary remains an open issue in mainstream economics. A range of circumstances may act against government action. These involve the cost of managing it, the ability to envisage an adequate solution to extant problems and the reliability of policymakers. The relevance of these issues is not central to the present discussion, which only cares to explain what policy consists of according to the mainstream.

INTERDEPENDENCE AND POLICY: A HETERODOX APPROACH

The Walrasian view is definitely restrictive in that it disregards that economic agents interact with each other, so that their choices do not depend on relative prices alone. Truly, the real economy does not match the abstract compactness of this theoretical model. A range of circumstances – typically, market failures - provide a less streamlined view of the economy. Their existence is beyond doubt. The issue is whether they undermine the abstract theoretical model. In other terms, are they mere exceptions to the general rule or do they signal that the theory fails to appreciate important features of real economies? Better said, are those circumstances "market failures" or "theoretical failures"? One way to deal with this issue is to focus on interdependence among economic actors and between the economy and the rest of society.

Agents may influence the decisions of other agents through advertisements[3]. In some instances, this action may consist in more or less surreptitiously convincing potential buyers that one product fits their needs better than another (Packard 1957). Sometimes the aim is to generate wants that are independent of needs. In other instances, advertisements try to conform to motives that transcend the goods. These motives may consist in the need people have to define their social status relative to others. Social status, in turn, may relate to a range of elements, such as income (Veblen 1994), fashion (Gladwell 1997), race and gender (hooks 1997). The relation between pressure to buy and the structure of society is twofold. On the one hand, advertisements reflect existing values. On the other, although they merely aim at selling products, they contribute to how people make sense of the reality they live in and to the values they have. Advertisements do not just reflect society. They reinforce some values rather than others.

This perspective leads to two remarks. First, it suggests that producers do not adapt to what consumers want but they contribute to a sequential interaction with consumers that eventually shapes perceptions of reality and values. Second, since what consumers want depends – at least to some extent - on what firms do, this raises the question what goals firms pursue. A typical answer might be that firms must guarantee that demand for their products is consistent with their desired degree of capacity utilization and with profitability. Following this perspective, however, what consumers want is functional to profit, not the other way round.

Another instance where interdependence is relevant is in the provision of goods. Consider public goods, a typical "market failure". Although they meet the needs of individuals – street lighting, for instance – it is not possible to assess the preferences of those individuals through the price system. The problem is that, while people can enjoy a public good independently of others, the provision of that good depends on their interdependent decisions to pay for it (Samuelson 1954). They may act as self-interested individuals but, in the light of extant values and institutions, they may also choose to seek a common solution.

Interdependence has greater implications with collective goods, that is, goods that do not merely satisfy individual needs but the needs of a community as a whole. An example is a monument that enhances values such as nationalism or self-sacrifice in order to meet a community's need for unity and mutual solidarity[4]. Collective needs have little to do with individual preferences. They are related to social values and may involve a variety of issues, depending on what a society's priorities are. Consider the natural environment: Although individuals might appreciate certain products, the community as a whole – thus, those same people but with a focus on social welfare - might ban them because their production, consumption or the waste they involve disrupts the ecosystem. Under these circumstances, the very composition of output is a collective good. This underscores that what a society deems relevant from a collective perspective affects the very nature of the economy.

Social justice has similar implications. It may consist in protecting individual liberty, that is, the right to pursue one's goals independently of how this affects the distribution of income and wealth and, more generally, the living conditions of others. Alternatively, it may consist in claiming that everybody has basic rights, such as the right to an education, to a healthy life and, more generally, to decent living conditions. This latter notion implies that a set of collective actions are required that may or may not be consistent with private economic concerns[5]. Social justice is a collective good in that it meets a community's needs for a good life. Here, too, depending on what values prevail, a different composition of output ensues. This is not a merely technical matter. It has to do with what people deem necessary in order to live together. It reflects interdependence but it also affects it. People are able to interact differently according to their health, their education and their more general living conditions.

So far, the discussion focused on the consumption of goods. Interdependence occurs also in their provision. Agents may interact through organizations such as firms. Typically, what characterizes the organization of a firm is that employers structure different tasks through command rather than by bargaining. Sometimes command is not enough. Workers are expected to solve problems and actively contribute to the firm's innovative competences. Incentives – thus relative prices – may be functional to this end but it is often more important to involve workers in the overall entrepreneurial project by creating a corporate culture. At the very least, corporate culture establishes an interdependence – in terms of shared values and goals - that complements relative prices in the coordination of production.

An alternative situation is when workers are expected to carry out their tasks in a passive way. Involvement may not be necessary but prevention of shirking is. Monitoring, therefore, becomes central to the organization of a firm. It may occur directly: workers are arranged in such a way that it is easy to look at them and check what they do. It may occur indirectly, by arranging tasks so that workers are forced to meet production requirements. Taylorism is one such case. It determines technical constraints among different tasks so that workers must comply with the timing of production decided by managers.

Thus, the organization of production is a case of structured interdependence among workers and between workers and management.

Conventional[6] views of production are that technology exogenously determines what workers must do. Workers choose whether to work or not, depending on how much they are paid. Employers decide how much to produce in relation to technology and to the availability of workers. The existence of organizations provides a different perspective. Firms may shape the way they are organized according to different goals. They may care to outcompete other firms or simply carve out their own market niche. In order to do this they may focus on innovation and qualitative requirements or cut (labor) costs so as to charge low prices. Depending on these strategies, they shape tasks to discipline or, alternatively, to involve workers[7]. As a result, organizations, and the ways they arrange the use of resources, are not neutral. Furthermore, different organizational arrangements involve different technological requirements, which suggests that technology, far from being neutral, is functional to interdependence[8].

Although individual firms may be constrained by economic circumstances that they cannot affect directly, firms as a whole establish institutions and act upon culture. Their strategies cannot be traced back to a unique set of relative prices – in that they codetermine them through their strategies - nor to given consumer preferences – because they codetermine these as well. Their activity consists of a sequential interaction with the rest of the economy.

Workers, like firms, may behave in different ways. They may be completely opportunistic or share the business projects of their firms. They may be prone to discipline or disrespectful of hierarchy. In so far as these elements depend on historical and cultural circumstances, the above mentioned business strategies will reflect the latter. It is reasonable that they will also feed back on those circumstances and, consequently, on the way workers behave. Thus, industrial relations may be substantially peaceful or marked by conflict. Workers may comply with business requirements or they may unite to achieve shared goals that clash with those of other sections of the economy.

As one looks at these characteristics of economic activity, it is ever more difficult to consider them within a market failures framework. They point to an interaction between strictly economic decisions – what allows provisioning - and decisions that have to do with the overall organization of society. Economic choices are not independent of the society to which they relate. They reflect its values and its institutions. Society frames the economy. The economy, in turn, has requirements of its own. In order to meet them, it frames social and societal institutions. Institutions matter for the economy even when they are not strictly related to production, consumption or distribution. In more abstract terms, they reflect the systemic openness of the economy as opposed to the closure that the mainstream approach implicitly assumes (Chick 1995, 2017; Chick and Dow 2001, 2005; Dow 1985, 2005; Lawson 1997, 2006, 2019).

The systemic openness of the economy – its interdependence with the society it is a part of – raises a coordination issue. Prices are a component in the coordination of economic activity but, from the perspective here outlined, they depend on how the economy evolves. In turn, this evolution depends on historically and culturally contingent institutions. It is possible to claim that some of these institutions actually prevent prices from coordinating the economy (North 1990; Hayek 1937, 1945). The problem is that – precisely because of their interdependence with existing institutions – whatever coordination prices were to achieve, it would not be based on the information-signaling mechanism that neoclassical theory or Austrian theory theorize. Such a coordination would simply imply that the institutions and the values that prices reflect must prevail over other institutions or values, such as democracy or religion. A slightly different perspective is that an orderly outcome is possible because some institutions prevail over others through a selection and retention process (Dopfer & Potts 2008). The implicit assumption, here, is that a selection mechanism exists that transcends existing rules. What such a mechanism should consist of remains an open issue.

Systemic openness does not merely extend the scope for coordination from markets to a broader set of relations. It involves the existence of a multiplicity of variables whose interaction is subject to a great many circumstances. Nothing warrants their consistency, even though this situation need not involve chaos (Dow 2005). Although there is no meta-coordinating instance that warrants the emergence of order, the economy and the society it is a part of are structured by their institutions. This implies that some type of order may occur. It may be temporary, as when stability is destabilizing (Minsky 1986). It may be partial, in the sense that it involves only a subsystem of society: the 2007-8 financial crisis affected the economy but not the polity of most of the countries involved.

Let us consider what this implies for policy. First, policy structures interdependence. Little matters whether it does so explicitly or implicitly: it allows certain priorities and rights to prevail over others, as is the case with the composition of output or with the notion of freedom it supports. Second, since it interacts with the overall features of society, it is historically contingent. Third, its goals may include not only output but also, e.g., the achievement of Maslow's higher-level needs, Aristotle's *eudaimonia* or Sen's (1985, 2000) capabilities. Thus, the main issue it must deal with is not to achieve efficiency but to decide what efficiency to pursue[9]. Development has a different meaning, in this perspective. Depending on what policy goals are deemed important, it may consist in a structural change of the economy to increase output or to change its composition. It may also consist in a change in the organization of production that ameliorates working – or, more generally, living - conditions, even when this involves a lower output. It may involve metrics other than prices, such as life expectancy, food insecurity, access to health, education and social security services, just to mention a few[10].

ECONOMIC POLICY AND OPEN SYSTEMS

The above discussion of the economy as an open system points out that the sequential interaction between the economy and the rest of society involves an evolutionary process whereby changes in one section affect changes in the other. It also points out that the structure of an economy is not given once and for all. Policy may be a means of change.

The conventional view of economic policy is that it requires two elements (Tinbergen 1967): knowledge of economic theory and a social welfare function. The former identifies the scope for government action. The latter sets out the policy priorities. The two elements involve two different actors. The first one is economists. They know economic theory and are able to point out what technical constraints government must acknowledge when it devises its policies. The second one is less straightforward. In the easiest case, it is a benevolent dictator. In a more realistic one, it can be voters or their representatives. Leaving aside the case where policymakers pursue goals other than those of a social welfare function – which is discussed further on – it is important to understand what assumptions underlie this somewhat standard approach.

A key assumption in the mainstream is that, much like consumer preferences, policy preferences are given. From the analytical perspective followed here, this is a very strong assumption. A more plausible one is that, much like consumer preferences, priorities change. Truly, the way people understand reality – make sense of it - is not a mechanical process. It depends on a range of circumstances, such as the cultural environment they are born in, their education, the heuristics they developed over their lifetime, the information and the images of reality that they have access to (Boulding 1961; Simon 1978). It is nevertheless the case that major (economic) institutional changes eventually feed back on people's views (Hodgson 2002)[11], thus on their preferences and priorities.

Another assumption in the conventional policy model is that available economic theory allows policymakers to foresee the outcome of their policies. Ideally, this suggests that government action can allow society gradually to achieve its goals. For instance, it can overcome the struggle for subsistence and pursue the expansion of everybody's capabilities, that is, the increasing opportunity for people to choose how to conduct their lives.

Policy, however, does not involve a mechanistic process, whereby its action inevitably leads to a predictable outcome. It is itself part of the evolutionary process depicted above. The variables involved – both at the individual and at the collective level - need not be mutually consistent. Inconsistencies may relate to the different dimensions of a person's life. Individuals have different identities (Davis 2009, 2011, 2015; Gallois, Hédoin 2017; Hogg, Terry, White 1995; Kirman and Teschl 2006; Sen 1986, 1999). For instance, being a parent who wishes to spend time with their children may clash with the need to work and receive an income. Depending on which identity prevails, a policy that reduces working time may lead the worker either to seek a second job, in order to earn more, or to devote more time to family relations.

Inconsistencies may also consist of conflicts of interest among economic actors and classes. As mentioned above, policy determines a system of rights. Rights determine opportunities for someone but at the expense of someone else's opportunities. For instance, the right not to work more than a certain number of hours per day precludes a firm's possibility to take advantage of a longer working day or week. It is, therefore, reasonable to believe that those who suffer the consequences of a given system of rights will try to bypass or change it. They may do so by proposing a different view of the social welfare function. They may also take advantage of the economic and political power they have and force decisions upon the rest of society[12].

In the absence of a general coordinating instance, it is not possible to have exact knowledge of how policy will affect people's concerns and how their reactions will feed back on the evolutionary process. Consequently, policy may lead to a variety of unpredictable changes. This accounts for the importance that uncertainty has for economic decisions (Keynes 1964).

This conclusion raises the issue to what extent the conventional view of economic policy is appropriate. As mentioned above, the claim that policymakers can rely both on a given economic knowledge and on a given social welfare function is very strong. Truly, some policy measures may have such a limited field of action that they are unlikely to feed back on these determinants unless something special happens: consider security requirements for aircrafts. On the other hand, other measures significantly affect people's lives. Working time, for instance, affects the time one has for activities other than work: care, leisure, active citizenship, etc. As mentioned above, these changes eventually feed back on people's habits and the way they interact. In turn, this affects how they perceive and interpret their reality – the way things are.

These circumstances suggest that a linear causation approach to economic policy should be treated with caution. It is reasonable to believe that economists will need to acknowledge whatever change occurred in the economy and, consequently, will adapt their models. The social welfare function is a more complicated issue.

When Tinbergen formulated his theory of economic policy, he assumed that policymakers acted according to their own social welfare function. This assumption was important because it allowed him to focus on how to conduct policy measures without having to deal with the discussions concerning the relation between individual and collective preferences. It also implied that policymakers could easily assess whether policy was successful or not. Despite its theoretical convenience, however, this assumption needs to be relaxed.

Critics of the "benevolent dictator" assumption argued that policymakers may not comply with a social welfare function that the members of society share. In the extreme case, this divergence may be due to a dictatorial government. More generally, there are various reasons why policymakers in a formal democracy may fail adequately to reflect what voters want. Voters may be inadequately informed. Policymaking may involve moral hazard. Above all, voters may vote for a political program – what potential policymakers consider the appropriate social welfare function - because they agree with most, but not all, of its items.

According to the mainstream, the gap between what policymakers purposefully do and what people want ultimately depends on two circumstances: coercion or incomplete information. Neither one prevents people from knowing what they want. Substantially - or, at the very least, boundedly - rational agents can decide what their social welfare function is. It may be explicit or implicit (tacit) but the upshot is that, even though bounded rationality may prevent full-fledged consistency, it is consistent enough for people to assess what policymakers do. Despite informational drawbacks, they are able to check whether a government is making them better or worse off[13]. This suggests that even dictators are subject to scrutiny and may eventually be toppled.

Contrary to the mainstream, members of a society may be unable to appreciate what their social welfare consists of, independently of the loose link with policymakers. The situation is similar to that of consumers discussed above. Much like consumption may be distorted by advertisements, policy goals may be distorted by propaganda and what Dugger and Sherman (2000) refer to as enabling myths. More interestingly, policy preferences may consist in establishing one's position within social hierarchies. Thus, people may care to distinguish themselves from the less fortunate segments of society by reinforcing a social stratification that ultimately is most beneficial for other sectors – the wealthiest – of society[14]. Under these circumstances, formal democracy may maintain, and possibly reinforce, a gap between social needs and social wants.

A further problem is the inconsistency between different needs. As mentioned above, people have different identities. Each identity involves different values and preferences, which need not be mutually consistent. Inconsistencies may be tacit in that they do not emerge in day-by-day life. When they do emerge, this may have two types of consequences. In the easiest case, a salient identity prevails over the others (Trepte and Loy 2017). Alternatively, individuals may need to reassess their overall self-identification: not only their specific identities but also how these are hierarchically arranged.

This perspective acknowledges that people may be persistently inconsistent. It is much in line with Simon's (2004) notion of procedural rationality, whereby individuals follow a step-by-step process to achieve a "satisficing" solution to a specific problem. It does not warrant overall consistency. Quite to the contrary, it suggests that identity reassessments may change the outlook people have of their environment and of how they situate themselves within it. It potentially involves a greater variability in the determination of social welfare functions.

Summing up, the systemic openness of the economy involves two major differences from the conventional theory of economic policy. First, the economy can change in a variety of unpredictable ways. Major policy measures can change how people interact among each other, how they relate to the economy and how they relate to policy itself. This means that policymakers cannot rely on an economic theory viewed as a series of incremental improvements in the understanding of given economic relations. Second, people need not be fully aware of their needs. Furthermore, although they need not passively adapt to changing economic conditions, they nonetheless can change their individual goals and their policy preferences along with the economy. Under some circumstances, even the way they self-identify may change.

These two differences suggest that the identification of policy measures does not consist in a mere deduction from a given economic theory. It involves a reassessment of theory itself, in relation to how the economy changes. Following Carabelli and Cedrini's (2015) reading of Keynes, economists "must let theories evolve when (logical) judgments of relevance change with varying times and circumstances." (ibid: 513). It also suggests that social welfare preferences change. The linear causation underlying the conventional theory of economic policy may be inadequate when significant economic change is involved.

POLICY AND NEOLIBERALISM

The discussion above pointed out that mainstream economics views the economy as a set of relations coordinated by prices, with institutions possibly playing a complementary role. Policy, according to this view, may improve or worsen how prices operate. Consequently, economic performance – the allocation of resources - may be more or less efficient. This applies to both minor and major measures as well as to short run and long run ones.

The alternative view is that institutions do not just complement prices. They can either structure the way prices operate – as when a system of rights structures economic transactions - or even substitute them, as in the case of a national health system. Coordination of the economy, therefore, can occur in a variety of ways. The goals assigned to the economy may vary and there is no unique criterion to assess economic performance. Assessment criteria depend on the goals pursued.

These two views apparently reflect the traditional ideological divide between liberal and policy-oriented approaches, based on different views about the stability and efficiency of price-coordinated markets. This distinction is outdated, however. Mainstream economics may well include traditional liberal views, based on the unique coordinating role of prices. As the section on the mainstream pointed out, however, it also includes a different approach, according to which institutions complement, or make up for, the inadequate coordinating function of prices[15]. This theoretical qualification accounts for the difference between liberalism and neoliberalism[16]. The former assumes prices are given and should not be interfered with. The latter believes that the institutional structure of the economy prevents prices from operating as they should. As a result, policy must establish the institutions that are most appropriate for prices to function (Lemke 2001; see also Foucault 2008).

The neoliberal approach raises two issues. The first one has to do with the set of rules that make up the legal-economic nexus, that is, the rules that underlie the functioning of the price mechanism: who can carry out a transaction, what can be transacted and how to carry out and, if necessary, enforce the transaction. Since these rules are a pre-requisite for prices to function, each legal-economic nexus is potentially conducive to a Pareto-efficient allocation in the strict sense that it is not possible to make someone better off other that at the expense of someone else. If this is true, however, an infinity of potentially efficient resource allocations is associated to an infinity of potential nexuses. The choice of a nexus does not depend on efficiency. It is a matter of value judgment. It has to do with who's rights will prevail.

The second issue is that, if price-centered coordination is to make any sense, the above rules should be consistent with the information-transmitting function of prices. Compliance with this requirement is anything but straightforward. Let us consider firms. In so far as they represent a means to make up for the inadequacy of price coordination, they may represent a "relatively efficient" - e.g. profitable - solution for the economic agents who set them up. By definition, however, the existence of a firm implies that there are two different types of coordination: within the firm and between the firm and other agents. This boundary implies that there is no continuity in the flow of information within the firm and outside of the firm. The coexistence of two types of coordinating instances precludes the completeness of the market. Thus, a firm may be "relatively efficient" from a businessperson's perspective - because it makes up for the market's high transaction costs - but it is inefficient from a market perspective because it interferes with the allocative function of prices. A typical outcome can be that other businesspersons will turn out to be "relatively inefficient" even though they complied with relative prices[17]. This argument is reminiscent of the Second Best Theorem, which suggests that there may be no unique optimal solution to market failures. Just as in the discussion of the legal-economic nexus, the choice of the proper price-cum-institutions setup is a matter of value judgment.

Similar conclusions apply when the assumption is that prices do not provide for the static allocation of resources but are the means to achieve dynamic efficiency. Following this approach, entrepreneurs use prices to identify potential innovations, which will be both profitable for them and satisfactory for consumers. The problem with this view is that those same potential innovations may prejudge the transparency of the price mechanism and their dynamic function.

The theoretical problem with the neoliberal account is that institutions do not eliminate interdependence. They inevitably adapt it to the requirements of specific sections of the economy. This is the difference between price allocation and price-cum-institutions allocation. Confusion between these two concepts leads to a major misunderstanding of neoliberal policies. The fact that they make some sections of society better off than others is not (just) because policymakers are biased. Despite its technocratic jargon, the neoliberal perspective cannot but lead to this choice.

Since neoliberal policies do not aim at reinstating a "natural" price system, it is important to focus on what they are actually pursuing. What characterizes them is that they trust in institutional change as a means to substitute price-centered choices for social rights-based rules. This means that welfare policies, which are supposed to ensure money transfers and/or services independently of primary income distribution, are appropriate only if they help people who are mentally or physically disadvantaged. Human solidarity is reasonable provided it does not prejudge price-centered coordination.

Neoliberal policies do not act directly on the extant distribution of income and wealth. Consequently, while they seem to establish a neutral price-centered playing field for economic agents, they maintain distributional disparities and downplay the cumulative implications that they involve. It is no wonder, therefore, that distributional disparities increased during the past decades.

This situation points to an apparent paradox. If only a minority benefits from these policies, why do people still vote for neoliberal policymakers? The previous section introduced the main elements for an adequate treatment of this issue. It argued that policy affects not only the structure of economic – and social - relations but also the way people understand and situate themselves within those relations. Therefore, the question is how these general considerations account for such unexpected behavior.

Neoliberal policy aims to establish institutions that support prices as coordinating instances of the economy but the prices it confides in are those that are most similar to those of a neoclassical market. Economic agents - businesses, households, workers - must be self-interested. They must not be collective agents, that is, agents that pursue other types of goals. While a minimal state is inevitable for the provision of essential public goods - police, legal and judicial systems and the military – all other functions generally carried out by governments must – or should - be devolved to private agents. This strategy, which reduces the role of the welfare state, implies that people can access education, health and other features of decent living conditions only to the extent that they are able to pay for them. They have the right to interact on markets as individuals, not as members of a community. Socially concerned policymakers, for their part, are forced to acknowledge that "the market" has its rules and that any attempt to contrast it may determine the reactions discussed above with regard to full employment policies.

This approach applies to other collective agents, like trade unions. Unions organize workers to contract wages and other aspects of people's jobs by availing themselves of their bargaining power, which depends on collective action, typically the threat of strikes. Neoliberalism, on the contrary, conceives only of individual bargaining power, based on the characteristics of the commodity sold on the labor market.

The overall aim of neoliberal policies is to approximate a market where individuals are isolated much like the homo oeconomicus of neoclassical theory. It has three major implications. First, it increases the relative bargaining power of businesses relative to workers. Consequently, workers must "adapt" to the labor market. As long as there is unemployment, the asymmetric bargaining power between business and workers implies a redistribution of income, so that a worker must either work more to achieve the same income or earn less than in the past. In the first case, this will prevent that person from dedicating time to other activities such as care, human relations and social commitments. In the second case, it will determine an impoverishment in terms of available income. Either way, the outcome is negative for the worker.

Second, it disrupts all those institutions that make people feel they are part of a community. This not only prevents unions from pressing for an alternative. It prevents people from thinking that an alternative to the status quo is possible.

Third, it holds individuals responsible for their economic success or failure. The negative economic outcome workers are confronted with depends, according to neoliberal ideology, on their inability or unwillingness to do any better. This view is reinforced by the absence of alternative policy outlooks. This is of no minor consequence. Individual economic failure may be difficult to deal with, because it undermines one's identity not only as a worker - or, in some instances, as a businessperson – but as a breadwinner and as a person who has a specific social role and status. This is likely to determine the reactions mentioned in the previous section. The individuals involved are likely to reconsider their identities and the way they situate themselves within the economy and society. They may do so in a variety of ways. Two extreme reactions deserve to be discussed. They both involve the internalization of "market rules" and the idea that there is no alternative to the extant economy.

The first one is that individuals acknowledge that "that's how things are" and realize that they will have to live with that. This is a typically individual solution in that it identifies two determinants of the negative situation one is in: an impersonal economy and the person's inclination to deal with it.

The second reaction is that the individual realizes that other people are in the same (negative) situation and identifies with them. Self-identification, here, is not an intellectual process. More dramatically, it may well signal a discontinuity in an individual's personal identity narrative, that is, in the cognitive process that allows an individual to (try to) provide a unified view of her different individual identities[18]. More specifically, it does not consist in understanding what the causes of the problem are and eventually joining people who care to find a solution. Based on social dynamics, the process goes the other way round. It begins with self-identification, which is an attempt to solve the cognitive dissonance, and consequent identity crisis, that the economic problem caused. The self-identification is determined by an in-group out-group dynamic (Tajfel 1981), which consist in viewing the out-group as the people who are at the root of the problem. These can be politicians or bankers, foreign governments, immigrants, specific ethnic or religious groups. Note that, since market rules are taken for granted, the cause of the economic problem must be people – the out-group - rather than the structural features of the economy. Laying the blame on specific groups of people ultimately minimizes the institutional nature of the problem.

The aim of this brief outline is not to provide a thorough account of the effects of neoliberal policies, although much of what occurs in many countries is consistent with the depicted reactions. What it does care to show is that (neoliberal) policies feed back on how people view the economy and on social consensus. The institutions neoliberal policy establishes tend to reinforce the ideology underlying it.

This pattern of self-reinforcing consensus – which accounts for the paradox of voter consensus mentioned above – reflects the emasculation of countervailing social actors such as unions and other intermediate solidarity-centered organizations. It need not mean that neoliberalism will remain forever. As a rule, systemic openness suggests that many patterns of sub-system dynamics may occur. Indeed, there have been various reactions to the status quo, over time. In 2019, there was the *gilet jaune* rebellion in France. In Chile, that same year, an apparently trivial subway ticket hike led to dramatic protests. The fact is that neoliberal policies tend to exacerbate what Karl Polanyi (1944) called the "double movement", that is, the clash between the rationale of a price-centered coordination of the economy and the inextinguishable tension toward a more humane society.

FUTURE RESEARCH DIRECTIONS

The recent Covid 19 crisis stressed how interdependence undermines the centrality of prices in economics. At the interpersonal level, the lockdown that followed the pandemic was based on the idea that physical distancing prevented someone not only from catching the virus but from transmitting it. Thus, while some libertarians contended that they were free to do as they deemed best, most people realized that there was no way to solve the pandemic other than through a collective involvement. In some cases this acknowledgement that people needed to act together in order to overcome this collective problem led to the establishment of mutual aid networks (Sitrin & Colectiva Sembrar 2020).

At the domestic policy level several governments were forced to acknowledge that they had to provide subsidies to those social sectors that were dramatically affected by the economic consequences of the lockdown. Any link between income and contribution to output was pointless, under those circumstances. The government was expected to guarantee the provision of a collective good – living conditions - to the community.

At the international level, despite attempts to close all types of boundaries, governments were forced to realize that, unless all countries were able to overcome their domestic pandemic, nobody would have overcome the global pandemic. It is no wonder that, aside from some exceptions, the overall approach within the European Union and the Eurosystem was much more cooperative than ten years before, at the time of the sovereign debt crises.

The interdependence outlined at these different levels – personal, domestic and international – raised the issue of what arrangements were required to ensure the survival of communities. What was convenient for single actors might easily be detrimental for the community as a whole. Consider the decision concerning which economic activities were "essential" and could not be shut down. These activities were supposed to guarantee the necessities of life for the population but they involved a risk of contagion for the workers who provided those goods and services. A price-centered coordination of this choice neglected the interdependence underlying contagion.

The financial requirements underlying government policies pointed to a set of alternatives for public debt: private financial markets, international agencies or central banks. While there is an open debate on the nature of money and the scope of central banking, the key issue was that neither the risk of inflation nor the profitability of finance could constrain public action. Some kind of institutional change was required to deal with issues that had little to do with the allocation of resources. In other terms, whether what was needed to prevent the rise in interest rate spreads was an expansionary monetary policy, a greater involvement of intergovernmental agencies or bounds on the functioning of financial markets, the main issue was to deal with problems – those mentioned above - that transcended price-centered decisions.

These policy issues suggest that more research is required to understand the implications of systemic openness for the functioning of an economy. This involves at least three theoretical issues. First, what is needed to coordinate the economy? Since coordination may occur in a variety of ways, with prices being only one of them, the theoretical problem that economic policy must address is how institutions relate to prices, which ones are essential for the stability of a society over time and, conversely, what institutional changes are possible to achieve a desirable – possibly more humane - society. Second, how can, and should, coordination be carried out? Is it just a technical issue or does it involve the consensus or even participation of the people involved? Who is supposed to assess the performance of the economy? Third, what does performance consist of? Since no criterion is given a priori, the issue is not to conform to one criterion – e.g., prices - but to understand what criteria exist and should be pursued. The insights provided by various authors cited above suggest that research along these lines does not have to begin from scratch. They also suggest that it may be an exciting field of inquiry.

CONCLUSION

There are different ways to conceive of the economy and of how it relates to society. They lead to different perspectives on what economic policy can consist of. The chapter distinguished the mainstream's reliance on prices, and on the institutions that complement them, from the heterodox emphasis on institutions as a prerequisite for any economy. It contended that this distinction reflects different views of interdependence within the economy and between the economy and society. The distinction relates to whether the economy is conceived of as an open or a closed system.

In an open systems perspective, coordination – including economic policy - acts upon the structure of economic relations but it also affects how people perceive the economy, interpret its requirements and ultimately accept or attempt to change its rules. It may eventually lead to changes in electoral and social consensus. Although systemic openness need not involve complete interdependence among different aspects of reality, it nevertheless implies that the long-run effects of policy, especially when it is not restricted to very specific aspects of the economy, act upon the social and societal environment that encompasses economic relations. Based on this approach, let us go back to the problems outlined in this chapter's introduction.

In what sense was the failure to foresee the Great Financial Crisis a major shortcoming in economics? The discussion in the previous sections suggests that there is no unique and compact "economics". It would therefore be misleading to claim that economics – rather than one of its strands of thought - failed.

Some economists believe it is possible to predict the future of the economy because they conceive of it as a closed system. Unsurprisingly, they were the most surprised by the crisis (Andrews 2008). It is, therefore, no wonder that many of them sought to explain it as an exceptional and unpredictable event: a "black swan" (Taleb 2007). Conversely, an open systems perspective suggests that, owing to the multifarious interaction among strictly economic and societal variables, prediction is a doubtful task, although it does not preclude the identification of patterns and possible outcomes.

What are the implications of the Great Financial Crisis for economic policy? The conventional approach, as discussed above, is to provide a model of the economy and to discuss how positive or negative incentives and existing regulations affect efficiency. For instance, a typical explanation of the Crisis focuses on how regulation of the financial sector led to the expansion of subprime loans. This is not wrong but one should ask to what extent it is the most insightful issue, that is, whether it is an important detail of a broader problem. For instance, a different approach to the crisis might be to ask why subprime loans were requested in the first place: why distribution of income makes it so risky for some households to buy a house; why there is no public housing for low-income households. Note that these issues do not exclude the former one. Indeed, they are likely to encompass it. A priori there is no reason why these more extensive accounts should be less relevant.

Following the open systems perspective outlined so far, there is no unique economy, not to speak of a unique market. Since economic performance depends on how policy frames the economy, both types of questions – the "restrictive" and the "extensive" - are reasonable. Granted that, a priori, they may both be plausible, which one should be investigated depends not on a technical statement but on a value judgment. What is at issue is what part of the institutional system they believe should not change. Doubtless, dealing with financial regulation may be easier in that it is a more restricted issue than distribution. It is questionable, however, that economists should avoid envisaging economic and societal improvements only because dealing with them is more difficult.

A different way to look at this issue is to focus on the metrics used. A discussion of issues such as income distribution, precarious living conditions or welfare services may be conventionally carried out in terms of a given price-centered metric, the underlying assumption being that those prices measure the resources available to achieve the desired goals. The alternative perspective is that policy can determine institutional changes – thus also different relative prices – that enable the achievement of a variety of goals such as full employment, distribution or welfare services (Minsky 1973; Tcherneva 2012)[19]. This does not to mean that these goals are easy to achieve. It means that the constraints they face may be cultural, institutional and political but not technical.

What all this leads to is that, before economists search for new theoretical tools to deal with their shortcomings, they should be aware that many tools are already available, provided they are willing to acknowledge their existence. In turn, this requires that they keep in mind the answer that Alice in Wonderland's Cheshire cat provides to Alice's question: "'Would you tell me, please, which way I ought to go from here?' 'That depends a good deal on where you want to get to,' said the Cat."

REFERENCES

Andrews, E. L. (2008). Greenspan Concedes Error on Regulation. *The New York Times*. https://www.nytimes.com/2008/10/24/business/economy/24panel.html

Boulding, K. E. (1961). *The image: Knowledge in life and society*. University of Michigan.

Bresser-Pereira, L. C. (2020). Financing Covid-19, the inflation and the fiscal constraint. *The Forum for Social Economics*, *49*(3).

Bromley, D. W. (1989). *Economic interests and institutions: The conceptual foundations of public policy*. Blackwell.

Carabelli, A. M. (1988). *On Keynes's Method*. St. Martin's Press. doi:10.1007/978-1-349-19414-8

Carabelli, A. M., & Cedrini, M. A. (2015). From Theory to Policy? Keynes's Distinction between Apparatus of Thought and Apparatus of Action, with an Eye to the European Debt Crisis. *Challenge*, *58*(6), 509–531. doi:10.1080/05775132.2015.1105666

Chick, V. (1995). "Order out of Chaos" in Economics? In S. Dow & J. Hillard (Eds.), *Keynes, knowledge and uncertainty* (pp. 25–42). Edward Elgar.

Chick, V. (2017). On Open Systems. In L.-P. Rochon & S. Rossi (Eds.), Post-Keynesian Economics. Volume 1. Issues in Methodology (pp. 124–137). Edward Elgar.

Chick, V., & Dow, S. (2005). The meaning of open systems. *Journal of Economic Methodology*, *12*(3), 363–381. doi:10.1080/13501780500223585

Chick, V., & Dow, S. C. (2001). Formalism, logic and reality: A Keynesian analysis. *Cambridge Journal of Economics*, *25*(6), 705–721. doi:10.1093/cje/25.6.705

Coase, R. H. (1988). *The firm, the market, and the law*. The University of Chicago Press.

Coase, R. H. (1988a). The Nature of the Firm. Academic Press.

Coase, R. H. (1988b). The Problem of Social Cost. Academic Press.

Crouch, C. (2011). The strange non-death of neoliberalism. *Polity*.

Davis, J. B. (2009). Identity and Individual Economic Agents: A Narrative Approach. *Review of Social Economy*, *67*(1), 71–94. doi:10.1080/00346760802431009

Davis, J. B. (2011). *Individuals and identity in economics*. Cambridge university press.

Davis, J. B. (2015). Stratification economics and identity economics. *Cambridge Journal of Economics*, *39*(5), 1215–1229. doi:10.1093/cje/beu071

Dopfer, K., & Potts, J. (2008). *The General Theory of Economic Evolution*. Routledge.

Dow, S. C. (1985). *Macroeconomic thought: A methodological approach*. Basil Blackwell.

Dow, S. C. (2005). Axioms and Babylonian thought: A reply. *Journal of Post Keynesian Economics*, *27*(3), 385–391.

Dugger, W. M., & Sherman, H. J. (2000). *Reclaiming evolution: A dialogue between marxism and institutionalism on social change*. Routledge. doi:10.4324/9780203160589

Elsner, W., Heinrich, T., & Schwardt, H. (2015). *The microeconomics of complex economies: Evolutionary, institutional, neoclassical, and complexity perspectives*. Academic Press. doi:10.1016/B978-0-12-411585-9.00001-4

Fiorentini, R. (2015). Neoliberal Policies, Income Distribution Inequality and the Financial Crisis. *The Forum for Social Economics*, *44*(2), 115–132. doi:10.1080/07360932.2014.951376

Foucault, M. (2008). *The birth of biopolitics: Lectures at the Collège de France, 1978-79. Palgrave Macmillan* (M. Senellart, Ed.).

Frank, T. (2005). *What's the matter with Kansas? How conservatives won the heart of America*. Henry Holt.

Freeman, J. (2018). *Behemoth: A history of the factory and the making of the modern world*. Norton.

Gallois, F., & Hédoin, C. (2017). From Identity to Agency in Positive and Normative Economics. *The Forum for Social Economics*, 1–17. doi:10.1080/07360932.2017.1394897

George, S. (1999, March 24). *A Short History of Neoliberalism*. Transnational Institute. https://www.tni.org/en/article/short-history-neoliberalism

Gladwell, M. (1997, March 17). The Coolhunt. *The New Yorker*. https://www.newyorker.com/magazine/1997/03/17/the-coolhunt

Harvey, D. (2005). *A brief history of neoliberalism*. Oxford University Press.

Hayden, F. G. (2018). Using the Social Fabric Matrix to Establish Corporate Accounting Consistent with Normative Criteria Regarding Climate Change. *The Forum for Social Economics*, *47*(1), 64–86. doi:10.1080/07360932.2014.1002517

Hayek, F. A. von. (1937). Economics and knowledge. *Economica, 4*, 33–54.

Hodgson, G. M. (2002). Reconstitutive Downward Causation: Social Structure and the Development of Individual Agency. In E. Fullbrook (Ed.), *Intersubjectivity in economics: Agents and structures* (pp. 159–180). Routledge.

Hodgson, G. M. (2006). What Are Institutions? *Journal of Economic Issues*, *40*(1), 1–25. doi:10.1080/00213624.2006.11506879

Hogg, M. A., Terry, D., & White, K. M. (1995). A Tale of Two Theories: A Critical Comparison of Identity Theory with Social Identity Theory. *Social Psychology Quarterly*, 58.

hooks, b. (1992). Selling Hot Pussy: Representations of Black Female Sexuality in the Cultural Marketplace. In Writing on the Body. Female Embodiment and Feminist Theory. South End Press.

Kalecki, M. (1990). Political Aspects of Full Employment. In M. Kalecki (Ed.), Collected works of Michal Kalecki. Volume 1. Capitalism: Business cycles and full employment (pp. 347–356). Oxford University Press.

Kapp, K. W. (2000). *The social costs of business enterprise*. Spokesman.

Keen, S. (1995). Finance and economic breakdown: Modeling Minsky's financial instability hypothesis. *Journal of Post Keynesian Economics, 17*(4), 607–635. doi:10.1080/01603477.1995.11490053

Keynes, J. M. (1964). *The general theory of employment interest and money*. Macmillan & Co.

Kirman, A., & Teschl, M. (2006). Searching for identity in the capability space. *Journal of Economic Methodology, 13*(3), 299–325. doi:10.1080/13501780600908200

Komlos, J. (2019). Foundations of real-world economics: What every economics student needs to know (2nd ed.). Routledge.

Koslowski, P. (Ed.). (1998). *The social market economy: Theory and ethics of the economic order*. Springer. doi:10.1007/978-3-642-72129-8

Lawson, T. (1997). *Economics and reality*. Routledge. doi:10.4324/9780203195390

Lawson, T. (2006). The Nature of Heterodox Economics. *Cambridge Journal of Economics, 30*(4), 483–505. doi:10.1093/cje/bei093

Lawson, T. (2019). *The nature of social reality: Issues in social ontology*. Routledge. doi:10.4324/9780429199035

Lemke, T. (2001). "The birth of bio-politics": Michel Foucault's lecture at the Collège de France on neo-liberal governmentality. *Economy and Society, 30*(2), 190–207. doi:10.1080/03085140120042271

Minsky, H. P. (1973). The Strategy of Economic Policy and Income Distribution. *The Annals of the American Academy of Political and Social Science, 409*(1), 92–101. doi:10.1177/000271627340900110

Minsky, H. P. (1984). *Can "it" happen again? Essays on instability and finance*. Sharpe.

Minsky, H. P. (1986). *Stabilizing an unstable economy*. Yale University Press.

Mirowski, P., & Plehwe, D. (Eds.). (2009). *The Road from Mont Pelerin: The Making of the Neoliberal Thought Collective*. Harvard University Press. doi:10.4159/9780674054264

Mudge, S. L. (2008). What is neo-liberalism? *Socio-economic Review, 6*(4), 703–731. doi:10.1093er/mwn016

Musgrave, R. A. (2008). Merit goods. In The new Palgrave dictionary of economics. Academic Press.

North, D. C. (1990). *Institutions, institutional change and economic performance*. Cambridge university press. doi:10.1017/CBO9780511808678

North, D. C. (2005). *Understanding the process of economic change*. Princeton University press. doi:10.1515/9781400829484

Okun, A. M. (1975). *Equality and efficiency, the big tradeoff*. The Brookings Institution.

Packard, V. (1957). *The hidden persuaders*. McKay.

Polanyi, K. (1944). *The great transformation*. Rinehart & Company.

Polanyi, K. (1957). The Economy as an Instituted Process. In *Trade and market in the early empires: Economies in history and theory*. Free Press.

Posner, R. A. (2009). *A failure of capitalism: The crisis of '08 and the descent into depression*. Harvard University Press.

Ramazzotti, P. (2018). Public Goods beyond Markets. *Review of Political Economy, 30*(4), 573-594.

Ramazzotti, P. (2020a). Economic Policy, Social Identity and Social Consensus. *American Review of Political Economy*, *49*(2).

Ramazzotti, P. (2020b). Economic Policy. Social Identity and Social Consensus. *International Journal of Political Economy*, *14*(1), 139-152.

Ramazzotti, P., Frigato, P., & Elsner, W. (Eds.). (2012). *Social costs today: Institutional analyses of the present crises*. Routledge.

Rawls, J. (2005). *A Theory of Justice*. Harvard University Press.

Röpke, W. (1960). *A humane economy: The social framework of the free market. H.* Regnery.

Rothschild, K. W. (2009). Neoliberalism, EU and the Evaluation of Policies. *Review of Political Economy*, *21*(2), 213–225. doi:10.1080/09538250902834038

Samuels, W., & Schmid, A. A. (n.d.). The Concept of Cost in Economics. In The economy as a process of valuation. Edward Elgar.

Samuelson, P. A. (1954). The pure theory of public expenditure. *The Review of Economics and Statistics*, *36*(4), 387–389. doi:10.2307/1925895

Sen, A. (1985). *Commodities and capabilities*. North-Holland.

Sen, A. (1986). Rationality, Interest, and Identity. In A. Foxley, M. S. McPherson, & G. O'Donnell (Eds.), *Development, Democracy, and the Art of Trespassing: Essays in Honor of Albert O. Hirschman* (pp. 355–373). University of Notre Dame Press.

Sen, A. (1999). The Possibility of Social Choice. *The American Economic Review*, *89*(3), 349–378. doi:10.1257/aer.89.3.349

Sen, A. (2000). *Development as freedom*. Anchor books.

Simon, H. A. (1978). Rationality as Process and as Product of Thought. *The American Economic Review*, *68*(2), 1–16.

Simon, H. A. (2004). From Substantive to Procedural Rationality. In M. Egidi & S. Rizzello (Eds.), Cognitive economics. Volume 1 (pp. 304–323). Elgar Reference Collection.

Sitrin, M., & Sembrar, C. (Eds.). (2020). *Pandemic Solidarity*. Pluto Books.

Stiglitz, J. E. (2013). *The Price of Inequality*. Penguin. doi:10.1111/npqu.11358

Tajfel, H. (1981). *Human groups and social categories: Studies in social psychology*. Cambridge university press.

Taleb, N. N. (2007). *The Black Swan: the impact of the highly improbable*. Penguin.

Tcherneva, P. R. (2012). *Beyond Full Employment: The Employer of Last Resort as an Institution for Change*. Levy Economics Institute of Bard College Working Paper No. 732.

Thomasberger, C. (2015). Europe at a Crossroads: Failed Ideas, Fictional Facts, and Fatal Consequences. *The Forum for Social Economics*, *44*(2), 179–200. doi:10.1080/07360932.2014.951379

Tinbergen, J. (1967). *Economic policy: Principles and design (4. revised printing)*. North-Holland.

Trepte, S., & Loy, L. S. (2017). Social Identity Theory and Self-Categorization Theory. In P. Rössler, C. A. Hoffner, & L. van Zoonen (Eds.), *The International Encyclopedia of Media Effects* (pp. 1–13). John Wiley & Sons, Inc. doi:10.1002/9781118783764.wbieme0088

Vanberg, V. J. (2001). *The constitution of markets: Essays in political economy*. Routledge. doi:10.4324/9780203443415

Veblen, T. (1994). *The theory of the leisure class*. Cofide.

von Hayek, F. A. (1945). The use of knowledge in society. *The American Economic Review*, *35*, 519–530.

Williamson, O. E. (1985). *The economic institutions of capitalism: Firms, markets, relational contracting*. Collier Macmillan.

Williamson, O. E. (1993). Contested Exchange versus the Governance of Contractual Relations. *The Journal of Economic Perspectives*, *7*(1), 103–108. doi:10.1257/jep.7.1.103

Williamson, O. E. (1998). Transaction Cost Economics: How It Works: Where It Is Headed. *De Economist*, *146*(1), 23–58. doi:10.1023/A:1003263908567

Williamson, O. E. (2000). The New Institutional Economics: Taking Stock, Looking Ahead. *Journal of Economic Literature*, *38*(3), 595–613. doi:10.1257/jel.38.3.595

KEY TERMS AND DEFINITIONS

Collective Good: A good that meets the needs of a community as a whole. The community is viewed not as the mere sum of the individuals that comprise it but also as the outcome of their interaction.

Heterox Economics: In this chapter it is an open systems approach as defined below.

Institution: As pointed out in note 1, it is a system of established and embedded social rules that structures social interactions.

Mainstream Economics: In this chapter it is a closed systems approach as defined below.

Neoliberalism: In this chapter it is a policy approach to the economy. It acknowledges the importance of institutional arrangements that allow price-centered coordination, albeit in a market that does not have the ideal advantages depicted by (Walrasian) general equilibrium theory.

Open/Closed Systems: A closed system, in this chapter, is a system that can function according to its own rules, independently of the rules of its surrounding environment. An economy conceived of as a closed system operates independently of the features of the society it is a part of. When society interferes with the rules of the economy, this appears as an exogenous shock. An open system, conversely, is one that interacts with its surrounding environment. When the economy is conceived of as an open system, society affects the rules of the economy and economy feeds back on the rules of society.

Social: In general, it is something that relates to society. In a closed system perspective, it encompasses societal relations as opposed to strictly economic relations: consider the use of the term "social cost" in Coase 1988b. In an open system perspective, there is no clear boundary between society and the economy so that social includes both: consider the use of the term "social cost" in Kapp (2000). In this chapter, whether the term is used according to one perspective or the other depends on the context.

ENDNOTES

1. "Institutions are systems of established and embedded social rules that structure social interactions." (Hodgson 2006: 18).
2. Note that, although public discourse generally considers that the economy is supposed to achieve growth and economic sustainability (profitability), what this framework suggests is that the extent to which it actually does so depends on how efficiently agents use resources.
3. The mainstream explanation for this is that information is imperfect and/or economic agents are boundedly rational.
4. Musgrave (2008) termed them merit goods. "Collective" appears to be a more encompassing term (see Ramazzotti 2018).
5. Consider the reactions to the Covid 19 lockdown. While most people acknowledged that restrictions were necessary for general welfare, others claimed that the lockdown was a violation of their individual liberty to act and move as they deemed best.
6. The term conventional refers to prevailing views that overlap the basic approaches here outlined.
7. Note that the distinction between discipline and involvement is less rigid that one may expect. Freeman (2018) points out: "Henry Ford's rural Protestant moralism, with its stress on thrift, sexual rectitude, and spurning of alcohol and tobacco, prescribed a way of life that Ford executives [...] saw as necessary for the physical and psychological demands of mass production." (p. 131). He adds Antonio Gramsci's comment that "the inspection services created by some firms to control the 'morality' of their workers are necessities of the new methods of work [in that they aim to create] a new type of worker and a new type of man." (p. 132; text in brackets added by the author).
8. "(T)echnology can be driven by such different objectives as immediate registered-cost minimization; positioning for future research and development opportunities; and, *inter alia*, control of the workplace and of the labor force." (Samuels and Schmidt 1997: 221).
9. "The issue is not one of being efficient or inefficient in the abstract, but of being efficient or inefficient with respect to a particular purpose or objective. If monetized net national income is the sole operative objective then certain institutional arrangements (such as encouraging the free and unfettered discharge of industrial wastes into air and water) are efficient for that purpose. On the other hand, if a clean environment and net national income are relevant objectives, then a different institutional structure (one that involves a different form of garbage disposal) is the efficient institutional setup. It is not possible to define efficiency without first specifying the objective to be pursued." (Bromley 1989: 79).

10 These indicators are often uncorrelated with aggregate income. See Komlos (2019; Chapter 2) for a detailed survey of these and other variables in the specific case of the USA. Kapp (2000) and Hayden (2018) provide possible tools for a policy that takes account of these variables while not subordinating them to output.

11 Hodgson has partially revised his views. See: http://www.geoffrey-hodgson.info/downward-causation.htm (accessed 5 May 2020).

12 Kalecki (1990: 355) points out that if, following an expansionary policy to overcome a slump, policy were to try to "maintain the high level of employment reached in the subsequent boom, strong opposition by business leaders is likely to be encountered. [...] lasting full employment is not at all to their liking. The workers would 'get out of hand' and the 'captains of industry' would be anxious to 'teach them a lesson'".

13 This view underlies Abraham Lincoln's famous remark that "You can fool some of the people all of the time, and all of the people some of the time, but you cannot fool all of the people all of the time".

14 Frank (2005) provides a vivid illustration of this phenomenon.

15 The major contributions to this approach come from New Institutionalism (Coase 1988; Williamson 1985, 1993, 1998, 2000; North 1990, 2005), Constitutional Political Economy (Vanberg 2001), Ordoliberalism (Röpke 1960) and the proponents of a Social Market Economy (Koslowski 1998).

16 On the ideological features of neoliberalism see George (1999), Mudge (2008), Mirowski and Plehwe (2009) and Thomasberger (2015). Crouch (2011), Harvey (2005), Rothschild (2009), Stiglitz (2013) and Fiorentini (2015) discuss its practical features.

17 An example is when a firm that internalizes information in order to protect its knowledge-related competitive advantage.

18 "Individuals' narratives about themselves are thus what they regard as their personal identities, or their identities as they themselves see them." (Davis 2009: 83).

19 A broader list is in the last paragraph of the section on interdependence and policy.

Chapter 4
A Minsky-Levy-Kalecki Model

Romar Correa
University of Mumbai, India

ABSTRACT

The authors add the monetary insights of Hyman Minsky to the 'real' Kalecki-Levy equation. The latter is embedded in the economics of Keynes and the former is expanded in the spirit of Minsky. They present their structural connections in a four-quadrant diagram as well as within a stock-flow-consistent model. The motivation arises from history and the revitalisation of the real bills doctrine. Accordingly, they make the case for the productive monetary emissions of a central bank acting in concert with the community of commercial banks. They define money as the emission of credit in the 'first moment' of the circuit. It is simultaneously the wage bill. Workers will consume basics and are free to prefer liquidity in the form of bank deposits. The latter they label cash or currency and a firewall separates it from money. The objective is the increase in output and employment called upon by the milieu in all countries of the world in which the 'dark forces' of uncertainty and pessimism have taken over. The policy stance is embellished by the introduction of central bank digital money.

INTRODUCTION

The introductory lecture in macroeconomics introduces the student to the breakup of GDP into consumption goods and investment goods. Thereafter, a representative agent is assumed to drive the consumption stream by maximizing her utility over time. Income not consumed is saved and then invested. Bounded rationality might be introduced and, lately, agents are behavioral in the models. Macro is founded on micro. Michal Kalecki drew attention to the dual breakup of national income into wages and profits. Backing each are classes this time, wages and capitalists that connect with the data. The connection with the textbook division of GDP into consumption and investment is the subdivision of the former into the consumption of Basics by the working class and the consumption of Luxuries by the capitalist class and, correspondingly, the division of the Investment Goods Department into capital goods used as inputs in Basics and Luxury Goods production respectively. The research programme is progressive as scholars worry about the collapsing of both classes into a rentier class. Workers who cannot find jobs are forced to flip their miniscule assets. Capitalists find it more lucrative to speculate in financial markets rather

DOI: 10.4018/978-1-7998-4933-9.ch004

than produce and invest in the goods market. The aggregates are manipulated to derive theorems like the realization problem of Marx or, equivalently, the problem of effective demand of Keynes.

Money in Kalecki was implicit, at best, with no more than the rate of interest figuring in the development of the theory. However, the identical starting point above is the launching pad of the theory of the monetary circuit actively researched mainly in Italy and France (Cencini, 2017, is a summary in a festschrift to Bernard Schmitt, the pioneer of a school in France). In short, the macroeconomic identity referred to must be underwritten by the advances of money that back the wages paid out to workers that produce goods and services (Mallorquin, 2019). The circuit is opened by the visit of the manager of a firm to a bank or a bank that ferrets out a profitable idea from the population of entrepreneurs and pursues it. New schemes or novel ways or green technologies will not possess probability distributions nor meet credit norms. Indeed, capital adequacy norms like those of Basel II have acted as an incentive opposite to truth telling as banks subvert them to preserve their bottom lines (Goodhart, 2018).The bigger the banks the harder they are falling in our times and the handshake between local and community bank manager and the environmentally-kind businesswoman, for instance, must be strong. In the Minsky archives at the Jerome Levy Institute in New York, numerous jottings will be found where the skills of scrutiny and audit of the bank manager are emphasized. When the credit line is drawn upon through an overdraft facility, the "first moment" in the circuit is initiated in the terminology of Schmitt. Production takes place and Basics, goods consumed by workers in the production process, are sold. The "second moment" is concluded. The sales circle back as revenues to firms who proceed to repay their loans to banks. The "third moment" is the closing of the accounts. The savings of workers and the financing of capital goods must be recorded in separate accounts in banks or financial institutions. Nothing in the account predisposes the adjunct 'commercial' or 'central' to the bank. In fact, Central Banks (CBs, hereafter), relatively young entrants on to the arena of production and finance, emerged from the community of commercial banks of longer standing as a result of the exigencies of extraordinary circumstances like the aftermaths of wars. CBs were leaders of the pack of banks and the connection between the two remained intimate and constructive, devoted to the joint primary task of screening and monitoring the writing up and drawing down of credit balances.

Returning to our macroeconomic identity, we observe the secular decline of the wage bill. Both its components, the wage rate and the number of workers have been on a steady downward trend for decades. Reverting to aggregate output, the left-hand side, nations worldwide are working far below their production possibility frontiers both in terms of levels and annual rates of growth. The conclusion is that profits from the production of goods and services, the remaining element on the right-hand side, must also be inefficiently low and not growing. Thomas Piketty lumps profits and rents in his popular book. However, rents are a drag on aggregate output and are best conceptualized independently (Vahabi, 2019). Modern capitalism is a "re-feudalization" rather than the next stage of classical capitalism. The top 20% or the upper middle class anywhere are a "new nobility" or "dominant rank or elite". The egalitarian measure of a tax on inheritance or capital gains stares the policy maker in the face. Kalecki made the case for a tax on Inessentials or Non Basics. Consequently, the contribution of Jerome Levy to the Kalecki identity, breaking up profits into distributed profits and retained profits, is salutary. The former is dividends to shareholders, the latter is for the ostensible purpose of ploughback into fresh investment plans. The first in the form of share buybacks as part of a financial circuit has taken on a life of its own as the arbitrage principle joins production firms and financial firms. The depletion of the second as the propensity to invest has correspondingly deteriorated has long been a driver of critiques of the "shareholder value maximization" model. Incentives get distorted when stock options reward managers for positive market valuations but do not penalize them for negative outcomes. The woeful implication for society is the absence of provision for the future in capital goods. A contender for the Presidential crown in America who had to withdraw, Elizabeth Warren, framed an Accountable Capitalism Act in August 2018 as a robust antidote to this model (Vogel, 2019). She was inspired by the sight of financial executives manipulating the performance of companies and then exercising their options. The canonical Japanese structure was used as a sounding board. Experienced insiders sit on corporate boards and their mandate is worker skilling exercises, efforts at reducing the cost of capital, increasing quality control. In good times and bad, the clarion call is "voice" and not "exit". Thereby, "loyalty" emerges. Workers and capitalists are partners and renegotiate relations, not abandon them, in a downturn.

Hyman Minsky was vigorous and pioneering in making his case for the "Big Bank" to pull economies out of a chronic slump. With his deep insights into the essentials of the monetary process he proposed 100% Reserves Banking. Commercial bank money was to be CB money. The expressions "failure-proof" or "risk-free" are commonly used to describe the arrangement for obvious reasons. The expectation was that infamous runs on banks prompted by the 'news' and rumors would be a thing of the past because people would be secure in the knowledge of the safety of their deposits. Liquidity would be deleted from the emergency manual of central banking. Despite this, the capitalist economy was prone to financial collapses and Minsky repeatedly wrote of the "Lender of Last Resort" function of the CB which must be on eternal standby.

Both Levy-Kalecki and Minsky drew upon and extended the economics of Keynes. The connection of the former with the General Theory is close and, therefore, state intervention is expected to deal with the vicissitudes of the cycle. Public expenditure, best exemplified in public works, is the calling card of Post Keynesian economics. Minsky, in contrast, wrote extensively and critically about the Federal Reserve and, in this case, a relation with Keynes' The Treatise on Money is easier to find. Since mainstream policy is monetary policy we are inspired to develop this connection as an alternative. All the same, we connect both perspectives, monetary and fiscal, in a four- quadrant diagram which is a structural display of a capitalist economy.

Our modus operandi contrasts with the standard method of proceeding with the specification of the choice problem of a representative agent. We elaborate on the distinction in the next section with the theme of this edited volume in focus.

BRIDGING MICROECONOMICS AND MACROECONOMICS

The familiar micro-grounded story concludes with the theorems and welfare implications of general equilibrium theory. The classical dichotomy between the real and the monetary holds and money is neutral and even super neutral. Data of an individual country is used to simulate a natural rate of unemployment and a natural rate of interest. These are yardsticks to determine the departure of the economy from the market-clearing outcome. When the Friedman rule pinning the growth rate of the stock of money to the rate of growth of output and the population growth rate is violated, the result is inflation. Inflation is a monetary phenomenon. Formulae like the Taylor rule are derived from the model as feedback rules to guide the hands of central bankers. The short-term interest rate is the instrument and the inflation rate is the target.

It is well known that this neat policy package has begun to fray as inflation is beaten and shows no signs of coming to life. The interest rate knows no lower bound in the quest to ignite investment plans.

Perceptive scholars within the establishment have begun to feel that there is something amiss in the workhorse model and not a few of these would welcome a return to Keynes and the recapture the special language of the aggregative structure of economies. A historical landmark in this enterprise is the locus classicus in macroeconomics transcribed by Godley and Cripps (1983). From the word go, the economy is described in the form of debt taking and debt giving. The economy is a monetary entity. Later in the book the nominal variables are translated into "widgets" for the purpose of formulating costs and prices and inflationary processes. Inflation is a non-monetary phenomenon. On identical tracks, according to one interpretation, Minsky follows Marx in theorizing that real variables can only be computed ex post in a monetary economy (Bellofiore, 2020). In a production economy both the private sector and the public sector are joined in a nexus of money inflows and money outflows connecting stocks and flows. We display the interlinkages in a stock-flow-consistent matrix below. Since the state is an element in the matrix it can control the related elements. Minsky was optimistic about the flowering of innovative schemes of production and employment outside the calculus of the market and the private sector. Finally, consumption must be directed. Policy must control not just the level but also the composition of output.

A radical approach to theory and policy can be pushed from within the establishment as well. Thus, in one scheme to ameliorate the current distress of England or, indeed, any country, the price level is recommended as a substitute target for the inflation rate (Barwell et al, 2020). If the price level is a government target variable, the price-taking or, indeed, price-making assumption of the basic theory is called into question. Since, in the non-neoclassical framework, costs make prices, wage formation would also appear in the radar of the policy makers calling for implicit wage-price guidelines or incomes policy. Secondly, both the short end and the long rate were to be grasped in "forward guidance". The central bank was expected to reestablish control of the term structure of interest rates to the end of the optimal output-inflation tradeoff. The yield targets would be published and market practitioners entrusted with the task of implementing the plan of the CB. Underlying it all is the appreciation of Keynes' "radical uncertainty" by former Bank of England Governor Mervyn King.

A corollary of the inflation-fighting task entrusted to the CB by the establishment is its autonomy for the purpose. Its separation from the government Treasury is often enshrined in law. The fiscal authorities are expected to obey the precepts of Econ 101 and confine themselves to addressing the problem of externalities and public goods. In the coursework, they are expected to be no different from individuals and balance their budgets as a transversality condition at least. However extraordinary the circumstances calling for massive government expenditure, Ricardian equivalence rumbles under the surface of the theory-policy terrain. The logic of backward induction is used to argue that beneficiaries of government largesse today will calculate the increased taxes they will have to pay on the morrow and so will modify their lifetime plans accordingly. The net effect of the hike in Treasury spending will be zero in the long run. In contrast, the architects of the English report under consideration seem to be indulging in forward induction in advocating the transfer of present resources across the private sector by taxation and to future generations by the issuance of debt. A second shibboleth dismissed by the authors of the report is another statute that has been codified, that CBs should not purchase government bonds directly. Indeed, the three scholars go as far as recommending the Bank of England as "market maker of last resort". They do no more than remind readers, as we have done, of the origins of CBs in history where balance sheet guidance was sought to assist the state in unique circumstances. The twist in the modern scheme is that the large-scale asset purchase was to be the following up of detailed design, not a mechanical injection of bank reserves. The monetary and fiscal authorities had to coordinate on conditions and clauses underlying the purchase of government securities.

Before we proceed to the geometry and the accountancy of our model, we continue with the motivation of our treatment in history.

PAST AND PRESENT

After falling into disuse for decades, the Real Bills doctrine is experiencing a comeback. The rolling out of goods and services from conveyor belts occupying large numbers of workers and supported by banks is an inspiring metaphor though the case is not confined to manufacturing. The origins of the doctrine lay in the join of commercial and central banking. The discounting of eligible paper was the bread-and-butter axis for the connection. Over time, the discount window took on a shaded hue and the discount rate came to be a penal rate. Post-2008, the window is sought to be opened to the light but the threat of a bad reputation is proving hard to banish. For instance, banks have been chary of using the Federal Reserve Discount Window (DW) (Armantier et al, 2011). The stigma attached to the DW has pushed them to more expensive sources of funds even when shortages of liquidity were severe. The stain on the reputation of a bank following a trip to the CB is not rubbing off and blocks the ability of the Fed to supply funds to banks during period of crisis. The following recounting of episodes is illuminating by way of contrast.

The monetary structure of the British economy was constructed on transactions- based credit but transformed into personal credit by the end of the war (Sissoko, 2019). The Bank of England was centered around supporting British industry and not the demands of the government. A sophisticated system of auditing was developed so as to monitor exposures to discounters and acceptors. The application of the Real Bills doctrine in the second half of the 18th century aided a vibrant development of the banking industry as a consequence. The instrument was a bill of exchange that was negotiable because it backed a verifiable commercial transaction. A bill was stamped thrice; by the issuer, the acceptor, the discounter. The issuer had an intimate relationship with the acceptor that enabled the former to draw a bill on the latter. Discounters were not permitted to broker or trade securities on the stock exchange. The doctrine imposed constraints on bank lending. What evolved over time, in contrast, were accommodation bills that did not represent trade in goods and services but only liquidity to the recipient. Early in the next century, the holder of the bill had only to prove that she had added value to the instrument in order to receive payment. English law contributed to these bills developing into "perfectly flexible currency". Transaction-based credit was extinguished upon the sale of goods. With accommodation credit, on the other hand, notes were rolled over. Convertibility being absent, every discount of such a bill became an addition to the supply of money which caused inflation which, in turn, increased the demand for the bills.

After 1945, instead of primarily reacting to market demands for liquidity by providing reserves, the Fed governed real-time overdraft policy (Walter & Wansleben, 2018). While a market interest rate proxying the cost of liquidity existed, the discount rate, the lending rate of the Fed, was evolving to the represent the true cost of (re)financing. It was the nominal anchor that market participants began to use in order to estimate their long-term costs instead of the calculation of intertemporal real costs provided by the market. For much of the 20th century, the Bank of England intervened in money markets via the purchase and sale of government and private paper of different maturities. These trades were effected by small institutions called Discount Houses that were conduits between the CB and commercial banks.

As promised in the first section, we assemble the elements in the economics of Keynes in a diagram displaying a short-run equilibrium which is a point of effective demand and a situation of involuntary unemployment.

A MINSKY-LEVY-KALECKI MODEL

Algebra

We work with the following representation of the Kalecki-Levy equation (Nachane, 2018, p 32).

π (corporate profits) = I (investment) + D (dividends) – [H_S (household savings) + G_S (government saving)] (1)

Nachane develops the long-run treatment of this identity where corporate profits are assumed to be zero. We are concerned with the short run and a regime in which profits are positive. Recalling our intuition, three of the four elements on the right-hand side of the equation above are subpar. The disbursal of dividends remains the sine qua non of the modern business enterprise, an aspect of so-called "short termism". Nachane proceeds to embed the equation in an Economics of Keynes perspective that embraces the Treatise on Money and the General Theory.

According to Keynes, the aggregate demand price (ADP) corresponding to a level of employment E is the sum total of proceeds expected from the sale of output Y producible by E (Nachane, 2018, p 34). That is, ADP = PY = PY(E). In the General Theory, Keynes assumed the price level, P, to be constant and a state of generalized excess capacity. Diminishing returns to employment are assumed and reflected in the shape of the curve in the figure. The aggregate supply price (ASP) corresponding to a level of employment E is the total costs involved in producing the output corresponding to E. Denoting the corresponding level of average costs by AC, we have ASP = AC.E. AC is likely to rise with employment as wages and rentals on capital go up. Consequently, the ASP curve has the shape depicted in the diagram till the point of full employment when the curve becomes infinitely inelastic. TR is total revenue and TC total cost and in the long run they are equal. If average costs are constant, we have TC = Y, the 45^0 line in the first quadrant. Finally, TR is divided into consumption, C, and investment, I. Government expenditure, G, is not included.

Minsky's macroeconomic model has the following structure which we proceed to modify based on the current conjuncture and the notion of firewalls (Minsky, 1986). The subscripts S and D in the diagram denote supply and demand respectively. According to Minsky, a portfolio balance expression or the liquidity preference relation yields a value of P_K, the market price of existing real capital, for every level of money M. Our model, in contrast, is not behavioural. In that, we are not far from the Master because Keynes allegedly did not care to specify three independent relationships for the propensity to consume, the marginal efficiency of capital, and the interest rate (Wray, 2018). Equilibrium is the "instantaneous" determination of income brought about by a particular concatenation of the three variables. Entrepreneurs are covert and are confronted with the choice between committing their resources into capital goods or holding cash. In a trough of investment activity, we assume that the CB and the network of banks work on both sides of the market, the demand for and the supply of capital goods. Also, we confine the term money to credit extended (and wages created thereby) by the community of banks. Returning to Minsky's formulation, $P_K = L(M, K)$. In his equation, there is a bar on K. Dropping the bar and checking out our CB as lender of first resort we have the following comparative static result. An increase in the stock of money is assumed to raise the price of capital and an increase in the stock of capital is expected to lower its price. Using the implicit function theorem,

$$\frac{dK}{dM} = -\frac{\frac{\partial L}{\partial M}}{\frac{\partial L}{\partial K}} = -\frac{+}{-} = + \tag{2}$$

The result connects with a line of thinking in current Marxian economics according to which the primal attention given to the accumulation of capital must be girded by the money process. Riccardo Bellofiore, for one, is hard at work researching a money value theory of labour. The marginal efficiency of capital (MEC) is substituted for P_K in Minsky's description. This is the turbulent equation in the system, shifting downward whenever a wave of pessimism overcomes investors. Animal spirits, in short, is the inverse of liquidity preference (Mallorquin, 2019). However, Keynes was unequivocal that functionaries of the state could do the job of computing quasi-rents during the lifetime of capital assets as competently as private entrepreneurs. In addition, in our case builders of capital goods not less than buyers of capital goods perform the present-value calculations of the MEC schedule. Secondly, liquidity, we will elaborate, is not in jeopardy with checking accounts with the CB. In short, we do not need the Keynes- Minsky tradeoff between "real investment" which expands "productive capacities" and liquidity preference. Minsky concludes with the following sequence: With P_{ID} the demand price of a unit of investment and PIS the supply price of a unit of investment, $P_{ID} = P_K$. Given the wage bill, Investment adjusts so that so that $P_{IS} = P_K$. Given Investment, Consumption and Income are determined in Y = C + I and $P_{IS} = P_{ID}$ and $M_D = M_S$. In our case, however, the first step is given by

$$M = P_{ID}I = P_{IS}I = P_KI \tag{3}$$

This process is displayed in the second and third quadrants of our diagram.

Keynes' capital theory, it is claimed, leads to a CB theory of the rate of profit (Spahn, 2019). The proposition that CB actions determine the real rate of interest even in the long run is well-established. The MEC schedule is reproduced in the third quadrant of the diagram and is represented by Minsky as follows $P_{ID} = \Sigma Q_t/(1+r_t)$. Compare with our equation 3. In Minsky's case, some Qs occur in upturns and some in downturns. The former might be represented by positive numbers and the latter by negative numbers. A present value or the demand price of capital (or the supply price of capital) cannot be a negative number but even in the case of a finite sum we can entertain a negative interest rate in the denominator to match the negative net profits in the numerator in the case of bad year, delivering a positive number. The negative interest rate here would be endogenous and a characteristic of investment plans unlike the policy rate that has motivated CBs in different countries. CBs continue to test the waters of the zero lower bound to interest rates to no effect. Their resolve is strengthened by some of the weightiest names in mainstream macroeconomics who pronounce that interest rates must be 'deeply negative' in the current milieu. They are unaware of the practical wisdom of Keynes. When prospects are completely bleak, policymakers can push interest rates to the floor to no avail. We have broken with the standard narrative of a given stock of capital and a market interest rate. The CB here sets the long-term interest rate. In the literature on the foundations of expectations formation, a distinction has been drawn between the "present future" and the "future present" (Watter, 2019). The former are potential futures projected on the basis of various scenarios written in the present. The latter is the actual present that will ensue at a future point in time. An illustration of the former is the building up (wherever absent) and manipulation of the yield curve. CBs set the short end of the curve and, as pointed out, 'forward guidance' has denoted 'operation twists' which means attempting to determine the long end as well. The intent, in other words, is for the public and the CB to coalesce their respective models of the future into the discipline of a unified model. No congruence with the economy is expected. As an example of the latter, in the 1920s the 'term structure of interest rates' entailed an adherence to the so-called free reserves doctrine which consisted of closely scrutinizing the item in the balance sheets of banks to detect early signs of abnormality in the movement of asset prices. The Fed would intervene to sterilize the changes in idle reserves through OMOS, restoring normalcy in the growth path of the money supply and to the formation of expectations. The discount window was pivotal here, setting bounds and displaying the concrete evidence of the movement of M.

The wage rate is given in the Minsky order traced above. An institutional structure underpins wage repression (Taylor, 2019). Laws and informal rules of the game have militated against labor. Already noted, the share of labor in national value added has fallen because of the demise of collective bargaining and the increasing hostility of business attitudes towards the working class. Falling or stable wages are aggravated by non-poaching and non-competition clauses in employee contracts which restrict job opportunities outside a company for a worker who quits. These divide-and-rule policies are easy to implement in an increasingly fragmented labor market.

Our monetary circuit, in contrast, originates with a wage bill and the increase in employment is depicted in the fourth quadrant in the diagram. Once again, there is a bar on the wage rate in Minsky's investment function which we drop in the reproduction, $I = I(P_K, W)$. Lifting the bar, we confirm that our CB is a 'People's CB'. An increase in the price of the capital stock is expected to increase the inducement to invest. The other partial derivative in the numerator below has been addressed in equation 2. An increase in the wage rate is assumed to decrease the propensity to invest. Using the implicit function theorem,

$$\frac{dW}{dM} = -\frac{\frac{dI}{dM}}{\frac{dI}{dW}} = -\frac{\frac{\partial I}{\partial P_K} \cdot \frac{\partial P_K}{\partial M}}{\frac{\partial I}{\partial W}} = -\frac{+.+}{-} = + \tag{4}$$

Also, we endorse the origins of the monetary circuit. The function must be invertible. Money causes an increase in wage disbursements so as to employ workers and kickstart the production process. As well, the wage contract is ab novo and can only be written up with a fresh emission of bank money. Workers will consume a major portion of their incomes and deposit some into their saving accounts with banks or financial institutions. We term this latter item cash or currency.

All the elements are depicted in the picture below. We have joined two diagrams in Nachane, 2018, (pp 34-35) to form quadrants 1 and 4. In addition, an independent fiscal authority could announce and implement a public works programme which would move the initial point of equilibrium to the right-hand side of the horizontal axis in quadrants 1 and 4. No change would take place in quadrants 2 and 3

Figure 1. The Minsky-Kalecki-Levy Model

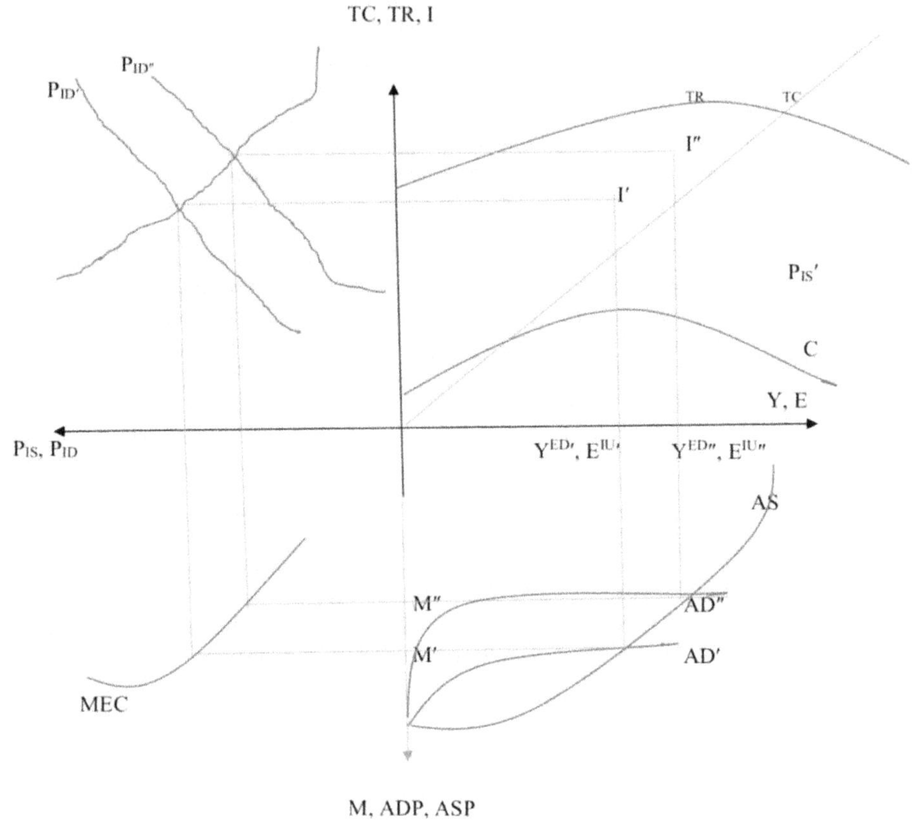

but it is natural to think, as Minsky did, of the "Big Bank" and "Big Government" acting in concert to lift economies out of the pit of a recession.

The primes denote an initial equilibrium. The common points on the x axis are points of effective demand (the first quadrant) and points of involuntary unemployment (the fourth quadrant). In the market for capital goods in the second quadrant, the demand curve tends to get perfectly elastic with regard to price increases at the higher end signifying Kalecki's principle of "increasing risk". By the same token, suppliers of capital goods are likely to succumb to a wave of optimism as the price of plant and machinery rises leading to an inelastic portion in that region. Minsky offered the possibility of demand and supply curves not intersecting anywhere. It is precisely the task of the "Big Bank" to umpire the plans of both demanders and suppliers of capital goods towards interior solutions. Corresponding to the kinked portion of the curves, in the second quadrant we have a truncation of the MEC curve, now constructed by the government as entrepreneur, in the third quadrant. We are prompted to label the situation an illiquidity trap. Our policy activism in the present originates in quadrant three with expansionary monetary policy and a new equilibrium depicted by double primes.

Stock-Flow-Consistent (SFC) Accounts

An alternative classificatory device to employ to make our case is SFC modeling as exemplified in Godley and Lavoie's (2007) classic. The modeling style goes back at least to François Quesnay, to his depiction of social interactions in the form of a financial transactions matrix. A similar but different research agenda is Ricardo-Marx-Leontief input-output economics. The elements of the matrix in this case are technological coefficients. Common to both bases is classes and not individuals. In common academics economics parlance, the requirement of rigor is the discipline of microeconomics. The rigor of SFC economics, in contrast, is scrupulous adherence to the principle of double- entry bookkeeping. Any entry must be matched with the same magnitude and a different sign elsewhere so that the terms add up to zero. In the box below, both commercial banks and the CB are subsumed as one and depicted in the bracketed items. In like manner, the CB and government are not independent. Profits of firms can be distributed as dividends or retained for the purpose of investment. The box above the dotted line is a snapshot of the economy. We have assumed one-period loan contracts with the loan rate strictly dominating the deposit rate which we have dropped.

Table 1. The Minsky-Kalecki-Levy Accounts

	Households	Firms		Banks	Government	Σ
		Current	Capital			
Consumption	-C	+C				0
Investment		+I	-I			0
Government Expenditures		+G			-G	0
Wages	+WB	-WB				0
Profits	+FD	-F	+FU			0
Taxes	-T				+T	0
Loan interest		$-r_{-1}L_{-1}$		$+r_{-1}L_{-1}$	$(+r_{-1}L_{-1})$	0
Deposits	+D			-D	(-D)	0
Changes in loans			+ ΔL	-ΔL		0
Changes in money				+ΔM	-ΔM	0
Changes in cash	-ΔD			+ΔD		0
Σ	0	0	0	0	0	

In general, an indecomposable matrix does not indicate the origin and direction of causal arrows. Notions of discretion of the monetary authorities, endogeneity of money, and the like are central to the discussion, though, and we use the notion of Directed Acyclic Graphs (DAGs) to illuminate the causal mechanisms involved in our model (Imbens, 2019). To be sure, the framework does not offer a underlying context, is not able to answer the question 'Why?'. For instance, the question 'Why did employment and wages fall during the Great Recession?' is a reverse causal inference question. A forward causal question is 'Can monetary and fiscal policy increase employment and wages'? Denoting the monetary authorities by MA and bringing in the price of capital from the diagram,

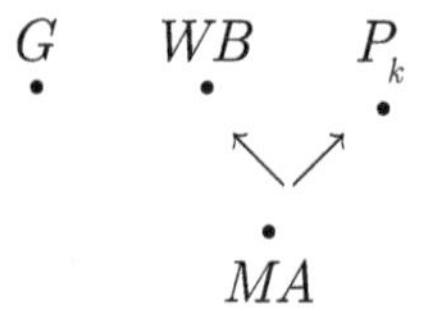

We have four nodes above and directed edges (arrows) connecting them. Now while an increase in wages and employment cause an increase in the market price of capital, the monetary authority is an observed confounder. The MA is the parent of WB and P_K while both are its children. P_K, according to the definition, has two parents, MA and WB. In our context, the endogeneity of WB arises from the employment of idle hands at a dignified wage and the anticipated effect of an employment-guarantee scheme on P_K. In traditional jargon, G is an instrumental variable because it satisfies the monotonicity requirement in having a positive effect, in this case on WB, indirectly effecting P_K. Another joining of the components is Keynes' "socialization of investment" (Wray, 2018). Keynes prognosticated that government spending would need to finance a larger and larger portion of the creation of resources in the modern economy. Correspondingly, government works programs would need to step in when the private sector employment was flagging. Income from work should replace transfer payments. Finally, public sector spending would increase stability when it was underwritten by money, a safe asset.

As in the case of the diagram, CB advances on the right-hand side at the bottom of the matrix originate the monetary process. The virtuous emission of money is cordoned off from the cash or currency that may be deposited by wage earners, the recipients of the loans taken out by firms. We use the emerging institution of CB digital currency to fortify the firewall drawn in with dotted lines between money and cash. Finally, the cordoning off also respects the accounting separation of the French circuit school. In any event, the institution of public digital money presses urgently as private digital money disruptions threaten to wreak havoc on social processes (DeNederlandscheBank, 2020). The demand for safe public money increases sharply under conditions of uncertainty. Our case is strengthened by the connection sought to be made between public digital money and the increased role of the commercial banking sector in the 20th century.

CENTRAL BANK DIGITAL MONEY (CBDM)

Central Bankers are coming alive to the implications of the 4th Industrial Revolution (Poloz, 2019). The term was coined by Klaus Schwab of the WEF. The common core with the first three are the massive displacement of labour, falling prices, and inflation. To these, digitalization is added. The development of digital money cannot be left to the private sector. Underpinning its evolution is a regime of wage repression and rentier payoff maximization (Juškaitė, Šisaudinis & Reichenbachas, 2019). Under active pricing, a CB could administer a time-variable discount rate on reserves.

Digital currency is already in existence in the form of bank reserves (Meaning et al, 2018; Sigitas, 2019). They are electronic and account-based, not token-based. In addition, as they are not founded on distributed ledgers nor other cryptographic formats they do not meet the definition of a cryptocurrency. They command a rate of return and are not imbued with universal access. Juškaitė et al distinguish between "general-purpose money" which is accessible to people at large, coterminous with cash and bank deposits, and "wholesale money" which are reserve accounts only open to firms through the intermediation of banks. In a similar vein, a distinction between a "retail CBDC" (RCBDC) and a "wholesale CBDC" (WCBDC) has been made (Mondello, Sinelnikova, & Trunin, 2020; Pfister, 2019). A RCBDC need not use a blockchain although the blockchain in this case would be "non-permissioned". The costs are higher and transactions are slow and energy-intensive. Transaction costs in the case of WCBDC, on the other hand, would be lower. In these "permissioned" blockchains, information is not available to the public but confined to a limited number of "nodes". Transactions would operate intra-day and the locus of monetary policy would reside here. While WCBDC would circulate outside the books of the CB, they could always be tracked through the distributed ledger. RCBDC is failsafe and perfectly liquid and meets the democratic mandate of CBs (Woodruff, 2019). It depends on the preference of the public vis-à-vis risk- and return-dominating financial instruments. Currency is exogenous. Tobin advocated "deposited currency accounts" according to which individuals would have direct access to their CBDC accounts through the medium of banks (Fegatelli, 2019). His motivation, following the huge drawdowns in his time, was the protection of deposit insurance. As in the Euro area, a well-oiled RTGS system would deliver. With the commercial bank-CB continuum, the threat of CBs crowding out commercial banks through competition would not arise. Commercial banks, if anything, would earn fees and commissions. Banks are not financial intermediaries but creators of money so the prognosis of disintermediation does not apply anyway. One scenario is two "fiat currencies" separated by a firewall. The reserves and currency accounts would each pay their charges, the interest on the former exceeding that of the latter. Correspondingly, banks would manage their separate reserve and currency accounts at the CB differently. WCBDC, on the other hand, is the outcome of the monetary process and is a feedback from the state of the economy. Money is endogenous. Accordingly, along with Juškaitė and coauthors we prefer the term CBDM ("central bank digital money") to CBDC (central bank digital currency).

FUTURE RESEARCH DIRECTIONS

Academics must come to grips with two concerns that all citizens of planet Earth obsess about. The ravages of climate change are already being felt. Secondly, digital technology and artificial intelligence is displacing labour in the production process. At the same time, the critical role played by health care and medical workers has flowered manifold. Robots will never be able to substitute for empathy and kindness. Thus, economists will need to build long-term models that incorporate green investments and production functions with computers and clouds as arguments. The private sector is unlikely to be forthcoming for reasons to do with technical scale and global reach as well as the futility of stochastic calculus in this matter. We need refurbished and exacting government investment and a radically revitalised public sector. Bank nationalisation must be reintroduced after unlearning the errors of yesteryear. One concept that would connect the elements and is a discussion point after years of disuse is the Real Bills Doctrine. Members of the erstwhile working class would hold the paper and share in the proceeds of rejuvenated economic growth.

CONCLUSION

Levy and Kalecki were pioneers in the structuralist tradition of macroeconomic model building. Economies malfunctioned, in general, and the state was a "built-in" or "automatic" stabilizer. With Abba Lerner, the chord connecting individual incentives and public outcomes was cut. In a Depression, the Treasury must do whatever it takes to effect a massive airlift of the economy. The money supply was a horizontal curve, responding to the compulsions of the capitalist dynamic. Neoclassical or new Keynesian policy, we have noted, is congruent with monetary policy and, quantitative easing notwithstanding, has meant lowering the overnight rate. Since pushing on that string has gone as far as it can go, our primary motivation has been a rewrite of monetary policy inspired by history and non-neoclassical macroeconomics. For the purpose, we have turned to Minsky for whom monetary (and financial) arrangements were at the forefront. Minsky and Levy and Kalecki built their edifices around the scaffolding erected by the architect Keynes. In the end, a stubborn recession must be countered by both cylinders firing, the Treasury and the Monetary Authority. We have focused on the latter in the form of the CB returning to its origins in commercial banking in inviting and vetting projects whose social value are in excess of their putative private profits. The works might be hard infrastructure like roads and irrigation schemes or soft infrastructure like the 'care industry' broadly conceived. Profits would be earned as would be wages. Some portion of the latter would be deposited in riskless liquid reserves with the CB or in risky financial institutions. Digital technology can take the place of the Chinese walls of yesteryear.

ACKNOWLEDGMENT

The first draft of the paper was presented at a National Symposium on the Indian Economy: Challenges and Prospects, Goa University, February 6-7, 2020. The opportunity and hospitality provided by Professor Pranab Mukhopadhyay are gratefully acknowledged. I thank two anonymous referees whose comments led to a more detailed and extended paper. I assume charge of any obfuscations that remain.

REFERENCES

Armantier, O., Ghysels, E., Sarkar, A. & Shrader, J. (2011, Aug. 31). *Is there Stigma to Discount Window Borrowing*. Federal Reserve Bank of New York, Liberty Street Economics.

Barwell, R., Chadha, J. S., & Greely, M. (2020). *Monetary Policy in Troubled Times: New Governor, New Agenda*. National Institute of Economic and Social Research Occasional Paper LIX.

Bellofiore, R. (2020). Hyman Minsky at 100: Was Minsky a Communist? *Monthly Review (New York, N.Y.)*, *71*(10).

Cencini, A. (2017). Introduction. In J.-L. Bailly, A. Cencini, & S. Rossi (Eds.), *Quantum Macroeconomics: The legacy of Bernard Schmitt* (pp. 1–20). Routledge.

DeNederlandschebank. (2020). *Central Bank Digital Currency* (Vol. 20-01). DeNederlandschebank Occasional Studies.

Fegatelli, P. (2019). *Central Bank Digital Currencies: The Case of Universal Central Bank Reserves.* Banque Centrale Du Luxembourg Working Paper No 130.

Godley, W., & Cripps, F. (1983). *Macroeconomics*. Oxford: Oxford University Press.

Godley, W., & Lavoie, M. (2007). *Monetary Economics*. Basingstoke, Hampshire: Palgrave Macmillan.

Goodhart, C.A.E. (2018). *Central Bank policies in recent years*. LSE Research Online.

Imbens, G. (2019). *Potential outcome and Directed Acyclic Graph Approaches to Causality: Relevance for empirical practice in economics*. NBER Working Paper 26104.

Juškaitė, A., Sigitas, Š., & Reichenbachas, T. (2019). *CBDC – in a whirlpool of discussion.* Lietuvos Bankas Occasional Paper No 29/2019.

Mallorquin, C. (2019). *How economics forgot power.* Universidad Autónoma de Cuidad Juárez.

Meaning, J., Dyson, B., Barker, J., & Clayton, E. (2018). *Broadening narrow money; monetary policy with a central bank digital currency*. Bank of England Staff Working Paper No 724.

Minsky, H. (1986). *Stabilizing an Unstable Economy*. Yale University Press.

Mondello, G., Sinelnikova, E., & Trunin, P. (2020). *Taking on Board the Long-Term Horizon in Financial and Accounting Literature*. GREDEG Working Paper No 2020-02, Université Côte D'Azur.

Nachane, D. (2018). *Critique of the New Consensus Macroeconomics and Implications for India*. Springer. doi:10.1007/978-81-322-3920-8

Pfister, C. (2019). *Central Bank Digital Currency: One, Two or None?* Banque de France Working Paper #72.

Poloz, S. S. (2019). *Technological Progress and Monetary Policy: Managing the Fourth Industrial Revolution*. Bank of Canada Staff Discussion Paper 2019-11.

Sigitas, Š. (2019). *Digital Currencies and Central Banking: A Sense of Déjà Vu*. Bank of Lithuania Occasional Paper No 26/2019.

Sissoko, C. (2019). *The Monetary Foundations of Britain's Early 19th Century Ascendancy*. Economics Working Paper 1906, University of West England, Bristol.

Spahn, P. (2019). *Keynesian capital theory: Declining interest rates and persisting profits*. Hohenheim Discussion Paper in Business, Economics and Social Sciences No 10-2019.

Taylor, L. (2019). Central Bankers, Inflation, and the Next Recession. Institute for New Economic Thinking.

Vahabi, M. (2019). *A Review of Péter Mihályi and Iván Szelényi, 2019, Rent-Seeking, Profits, Wages and Inequality, the Top 20%*. Palgrave Macmillan.

Vogel, S. K. (2019). Japan's Ambivalent Pursuit of Shareholder Capitalism. *Politics & Society*, *47*(1), 114–117. doi:10.1177/0032329218825160

Watter, T. (2019). The Janus face of Inflation Targeting: how governing through standardized expectations decouples monetary policy implementation from the future. *Futures past: Economic Forecasting in the 20th and 21st century*.

Watter, T., & Wansleben, L. (2018). How Central Bankers Learned to Love Financialization: The Fed, the Bank, and the Enlisting of Unfettered Markets in the Conduct of Monetary Policy. *Socio- Economic Review*.

Woodruff, D. M. (2019). To democratize finance, democratize central banking. *Politics & Society*, *47*(4), 539–610. doi:10.1177/0032329219879275

Wray, L. R. (2018). *Functional Finance: A Comparison of the Evolution of the Positions of Hyman Minsky and Abba Lerner*. Levy Economics Institute of Bard College Working Paper 900.

ADDITIONAL READING

Minsky, H. (2008). *John Maynard Keynes*. McGraw-Hill.

Minsky, H. (2015). *Can "it" Happen Again? Essays on Instability and Finance*. Routledge. doi:10.4324/9781315705972

Tcherneva, P.T. (2020). Guaranteeing Employment During the Pandemic and Beyond. Levy Economics Institute of Bard College Policy Note 2020/4.

van Veen, T. (2020). Have Macroeconomic Models Lost Their Connection with Economic Reality? CESifo Working Paper 8256.

KEY TERMS AND DEFINITIONS

Employer of First Resort: The government offering employment particularly in soft infrastructure like health but not excluding hard infrastructure like roads, traditionally the domain of public investment.

Illiquidity Trap: The truncation of the marginal efficiency of capital schedule at the point of the perfect elasticity of the demand curve and the perfect inelasticity of the supply curve for capital.

Lender of First Resort: The Central Bank originating lending for green investments when the private sector is not forthcoming for reasons that include uncertainty and high costs.

Chapter 5
Panel Non-Stationarity Methods in Macro- and Microeconomic Studies

Georgi Marinov
University of Economics, Varna, Bulgaria

ABSTRACT

Panel data analysis aims to overcome the weaknesses of its alternatives: country-by-country analysis is usually based on short samples, there is a significant country-specific distortion in the data, and it leads to biased estimates, and the cross-section analysis neglects the time dimension. In last two decades, tests for non-stationary panels sparked a large body of literature both on tests theory and on various empirical studies in multiple areas of micro- and macroeconomic research. The most popular studies include topics such as growth, finance, exchange rates, fiscal matters, and international trade, but also popular are studies in tourism, energy, resource demand and supply, IT and technology spreading, politics, inflation, international trade and current accounts, stock markets, etc.

INTRODUCTION

Data in macroeconomics is often comprised of short series, therefore the usage of tests for non-stationarity can lead to suspicious results. In microeconomics the situation is similar in many cases. The emergence of panel non-stationarity methods in the last decades gives the researcher the opportunity to explore for non-stationarity even shorter series. Panel tests are considered as more powerful than their time series counterparts. Combined with broader accessibility of data, especially from international sources as the World Bank, IMF, UN etc., a big number of studies appears for all types of countries and in various areas. Many countries provide more detailed data on their economies, making panel data studies feasible.

Theory behind the panel tests on non-stationary data has been developed mainly in the 1990s and up to 2008-2009. The first attempts to treat panel data were made parallel to the time series non-stationarity tests, in the late 1980s. Seminal papers by Levin and Lin (1993) and Im, Pesaran and Shin (1995) were

DOI: 10.4018/978-1-7998-4933-9.ch005

followed by vast literature on panel unit root tests and panel tests for cointegration. In its majority, panel literature is developed as some generalization of non-stationarity in time series.

However, there are two major problems with panel tests: the cross-sectional dependence and the unexplored small sample properties of the tests. The former problem consists in the fact that the early tests rely on independence in the N-dimension, which is almost never the case with real world data. In approaching this problem, tests are divided in "first generation" and "second generation" types. The latter problem is addressed mainly with bootstrap methods and other simulations.

The use of panel tests has recently become a common practice in economic studies, panel data has turned into a de facto standard in many cases. In the 2000s, the main panel tests on unit roots and cointegration were included in the popular econometric software packages, today they are an integral part of the software, and since then numerous papers using panel data and tests have appeared.

Panel methods have been applied in various macro- and microeconomic studies, to name but a few areas and titles: economic growth, inflation and other general issues; money demand and exchange rates; investment; fiscal policy; energy; environmental issues; trade and integration; development studies; labour studies; various sectoral studies. Most of the popular panel studies appear to be in the field of macroeconomics, however panel methods prove to be especially useful for studying some microeconomic topics as well, notably the market failures areas, and papers on ecology, energy, and resource allocation and use are among the most cited ones with panel methodology.

The rest of this chapter is organized as follows: section 2 presents the most popular tests, section 3 presents some of the popular areas of research, section 4 gives some future research directions, section 5 concludes.

TESTS FOR PANEL NON-STATIONARITY

Panel Unit Root Tests

Pioneering work in panel data on exploiting the information from cross-sectional dimensions in inferring non-stationarity is contributed to Quah (1994), who derives the normality of some cases of unit root regression in panels, demonstrating that coefficient estimators have a mixture of standard normal and Dickey-Fuller-Phillips asymptotics. Also found is that the standard normal distribution is a good approximation of both large N, small T, and large N, large T cases. This initial work is soon followed by a multitude of practical tests.

Levin, Lin and Chu (LLC) Test

Levin et al. (2002) develop a theory and a test (LLC) for panels where weak stationarity is violated by unit roots within each individual time-series. The test is based on the asymptotic theory, therefore it is applicable for relatively large panels. The proposed test statistic is a modified t-statistic, based on the normality of unit root t-statistic for a model with no individual fixed effects and independent and identically distributed disturbances derived by Quah (1994).

The test statistics have limiting normal distributions, but are "super-consistent", they converge faster as the time dimension grows, unlike the case of stationary data.

Considered is a *NxT* panel of *N* individuals with *T* periods observed, *i=1...N, t=1...T*. As a data generating process the standard dynamic model for panel data is used:

$$y_t = \rho y_{it-1} + \delta_0 + \delta_1 t + \eta_i + v_t + \varepsilon_{it},$$

where the last three terms, the individual-specific effect η_i, the time-specific effect v_t and the idiosyncratic disturbance ε_{it} are mutually independent random variables with zero mean.

The Monte Carlo simulations in Levin et al. (2002) show that the normal distribution is a fairly good approximation of the empirical distribution of the test statistic in relatively small samples, therefore the panel approach leads to significantly more powerful tests, compared to univariate tests.

The LLC test has a null hypothesis that each individual time series contains a unit root against the alternative of stationarity in each series. The model used is:

$$\Delta y_t = \rho y_{it-1} + \sum_{L=1}^{p_i} \theta_{iL} \Delta y_{it-L} + \alpha_{mi} d_{mt} + \varepsilon_{it}, m = 1, 2, 3,$$

where d_{mt} denotes the deterministic variables with their coefficients a_{mi} for three particular models: with no constant and trend, with a trend, and with constant and trend *(m=1, 2, 3)* and p_i is the (possibly unknown) lag order, permitted to vary across individuals.

The test is performed in three steps: in the first step, ADF regression is implemented, in the second step the ratio of long-run to short-run standard deviations is estimated, in the third step the panel test statistics is calculated, by pooling all cross sectional and time series observations. The test statistics has a standard normal distribution under the null for the model without constant or trend, but it diverges to negative infinity for the other models, however adjusted statistics is easy to calculate.

Since the test is a test on pooled data, it has strong restrictions - it requires ρ to be homogeneous across the individual series, which is not often a fact in practical cases.

Im, Pesaran and Shin (IPS) Test

Im et al. (2003) propose an alternative testing procedure, allowing ρ to vary across individual series. They suggest to take the average of the *t*-statistics in ADF tests, with the null hypothesis of unit roots in all individual series against the alternative of stationarity in some of the series. Under the null, the test statistics has a standard normal distribution after a simple correction, values for the correction are obtained with Monte Carlo simulations and presented in their paper. However, for unbalanced panels simulations have to be run by the researcher, this is also needed for cases where different lags for individual series are used.

Im et al. (2003) show their test is more powerful than the LLC test in smaller panels. However the results have to be interpreted carefully, due to the heterogeneous nature of the alternative hypothesis.

Maddala and Wu (MW) Test

Maddala and Wu (1999) propose a Fisher (1932) type test on *p*-values from univariate unit root tests from the individual series. The MW test combines the evidence from several tests. Instead to combine the test statistics, as in the IPS test, they suggest combining of the significance levels of the test statistics. Their idea is that in the case where the test statistics is continuous, its significance levels π_i are independent uniform *(0,1)* variables, and a combination of them has χ^2 distribution. They propose as test statistics a Fisher type statistics:

$$\lambda = -2\sum_{i=1}^{N} log_e \pi_i ,$$

which has a χ^2 distribution with *2N* degrees of freedom. The null hypothesis is presence of unit roots in all individual series, against alternative of stationarity in some of the series.

The MW test is simple and universally applicable, it is applicable also to panel cointegration tests. However, presence of a correlation among test statistics for different individual series is a problem leading to loss in power.

Hadri (H) Test

The H test by Hadri (2000) is a panel extension of the Kwiatkowski et al. (1992) univariate test. Unlike the previous tests, the null is stationarity in all series, against alternative of unit root in panel data. The test is a residual-based Lagrange multiplier test. The regression used is:

$$y_{it} = \alpha_i + \gamma_i t + \sum_{t=1}^{T} u_{it} + \varepsilon_{it},$$

where the first two terms are the deterministic components (constant and trend), ε_{it} is white noise, and $\sum_{t=1}^{T} u_{it}$ is random walk. Under the null of stationarity the variance of the random walk component is zero. The test statistics is $\frac{\sigma_u}{\sigma_\varepsilon}$ and has a standard normal distribution.

Choi (Choi) Test

The main idea in Choi (2001) is to combine *p*-values of unit root tests applied to each group, as a type of meta-analysis. Choi's approach is similar to MW, but additional tests are also proposed. The tests can be used for testing various null hypotheses - non-stationarity, stationarity, and also cointegration, after modifying the respective tests by adjusting the hypotheses, conditions and models. For short time dimensions, a bootstrap procedure is proposed.

"Second Generation" Panel Unit Root Tests

If there is a cross-sectional correlation in the series, the size of the tests is distorted.

The main problem of the "first generation" tests - LLC, IPS and MW, is that they would asymptotically always reject the null hypothesis on non-stationarity when it is true, as found by Banerjee, Marcellino and Osbat (2004).

Newer, "second generation" tests address the cross-sectional correlation by proposing various possible solutions - good overviews can be found in Hurlin and Mignon (2007), Hlouskova and Wagner (2006) and Wagner and Hlouskova (2009). For a more mathematical representation see Banerjee (2008).

The most popular approach with newer tests is first to estimate and eliminate the common driving factors of cross-sectional dependence and then to perform the panel unit root tests on the "de-factored" residuals. This is the core of the PANIC ("panel analysis of non-stationarity in idiosyncratic and common components") approach of Bai and Ng (2004). They use a data generating process where data is composed of three parts - deterministic, common multivariate factor and an idiosyncratic component. Their proposal is to test for unit roots separately for the common factor and for the idiosyncratic component.

Panel Cointegration Tests

As with cointegration in time series, the two main approaches are to use single equation models (extending the Engle-Granger approach to panel data, with residual-based tests for the null of non-cointegration and residual-based tests for the null of cointegration), and to estimate cointegrating vectors (extending the Johansen approach).

Pedroni (P) Test

Pedroni (1999, 2004) proposes several test statistics based on the Engle-Granger cointegration approach. Four of the statistics are in the "within-dimension": Panel *v*-Statistic, Panel *rho*-Statistic, Panel *PP*-Statistic, Panel *ADF*-Statistic; and three are in the "between-dimension": Group *rho*-Statistic, Group *PP*-Statistic, Group *ADF*-Statistic. All of them are asymptotically normal.

Kao and Chiang (KC) Test

Kao and Chiang (2000) use three models - bias-corrected OLS, fully-modified OLS (FMOLS), and dynamic OLS (DOLS) to propose asymptotically efficient estimators of the cointegrating vector in the presence of cross-sectional dependence. The main assumption is long-term covariance across cross-section.

Since the bias-corrected OLS has poor performance, mainly FMOLS and DOLS are used. The testing for panel cointegration itself is in fact testing the stationarity of the residuals. Similar is the Pedroni (2000) test.

Other popular tests are Gengenbach et al. (2006), Westerlund (2005) and Larson, Lyhagen and Lothgren (2001). The Kapetanios, Pesaran and Yamagata (2011) test seems to be very promising - see Choi (2013) and Pedroni (2019) for details and excellent technical overviews.

SOME RECENT AREAS OF RESEARCH WITH PANEL DATA

PPP and REER

Purchasing power parity (PPP) and real exchange rates (REER) are among the principal working areas for panel unit root and panel cointegration tests. Like with many other economic variables, starting point is the non-stationary nature of the exchange rates. The magnitude of forex markets, combined

Table 1. Selected Panel Unit Root and Cointegration Tests

PH - Phillips and Hansen (1990) P - Pedroni (1996, 1999, 2004) P00 - Pedroni (2000) LL - Larson and Lyhagen (2007) BM - Breitung and Meyer (1994) Q - Quah (1994) H - Hadri (2000) MS - Mark and Sul (2003) Pes - Pesaran (2007) PSS - Pesaran, Shin and Smith (1999) W - Westerlund (2007) K - Kao (1999) MW - Maddala and Wu (1999) Choi - Choi (2001) BN - Bai and Ng (2004) LS - Lee and Strazich (2003) AB - Arrellano and Bover (1995) ULLC - Breitung (2000) PS - Phillips and Sul (2003) MP - Moon and Pesaran (2004) KPY - Kapetanios, Pesaran and Yamagata (2011) B - Breitung (2005) LLL - Larsson, Lyhagen and Lothgren (2001) C - Carrion-i-Silvestre (2005) MK - McCoskey and Kao (1998) CS - Chang and Song (2009) HK - Hadri and Kurozumi (2012) BB - Blundell and Bond (1988) K - Kao (1999) AM - Agosin and Mayer (2000) HV - Hurlin and Venet (2001) PY - Pesaran and Yamagata (2008) DH - Dumitrescu and Hurlin (2012) GH - Gregory and Hansen (1996) DIF - Di Iorio and Fachin (2010) WE - Westerlund and Edgerton (2008) G - Gengenbach et al. (2009) PS - Pelgrin and Schich (2004) PSS - Pesaran, Shin and Smith (1999) PM - Phillips and Moon (1999) KC - Kao and Chiang (2001) HT - Harris and Tzavalis (1999) ASB - Alam, Sultana and Butt (2010)

Note: Further in the text these abbreviations are used to show the usage of the tests in empirical studies.

with the popularity of forex operations among investors, brings additional "common sense" arguments to support the non-stationarity of exchange rates. Both nominal exchange rates and price levels are well documented to be integrated processes.

Therefore testing for cointegration relationship between them makes sense. Pedroni (2004) represents the most used model as a test for presence of unit roots in the residuals of:

$$s_{it} = \alpha_i + \beta_i p_{it} + e_{it},$$

where s_{it} is the log nominal exchange rate of country *i* to the numeraire currency (most used is *USD*, but studies towards the *DEM* or the *EUR* do exist), and p_{it} is the log price level differential between country *i* and the numeraire, for period *t*. Often the countries share common disturbances which have to be taken in consideration, so that common time dummies δ_t can be added to the model:

$$s_{it} = \alpha_i + \delta_t + \beta_i p_{it} + e_{it} ,$$

The narrow interpretation of PPP suggests that under long run equilibrium β_i is necessarily equal to one. However, different theories explaining the non-unity of β_i exist, even if long term tendency towards equilibrium is present.

PPP is also the theoretical base for REER. As explained in Jacobson, Lyhagen, Larsson, and Nessén (2008), according to the PPP hypothesis, real exchange rates have to be stationary, so that persistent deviations from the "equilibrium level" can not exist. REER is defined as the relative price of traded goods to non-traded goods in the local economy:

$$REER = \frac{P_T}{P_{NT}} ,$$

where P_T and P_{NT} are the price indexes in local currency for tradable and non-tradable goods, respectively.

REER is believed to reflect the country's competitiveness, with a fall in REER (appreciation) indicating deterioration of competitiveness, and vice versa, a rise in REER (depreciation) indicating improvement of competitiveness.

Although exchange rates data is relatively easy to obtain in the form of long series, with multiple data observations, most popular studies focus on macroeconomic aspects of exchange rates and therefore researchers use relatively small panels.

The combined impact of data availability for exchange rates and price levels and the explored country groups effects leads to a situation where the analyzed panels are small *N*, large *T* panels. For those type of panels theory suggests the usage of time series, not panel techniques, as a more suitable approach. Mixed results with panel tests in exchange rates studies is one of the outcomes. Most researchers use mainly the older, "first generation" tests, which do not fully capture the cross section interdependencies.

FDI

Panel studies of foreign direct investment (FDI) exist primarily in relation with unemployment, growth and income, these being the most interesting variables from the economic policy point of view. In the typical case, FDI creates new working places and raises the technological level of the recipient economy by bringing new know-how and equipment. Efforts to attract FDI are high on the political agenda of many countries.

Inward FDI can contribute to employment, and to encourage supplier firms, acting as an accelerator for the economy, but at the same time FDI may displace local producers and contribute to the overcrowding of urban areas.

Table 2. Selected Empirical Panel Studies on PPP and REER

Authors	Instruments	Data	Results
Canzoneri, Cumby and Diba (1999)	PH, P, IPS	1970-1991, 13 countries	large and long-lived deviations from PPP for USD
Égert (2002)	P00, IPS	1991-2001, 5 countries	PPP holds for tradable goods, but it does not fully explain the REERs
Jacobson, Lyhagen, Larsson, and Nessén (2008)	P, LL	1974-2000, 4 countries	PPP does not hold, but may be a reasonable approximation
Breitung and Candelon (2005)	P, BM, LLC, IPS	1981-2001, 10 countries	PPP is relevant for countries with flexible rates, but not for pegged
Chen, Shen and Wang (2007)	P, Q, LLC, IPS, H	1992-1999, 16 countries	Big Mac price supports PPP stronger than CPI
Basher and Mohsin (2004)	P00, LLC, IPS	1980-1999, 10 countries	PPP does not hold
Égert, Drine, Lommatzsch, and Rault (2003)	P00, LLC, IPS	1995-2000, 9 countries	mixed results
Drine and Rault (2004)	P, Q, LLC, IPS	1983-1997, 6 countries	empirical rejection of the BS hypothesis
Hassan and Holmes (2013)	P, P00, MS, Pes, W, LLC, IPS	1987-2010, 24 countries	causality between remittances and REER
Mark and Sul (2001)	MS	1973-1997, 19 countries	monetary fundamentals dominate over PPP
MacDonald and Vieira (2010)	P, K, LLC, IPS, MW, Choi	1980-2004, 90 countries	more real depreciated exchange rate helps GDP growth
Béreau, Villavicencio, and Mignon (2012)	BN, PSS, P, K, LS, AB	1980-2007, 32 countries	overvaluations negatively affect growth
Hlouskova and Osbat (2009)	P, P00, W, KPY, LLL, LLC, ULLC, IPS, MW, PS, MP	1995-2008, 50 countries	estimates of "equilibrium exchange rates" are relatively robust
Basher and Westerlund (2009)	W, C	1973-1997, 19 countries	the monetary model seems to hold if cross-country dependence and structural breaks are not ignored
Maeso-Fernandez, Osbat and Schnatz (2006)	P00, K, Pes, IPS, H, MK	1975-2002, 25 countries	REER depends on income, government spending, and openness
Erdem, Nazlioglu and Erdem (2010)	P, P00, W, LLC, IPS, B	1980-2005, 21 countries	over time, trade is much more closely linked to income and exchange-rate uncertainty than to the level of the exchange rate
Ojo and Alege (2014)	P, K, W, LLC, IPS, AB	1995-2007, 40 countries	right policy on exchange rate determinants can attenuate fluctuations
Bahmani-Oskooee and Miteza (2006)	P, LLC, IPS	1988-1997, 42 countries	in the long-run, devaluations are contractionary
Bénassy-Quéré, Béreau and Mignon (2009)	P, LLC, H, IPS, MW	1980-2004, 15 countries	BEER estimations are quite robust
Mehmood and Younas (2019)	K, IPS	2000-2017, 5 countries	two-way causality between exchange rate and price differential

As Mucuk and Demirsel (2013) resume, in most cases there is a long term causal relationship from FDI to unemployment. Herzer et al. (2014) advert that FDI may undermine efforts to narrow income gaps.

Despite the availability of data about FDI for many countries, most of the studies concentrate on relatively small (in the N dimension) panels. Different views about the role and importance of FDI in different countries, combined with the need to account for regional patterns, can be the reason for the usage of small N panels, with bigger groups of countries being intrinsically incompatible. "First generation" tests prevail also in FDI studies. However, given the regional specifics, usage of newer tests can be a plus.

The Feldstein-Horioka Puzzle

Feldstein and Horioka (1979) present evidence that despite the expectations that in the times of globalization perfect or near to perfect capital mobility exists, in fact the data on savings and investments in OECD countries shows almost equal corresponding differences in domestic savings and domestic investments. Therefore the existence of international capital mobility has to be excluded, or at least it has to be put under question. In their original paper, Feldstein and Horioka (1979) apply an ordinary panel regression model on the ratios of investment and savings to GDP in the following form:

$$\left(\frac{I}{Y}\right)_i = \alpha + \beta\left(\frac{S}{Y}\right)_i,$$

where I are the investments, S are the savings, and Y is the GDP of the respective countries.

With perfect capital mobility, an increase in the savings in one of the countries would cause increases in investment in all other countries. They explore data for 15 years and 21 OECD countries and find β to be 0.89 when gross savings and investments are used and 0.94 when net savings and investments are used. Application of models with higher detailisation leads to similar results. This high correlation is believed to be a proof for the lack of capital mobility - all capitals are used domestically.

For the next decades, these findings became an intensively researched topic, see Coakley, Kulasi and Smith (1998) for an excellent overview of literature. Earlier studies do not account for the possible non-stationarity of the used variables, but if panel non-stationarity methods are applied, results become more authentic.

Unlike other macroeconomic issues, the Feldstein-Horioka puzzle seems to be reliably solved with the help of panel non-stationarity methods. As an indirect proof of that statement one can consider the lack of interest to this topic in the last decade, the latest significant papers being published around 2010.

Fiscal Matters

Fiscal policy is regarded as one of the major instruments to influence the economy, especially in providing stable macro-environment for growth.

Among the main topics in the fiscal matters studies is the institutional efficiency, with institutions having a special role in maintaining the framework for growth. In most empirical studies explored are the possible long-term relationships among growth, institutions, and fiscal policy.

Tax smoothing, optimizing tax revenues, spending path and spending distortions, links to interest rates and monetary policy are among other questions of interest.

Table 3. Selected Empirical Panel Studies on FDI

Authors	Instruments	Data	Results
Chintrakarn, Herzer and Nunnenkamp (2012)	LLL, P, B, P00, Pes, LLC, IPS, CIPS	1977-2001, 48 US states	there is considerable heterogeneity in the long-run effects of FDI on income inequality across states
Rizvi and Nishat (2009)	P, IPS, AM	1985-2008, 3 countries	FDI enhancement policies must be supplemented by the other measure to stimulate employment growth
Herzer, Hühne and Nunnenkamp (2014)	P, K, KC, P00, LLC	1980-2000, 5 countries	FDI contributed to widening income gaps
Asghar, Nasreen and Rehman (2011)	LLL, P00, HV, LLC, IPS	1983-2008, 14 countries	existence of long-run relationship between FDI and growth
Lee and Chang (2009)	P, P00, LLL, LLC, IPS, H	1970-2002, 37 countries	fairly strong long-run relationship among FDI and financial development indicators
Agrawal (2015)	P, LLC, IPS	1989-2012, 5 countries	bidirectional causality FDI-growth
Hudea and Stancu (2012)	P, LLC, B, IPS, MW, Choi	1993-2009, 7 countries	bidirectional causality FDI-GDP
Apergis, Katrakilidis and Tabakis (2006)	P, Pes, IPS	1992-2002, 30 countries	significant two way dynamic relationship between FDI and domestic investment
De Vita and Kyaw (2008)	P, LL, IPS	1990-2004, 32 countries	for FDI flows, domestic productivity growth increases considerably a developing country's attractiveness for investment while foreign output growth exerts a significantly negative influence
Eregha (2012)	P, K, IPS, LLC, B, H, Choi	1970-2008, 10 countries	FDI inflow crowds out domestic investment in the region during the sample period
Herzer (2008)	GH	1971-2005, 14 countries	FDI has positive long-run effects on domestic output
Sothan (2016)	P, K, LLC, IPS, MW	1980-2013, 21 countries	FDI and exports are really important contributors of long-run growth
Herzer and Donaubauer (2018)	KC, P, Pes	1981-2011, 70 countries	long-run effect of FDI on TFP is significantly negative on average in developing countries
Mucuk and Demirsel (2013)	P, KC, LLC, IPS, H	1981-2009, 7 countries	FDI and unemployment are cointegrated in the long run
Bayar and Gavriletea (2018)	PY, DH, W, P00, CIPS, MW	1996-2015, 11 countries	a developed financial system leads a country to attract more FDI inflows
Zdravković, Đukić and Bradić-Martinović (2017)	P, P00, KC, CIPS, LLC, IPS	2000-2014, 17 countries	mixed results
Al-Iriani (2007)	P, AB, IPS,	1970-2004, 6 countries	FDI has been an important factor in growth
Pradhan (2009)	P, LLC, IPS	1970-2007, 5 countries	high level of FDI can generate high level of growth and vice versa
Kizilkaya, Ay and Akar (2016)	P, P00, MW, LLC	2000-2013, 39 countries	positive relationship among long term FDI, human capital, economic freedom and growth
Erdal and Göçer (2015)	DH, MW, B	1996-2013, 10 countries	FDI contribute to speed up R&D and innovation
Ponce and Alvarado (2019)	P, Pes, W, DH, LLC, IPS	1980-2017, 100 countries	FDI flows, trade, and urban concentration play an important role in determining air pollution levels
Kim (2019)	P, LLC, IPS	1980-2013, 87 countries	FDI inflows do not cause an increase in CO2 emissions in the short run

Panel non-stationarity tests seem to be useful instruments in exploring fiscal policy effects and feasibility of fiscal measures. However, in most of the studies, even in newer ones, "first generation" tests are used. Given the specifics of the fiscal matters and their linkage to the political structure of the country, the usage of relatively small panels should not be a surprise.

Table 4. Selected Papers on Feldstein-Horioka Puzzle

Authors	Instruments	Data	Results
Herwartz and Xu (2009)	PS	1971-2002, 97 countries	savings-investment relation might be also subject to other economic forces
Banerjee and Zanghieri (2003)	P, BN, LLC, IPS, MW	1960-2002, 14 countries	mixed results
Ho (2002)	KC	1961-1997, 20 countries	cointegration is strongly rejected
Di Iorio and Fachin (2010)	GH, DIF	1970-2007, 18 countries	the null hypothesis of no cointegration is not rejected
Bangake and Eggoh (2011)	K, P00, PSS, LLC	1970-2006, 37 countries	savings and investment are non-stationary and cointegrated
Murthy (2009)	P00, LLC, IPS, MW	1960-2002, 14 countries	F-H puzzle is not valid
Coakley, Fuertes and Spagnolo (2001)	PM	1980-2000, 12 countries	slope coefficient consistent with long run capital mobility
Murthy (2007)	LLL, IPS, MW, B, H	1960-2002, 14 countries	F-H puzzle is not valid
Kim (2004)	P, P00, K, LLC, IPS	1960-1998, 48 countries	capitals are mobile across countries
Pelgrin and Schich (2004)	P, K, PSS, MW, BN	1960-1999, 20 countries	S and I are cointegrated

Various Growth-Related Issues

Economic growth is of utmost interest in macroeconomic studies, especially given its importance for policymakers. Panel non-stationarity tests can contribute to the debate about the endogeneity of growth, in supplying suitable instruments for handling possible integrated variables, as well as the related evidence. Growth-related issues prove to be a very popular field of macroeconomic research with use of panel data. Growth studies with panel data are multi-faceted, exploring various linkages, even linkages between growth and appearingly non-explorable variables as democracy and religion.

Growth studies are among the areas where large N panels can be used. Data availability from international sources like the World Bank or OECD strongly contributes to the feasibility of this type of studies.

Various Ecology and Energy Issues

Ecology and energy are among the areas, where market failures appear. Given their importance for growth, this is the field in microeconomic research where panel studies have their natural application. Ecology and energy papers are the most cited papers with panel non-stationarity tests, a contribution to this fact has also been the growing interest in environment and pollution topics.

FUTURE RESEARCH DIRECTIONS

For what concerns theory, some of the panel non-stationarity tests have become very popular, however their applicability continues to have its limits. Testing is reliable enough only for relatively long series, because the test theory lies in many cases on assumptions of asymptotics. Therefore small sample prop-

Table 5. Selected Papers on Fiscal Matters

Authors	Instruments	Data	Results
Abdullah (2020)	P, P00, LLC, IPS, MW	1982-2001, 13 countries	fiscal policy is practically possible and can be effective in influencing the real per capita GDP
Nieh and Ho (2006)	KC, B, IPS, HT, H	1980-2000, 23 countries	empirical results justify the Keynesian plea for expansionary fiscal policy
Alam, Sultana and Butt (2010)	ASB, IPS	1970-2005, 10 countries	expenditures in the social sector can increase economic growth
Westerlund, Mahdavi and Firoozi (2011)	W, KC	1963-1997, 50 US states	expenditures seem to bear the adjustment burden in response to budgetary disequilibria
Lamartina and Zaghini (2011)	P, K, LLC, B, IPS, MW, H, CIPS	1970-2006, 23 countries	widespread validity of the Wagner's law
Jäger and Schmidt (2016)	P, K, KC, LLC, IPS, MW, CIPS	1971-2007, 13 countries	share of elderly voters and public investment rates are cointegrated and negatively correlated
Claeys (2007)	P, LL, IPS	1970-2001, 14 countries	at the European level, panel cointegration tests indicate European fiscal authorities have maintained sustainable fiscal policies
Christopoulos and Tsionas (2003)	P, P00, IPS, LL, HT	1970-1999, 11 countries	long run negative relationship between government spending and government deficits
Mehrara, Pahlavani and Elyasi (2011)	K, LLC, IPS	1995-2008, 40 countries	bidirectional causal relation between government revenues and government expenditures
Bujang, Hakim and Ahmad (2013)	K, LLC, IPS, MW	2000-2009, 48 countries	tax can be an important tool to recover the current recession or economic slowdown
Mitrovic et al. (2019)	W, PSS, Pes	1995-2018, 25 countries	public debt is integrated of level one
Lin and Kueh (2019)	P, LLC, IPS	1990-2016, 6 countries	handling optimal debt is very important to overcome the unbalances of fiscal and current account
Mohammadi Khyareh (2019)	P, K, LLC, IPS, MW	2000-2010, 31 countries	corruption has a negative impact on all three stages of entrepreneurial motivation, tax evasion has a negative effect on established entrepreneurship

erties of the tests, and especially under presence of cross-sectional dependence continue to be the most important problem to solve with panel data.

Further exploration of the tests which allow for unbalanced panels seem also be very promising, given the limited availability of data in some important areas, where data from countries of different groups has to be studied. Another interesting direction of development is the exploration of nonlinear panel data models, because parameter estimation in panel models is more reliable than in time series models.

In applied modeling, re-evaluation of previous panel studies by using more recent techniques can bring surprising results. Special attention require studies of the circular economy and the sustainable

Table 6. Selected Papers on Growth Related Issues

Authors	Instruments	Data	Results
Mehrara and Musai (2013)	P, LLC, IPS	1970-2010, 101 countries	long-run relationship between human capital and GDP
Jaunky (2013)	P, W, Pes, BB, HK, CS, LLC, IPS, H	1980-2005, 28 countries	long-run relationship between democracy and growth
Ee (2016)	P, KC, LLC, IPS, MW	1985-2014, 3 countries	highly significant export-led growth effect
Demetriades and James (2011)	P, W, Pes, LLC	1975-2006, 18 countries	finance does not lead economic growth in SSA
Cavalcanti, Mohaddes and Raissi (2011)	P, P00, Pes, CIPS	1980-2006, 53 countries	the effect of oil abundance on real income is significantly positive
Asteriou and Price (2005)	P, PSS, IPS	1966-1992, 59 countries	uncertainty reduces both investment and growth
Hossain and Mitra (2013)	K, LLC, IPS, MW, Choi	1974-2009, 33 countries	Long-run causal relationships from growth to trade openness, domestic investment and government spending
Mitra, Hossain and Hossain (2015)	K, LLC, IPS, MW, Choi	1971-2010, 13 countries	effects of foreign aid on growth are significantly negative
Donaubauer (2014)	P, K, KC, IPS, MW	1970-2012, 63 countries	in the long-run and on average, aid and FDI are negatively correlated
Martins (2011)	P, K, W, LLC, IPS, MW, H, Pes, B	1970-2007, 59 countries	macroeconomic management of aid inflows in Africa has been better than often suggested by comparable exercises
Herzer and Nunnenkamp (2012)	P, K, Pes, P00, IPS, CIPS	1970-1995, 21 countries	aid exerts an inequality increasing effect on income distribution
Moolio and Kong (2016)	P, K, P00, KC, LLC, B, IPS, MW	1997-2014, 4 countries	foreign aid and GDP cointegrate
Chowdhury and Das (2011)	P, LLC, IPS, MW	1976-2008, 5 countries	positive relationship between aid and growth
Neelankavil, Stevans and Roman Jr (2012)	K, B, LLC, IPS, MW	1990-2007, 37 countries	FDI is not very important in explaining real GDP over the long-run
Alam and Sumon (2020)	P, KC, LLC, IPS, MW	1990-2017, 15 countries	bidirectional causality between trade and economic growth
Bluszcz and Manowska (2019)	P, K	2006-2017, 5 countries	causality of gross domestic product growth for developing countries

development, where there is scarcity of data on the one hand, and a big social and economic importance on the other hand.

CONCLUSION

Panel non-stationarity tests emerged since the early 1990s, and in the recent years they became some of the primary instruments to study various micro- and macroeconomic issues. The main reason for

Table 7. Selected Papers on Energy and Ecology Issues

Authors	Instruments	Data	Results
Uddin et al. (2017)	P, P00, KC, LLC, IPS, MW, Choi	1991-2012, 27 countries	sustained economic growth is a necessary, but not sufficient, condition to safeguard the environment
Charfeddine and Mrabet (2017)	P, P00, KC, LLC, IPS	1975-2007, 15 countries	strong evidence for long run relationship between all panel variables
Hamit-Haggar (2012)	P, Pes, LLC, IPS, H, Choi, MW	1990-2007, 21 Canadian industrial sectors	strong evidence of a long-run relationship between greenhouse gas emissions and energy consumption
Destek and Sarkodie (2019)	DH, Pes	1977-2013, 11 countries	increased levels of energy use lead to an increase in ecological footprint
Dinda and Coondoo (2006)	IPS	1960-1990, 88 countries	results suggest that openness reduces CO2 emission in Western Europe and Europe as a whole, whereas it increases emission in Africa, Central America
Rauf et al. (2018)	P, K, DH, LLC, IPS	1980-2016, 47 countries	all the regressors positively and significantly impacted environmental quality, except for trade openness, which had a negative impact on CO2 emissions
Charfeddine (2017)	GH, C	1970-2015, 1 country	strong evidence of a U-shaped relationship between the Ecological Footprint and real GDP per capita
Danish, Ulucak and Khan (2020)	W, Pes, DH	1992-2016, 5 countries	natural resources and ECF granger cause each other
Lee and Lee (2009)	P, AB	1971-2003, 109 countries	the per capita CO2 emissions and real GDP per capita in the sample countries are a mixture of I(0) and I(1) processes and the generally used panel root tests could lead to misleading inferences
Nathaniel et al. (2020)	P, Pes, W, CIPS, LLC, MW	1990-2016, 13 countries	renewable energy does not contribute meaningfully to environmental quality in about 84% of the countries sampled. On the other hand, non-RE consumption contributes about 17% of environmental deterioration in the region

their popularity is that these instruments help to overcome the problems resulting from the possible integrated nature of many economic variables. Panel methods are most valuable in cases where data is scarce, resulting in short series, i.e. in macroeconomic studies. In this chapter only a very small part of the vast literature was presented. Further areas of intensive research with panel data are tourism, resource demand and supply, IT and technology spreading, politics, inflation, international trade and current accounts, stock markets etc.

Recent versions of econometric software include many of the panel instruments, therefore the popularity of panel studies can be expected to grow even further in the future.

REFERENCES

Abdullah, H. (2020). Fiscal policy, institutions, and economic growth in Asian countries: Evidence from Pedroni's Cointegration approach. *Malaysian Management Journal*, *12*(1-2), 117–135.

Agrawal, G. (2015). Foreign direct investment and economic growth in BRICS economies: A panel data analysis. *Journal of Economics. Business and Management*, *3*(4), 421–424. doi:10.7763/JOEBM.2015.V3.221

Al-Iriani, M. (2007). Foreign direct investment and economic growth in the GCC countries: A causality investigation using heterogeneous panel analysis. *Topics in Middle Eastern and North African Economies*, 9.

Alam, K. J., & Sumon, K. K. (2020). Causal Relationship between Trade Openness and Economic Growth: A Panel Data Analysis of Asian Countries. *International Journal of Economics and Financial Issues*, *10*(1), 118–126. doi:10.32479/ijefi.8657

Alam, S., Sultana, A., & Butt, M. S. (2010). Does social expenditures promote economic growth? A multivariate panel cointegration analysis for Asian Countries. *European Journal of Soil Science*, *14*(1), 44–54.

Apergis, N., Katrakilidis, C. P., & Tabakis, N. M. (2006). Dynamic linkages between FDI inflows and domestic investment: A panel cointegration approach. *Atlantic Economic Journal*, *34*(4), 385–394. doi:10.100711293-006-9026-x

Asghar, N., Nasreen, S., & Rehman, H. (2011). Relationship between FDI and economic growth in selected Asian countries: A panel data analysis. *Review of Economics & Finance*, *2*, 84–96.

Asteriou, D., & Price, S. (2005). Uncertainty, investment and economic growth: Evidence from a dynamic panel. *Review of Development Economics*, *9*(2), 277–288. doi:10.1111/j.1467-9361.2005.00276.x

Bahmani-Oskooee, M., & Miteza, I. (2006). Are devaluations contractionary? Evidence from panel cointegration. *Economic Issues*, *11*(1), 49–64.

Bai, J., & Ng, S. (2004). A PANIC attack on unit roots and cointegration. *Econometrica*, *72*(4), 1127–1177. doi:10.1111/j.1468-0262.2004.00528.x

Baltagi, B. (2008). *Econometric analysis of panel data*. John Wiley & Sons.

Banerjee, A., Marcellino, M., & Osbat, C. (2004). Some cautions on the use of panel methods for integrated series of macroeconomic data. *The Econometrics Journal*, *7*(2), 322–340. doi:10.1111/j.1368-423X.2004.00133.x

Banerjee, A., & Zanghieri, P. (2003). *A new look at the Feldstein-Horioka puzzle using an integrated panel* (Vol. 22). CEPII.

Bangake, C., & Eggoh, J. C. (2011). The Feldstein–Horioka puzzle in African countries: A panel cointegration analysis. *Economic Modelling*, *28*(3), 939–947. doi:10.1016/j.econmod.2010.11.011

Basher, S. A., & Mohsin, M. (2004). PPP tests in cointegrated panels: Evidence from Asian developing countries. *Applied Economics Letters*, *11*(3), 163–166. doi:10.1080/1350485042000203788

Basher, S. A., & Westerlund, J. (2009). Panel cointegration and the monetary exchange rate model. *Economic Modelling*, *26*(2), 506–513. doi:10.1016/j.econmod.2008.10.006

Bayar, Y., & Gavriletea, M. D. (2018). Foreign direct investment inflows and financial development in Central and Eastern European Union countries: A panel cointegration and causality. *International Journal of Financial Studies*, *6*(2), 55. doi:10.3390/ijfs6020055

Bénassy-Quéré, A., Béreau, S., & Mignon, V. (2009). Robust estimations of equilibrium exchange rates within the G20: A panel BEER approach. *Scottish Journal of Political Economy*, *56*(5), 608–633. doi:10.1111/j.1467-9485.2009.00500.x

Béreau, S., Villavicencio, A. L., & Mignon, V. (2012). Currency misalignments and growth: A new look using nonlinear panel data methods. *Applied Economics*, *44*(27), 3503–3511. doi:10.1080/00036846.2011.577022

Bluszcz, A., & Manowska, A. (2019). Panel Analysis to Investigate the Relationship Between Economic Growth, Import, Consumption of Materials and Energy. In *IOP Conference Series: Earth and Environmental Science* (Vol. 362, No. 1, p. 012153). IOP Publishing. 10.1088/1755-1315/362/1/012153

Breitung, J., & Candelon, B. (2005). Purchasing power parity during currency crises: A panel unit root test under structural breaks. *Review of World Economics*, *141*(1), 124–140. doi:10.100710290-005-0018-8

Bujang, I., Hakim, T. A., & Ahmad, I. (2013). Tax structure and economic indicators in developing and high-income OECD countries: Panel cointegration analysis. *Procedia Economics and Finance*, *7*(13), 164–173. doi:10.1016/S2212-5671(13)00231-1

Canzoneri, M. B., Cumby, R. E., & Diba, B. (1999). Relative labor productivity and the real exchange rate in the long run: Evidence for a panel of OECD countries. *Journal of International Economics*, *47*(2), 245–266. doi:10.1016/S0022-1996(98)00021-X

Cavalcanti, T. V. D. V., Mohaddes, K., & Raissi, M. (2011). Growth, development and natural resources: New evidence using a heterogeneous panel analysis. *The Quarterly Review of Economics and Finance*, *51*(4), 305–318. doi:10.1016/j.qref.2011.07.007

Charfeddine, L. (2017). The impact of energy consumption and economic development on Ecological Footprint and CO2 emissions: Evidence from a Markov Switching Equilibrium Correction Model. *Energy Economics*, *65*, 355–374. doi:10.1016/j.eneco.2017.05.009

Charfeddine, L., & Mrabet, Z. (2017). The impact of economic development and social-political factors on ecological footprint: A panel data analysis for 15 MENA countries. *Renewable & Sustainable Energy Reviews*, *76*, 138–154. doi:10.1016/j.rser.2017.03.031

Chen, C. F., Shen, C. H., & Wang, C. A. A. (2007). Does PPP hold for Big Mac price or consumer price index? Evidence from panel cointegration. *Economic Bulletin*, *6*(16), 1–15.

Chintrakarn, P., Herzer, D., & Nunnenkamp, P. (2012). FDI and income inequality: Evidence from a panel of US states. *Economic Inquiry*, *50*(3), 788–801. doi:10.1111/j.1465-7295.2011.00384.x

Choi, I. (2001). Unit root tests for panel data. *Journal of International Money and Finance*, *20*(2), 249–272. doi:10.1016/S0261-5606(00)00048-6

Choi, I. (2013). *Panel Cointegration.* Working Papers 1208, Research Institute for Market Economy, Sogang University.

Chowdhury, M., & Das, A. (2011). Aid-growth nexus in south Asia: Evidence from time series and panel cointegration. *Research in Applied Economics*, *3*(1), 1. doi:10.5296/rae.v3i1.601

Christopoulos, D. K., & Tsionas, E. G. (2003). Testing the Buchanan-Wagner hypothesis: European evidence from panel unit root and cointegration tests. *Public Choice*, *115*(3-4), 439–453. doi:10.1023/A:1024213614689

Claeys, P. (2007). Sustainability of EU fiscal policies: A panel test. *Journal of Economic Integration*, 112-127.

Coakley, J., Fuertes, A. M., & Spagnolo, F. (2001). *The Feldstein-Horioka puzzle is not as bad as you think.* Birkbeck College, Department of Economics.

Coakley, J., Kulasi, F., & Smith, R. (1998). The Feldstein–Horioka puzzle and capital mobility: A review. *International Journal of Finance & Economics*, *3*(2), 169–188. doi:10.1002/(SICI)1099-1158(199804)3:2<169::AID-IJFE74>3.0.CO;2-H

Danish, U., Ulucak, R., & Khan, S. U.-D. (2020). Determinants of the ecological footprint: Role of renewable energy, natural resources, and urbanization. *Sustainable Cities and Society*, *54*, 101996. doi:10.1016/j.scs.2019.101996

De Vita, G., & Kyaw, K. S. (2008). Determinants of FDI and portfolio flows to developing countries: A panel cointegration analysis. *European Journal of Economics. Finance and Administrative Sciences*, *13*(13), 161–168.

Demetriades, P. O., & James, G. A. (2011). Finance and growth in Africa: The broken link. *Economics Letters*, *113*(3), 263–265. doi:10.1016/j.econlet.2011.08.007

Destek, M. A., & Sarkodie, S. A. (2019). Investigation of environmental Kuznets curve for ecological footprint: The role of energy and financial development. *The Science of the Total Environment*, *650*, 2483–2489. doi:10.1016/j.scitotenv.2018.10.017 PMID:30293003

Di Iorio, F., & Fachin, S. (2010). *Savings and Investments in the OECD, 1970-2007: a Panel Cointegration test with breaks.* Academic Press.

Dinda, S., & Coondoo, D. (2006). Income and emission: A panel data-based cointegration analysis. *Ecological Economics*, *57*(2), 167–181. doi:10.1016/j.ecolecon.2005.03.028

Donaubauer, J. (2014). Does foreign aid really attract foreign investors? New evidence from panel cointegration. *Applied Economics Letters*, *21*(15), 1094–1098. doi:10.1080/13504851.2014.909570

Drine, I., & Rault, C. (2004). Does the Balassa-Samuelson hypothesis hold for Asian countries? An empirical analysis using panel data and cointegration tests. *Applied Econometrics and International Development, 4*(4).

Ee, C. Y. (2016). Export-led growth hypothesis: Empirical evidence from selected Sub-Saharan African countries. *Procedia Economics and Finance, 35*(2), 232–240. doi:10.1016/S2212-5671(16)00029-0

Égert, B. (2002). Investigating the Balassa-Samuelson hypothesis in the transition: Do we understand what we see? A panel study. *Economics of Transition, 10*(2), 273–309. doi:10.1111/1468-0351.00112

Égert, B., Drine, I., Lommatzsch, K., & Rault, C. (2003). The Balassa–Samuelson effect in Central and Eastern Europe: Myth or reality? *Journal of Comparative Economics, 31*(3), 552–572. doi:10.1016/S0147-5967(03)00051-9

Erdal, L., & Göçer, İ. (2015). The effects of foreign direct investment on R&D and innovations: Panel data analysis for developing Asian countries. *Procedia: Social and Behavioral Sciences, 195*(3), 749–758. doi:10.1016/j.sbspro.2015.06.469

Erdem, E., Nazlioglu, S., & Erdem, C. (2010). Exchange rate uncertainty and agricultural trade: Panel cointegration analysis for Turkey. *Agricultural Economics, 41*(6), 537–543. doi:10.1111/j.1574-0862.2010.00469.x

Eregha, P. B. (2012). The dynamic linkages between foreign direct investment and domestic investment in ECOWAS countries: A panel cointegration analysis. *African Development Review, 24*(3), 208–220. doi:10.1111/j.1467-8268.2012.00317.x

Feldstein, M., & Horioka, C. (1980). Domestic Saving and International Capital Flows. *Economic Journal (London), 90*(358), 314–329. doi:10.2307/2231790

Feldstein, M. S., & Horioka, C. Y. (1979). *Domestic savings and international capital flows.* NBER Working paper nr. 310.

Fisher, S. R. A. (1932). *Statistical Methods for Research Workers*. Oliver and Boyd.

Gengenbach, C., Palm, F. C., & Urbain, J. P. (2006). Cointegration testing in panels with common factors. *Oxford Bulletin of Economics and Statistics, 68*, 683–719. doi:10.1111/j.1468-0084.2006.00452.x

Hadri, K. (2000). Testing for stationarity in heterogeneous panel data. *The Econometrics Journal, 3*(2), 148–161. doi:10.1111/1368-423X.00043

Hamit-Haggar, M. (2012). Greenhouse gas emissions, energy consumption and economic growth: A panel cointegration analysis from Canadian industrial sector perspective. *Energy Economics, 34*(1), 358–364. doi:10.1016/j.eneco.2011.06.005

Hassan, G. M., & Holmes, M. J. (2013). Remittances and the real effective exchange rate. *Applied Economics, 45*(35), 4959–4970. doi:10.1080/00036846.2013.808311

Herwartz, H., & Xu, F. (2009). Panel data model comparison for empirical saving-investment relations. *Applied Economics Letters, 16*(8), 803–807. doi:10.1080/13504850701221949

Herzer, D. (2008). The long-run relationship between outward FDI and domestic output: Evidence from panel data. *Economics Letters, 100*(1), 146–149. doi:10.1016/j.econlet.2007.12.004

Herzer, D., & Donaubauer, J. (2018). The long-run effect of foreign direct investment on total factor productivity in developing countries: A panel cointegration analysis. *Empirical Economics, 54*(2), 309–342. doi:10.100700181-016-1206-1

Herzer, D., Hühne, P., & Nunnenkamp, P. (2014). FDI and Income Inequality—Evidence from Latin American Economies. *Review of Development Economics, 18*(4), 778–793. doi:10.1111/rode.12118

Herzer, D., & Nunnenkamp, P. (2012). The effect of foreign aid on income inequality: Evidence from panel cointegration. *Structural Change and Economic Dynamics, 23*(3), 245–255. doi:10.1016/j.strueco.2012.04.002

Hlouskova, J., & Osbat, C. (2009). *Panel cointegration approaches to estimating equilibrium real exchange rates-separating the wheat from the chaff.* European Central Bank.

Hlouskova, J., & Wagner, M. (2006). The performance of panel unit root and stationarity tests: Results from a large scale simulation study. *Econometric Reviews, 25*(1), 85–116. doi:10.1080/07474930500545504

Ho, T. W. (2002). The Feldstein–Horioka puzzle revisited. *Journal of International Money and Finance, 21*(4), 555–564. doi:10.1016/S0261-5606(02)00005-0

Hossain, M. S., & Mitra, R. (2013). The determinants of economic growth in Africa: A dynamic causality and panel cointegration analysis. *Economic Analysis and Policy, 43*(2), 217–226. doi:10.1016/S0313-5926(13)50019-1

Hudea, O. S., & Stancu, S. (2012). Foreign direct investments, technology transfer and economic growth. A panel approach. *Romanian Journal of Economic Forecasting, 15*(2), 85–102.

Hurlin, C., & Mignon, V. (2007). *Second generation panel unit root tests.* Academic Press.

Im, K. S., Pesaran, M. H., & Shin, Y. (1995). *Testing for unit roots in dynamic heterogeneous panels.* Department of Applied Economics working paper, 9526.

Im, K. S., Pesaran, M. H., & Shin, Y. (2003). Testing for unit roots in heterogeneous panels. *Journal of Econometrics, 115*(1), 53–74. doi:10.1016/S0304-4076(03)00092-7

Jacobson, T., Lyhagen, J., Larsson, R., & Nessén, M. (2002). *Inflation, exchange rates and PPP in a multivariate panel cointegration model* (No. 145). Sveriges Riksbank Working Paper Series.

Jacobson, T., Lyhagen, J., Larsson, R., & Nessén, M. (2007). Inflation, exchange rates and PPP in a multivariate panel cointegration model. *The Econometrics Journal, 10*, 1–21.

Jacobson, T., Lyhagen, J., Larsson, R., & Nessén, M. (2008). Inflation, exchange rates and PPP in a multivariate panel cointegration model. *The Econometrics Journal, 11*(1), 58–79. doi:10.1111/j.1368-423X.2008.00231.x

Jäger, P., & Schmidt, T. (2016). The political economy of public investment when population is aging: A panel cointegration analysis. *European Journal of Political Economy, 43*, 145–158. doi:10.1016/j.ejpoleco.2016.04.004

Jaunky, V. C. (2013). Democracy and economic growth in Sub-Saharan Africa: A panel data approach. *Empirical Economics*, *45*(2), 987–1008. doi:10.100700181-012-0633-x

Kao, C. (1999). Spurious regression and residual-based tests for cointegration in panel data. *Journal of Econometrics*, *90*(1), 1–44. doi:10.1016/S0304-4076(98)00023-2

Kapetanios, G., Pesaran, M. H., & Yamagata, T. (2011). Panels with non-stationary multifactor error structures. *Journal of Econometrics*, *160*(2), 326–348. doi:10.1016/j.jeconom.2010.10.001

Kim, H. (2004). *The Measurement of International Capital Mobility Using Panel Cointegration Estimators*. Academic Press.

Kim, S. (2019). CO2 Emissions, Foreign Direct Investments, Energy Consumption, and GDP in Developing Countries: A More Comprehensive Study using Panel Vector Error Correction Model. *Korean Economic Review*, *35*, 5–24.

Kizilkaya, O., Ay, A., & Akar, G. (2016). Dynamic relationship among foreign direct investments, human capital, economic freedom and economic growth: Evidence from panel cointegration and panel causality analysis. *Theoretical & Applied Economics, 23*(3).

Kwiatkowski, D., Phillips, P. C., Schmidt, P., & Shin, Y. (1992). Testing the null hypothesis of stationarity against the alternative of a unit root. *Journal of Econometrics*, *54*(1-3), 159–178. doi:10.1016/0304-4076(92)90104-Y

Lamartina, S., & Zaghini, A. (2011). Increasing public expenditure: Wagner's Law in OECD countries. *German Economic Review*, *12*(2), 149–164. doi:10.1111/j.1468-0475.2010.00517.x

Larsson, R., Lyhagen, J., & Löthgren, M. (2001). Likelihood-based cointegration tests in heterogeneous panels. *The Econometrics Journal*, *4*(1), 109–142. doi:10.1111/1368-423X.00059

Lee, C. C., & Chang, C. P. (2009). FDI, financial development, and economic growth: International evidence. *Journal of Applied Econometrics*, *12*(2), 249–271.

Lee, C. C., & Lee, J. D. (2009). Income and CO2 emissions: Evidence from panel unit root and cointegration tests. *Energy Policy*, *37*(2), 413–423. doi:10.1016/j.enpol.2008.09.053

Levin, A., & Lin, C. F. (1993). *Unit root tests in panel data: new results.* University of California at San Diego, Economics Working Paper Series.

Levin, A., Lin, C. F., & Chu, C. S. J. (2002). Unit root tests in panel data: Asymptotic and finite-sample properties. *Journal of Econometrics*, *108*(1), 1–24. doi:10.1016/S0304-4076(01)00098-7

Lin, S. X., & Kueh, J. (2019). Twin Deficits and Debts in 6 ASEAN Countries: A Panel Approach. *International Journal of Academic Research in Business and Social Sciences*, *9*(7), 550–559. doi:10.6007/IJARBSS/v9-i7/6147

MacDonald, R., & Vieira, F. V. (2010). *A panel data investigation of real exchange rate misalignment and growth,* CESifo Working paper no. 3061.

Maddala, G. S., & Wu, S. (1999). A comparative study of unit root tests with panel data and a new simple test. *Oxford Bulletin of Economics and Statistics*, *61*(S1), 631–652. doi:10.1111/1468-0084.0610s1631

Maeso-Fernandez, F., Osbat, C., & Schnatz, B. (2006). Towards the estimation of equilibrium exchange rates for transition economies: Methodological issues and a panel cointegration perspective. *Journal of Comparative Economics*, *34*(3), 499–517. doi:10.1016/j.jce.2006.05.003

Mark, N. C., & Sul, D. (2001). Nominal exchange rates and monetary fundamentals: Evidence from a small post-Bretton Woods panel. *Journal of International Economics*, *53*(1), 29–52. doi:10.1016/S0022-1996(00)00052-0

Martins, P. M. (2011). Aid absorption and spending in Africa: A panel cointegration approach. *The Journal of Development Studies*, *47*(12), 1925–1953. doi:10.1080/00220388.2011.579115

Mehmood, R., & Younas, Z. (2019). Purchasing Power Parity Hold in Major SAARC Countries? Panel Cointegration Analysis. *Quarterly Journal of Econometrics Research*, *5*(1), 1–16. doi:10.18488/journal.88.2019.51.1.16

Mehrara, M., & Musai, M. (2013). The causality between capital formation and economic growth in MENA region. *International Letters of Social and Humanistic Sciences*, *8*, 1–7. doi:10.18052/www.scipress.com/ILSHS.8.1

Mehrara, M., Pahlavani, M., & Elyasi, Y. (2011). Government revenue and government expenditure nexus in Asian countries: Panel cointegration and causality. *International Journal of Business and Social Science*, *2*(7), 199–207.

Mitra, R., Hossain, M. S., & Hossain, M. I. (2015). Aid and per-capita economic growth in Asia: A panel cointegration tests. *Economic Bulletin*, *35*(3), 1693–1699.

Mitrović, R. D., Glavaški, O., & Pucar, E. B. (2019). Fiscal Sustainability in Flow Model: Panel Cointegration Approach for the EU-28. *Ovidius University Annals, Series Economic Sciences, 19*(1).

Mohammadi Khyareh, M. (2019). A cointegration analysis of tax evasion, corruption and entrepreneurship in OECD countries. *Economic research-. Ekonomska Istrazivanja*, *32*(1), 3627–3646. doi:10.1080/1331677X.2019.1674175

Moolio, P., & Kong, S. (2016). Foreign aid and economic growth: Panel cointegration analysis for Cambodia, Lao PDR, Myanmar, and Vietnam. *Athens Journal of Business and Economics*, *2*(4), 417–428. doi:10.30958/ajbe.2.4.6

Mucuk, M., & Demirsel, M. T. (2013). The effect of foreign direct investments on unemployment: Evidence from panel data for seven developing countries. *Journal of Business Economics and Finance*, *2*(3), 53–66.

Murthy, N. V. (2007). Feldstein Horioka puzzle in Latin American and Caribbean countries: Evidence from likelihood-based cointegration tests in heterogeneous panels. *International Research Journal of Finance and Economics*, *11*, 112–122.

Murthy, N. V. (2009). The Feldstein–Horioka puzzle in Latin American and Caribbean countries: A panel cointegration analysis. *Journal of Economics and Finance*, *33*(2), 176–188. doi:10.100712197-008-9051-5

Nathaniel, S., Anyanwu, O., & Shah, M. (2020). Renewable energy, urbanization, and ecological footprint in the Middle East and North Africa region. *Environmental Science and Pollution Research International*, *27*(13), 1–13. doi:10.100711356-020-08017-7 PMID:32043254

Neelankavil, J. P., Stevans, L. K., & Roman, F. L. Jr. (2012). Correlates of economic growth in developing countries: A panel cointegration approach. *International Review of Applied Economics*, *26*(1), 83–96. doi:10.1080/02692171.2011.557048

Nieh, C. C., & Ho, T. W. (2006). Does the expansionary government spending crowd out the private consumption?: Cointegration analysis in panel data. *The Quarterly Review of Economics and Finance*, *46*(1), 133–148. doi:10.1016/j.qref.2004.11.004

Ojo, A. T., & Alege, P. O. (2014). Exchange rate fluctuations and macroeconomic performance in sub-Saharan Africa: A dynamic panel cointegration analysis. *Asian Economic and Financial Review*, *4*(11), 1573.

Pedroni, P. (1999). Critical values for cointegration tests in heterogeneous panels with multiple regressors. *Oxford Bulletin of Economics and Statistics*, *61*(s1, S1), 653–670. doi:10.1111/1468-0084.61.s1.14

Pedroni, P. (2000). Fully modified OLS for heterogeneous cointegrated panels. *Advances in Econometrics*, *15*, 93–130. doi:10.1016/S0731-9053(00)15004-2

Pedroni, P. (2004). Panel cointegration: Asymptotic and finite sample properties of pooled time series tests with an application to the PPP hypothesis. *Econometric Theory*, *20*(3), 597–625. doi:10.1017/S0266466604203073

Pedroni, P. (2019). Panel Cointegration Techniques and Open Challenges. In Panel Data Econometrics (pp. 251-287). Academic Press. doi:10.1016/B978-0-12-814367-4.00010-1

Pelgrin, F., & Schich, S. (2004). *National saving-investment dynamics and international capital mobility*. Working Paper 2004-14, Bank of Canada.

Pesaran, M. H. (2007). A pair-wise approach to testing for output and growth convergence. *Journal of Econometrics*, *138*(1), 312–355. doi:10.1016/j.jeconom.2006.05.024

Ponce, P., & Alvarado, R. (2019). Air pollution, output, FDI, trade openness, and urbanization: Evidence using DOLS and PDOLS cointegration techniques and causality. *Environmental Science and Pollution Research International*, *26*(19), 19843–19858. doi:10.100711356-019-05405-6 PMID:31090009

Pradhan, R. P. (2009). The FDI-led-growth hypothesis in ASEAN-5 countries: Evidence from cointegrated panel analysis. *International Journal of Business and Management*, *4*(12), 153–164. doi:10.5539/ijbm.v4n12p153

Quah, D. (1994). Exploiting cross-section variation for unit root inference in dynamic data. *Economics Letters*, *44*(1-2), 9–19. doi:10.1016/0165-1765(93)00302-5

Rauf, A., Liu, X., Amin, W., Ozturk, I., Rehman, O. U., & Sarwar, S. (2018). Energy and ecological sustainability: Challenges and panoramas in belt and road initiative countries. *Sustainability*, *10*(8), 2743. doi:10.3390u10082743

Rizvi, S. Z. A., & Nishat, M. (2009). The impact of foreign direct investment on employment opportunities: Panel data analysis: Empirical evidence from Pakistan, India and China. *Pakistan Development Review*, *48*(4II), 841–851. doi:10.30541/v48i4IIpp.841-851

Sothan, S. (2016). Foreign direct investment, exports, and long-run economic growth in Asia: Panel cointegration and causality analysis. *International Journal of Economics and Finance*, *8*(1), 26–37. doi:10.5539/ijef.v8n1p26

Uddin, G. A., Salahuddin, M., Alam, K., & Gow, J. (2017). Ecological footprint and real income: Panel data evidence from the 27 highest emitting countries. *Ecological Indicators*, *77*, 166–175. doi:10.1016/j.ecolind.2017.01.003

Wagner, M., & Hlouskova, J. (2009). The performance of panel cointegration methods: Results from a large scale simulation study. *Econometric Reviews*, *29*(2), 182–223. doi:10.1080/07474930903382182

Westerlund, J. (2005). A panel CUSUM test of the null of cointegration. *Oxford Bulletin of Economics and Statistics*, *67*(2), 231–262. doi:10.1111/j.1468-0084.2004.00118.x

Westerlund, J., Mahdavi, S., & Firoozi, F. (2011). The tax-spending nexus: Evidence from a panel of US state–local governments. *Economic Modelling*, *28*(3), 885–890. doi:10.1016/j.econmod.2010.10.016

Zdravković, A., Đukić, M., & Bradić-Martinović, A. (2017). Impact of FDI on unemployment in transition countries: Panel cointegration approach. *Industrija*, *45*(1), 161–174. doi:10.5937/industrija45-13548

ADDITIONAL READING

Arellano, M. (2003). *Panel data econometrics*. Oxford university press. doi:10.1093/0199245282.001.0001

Baltagi, B. H. (Ed.). (2015). *The Oxford handbook of panel data*. Oxford Handbooks. doi:10.1093/oxfordhb/9780199940042.001.0001

Croissant, Y., & Millo, G. (2019). *Panel data econometrics with R*. John Wiley and Sons, Incorporated.

Hatemi-J, A. (2020). Hidden panel cointegration. *Journal of King Saud University-Science*, *32*(1), 507–510. doi:10.1016/j.jksus.2018.07.011

Hsiao, C. (2014). *Analysis of panel data (No. 54)*. Cambridge university press. doi:10.1017/CBO9781139839327

Okui, R., & Yanagi, T. (2019). Panel data analysis with heterogeneous dynamics. *Journal of Econometrics*, *212*(2), 451–475. doi:10.1016/j.jeconom.2019.04.036

Sarafidis, V., & Wansbeek, T. (2020). *Celebrating 40 Years of Panel Data Analysis: Past, Present and Future (No. 6/20)*. Monash University, Department of Econometrics and Business Statistics.

Tsionas, M. (Ed.). (2019). *Panel Data Econometrics: Empirical Applications*. Academic Press.

KEY TERMS AND DEFINITIONS

Cross-Sectional Dependence: Time series for different cross-section units are correlated, as a result either from unobserved factors, or from spatial or spillover effects. Cross-sectional dependence is defined also as "weak" or "strong" (resulting from "weak" or "strong" common factors).

Non-Stationary Panel: A panel data set where some (or all) of the time series contain unit roots.

Panel Cointegration: Some (or all) of the non-stationary time series in the panel have a stable, long-run relationship.

Panel Data: A data set with both cross-sectional and time series dimension. If all cross-sectional units are observed for the whole time period, the panel is *balanced*. Otherwise, if the time series for some of the cross-section units are not of the same length and there are missing values, the panel is *unbalanced*.

Chapter 6
Second Generation Reforms:
From Macroeconomics to Microeconomics

Mikail Kar
Bursa Uludag University, Turkey

ABSTRACT

Economic reforms include comprehensive and radical changes in the functioning of the economic system and its main rules. There is no clear and generally accepted classification of economic reforms in the literature. In this study, economic reforms are analyzed by classifying them as first-generation reforms and second-generation reforms. First-generation reforms are made in macroeconomics for the purposes of eliminating macroeconomic imbalances, ensuring stability, controlling inflation, ensuring fiscal and monetary discipline, reducing public debt. Second-generation reforms are microeconomic reforms, which include strengthening the infrastructure of the market economy, increasing efficiency, enhancing the competitive power, and strengthening the institutional infrastructure that creates competitive markets. The aim of this study is to examine the theoretical framework of first-generation and second-generation reforms in line with macroeconomic and microeconomic expectations and to explain and discuss the main areas of second-generation reforms.

INTRODUCTION

Reform means a planned and informed radical change, correction, reclamation, and improvement to make the current situation better. Reform in the economic approach is a radical change process that increases living standards, improves well-being and increases resistance against shocks in order to provide permanent and long-term improvement and solutions. In other words, economic reforms include comprehensive and radical changes in the functioning of the economic system and its main rules. In this respect, economic reforms aim to support economic growth and development by making changes in the areas that are currently problematic or which are predicted to cause problems in the future. Economic reforms aim to provide long-term and permanent improvements in the legal framework, in the functioning of markets or in the structure of economic institutions, rather than short-term and temporary solutions.

DOI: 10.4018/978-1-7998-4933-9.ch006

Although there is no clear and accepted general definition and distinction in the literature in the classification of economic reforms, the approach that divides reforms into two main groups, first-generation reforms, and second-generation reforms, is preferred in this study. First-generation reforms refer to the reforms in monetary and fiscal policies, which are in the field of macroeconomics, with the aim of eliminating economic imbalances, ensuring stability, lowering interest rates, controlling inflation, ensuring fiscal and monetary discipline, and reducing public debt. Second-generation reforms are microeconomic reforms that strengthen the infrastructure of the market economy, increase efficiency, increase competitiveness, create competitive markets and renew the institutional infrastructure. As problems in macroeconomic fields are more visible and easier to intervene, authorities primarily focus on first-generation reforms. With these reforms, basic problems have been tried to be solved and important progress has been made. However, in order to protect and improve the success achieved with the first generation reforms and to eliminate the detected deficiencies, it should be supported with the second generation reforms. Without second-generation reforms, the sustainability of macro-economic development is unrealistic. In other words, second-generation micro reforms must be implemented in order to make the macroeconomic gains permanent and sustainable. If this complementarity relationship is ignored, the maintenance of macroeconomic stability will be compromised, and the improvement in macroeconomic indicators will not contribute to the expected prosperity of producers and consumers on a micro-scale (Forsyth, 1992; Gregory, 1992; Jones, 1994; Pastor & Carol, 1999; Naim, 1995).

The aim of this study is to examine the theoretical framework of first-generation and second-generation reforms in line with macroeconomic and microeconomic expectations and to explain and discuss the main areas of second-generation reforms. Following this introduction, where the concept of reform is discussed, the process of the emergence of economic reforms is covered in the second part. In the third part, first and second-generation reforms are defined and in the fourth part, the transition process from first-generation reforms to second-generation reforms is evaluated by explaining the differences between first-generation and second-generation reforms. In the fifth part, where the areas of second-generation reforms are discussed, the reforms that have to be done and done are discussed in detail in five different basic areas. In the conclusion, a general evaluation of the study is made.

ECONOMIC REFORMS AND EMERGENCE PROCESS

The place and relations of the state and market in the economic structure have been discussed throughout the history of economic and there have often been differences of opinion in the policies to be adopted in this context. At the point of economic growth and development, the most important turning point in the debates on the place and relation of market and state was the Keynesian Revolution, which offered a recipe for a solution to the 1929 crisis. Keynes argued that the assumptions of the classical theory are valid only for particular situations, arguing that it does not reflect the characteristics of the society lived in, and as a result, he claimed that the classical approach has a weak link with the real world and cannot solve the problems of the real world. According to the Keynesian approach, when market failures occur, the deteriorating equilibrium can be recreated not by the free movement of market forces but by the intervention of the state in economic life through macroeconomic policies. During the period from 1929 to the 1970s, state intervention was seen as salvation for developing countries, and the state's influence in the economy gradually increased. During these periods, rapid economic growth, high levels of employment and price stability were maintained together (Milonakis & Fine, 2009; Davidson, 2004; Gore, 2000; Rodrik, 2006; Williamson, 2003; Williamson, 2000; Harvey, 2005).

The oil crises of the 1970s changed the economic balances and made Keynesian policies controversial, which were insufficient to find solutions. Since this date, the approach that the main source of economic problems is the insufficient operation of the free market mechanism has started to come to the agenda with strong statements. After the oil shock of 1973, Neo-classical economists claimed that the main source of underdevelopment was state interventions that immobilized market forces and thus prevented economic development. According to neo-classicalists, it is not the market failures that require state intervention that is responsible for the problems experienced by underdeveloped countries, but the undisciplined state interventions that leave the country facing extremely high inflation rates and state debts. The basic suggestion of the Neo-Classics is that the state should withdraw its hand from the market by sticking to the basic principles of the market. It is believed that underdeveloped countries can achieve their economic development if this recommendation is followed. In other words, the main claim of the neoliberal approach is that underdevelopment arises from poor resource distribution caused by excessive state intervention and erroneous price policies and that the economy can only provide optimal resource distribution by the free market, and world welfare will increase if the economy is left to the market mechanism (Jessop, 2002; Davidson, 2004; Williamson, 2000; Harvey, 2005).

The external shocks that continued to occur in the early 1980s, especially the debt crises, affected the underdeveloped countries significantly. US-based financial institutions have created a pro-market and anti-government recipe for the world crises that started from Latin America. Beginning in mid-1980, the US Treasury, the IMF and the World Bank, leading lenders, demanded that developing countries implement a series of market-oriented policies in response to the aid they provided. In other words, a link has been established between the implementation of a specific policy series proposed by international economic institutions for economic growth and development, and financial aid to be provided. The new exit path proposed by international economic institutions for the growing debt crisis of developing countries is not only the implementation of short-term stability measures but also the implementation of "structural adjustment programs" that make it possible to address the economic development of these countries within the framework of a new economic policy. In other words, until the beginning of 1980, these institutions demanded the implementation of macroeconomic stability-based policies in order to overcome the problems of developing countries of foreign debt and the balance of payments (Milonakis & Fine, 2009)

After the mid-1980s, the structural adjustment model consisting of Neo-liberal economic policy measures, called the "Washington Consensus" was introduced upon the deepening of the existing problems of developing countries. On the basis of this model, the market is seen as the most basic mechanism for allocating scarce resources and sustaining rapid economic growth. Instead of interventionist and protectionist economic measures, it is essential that liberalization in all areas of the economy and reducing the economic role of the state is essential. The Washington Consensus, a series of economic policies agreed upon by the IMF, the World Bank, and the US Treasury, was originally developed for Latin American countries in debt crisis and later became recommended for all developing countries. The Washington Consensus is an output of the assumption that state interventions are the source of the problem rather than a solution, and its main proposal is to systematically reduce the state's interventions to the economy. For developing countries, the Washington Consensus emphasizes the need for macro-economic and financial policies, competitive exchange rates, financial liberalization, privatization, and deregulation. Since the aim is to ensure efficient distribution of resources, it is accepted that the free movement of market forces will create the market price that will provide this efficiency (Williamson, 2003; Rodrik, 2001; Jessop, 2002; Milonakis & Fine, 2009).

The general approach to the Washington Consensus is that it is very costly to diverge from neo-liberal economic policies at the point of the world and that the countries implementing these policies have grown and developed, and otherwise growth is unsustainable. It is argued that under the enrichment of developed countries there is free trade and free finance movements and that state interventions in developing countries impede economic growth and development. If developing countries want to achieve economic growth and development, they need to go under the supervision of international organizations and policy-independent regulatory and supervisory institutions. The control of the economic system by the government in these countries will have adverse consequences due to the pressure it will create. Managing the system with policies and pressures arising from power anxiety results in irreparable consequences. Public investments should be made with an encouraging approach, not an inhibitory manner, and public companies that have been the center of inefficiency and waste should be privatized. The main idea behind the neo-liberal Washington Consensus is that the state is wasting resources and acting irrationally. In return, individuals are rational and development occurs at the highest level when individuals are able to move freely, without interference with their preferences. The optimal distribution and efficient use of resources can only be achieved under free competitive market conditions, and the more a country opens out, the higher the growth rate and the more permanent it will be. In other words, according to the Washington Consensus, the central role in economic development is not the state but the market (Davidson, 2004; Gore, 2000; Rodrik, 2001; Harvey, 2005).

These neoliberal policies, which developed countries applied as much as they wanted with their preferences, were forced into many developing countries in need of financial assistance in exchange for economic aid. Until the late 1990s, it was thought that the implementation of the Washington Consensus would be sufficient for economic growth and development. Many empirical studies have reached conclusions that reveal the success of Neo-liberal policies in these years. However, this positive atmosphere left its place to criticism towards the end of the 1990s. Although many countries have implemented reforms imposed by the Washington Consensus, liberalization of capital movements, the realization of privatizations, liberalization of the markets, and control of budget deficits by ensuring fiscal discipline, they have not achieved and sustained the expected economic growth. As countries failed to reach the level of growth and development they wanted, their economic vulnerabilities also increased. The dominance of the Washington Consensus in the economic approach has been shaken and debatable. The Washington Consensus initially helped Latin American countries recover from the debt crisis but failed to achieve the expected economic growth. These policies also caused the East Asian crisis that coincided with the end of the 1990s with their impact on financial markets. The reforms were not able to achieve a remarkable poverty reduction and economic development and growth, especially in underdeveloped low-income countries. Evaluations have been made that the Washington Consensus does not address macroeconomic stability in all its aspects and looks with very narrow patterns and broad assumptions (Davidson, 2004; Rodrik, 2006; Williamson, 2000; Harvey, 2005; Milonakis & Fine, 2009).

Ineffective and misdirected programs, combined with the crises in the 1990s, have been the source of constant deterioration in wages, employment and social conditions in many countries. Therefore, there was a need to revise state-market interaction, redefine market elements and re-determine their functions, that is, to correct the Washington Consensus policies and to develop new economic growth and development-centered approaches. As a result of these discussions, the failure of the Washington Consensus was relatively accepted, but there was no general rejection. After all, a new synthesis, called the "Post Washington Consensus" and which criticizes the Washington Consensus, has been introduced. Depending on the political criticism, it has been stated that some innovations should be made on subjects such as institutions, income distribution, fighting poverty, social policies and effective financial markets (Williamson, 2003). Stiglitz and Dani Rodrik have been leading economists in the Washington Consensus criticism and in determining the Post Washington Consensus policies.

The Post Washington Consensus offers solutions that center the market and the rational individual, just like the previous Consensus. Assumptions that acknowledge that individualism, utilitarianism, and exchange are part of human nature continue here as well. Some economists do not see a fundamental difference between the Washington Compromise and the Post Washington Consensus as there is no softening in the role of the state, redistribution policies, the functioning of the free market, and free trade. Dani Rodrik states that in the face of the failures caused by the Washington Consensus, a strengthened and expanded Washington Consensus is needed, with the creation of institutional pillars of market economies by moving beyond liberalization and privatization. Rodrik does not reject the Washington Consensus but states that it needs to be reformed, such as legal, institutional and political reforms, in order to succeed. Stiglitz supported an understanding of interventionism in which the state had limited control over the markets and became the representative of the Post Washington Consensus by making criticisms targeting the Washington Consensus. According to Stiglitz, in the new structure that is being formed, the state and the markets should be seen as complementary rather than substitutes, and therefore governments should be treated as institutions that help create free markets (Stiglitz, 1997; Rodrik, 2006; Rodrik, 2001).

The Washington Consensus places greater emphasis on public failures and measures to address public failures in reforms, while the risk and information gaps in the Post Washington Consensus are addressed more. The Post Washington Consensus treats potential interventions more cautiously and sees the cause of any intervention as market failures that need to be fixed. It is claimed that the problem of information is one of the main problems that cause intervention. According to the basic assumption of the Washington Consensus, macroeconomic stability, privatization and liberalization are sufficient for good economic performance. The Post Washington Consensus acknowledged that poverty can be overcome with increased economic growth. The Post Washington Consensus emphasizes the need for various institutions for a good and efficient functioning of the market mechanism and that some of the government's interventions on the market can make a positive contribution. As a result, the Post Washington Consensus was created in an effort to compensate for the shortcomings of the Washington Consensus that were exposed to both theoretical and political levels.

The Post Washington Consensus has a broader set of goals and tools than the Washington Consensus. In addition to economic growth, it has introduced further objectives such as improved standard of living, sustainable development, egalitarian and democratic development. Privatization, liberalization, competitive markets and functioning financial systems are important to achieve sustainable results. Human capital and research and development are two important elements of economic growth and development. In the Post Washington Consensus, market failure is very important and is expected to be corrected through active government intervention. The relationship constructed as market anti-government in the Washington Consensus was transformed into a balanced relationship in the Post Washington Consensus, and market failures were presented as problems that could be corrected by non-market institutions. The Post Washington Consensus has the idea that market failures are not an incidental phenomenon, and state intervention to the extent of correcting this will ensure the efficient functioning of the market system. The Washington Consensus argues that markets will operate effectively if left to their own. Post Washington

Consensus focuses on why markets will not work well. In the Washington Consensus, greater emphasis is placed on public failures, and measures to address them are highlighted in reforms, while in the Post Washington Consensus the risk and information gaps are more emphasized.

In the first period of the Post Washington Consensus, many people supported this idea by thinking that these ideas have the potential to correct the mistakes of the Washington Consensus, but the inadequacies of the framework were also criticized. An important part of the criticisms of the Post Washington Consensus is that it has the same methodological basis as the Washington Consensus. In both consensuses, it approaches the developing countries with the same recommendations. The reforms proposed by both systems include the same elements and are extremely conservative in fiscal and monetary policies. The difference between the two consensuses is only related to the speed, depth, and method of reforms. Analysis of the successes and failures, supports and criticism, improvements and deteriorations from the Washington and Post Washington Consensus results led to the shaping of microeconomic reforms, the second generation reforms (Stiglitz, 1997; Rodrik, 2006; Rodrik, 2001).

CLASSIFICATION OF ECONOMIC REFORMS

Although there is no clear and accepted general distinction in the literature in the classification of economic reforms, the approach that divides reforms into two main groups, first-generation reforms and second-generation reforms, is preferred in this study.

First Generation Reforms

First-generation reforms refer to reforms in the field of macroeconomics, such as eliminating macroeconomic imbalances, ensuring stability, lowering interest rates, controlling inflation, ensuring fiscal and monetary discipline, and lowering public debt. The first-generation reforms aim to implement monetary policy in a way that ensures price stability and fiscal policy in a way that captures a sustainable level of deficit. In other words, the first-generation reforms include institutionalizing fiscal discipline and maintaining monetary discipline through independent monetary policy.

In first-generation reforms, accelerating growth and lowering inflation are two main priorities. Changing macroeconomic rules, reducing the scale and scope of the state, and reducing protectionism constitute the strategy of these reforms. First-generation reforms have been introduced with the aim of finding solutions to problems such as macroeconomic imbalances, instability, high interest, high inflation, financial and monetary discipline, and high public debt. These include reducing government expenditures, regulating the tax system, ensuring price liberalization, privatization, reducing protectionism, reducing regulations for markets and the private sector, and focusing on liberalization in foreign trade and foreign investments. Aims and strategies have enabled first-generation reforms to focus on reducing market regulations, accelerating privatizations, liberalizing foreign direct investment, reducing government spending, upgrading the tax system, and removing price regulations. In first-generation reforms, international institutions such as IMF and WB, central banks, government, and local financial institutions are emerging as actors of the reform process. The preparation and implementation of first-generation reforms are relatively easy and simple. In addition, one of the most important features of the first generation reforms and the reason for its preference is its ability to show its effects in a short time (Forsyth, 1992; Gregory, 1992; Jones, 1994; Pastor & Carol, 1999; Naim, 1995).

Second Generation Reforms

Second-generation reforms are microeconomic reforms that strengthen the infrastructure of the market economy, increase efficiency, create competitive markets and renew the institutional infrastructure. Second-generation reforms are mainly focused on structural transformation. These reforms include a growth strategy based on the production economy and a solution to employment and the steps to be taken to strengthen this strategy. In other words, second-generation reforms are essentially based on changing the rules and institutional infrastructure. With the second-generation reforms, it is aimed to provide more reliable and sustainable results by supporting first-generation reforms by providing human capital accumulation, increasing the quality of labor, promoting technology and innovation, increasing productivity, creating a competitive and free-market environment, and improving infrastructure.

These reforms are sometimes referred to as micro-economic reforms and structural reforms, albeit with minor differences. Within the scope of these reforms, it is desired to establish a sustainable growth environment by reducing the role of the public in the economy, creating a more effective and transparent public administration, following a more effective support policy in the agricultural sector and establishing a strong banking system that will perform the function of transferring resources to the real sector. Second-generation reforms are micro-focused reforms that, on the one hand, maintain fiscal discipline and monetary policy, on the other, strengthen the infrastructure of the free market economy, increase efficiency and increase competitiveness. Second-generation reforms are shifting from rule change to institutional change by introducing a strategy based on the production economy, providing solutions to unemployment, reducing the informal economy, increasing efficiency and quality in public services, promoting technological development and innovation, supporting entrepreneurship, and eliminating rigidity. So second-generation reforms actually involve institutionalization in all structures to preserve and improve the progress achieved through first-generation reforms. Second-generation reforms are reforms that remove barriers to firms and open up investments, affect production techniques, increase competition and encourage efficiency. In other words, second-generation reforms, on the one hand, protect the foundations of macroeconomic stability, on the other hand, are micro-focused reform movements that strengthen the institutional infrastructure of the free market economy and offer appropriate incentives for economic actors to move towards more productive activities. Through these reforms, financial balances will be maintained, high growth rates will be maintained in price stability, an increase in investments financed by internal resources will increase employment opportunities, and a highly efficient industrial structure will be created, with education and R & D activities contribute to (Forsyth, 1992; Gregory, 1992; Jones, 1994; Pastor & Carol, 1999; Naim, 1995).

THE TRANSITION FROM FIRST TO SECOND GENERATION REFORMS: THE IMPORTANCE OF MICRO-ECONOMIC REFORMS

While the priority of first-generation reforms is to provide macroeconomic stability, accelerate growth and reduce inflation by creating price stability, the main purpose of second-generation reforms is to maintain macroeconomic stability and high growth rates and to increase international competitiveness and social development. While first-generation reforms use strategies such as changing macroeconomic rules, reducing the state and reducing protectionism to achieve their goals, second-generation reforms act with strategies of renewing and establishing new institutions, strengthening the foundations of the free market economy, raising the competitiveness of the private sector, improving public services such as education and health, ensuring integration into the global structure. Despite macroeconomic reform areas, reforms are made within the scope of second-generation reforms regarding the labor market, public structure, education system, capacity of independent regulatory institutions, tax administration and competitive structure of the market. Second-generation reforms are technically and administratively complex and the impact of second-generation reforms appears in the longer term compared to first-generation reforms. In the first generation reforms, there are more clear and fewer actors such as the government, central bank and international financial institutions, while in the second generation reforms many other actors that are not easy to act together such as municipalities, non-governmental organizations, unions, chambers, and private sector organizations are included in the reform process. First-generation reforms target the whole society in general, the cost of reform is felt in time and affects the whole society, and the resulting return is clearly shared by the whole society. However, in the second generation reforms, different segments of the society are affected in different ways, the costs of the reforms are paid at the beginning and these costs are not distributed equally among the actors. Moreover, the emergence of the returns from the second generation reforms requires a long term and these returns are not shared equally among the actors.

The realization of the second generation reforms requires a more detailed and meticulously prepared program and implementation skills compared to the first generation reforms. In order to achieve the expected outcome of the second-generation reforms, the internalization of the main goal by all institutions, ensuring broad social consensus, locking all institutions in harmony and coordination to the same goal, achieving a consensus on the political and administrative system, conducting the reform process transparently and developing social solidarity mechanisms taking into account the costs are very important. In this respect, the resistance faced by the government during the second generation reforms is much more than the difficulties it faced during the first generation reforms. For these reasons, governments prefer first-generation reforms considering their political future. Only approaches that can make long-term plans and are committed to their economic goals can realize second-generation reforms in real terms.

First-generation reforms and second-generation reforms should be considered complementary rather than substitutes. The reason for the emergence of the second generation reform process is that after the successful results of the first generation reform process for a certain period of time, reforms that increase competition and efficiency are needed for the sustainability of growth and development. The shortcomings and failures of macroeconomic reforms have been tried to overcome with new macroeconomic reforms from time to time, but over time, it has been understood that the basic deficiency is that the reform process is not supported by microeconomic reforms. For example, the failures and shortcomings of the reforms dictated to the developing countries with the Washington Consensus were tried to be resolved with the Post Washington Consensus, which was not very different in terms of approach, and as a result, it also failed. So ultimately, achieving economic targets with only macroeconomic policies is not sustainable in the long run. In order for macroeconomic reforms to have positive results, it has been accepted later that microeconomic reforms should be fully realized. In order to get the expected output from economic policies, first-generation and second-generation reforms must be carried out together as complementary and supporter of each other. First-generation reforms are more often preferred because imbalances in the macro areas are more visible and easier to prepare and implement first-generation reforms. However, experience has shown that it is impossible for first-generation reforms, which are carried out without second-generation reforms, to yield long-term and permanent results (Forsyth, 1992; Gregory, 1992; Jones, 1994; Pastor & Carol, 1999; Naim, 1995).

SECOND GENERATION REFORM AREAS

Second generation reform areas can be expressed in many and diverse areas, but this study addresses reforms related to product markets, employment, the informal economy, tax systems, and research and development (R&D) activities. Here, the problems in the related fields are mentioned and the second generation microeconomic reforms that are made and need to be done in order to find solutions to these problems are explained.

Product Markets Reforms

The main objective of the economic approaches of all countries is to create a market-oriented, competitive manufacturing economy where the private sector is active and to ensure continuous and stable growth in exports. Second generation microeconomic reforms related to product markets play an important role in achieving this goal. The reforms related to the product markets refer to microeconomic reform policies that increase competition in the goods and services markets, facilitate entry and exit to the markets, strengthen productivity and prevent monopolistic trends. The main objective of these reforms is to open the relevant market to domestic and foreign competitors, to facilitate and encourage entrances and exits by removing barriers to entrepreneurship, and to increase competition in the market by ensuring fair, understandable and transparent competition among firms. Product market reforms increase competition and ensure the reallocation of resources between and within companies, thereby increasing efficiency and positively affecting productivity performance. Product market reforms have a significant impact on the market entry and exit rate, and this effect is very important for the market to have a competitive structure. The increasing number of competitors in the market, or at least the threat of new entries, in itself enables the market to operate with more competitive approaches. Weakening the market power of incumbent firms and increasing competitive policies bring the market price closer to marginal costs. Firms working with low efficiency with the freedom of entry and exit leave the market, while firms that work more efficiently find a chance to enter the market and gain market share (Harrison, 2004; Nicoletti & Scarpetta, 2005; Duval & Elmeskov, 2006; Berger & Danninger, 2007; Griffith et al., 2007).

Reforms based on the goods and services markets can be directed towards certain sectors as well as for the general economy. For example, reducing bureaucratic obstacles that make it difficult to establish firms contribute to strengthening the competitive environment across the economy, while reforms to increase permits to encourage entry in the telecommunications market are market-specific policies. Since the obstacles that weaken competition in different sectors can be different, microeconomic reform proposals for these can also be sector-specific. When the second generation reforms on markets are considered, it is seen that markets such as communication, transport and energy markets, which have natural monopoly characteristics and are called network industries, have an important place. Because these markets contain externalities and the economic scale is large, when they are left to the market mechanism by their nature, they turn into inefficient and ineffective structures, rather than competitive and efficient balances. While competition arising from foreign trade in the goods markets automatically enforces a certain competition discipline, it is more common in service sectors, where this enforcement is weaker, that distract the industry from competition. Regulations such as leaving some services to a limited number of permit holders without need, price regulations, limiting service imports and restricting the entry of large stores to the sector in order to protect small businesses in the retail sector are various practices that prevent competition in the service sector. In this respect, through second-generation reforms, the service sectors are tried to be cleared of these negative factors and brought to competitive structures. In sectors where the state is a producer, there is a great deal of inefficiency. Since there is no obligation to make a profit, public enterprises are not able to adopt competitive approaches as much as the private sector, and in this case, creates a great deal of inefficiency in production. For this reason, leaving the economic activity to the private sector, especially in areas where the private sector can operate, is another second-generation reform area. However, only increasing the privatizations did not provide the expected results from these markets. It should be ensured that the market is left to as many private companies as possible and that it is encouraged at its new entrances through the reforms to be carried out, in order to enable a competitive structure in these markets (Harrison, 2004; Berger & Danninger, 2007; Griffith et al., 2007; Fiori et al., 2012).

Countries have realized the necessity of second-generation microeconomic reforms related to the product markets, especially when the Washington and Post Washington Consensus did not achieve the expected results. Within the scope of second-generation reforms, in order to reach economic goals, there are many change and transformation movements, some of which are stated below. With these reforms, it is aimed to make product markets the main sector that drives economic growth. Transformation into a structure that will adapt to international competition is supported by focusing on high added-value products and activities in labor-intensive traditional sectors. In order to prevent unfair competition in products manufactured with advanced technology, compliance with international technical legislation should be realized and market surveillance and control systems should be strengthened in order to prevent the supply and circulation of non-compliant goods to the market. By providing technology transfers to companies on a sectoral basis, measures are taken to facilitate their access to finance. Transforming the small tradesmen and craftsmen-oriented structure of the trade into a modern structure through scaling-up policies is encouraged, and it is supported to improve product quality, to develop financing resources and tools, and to increase cooperation and electronic commerce opportunities. Investments are directed to areas that have high competitive power and can create more added value, rather than those with low competitiveness. Policies to promote competitive areas of activity and strategies to remove obstacles to doing business are being developed. Organized industrial zones and technology development zones are established to meet the physical infrastructure and technology needs encountered in the industry to improve the investment environment at the micro-level. Reforms are carried out for the establishment of the company electronically, reducing the establishment costs as well as the elimination of the problems experienced during the liquidation of the company. Under these reforms, firms' access to finance is facilitated, registration costs are reduced, the number of licenses required to register and work is reduced, and the duration of bankruptcy procedures is reduced (Harrison, 2004; Nicoletti & Scarpetta, 2005; Duval & Elmeskov, 2006; Berger & Danninger, 2007; Griffith et al., 2007; Fiori et al., 2012).

Employment Reforms

Employment, emerging as a result of the production process, is considered as one of the most important economic issues of developed and developing societies. Countries are intervening in labor markets with a series of reform policies to increase employment, provide jobs for everyone who wants to work, improve labor quality and productivity, harmonize labor supply and demand, and solve the problems posed by unemployment. At this point, each country evaluates its own economic and social conditions and needs and implements second-generation microeconomic reforms related to the labor market in various fields of motivation, different scope and in different areas. Years of experience have shown that macroeconomic policies cannot improve employment opportunities after a certain point unless the labor market is supported by microeconomic reforms. In reforms related to labor markets, there are many and various reasons and targets such as decreasing labor costs, providing flexibility by eliminating rigidities, increasing active employment measures and preventing informal employment. The main goal of employment policies is to reduce the loss of parties in the labor market and to ensure that the increasingly complex labor market becomes orderly (Albrecht et al., 2009; Bertola et al., 1999; Vlandas, 2013; Ahsan & Pages, 2009).

Labor costs are often discussed in second-generation microeconomic reform policies regarding employment as one of the most important factors determining the course of employment. The high labor cost restricts the increase in employment by reducing the competitiveness of firms and affects productivity and causes the rate of unregistered employment to increase. Since decision-making authorities want to increase employment and production, they have to develop policies to reduce labor costs in a way that makes labor employment attractive. The high cost of labor causes employers to be cautious about hiring workers, and instead of hiring new staff and increasing employment, they look for ways to increase their working time or increase productivity. Thus, the level of employment decreases and unemployment increases. Reducing labor costs will help create the desired level of employment and reduce informal employment (Albrecht et al., 2009; Bertola et al., 1999; Vlandas, 2013; Ahsan & Pages, 2009).

One of the reform areas related to employment is the steps taken to provide flexibility by eliminating the rigidities in the labor markets. One of the most important tools for balancing labor supply and demand, maintaining the competitiveness of companies and ensuring sustainable growth is creating a flexible labor market. The rigidity of the labor market, informality, and inactive job search processes cause the labor force to be unable to find a job. Firms' difficulties and high costs in hiring and firing weaken competitiveness and limit employment increases. On the other hand, since the lack of workers 'job security will pose a risk for social peace, it is aimed to encourage employment by reducing unemployment, to increase the enterprises' competitiveness and to encourage employment by bringing certain measures to employees. Measures such as facilitating employment contracts, providing opportunities for working from home, differentiating working hours, unemployment insurance and increasing the efficiency of employment agencies are solutions that will increase flexibility in the labor market. Unemployment insurance is an important tool for workers to have income security inflexible labor markets, but in cases where unemployment insurance payments are high and the payment period is long, people have the risk of getting their livelihood from unemployment insurance instead of looking for a job. Therefore, the limited amount of unemployment insurance payments in terms of duration and amount is important in terms of encouraging the beneficiaries of unemployment insurance to stay in the labor market (Ahsan & Pages, 2009; Pissarides, 1997).

The decision-making authority intervenes in the labor markets with active policies along with passive policies and tries to eliminate the unemployment or the negative effects of unemployment. The main purpose of active employment policies can be expressed as increasing employment opportunities for job seekers and improving the matching of unemployed and vacant jobs. The development of active employment policies increases the employability of individuals and plays a key role in the success of labor market reforms. Programs such as vocational training programs, job and vocational counseling, on-the-job training programs are examples of active labor market policy tools. Passive labor policies, such as unemployment insurance, prevent people from falling into poverty when they are unemployed, while active labor market policies help individuals enter the labor market or remain in the labor market. Determining the number of job vacancies and qualifications required will increase the effectiveness of organizing appropriate vocational training programs and directing job seekers to suitable jobs. Encouraging or enforcing the participation of individuals benefiting from unemployment insurance in active labor market programs will contribute significantly to the increase in efficiency in the labor market. To help individuals choose the most suitable job and profession by comparing their characteristics with the qualifications and conditions required by the professions and workplaces, organizing workforce courses to help unemployed people to find jobs or start their own businesses, to work towards increasing women's employment in the labor market, making the unskilled workforce qualified for the labor market, providing consultancy and training services for the unemployed to be re-employed, conducting training activities in enterprises to increase the productivity and performance of the workforce is among the main topics of active workforce programs. The concentration of active labor market programs in social segments with more limited employment opportunities, such as young people, women, people with disabilities and ex-convicts, will increase the benefits of these programs. Active employment programs provide structural transformation by increasing the quality of labor supply in combating structural unemployment caused by economic differentiation. In other words, with the active employment programs, individuals are tried to gain the most updated version of the qualifications required by the labor market (Vlandas, 2013; Bonoli, 2010).

In today's world of intense competition, on the one hand, while unemployment rates are rising, many businesses need a qualified, professionally trained workforce. In order to meet the need for trained intermediaries and to minimize the loss of products and labor, various training, courses and certificate programs are provided in the areas required in the labor market. Aware of this fact, action plans have to be developed and policies have to be put forward to meet the need for qualified personnel in the labor market and facilitate the employment of the unemployed within the understanding of lifelong education. Vocational courses opened for this purpose increase the employment possibilities of unemployed people who want to improve their vocational qualifications, by increasing their qualifications according to the requirements of the labor market. Employment-guaranteed workforce training courses are courses aimed at employing unemployed people who do not have a valid profession in the labor market, by training them in the qualifications required by the market. By reviewing the existing education programs in vocational education and higher education, it is ensured that the education programs to be opened are determined in line with the need for labor quality.

Informal employment is one of the important issues taken into consideration in the second generation microeconomic reforms regarding the labor markets. Informal employment refers to the fact that the work or the wages and earnings of the employees working or employed on their behalf are never reported to the relevant public institutions or underreported in terms of days or wages. Informal employment basically arises due to reasons such as paying lower wages, avoiding tax and social security premiums, avoiding compensation in layoffs, and avoiding legal obligations. Informal employment causes unfair competition, losses in public revenues such as tax and social security premium, deprivation of rights arising from social security and labor law and social policy ineffectiveness. When the causes of informal employment are examined all over the world, rapid population growth, interregional development differences, high share of agriculture in employment, migration, urbanization, unfair distribution of income, poverty, high unemployment, high labor costs, low education level, the structure and low competitiveness of the industry, high tax rates and inability to collect taxes fairly, frequent changes in social security and tax laws, early retirement, dissatisfaction with social security institutions services, lack of coordination and cooperation between public institutions are encountered. In solving the problem of informal employment, generalizing access to education, flexing labor market legislation, facilitating the transition to formal employment by providing legal and financial opportunities to unregistered workers, reducing the tax and social security burden on the labor force, in some cases, subsidizing the costs on the employer and unregistered employment punishment are effective methods (Anand & Khera, 2016; Albrecht et al., 2009).

Informal Economy Reforms

The informal economy, which hides from the state, is not registered, cannot be controlled and therefore does not contribute to the official GNP, is one of the important economic problems that must be resolved, even if it occurs in different dimensions and in different reasons and forms depending on the economic, political and social structures of the countries. The informal economy is an important structural problem of economic life for many developing countries. Macroeconomic instabilities, high tax and premium rates, administrative, financial and legal burdens, the small scale of enterprises, high bureaucratic formalities, high use of cash, the ineffectiveness of the control system causes the unregistered economic activities to emerge. Various measures need to be taken in order to register the informal economy, which has negative economic and social consequences. In the informal economy, there are no documents related to economic activity, or with the documents that do not reflect the truth, the economic transaction carried out is taken out of the formal economy by hiding it completely or partially from the state and other persons related to the company. The causes of the informal economy differ from country to country, depending on financial, economic, political, legal and social factors, but in the economic literature, underdevelopment of the economy, high tax rates, high inflation and increase in unit labor costs, increase in regulations in the formal economy, weekly working hours reduction, early retirement, and disruption of tax payment are among the main reasons. Although the size of the informal economy may change depending on the economy being developed or underdeveloped, the economic policies followed, the crises experienced, the instability, the limited employment and income opportunities in the formal economy, knowing the causes of the informal economy is important to prevent or reduce its share in the economy. Since the informal economy does not enter official records, economic indicators such as inflation, unemployment, growth rates and income levels in the formal economy are different than they actually are and the analyses developed accordingly cause unreliable estimates. Therefore, economic policies such as growth, development, fairness in income distribution and employment creation, which will be developed based on these analyses and forecasts, will also produce unexpected and incorrect results. Informal economy makes informal firms more advantageous compared to formal firms with more competitive prices, destroys the competitive structure of the market and creates an unfair competitive environment against the formal economy. Thus, it prevents the expected positive results from the competitive system, promotes the shift of resources to non-taxed sectors and disrupts the efficiency in resource allocation.

Success in combating the informal economy and reducing informality depend on ensuring cooperation and coordination between institutions and obtaining public support by establishing an effective monitoring and evaluation system. Therefore, the efficiency of inspections is increased by improving the human and technological infrastructure of public administrations, and it is aimed to explain the losses of the informal economy to people. In the fight against informality, it is aimed to implement practices for strengthening and activating the audit dimension by increasing social sensitivity and making necessary legal arrangements.

A strategy to fight against the informal economy should be prepared in order to detect the losses of the informal economy, raise the awareness of the society, encourage registration, simplify the legislation and procedures, develop effective control and penal system and strengthen data sharing among the relevant institutions. With this plan, it should be aimed to encourage registered activities, strengthen audit capacity and ensure institutional and social consensus. To this end, efforts are being made to a gradual reduction of administrative, financial and legal obligations in line with budgetary possibilities, increasing financing opportunities for registered businesses, reducing bureaucratic formalities by simplifying the legislation on work and working life, promoting the institutionalization of enterprises, improving public services for registered businesses and individuals, increasing flexibility in business life and labor market. Cooperation and coordination between institutions fighting against informality should be ensured, and all kinds of amnesty and debt structuring practices that reward the informal economy, shake the trust in the public and encourage informality should be removed. At the point of blocking the informality, topics such as information and awareness-raising activities, reducing bureaucracy, ensuring inter-agency coordination, conducting effective and deterrent audits, making social security services attractive should be carefully considered without preference to the other (Djankov et al., 2002; Farrell, 2004; Gerxhani, 2003; Oviedo et al., 2008; Perry et al., 2007).

Tax Systems Reforms

Reforms related to tax systems basically refer to the deep-rooted regulatory and improvement movements in the whole tax systems and the components that make up the whole in order to achieve economic and social goals. With tax system reforms, justice and equality are expected to be achieved in the distribution of tax burdens in society. Depending on the changing economic, financial, social, political and administrative conditions of the countries, it is a common phenomenon to reform the tax systems according to the economic and social needs of all countries. With the tax reform, it is aimed to make the tax system suitable for the economic, financial and social development of the society, to adopt modern tax practices, to ensure that tax revenues are obtained at the desired level and to rearrange the distribution of tax burdens. Ensuring efficiency in both the collection of public revenues and distribution of public resources and designing public income/expenditure policies taking into account the basic economic and social objectives play an important role in achieving sustainable macroeconomic goals.

In order to achieve effective and successful tax reform, first of all, a realistic and appropriate tax policy must be determined. Tax reform should be an efficient and uncomplicated arrangement that reduces costs, increases the tax base by lowering tax rates, prevents tax evasion, increases the credibility of political authority by ensuring impartiality, pays as much as everyone earns. The more the tax base is expanded through the Reform, the easier it will be to distribute the tax burden fairly and balanced and to reduce marginal tax rates.

The expansion of the tax base stands out as one of the most important issues in the reform of tax systems. Expanding the tax base, taxation of non-taxable income, expenditure or wealth items and recording of the informal economy ensure that tax rates can be reduced without decreasing total tax revenues, thereby reducing the negative impact of taxes on the economy. At this point, countries seek to establish a simple, understandable and long-term system that expands their tax base, strengthens their tax collection and audit units, increases data collection and review capacity, reduces tax evasion and informality, reduces the time and monetary costs of taxpayers (Bird, 2004; Perret et al., 2016; Profeta, 2003).

Research and Development (R&D) Activities Reforms

In today's fast-changing and globalizing world, companies need to constantly change and renew their products, services and production methods in order to survive in an intense and dynamic competitive environment. In other words, firms' increasing their competitiveness and ensuring their sustainability dependent on revealing originality and innovation in production information. It is the only way for companies to follow innovations closely or to be the pioneers of innovations themselves in order to be successful. The only way to ensure innovation is intense and efficient R&D activities. R&D activities are regular works to obtain new information that will enable the development of science and technology or to produce new materials, products or tools with existing information, to create new systems, processes, and services, including software production, or to develop existing ones. It is not possible to develop new products and processes, to keep up with the developments of competitors, to reduce production costs, to increase efficiency and to develop existing production techniques by finding new production techniques without making the necessary importance and investment in R&D activities. For these reasons, governments should develop policies that support and encourage research and development activities. Efforts are being made to establish an education and training infrastructure that will encourage and guide young people to science and technology and encourage innovation. These policies are carried out within the framework of the establishment of competent brainpower potential and the implementation of mechanisms and support programs that encourage young people to move towards innovation and to enable them to easily access information and information resources at the international or national level. It is vital for economic growth and development to enforce research and financial support programs that will increase the country's research and development volume and competence, and to develop and support mechanisms that will enable competence in science and technology to enter the fields of economic activity.

The level of the countries in the world in terms of science and technology is determined by factors such as the size of the R & D activities carried out, the share of R & D expenditures in GNP and the number of expert researchers employed. Countries, that want to grow and develop, support R&D studies with a large amount of funds to produce technological information, raise product quality and standards, reduce production costs, make the economy competitive at an international level, efficiently evaluate qualified manpower. It can be said that economic efficiency, growth rate, and employment level cannot be increased in the long term and permanently without supporting and developing R&D activities. The main objectives of R&D incentives are to produce technological information, to innovate in product and production processes, to increase product quality and standard, to increase productivity, to reduce production costs, to commercialize technological knowledge, to increase technology-intensive productions and investments, to increase foreign direct investment and to increase employment of R&D personnel and qualified labor force. With the policies created, it is aimed to generate information, transform information into value, and carry innovation into every area of products, systems, processes, and marketing. It is necessary to produce new ideas that the new world needs and will demand in the future and to be able to generate economic returns by commercializing these innovations. These efforts and studies have an important role on economic growth, prosperity growth and regional development. In addition, with the R&D activities, the technology capability is tried to be increased on the one hand, and on the other hand, projects that will create vitality in the economy and create new employment areas are implemented.

Within the scope of second-generation reforms, policies have been developed to increase the share of R&D expenditures in GNP and to increase the private sector's weight in this share. With the awareness of science and technology, the number of qualified researchers has been increased and research institutes and universities have been developed. To this end, technology development zones have been established and strengthened, and monitoring and impact assessment studies on R&D activities have been carried out. In this context, supports provided to companies for strengthening R&D capacity and protection of intellectual property rights has been expanded. University-industry cooperation and research centers were supported to strengthen R&D-based production capabilities. In order to support products based on university-industry cooperation and local specialization, technology transfer centers have been established to transfer the information formed as a result of R&D activities to industry and production by implementing sectoral organized industrial zones in appropriate regions. In addition, the establishment of the private sector and non-governmental organizations to support consultancy on technology selection, transfer and management were also supported.

FUTURE RESEARCH DIRECTIONS

This study discusses second-generation microeconomic reforms in general and with basic topics. The study can be improved by discussing second-generation microeconomic reforms specific to certain markets. In addition, the effects of second-generation microeconomic reforms should be analyzed empirically as data sets develop over time. Examples showing the positive and negative effects of the reforms in key markets with empirical results should be increased. Examples of similar countries that have implemented and have not implemented second-generation microeconomic reforms can be compared with analysis. Identifying the effects of the reforms through empirical analysis is important for guiding policymakers in their decisions and steps.

CONCLUSION

Developed and developing countries have always kept economic reforms on their agenda in order to ensure economic development, maintain their economic performance and improve their living standards. For this purpose, priority has been given to first generation reforms which is main purpose is to provide macroeconomic stability and which are easier to prepare and implement technically and administratively. With these first generation reforms, problems such as macroeconomic imbalances, instability, high interest rates, high inflation rates, financial and monetary discipline, and high public debt were tried to be solved. In this context, strategies such as changing macroeconomic rules, reducing the economic activities of the state and reducing protectionism were implemented. After the first generation reforms were implemented, new searches started with the slowdown in their success, their deficiencies becoming clearer and their inadequacy in reaching the targets. In order to sustain growth and development and increase international competitiveness and social development, reforms that strengthen the infrastructure of the market economy, increase efficiency and increase competitiveness were needed. At this point, countries have started to implement micro-economic reforms, which are called second-generation reforms. With the second generation reforms, countries have changed from rule change to institutional change by introducing a strategy based on the production economy, providing solutions to unemployment, reducing the informal economy, increasing efficiency and quality in public services, promoting technical development and innovation, supporting entrepreneurship and eliminating rigidity. In this context, second generation reforms are used in the economic system as a complement, not a substitute for first generation reforms.

Within the scope of the second generation micro reforms, reforms are made in many areas, but the most subject areas of reforms are product markets, employment, informal economy, tax systems and research and development activities. Within the scope of reforms regarding product markets, it is aimed to increase competition in the goods and services markets by facilitating entry and exit to the markets, strengthening efficiency and preventing monopolistic tendencies. In second generation micro reforms regarding employment, there are many reasons and targets such as decreasing labor costs, providing flexibility by eliminating rigidities, increasing active employment measures and preventing informal employment. With the micro reforms related to the tax system, it is aimed to make the tax system suitable for the economic, financial and social development of the society, to adopt modern tax practices and to obtain the tax revenues at the desired level and to rearrange the tax burden distribution. Reforms supporting the aim of obtaining new information that will enable the development of science and technology or producing new materials, products or tools with existing information, and creating new systems, processes, and services or developing existing ones are carried out within the scope of second-generation micro reforms related to research and development activities.

There is considerable assessment of the inadequacy of first-generation reforms and the need for second-generation reforms. The main conclusion to be drawn from these discussions is that economic reforms are a long process with stages and both generations of reforms are indispensable and irreplaceable parts of this long process. It is impossible for first-generation reforms carried out without second-generation reforms to yield long-term and permanent results alone, and it is pointless to attempt second-generation reforms without first-generation reforms.

REFERENCES

Ahsan, A., & Pagés, C. (2009). Are all labor regulations equal? Evidence from Indian manufacturing. *Journal of Comparative Economics*, *37*(1), 62–75. doi:10.1016/j.jce.2008.09.001

Albrecht, J., Navarro, L., & Vroman, S. (2009). The effects of labour market policies in an economy with an informal sector. *Economic Journal (London)*, *119*(539), 1105–1129. doi:10.1111/j.1468-0297.2009.02268.x

Anand, R., & Khera, P. (2016). *Macroeconomic impact of product and labor market reform on informality and unemployment in India.* IMF Working Paper. Washington, DC: International Monetary Fund, WP/16/47.

Berger, H., & Danninger, S. (2007). The employment effects of labor and product markets deregulation and their implications for structural reform. *IMF Staff Papers*, *54*(3), 591–619. doi:10.1057/palgrave.imfsp.9450014

Bertola, G., Boeri, T., & Cazes, S. (1999). Employment protection and labor market adjustment in OECD countries: evolving institutions and variable enforcement. Employment and Training Papers International Labor Organization, Geneva, No. 48.

Bird, R. M. (2004, Feb.). Managing tax reform. *International Bureau of Fiscal Documentation Bulletin.*

Bonoli, G. (2010). The political economy of active labour market policy. *Politics & Society*, *38*(4), 435–457. doi:10.1177/0032329210381235

Davidson, P. (2004). A post Keynesian view of the Washington consensus and how to improve it. *Journal of Post Keynesian Economics*, *27*(2), 207–230.

Djankov, S., Lieberman, I., Mukherjee, J., & Nenova, T. (2002). *Going informal: benefits and costs", mimeo*. The World Bank.

Duval, R., & Elmeskov, J. (2006). *The effects of EMU structural reforms in labour and product markets*. ECB Working Paper Series, No. 596.

Elmeskov, J., Martin, J., & Scarpetta, S. (1998). Key lessons for labour market reforms: Evidence from OECD countries' experiences. *Swedish Economic Policy Review*, *5*, 2.

Farrell, D. (2004). The hidden dangers of the informal economy. *The McKinsey Quarterly*, 3.

Fiori, G., Nicoletti, G., Scarpetta, S., & Schiantarelli, F. (2012). Employment effects of product and labor market reforms; are there synergies? *Economic Journal (London)*, *122*(558), 79–104. doi:10.1111/j.1468-0297.2011.02494.x

Forsyth, P. (1992). A perspective on microeconomic reform. In P. Forsyth (Ed.), *Microeconomic Reform in Australia*. Allen and Unwin.

Gerxhani, K. (2003). *The Informal Sector in Developed and Less Developed Countries. Amsterdam Institute for Advanced Labour Studies*. University of Amsterdam.

Gore, C. (2000). The Rise and fall of the washington consensus as a paradigma for developing countries. *World Development*, *28*(5), 789–804. doi:10.1016/S0305-750X(99)00160-6

Gregory, R. G. (1992). An ovetview ofmicroeconomic reform. In P. J. Forsyth (Ed.), *Microeconomic Reform in Australia*. Allen and Unwin.

Griffith, R., Harrison, R., & Macartney, G. (2007). Product market reforms, labor market institutions and unemployment. *Economic Journal (London)*, *117*(519), 142–166. doi:10.1111/j.1468-0297.2007.02039.x

Harrison, A. E. (1994). Productivity, imperfect competition and trade reform. Theory and evidence. *Journal of International Economics*, *36*(1-2), 53–73. doi:10.1016/0022-1996(94)90057-4

Harvey, D. (2005). *A brief history of neoliberalism*. Oxford University Press.

Jessop, B. (2002). Liberalism, neoliberalism, and urban governance: A state–theoretical perspective. *Antipode*, *34*(3), 452–472. doi:10.1111/1467-8330.00250

Jones, R. (1994). *Australian Microeconomic Policies*. Prentice Hall.

Manuel, P., & Carol, W. (1999). The politics of second-generation reform. *Journal of Democracy*, *10*(3), 34–48. doi:10.1353/jod.1999.0052

Milonakis, D., & Fine, B. (2009). *From Political Economy to Economics: Method, the Social and the Historical in the Evolution of Economic Theory*. Routledge. doi:10.4324/9780203887110

Naim, M. (1995). Latin America: The second stage of reform. In Economic Reform and Democracy. Baltimore, MD: Johns Hopkins University Press.

Nicoletti, G., & Scarpetta, S. (2005). *Product market reforms and employment in the OECD countries.* OECD Economics Department Working Papers, No. 472.

Oviedo, A. M., Thomas, M. R., & Ozdemir, K. (2008). *Economic informality: causes, costs, and policies – a literature survey*. The World Bank.

Perret, S., Brys, B., Alastair, T., & Pierce, O. (2016). *Tax design for Inclusive Economic Growth.* OECD Taxation Working Paper, No. 24.

Perry, G., Arias, O., Fajnzylber, P., Maloney, W., Mason, A., & Saavedra, J. (2007). *Informality: Exit and exclusion*. The World Bank. doi:10.1596/978-0-8213-7092-6

Pissarides, C. (1997). The need for labour market flexibility in a European economic and monetary union. *Swedish Economic Policy Review*, *4*, 513–546.

Profeta, P. (2003). Political support and tax reforms with an application to Italy. *Public Choice*, *131*(1-2), 141–155. doi:10.100711127-006-9110-4

Rodrik, D. (2001). *The Global Governance of Trade- As if Development Really Mattered.* http://www.giszpenc.com/globalciv/rodrik1.pdf

Rodrik, D. (2006). Goodbye Washington consensus, hello Washington confusion? A review of the world bank's economic growth in the 1990s: Learning from a decade of reform. *Journal of Economic Literature*, *44*(4), 973–987. doi:10.1257/jel.44.4.973

Stiglitz, J. E. (1997). *An agenda for development for the twenty-first century*. https://documents.worldbank.org/curated/en/503521538245109923/pdf/An-agenda-for-development-for-the-twenty-first-century.pdf

Vlandas, T. (2013). Mixing apples with oranges? Partisanship and active labour market policies in Europe. *Journal of European Social Policy*, *23*(1), 3–20. doi:10.1177/0958928712463161

Williamson, J. (2000). What should the world bank think about the Washington consensus? *The World Bank Research Observer*, *15*(2), 251–264. doi:10.1093/wbro/15.2.251

Williamson, J. (2003). The Washington Consensus and beyond. *Economic and Political Weekly*, *38*(15), 1475–1481.

Williamson, J. (2005). The strange history of the Washington consensus. *Journal of Post Keynesian Economics*, *27*(2), 195–206.

ADDITIONAL READING

Basanes, F., & Willig, R. (2002). *Second-generation reforms in infrastructure services*. Inter-American Development Bank.

Betcherman, G. (2014). Designing labor market regulations in developing countries. *IZA World of Labor, 2014*, 57. doi:10.15185/izawol.57

Bordon, A. R., Ebeke, C., & Shirono, K. (2016). When do structural reforms work? On the role of business cycle and macroeconomic policies. *IMF working paper*, 16/62

Caballero, R. J., Cowan, K. N., Engel, E. M., & Micco, A. (2004). Effective labor regulation and microeconomic flexibility. *NBER Working Paper No. 10744*.

Eggertsson, G., Ferrero, A., & Raffo, A. (2014). Can structural reforms help Europe? *Journal of Monetary Economics*, *61*, 2–22. doi:10.1016/j.jmoneco.2013.11.006

Lora, E. (2012). Structural reform in Latin America: What has been reformed and how to measure it. *IDB Working Paper Series No. 346, Inter-American Development Bank*, Washington, DC.

Lusinyan, L. (2018). Assessing the impact of structural reforms through a supply-side framework: The case of Argentina. *IMF Working Paper 18/183, International Monetary Fund*, Washington, DC.

Rodrik, D. (1996). Understanding economic policy reform. *Journal of Economic Literature*, *34*(1), 9–41.

Rodrik, D. (2009). *One economics, many recipes: Globalization, institutions, and economic growth*. Princeton Univerity Press.

Williamson, J. (1994). *The political economy of policy reform* (J. Williamson, Ed.). Institute for International Economics.

KEY TERMS AND DEFINITIONS

Economic Reforms: A radical change process that increases living standards, improves well-being, and increases resistance against shocks in order to provide permanent and long-term improvement and solutions.

Employment Reforms: It is the reform policies that increase employment, provide jobs for everyone who wants to work, improve labor quality and productivity, harmonize labor supply and demand, and solve the problems posed by unemployment.

First Generation Reforms: Reforms that aim to implement monetary policy in a way that ensures price stability and fiscal policy in a way that captures a sustainable level of deficit.

Macroeconomic Reforms: Economic reforms that fall under the scrutiny of macroeconomics.

Microeconomic Reforms: Economic reforms that fall under the scrutiny of microeconomics.

Product Market Reforms: It is the reform policies that increase competition in the goods and services markets, facilitate entry and exit to the markets, strengthen productivity, and prevent monopolistic trends.

Reforms: A planned and informed radical change, correction, reclamation, and improvement to make the current situation better.

Second Generation Reforms: Reforms that strengthen the infrastructure of the market economy, increase efficiency, create competitive markets, and renew the institutional infrastructure.

Structural Reforms: It is the restructuring of the economic system so that it can work more efficiently and make it more resistant to shocks.

Chapter 7
The Money as the Necessary Link Between Micro and Macro Levels

Gancho Ganchev
South-West University "Neofit Rilski", Bulgaria

ABSTRACT

The aim of the chapter is to introduce money as the necessary link between micro and macro levels. The author starts with a critical appraisal of the neoclassical monetary theory paradigm. The opening argument is that it is not possible to separate the relative prices and price level formation. The interdependence between the price of money and the prices of all the other goods leads to the conclusion of the gross complementarity of money what violates the gross substitutability principle. Further, it is argued that the function of money as medium of exchange in a decentralized monetary economy is only possible under cyclic sequencing of bilateral exchanges. The latter means that new macroeconomic constraint is added to the conventional micro equilibrium requirements. The macro constraint makes possible to derive the individual utility functions from macro variables such as the income velocity of money and the price level. The macro constraint allows also for optimal solutions under the second-best conditions.

INTRODUCTION

The neoclassical economics is based on just two main concepts- the principle of the methodological individualism and the idea of the general equilibrium (see for critique Colander 2000). The proof that the decentralized exchange between self-interested economic agents converges to simultaneous equilibrium on all markets is the core objective and the main result of the neoclassical research program. This reductionist approach regards the macro level (the economic system as a whole) as a simple consequence of the micro foundations (endowments and objectives of the economic agents) without any feedback from macro to micro level. In other words, there are no parameters, reflecting the functional state of the system, that affect in turn the individual players. The prices balance the supply and demand on inter-

DOI: 10.4018/978-1-7998-4933-9.ch007

dependent markets, but this interdependence does not reflect the additional conditions and constraints, guarantying the wholeness of the economic system. These additional conditions are related to money.

Without competitive equilibrium, derived straightforwardly from the bottom up, the whole structure of the neoclassical economics would change. In fact, the justification of the general equilibrium comes at a high price. The competitive equilibrium is still a kind of multilateral barter exchange, excluding any meaningful role for money. In addition, the mathematical proof that general equilibrium exists in some mathematical sense does not mean that it's actually feasible in our finite world (see Boylan and O'Gorman 2018).

The famous micro foundations of the neoclassical models are introduced without elucidation of how so many unrelated activities are coordinated in order to form a single rational representative individual (Bergh and Gowdy, 2003). Furthermore, the exchange of composite goods between two or three archetypal players does not really require monetary intermediation. In contrast, the synchronization of actions, allowing big number of participants to behave in a coordinated way can ultimately be carried out only via the circulation of money, as it is demonstrated in this chapter.

The main problem of the neoclassical general equilibrium approach is the money market and the connection between money market equilibrium and the rest of the economy. Not only the money market is ill defined, but the price of money is presumed to be equal to unity and the equilibrium is derived not constructively, via money market behavior itself, but implicitly, by bringing into play the so called Walras Law.

Without explicit introduction of all functions of money, namely medium of exchange, numéraire (unit of account), standard of differed payments and store of value, it is not possible to create credible theory of contemporary decentralized money intermediated economies (Ganchev 2015). The objective of the present study is twofold. On the one hand, we intend to prove, that in an economy with money, purely decentralized equilibrium convergence is not possible, money market does not obey the gross substitutability rule. On the other hand, it will be demonstrated, that macro parameters affect micro behavior, so the neoclassical reductionism is not relevant.

The actual decentralized economic systems, not converging to equilibrium, but subject to periodic boom and bust cycles, are quite different, contrasted to neoclassical equilibrium oriented economies. In the genuine neoclassical world, the decentralized capitalist economies are stable; the external shocks are absorbed by markets. In the non-so neoclassical setting, the markets themselves generate instability; the stabilization is brought about externally, via macroeconomic policy. This explains why the empirical DSGE models need so many artificial external shocks in order to fit the data (see for details Romer 2016). From the point of view of the political economics, there are just two ways to deal with economic instability. The first is the radical transformation of capitalist societies in the sense of Marx and the second, suggested by Keynes, consists of reforming and regulating capitalism. In the modern context, only the second alternative seems feasible.

The concrete results of the present chapter can be summarized as follows.

The value (price) of money must be determined in a system of simultaneous equations together with the prices of all the other goods, so the general equilibrium models should not be normalized. Deriving relative prices and the price level are the two sides of the same coin. Inflation (deflation) is viewed as macro disequilibrium indicator. Therefore, it is deduced, that decentralized monetary economies are self-regulating via inflation-deflation cycles, but not converging to equilibrium.

Stabilization monetary and fiscal policies are necessary, though not sufficient, for general equilibrium convergence and optimal resource allocation. The income velocity of money is introduced not as datum, but as an eigenvalue of the so-called matrix of bilateral velocities. Thus, the velocity of money is the same for all agents and depends on the systemic parameters of the economy (the connectedness between agents via payments). If the matrix of bilateral velocities is indecomposable and cyclic (this simply means that there are no groups of agents that do not obtain monetary payments from other agents, plus possibility for cyclic sequencing of payments), closed monetary rotations exist. In other words, the cyclic nature of the matrix of velocities is a necessary condition for the existence of money intermediated exchange. The interpretation is that the cyclic sequencing of bilateral exchanges is an additional macroeconomic constraint to the economy. In such a system, the individual utility functions depend on macroeconomic parameters such as the income velocity of money and the price level.

The chapter consists of six parts. The second part discusses the general equilibrium approach to money. The third part is dedicated to the definition of money market, stability and coordination. The fourth paragraph is focused on the impact of macro variables such as price level and income velocity of money on the micro behavior (utility functions). The fifth section briefly deals with economic growth and development. Conclusions are summarized in the last part. In addition, the chapter includes four appendices- the first is about the disequilibrium, related to money; the second deals with the relative prices and the price of money; the third includes special part about the velocity of money and the impact of macro variables on the individual utility functions; and the fourth appendix briefly deals with the directed graphs' interpretation of the monetary circulation.

The General Equilibrium and The Money: The Conventional Tautology

The neoclassical theorists had never been enthusiastic about actually introducing money and money market in the exchange system. Since however general equilibrium is hardly possible without some kind of individual goods mutual comparability, the neoclassicals focused their attention on such metaphysical subjects, as homogeneity postulate (see for example Takayama 1990) and money neutrality (Lucas 1995). Both homogeneity and neutrality are quite appropriate in order to pledge commensurability among goods, without any tangible impact on the exchange and production. Yet this disregards the fact, that equally in physics and economics, it is not possible to measure an object, without affecting it.

Following these two basic neoclassical assumptions, the price of money is artificially fixed, before the existence of equilibrium is actually proved. This can be done in two ways. The first variant is simply to fix the price of money to unity (Walras 1874). The second option is to fix not the price of money, but the price level (the index of all prices) to unity. The latter variant is obviously equivalent to the first since the price of money is the inverse of price level.

Walras explicitly states that we should measure the monetary prices in terms of monetary units and not in terms of the exchange value of the monetary unit. This is acceptable in the case of hypothetical simultaneous barter exchange at equilibrium prices. However, if we swap goods for money and vice versa and the exchange system is not in equilibrium, we are interested in knowing not only the monetary prices of the specific goods and services, but the exchange value of money itself, since the latter, according to Pigou (1917), is nothing but an expression of the inverse of the sum of the prices of all exchanged goods in terms of money and consequently affects the outcome of the exchange. This means that in disequilibrium situations we should abandon the Walrasian postulate about fixing the exchange value of money to unity. The convergence to equilibrium is thus simultaneous adjustment of all prices, including that of money. This is true even if the role of money is reduced to the unit of account function. In the case when money fulfils the more demanding means of exchange role, the convergence to equilibrium is even not feasible (see Appendix 1).

To put it differently, if the price of money and all the other prices are interdependent, we cannot fix one of the prices in advance. Yet, the particularity of the exchange value of money is that it consists of combination of all the outstanding prices. Therefore, the price of money combines micro and macro features.

If all markets, including that of money, are in equilibrium, then homogeneity hypothesis holds in the sense that if we multiply all prices by factor k (¥>k>0) supply and demand functions remain unaltered. However, even in such a case, if all prices include the price (exchange value) of money, then it is simply impossible to multiply every single price by the same factor (the price of money moves in opposite direction to all the other prices). That's why the more sophisticated adepts of the neoclassical school acknowledge that homogeneity can be applied to all goods, except money (Modigliani, 1944), but some authors (Lange 1942; Patinkin 1947; 1949) object that if homogeneity is applied to all but one price, then according to Walras Law, equilibrium on non-money markets, combined with the Cambridge money demand equation, would imply that money market is also homogenous of degree zero.

There is another logical conundrum. In order to preserve the neutrality and homogeneity, the neoclassical theorist (with the somewhat paradoxical exception of Walras himself) separate the processes of deriving relative prices and the price level. This is necessary in order to prove the existence of equilibrium without money and next to prove that money market is also in equilibrium. According to Fisher (1963), the procedure includes two steps. First, the real sector determines equilibrium relative prices and quantities, exchanged at equilibrium, usually via some variant of tâtonnement process. Tâtonnement, or groping, is the process of finding the market clearing prices for all commodities. Then money market is introduced and the equilibrium price level is derived. In other words, the relative prices are established without any relation to the money market itself.

This is clearly false. If we have only two goods, the relative price can be easily determined, since one of the goods can be viewed as money. However, if we have more than two goods, the relative prices can be expressed only in terms of bilateral exchange proportions, forming a system, analogous to the system of bilateral exchange rates.

Such systems obey consistency rule excluding arbitrage profits and any good's bilateral exchange proportions against all the other goods contain all information about the entire number of cross exchange proportions, as Walras himself once demonstrated. This means that in such a system any good, exchangeable directly or indirectly against all the other goods, may be viewed as numéraire. In mathematical terms this means that the matrix of relative prices must be indecomposable (what is the usual condition of input-output and general equilibrium analysis) and imprimitive (cyclic), what is against the standard general equilibrium features, see the Appendix 2 for details.

Further, because according to Pigou's definition, the value of money is nothing but the inverse of the price level, it can be expressed in terms of any exchangeable good. Consequently, by determining relative prices we fix the price level(s) and since the price level includes all prices, it defines relative prices. The relative commodity prices and the price of money can be derived only simultaneously.

All this has an important consequence. The conditions, necessary for the derivation of price level and relative prices, imply also the existence of closed monetary circulation paths integrating all agents and markets. This means that the functions of money as numéraire and means of exchange can be fulfilled only jointly. What is crucial in order to secure trade commensurability is not the participation of individual goods in direct multilateral barter exchange (such an exchange is neither necessary nor possible), but the involvement in closed monetary cycles.

To resume, if there is an equilibrium in terms of relative prices, at least one of the exchanged goods can be defined as numéraire and any separate money equation is superfluous. On the contrary, fixing the price of money means that we can analyze only $n - 1$ equations, were n is the number of markets. Under normalized price system and with the assumption that all final production is consumed, it can be proved that general equilibrium exists (McKenzie 1959). In particular, since all markets with the exception of that of money are in equilibrium, then according to Walras' Law the money market should also be in balance. This is an obvious example of logically unacceptable circular reasoning (Ganchev 2015; see also from a somewhat different perspective Area 2015).

Following this way of thinking, we are able to formulate regularity that can be termed Inverse Walras' Law. This law consists of straightforward deduction that if we fix the price of money we implicitly fix all prices (see for argumentation Appendix 2). But any price can be fixed if and only if supply equals demand. Consequently, by settling the price of money at unity we tacitly assume that the general equilibrium already exists. Thus the Inverse Walras' Law transforms all theoretical constructions deriving general equilibrium on the basis of conventional Walras' Law into tautologies.

The Walras himself, as an originator of the general equilibrium analysis, was aware of these contradictions. In fact, he suggested two variants of his model. The first reduced the role of money to a numéraire. This is the traditional general equilibrium assumption. The second variant introduced the main functions of money and allowed for simultaneous determination of relative prices and the price level, the money market being associated with the short-term credit market. In his Théorie de la monnaie (1886), published after the first edition of the Eléments de l'économie politique pure, Walras, under the influence of Jevons, admitted that the exchange value of money is not stable and even suggested a variant of monetary policy that could stabilize the price level. Walras, however, finally opted for the first variant, because he was conscious of the instability that the introduction of money will add to his model (see for discussion Schumpeter 1954).

Another typical inaccuracy of the neoclassical and Austrian economics (see Wicksel 1934 and Hayek 1931) is the lack of discrimination between the money market as a kind of macroeconomic device and the short-term funds market. Money is always an instrument of short terms financing at micro level via bilateral exchange, so money market is interdependent, but not identical, to short-term funds market. Viewing the interest rate as a price of money allows us to establish connection between real and the monetary dimensions of the economy via the chain saving-investment-commodity market-consumption, but does not resolve the problem of general equilibrium system of equations inconsistency.

Some neoclassical authors diverge from these schemes. They assume that relative prices can be money intermediated. In this case, the system starts at some price level determined by the optimizing behavior of economic agents (utility and profit maximization) and gradually converges to equilibrium. Initially transactions take place at non-equilibrium prices. The proof of equilibrium convergence however is also based on the inconsistent hypothesis of fixed price of money (see for example Friedman 1979; Arrow and Hahn 1972). So this divergence from the traditional general equilibrium approach does not really add anything new.

The analysis of normalized price systems nevertheless cannot ignore the fact, that the swings of value of money influence the real economy. Scitovsky (1941), Haberler (1946), Pigou (1943) and later Patinkin (1965), claim that the change of price level affects the purchasing power of money stock and thus provokes the so called real balance or wealth effect. The interesting thing about this concept is that in spite of investigating the impact of the value of money variations on the demand for money via the money market, the neoclassical authors investigate the role of money as a store of value. In other words, they focus on stock effects, underestimating the direct flow dimensions of equilibrium convergence.

The real balance effect simply means, that if the price level goes up, the real money balances decline, so the economic agents become poorer and cut their purchases of goods and services. The underlying idea is that this type of behavior is self-regulating, as far as is in the case of inflation the wealth effect will help to decelerate the price level escalation via reduced spending and in the case of deflation, it will ease the restoration of demand.

The real balance effect is criticized from two standpoints. First, it is argued that wealth effect is too weak to influence the economy in a noteworthy way and second, it does not take into account the so-called inter-temporal substitution effect (Grandmont 1985). The latter states that the expected future rate of inflation affects the current demand and can either strengthen or abate the wealth effect. So, the equilibrium convergence is not certain. Both wealth and inter-temporal substitution effects however do not opt for the most natural way of dealing with the problem, which is to take into account the response of the economic agents to the variations of the exchange value of money, as it's carried out with all the other markets.

From the point of view of the concept of the general equilibrium, the unit of account function of money should be derived from the price or the value of money. In terms of numéraire we are free to choose any quantity of money as unit of account without loss of generality, especially in the case of commodity money. But it does not mean that we can randomly fix the price of that unit. The price of money, as already emphasized, is nothing but an expression of the inverse of the sum of prices of all exchanged goods in terms of money. This price can be determined either by market forces or via central bank monetary policy. We can see again that the value (price) of money is determined by the system as a whole or "the money market" is a kind of global market, were we exchange money against all the other goods. This market operates by the way of all the other individual goods markets.

We should also take into account that any change in the value of money is simultaneously a change in the purchasing power of the monetary unit (see for details Schumpeter 1954). The converse is also true- if we modify the monetary unit we change ceteris paribus its' purchasing power. So in terms of exchange proportions we cannot distinguish between exchange value and unit of account variations (see for details Appendix 2). The equivalence between unit and exchange value changes can be illustrated by the Irving Fisher "compensated dollar" proposal. The idea was to stabilize the purchasing power of the dollar by increasing the gold content of the American currency when the prices were going up and by diminishing the amount of gold per dollar when prices fall (JEC 2004).

The monetary unit as a kind of measure of market prices has another singularity. The value or the scale of this measure is determined after the measurement had already taken place, because the value of money is a function of all prices. As a result, we face uncertainty, inherent to decentralized exchange. The reason for this is the interaction between the instrument of measurement (money) and the subject of measurement (goods and services). Theoretically, this inconsistency can be avoided if we base our analysis on a system of simultaneous equations, but in practice there will always be some "time inconsistency", since the transfer of information from micro to macro level and backward always takes time.

The traditional functions of money, introduced in all textbooks, are not as obvious as they may seem. For example, the function of medium of exchange implies not only elimination of the double coincidence of wants (Jevons, 1875), as commonly supposed, but that money completes closed cycles incorporating all markets and economic agents. The existence of such cycles is not evident and is strongly dependent upon the parameters of the respective economic system (Ganchev 2013; see also about similar ideas Nenovsky 2002). In other words, the function of the medium of exchange has complex systemic nature.

The medium of exchange implies also elements of short-term financing. Under money intermediated exchange the seller does not obtain immediately the goods or services he needs, but respective some of money. Therefore, the seller lends to his counterpart what he trades, money being instrument of financing. Thus money is a kind of reverse promissory note, i.e. it is a collective obligation not to pay, but to accept pecuniary payment from any bearer. For the seller the exchange is completed and the lending is reimbursed only after he buys the goods he wants, though this does not close the circuit.

On the contrary, the next seller is taking the relay (see for discussion Marx 1887). Consequently, the exchange process must be infinite (see Appendix 1 and Appendix 4) since otherwise the last seller will remain unsatisfied. There are just too possibilities for infinite process- existence of endless number of participants or formation of closed paths (cycles). Only the second variant is workable. The monetary circulation is never ending closed succession of short term lending and refunding. Thus any finite theory of money is inconsistent.

This line of thinking has another unexpected consequence. Theory of pure exchange excludes money since such exchange is finite unless economic agents dispose with unlimited endowments. The source of such endowments can only be continuous production and re-production. So money is fundamentally linked to production what is demonstrated with somewhat different arguments by money circuit theorists (see for example Graziani 2003; Rochon and Rossi, 2006). The connection between money and production and infinite circulation is present also in the works, related to evolutionary approach to money (Kyiotaki and Wright 1989). The circuitists suggest another solution, namely that money is created and destroyed in the process of bank lending and repayment of loans (Graziani 2003). This simply means that closed cycles necessarily exist in order to repay the loans, but that the completion of the cycle ends this cycle and requires new sequence of money creation and destruction.

The other two traditional functions of money (standard of deferred payments and store of value) are also surprisingly systemic and non-quantitative (Copeland 1952). Standard of deferred payments merely implies that all debts and other payments due in the future should be paid in nominal terms if the contracts do not include some kind of indexing. This indicates that future variations of the exchange value of money affect the real burden of debts. As a result, the nominal level of all existing financial obligations is not neutral. In line with current trends of the exchange value of money (inflation or deflation), income is redistributed between net lenders and borrowers. If the nominal amounts of money and other financial assets are indexed to inflation, then they can be considered unbiased. Yet in such a case the real quantity of money cannot adjust to the variations of the exchange value of money, so the system does not possess a feedback and is not self-regulating.

The function of store of value is a mirror image of the mission of standard of deferred payments. The money as a store of value is also non neutral vis-à-vis the variations of the exchange value of money. What's more, this role is necessary from the point of view of the medium of exchange function. Money transmits provisionally purchasing power from one market to another. However, exactly this particularity makes (gold like) money inefficient in general equilibrium models (see Dubey, Geanacoplos and Shubik 2003).

Money has both micro and macroeconomic foundations. The elimination of double coincidence of wants and the store of value are two functions that have predominantly micro economic nature. The roles of medium of exchange, unit of account and standard of deferred payments are defined at the level of the economy as whole. The nature of money can be understood if both micro and macro foundations are considered concomitantly. Such an approach is in contrast to the neoclassical view, based on reductionist principle, postulating, that macroeconomic features must be derived solely from microeconomic assumptions (Janssen 2008). The latter is clearly not possible in the case of money.

The Macroeconomic Nature of Money Market

In any economy, based on monetary circulation, the effective demand for money can come only from agents, selling goods and services. The buyers consequently supply money. If we take into account credit and capital markets, then the effective demand for money includes the borrowers and supply of money- the lenders. The inclusion of financial markets is equivalent to restructuring of present demand and inclusion of implicit forward markets. The so described flow approach to money market is obviously related to the changes of money stocks- if, for example, the demand for money exceeds supply, the price will increase (deflation) and economic agents will increase their money stocks. This understanding of the money market is similar to the definition of forex market. The latter is not accidental, since the exchange rate is nothing, but the external price of money.

In our formulation the money market is simply a linkage between aggregate supply (demand for money) and aggregate demand (supply of money), eventually augmented with financial markets. Such definition is not necessarily new. It was John Stuart Mill who admitted that in periods of oversupply of all commodities there should be an under-supply of money (Mill 1888). The price of money is linked to the inverse of the sum of the prices of all exchanged goods in terms of money. In such a system the equilibrium on all individual markets depends directly on the aggregate equilibrium. The money market is thus entangled with all the other markets, it's the link between micro and macro level.

This understanding of the supply and the demand for money has interesting connection to Walras Law. The problem is that the traditional neoclassical understanding of Walras Law excludes by definition the existence of macroeconomic disequilibrium (see for details Heise 2017), only mutually offsetting excess demand and supply on individual markets can exist. Since macroeconomic imbalances are important part of economic reality, the present formulation of money market allows combination of micro and macro-economic disequilibrium.

The present line of thinking corresponds also to the Keynesian idea that the theory of money should be "a theory of the output as whole" (Keynes 1936). Another consequence of our formulation is the deduction that inflation and deflation reflect the existence of macroeconomic disequilibrium, oversupply and over demand for money respectively.

The proposed definition of demand and supply of money disagrees with the traditional formulation, identifying the supply of money with the quantity of money in the economy and the demand with the desired sum of money (see for discussion Yeager (1986). The connection between our definition and the conventional one is that if there is disequilibrium in the traditional sense, then this imbalance can be eliminated only via adjustments of the effective demand. For example, in the absence of central bank monetary policy, the oversupply of money in the conventional sense can be eradicated only by spending it. This will result in inflation, increased production or both, depending on price elasticity of demand. The deflation episode after the global financial crisis of 2007-2008 can be viewed as an over demand for liquidity, driven by high risk expectations.

The conventional understanding of demand, supply and equilibrium on money market is built on stocks, while effective money demand implies flows. The variations of the exchange value of money trigger stock-flow adjustments, money has both stock and flow dimensions. The flow dimension of money (the effective demand for money) has as counterpart the income generation (or redistribution) process in the real economy. The flow feature is an intersection between the real and the monetary sectors.

Therefore, money is neither neutral (since monetary stock-flow adjustments take place via income generation process) nor homogenous (the price of money variations move against the general price level). Unfortunately, the flow component of money market adjustment is usually omitted from the neoclassical economic analysis. This is serious shortcoming, since no stock adjustment is possible without flow variation. Reducing money to stock is in the origin of the classical dichotomy misapprehension.

The neoclassical loanable funds theory is an exception to this rule. However, this flow approach to money is limited to saving-investment relationship (Mankiw 2010). It does not define the exchange value of money and introduces the interest rate as a price of money (loanable funds).

Another attempt to avoid the problem of equilibrium convergence in a monetary economy and to justify the presence of money under neoclassical setting is the transaction costs approach. The basic idea is that money emerges spontaneously as an instrument of reducing transaction costs (Niehans 1969). While we can agree that money reduce frictions, we must emphasize that transaction costs are complementary to the circulation of money and are not therefore independent explanation of disequilibrium properties of markets.

Resolving the problem can be done with the help of a simple heuristic economic model (see Ganchev 2015). This model is based on the connection between the demand for money and the price level and arrives at the conclusion, that money intermediated systems do not converge to equilibrium, but accomplish inflation-deflation cycles.

The same conclusion can be drawn on the basis of the gross substitutability. It is well known, that gross substitutability between all exchanged goods is necessary and sufficient condition for general equilibrium convergence (Arrow, Block, and Hurwicz 1959). In the case of money market, if the latter is included in a system concurrently with all the other markets, this would imply $\partial x_i / \partial p_m > 0$ for all goods, were x_i is the volume of demand for the good i and p_m is the price of money (the inverse of the price level).

This condition is clearly not satisfied in the case of the reaction of the demand for normal goods to the changes of the price of money (an increase of the price of money (deflation) implies decrease of demand for all the other items and vice versa- the decline of the price of money (inflation) means rise of demand on the rest of the markets, or to put it differently, $\partial x_i / \partial p_m < 0$. Money is not substitute to any product; it's rather a complement to all goods in exchange and production (everything is obtained via money). In the case of money we replace the gross substitutability with gross complementarity of money.

This has three important consequences.

First, money is not neutral; its price affects the demand for the rest of the goods.
Second, the decentralized money intermediated general equilibrium convergence is not feasible.
Third, there is interdependence between micro level (goods prices) and macro level (the price of money).

The conclusion about the gross complementarity (or negative substitutability) of money is not obvious. It is usually assumed that money has zero (or negligible) elasticity of substitution and that the variations of the price of money are neutral in the sense that "the demand for a store of value, in an uncertain world, does not generate the demand to commit resources" (see Davidson 1972). In contrast, we accept that the increase of the price of money (deflation) affects negatively investment and consumption, while inflation has the opposite effect.

The theory of money is strongly related to the theory of the second best. Since the decentralized general equilibrium is not feasible in monetary economies, the problem emerges of how economic policy should be modified in order to attain social optimum. The interesting point is that the rational solutions under the generalized second best conditions require complementarity between money (numéraire) and all the other goods (see for details Lipsey and Lancaster 1956-1957). Here the term numéraire means unit of account, the benchmark good in which the prices are fixed.

To conclude, the equilibrium convergence is not a genuine property of the decentralized money intermediated economic systems. The simple aggregation of individual optimizing behavior does not guarantee optimal outcome of the system as whole. Decentralized coordination can bring about only self-regulation and interdependence, but not optimization. The general equilibrium and the optimal allocation of resources are external concepts, in the sense that no individual economic agent, excluding centralized institutions, is looking for general equilibrium or for socially optimal allocation. For themselves, these attributes require intelligent design, purposeful formation of institutions, securing socially preferable economic outcomes.

The General Equilibrium: Bottom Up Versus Top Down

As Aristotle once admitted, its money, that makes human society possible (Aristotle, Nicomachean Ethics). Money integrates economic systems, based on decentralized exchange. On the other hand, centrally planned economies also need money and central banks. So the role of money is not limited to decentralized economic systems. Furthermore, money can be viewed as structural device creating feedback from macro to micro level.

As mentioned, the basic methodological assumption of the classical general equilibrium approach is that it is possible to derive the macroeconomic behavior of the system from the micro parameters- preferences, utility and profit maximization, endowments, supply conditions and so on. This is a result of the enactment of the so called methodological individualism principle, because only the individuals can be treated as agents in a course of subjectively understandable action (Weber 1922). However, the very way of describing the general equilibrium via system of simultaneous equations implying interdependence between markets and introducing money as medium of exchange, allows for alternative interpretation of the latter, namely as state determined by the parameters of the system as whole. These problems are discussed in details in Appendix 3.

We start with the assumption that the economy is producing below its production possibility frontier. Secondly, the economic agents are endowed with indirect utility functions, so that the utility they derive via exchange depends on the income and the relative prices. The question is how the monetary prices of individual goods are "discovered" in the process of exchange. The neoclassical analysis relies on mechanisms such as "tâtonnement" which are not well defined. We can suggest an alternative, monetary circulation based mechanism.

We argue in Appendix 3 that the utility of any economic agent depends on the price level and velocity. This is so because the income velocity contains information about individual agents' money endowments and income (since individual money endowments multiplied by velocity equal individual income, the latter is also known); the price level is derived simultaneously with the relative prices. In this way price level and velocity determine the relative prices and income, so we obtain an individual indirect utility function, determined by macroeconomic variables, contrary to neoclassical bottom up approach. This means that macroeconomic fluctuations generated by the instability of the monetary general equilibrium, affect the micro behavior.

Furthermore, we can critically asses not only the thesis of micro foundations of macro theory, but the related approach of the so called representative agents, being part of virtually all neoclassical models. The fundamental flaw of this anthropomorphic concept is that it imposes human-like features to collective, impersonal objects. Any representative consumer for example, as a kind of "collective individual", maybe assumed to have non-transitive preferences, as in the case of collective decision making, with unpredictable consequences for utility maximization. The problem of individual preferences aggregation is extremely complex (see Schofield 1996) and the legitimacy of representative agents paradigm casts serious doubts. If we add to the possible non-transitivity of collective preferences the impact of macro variables on micro behavior, we obtain a potentially unpredictable behavior of economic systems.

The only gap in our way of reasoning is the absence of financial system. We can however fill this gap in a minimalist way. The role of the financial system is to connect saving to investment. So it increases the present demand for investment goods and future demand for consumption and investment goods. By buying financial instruments we increase the future demand and divert the present demand from consumption to investment goods. Consequently adding financial markets is equivalent to restructuring present demand and adjoining forward markets. This transformation also decelerates income velocity of money (economic agents need longer cycles to generate comparatively less income) and affects money holdings. So our concept can successfully include financial intermediation via increasing the number of markets with implicit forward markets. Creating additional markets means adding new connections to the already existing network what in principle can increase the probability of closed monetary cycles.

It must be added also, that financial markets amplify instability. As Shiller (2000) admits, the so called "feedback loops" play important role in the propagation of bubbles. Essentially these loops are based on the observation that asset price increase lead to greater investor enthusiasm and subsequently to higher demand and further price escalation. In theoretical terms this means that financial markets, in the same way as money market, do not obey the gross substitutability principle.

Another problem is the formation of closed monetary cycles. The conscious construction of such cycles (in terms of graphs theory these are Hamiltonian cycles or cycles that include once all vertices of the respective graph), in a centrally planned economy for example, is not feasible. In particular, if a computer is able to calculate 10 000 cycles per second, it will take about 18 seconds to calculate the cycles between 10 vertices (economic agents), 50 days for 15 vertices, two years for 16, and 193,000 years for twenty vertices (Ganchev 2013).

However, if we change the approach and view the configuration of Hamiltonian cycles as random process of selecting new edges (bilateral monetary payment for goods, services and financial instruments) connecting vertices (economic agents), then the graphs of a size marginally less than a certain ceiling are unlikely to have a given property (Hamiltonian cycles), whereas graphs with slightly more edges are almost guaranteed to have it (this is referred to as phase transition, see Brunet 2005). In terms of complex money intermediated economic systems this attribute can be qualified as the paradox of uncertainty, since the existence of random elements (uncertain money intermediated exchanges) is the basis of almost sure systems of closed integrating cycles, while conscious efforts of constructing "sure" configurations, are hopeless. Key role of closing the monetary cycles in the complex economic systems play the financial intermediation, since it can redistribute and even reverse currency flows between economic agents.

The uncertainty of monetary cycles goes hand I hand with the already discussed complementarity of money. The complementarity and uncertainty exclude the first best economic policy solutions. In the same time however, the complementarity of money is a necessary precondition for optimal second best solutions.

Economic Growth and Development: The Role of Money

The role of money, banking and financial markets is crucial from the point of view of growth and development. Monetary factors can be divided in two main strands- cyclical stabilization and long term structural shifts.

Since decentralized monetary economies do not mechanically converge to equilibrium, but are prone to inflation-deflation cycles, the role of the central banks' monetary policy is of crucial importance. Given the non-neutrality of money, the monetary policy has necessarily two dimensions- inflation targeting and full employment. Therefore the most part of the leading central banks, such as Fed and BOE, have explicit double mandate (see for details Baker, Rawlins and Stein 2017). What is interesting, the implementation of the inflation targeting affects not only the general price level, but the relative prices too (see Cantelmo and Melina 2017).

Econometric research confirms also the existence of positive correlation between inflation and cyclical income, interpreted as Phillips curve over business cycles (Katagiri 2018). On global level, the origins of the financial crises are related not only to price-quantities adjustments, but to causes deeply rooted in the financial sector- the bursting of leveraged bubbles in developed market economies and vulnerabilities in emerging markets related to lengthy booms in credit and asset prices combined, with growing weaknesses in the corporate and external sectors (see for details Basu, Chamon and Crowe 2017).

Minsky (1992) attributes the instability of capitalist economies to the Keynesian capital development. The main feature of such development is the exchange of present for future money. Typically the capitalist economies are going through hedge, speculative and Ponzi game financing. The empirical research confirms the connection between the macroeconomic Minsky cycle of optimism and the micro behavior of individual banks (Espinoza, Segoviano, and Yan 2020).

The long run growth is inevitably related to capital accumulation. The accumulation of capital, in turn, is impossible without the store of value function of money. Money intermediate not only the exchange of goods and services, but the investment in long term financial assets, such as saving deposits, bonds and shares. On the one hand, financial markets aggregate micro economic parameters, related to time preferences and optimizing behavior of individual economic agents, but, on the other the systemic variables (interest rates, financial markets indices, income velocity of money, inflation) provide feedback towards micro level.

The classical growth models, based on accumulation of capital, reflect the role of money and financial markets only indirectly, via the connection between saving and investment. The same applies in principle to the more recent endogenous growth models, considering not only the physical capital stock, but technological progress, human capital and other factors (Romer 1989; Jones 2019).

The dynamic stochastic general equilibrium models are probably the most sophisticated instruments of dealing with the complexities of economic growth. They include households, production, banking, finance, monetary policy, external sector and other segments of the economy (see for example Vitek 2017). The main feature of these models are the external shocks, which are necessary in order to gauge the unevenness of the economic growth. In other words, the volatility of capitalist economies, brought about by the money, is exogenous factor from the point of view of this approach to economic analysis and forecasting. While useful for projecting economic dynamics, these models do little for improving our understanding of causal interconnections of economic systems development.

So growth and development are unstable processes, the instability being brought about by money. The solution requires the introduction of both anticyclical and structural policies.

FUTURE RESEARCH DIRECTIONS

Paradoxically enough the main direction for future research is supposed to be the field of international monetary economics. Up to now, one of the main focal points of the theoretical and the empirical research in the international monetary economics was the optimum currency areas theory, or, in other words, the question of interest was how to reduce the number of currencies circulating in the world economy. However, the interrogation about why we have many monetary units and not a single one is of much greater theoretical and practical interest, especially after the emergence of the crypto currencies. The answer to this question is obviously related to the extreme complexity of the world economy and the existence of nation-states with different economic policies. The formation of closed circulation paths directly on world level is thus virtually impossible. Nonetheless, there is a more fundamental reason. The price of money, or the inverse of price level, is difficult to measure indoor. The central banks are typically relying on different variants of consumer price indices. Still there is no explicit market based decentralized mechanism of identifying the exchange value of money, at least internally. The existence of many currencies, forex markets and exchange rates respectively, transforms the situation fundamentally. As far as we can expect that in the long run the exchange rates converge to the purchasing power parities, we obtain an objective measure of the relative price of money. Therefore, the presence of multitude of currencies is a necessary precondition for the fulfilment of the unit of account function of money. Accordingly, the money is not only the link between micro and macro level, but also the tie amongst internal and external equilibrium. The internal and the external exchange values of money are mutually interrelated and cannot exist separately. This raises many fundamental conceptual and functional questions, requiring further research.

CONCLUSION

The main conclusion of the present study is twofold. On the one hand, the decentralized money intermediated economic systems do not possess equilibrium convergence features and can be either self-regulating (performing inflation-deflation cycles) or central bank-fiscal policies controlled. Adding complex banking and financial systems increases the possibility of closing monetary cycles, on the one hand, but may worsen the situation via the negative feedback loops. So the financialization requires additional supervision and regulation. In the same time, the instability, generated by money, is the only way of constructing complex exchange structures, what can be called the paradox of uncertainty.

The necessary existence of closed monetary paths is another finding of the present investigation. This follows from the specific requirement of connectedness of markets, involved in the exchange. The individual goods become mutually comparable only if they belong to some closed monetary cycle. Cycles can exist only in productive economy, so the theory of money is necessarily related to production.

The functions of means of exchange and unit of account are fulfilled jointly. Money cannot be defined against itself, but against all the other goods. We introduce the so called Inverse Walras Low consisting of inference that if we fix the price of money then all prices are fixed. The money market is macroeconomic device by definition and can be viewed as balance between aggregate supply and aggregate demand. It follows also that relative prices and the price level can be defined only simultaneously. In practice, the value of money (inverse of price level) is defined after the individual price discovery had taken place. This fundamental dichotomy between the unit own exchange value and the results of evaluation of the rest of the goods is inbuilt for all types of decentralized money intermediated exchange.

Only via implementation of some kind of monetary targeting (in terms of inflation or price level, plus full employment), based on purposeful monetary and fiscal policies, one can reduce the uncertainty to some acceptable degrees. The substitution of neutrality for uncertainty implies that the process of price formation, including the stabilization of the exchange value of money, has an impact on the real economy. The income velocity of money is an example of macroeconomic variable that depends on every economic agent behavior, but cannot be reduced to micro level being related to the need for cyclical sequencing of exchanges. Inflation, on the contrary, is macroeconomic disequilibrium variable, affecting directly the micro level. We can go further and reject the principle of methodological individualism since we can derive the micro behavior (utility functions) from macro parameters as demonstrated in the fourth paragraph.

Another aspect of the fundamental uncertainty inherent to monetary economies is the Keynesian liquidity preference theory. For Keynes (1936) the primary problem the economic agents face is the dilemma whether or not to "convert deferred command over specific goods into immediate command over goods in general". This Keynesian problem is nothing, but a particular formulation of the maximum entropy principle. The latter reflects behavior "maximally noncommittal with regard to missing information" (Jaynes 1957) and represents a rational response to situations with unknown probabilities.

Accumulation of liquidity implies exactly no commitment to missing information and takes the form of "command over goods in general". Money allows individuals to take advantage of viable events with indefinite likelihood. Note that liquidity is related not to risk, as usual (see for example Tobin 1958), but to broader concept of uncertainty. All Keynesian motives of holding money (transactional, precautionary, speculative and finance) indicate such faltering states. Ultimately, money may be defined as the liquid financial asset allowing for flexible decentralized exchange intermediation under uncertainty. The paradox of uncertainty ultimately means that certain fuzziness of economic exchange relations is not an imperfection, but a necessary attribute of developing complex financial structures, since elaborate sure constructions are not feasible.

From political economy point of view, we can draw two key conclusions. First, complex command economies with detailed central planning are not likely to endure since intricate cycles are difficult to construct intentionally. Second, complex decentralized money intermediated economies are viable, but unstable, prone to boom and bust cycles. The development of more and more complex societies requires combination of decentralized uncertainty braking initiatives and purposeful centralized macroeconomic regulation, fostering predictability and efficiency.

In terms of the main purpose of the present chapter, all the discussed attributes of money- cycles, complementarity, uncertainty finally leads to the conclusion, that money introduce additional constraint to the economic exchange- the constraint of exchangeability of the goods and services subject to production and trade. This means that the exchanges should be sequenced in cycles, with the velocity of money being the macroeconomic parameter allowing for closing such cycles. The velocity, together with the price level is sufficient statistics for utility maximization. It must be emphasized however that income velocity of money in the present chapter is complex variable, associated with the eigenvector of the economic agent's money endowments. The price level in turn is determined together with the relative prices.

Finally, we obtain a concept of decentralized economic system, subject to uncertainty and instability. In such a system the macroeconomic parameters affect the micro behavior and add uncertainty, on the one hand, but on the other, macro-economic regulation is both desirable and feasible.

REFERENCES

Area, N. T. (2015). The Validity of Walras' Law in a Monetary Exchange Economy: Money, Prices and the Integration of Monetary and Value Theory. *Iberian Journal of the History of Economic Thought, 2*(2), 101–114.

Aristotle. (350 BC). *Nicomachean Ethics* (W. D. Ross, Trans.). https://www.constitution.org/ari/ethic_00.htm

Arrow, K. J., Block, H. D., & Hurwicz, L. (1959). On the Stability of the Competitive Equilibrium. Econometrica, 27.

Arrow, K. J., & Hahn, F. H. (1972). *General Competitive Analysis*. Holden-Day.

Baker, D., Rawlins, S., & Stein, D. (2017). *The Full Employment Mandate of the Federal Reserve: Its Origins and Importance*. CEPR, Fed Up and CPD. https://cepr.net/images/stories/reports/full-employment-mandate-2017-07.pdf

Basu, S. S., Chamon, M., & Crowe, C. (2017). *IMF, A Model to Assess the Probabilities of Growth, Fiscal, and Financial Crises*. WP/17/282.

Bergh, J. C. J. M., & Gowdy, J. M. (2003). The Microfoundations of Macroeconomics: An Evolutionary Perspective. *Cambridge Journal of Economics, 2003*(27), 65–84. doi:10.1093/cje/27.1.65

Bordo, M. D., Dittmar, R., & Gavin, T. W. (2007). *Gold, Fiat Money and Price Stability*. Federal Reserve Bank of St. Louis, Working Paper Series, Working Paper 2003-014D.

Boylan & O'Gorman. (2018). Philosophy of Mathematics and Economics Image, Context and Perspective. Routledge.

Brunet, G. (2005). A Brief Introduction to Hamilton Cycles in Random Graphs. Department of Computer Science University of Toronto.

Cagan, P. (1984). The Report of the Gold Commission (1982). *Carnegie Conference Series on Public Policy, 20*, 247–268. doi:10.1016/0167-2231(84)90050-2

Cantelmo, A., & Melina, G. (2017). *Monetary Policy and the Relative Price of Durable Goods*. IMF, WP/17/290.

Cassel, G. (1918). Abnormal Deviations in International Exchanges. *Economic Journal (London), 28*(112), 413–415. doi:10.2307/2223329

Clower, R. W. (1967). A Reconsideration of the Micro foundations of the Monetary Theory, Western. *Economic Journal (London)*, *6*(4), 1–8.

Clower, R. W., & Howitt, P. W. (1978, June). The Transaction Theory of the Demand for Money: A Reconsideration. *Journal of Political Economy*, *86*(3), 449–466. doi:10.1086/260681

Colander, D. (2000). The Death of Neoclassical Economics. *Journal of the History of Economic Thought*, *22*(2), 127–143. doi:10.1080/10427710050025330

Copeland, M. A. (1952). The Quantitative Functions of Money. In *A Study of Money flows in The United States*. NBER. https://www.nber.org/books/cope52-1

Davidson, P. (1972, March). Money and the Real World. *Economic Journal (London)*, *82*(325), 101–115. doi:10.2307/2230209

Dixon, R. (2017). *Walras' Law*. https://www.online.fbe.unimelb.edu.au/WalrasLaw.pdf

Dubey, P., Geanacoplos, J., & Shubik, M. (2003). Is Gold an Efficient Store of Value? *Economic Theory*, *21*(4), 767–782. doi:10.100700199-002-0266-y

Espinoza, R. A., Segoviano, M. A., & Yan, J. (2020). *Systemic Risk Modeling: How Theory Can Meet Statistics*. IMF, WP/20/54.

Fisher, I. (1963). *The Purchasing Power of Money* (rev. ed.). Kelley.

Friedman, D. (1979). Money-Mediated Disequilibrium in a Pure Exchange Economy. *Journal of Mathematical Economics*, *6*(2), 149–167. doi:10.1016/0304-4068(79)90004-1

Ganchev, G.T. (2013). *The Theory of Monetary Circuit*. Economic Thought No. 1/2013.

Ganchev, G. T. (2015). Towards Holistic Theory of Money: Overcoming Twentieth Century Neoclassical Monetary Paradigm. Economic Studies, 4, 3-24.

Grandmont, J. M. (1985). *Money and Value: A Reconsideration of Classical and Neoclassical Monetary Theories*. Cambridge University Press.

Graziani, A. (2003). *The Monetary Theory of Production*. Cambridge University Press. doi:10.1017/CBO9780511493546

Gurley, J. G., & Shaw, E. S. (1960). *Banking in a Theory of Finance*. The Brookings Institution.

Haberler, G. (1946). *Prosperity and Depression: A Theoretical Analysis of Cyclical Movements* (3rd ed.). United Nations.

Hayek, F. (1931). *Prices and Production*. Routledge.

Heise, A. (2017). Walras' Law in the Context of Pre-Analytic Visions. *Economic Thought*, *6*(1), 83–96.

Janssen, M. (2008). Microfoundations. In The New Palgrave Dictionary of Economics (2nd ed.). Academic Press.

Jaynes, E. T. (1957). Information Theory and Statistical Mechanics. *Physical Review*, *106*(4), 620–630. doi:10.1103/PhysRev.106.620

JEC. (2004). *Price Stability and Inflation Targets, a Joint Economic Committee Study*. United States Congress.

Jevons, W. S. (1875). *Money and the Mechanism of Exchange*. London: Macmillan.

Jones, C. I. (2019). Paul Romer: Ideas, Nonrivalry, and Endogenous Growth. *The Scandinavian Journal of Economics*, *121*(3), 859–883. doi:10.1111joe.12370

Kaldor, N. (1964). The problem of international liquidity. In Further Essays on Applied Economics. London: Duckworth.

Katagiri, M. (2018). *Equilibrium Yield Curve, the Phillips Curve, and Monetary Policy*. IMF, WP/18/242.

Keynes, J. M. (1936). *The General Theory of Employment, Interest and Money*. Macmillan.

Kyiotaki, N., & Wright, R. (1989). On Money as Medium of Exchange. *Journal of Political Economy*, *97*(4), 927–954. doi:10.1086/261634

Lange, O. (1942). Say's Law: a Restatement and criticism. In Studies in Mathematical Economics and Econometrics. Academic Press.

Lipsey, R. G., & Lancaster, K. (1956-1957). The General Theory of Second Best. *The Review of Economic Studies*, *24*(1), 11–32. doi:10.2307/2296233

Lucas, R. E. Jr. (1973, June). Some International Evidence on Output-Inflation Tradeoffs. *The American Economic Review*, *63*, 326–344.

Lucas, R. E. Jr. (1995). *Monetary Neutrality*. Prize Lecture, December 7, 1995, Economic Sciences.

Mankiw, G. N. (2010). Macroeconomics. New York: Worth Publishers.

Marshall, A. (1886). Answers to Questions on the Subject of Currency and Prices, circulated by the Royal Commission on the Depression of Trade and Industry, Third Report. In J. M. Keynes (Ed.), *Official Papers by Alfred Marshall*. Macmillan.

Marx, K. (1887). Capital. Progress Publishers.

McKenzie, L. W. (1959, January). On the Existence of General Equilibrium for a Competitive Market. *Econometrica*, *27*(1), 1–41. doi:10.2307/1907777

Mill, J. S. (1888). Principles of Political Economy with Some of their Applications to Social Philosophy (6th ed.). London: Longmans, Green, Reader & Dyer.

Minsky, H. P. (1992). *The Financial Instability Hypothesis*. The Jerome Economics Institute of Bard College, Working Paper No. 74.

Modigliani, F. (1944). Liquidity Preference and the Theory of Interest and Money. *Econometrica*, *12*(1), 45–88. doi:10.2307/1905567

Nenovsky, N. (2002). *Improving Monetary Theory in Post-communist Countries- Looking Back to Cantillon*. BNB, Discussion Papers.

Niehans, J. (1969). Money in a Static Theory of Optimal Payments Arrangements. *Journal of Money, Credit and Banking*, *1*, 706–726. doi:10.2307/1991447

Patinkin, D. (1947). *On the Consistency of Economic Models: A Theory of Involuntary Unemployment* (Doctoral dissertation). University of Chicago.

Patinkin, D. (1949). Involuntary Unemployment and the Keynesian Supply Function. *Economic Journal (London)*, *59*(235), 361–383. doi:10.2307/2226869

Patinkin, D. (1965). *Money, Interest and Prices* (2nd ed.). Harper and Row.

Pigou, A. C. (1917). The Value of Money. *The Quarterly Journal of Economics*, *32*(1), 38–65. doi:10.2307/1885078

Pigou, A. C. (1923). The Foreign Exchanges. *The Quarterly Journal of Economics*, *37*(1), 52–74. doi:10.2307/1885909

Pigou, A. C. (1943, December). The Classical Stationary State. *Economic Journal (London)*, *53*(212), 343–351. doi:10.2307/2226394

Piketty, T. (2013). *Le capital au XXIème siècle*. Edition du Seuil, Paris XIV.

Polanyi, K. (1944). *The Great Transformation*. Rinehart & Company, Inc.

Rochon, L. P., & Rossi, S. (2006). *Endogenous money: the evolutionary versus revolutionary views*. Centro di studi bancari Villa Negroni-RME LAB Research Laboratory of Monetary Economics.

Romer, M. P. (1989). *Endogenous Technological Change*. NBER Working Paper #3210.

Romer, M. P. (2016). *The Trouble with Macroeconomics*. Delivered January 5, 2016 as the Commons Memorial Lecture of the Omicron Delta Epsilon Society. https://www.law.yale.edu/system/files/area/.../leo16_romer.pdf

Samuelson, P. A. (1939). Interaction between the Multiplier Analysis and the Principle of Acceleration. *The Review of Economics and Statistics*, *21*(2), 75–78. doi:10.2307/1927758

Schofield N. (1996). Introduction: Research Programs in Preferences and Beliefs Aggregation. In *Collective Decision-Making: Social Choice and Political Economy*. Springer Science+Business LLC.

Schumpeter, J. A. (1954). *History of Economic Analysis*. Routledge.

Scitovsky, T. (1941, February). Capital Accumulation, Employment and Price Rigidity. *The Review of Economic Studies*, *8*(2), 69–88. doi:10.2307/2967464

Sen, A. (1977, October). On Weights and Measures: Informational Constraints in Social Welfare Analysis. *Econometrics*, *45*(7), 1539–1572. doi:10.2307/1913949

Shiller, R. J. (2000). *Irrational Exuberance*. Princeton University Press.

Takayama, A. (1990). *Mathematical Economics* (2nd ed.). Cambridge University Press.

Tobin, J. (1958, February). Liquidity Preference as Behavior towards. *Risk (Concord, NH)*, *25*(2), 65–86.

Ussher, L. J. (2009, July). Global Imbalances and the Key Currency Regime: The Case for a Commodity Reserve Currency. *Review of Political Economy*, *21*(3), 403–421. doi:10.1080/09538250903073461

Vitek, F. (2017). *Policy, Risk and Spillover Analysis in the World Economy: A Panel Dynamic Stochastic General Equilibrium Approach*. IMF, WP/17/89.

Walras, L. (1874). *Elements of Pure Economics* (1926 ed.). Allen & Unwin.

Walras, L. (1886). Theorie de la monnaie. Academic Press.

Weber, M. (1922). Economy and Society. University of California Press.

White, L. H. (2008). *Is the Gold Standard Still the Gold Standard Among Monetary Systems?* Cato Institute Briefing Papers, No 100.

Wicksell, K. (1898). Interest and prices (R. F. Khan, Trans.). London: Macmillan.

Wicksell, K. (1931). *Lectures on Political Economy*. Routledge. (Original work published 1901)

Yeager, L. (1986, Fall). The Significance of Monetary Disequilibrium. *The Cato Journal*, *6*(2), 369–420.

KEY TERMS AND DEFINITIONS

Equilibrium Convergence: In economic theory general equilibrium concept attempts to explain the behavior of supply, demand, and prices in a whole economy with many interacting markets, by seeking to prove that the interaction of demand and supply will result in an overall convergence to general equilibrium.

Imprimitive (Cyclic) Matrices: In the context of the present chapter, the matrix A is imprimitive or cyclic if any industry (market) which belongs to the J_i- group of industries or markets does not use the outputs or does not purchase products of J_{i-1} group of industries or markets and does not use the outputs (sails) of any other group of industries as inputs (purchases). The respective matrix may have several such decompositions.

Income Velocity of Money: In monetary theory by income velocity of money, we understand the number of times one unit of currency is spent over a given period of time. It is indicative of how much economic activity occurs at a certain level of money supply.

Macroeconomic Regulation: The macroeconomic regulation is understood as set of government and central bank policies aiming at price stability, full employment, stable growth, external equilibrium, high living standards, reduction in poverty, high productivity and so on.

Money: Money is viewed a medium of exchange that market participants use to engage in transactions for goods and services. The other functions the money is supposed to fulfil are the unit of account, the standard of differed payments and the store of value.

Value of Money: The internal value of money is understood in this chapter as the inverse of the price level or its purchasing power. The external value of any currency is its exchange rate, converging in the long run to the purchasing power parity between any pair of monetary units. The internal and external values of money are mutually interconnected.

Walras Law: Walras's law affirms that the sum of the values of excess demands (supplies) across all markets must equal zero, whether or not the economy is in a general equilibrium, consequently if all but one markets are in equilibrium, the additional (money) market is also balanced.

APPENDIX 1

We define a pure exchange Walrasian system. It is based on the so called Walrasian identity, that is on the assumption, that the monetary value of all planned market purchases are identically equal to the monetary value of all planned market sales (see Dixon 2017). Walras' identity also implies that if there is an excess demand for any particular good, there must be a corresponding excess supply for at least one other good. This is based on the conjecture that the economic agents possess some endowments of goods that they plan to sell and to buy equal amounts of goods in monetary terms.

Consider a barter exchange economy with n agents and m goods. For every agent K_i is his (her) initial endowment vector and x_i is his demand function, depending on the prevailing price vector p and demand ($x_i = x_i(p, p \cdot K_i)$), determined by the sale of endowments $(p \cdot K_i)$..

So, by definition the excess demand function *z(p)* in monetary terms is:

$$p \cdot z(p) = \sum_{i=1}^{n} \left(p \cdot x_i \left(p, p \cdot K_i \right) - p \cdot K_i \right)$$

If money fulfils only the function of a numeraire, we can assume that $p \cdot x = p \cdot K_i$ and the Walras Law holds ($p \cdot z(p) = 0$). If however we introduce an additional constraint, the so called Clower Rule- "money buys goods and goods buy money; but goods do not buy goods" (Clower, 1967), then the excess demand function takes the following form:

$$p \cdot z(p) = \sum_{i=1}^{n} \left(p \cdot x_i \left(p, p \cdot K_i \right) + m_i - p \cdot K_i \right)$$

Where m_i is the monetary endowment of the respective economic agent. Under the Clower Rule the effective demand depends only on economic agents' money residues and the total demand includes also the revenues from selling the goods. Now even if $\sum_{i=1}^{n} p \cdot x = \sum_{i=1}^{n} p \cdot K_i$ the excess demand is $p \cdot z(p) = \sum_{i=1}^{n} m_i = M$. This is so, because if some agent, say i, spends its money endowment, the respective sum does not disappear, but becomes part of the money holding of another agent, say j, thus in our model M (the total amount of money) is constant. Since, in addition, the purchases of every agent equal sells, the individual money holdings remain invariable. Therefore, if money fulfils more complicated functions, such as means of exchange (in order to avoid the requirement of the double coincidence of wants), the Walras Law does not hold. From this several important consequences follow- first, general equilibrium is unfeasible; second, macroeconomic disequilibrium is possible; third, the Walras symmetry does not hold and fourth, the monetary circulation must be infinite.

APPENDIX 2

We start the exposition by introducing the square n-matrix of relative prices A. The elements a_{ij} of this matrix are defined in a similar manner as in the case of input-output analysis, i.e. they represent the quantity of good i exchanged for unit of good j, or elements a_{ij} stand for the price of j in terms of i. All elements are non-negative, or $a_{ij} \geq 0$.
Proposition: The necessary condition for the existence of price level in terms of all exchanged goods is the matrix A to be indecomposable and the sufficient requirement is the above matrix to be in addition imprimitive.

Proof of necessity:

We start with the definition of indecomposable matrix using the notation of Takayma (1990). Matrix A is called decomposable if there exists partition $\{J,K\}$ of $N= \{1,2,3,\ldots,n\}$, such that $N = J \cup K$ and $J \cap K = \varnothing$ with $J \neq \varnothing$ and $K \neq \varnothing$ and $a_{ij}=0$ for $i \in K$ and $j \in J$. The equality $a_{ij}=0$ means that there is no exchange between goods i and j. This decomposition is interpreted in the sense that the market is partitioned into two groups, the J group and K group. Goods that belong to J group are not exchanged for goods belonging to K group. From the definition of decomposability if follows that if the matrix A is indecomposable, then the above partition does not exist so $J \cap K \neq \varnothing$ and there are no groups of goods that are not connected via exchange. This condition is obviously necessary in order to be able to express all prices in terms of one good, representing the price level.
The proof of sufficiency is more complicated and is related to imprimitive or cyclic square matrices. An $n \times n$ indecomposable matrix A is called imprimitive if:

There exists a partition $\{J_1, J_2, \ldots, J_m\}$ of $N \equiv \{1,2,\ldots,n\}$ such that

$$N = J_1 \cup J_2 \cup \ldots \cup J_m, J_i \cap J_j = \varnothing (i \neq j), J_i = \varnothing, i = 1,2,\ldots,m, and$$

$$a_{ij} = 0 (i \notin J_{i-1}, j \in J_i), and \sum\nolimits_{i \in J_{i-1}} a_{ij} > 0 (j \in J_i), i = 1,2,\ldots m.$$

In other words, the fact that A is imprimitive means that any market which belongs to the J_i-group of goods does exchange its goods against the J_{i-1}-group of markets but does not exchange its goods against any other group of markets. We assume further, that the elements J_i include only one good, so $m=n$. This implies that we can order markets in succession such that the good numbered $n-1$ is exchanged for the good n and the nth good is exchanged back against the first good thus closing the cycle. The so defined arrangement does not assume explicitly the existence of monetary circulation, but is a necessary precondition for it. The matrix may have several such decompositions. We can write $a_{n,1} = a_{1,2}a_{2,3}a_{3,4}\ldots a_{n-1,n}$. The latter equation reflects the arbitrage conditions requiring that the sequence of exchanges returning to the initial bilateral price does not yield any profit. This simply means that we have a price level in terms of n in the sense that all prices are cyclically interdependent and any bilateral price hinges on all the other prices. Note that we can eventually write $a_{n,1} = 1 / a_{1,n}$, what means that the price level in terms of n is the inverse of the price of n in terms of all the other goods, if we assume the existence of an opposite cycle. The same applies to all the other goods since we can start the cycle with an arbitrary a_{ij}, i.e. we can have price level in terms of any good. This completes the sufficiency.

Q.E.D.

All this simply means that if we have adequate system of relative prices, the respective price level is also defined and vice versa. It follows also, that if the price of money is fixed (as virtually all neoclassical models assume), then all prices are also fixed. Thus, we cannot separate the price level definition and the relative prices formation. As a result, money is not neutral and prices, including the price of money, are not homogenous, since the price of the good, which is chosen as numéraire is inversely related to all the other prices.

This indicates also that isolating money as separate good, outside the system of simultaneous equations, is wrong.

Including money however also creates problems, especially if our objective is to prove the existence and the stability of the general equilibrium. The main difficulty is the requirement that price matrix A must be imprimitive. This contradicts the traditional approach to equilibrium. From the matrix theory we know, that a non-negative indecomposable matrix is primitive if it has at least one diagonal element which is positive (Takayama 1990). In the case of price matrix A this condition may be fulfilled if one the goods' prices is defined vis-à-vis itself. By subtracting the money market from the system of markets and by fixing illegitimately its price to unity, the neoclassical economists are doing exactly this.

It is true, that in the case of commodity money we can arbitrary fix the quantity of the respective good that is used as numéraire. For example, the official gold content of the US dollar maybe fixed as $\frac{1}{38}$ troy ounces per dollar or equivalently 38 dollars per troy ounce. However, this does not mean that the relative price of the troy ounce in terms of the other goods and the price (the inverse of the purchasing power) of the dollar are fixed, because the exchange proportions between gold (dollar) and the other commodities vary according to supply and demand conditions.

Fixing the value of money is the actual reason behind the famous compensated dollar proposal of I. Fisher, i.e. we can have stable price of money only if we vary the weight of the unit. Any change of the purchasing power of the dollar modifies its real gold content and vice versa, so that we cannot distinguish between unit and price change if we observe only the purchasing power of money.

It is interesting that A. Sen (1977) comes to similar conclusion in the case of cardinal full comparability of personal welfares in the sense that it is impossible to distinguish between welfare and unit of measurement changes. The self-referential way of fixing the price of money is at the origin of the inconsistency of the neoclassical theory of money. Money can be defined only in respect to all the other goods. Finally, if we fix the price level to unity, the matrix A can be artificially defined as primitive, but we cannot express the relative prices and the price level in a consistent way.

To support Fishers recommendations we should admit, that the predisposition for persisting alternating declines and increases in prices is a basic characteristic of gold standard (Cagan 1984). At an earlier time the instability of the exchange value of gold was discussed by Marshall (1886) and Jevons (1875), who supported the so called "tabular standard", a predecessor of the modern monetary targeting. Theoretical simulations, based on DSGE model, including gold sector (see Bordo, Dittmar and Gavin 2007), generally confirm these observations. Both inflation and price level targeting provide more short-run price stability than does the gold standard.

APPENDIX 3

Monetary economy or economy were the exchange is intermediated by money can be only economy with production since pure exchange means that after the exchange agents with remaining money stocks are unable to use them in any meaningful way. Only closed cycles of money circulation transforms the latter into useful device. Circulation in turn is impossible but under repeated productive cycles. Circulation and velocity of circulation in particular is key variable reflecting the reproductive parameters of the economy. So the income velocity of money is the way the production is introduced in this chapter. We start with the assumption that the economy is producing below its production possibility frontier. Second, the economic agents are endowed with indirect utility functions, so the utility they derive via exchange depends on income and the relative prices. The question is how the monetary prices of individual goods are "discovered" in the process of exchange. The neoclassical analysis relies on mechanisms such as "tâtonnement" which are not well defined. We can suggest an alternative, monetary circulation based mechanism.

Suppose we have n economic agents and m goods (including money), produced and exchanged between agents with the intermediation of money. For a given time period every agent performs v_{ij} number of payments (i.e. the volume of payments divided by money endowments of agent i) vis-à-vis the other participants in the exchange. The square matrix $V=[v_{ij}]$ describes the exchange between agents. The matrix V is nonnegative and indecomposable by definition. Every economic agent possess some quantity of money m_i so we have $m_1 + m_2 + \ldots m_i + \ldots m_n = M$. In principle the quantity of money per agent varies with the time since the participants spend money and receive payments.

Further we can write $V \cdot m = \lambda m$, were λ is the eigenvalue of the matrix V and m is the eigenvector of average monetary endowments. Obviously we have also

$$\lambda m = \lambda m_1 + \lambda m_2 + \ldots \lambda m_n = \lambda \left(m_1 + m_2 + \ldots m_n \right) = \lambda M .$$

We interpret λ as the (macroeconomic) velocity of money. The meaning of the fact the income velocity of money is an eigenvalue (Frobenius root) of the matrix of the bilateral velocities is that in such a case every economic agent can generate income $y_i = m_i \lambda$. In other words, velocity as eigenvalue presupposes a coordination of bilateral exchanges that allows for the participation of all agents in proportion to their average money holdings. Without such condition money intermediated exchange including all agents and reproducing their money endowments via closed circulation cycles, would not be possible.

Since the money is spent in exchange for goods, the velocity of money, taking into account the price level, determines the physical quantity of goods produced and exchanged between agents and the monetary value of that exchange. So given the velocity and the price level, we have also relative prices. Finally we introduce indirect utility function of the following type $f_i \left(P, m, \lambda \right) = v_i \left(p, y_i \right) = u_i \left(x \left(p, y_i \right) \right)$, where P is the price level, m is vector of average quantities of money per economic agent, λ stands for the macroeconomic velocity of money, p is the vector of relative prices and y_i is the income of agent i. Further we can write $f_i(P,m,\lambda)=F_i(P,\lambda)$ since m is an eigenvector associated with λ.

The eigenvector m is unique up to a scalar multiple, that's why we need the price level P to determine the real quantity of money endowments. Note also that according to Appendix 2, if the economic agents observe the relative prices they observe also the price level and vice versa. Thus the utility of any economic agent depends on the price level and velocity. Finally, we obtain an individual utility function depending on macroeconomic variables, contrary to neoclassical bottom up approach.

The derivation of the income velocity of money as a characteristic root of the matrix of bilateral velocities means, that the velocity of money is an extremely important macroeconomic device, directly dependent on the micro level, but irreducible to it. The latter follows from the fact, that the velocity reflects the macroeconomic requirement for cyclical sequencing of individual exchanges. It means also, that any particular velocity is associated with the respective money endowments (the eigenvector m).

In principle, the velocity should be considered unobservable and especially volatile variable. The empirical velocities are approximations.

APPENDIX 4

We start our exposition with the equation of exchange $Mv=Py$ where M, v, P and y are as usual the quantity of money, the velocity, the price level and the real income. While the right hand side of the equation of exchange is more or less obvious, the left hand side is not trivial. The problem is the velocity of money, which has different interpretations. Our approach is based on the introduction of the matrix of bilateral velocities V as in Appendix 3.

The matrix $V=[V_{ij}]$ is obviously non-negative and indecomposable, since it is assumed by definition that there are no groups of agents that are not connected via exchange to the other participants.

Another interpretation of indecomposable (irreducible) matrices is in terms of directed graphs. We associate with every matrix V a graph G_v with n vertices. The elements v_{ij} correspond to the edges of the graph. The matrix V is irreducible if and only if the graph G_v is strongly connected. Further, a directed graph is defined as strongly connected if there exists a path in each direction between each pair of vertices of the graph. This means that cycles, including all vertices (economic agents), exist, what corresponds to the circulation of money in a productive economy.

Chapter 8
Personal Income Taxation and Its Effects on Economic Development and Growth

Bistra Svetlozarova Nikolova
University of Economics, Varna, Bulgaria

ABSTRACT

This chapter reviews traditional and contemporary concepts of income taxation and their effects on economic development and growth. The author focuses on discussion issues related to the contemporary concepts of income taxation. The author also considers modern functions of personal income taxes relating to environmental protection and income inequality mitigation. Additionally, the author studies the potential of personal income taxation to apply as an instrument for maintaining sustainable economic development and social stability. This chapter analyzes the effects of progressive and proportional personal income taxation on economic development and growth. It presents a technological model of inspections and audits with the aim of improving the tax and social security control of individuals.

INTRODUCTION

Personal income taxation occupies a central position in the tax system. Additionally, it is one of the most discussed topics during the tax policy implementation since it has a significant impact on economic development and growth. Regardless of the usage of different methods of assessment and different sources of information, results of scientific research (Staykov, 2016) show that tax level has serious effects on economic growth. This is true even after researchers have eliminated the impact of factors such as government expenditure, business cycle development, and monetary policies.

Tax subjects, syndicates, any representation organizations of employers, government, and political parties, demonstrate heightened interest and sensitivity to income taxation of individuals and social security contributions. All of them have certain interests in the said aspects, which are often contradictory. For that reason, it is usually hard to reach a consensus on income taxation of individuals and social security contributions, and any decisions taken are regularly reconsidered and subject to changes in order to en-

DOI: 10.4018/978-1-7998-4933-9.ch008

courage economic development and growth. Moreover, in the contemporary socio-economic conditions, issues such as income inequality, the harmful effect on the environment, and disturbance of ecological equilibrium come to the forefront of conversations. Thus, efforts of scientists and the government aim at ensuring conditions of sustainable economic development and growth through the implementation of the macroeconomic and tax policy. Stiglitz (2012) points out that the nature of growth is what is significant, and thus, the aspiration should focus on such growth that does not aggravate people's welfare and jeopardize environment.

The issue of finding a balance between economic effectiveness and social justice regarding taxation is related to the aim of ensuring both growth and sustainable economic development at the same time. Hristov (2014) points out that the supporters of the concept of the "minimal state" defend the thesis of limited state participation in the economy, low taxes and reduced government spending, which, according to them, stimulates economic growth and welfare of society. In this way, the funds will remain available to the private sector, which is considered to be able to spend them efficiently. This will reduce budget expenditures and the role of the state in the economy. Instead, Stiglitz (2012) proposes an alternative approach to stimulating the economy: simultaneously increasing taxes and spending so that the current account deficit remains unchanged. According to him, such a strategy will be based on a proven principle called the balanced budget multiplier. He acknowledges that taxes "suffocate" the economy, but costs stimulate it, and points out that the stimulus effect is significantly greater than the contraction effect of the economy. Stiglitz argues for the need to achieve greater economic efficiency and more equality at the same time. In this regard, he recommends the introduction of progressive income taxes. The author gives Scandinavian countries as a positive example of a nation's prosperity in the utmost degree in modern conditions, where the state's role in economy is enhanced through active redistribution of income and significant investments in public goods. The alternative for economic development, which Stiglitz argues, requires a better balance between the state and the markets. He believes that in these alternative frameworks, one of the roles played by the state is to redistribute income, especially if the results of market processes are highly contradictory. Soldatos (2016, p. 261) states: „There appears to be in operation a New Keynesian version of the national and international economy. Should tax policy be conducted as prescribed by this school of thought? The answer to this question lies beyond the scope of this paper, but one thing the spirit of the whole discussion makes sure is that taxation should be (i) inspired by the overall macroeconomic policy, (ii) accompanied by anti-monopoly policy. It is the spirit of the quest for efficiency as the driving force behind income and wealth redistribution, which is welfare-enhancing by itself and by sustaining economic growth."

This chapter looks at current issues related to personal income taxation step by step. First, the author studies the role and functions of personal income taxation in the context of modern requirements for sustainable economic development and growth. Second, the author deduces any advantages and shortcomings of the application of progressive and proportional income taxation. Thirdly, the author examines the potential of increasing the effectiveness and efficiency of tax control over personal income taxation through improving implementation process.

BACKGROUND

Two main economic paradigms - Keynesian and Neoclassical economics, have strongly influenced the formation of modern views and policies related to economic growth. Each of them has many followers.

Both theoretical directions seek a solution to the problems in the development of the market economy. The main difference between them is the understanding of the need for state intervention in the economy. The current challenges arising from globalization give a new impetus to economic thought in the search for concepts to ensure sustainable economic development and growth.

Keynesianism developed widely in the 1930s, in connection with the need to justify decisions to overcome the sharp decline in production, high unemployment and inflation as a result of the Great Depression. John Keynes disputes neoclassical assumption that free markets will automatically provide full employment. He believes that the state must intervene in the economy to ensure increased aggregate demand and investment growth. In Keynes's theory, the study of the multiplier takes up an important place. According to him, there is a stable relationship between investment growth and national income. Thus, each investment cost generates subsequent income.

Aggregate demand, such as the amount of consumer demand, investment demand and government spending, is seen by Keynes as a major factor in economic development. He argues the need for government intervention to increase aggregate demand (aggregate costs) in order to achieve full employment in the economy. In this regard, according to Sedlarski (2013), two approaches to Keynesian economic policy are possible.

1. **Increase in government expenditures in the form of government investments and transfer payments**: pensions, grants, scholarships, etc., which are directed by the government to generate income for certain groups of the population, as well as subsidies to enterprises. Increased government spending can be financed in two ways:
    a. By raising taxes. This will have a positive effect on the economy, as households save part of the income they have at their disposal, and the state is expected to spend the collected tax funds appropriately, which will cause a multiplier increase in national income.
    b. Through credit (deficit) financing. The multiplier effect of government spending on income will lead to an increase in tax revenues in the future, as a percentage of increased income. This will allow for accelerated debt repayment.
2. **Regulation of propensity to consume**: Such an effect is possible through the tax system by reducing the tax burden, which will lead to an increase in funds in the private sector, and hence to an increase in effective demand.

As can be seen from the concepts presented so far, Keynes relies on the budgetary (fiscal) regulation of investment activity to increase employment and income. His views had a significant impact on economics and practice for three to four decades until the 1970s, when leading economies faced new economic crises that diminished confidence in Keynesian theory. Criticism of state regulatory intervention in the economy by neoclassical economists who do not believe in the ability of governments to regulate the economic cycle with fiscal policy is growing. Neoclassical theory seeks the basic explanation of economic phenomena at the level of individual behavior, accepting it as rational. At the heart of this theory is the model of perfect competition.

The modern neoclassical thought is associated with Milton Friedman's views and the economic doctrine of monetarism, the "economy of supply" and "rational expectations." Monetarists support the thesis of market efficiency and minimal government intervention in the economy, with the exception of money supply. They insist on a tight monetary policy in order to limit inflation, which they see as a major problem of the self-regulating market mechanism. They see money and monetary policy as the most effective means of regulating the market economy. They believe that the increase in money supply from the Central Bank causes a fall in interest rates. This forces the private sector to look for an opportunity to dispose of excess cash reserves as they depreciate which increases the demand for goods and services and thus revives production. According to monetarists, for a short period of time monetary changes affect primarily production and GDP, and for a long period of time the growth of money supply mainly affects the price level.

The ideas of Ludwig Mises and Friedrich Hayek, which are associated with neoliberalism, are also popular in modern economic theory. This is an ideology based on economic liberalism. It is oriented towards economic decisions based on neoclassical economic theories. Representatives of this economic direction criticize the intervention of the state and consider the market as the best regulator of the economy. At the same time, they accept the idea of social orientation of the market economy and allow the negative results of free competition to be eliminated through minimal state intervention.

With changing economic conditions, Keynesianism is evolving. Thus, in economic thought, the views of Neo-Keynesian economics began to take shape. Its representatives are John Hicks, Paul Samuelson, Joseph Stiglitz, Paul Krugman and others. Neo-Keynesians focus on the problems of economic growth and advocate for a systematic and direct impact of the state on the economy. Özlen Hiç (2019) distinguishes between Neo-Keynesianism and the New Keynesian Economy. He points out that "neo" - Keynesian economists, as followers of Keynesianism, have worked only with macroeconomic analysis. In contrast, the New Keynesian economists, like the New Classical economists, have incorporated microeconomic analysis into their macroeconomic system. For this reason, New Keynesian economists differ from Neo-Keynesians in their "methodology." The author (2019, p. 1025) points out: „New Keynesian Economics provide the consistency between the micro- and macro-analysis and seem to be more realistic and valid for the developing countries. The representatives of the New Keynesian Economics are Alan S. Blinder, N. Gregory Mankiw, John Taylor and David Romer." Post-Keynesian economics is a branch of economic thought that also derives from the general theory of John Keynes. Its representatives include Joan Robinson, Nicholas Caldor and others. They pay more attention to issues of income distribution in society.

The overview of economic views can be summarized as follows:

- **Followers of Keynesian economics thought**: They assert greater state intervention in the economy and are more in favor of pursuing expansionist fiscal policies to increase government spending than economists with neoclassical views. The first group of economists also advocated the need to introduce a progressive tax system and strengthen the redistributive functions of the state, which makes it possible to bring fairness to income taxation.
- **Representatives of Neoclassical economic thought**: They believe that markets are capable of self-regulation and insist on the need for minimal government intervention in the economy. In this regard, they are more in favor of pursuing a restrictive fiscal policy to reduce government spending and distain a small part of income through the tax system, so that more funds can remain at the disposal of the private sector, which is considered that is able to use them in the most effective way.

The onset of the global financial and economic crisis in 2008 revived Keynesian ideas to overcome its effects and stimulate economic growth through more active government intervention. However, in this period there is no lack of advocates of the effectiveness of monetary policy as a means of overcoming the crisis. For example, Frederic Mishkin, criticized Paul Krugman's distrust, expressed in the pages of the New York Times (Krugman, 2008), of using "the usual tools of monetary policy – above all the Federal Reserve's ability to pump up the economy by cutting interest rates". Mishkin (2009, p. 573) points out: "I will argue that, to the contrary, financial crises of the type we have been experiencing provide a strong argument for even more aggressive monetary policy easing than normal." In its current economic development forecast, the International Monetary Fund (IMF) warns that under the blows of the coronavirus pandemic (Covid-19), the world economy is facing the worst years since the Great Depression. It is likely that this will make the relevant possibilities for solving global economic problems through the tried and tested Keynesian tools and will put at the heart of the economic debate the Keynesian ideas adapted to modern times.

In addition to theoretical interpretations of the views of Keynesian and Neoclassical economics, the results of empirical research have been used in the development of this chapter. The most important of them are as follows: inequalities overcoming (of the European Commission); pre-history, introduction, and results of the flat tax in Bulgaria, as well as inequality dynamics and causes in the country (of the Bulgarian Institute for Market Economics); and the effectiveness of progressive income taxation (of the Center for Economic Studies and Ifo Institute [CESifo], Munich). The author uses the European Commission's statistical data of tax rates and tax income in the member countries of the European Union (EU) for the period 2003-2019. Furthermore, the author studies methodical instructions on carrying out inspections and audits on individuals by the National Revenue Agency authorities in Bulgaria.

CONTEMPORARY ROLE AND FUNCTIONS OF PERSONAL INCOME TAXES

From macroeconomic point of view, a traditional approach to studying personal income taxes is to relate them to economic growth and search for their relationship. In view of the scientific and practical needs, nowadays it would be useful to also examine the impact of personal income taxes on sustainable economic development. A starting point of such bilateral study is the explanation of the relevant tax functions. As a part of the tax policy, personal income taxation performs three main functions:

- **Fiscal (f):** It provides the necessary finance for functioning of the state and creation of public goods.
- **Social (f):** It re-distributes the income of individual taxpayers and affects social processes.
- **Economic (f):** It has an impact on employment, economic development and growth.

Personal income taxes form a traditional part of any modern tax system. At present, it is typical of them that their fiscal function has a less important role than their social and economic functions.

The reduction of personal income taxes may be an instrument to encourage higher employment levels and to provoke desired social effects. The European Commission's information documents (2017a) state that reduced taxes on the employment income of vulnerable and more sensitive groups, like employed persons earning low income or the second working household members, may contribute to the employment level rise while reducing poverty and social exclusion at the same time. Governments should search for a way of funding such reductions because not all countries have sufficient fiscal space to be able to consider personal income tax reduction without adequate compensation. In that relation, the tax burden shifting to other tax bases is a possible option. The high levels of personal income taxes along with the relatively low tax burden of any taxes on consumption, regular taxes on properties and ecological taxes, may be indicators of the possibility of moving tax burden from employment income. From the point of view of economic growth, researchers consider certain types of tax bases to be less harmful than income taxes, such as taxes on consumption, regular taxes on residential properties, and ecological taxes.

Tax burden shifting from personal income taxes to any other appropriate taxes through the tax policy being implemented may not only reduce the barriers to economic growth but also facilitate sustainable development and social stability. For example, in case taxation burden is shifted to indirect taxes, increased income and consumption will also ensure increased budget income. Moreover, indirect taxes distribute tax burden according to the actual consumption of the tax subjects, and thus justice is achieved in taxation. Readers should take into account that where the role of indirect taxes in a tax system grows at the expense of direct taxes, the provision of higher income in the budget is possible in the conditions of economic growth because the income and consumption have grown. Thus, such approach would have a negative effect in an economic crisis and depression. The accumulation of tax income from real estate taxation at the expense of employment income also introduces some justice in the tax policy due to its implementation since tax burden is shifted to wealthy people owning or using them. Tax burden shifting from personal income taxes to ecological taxes, in its turn, may introduce justice in taxation and assist in limiting the harmful impact on environment.

The aspiration for ensuring sustainable development and growth is related to maintaining fiscal stability in individual countries, which turns the attention to the "grey economy" and the search of methods of its restriction. A large proportion of the economic studies assume that taxes and social security contributions forms the main cause of the occurrence of the "grey sector." Specialized publications (Iliev, 2013) state that the bigger the difference between the total labor expenses and the salaries after taxation is received, the higher the stimulus for avoiding such difference and work in the informal sector is. A tax wedge arises from that difference, which depends on the social security system's peculiarities and may consist of personal income tax (paid by the employee) and social security contributions (paid by both the employer and the employee).

Furthermore, researchers have determined that the higher the tax wedge values are, the larger the possibility of extending the informal sector at the expense of the formal one is. The tax wedge affects the employment of mainly low qualified (low paid) employees since the negative effect of the tax and social security burden on them is strongest. Thus, the possibility of such people moving to the "grey sector" is very high, and that puts them in a particularly unfavorable social position because the people working in that sector suffer numerous negative effects, such as non-compliance with the labor standards set and lack of social protection through the social security system. Depending on the tax wedge model, the "grey economy" should have low values in countries of low levels of labor taxation, and vice versa, in countries where the tax wedge has the highest values, studies should report a large share of the "grey sector." Practically, that is not confirmed by the data regarding some EU countries. For instance, the level of tax and social security burden in Bulgaria is low compared to the other EU countries, but it reports a relatively large share of "grey economy." Additionally, in countries like Belgium and Sweden, where taxes and social security contributions are high, have a relatively low share of the "grey economy."

The above discrepancy between the tax wedge model and the practice in EU countries may be explained by the existence of other factors favoring the "grey economy" development, such as level of corruption, trust in institutions, legal regulations, and levels of bureaucracy. Such a combination of factors varies among countries, and is not a generally valid model of the factors that have an effect on development of "grey economy". So, apart from the tax and social security burden, researchers should also take into account the influence of those factors on the level of "grey economy." Iliev (2013) state that, the tax wedge does not have to be the only or leading factor determining the development of informal employment. The author also state that there is not an established generally valid combination of influencing factors, and therefore the approach to each economy should be individual.

In case researchers study the impact of personal income taxation and social security contributions on the "grey economy", they should pay attention to the social security system and especially to the relation of employees' social security contributions that they currently pay and any future compensation guaranteed to them by such contributions. The persons' assessment of the quality of any social benefits they receive or will receive against the social security contributions that they pay is very important in that regard. Hazans (2011) holds that the granting of a wider scope of social benefits of good quality limits the "grey sector." In addition, where the demographic indicators are aggravated tangibly (the persons making social security contributions become less, and the number of retired people rises) and a cost-covering type of social security system functions predominantly, where pensions are paid by the principle of solidarity and not based on preliminary accumulated funds in personal accounts, distrust may cause the people's willingness to move to the "grey sector." Therefore, the transition to the "grey economy" may be a result of distrust in the pension insurance system functioning and unwillingness to pay social security contributions even at low levels of the personal income tax because the income forms the base for both levying the tax and charging the social security contributions. Thus, researchers should apply a complex approach to the searching for any reasons for expanding the "grey sector" and undermines the financial stability and legality in the state.

Personal income taxes may play a role in encouraging individuals' labor activity and entrepreneurship and consequently, causing economic growth, in which the economic function of taxes, is performed. In addition to these roles, personal income taxes may also be considered as an instrument of introducing social justice and stability to the society. Such effects represent an expression of the social function of taxes. They are achieved, for example, when the government redistributes the income of more highly paid persons and households to poorer ones through progressive taxation scales, introduction of non-taxable minimum, tax relief, and stimuli for personal income taxation.

In theory, researchers usually see progressive income taxation as an instrument of mitigating social inequality and increasing public welfare, since the people earning lower income pay a lower percentage of that tax compared to the ones with higher income. Progressive taxation enhances economic activity, as well as consumption among the groups with lower income. The application of progressive scales to personal income taxation leads to increased tax revenue in the budget due to the higher tax rate taxation of the higher income. Thus, the progressive tax allows the government to incur additional public expenditure for financing health care, education, science, culture, infrastructure, government administration, national security, and defense, which extends the access of poor people and persons in risk of social exclusion to such benefits. Progressive tax also allows for improvement of public order and security, increases in public investments and public goods available to everyone. These public goods may include new ambulances, public transport, medical equipment, and refurbished schools and kindergartens. Thus, progressive taxation helps to reduce the confrontation among various social groups in the society. Most of the EU member countries apply progressive income taxation. All countries that have introduced the so-called "flat tax" are situated in Central and Eastern Europe. According to the European Commission (2019), for example, by 2019 the rate of this tax is as follows: Bulgaria (10%), Hungary (15%), Romania (10%) and Estonia (20%).

GDP distribution is carried out through the revenue tax and social security system, and that distribution is continued and completed by the system of government expenditure. Thus, justice is introduced into the society, making up to some extent for the income inequality resulting from the market mechanism operation. Researchers assume the state's role in the society is measured by the value of public expenditure to the GDP level (Hristov, 2014). In theory, there is no consensus on state intervention in the economy. Economists with neoclassical ideas defend the thesis of limited state participation in the economy and believe that low taxes and reduced government spending have a positive impact on economic growth. Proponents of the "minimal state" concept, such as Friedrich Hayek (Austrian School) and Milton Friedman (Chicago School), affirm the ability of the market economy to self-regulate and advocate a restrictive policy to reduce government spending. Keynesian economists are in favor of greater government intervention in the economy and believe that public spending stimulates economic growth. These views are related to the concept of a steady increase in government spending, known as Wagner's law. According to him, the state is increasing its activity, which leads to an increase in public spending due to the emergence of new needs to be met and the desire to increase the welfare of citizens. Joseph Stiglitz (2012), a contemporary follower of the Keynesian paradigm, proposes reasoned economic growth programs based on public investment in infrastructure, education, and technology that are expected to expand the economy and make private investment even more attractive. He believes that the viability of the modern economy depends heavily on a well-functioning public sector, as the government creates the internal and external infrastructure that allows society and the economy to function. If the government does not provide investment in public goods, such as roads, ports, education or basic research, then normal business may not prosper.

From the point of view of any potential of the public sector expansion, active social policy, and the higher standard of living of the EU countries' population, good practical results are achieved in those countries where public expenditure is high, (i.e., state interference is high). France, Belgium, Sweden, Denmark and Austria have relatively high levels of government spending that is permanently over 50% of GDP. In comparison, due to the low tax income in Bulgaria (the highest income tax rate of 10% is the lowest in EU), the country is unable to implement an active social policy and offer various social services. Adding also the application of proportional personal income taxation with no non-taxable minimum income since 2008, the opportunities of achieving positive social effects and social justice through personal income taxation in the country are considerably limited. The introduction of a non-taxable minimum income for individuals' income taxation may create justice in personal income taxation, whether progressive or proportional (with a flat tax). Moreover, the financial stimuli of the tax subjects with the lowest income for shifting to the "grey sector" would be reduced that way.

The maintenance of low levels of income taxes for the individuals and the business, of the social security contributions and of the expenses for salaries is typical of the export-orientated growth strategy, in which the attention is drawn to the achievement of "cost competitiveness" and attractiveness for external investors (Vladimirov, 2015). Such a policy, in which the level of salaries lags behind the labor productivity and the level of income taxes and social security contributions is low, leads to reduced budget revenues and, consequently, to reduced public spending. All that causes higher income inequality and social tension. In addition, it may provoke emigration of young people and qualified professionals seeking better labor remuneration and social comfort abroad. Therefore, researchers should take into account that maintaining low income and social security contributions and using them as an instrument of attracting foreign investments creates numerous negative effects that restrict domestic demand and its role as a driver of economic development and growth. In the present situation with an economy based on knowledge, the intensified income inequality limits the opportunities of investment in human resources. For this reason, turns out to be an obstacle to productivity and economic growth (Mavrov, 2017).

If the government desires encouragement of the economic growth and foreign investments, the "dual income tax" model may be applied to avoid such negative effects. This model combines proportional low corporate income taxation with progressive personal income taxation (Galabov, 2009). The developed EU countries may be an example of the optimization of taxation and tax rates, in which the corporate income tax (CIT) rates are significantly lower compared to those of the personal income tax (PIT) for the period 2003-2019. For example, according to the European Commission (2019), CIT in Belgium is 34% to 29.6%, whereas progressive PIT is 53.7% to 53.1%; CIT in Germany is 39.6% to 29.9%, whereas progressive PIT is 51.2% to 47.5%; CIT in Denmark is 30% to 22%, whereas progressive PIT is 62.3% to 55.9% (European Commission, 2019). Thus, the developed EU member countries introduce justice in personal income taxation through the progressive individuals' income tax. Additionally, these countries maintain a stimulating ratio between the personal and corporate income tax rates in order to encourage the undertaking of entrepreneurial risk instead of work as a person employed under a labor contract.

The implementation of an active policy of income increase, including income increase through the introduction of a non-taxable minimum income for the lowest income in individuals' taxation and through the minimum salary mechanism, is an addition to the measures of ensuring social justice and stability in the society. The minimum salary increase should allow for 100% coverage of the poverty line and any social security contributions and personal income tax due to law. This will prevent people from moving into the "grey sector" or emigrating (losses of human resources). Unfair labor remuneration along with unfair taxation leads to social tension escalation, insecurity, and social exclusion. Vice versa, the harmonious rise of GDP and salaries brings more income into the budget from taxes and social security contributions, and thus provides additional funds for health care, education, science, pensions, innovations and investments, technological renovation of the economy, and work force quality (Ninov, 2014). The combination of these measures may expand the potential of domestic demand with its two basic components: household consumption and public spending as economic growth drives. In turn, family income taxation may create social justice because it takes into account the total amount of the annual individual income and the taxpayer's marital status, number of dependents, and number of children, among other factors. Researchers believe that family income taxation plays a positive role in supporting families and encouraging births, which helps in solving demographic problems (Kotsev et al., 2008).

James and Nobes (2015) assert that income taxation may influence people's willingness to get involved and invest in the acquisition of more productive skills or to start a more productive lob. Income taxation may also affect their willingness to have a more difficult job or strive for a promotion. Moreover, it is possible for income taxes to have an impact on the sum of incentives that parents give to their children for acquiring certain skills. Aleksieva (2016) believes that tax reduction stimulates people to work because most of their personal income remains for consumption and savings. On the other hand, redundancy expenses shrink due to the higher interest in employment. The seizure of economic subjects' income leads to lower consumption and savings. In a situation with low levels of income and high taxes, savings are the first to suffer from the negative effects. In turn, the low levels of savings limit the economic credit capacity and, indirectly, individuals face barriers to obtaining loan capital.

The theoretical assumptions suggest the existence of optimal level of taxation in accordance with the economy of each state ensures an effective scope of good quality public services (Vladimirov, 2011). Excessively high levels of income taxes have a retaining result on growth because the labor incentives decrease; they provoke attempts of tax avoidance and income hiding; they lower the level of savings and investments; and they delay the development of all factors of production. When tax levels are in the contemporary conditions of mobility of goods and services, people and funds are able to orientate labor and capital to countries with lower levels of taxation.

On the other hand, researchers should consider that not only excessively high levels but also excessively low levels may hinder economic growth. Tax revenue provides funds for the state to maintain infrastructure, conduct scientific research, and advance technical progress, among other things (i.e. for public spending promoting intelligent and long-lasting economic growth). Should tax levels be below their optimal levels, they may not provide sufficient funds for financing government expenditure to stimulate any potential economic development. The low level of taxation causes a disturbed budget balance resulting in increased deficit and higher government debt, which is an unfavorable condition of maintaining stability in public finances.

The importance of income policy is a consequence of the fact that personal income taxes take away a significant share of the individual income, resulting in income redistribution and civil consumption shrinking at the expense of the state's income. Actually, a considerable part of the funds accumulated through taxes is returned to the people through the government spending system. The tax amount determines individuals' purchasing power, and therefore demand, and thus employment and economic growth are also of extreme importance. For example, researchers may consider personal income tax as an instrument of direct household aid through reduced tax rate, introduced tax reliefs, reductions, and tax credits. The reduction of tax rates and tax reliefs have their strongest impact on any persons with minimum or low income (Aleksieva, 2016).

Apart from the fiscal, economic and social functions of personal income taxation, which the author has discussed so far, contemporary researchers may also distinguish some supplementary functions, such as ecological functions, which facilitate the achievement of sustainable economic development through personal income taxes. For this purpose, when the total annual tax base is determined, the following may be deducted as tax relief: any sum for using public transport instead of private vehicles; any sum for acquisition of a "passive house" type residential property; any sum for introducing ecological power sources in households; and any sum for acquisition of a new electric car. The complex nature of the functions (fiscal, economic, social and ecological) of personal income taxes turns them into an instrument of sustainable economic development.

Any issues related to the planet's preservation and the counteraction to climatic changes comes to the forefront at the modern stage of the socio-economic development. In this regard, the theme of the meeting of the World economic forum held in January 2020 in Davos was "Stakeholders for a cohesive and sustainable world", and the European Commission proposed the European Green Pact in combating climatic changes. Climate changes and aggravated environmental conditions jeopardize human existence globally. In order to overcome this challenge, Europe needs a new growth strategy that allows for the Union to become a modern, resource effective and competitive economy with no net emissions of greenhouse gases by 2050. The achievement of the European Green Pact's objectives needs considerable investments, which require the mobilization of both public and private sectors (European Union, 2019). In this context the contemporary role of personal income taxation stands out as an instrument that affects the tax subjects' behavior for achieving not only fiscal, economic, and social results but also ecological objectives. The above section provides a new perspective of the personal income taxation functions, and it may be deemed an instrument of implementing the sustainable economic development policy.

The complex approach in sustainable development research is the result of the crossing point of objectives related to three inter-related systems: environmental, economic and social (Barbier & Burgess, 2017). This is how the idea of the three "pillars of sustainable development" was formed. The tax policy regarding personal income taxation may be related to the concept of sustainable development in three main aspects:

- **Economic aspect:** Maintaining financial stability and low levels of unemployment is possible by the implementation of an adequate policy regarding income and individuals' taxation in order to encourage employment and economic development. This limits the "grey economy" and ensures the optimal payment of tax revenue and social security contributions in the budget.
- **Social aspect:** Reducing income inequality (introduction of non-taxable minimum income), and creating social justice and social stability by the personal income taxation (determination of optimal tax amounts and personal income taxation schemes).
- **Ecological aspect:** Encouraging tax subjects to facilitate environmental protection by choosing energy saving resources in households, constructing ecological residential properties, driving environment-friendly motor vehicles, and intensively using public transportation at the expense of private transportation.

Moffatt (2000) explores the methodology of the Environmental Footprint Concept, which is supported by environmental economists. According to him, the ecological footprint is an attempt to develop a biophysically based ecological economy. It approximates reality better than many economic expansionist models. The author (2000, p. 361) states: „We could also assume that the sustainable trajectories are equitable (although neo-classical economists have a different view on equity, usually Pareto optimality, than many ecological economists)." He states that if we want to be actively involved in the processes that make development sustainable, we need to establish indicators so that we know whether we are moving towards or moving away from a sustainable future. We also need to look at which trajectories are equitable, economically and ecologically desirable and achievable.

PROGRESSIVE AND PROPORTIONAL INCOME TAXATION

With progressive taxation system, the tax rate changes by a progression chosen in advance, and the tax liability increases progressively with the rise in the tax base. Such a taxation system leads changes the proportion of income set before taxation. Thus, Tsenova (2020) assume that progressive income taxation is more favorable for low income than high income. With the proportional taxation system, the tax rate remains the same, and the tax liability changes proportionately to the tax base change. This type of taxation does not cause any change in income proportion before and after taxation. Tsenova assume that this system to be acceptable for taxation of both high and low income, and it seems to be objective and fair. In addition to these two main systems of taxation, there is a regressive taxation, in which the tax rate decreases as income increases. For example, the patent tax has the character of a regressive taxation, as its amount is known in advance and does not change regardless of the realized turnover. Thus, the higher the turnover is, the lower the effective tax rate is. As positive aspects of regressive taxation can be pointed out, that it stimulate traders to expand their activities and reduce the opportunities for tax evasion. This chapter does not deal in detail with regressive taxation issues, but rather gives an idea of the regressive effect of the application of the proportional taxation system.

Adamov, Dimitrova, Nenkov and Petev (2013) state that income tax was introduced in all advanced, industrially developed countries (UK, Sweden, Japan, USA) in the beginning of 20th century. The German economist and financier Adolf Wagner asserts that the idea that taxes should have an effect on the distribution of national income and wealth in the name of greater justice. Thus, progressive income taxation becomes commonly applied and associated with the expectations of reducing any large differences in income and wealth (Kotsev et al., 2008). The main argument in favor of progression with the personal income tax is that social justice is achieved in that way (i.e., the state can re-distribute income from people and households paid higher to poorer ones through elaborated progressive taxation scales). The opponents of progressive income taxation hold that progressive taxation scales bring ineffectiveness into the economy since the high limit rates for groups with higher income hinder any incentives for labor and entrepreneurship of economic subjects.

However, the thesis against progressive income taxation is refuted by the results of some studies, (Corneo, 2000) which hold that if people care about their income status rather than their leisure time, they would devote a large share of their time to work. Progressive income taxation is useful by increasing individuals' ineffective low quantity of leisure time without changing their status. Other scientists (Cullen & Gordon, 2002) conclude that reduced personal tax rates actually lead to lower entrepreneurial activity, which is an important source of innovative ideas and economic growth, because it discourages any business risk undertaking and performance of independent entrepreneurial activity. Moreover, Cullen and Gordon (2002) note that poor countries often have minimum personal income taxes. Keeping in mind the considerations above, when a tax policy is implemented in its part regards personal income taxation the basic dilemma often is which to be given priority: justice when revenue to finance the state is collected or economic effectiveness.

According to the followers of proportional income taxation (the flat tax), justice may be achieved not only through the revenue system of public finance but also through the system of expenditure (i.e., through government spending, which has a less deforming impact on labor and economic growth incentives). In that sense, the same net redistribution in result of the progressive income tax may be achieved by taking away from everyone a sum proportional to the income (i.e., all income is taxed by the same tax rate) but, for the purpose of compensation, some individuals are granted government transfers in the form of social benefits, allowances, vouchers, and other preferences. Researchers state that income redistribution through government spending has some negative effects because any redistribution beyond the one implemented by the market mechanism gives rise to deformations and ineffectiveness. On top of that, any redistribution by the system of expenditure is related to huge administration costs as well.

In almost all countries that have introduced the flat tax, in which a single tax rate is used, income taxation begins above a certain non-taxable minimum income. Such a combination of non-taxable minimum income and a single tax rate actually ensures some kind of income taxation progressiveness. The progressive income taxation scale and non-taxable minimum income were cancelled in Bulgaria in the beginning of 2008. Currently, individuals' income taxation in the country is entirely proportional, and the regulated basic taxation rate on personal income is 10%, which is equal to the corporate income tax rate. Usually, in order to mitigate the flat tax effect and make it more socially acceptable, the government introduces a basic relief (non-taxable minimum income) and often some additional target reliefs, for instance, for families with children. Thus, the government achieves a fair transformation of the traditional progressive personal income tax into a proportional tax for individuals and compensates the lack of a higher number of tax amounts in the income taxation scale.

From theoretical point of view, the flat tax is related to the ideas of two American economists (Robert Hall and Alvin Rabushka) of the 1980s, and researchers consider it to be very close to the "supply-side economics" (Robert Mundell and Arthur Laffer) in its part related to income taxes. The original concept of Hall and Rabushka suggests an "integrated flat tax" on consumption, not income. The governments have not implemented it, though. What those economic ideas have in common is the negative attitude to the state interference in economy and the assessment that it is rather harmful since it causes deformation of the optimal proportions established on the market. Researchers consider that such interference discourages employment and entrepreneurship and encourages tax evasion, tax havens, illegal economy, and labor in a natural economy. All this leads to a weak economy and low economic growth. By these views, negative attitudes exist toward progressive taxation, especially with personal income taxes, which researchers deem an instrument of "aggressive" redistribution, killing stimuli and personal freedom. In Laffer's opinion, tax revenue is a product of both tax amounts and tax bases. Related to this, he has a positive attitude to expanding tax bases by restriction of various forms of tax reliefs and exemptions (Galabov, 2009).

Alberto Alesina and Silvia Ardagna (2010, p. 2) state: "It is fair to say that we know relatively little about the effect of fiscal policy on growth and in particular about the so called fiscal multipliers, namely how much one dollar of tax cuts or spending increases translates in terms of GDP. The issue is very politically charged as well, since right of center economists and policymakers believe in tax cuts and the left of center ones believe in spending increases. Unfortunately both sides can't be right at the same time!" George Pardee and Helen Pardee (2020, p. 32) come to the conclusion: „It insists that monetary and fiscal policies are most effective when used in tandem."

Unlike progressive taxation, in which the rate is variable, with the flat tax (also called "proportional tax"), the tax rate is constant, which researchers believe to be its advantage. Since the progression has no exact criterion, it is random and may reach confiscation even: how unequally unequal income should be taxed is an issue of social, moral, ethical values. In that sense, the reduction of tax levels by their consolidation causes progressiveness reduction and labor stimulus intensification. Galabov (2009) affirms that the progression and tax relief system makes taxation more complicated, and therefore they diminish the "tax consent" and tax collectability. Additionally, he holds that the high taxes on labor reduce the incentives for work, which refers more to the progressive income taxation, where income over certain thresholds is taxed at a higher tax rate. Since higher income is usually associated with higher educational attainment and/or skills, the progressive tax plays a penalizing role, which discourages investments in education and professional qualification and limits human resource development (Staykov, 2016).

Governments usually apply flat taxation to income taxation of individuals and corporate profit tax. Most often, the flat tax rate is low to promote collectability, employment, and entrepreneurial initiative. Galabov (2009) points out that the flat tax began to be applied in Europe at the end of the 20th century with its adoption by Estonia (1994, 26%). It was then introduced in Lithuania (1995, 33%), Latvia (1997, 25%), Russia (2001, 13%), Serbia (2003, 14%), and Ukraine (2004, 13%), Slovakia (2004, 19%), Romania (2005, 16%). The arguments in favor of the flat tax introduction are related to the potential of economic development acceleration and its use as an instrument of exiting the recession. Governments introduced a 10% flat tax in Bulgaria for corporate and personal income tax consecutively in 2007 and 2008 for the purpose of improving collectability, reducing the "grey sector" share, promoting economic growth by employment rise, and attracting of foreign investments. Over 20 countries have introduced a flat tax in the beginning of 2010, and most of them are ex-socialist countries. According to Galabov (2009) and the European Commission (2019), in 2008 government officials set the tax rate within the range from 10% of income (Bulgaria, Macedonia, Mongolia, Kyrgyzstan) to 35.7% of income (Iceland). Tax preferences and non-taxable minimum income are kept in many of these countries.

Galabov (2009) maintains that governments have introduced the "flat"-type taxes mainly in Eastern European countries. In his opinion, the reduction of maximum tax amounts does not result in considerable economic growth to expand the tax base, so any tax revenue may be compensated. He cites numerous empirical studies to support his argument that the relation between the labor supply and the reduction of maximum tax amounts is weak and sometimes missing. All data and authors confirm that one can't expect significant improvement of the Laffer's type effectiveness.

The positive results of the flat tax introduction are limited to some transparency intensification, simplification and cost-reduction of the tax collectability. For that reason, the proposal of introducing a flat rate in USA did not reach the implementation stage. The results of the flat tax introduction are poor in developing countries and those in transition to market economy. That is also confirmed by the data on Bulgaria regarding the share of personal income taxes in GDP: its values increased within the range of 2.6-3.3 in 2005-2017; its value is 3.0 prior to the flat rate introduction in 2007 (European Commission, 2019).

Galabov (2009) believes that any excessive reduction of the tax amounts causes a drop in the budget revenue and unfavorable tax burden distribution to the benefit of the wealthy people. Tax compliance may not be significantly improved while, the benefits of income tax evasion are much bigger than the sanctions expected, and tax control is weak. Upon the introduction of proportional taxation and removal of the non-taxable minimum income, the tax burden shifts to low-income and medium-income groups. Contrariwise, the application of progressive income taxation leads to tax burden redistribution, so fairer distribution of goods is achieved and a more stable society is created. Some studies state that if people are more sensitive to the disposable income, the progressive income taxation plays an effective role that is more important in the more egalitarian economy (Corneo, 2000). Regarding the tax practice established in most EU countries, researchers assume that the progressive taxation system is more suitable for individuals' income taxation, while the proportional one is appropriate for company profit taxation. The progressive and the proportional taxation systems are applied in various ways in the EU member countries. The Scandinavian countries and the Netherlands tax the income of individuals by the progressive system and the company profit by the proportional one (Tsenova, 2020). The older EU member countries, such as Germany, UK, France, Italy, Spain, Holland, Belgium, Austria, Portugal, Sweden, Finland, Ireland, Denmark, Greece, and Luxemburg, use progressive income taxation. All countries in the group of original EU member countries have a large share of the personal income tax in GDP, and the maximum tax rates are very high at approximately 50% of income.

Furthermore, there is a non-taxable minimum income in the income taxation system of these countries, which protects the low-income population. Apart from that, the governments provide tax relief that aims at reducing the tax burden in the lowest-income groups. According to the 2015 data, countries like Germany, Denmark, and Spain increased tax relief in the form of tax credit or any other reductions, France introduced a new tax credit for persons over 65, and Holland raised the tax credit for working parents. The rates of personal income taxes and the share of these taxes in GDP are twice as low in the new EU member countries compared to those in the other EU countries. Aleksieva (2016) lists Bulgaria, Malta, Cyprus, Romania, Estonia, Latvia, Lithuania, Hungary, Slovakia, Czech Republic, and Poland as examples of this effect. These countries apply both progressive and proportional income taxation. Flat tax was introduced in Bulgaria, Czech Republic, Estonia, Latvia, Lithuania, Romania and Hungary, and the non-taxable minimum income was removed in two of those countries (Bulgaria and Hungary).

Referring to the fundamental work Rudiments of Financial Science of Professor Petko Stoyanov, Hristoskov (2010) affirms that the application of progressive income taxation may be justified by two theories:

- **Sacrifice theory:** This theory originates from the term of marginal utility, according to which the value of any good decreases with its quantitative increase, and vice versa, the value increases with the reduction of the available resources of that good. In the context of taxation, the example given is that a tax in the sum of 2,000 BGN (20 percent of 10,000 BGN incomes) forms a much bigger sacrifice than a tax in the sum of 2,000 BGN (20 percent of 100,000 BGN incomes).
- **Theory of economic power:** This theory relates income taxation with the social minimum. If the social minimum is a constant average quantity, increased income and property status would leave at the disposal of the taxpayer ever increasing remainders for taxation above that minimum. For instance, in case of two people with annual income of 10,000 BGN and 100,000 BGN respectively, the ratio is 1:10. If one assumes that the social minimum was 5,000 BGN, the ratio between the remainders would be 1:19 (5,000:95,000). If there is a proportional tax of 20%, the taxpayer with lower income would pay 2,000 BGN, which would actually be a 40% tax on the remainder for taxation (2,000:5,000), and the one with higher income would pay 20,000 BGN, which would actually be a 21% tax on his remainder for taxation (20,000:95,000). Hristoskov (2010) points out that, governments apply progressive income taxation for eliminating this injustice. Moreover, he notes that high-income groups have the economic power to compensate the higher taxation of their income by earning extra income. However, earning additional income is impossible for low-income individuals. Vice versa, their taxation on an equal level with the high-income groups diminishes their economic power and pushes them into the poverty trap.

One could place a judgment on the justice of flat taxation if they compare the marginal utility of the share taken away by the personal income tax from wealthy individuals and from such with low income, since they would not deprive themselves of the same part of consumption as a result of taxation. The part taken away from any taxpayers with low income, although smaller in absolute value, has a larger marginal utility for them. Vice versa, the higher the income of a person is, the lower the marginal utility taken away from him at 10% taxation. Thus, although they pay in more in absolute value (compared with low-income taxpayers), for the high-income taxpayers are left with sufficient funds after income taxation in order to satisfy their basic vital needs and even consume luxury goods. Low-income individuals do not have the purchasing power of high-income taxpayers and consume mainly necessities. Therefore, the proportional taxation takes away a relatively small part of the wealthy people's income, and their disposable income remains much higher compared to low-income individuals. In this context, it becomes clear that the application of flat income taxes intensifies income inequality.

One may use the values of Gini coefficient for measuring income inequality in EU when that hypothesis is verified. The 2015 data shows that the coefficient has similar values before taxation (regardless of whether the taxes are progressive or flat) because they change considerably once the direct taxes and social transfers (including pensions) have been deducted. Thus, the countries that have the most effective social systems (Sweden, Denmark, Hungary) manage to reduce the values of the Gini coefficient by half unlike those (Bulgaria, Latvia, Estonia) where income redistribution by the tax and social security systems is poor (European Commission, 2017b). Thus, researchers conclude that efforts should be focused on enhancing the effectiveness of redistribution processes by the tax and social security policy in order to overcome income inequalities. Researchers should consider the effect of the "unemployment trap" d in that relation. The "unemployment trap" occurs in the case of generous programs of allowances, support of unemployed people, and heavy taxation of low-paid persons because there is a slight difference between the income from work and from allowances in such a case. Some studies (Pedersen & Smith, 2001) state that, the payment of unemployment allowances and social allowances for a long time makes the demotivation of involvement on the labor market higher, just like the high taxation of income from labor.

The European Commission considers the tax and social security policy to be an important instrument with the tangible effect of overcoming income inequality. The European Commission states that the social expenditure effect on equality reduction depends on the proper allocation of the spending. In that sense, keeping some of the allowances for people returning to work and diminishing the tax burden for those with the lowest income ensure that unemployed and inactive persons would have are positively incentivized to start working on a labor contract. The European Commission takes into account that the financial crisis and the necessity of public finance stabilization have an impact on the ability of the state to redistribute income. Thus, the governments decides progressive income taxation of individuals to be avoided in a number of EU countries, such as Latvia, Lithuania, Estonia, Bulgaria, and Romania (European Commission, 2017b), where the flat income taxation system operates.

Some specialized economic studies state that in view of budget and tax revenue, the introduction of flat tax on income actually plays the role of an anticyclic instrument of fiscal policy (budget stabilization) that, to some extent, makes up for any losses of budget revenue from other taxes in a situation of financial crisis (2009-2010). According to Nikolova (2016) positive effects of flat income tax for the budget may be sought in the "lightening of economy" and the reduction of informal labor relations. In particular, the effect of the introduction of flat tax and lower tax and social security burden is that it boosts the "lightening" of the income of working people by hiding their actual salary amounts compared to those who principally do not declare their income (Ganev, 2016). Other economists justify the flat tax advantages, maintaining that tax collectability may not be increased without tax rate reduction and

Table 1. Effects of the flat tax introduction

Positive effects of the flat tax
(+) the government taxes the various income at the same rate, which seems to be objective and fair; (+) it creates economic effectiveness since it does not eliminate the incentives for more labor and employment; (+) an anticyclic fiscal policy instrument partially makes up for the reduced budget revenue from other taxes in a situation of financial crisis; (+) more stimuli for declaring the actual salary amounts; (+) it facilitates the enhancement of revenue collectability from voluntary fulfillment of the tax obligations due to low tax rates and simplification of the tax system; (+) transparency intensification, simplification, and cost-reduction of the tax collectability.
Negative effects of the flat tax
(–) it may not solve the problem of income hiding entirely; (–) there is little evidence for a significant rise of revenue from personal income taxes in result of tax rate reduction; (–) reduced personal tax rates actually lead to less inventive for entrepreneurial activity because it discourages any business risk undertaking; (–) the tax burden shifts to low-income and medium-income groups, particularly if the non-taxable minimum income is removed; (–) it does not facilitate the creation of social justice by income redistribution and compensation of big income differences in the society.

tax system simplification (Angelov, 2016). Based on the findings discussed in this section, the author has formulated the following main results of the flat tax introduction, which are presented in Table 1.

The author concludes that when income inequality before and after taxation and social transfers does not change substantially, then the state does not redistribute national wealth in an efficient way to mitigate the gaping differences between the poor and the rich. Moreover, the focus on indirect taxes as revenue sources creates additional burden for people with lower income who spend everything they earn and give most of their income to the budget as Value added tax (VAT) and excises. Therefore, provided that the lowest income remains at critical levels and the tax and social security system does not manage to make up for the huge income inequality, the large share of people living in risk of poverty or social exclusion grows. This creates prerequisites for social tension and instability in society.

According to Hristov (2013), the views on inequality can be provisionally divided into two groups. The representatives of the first group find arguments to show the positive effects of inequality among separate groups of the population. Examples of this include the encouragement of investments and education. When inequality increases, the people with lower income invest more in education and have a stronger incentive to work. If taxes rise for the purpose of income redistribution in economy, the people lose these incentives. The representatives of the second group submit a series of arguments against inequality. They believe that big differences in income may prevent talented people from obtaining a good education and a chance of a career. Thus, the general potential productivity of the population and the opportunity for more intense economic growth in the long-term are reduced. Hristov (2013) cites studies conducted by the International Monetary Fund and the Asian Development Bank, stating that income inequality leads to slow growth and a financial crisis and an increase in the number of people living below the poverty threshold.

Based on the information above, and considering the strive for sustainable economic growth uniting the leading countries in the world, the author concludes that the efforts have been focused on mitigation of the negative effects of income inequality in recent years, and this tendency will intensify in the future. For this reason, one may expect extended state interference in economy and allocation of more funds for financing public activities and public goods, as well as more active income redistribution in the society by the tax and social security system.

TAX CONTROL OVER PERSONAL INCOME TAXATION

In order to increase the collection of personal income taxes by increasing the voluntary fulfillment of tax obligations in Bulgaria, more than 10 years ago, a tax policy was adopted as follows: the personal income tax rates are reduced, the individuals' taxation mechanism is simplified, and comfort is created during the fulfillment of their tax obligations. For instance, this could occur by submitting returns electronically containing data generated officially, which should be confirmed and supplemented by the person. Thus, governments seeks Laffer's type effect and tax compliance enhancement while stimulating the tax subjects' willingness to perform their tax obligations in a timely manner. That aspiration may be expressed in the application of a low-rate flat tax on individuals' income. For example, the government of Bulgaria has levied a single rate of 10% for income taxation since 2008. However, as has been clarified so far, there is no convincing empirical evidence that the introduction of a flat tax with a low flat rate leads to a significant increase in income tax revenues. Such a type of tax policy can't solve the problems regarding income hiding. This warrants research for the prerequisites for deviation from income taxation.

The author divides the prerequisites for the occurrence of offences and frauds at individuals' income taxation into three groups:

1. **Errors and omissions made by the tax liable persons (TLP), the employer, or the income payer, regarding return filing (filing compliance).** Individuals who should pay personal income taxes often have no obligations to do accounting, therefore they have not sufficient knowledge of the proper application of any tax regulations, nor do they have the habits needed to comply with the deadlines of fulfilling the tax and social security obligations. They are likely to enter incorrect and incomplete details while filling out their returns, to file no returns, or to miss the required deadline of their filing.

Employers and income payers may also make errors while working out salaries, social security contributions, and tax liabilities. This is possible even when specialized software is used for working out any salaries because a large share of the details is input manually, and an electronic system failure is also possible.

2. **Acts performed in bad faith by TLP, the employer or income payer, regarding a discrepancy between the liability declared and actually due (reporting compliance).** TLP often try to hide income in order to avoid paying taxes and social security contributions. Employers are also interested in hiding some of the income actually paid to any persons involved in the business in order to save the payment of contributions for social security and health care on that income. In other cases, where dishonest companies form fictitious business on paper, they account for and declare fictitious costs for salaries and consequently form relevant fictitious income.
3. **Payment failure of declared liabilities (payment compliance).** Individuals' tax illiteracy may become the reason for both filing failure of a tax return and payment failure of any tax liabilities in time. Employers and income payers may also fail to file the tax liabilities declared provided that the payment failure of declared taxes is not incriminated, and the Criminal Code refers exclusively to undeclared tax evasion. The expert knowledge on the prerequisites for the occurrence of offences and frauds relating to the individuals' income taxation allows the revenue authorities to formulate control hypotheses to be subjected to verification by appropriate control means based on data from relevant information sources. When controlling individuals' income, the revenue authorities may verification of two groups of control hypotheses.

First group: Logical hypotheses of incompliance of any reported and declared data with the tax regulations. For example, revenue authorities should check for this in case of advance payments made: whether they were determined correctly in compliance with the regulatory requirements, whether they were declared and paid within the term required.

Second group: Logical hypotheses of untrustworthiness of any reported and declared data. For example, where taxpayers declare their income in unusually low amounts, revenue authorities should investigate if there is a discrepancy between its amount and any costs for support and living, trips abroad, and property acquisition by the relevant individual (i.e., is there hidden income).

With insufficient tax capacity and a high level of corruption (for instance, in countries in transition to market economy), the government introduces low tax rates and simplifies the taxation mechanism by a flat tax in order to increase the income tax collectability. Having considered the complex nature of the prerequisites for deviation from income taxation discussed, one may not rely exclusively on any measures of encouraging the voluntary fulfillment of tax obligations in order to significantly increase the income tax collectability. However, the effectiveness and tax control results should also be improved by the application of modern methods of human resource management in the administration, enhancement of personal integrity and ethics, and improvement of the tax control technique and process.

To that effect, it would be expedient to also discuss **the indicators of offence and fraud commitment** related to income taxation (Foks, 1998). Researchers may deem the following indicators to be signs of committed offences and fraud:

- TLP does not keep or keeps any accounting books and documentation required irregularly.
- TLP made attempts to forge accounting documents and/or entries or they kept two sets of accounting books are kept;
- Refusal to present the accounting documentation or proved destruction of accounting documents.
- Failure to provide any information requested, to give explanations, or the entire taxpayer's behavior shows that he is unwilling to collaborate with the revenue authorities during the talk/meeting.
- TLP made incorrect, misleading, or inconsistent statements during the talk with the revenue authority.
- TLP presented a forged document or notarized declaration to justify a certain item on the tax return.
- Concealment of facts or documents.
- Replacement of accounting or any other documents.
- Not all revenue from the company business operations is deposited into a bank account, and at the same time, there are no sufficient grounds for arrest of a part of the cash proceeds.
- TLP is unwilling to assign some of the control over the cash proceeds of his employees, but the activity scales clearly demonstrate the necessity of doing so.
- Undertaking risky activity.
- TLP's personal living standard, including their maintenance costs and any assets accumulated, considerably exceed the declared income from the business.
- Any property purchased by the taxpayer is registered in the name of other persons.
- TLP makes statements favorable for his personality and behavior, but they can't justify them by any evidence.
- TLP is constantly late and postpones their business meetings, they fail to present any information requested, and they make no benevolent efforts to collaborate with the revenue authorities.

The implementation of a modern tax policy in income taxation based on encouragement of voluntary tax obligation fulfillment in the conditions of extended electronic services and information exchange does not cancel the necessity of efficient tax control over individuals' income taxation for the determination of their actual tax and social security liabilities and the performance of their obligations arisen from the tax and social security legislation. Thus, the author will briefly review a technological model of inspections and audits of individuals' income, which may facilitate the enhancement of tax control effectiveness and results in this aspect. This model consists of four stages and describes the technological sequence in which the revenue authorities may perform complex control actions during inspections and audits of individuals' income. The model is based on a study of the practice and procedural rules (Vlahov et al., 2007) of the tax and social security control authorities of the National Revenue Agency in Bulgaria.

Stage one: Determination of a person's property status and any expenses incurred by him: The revenue authorities consecutively determine the following at this stage:

- Any real estates, owned by a person in the country and abroad.
- Any movable property owned by a person.
- Any cash, securities, and shares owned by a person.
- Any support and living costs incurred by a person.

Stage two: Determination of a person's sources of income and funds: The revenue authorities consecutively determine the following at this stage:

- Any income received by them.
- Any loans from individuals and legal entities in the country and abroad, as well as any other specific sources of funds.

Stage three: Comparison between the properties owned, costs incurred, and any income received.

Stage four: Determination of any taxes and social security contributions due after the audit has been completed: The implementation of efficient tax control requires not only the tax offences and frauds in relation to income taxation to be determined but also an appropriate control impact to be formed to combat them reliably and to prevent this from occurring in other cases. Below, the author lists the basic measures:

1. Imposing administration fines and sanctions for offences relating to income taxation. Researchers believed administration fines to be most efficient when they are related to the amount of any income concealed or tax evaded (Pashev, 2006).
2. Recovery of any fiscal damage caused by evaded taxes along with any legal interest.
3. In case of concealed income and when such acts are incriminated authorities initiates court proceedings for seeking criminal responsibility from the perpetrator.
4. Creation of public culture for voluntary tax obligation fulfillment and intolerance to income concealment and tax evasion.
5. Initiation of legislative changes for the improvement of the tax regulations and the tax policy in relation to income taxation.

The enhancement of integrity and ethics in the institutions and in the society should also be added to the measures of improved control impact in income taxation because high tax collectability, based on actual earned income data, is incompatible with high levels of corruption.

SOLUTIONS AND RECOMMENDATIONS

During the elaboration of the modern tax policy supporting sustainable development, the focus should fall not on whether priority to be given to the principle of effectiveness in economy or whether to the principle of justice in taxation but rather on the issue of finding an efficient way of balancing these two approaches. For example, this could occur by applying the "dual income tax" model, which combines proportional low taxation of corporate income with progressive taxation of personal income, or, at least by introducing non-taxable minimum income into proportional taxation and optimizing the tax rate. In income taxation, researchers should not draw attention to the choice between progressive or proportional income taxation but rather to finding the optimal taxation level for each country – that is, a level that can ensure sufficient funding of qualitative public goods and thus, generate sustainable economic growth. The author recommends that governments introduce non-taxable minimum income and minimum salary fully covering the poverty line for compensating the negative effects of income inequality.

The maintenance of low levels of income taxes, social security contributions, and salary costs for the purpose of attracting foreign investments and economic growth causes a reduction in budget revenue. Therefore, this causes a reduction in public expenditure, which intensifies income inequality and forms a prerequisite for both social tension and intensified demographic problems. In order to avoid such negative effects, contemporary programs of sustainable economic development and growth should be based on public investments in various areas, such as infrastructure, science, education, ecology, innovations, and technologies.

FUTURE RESEARCH DIRECTIONS

From the point of view of contemporary requirements for ensuring sustainable economic development, it would be useful to comprehensively study any options of combating the negative environmental changes and mitigating income inequalities by the overall tax policy and not only by the personal income taxes. In addition, researchers may study any expected short-term and long-term effects of the tax policy being implemented. Researchers may also examine the impact of personal integrity and level of corruption on tax collectability as a whole and on personal income taxes, and in particular in relation to the role of the human factor in taxation.

CONCLUSION

Nowadays, apart from the traditional functions of personal income taxes, such as fiscal, economic and social, researchers may also distinguish an ecological function. This function can facilitate the achievement of ecological effects by appropriate tax relief. Traditionally, researchers consider personal income taxation to be an instrument of impact on economic growth. Its role and significance extend gradually, and it may be already seen as a factor for maintaining sustainable economic development and growth as well as for ensuring social justice and stability.

Considering the results of this study, the introduction of a flat income tax may be treated as an instrument of budget revenue stabilization in a situation of crisis (recession) because proceeds from personal income taxes remain a constant in such an economic situation. Researchers not consider the flat income tax to be a reliable means of limiting "gray economy", because it helps with the declaration and taxation of the actual income of those taxpayers who usually hide just some of it. However, it can't motivate income that is entirely hidden "to come to light." The application of a flat personal income tax may not be seen as a prime cause of income inequality occurrence, but there are sufficient grounds to assume that it is intensified by the said tax with all negative consequences arisen there from, such as intensified poverty and higher risk of social exclusion. As an argument in favor of proportional income taxation (the flat tax), the researchers usually point out that justice in taxation may be achieved not only through the revenue system of public finance but also through the system of government expenditure, which deforms the incentives for labor and economic growth less. Researchers should take into account in that relation that excessively low tax rates, typical of the flat tax system, give no opportunity to accumulate sufficient funds for funding public spending because the reduction of tax amounts does not lead to considerable economic growth to extend the tax base, so as to the tax revenue is compensated. Moreover, it is possible for social transfers not to be effective enough and fail in compensating the low-income groups of the population in a situation of a high level of corruption and bureaucratic systems.

The performance of the personal income taxation functions assumes implementation of effective and efficient tax and social security control. It may facilitate the minimization of offences and frauds regarding income taxes and social security contributions to the level of no threat to the state fiscal security. Such control is supposed not only to reveal any offences and determine any liabilities for taxes and social security contributions but also to form an overall control impact, including: recovery of any fiscal damage in full; imposing fines and sanctions with a prevention effect to future offences; seeking criminal responsibility in cases of frauds and income concealment; and legislation improvement in relation to income taxation and social security; creation of positive tax culture in the society facilitating the enhancement of collectability of personal income taxes and social security contributions.

REFERENCES

Adamov, V., Dimitrova, T., Nenkov, V. & Petev, M. (2013). *Tehnika na danachnoto oblagane*. Svishtov: SA "Tsenov".

Aleksieva, N. (2016). Danachnoto oblagane v stranite-chlenki na ES – spetsifichni harakteristiki, dinamika i tendentsii. *Godishen almanah "Nauchni izsledvania na doktoranti", 9*(11), 134-153.

Alesina, A., & Ardagna, S. (2010). Large changes in fiscal policy: taxes versus spending. *Tax Policy and the Economy, 24*(1), 1-37. Doi:10.3386/w15438

Angelov, G. (2016). Ploskiyat danak – kulminatsia na pragmatichni danachni reformi. In K. Hadzhinedelcheva (Ed.), *Plosak danak v Bulgaria. Predistoria, vavezhdane, rezultati* (pp. 37–48). I.P.I.

Barbier, E., & Burgess, J. (2017). *The Sustainable Development Goals and the systems approach to sustainability*. Discussion Paper. Economics. No. 2017-28.

Corneo, G. (2000). *The efficient side of progressive income taxation*. CESifo Working Paper No 364.

Cullen, J., & Gordon, R. (2002). *Taxes and entrepreneurial activity: Theory and evidence for the U.S.* NBER Working Paper No. 9015.

European Commission. (2017a). *Evropeyski semestar: Tematichen informatsionen document. Danachno oblagane*. European Commission.

European Commission. (2017b). *Evropeyski semestar: Tematichen informatsionen dokument. Preodolyavane na neravenstvata*. European Commission.

European Commission. (2019). *Taxation trends in Europe 2019*. European Commission.

European Union. (2019). *Evropeyski zelen pakt: stimuli za ikonomikata, podobryavane na zdraveto i kachestvoto na zhivot na horata*. Brussels, Belgium: European Union.

Foks, N., & Bergherm, D. (1998). *Metodi i tehniki za provezhdane na danachni revizii: Rabotna sreshta s instruktori ot Ministerstvo na finansite na SASht*. MF GUDA.

Galabov, N. (2009). Ploskiyat danak - teoria i praktika. *Ikonomicheska misal*, (2), 3-18.

Ganev, P. (2016). Plosak danak i tezhest varhu truda. In K. Hadzhinedelcheva (Ed.), *Plosak danak v Bulgaria. Predistoria, vavezhdane, rezultati* (pp. 73–83). I.P.I.

Hazans, M. (2011). *What explains prevalence of informal employment in European countries: The role of labor institutions, governance, immigrants and growth*. WB Working Paper No 5917.

Hiç, Ö. (2019). Evolution of New Keynesian Economics. *Procedia Computer Science, 158*(1), 1025-1032. Doi:10.1016/j.procs.2019.09.144

Hristoskov, Y. (2010). Ploskiyat danak (mitove i realnosti). *Ikonomicheski alternativi*, (5), 55-56.

Hristov, V. (2014). Danachna politika i danachni tendentsii v ES. *Nauchni trudove*, (14), 22-33.

Hristov, S. (2013). *Neravenstvoto v Bulgaria - dinamika, sravnitelen analiz i prichini*. Sofia: I.P.I.

Iliev, K. (2013). Danachno-osiguritelnata tezhest varhu truda i neformalnata zaetost v Bulgaria. In H. Blagoycheva (Ed.), Finansi i ustoychivo razvitie (pp. 62-70). Varna: Nauka i ikonomika.

James, S., & Nobes, C. (2015). *The economics of taxation: Principles, policy, and practice*. Fiscal Publications.

Kotsev, T. (2008). Lichno podohodno oblagane. In T. Vladimirova (Ed.), *Publichni finansi* (pp. 181–200). Steno.

Krugman, P. (2008, November 14). Depression Economics Returns. *New York Times*. Retrieved from www.nytimes.com/2008/11/14/opinion/14krugman.html

Mavrov, H. (2017). Dohodnoto neravenstvo, choveshki kapital i ikonomicheskia rastezh. In IPS: Sbornik s dokladi ot VIII mezhdunarodna nauchna konferentsia (pp. 269-274). Varna: Nauka i ikonomika.

Mishkin, F. (2009). Is Monetary Policy Effective during Financial Crises? *The American Economic Review*, *99*(2), 573–577. doi:10.1257/aer.99.2.573

Moffatt, I. (2000). Ecological footprints and sustainable development. *Ecological Economics, 32*(1) 359-362.

Nikolova, D. (2016). Plosak danak varhu dohodite i danachni prihodi. In K. Hadzhinedelcheva (Ed.), *Plosak danak v Bulgaria. Predistoria, vavezhdane, rezultati* (pp. 63–72). I.P.I.

Ninov, D. (2014). Kakav e i kakav tryabva da bade razmerat na minimalnata rabotna zaplata (MRZ) u nas sled vavezhdaneto na ploskia danak i premahvaneto na neoblagaemia minimum. *Sotsiologia i ikonomika*, (1), 43-54.

Pardee, G., & Pardee, H. (2020). Keynesian economics: Can it return if it never died? *Review of Keynesian Economics, Edward Elgar Publishing*, *8*(1), 23–35. doi:10.4337/roke.2020.01.03

Pashev, K. (2006). *Danachna politika i administratsia: Teoria i praktika*. Sofia: Univ. izd. "Sv. Kliment Ohridski".

Pedersen, P., & Smith, N. (2001). *Unemployment traps: Do financial dis-incentives matter?* IZA Discussion Paper No. 274.

Sedlarski, T. (2016). The 'Keynesian Revolution' in the History of Economic Thought. *Yearbook of St Kliment Ohridski University of Sofia*, *14*(1), 217–234.

Soldatos, G. (2016). The Laffer Curve, Efficiency, and Tax Policy: A Note. *Review of Economics*, *67*(3), 255–262. doi:10.1515/roe-2016-0006

Staykov, K. (2016). Plosak danak i korporativno oblagane. In K. Hadzhinedelcheva (Ed.), *Plosak danak v Bulgaria. Predistoria, vavezhdane, rezultati* (pp. 49–62). I.P.I.

Stiglitz, J. (2012). *The price of inequality: How today's divided society endangers our future*. W.W. Norton & Company.

Tsenova, L. (2020, February 20). *Kakvo predstavlyava sistemata na ploskia danak*. IK "Trud i pravo". Retrieved from http://trudipravo.bg/component/content/article?id=117

Vladimirov, V. (2011). *Fiskalna politika i makroikonomicheska stabilizatsia*. Steno.

Vladimirov, V. (2015). Alternativna politika za rastezh na ikonomikata. In IPS: Sbornik s dokladi ot mezhdunarodna nauchna konferentsia (pp. 29-35). Varna: Nauka i ikonomika.

Vlahov, I. (2007). Narachnik za izvarshvane na proverki i revizii na fizicheski litsa. Sofia: NAP.

ADDITIONAL READING

Bordo, M., & Rockoff, H. (2011). The Influence of Irving Fisher on Milton Friedman's Monetary Economics. NBER Working Paper No. 17267, 1-56. Doi:10.1017/S1053837213000047

Carroll, H.-E. Rider & Rosen. (2000). Personal Income Taxes and the Growth of Small Firms. NBER Working Paper No. 7980. Doi:10.3386/w7980

Fitoussi, J. & Stiglitz, J. (2009). The Ways Out of the Crisis and the Building of a More Cohesive World. OFCE No. 2009-17, 1-14.

Laidler, D. (2012). Milton Friedman's Contributions to Macroeconomics and their Influence. EPRI Working Paper No. 2012-2, 11-16.

Larsson, M., & Hanberger, A. (2015). Effects on sustainable development from large environmental programmes: A review of 16 evaluations. *Journal of Integrative Environmental Sciences*, *12*(2), 85–105. doi:10.1080/1943815X.2014.1001857

Sari-Aksakal, B. (2019). World Bank and Keynesian economics. *Business and Economics Research Journal, 10*(1), 77–94. doi:10.20409/berj.2019.156

Soubbotin, T. (2004). *Beyond Economic Growth: an Introduction to Sustainable Development*. The World Bank. doi:10.1596/0-8213-5933-9

Westley, C., Anderson, W., & Kjar, S. (2011). War and the Austrian School: Ludwig von Mises and Friedrich von Hayek. *The Economics of Peace and Security Journal, 6*(1), 28–33. doi:10.15355/epsj.6.1.28

KEY TERMS AND DEFINITIONS

Gini Coefficient: An economic indicator describing the difference between the income and welfare of the poor and the rich in the society. The "0" value shows a full equal standing, and the "1" value shows absolute lack of equal standing.

Gray (Informal) Economy: Market production of goods and services, whether legal or illegal, which is not included in the official statistics for GDP calculation.

"Laffer's Type" Effects: With a tax burden increase, the state revenue grows but to a certain point, and then any additional tax rate rise leads to a revenue reduction.

Public Goods: Accessible to anyone. Examples include the national security and defense, jurisdiction, state governance, education and scientific research, health care, social security, and infrastructure.

Social Justice: Solidarity in meeting risks and equality of opportunity, which can be achieved through the redistribution of income in a market economy, respect for human rights and the dignity of every individual in a democratic society.

Sustainable Development: Development satisfying the necessities of the present without taking away the chance of future generations to meet their own needs.

Tax Compliance: Voluntary compliance with the tax legislation measured by three indicators: filing a return (filing compliance), equivalence between the amount declared and the amount actually due (reporting compliance), and payments of any liabilities declared (payment compliance).

Tax Fraud: Multiple, systematic, or intentional violation of the tax law in which a taxpayer has made an intentional attempt to reduce the due amount of his tax following a plan contemplated in advance.

Tax Wedge: Any taxes and social security contributions on labor as a share in the labor costs.

Unemployment Trap: This arise in the case of generous benefits and assistance programs for the unemployed, on the one hand, and heavy taxation for the low-paid, on the other. In these cases, there is very little difference between income from work and income of the unemployed, which reduces the motivation to participate in the labor market.

Wagner Law: Public spending increases faster than the national production growth.

Chapter 9
Robots and Economics:
It Is More Complex Than It Seems

Josipa Višić
Faculty of Economics, Business and Tourism, University of Split, Croatia

ABSTRACT

Robotization will eventually transform the nature of doing business and economics in general. Therefore, the aim of this chapter is to provide a broader perspective on economic repercussions of robotization covering both microeconomic and macroeconomic aspects as well as other closely related sociological aspects. This broad perspective is needed for researchers, policy makers, as well as managers while contemplating changes as stirring as robotization. Further, the chapter deals with the issue of education of future economists in the context of robotization. In that sense, it emphasizes the need to make future economists more flexible, observant, and consequently, more efficient, regardless of their position on labor market. In that sense, the chapter serves as an alarm since existent (economic) lag between countries may become even bigger if it is not addresses in a timely manner.

INTRODUCTION

High pressure on productivity is surely an important factor for increasing investments in technological progress, especially investments in robotization and artificial intelligence (AI). Significant financial resources are being invested and robotics market is expanding rapidly. For instance, market size of the entire Japanese robot industry will reach 80 billion euros by 2035, of which service robots are projected to account for about half or 40 billion euros (Nitto, Taniyama, & Inagaki, 2017). More and more people use or are exposed to robots in various situations. In addition, augmented reality, artificial intelligence and technological singularity are no longer themes reserved only for science fiction movies. Therefore, it became common, a cliché even to discuss rapid technological changes and impact of robotization on labor market. There are many studies on possible impacts of robotization and AI on labor market and

DOI: 10.4018/978-1-7998-4933-9.ch009

there is a growing trend of research on human/worker – robot interaction. Further, analysis of robot market shows country-by-country differences in robotics development trends and differences in attitudes and acceptance of robots as well. In general, number of scientific studies dealing with different aspects and effects of technological progress is increasing.

Regardless of one's opinion on technological progress, it will transform the nature of doing business, labor market and economics in general and it will bring new life style and consequently various sociological side effects. The pace and depth of these changes is yet to be seen but traditional divide of sciences and consequently policy and educational programs might become outdated. One may find ideas like new doctrine on Space Economy (Dirican, 2015) a Luddite perspective and just go with the flow since somehow the economy has always adjusted and somehow in the future it always will (Allen, 2017). Others might overestimate the pace and influence of technological progress on business and labor market, but whatever stand one takes, existent changes cannot be ignored. In that manner, Šabanović (2010) proposes a mutual shaping of robotics and society since the public is put in the passive position of taking up technologies after they have been constructed in robotics laboratories. Further, Harari (2017) argues that AI revolution will not be a single event after which the job market and the educational system will settle into a new equilibrium. Rather, he believes it will be a cascade of ever-bigger disruptions.

Having all stated in mind, the aim of this chapter is to raise questions about the need to overcome traditional divide of humanities/social sciences and the natural/design sciences while both analyzing robotization and educating future employees and employers, with the accent on educating future economists. Next generation will need to cope with all consequences of technological progress, especially regarding robotization and AI. Although it is hard to precisely estimate when these changes will occur, it is almost certain that new generation of economists will eventually face them during their professional life. In other words, this chapter adds to the field in several ways. It addresses various issues that robotization and technological change bring out in economy, observed both from a microeconomic and macroeconomic perspective. This broad perspective is a novelty and is needed while contemplating changes as stirring as robotization. Further, chapter emphasizes the need to adjust education of future economists in context of diversified changes caused by robotization, which is, to the author's best knowledge, a completely new issue on both scientific and policy decision level. This issue is also connected to possible additional development problems in less developed countries if changes in education do not follow technological progress. Presented implications of robotization are a framework that should be broadened over time to include all aspects of economy and society that will change in the future due to technological progress and hopefully will add to the field observed from researchers', policy makers', managers' and educators' perspective.

Microeconomic Aspects of Robotization

There are multiple microeconomic implications of robotization that we should be aware of and some of them are obvious but some of them are not so direct. In that manner, this section addresses different aspects of robotization that are related either to a company or to an individual.

Increased use of robots and AI changes production in obvious manner. Robots are at the same time both inputs and outputs in a production process. Looking it from the input perspective, robots are utilized to perform tasks faster, more precisely, cheaper and often to do things that humans are not capable of doing, or it is just too dangerous for them to do it. Further, while thinking about too dangerous tasks form humans one must think beyond activities such as mine clearance since robots can be used in medicine when it is unsafe for nurses and doctors to have a direct contact with patients.1 Among these advantages, which are often mentioned when advocating for robots, Ivanov and Webster (2017) make an interesting point by emphasizing that unlike human employees who get bored by tedious, repetitive and intellectually unchallenging tasks, robots can entail long hours and unsafe/unhygienic conditions. Further, robots could possibly take over a range of tasks which require a lot of effort from humans (with negative health effects), do not correspond to the human diurnal rhythm (night work) or exceed the capabilities of old, sick and disabled people (Decker, Fisher, & Ott, 2017). Technological progress also enhances quality of products/services, sometimes making them safer to use since human error is now out of the equation.2 Companies that harness advantages of more efficient production may gain competitive advantage and if they recognize both the opportunities and threats of technological progress to competitiveness, they could climb the learning curves earlier rather than later (Manyika et al., 2017). Additionally, Stiglitz (2014) argues that labor-augmenting technological progress, such as robots are, reduces not only the direct labor costs, but indirect turnover (search and recruitment) costs as well. He adds to the theme by including externalities in the picture. Namely, a firm's decision to engage in robotization progress, and thus in less recruitment, imposes externalities on other market participants, both on workers (who must now search longer to find a job) and on other firms (who now may face a lower recruitment costs).

Closely related to the previous issue is an issue of using robots in production/providing services. Consequently, this raises a question of human workers being replaced with robots. This topic can be approached from different angles, and before dealing with an impact of robots on labor in terms of jobs and wages, it is important to distinguish between impact of robots on occupation and impact on activities. Almost every occupation has a partial automation potential and there are estimates that about half of all activities people are paid to do in the world's workforce could potentially be automated by adapting currently demonstrated technologies (Manyika et al., 2017). However, the pace and extent of technological progress, and thus its impact on workers, will vary across different occupations, wages and skill levels. It is on both on managers and workers to estimate to what extent robotization will affect a certain job. As Decker et al. (2017) stated, today the robot is increasingly able to perform not only manual and routine tasks but also non routine manual and cognitive tasks so areas of application for robots have expanded and they can be used to substitute even more job profiles than before and might help mitigate shortages within the labor market. Due to their capabilities, robots also increasingly act as collaborators of human labor, which means that robots do not necessarily substitute human labor, but complement it and, in specific areas, make it even more productive. Exactly this issue of robots working with or instead of humans is important to perceive before making conclusions on the impact of robots on human workers.

Use of robots in production means that workers need to be trained to use these robots. This is an important issue for managers while deciding on employment policy. It is necessary to assess what works the best - to fire old workers whose skills and knowledge are no longer sufficient, to employ new employees with suitable qualifications, to train existing workers, or all stated. Beside the need to train employees to use robots, there are other aspects of worker-robot interaction (WRI), which need to be addressed. Moniz and Krings (2016) gave an overview of changes related to research on both WRI and human-robot interaction in general. They showed how analyses of social dimensions derived from WRI firstly covered issues of industry safety, control systems and interface ergonomics and during time evolved to reflect on the interrelationship of robots with humans at work, its organizational models and underlying managerial strategies3. In other words, it became obvious that mangers will need to spend more time and effort thinking about multiple implications of using robots in order to handle limitations and interdependence of both, technology and human workers. Further, technological progress will require more resources spent on training and educating employees, dealing with how they feel while working with robots, referring to quality of working conditions, and finding ways how to increase creativity in work process.

Having in mind all implications of robot use in a production process, a final decision on adopting this sort of technical progress should be made after a cost-benefit analysis. Like any other investment, using robots as inputs causes costs, both direct and indirect. Ivanov and Webster (2017) offered a decision framework for travel, tourism and hospitality companies when deciding on adoption of robots, AI and service automation (RAISA). Although their work focused on these specific industries, it provides a solid starting point for any company thinking about the use of RAISA since they provided a list of both benefits and costs, observed from a financial and non-financial perspective. Additionally, they offered a list of various factors to check whether adoption of RAISA is beneficial to the company as well as advice on activities that companies need to undertake if they decide to use it. Many companies4 already use RAISA, and there are leading industries in annual installations of industrial robots (automotive, electrical/electronics, metal and machinery, plastic and chemical products and food industry)5 but there is no universal approach and each company should decide on technological improvements based on its specific situation.6 However, industries where human contact with clients and atmosphere while consuming a product/service is one of their key features should avoid it.7 In other words, robotization will provide significant opportunities for companies to capture value, but it will heighten competition. Therefore, companies need to pay a close attention to monitoring and evaluating effectiveness and efficiency of robot adoption. In that sense, measuring productivity as well needs to be adjusted to technological progress. Namely, development of artificial intelligence and its increased use in production will inevitably change the way we analyze productivity.

As well as when robots are inputs, robots as outputs raise many issues. Deciding on what to produce, or what kind of service to offer, requires a great deal of knowledge and ability to predict consumers' needs and preferences. For instance, there is an increasing market of nursing care robots developing fast since population is aging fast in high-income economies as Japan. This fact should be observed along with the fact that a personal nursing robot keeps an individual's integrity untainted since a person can take care of him/her self with the help of a nursing care robot. However, success of these products in Japan is not a random guess of robot producing companies8. Attitude toward robots is one of the major factors determining the success or failure of social robots that are expected to occupy our homes, offices, hospitals and schools, and culture is an important factor that affects these attitudes (Yasser & Toyoaki 2015). Bartneck et al. (2005) noticed that different cultures have a different exposure to robots through media or through personal experience. For instance, because of the popularity of games and robot anime, Japanese consumers feel greater familiarity with robots then US and European consumers, and tend to define a robot as a partner having a human-like shape and living with humans (Nitto et al., 2017). At the same time, it seems that Japanese people are concerned with the impact that robots might have on society since through the high exposure to robots, Japanese are more aware of robots' abilities and also their lack of abilities (Bartneck et al., 2005). Further, differences in attitudes toward robots among cultures might depend on the type of a respective robot. For example, in Germany consumers show a strong tendency to consider robots for industrial purposes and unlike in US feel strong resistance to the presence of robots in their households (Nitto et al., 2017)9.

Perceiving differences among consumers due to their cultural and demographical differences, as well as understanding certain aspects of psychology has always been crucial for economists. For example, along with issues arising from WRI, managers should not neglect various psychological aspects of developing a new product, a robot in this case. One possible aspect of economic implication of psychology is presented in example of raising Japanese market for personal nursing robots since it is a good example of well-detected consumers' needs and their willingness to adapt to a technological solution for their problems. Although there are significant differences among consumers' preferences, when it comes to attitudes of consumers to robots and their willingness to use them10, playing the right emotional card might overcome initial problems while expanding the market. For instance, personal nursing robots might overcome limitations in more traditional markets when it comes to taking care of elderly. At the same time they satisfy the urge (often imposed by culture and tradition) to keep elderly family members in respective household and meet all the needs of hectic everyday life with less and less time available for taking care of someone. Another aspect should be taken into account while making a decision about pouring huge amount of money in developing a new product/robot since it might not be well adopted by users. In that manner, Nitto et al. (2017) presented several studies that came to conclusion that as the appearance of robots moves from mechanical to human-like, their likeability increases. However, fifty years ago (in 1970) Japanese roboticist Masahiro Mori introduced a concept known as the "uncanny valley". This theory explains a paradox, which appears when robots reach a certain point where they look too human-like, to the extent that they evoke a sense of revulsion in most human beings (Nitto et al., 2017)11. Along with other differences among consumers' attitudes on robots, this phenomenon should also be addressed while developing a new robot12. Šabanović (2010) offered a possible solution to overcome problems arising from different attitudes toward robots. She proposed a mutual shaping of robots and society, i.e. moving a focus from dealing with how to adapt to technology to how to shape it. In other words, she recognized the importance of including potential users in the process of designing so that robotic technologies become more socially robust, rather than merely acceptable.

Analyzing robots as inputs or outputs obviously has multiple implications varying from issues that producers should tackle with, over those important to customers to those important for a whole society. Here presented themes are not all possible microeconomic repercussions of robotization. Just to get the idea how this story about robots could evolve even more, imagine if advanced concept of robots as future consumers, provided by Ivanov and Webster (2017), becomes a reality at a certain point in the future.

Macroeconomic Aspects of Robotization

Macroeconomic perspective of robotization is as complex as microeconomic and there are several issues that are going to be mentioned here. However, after dealing with pure macroeconomic implications of robotization, a few issues regarding robots that have manifold social implications will be address as well.

One of the obvious macroeconomic facts that should not be neglected is the robot market size. Even if we do not believe that technological progress will soon make robots a part of our everyday lives, financial numbers behind this industry force us to rethink that standpoint. On a global level, size of the market for industrial and non-industrial robots in 2017 was 39,3 billion US dollars, while the same source (Statista – The portal for statistics, 2019) provides an estimate for 2025 high as 498,6 billion US dollars. In other words, there are numerous data on different segments of robot market size and all of them make dilemmas about the economic significance of robots obsolete.

Inseparable from the robot market size is the issue of the impact of robotization on productivity and consequently on labor employment and wages. Unlike when it comes to employment, estimates regarding productivity are generally more positive. For instance, Muro and Scott (2015) made a parallel with Robert Solow's analysis of the impact of information technology on the economy, which at first did not show computer age in the productivity statistics. They build their case on Graetz and Michaels (2018) research that showed that the use of robots within manufacturing raised the annual growth of labor productivity and GDP by 0.36 and 0.37 percentage points, respectively, between 1993 and 2007. These numbers might not seem like a lot but it represents 10% of total GDP growth in the countries studied and 16% of labor productivity growth over that period13. However, when it comes to jobs, increased robot use raises many eyebrows since robots engaged in different chores replace many activities done by humans. As stated earlier, robots can make certain things better, faster, safer and cheaper than humans can, so in order to boost productivity, and consequently competitiveness, companies employ them. There is ongoing debate whether robots' productivity impacts are resulting in job losses. In that context, attitudes on impact of robots range from positive, in terms of liberating humans of manual labor and providing new business opportunities, to fear of making humans obsolete when society is fully robotised. Sachs and Kotlikoff (2012) go even further with dark forecast, stating that advances in machine productivity can indeed immiserate today's young and future generations. As many others, they believe that the income gap between skilled and unskilled workers will raise, but they also emphasize a generational effect. More precisely, raising the income of the older generation while lowering the income of the young will occur because the old have accumulated physical and human capital, while the young, initially unskilled workers, encounter an economy with less human and physical capital, which further drives down their wages.

Although it is hard to estimate precisely the impact of robots on number of available jobs, it is rational to expect the strongest influence in low-skilled and middle-skill jobs. However, Autor (2015) offers a more positive perspective by arguing that many of the middle-skill jobs, that will persist in the future, will combine routine technical tasks with the set of non-routine tasks in which workers hold comparative advantage: interpersonal interaction, adaptability, and problem solving. Therefore, his forecast on number of available jobs is optimistic, since many of the tasks currently bundled into these middle-skill jobs cannot easily be unbundled (with machines performing the middle-skill tasks and workers performing only low-skill residua) without a substantial drop in quality. Those advocating for robots argue that robotization does not lead to job loses, but rather to re-allocation of both jobs and tasks in which robots complement and augment human labor by performing routine and dangerous tasks (International Federation of Robotics, 2017)14. However, a more realistic estimate will probably confirm Graetz and Michaels (2018) findings that there is no significant relationship between the increased use of industrial robots and overall employment, although robots may be reducing the employment of low-skilled workers.

At first, it might seem simple – robots will increase productivity, which will result in more available jobs and higher wages. However, Allen (2017) makes a strong point by emphasizing the fact that the "future of work" significantly depends on where you are in the world. Hence, it is necessary to investigate the effect of technological change on work and production everywhere. Some argue that robots will not cause excessive labor supply due to aging of the world's population, but economies around the world are not uniform. Therefore, macroeconomic repercussions of robotization must be analyzed cautiously. An interesting point is made in Manyika et al. (2017), in which they argue that automation15 could boost productivity and help close the economic gap in the 20 largest economies by 2030. However, they distinguish three16 groups of countries depending on their demographic trends and growth inspirations. Evidently, automation or more precisely robotization, may offer different possibilities depending on country's economic strength and population age. As expected, paper by International Federation of Robotics (The Impact of Robots on Productivity, Employment and Jobs 2017) presented additional, possible positive impact of robots on countries' economies due to lower cost of production. They argue that automation could encourage companies to move their manufacturing closer to home and consolidate production, which will cause positive spillovers in other sectors and consequently will increase national competitiveness. Altogether, it is too soon to make a general conclusion about robots' impact, but Jimeno (2019) provided a suitable theoretical framework by emphasizing three effects of technological change: 1) displacement effect that decreases labor demand as human is replaced by machines, 2) productivity effect generated by the cost-reducing consequences of new technologies and 3) reinstatement effect referring to the creation of new tasks and new goods and services that require human labor. Time will show which effect prevailed in which country/economic region.

It is still impossible to estimate precisely the strength and impact of robots on different aspects of world economy, but there is a legitimate concern that economic inequality might increase. DeCanio (2016) focuses on jobs and wages and believes that expansion of AI capabilities is likely to depress wages over time, unless returns to robotic assets are broadly spread across population. Additional problem of inequality may arise among countries due to difference in their economic strength and ability to cope with technological progress. In other words, poor countries might become even poorer if they do not manage to catch up with all economic changes caused by robotization. However, this possible threat may be seen as an opportunity to narrow the gap between developed and developing countries. In that sense, Dias, Mills-Tettey, and Nanayakkara (2005) explored directions in which research and education in robotics and other advanced technology fields can benefit developing communities around the world. They see an innovative technology, and related higher educational initiatives between developed and developing countries, as a necessary tool for the empowerment of developing communities17. Further, for economists it is important to perceive possible applications of robots in not so obvious segments of economy as well. Closely related to previously mentioned differences between geographical areas, another possibility also offers a way to overcome some of the problems of less developed countries. For instance, there are areas in large numbers of countries that lack quality teachers due to money issues and/or undesirability of these areas for teachers to move there. Distant learning devices might, at least partially, solve this problem and even if one argues that this is not an economic issue, it surely has economic repercussions for respective country's economy and development.

When it comes to issue of inequality caused by robotization, some authors argue for taxation that will redistribute returns to robotic assets. Sachs and Kotlikoff (2012) believe that with the right choice of tax-and-transfer policies, all generations of workers can benefit from the advances in technology, while under laissez faire, only today's older generation benefits, and at the expense of all other generations. DeCanio (2016) however, believes that large-scale taxation and redistribution schemes would have adverse effects on effort and innovation. In other words, making one thing right might mess up the other. Further, taxation and redistribution schemes would strengthen government power to the point where economic outcomes would essentially be determined by the political process. Regrettably, when it comes to political decisions, it is almost a rule, rather than exception, that immediate results often get high priority while programs that project benefits in the long term are often considered less desirable.

Another interesting aspect of the impact of robotics on jobs and productivity is the fear of broader geopolitical and social shifts driven by issues such as trade policy and immigration that, overall, contribute to a sense of insecurity about the employment prospects of current and future workers (International Federation of Robotics, 2017). In other words, if robots cause significant changes in the labor market it may cause multiple economic, social and political consequences. Therefore, macroeconomists, as well as microeconomists, need to balance between possible positive and negative consequences of robotization.

Other Closely Related Sociological Aspects of Robotization

It might seem a bit off the topic to talk about social and ethical dimension of robotization, but economic effects of these radical changes in society should not be neglected. Technological progress changes the way we work and how we live our lives, and change is stressful (Harari, 2017). Therefore, once again, psychology confirms its importance. Aside from an altruistic point of view, taking care of mental health is an important economic issue due to its various implications on a both microeconomic and macroeconomic level18. Today it is difficult to estimate the speed and the depth of changes in society due to technological progress. Therefore, education of the future should also include development of mental flexibility along with development of critical and creative thinking. In a volatile economic environment, creative thinking is one of the factors that help individuals, companies and consequently countries to be ahead of all others. However, there is a decline in creative thinking that needs to be reversed (Kim, 2011).

Closely related to issue of creative thinking is STEM (science, technology, engineering and mathematics) movement in education. From an economic point of view, it is interesting to see how some countries are pouring huge amounts of money on STEM education. This might seem a bit short-sighted since human psychology, in terms of need to nurture creative thinking, might be a key hurdle to future technological changes. In that manner, some countries/institutions are trying to better integrate scientific thinking and the humanities by moving from STEM to STEAM (science, technology, engineering, arts and mathematics) (Cunha, 2016). This might be a good starting point to overcome possible problems, which may occur in the future if a technological progress is not followed by corresponding progress in other aspects of economy and society as a whole19. In other words, thinking about STEM, STEAM or any other concept referring to education, has significant macroeconomic implications since technologically challenged countries might lag behind even more if they do not address these issues in a timely manner.

Regarding possible impact of robots on jobs in the context of education, Harari (2017) makes an interesting point by saying that creating new jobs might prove easier than retraining people to fill them. Further, he believes that a huge useless class might appear, owing to both an absolute lack of jobs and a lack of relevant education and mental flexibility. Therefore, future human capital investment or education system at a national level must be at the heart of any long-term strategy for producing skills that are complemented rather than substituted by technological change (Autor, 2015). Thus, along with previously mentioned mental flexibility and critical and creative thinking, educational system and employees themselves, should strive to develop capabilities that are among the most difficult to automate, including creativity, understanding human emotions, managing and coaching others (Manyika et al., 2017). However, even if a majority of employees manage to cope with technological progress, there will always be a certain portion of population struggling if automation results in labor displacement. Beyond direct economic consequences of disequilibrium on a labor market, social aspects of technological progress are also important. In other words, significant changes on a labor market, caused by robotization and technological progress, have complex indirect economic implications. Having a large portion of unemployed population, due to incompatibility of their skills with the needs of existing/future jobs, calls for their retraining and changes in the educational system. However, retraining workers might take some time; meanwhile they might be out of work. In that manner, labor redeployment will be one of the most important societal challenges. It is not realistic to expect that technological change will suddenly put significant number of employees out of work, but economists should learn from the past when it comes to industrial revolutions20. Safety nets, providing social support to workers as they transition from one set of activities to another, might help employees to adjust to new age in the labor market.

Beyond these direct and indirect economic effects of robotization and technological changes, an economist must perceive that how people feel about their job, or the lack of it, reflects on every aspect of their lives. Having workers feel inadequate to adopt to changes becomes a complex issue whether you observe it strictly from an economic point of view in form of their lower productivity or with more feelings for general well-being of a population and worrying how their quality of lives decreased. This leads to another implication of robotization.

Technical progress, in terms of development of AI and robotics, also has an ethical dimension with economic implications. Question of ethics in economy is an old issue, and it is hard to find a conclusion since it is a philosophical question with more than one right answer. However, now it is possible to add some questions. Bossmann (2016) addressed several ethical issues in artificial intelligence and security is one of them. Proponents emphasize benefits of robots in production due to their greater efficiency; in services, they emphasize benefits on quality of life for robot users etc. However, a powerful technology can also be used for malicious purposes. For instance, producing robots to replace human soldiers, or producing autonomous weapons has a clear economic justification and at the same time, a strong ethical dilemma arises21. How do robots affect our behavior and interaction is another ethical question with both microeconomic and macroeconomic implications, beside those that are non-economic. Issue of privacy in the context of technological progress is not new, yet now it becomes even more important since development of AI and robots enables collecting all kinds of data on individuals rather easy.

In general, macroeconomists should be able to perceive opportunities provided by robotization and technological progress in a timely manner. At the same time, it is necessary to detect both direct and indirect effects of these changes since they might burden or slow down economic progress.

COULD FUTURE ECONOMISTS BRIDGE MICROECONOMICS AND MACROECONOMICS?

Beside the need to implement some degree of technical knowledge in education in general, education of economists is extremely important since today we are educating future decision makers in companies and governments. It is not about educating them about robots; it is about preparing them to be able to anticipate technological, economic and sociological changes so they can make rational decisions for themselves and for society as well. Future decision makers should be aware of unbreakable link between micro and macroeconomic decisions. Issue of anxiety related to increased usage of technology in private and business life can be used as an example. Usually technological improvements are implemented in companies in order to bring financial benefits and market advantage but quick changes and need to adopt fast sometimes cause employees to feel anxious. At first it seems like something not quite related to economics but it is as it affects employees' productivity and their productivity is strongly related to company's profitability. This impact goes further on macroeconomic level since companies pay taxes related to their profit level so less profit means less income from taxes i.e. less money in government funds used to cover all sorts of spending including health system that treats patients with anxiety as well. Another simplified example related to robotization might also show how complex is this connection between microeconomic and macroeconomic implications of a certain economic decision. If a country keeps its economy healthy, encouraging technological progress and invests significant amount of money in science by financing basic (fundamental) research, that country will be able to exploit its long term investment in a situation when it is dealing with global health problems. More precisely, respective country will have domestic companies and workers able to produce necessary medicine equipment. Consequently, since it will more easily adapt to health crises its economy will suffer less, companies will be able to earn profit, pay salaries and eventually companies and citizens will again fill up government's funds.

These two examples show how complex is the decision to invest in robots on both micro and macroeconomic level. On one side robots might cause different problems ranging from unemployment, psychological problems to negative sociological changes but at the same time they increase productivity, save lives doing dangerous tasks, help and entertain people. Therefore, (future) economists should be able to perceive how complex their decisions will be especially if we take into consideration pace of technological changes. In other words, like with any other decision, when it comes to robots cost-benefit analysis is necessary, especially when both sides of the coin are getting more complicated over time.22 Hence, it would be useful if future economists gain some knowledge on economic implications of robotization.23 This is especially important for future economists in countries that are not leaders in technological development, but should at least try to do their best while keeping up with changes in world economy. Namely, existing gap between countries might become even bigger if future economic changes in form of robotization and its repercussions are not at least perceived, if not adequately responded to. In that sense, education of economists becomes even more important and makes the story about economic implications of robotization even more complex.

FUTURE RESEARCH DIRECTIONS

Study limitations of this chapter will be addressed in future work on the issue and will include more detailed analysis of microeconomic and macroeconomic aspects of robotization significant for policy makers and managers. Additionally, more extensive research will be directed toward analysis of countries' economic characteristics related to: a) its technological progress and b) future economists' attitudes on robotization.

CONCLUSION

Robotization and related subjects cover manifold, complex issues ranging from clearly microeconomic and macroeconomic to those issues where lines between scientific fields are a bit blurry. It might seem perfunctory how these issues are covered in the chapter, but the idea was not to present all economic implications of robotization, yet to provide a frame for researchers, policy makers, managers and educators to develop as technological progress continues to change the world we live in. Further, additional aim of this chapter was to emphasize the importance of education of future economists. They should be able to perceive microeconomic and macroeconomic implications of their professional decisions, hopefully having both economic and noneconomic benefits in focus. Namely, impact of technology i.e. robots on each segment of our lives is rising so the need to broaden economists' mind-sets gets more and more important. Global economy and society is changing but cannot grow and develop if (future) decision makers are not educated to deal with the future. In that manner, researchers of economic aspects of robotization need to widen their perspective while policy makers and managers should consult results obtained from this growing field of study. Educators of future economists, on the other hand, should try to make them more flexible, observant and consequently more efficient, regardless of their position on labor market. It is easy to perceive obvious implications of any process, as well as when it comes to robotization, but those indirect and sometimes hard to perceive impacts have their economic and social consequences as well. Therefore, it is up to all stakeholders to provide a good starting point necessary to keep up with current changes and changes that are yet to come.

REFERENCES

Allen, R. C. (2017). Lessons from history for the future of work. *Nature*, *550*(7676), 321–324. doi:10.1038/550321a PMID:29052648

Autor, D. (2015). Why Are There Still So Many Jobs? The History and Future of Workplace Automation. *The Journal of Economic Perspectives*, *29*(3), 3–30. doi:10.1257/jep.29.3.3

Bartneck, C., Nomura, T., Kanda, T., Suzuki, T., & Kennsuke, K. (2005). Cultural Differences in Attitudes Towards Robots. In *Proceedings of the AISB Symposium on Robot Companions: Hard Problems And Open Challenges In Human-Robot Interaction* (pp. 1-4). Hatfield: Academic Press.

Bossmann, J. (2016). *Top 9 ethical issues in artificial intelligence*. World Economic Forum. Retrieved from https://www.weforum.org/agenda/2016/10/top-10-ethical-issues-in-artificial-intelligence/

Companies already replacing humans with robots. (2019). Retrieved from https://www.lovemoney.com/gallerylist/61607/companies-already-replacing-humans-with-robots

Crowe, S. (2019). *Top 5 countries using industrial robots in 2018*. Retrieved from https://www.therobotreport.com/top-5-countries-using-industrial-robots-2018/

Cunha, D. (2016). *The educational strategy that's turning students into unimaginative robots*. Retrieved from https://qz.com/605452/the-educational-strategy-thats-turning-students-into-unimaginative-robots/

Danaher, J., & McArthur, N. (Eds.). (2017). *Robot Sex: Social and Ethical Implications*. The MIT Press. doi:10.7551/mitpress/9780262036689.001.0001

DeCanio, S. J. (2016). Robots and humans–complements or substitutes? *Journal of Macroeconomics*, *49*, 280–291. doi:10.1016/j.jmacro.2016.08.003

Decker, M., Fischer, M., & Ott, I. (2017). Service Robotics and Human Labor: A first technology assessment of substitution and cooperation. *Robotics and Autonomous Systems*, *87*, 348–354. doi:10.1016/j.robot.2016.09.017

Dias, M. B., Mills-Tettey, G. A., & Nanayakkara, T. (2005). Robotics, Education, and Sustainable Development. In *Proceedings of the 2005 IEEE International Conference on Robotics and Automation* (pp. 4248 – 4253). Barcelona, Spain: IEEE. 10.1109/ROBOT.2005.1570773

Dirican, C. (2015). The Impacts of Robotics, Artificial Intelligence On Business and Economics. *Procedia: Social and Behavioral Sciences*, *195*, 564–573. doi:10.1016/j.sbspro.2015.06.134

Graetz, G., & Michaels, G. (2018). Robots at Work. *The Review of Economics and Statistics*, *100*(5), 753–768. doi:10.1162/rest_a_00754

Harari, Y. N. (2017). Reboot for the AI revolution. *Nature, 550*(7676), 324–327. doi:10.1038/550324a PMID:29052637

Ivanov, S. H., & Webster, C. (2017). *Adoption of robots, artificial intelligence and service automation by travel, tourism*. Paper presented at International Scientific Conference Contemporary tourism – traditions and innovations, Sofia University, Sofia, Bulgaria.

Jimeno, J. F. (2019). Fewer babies and more robots: Economic growth in a new era of demographic and technological changes. *SERIEs, 10*(2), 93–114. doi:10.100713209-019-0190-z

Katz, J. E., & Halpern, D. (2014). Attitudes towards robots suitability for various jobs as affected robot appearance. *Behaviour & Information Technology, 33*(9), 941–953. doi:10.1080/0144929X.2013.783115

Kim, K. H. (2011). The Creativity Crisis: The Decrease in Creative Thinking Scores on the Torrance Tests of Creative Thinking. *Creativity Research Journal, 23*(4), 285–295. doi:10.1080/10400419.2011.627805

Manyika, J., Chui, M., Miremadi, M., Bughin, J., George, K., Willmott, P., & Dewhurst, M. (2017). *A future that works: Automation, employment, and productivity*. McKinsey Global Institute. Retrieved from https://www.mckinsey.com/~/media/mckinsey/featured%20insights/Digital%20Disruption/Harnessing%20automation%20for%20a%20future%20that%20works/MGI-A-future-that-works-Executive-summary.ashx

Mendick, H., Berge, M., & Danielsson, A. (2017). A Critique of the Stem Pipeline: Young People's Identities in Sweden and Science Education Policy. *British Journal of Educational Studies, 65*(4), 481–497. doi:10.1080/00071005.2017.1300232

Moniz, A. B., & Krings, B.-A. (2016). Robots Working with Humans or Humans Working with Robots? Searching for Social Dimensions in New Human-Robot Interaction in Industry. *Societies (Basel, Switzerland), 6*(3), 1–23. doi:10.3390oc6030023

Muro, M., & Andes, S. (2015). Robots Seem to Be Improving Productivity, Not Costing Jobs. *Harvard Business Review*. Retrieved from https://hbr.org/2015/06/robots-seem-to-be-improving-productivity-not-costing-jobs

Nitto, H., Taniyama, D., & Inagaki, H. (2017). *Social Acceptance and Impact of Robots and Artificial Intelligence – Findings of Survey in Japan, the U.S. and Germany*. NRI Papers No. 211, Nomura Research Institute. Retrieved from https://www.nri.com/-/media/Corporate/en/Files/PDF/knowledge/report/cc/papers/2017/np2017211.pdf?la=en&hash=A730998FD55F6D58DF95F3479E3B709FC8EF83F4

Over 80% of Japanese positive about robotic nursing care. (2018). Retrieved from https://www.japantimes.co.jp/news/2018/11/15/national/80-japanese-positive-robotic-nursing-care/#article_history

Šabanović, S. (2010). Robots in society, society in robots: Mutual Shaping of Society and Technology as a Framework for Social Robot Design. *International Journal of Social Robotics, 2*(4), 439–450. doi:10.100712369-010-0066-7

Sachs, J., & Kotlikoff, L. (2012). *Smart Machines and Long-Term Misery*. Working Paper No. 18629, National Bureau of Economic Research.

Schwab, K. (2019). *The Fourth Industrial Revolution*. World Economic Forum. Retrieved from https://www.weforum.org/about/the-fourth-industrial-revolution-by-klaus-schwab

Stiglitz, J. E. (2014). *Unemployment And Innovation*. Working Paper No. 20670, National Bureau Of Economic Research. Retrieved from https://www.nber.org/papers/w20670

The International Federation of Robotics. (2017). *The Impact of Robots on Productivity, Employment and Jobs*. Retrieved from https://ifr.org/img/office/IFR_The_Impact_of_Robots_on_Employment.pdf

Wagner, I. (n.d.). *Global robotics market revenue 2017/2025*. Retrieved from https://www.statista.com/statistics/760190/worldwide-robotics-market-revenue/

Yasser, M., & Toyoaki, N. (2015). Cultural Difference in Back-Imitation's Effect on the Perception of Robot's Imitative Performance. *LNAI*, *9549*, 17-32.

ADDITIONAL READING

Backonja, U., Hall, A. K., Painter, I., Kneale, L., Lazar, A., Cakmak, M., Thompson, H. J., & Demiris, G. (2018). Comfort and Attitudes Towards Robots Among Young, Middle-Aged, and Older Adults: A Cross-Sectional Study. *Journal of Nursing Scholarship*, *50*(6), 623–633. doi:10.1111/jnu.12430 PMID:30230692

Benzell, S. G., Kotlikoff, L. J., LaGarda, G., & Sachs, J. D. (2015). Robots Are Us: Some Economics of Human Replacement. NBER Working Paper No. 20941. Retrieved from https://www.nber.org/papers/w20941.pdf

Cheng, H., Jia, R., Li, D., & Li, H. (2019). The Rise of Robots in China. *The Journal of Economic Perspectives*, *33*(2), 71–88. doi:10.1257/jep.33.2.71

Chiacchio, F., Petropoulos, G., & Pichler, D. (2018). The impact of industrial robots on EU employment and wages: A local labour market approach. Retrieved from https://bruegel.org/2018/04/the-impact-of-industrial-robots-on-eu-employment-and-wages-a-local-labour-market-approach/

Gnambs, T., & Appel, M. (2019). Are robots becoming unpopular? Changes in attitudes towards autonomous robotic systems in Europe. *Computers in Human Behavior*, *93*, 53–61. doi:10.1016/j.chb.2018.11.045

Humlum, A. (2019). Robot Adoption and Labor Market Dynamics Anders. Job Market Paper. Retrieved from https://static1.squarespace.com/static/5d35e72fcff15f0001b48fc2/t/5dcf78576d59eb44eac86f63/1573877848584/humlumJMP.pdf

Ivanov, S., & Webster, C. (2019). Robots in tourism: A research agenda for tourism economics. *Tourism Economics*, 1–21. doi:10.1177/1354816619879583

Leduc, S., & Liu, Z. (2020). Robots or Workers? A Macro Analysis of Automation and Labor Markets. Federal Reserve Bank of San Francisco Working Paper 2019-17. Retrieved from https://www.frbsf.org/economic-research/files/wp2019-17.pdf

KEY TERMS AND DEFINITIONS

Artificial Intelligence: An ability of a machine to imitate cognitive functions of a human being.

Augmented Reality: A way of altering experience of observing existing objects or environment done by various technological solutions that affect person's senses.

Automation: A process which describes using technology doing tasks without the help of humans.

Economist: A person who is a professional in economic issues related to individuals, organizations, or societies.

Robot: A machine that can independently perform one or more tasks. Robots can be divided into industrial and non-industrial robots.

Robotization: A process which describes robots doing tasks without the help of humans. It has more narrow meaning than automation.

ENDNOTES

1. Covid-19 pandemic is a great example of a situation when advanced robot technology can help nurses and doctors in different activities ranging from disinfecting hospital facilities (there are UV disinfection robots) to close contact with infected patients (e.g. robot nurse can help check patients' vital signs and ease the burden on healthcare workers while telemedicine robot allows doctors to consult with patients and hospital staff remotely).
2. There are surgical robot systems like da Vinci that assist doctors during surgeries.
3. Complex issue of working with robots raises multiple questions and further analysis of this subject should include Moniz and Krings (2016) paper due to its extensive literature overview.
4. For example: DHL, Tesla, Shiseido, Amazon, Walmart etc. Cf. https://www.lovemoney.com/gallerylist/61607/companies-already-replacing-humans-with-robots
5. Cf. https://www.therobotreport.com/top-5-countries-using-industrial-robots-2018/
6. Beside the fact that it is not easy to decide whether to invest in a certain technological improvement, situation can quickly change (cf. endnote no. 20).
7. For example, same approach to robots do not apply in case of a coffee shop with a mission to quickly serve as many guests that take coffee to go on their way to work and in a case of a coffee shop with a mission to provide a certain feeling while their guests enjoy coffee drinking it in that coffee shop.
8. Orix Living Corporation conducted a survey in November 2018 that covered 1,238 people aged 40 or above across Japan and results showed that over 80 percent of people hold positive views about receiving nursing care from robots. Cf. https://www.japantimes.co.jp/news/2018/11/15/national/80-japanese-positive-robotic-nursing-care/#article_history.
9. Katz and Halpern (2014) offer another interesting dimension by listing religiosity and avatar engagement as some of the variables considered to affect attitudes toward robots. These additional variables are mentioned beside culture, just to get an idea on complexity of the respective issue.
10. Cf. Katz and Halpern (2014).
11. Beside uncanny valley, a concept of technical singularity also raises many questions since it describes a situation where artificial intelligence gains greater thinking ability than all humans have.

12 Nitto, Taniyama, and Inagaki (2017) offer a detailed insight into differences among customers by presenting results of a research conducted on Japanese, U.S. and German consumers. Further, they provide additional information on consumers in China and France.

13 The research was performed on seventeen developed countries.

14 An extensive source of information and research studies arguing pro robots can be found in International Federation of Robotics paper (The Impact of Robots on Productivity, Employment and Jobs 2017). For instance, they argue that countries with the highest robot density, notably Germany and South Korea, have among the lowest unemployment rates.

15 Automation is a more general concept than robotization but regarding this issue, same logic applies.

16 Advanced economies with aging workforce (Australia, Canada, France, Germany, Italy, Japan, South Korea, the United Kingdom, and the United States), emerging economies with aging populations (Argentina, Brazil, China and Russia) and emerging economies with younger populations (India, Indonesia, Mexico, Nigeria, Saudi Arabia, South Africa, and Turkey).

17 They also presented an interesting fact that Professor Ray Reddy, one of the pioneers in robotics and AI, more than 30 years ago perceived challenges of the poor in this context and highlighted the necessity for innovative technology that will benefit poor.

18 Bartneck et al. (2005) raised a question of the effects of robot anxiety that are still largely unknown. With an increasing number of robots, they express concern that robot anxiety might become as important as computer anxiety is today and it is needless to mention financial effects of these health problems.

19 There are many aspects of STEM education with economic implications. For example, Mendick, Berge, and Danielsson (2017) criticize STEM pipeline model and science education policy in Sweden. Although they analyze a broader context of respective theme, economic aspects of science education policy are quite important when it comes to national resources in terms of creating a solid base of experts in different fields that can boost country's economy. Therefore, economists should also put an effort to make science education more in line with the needs of an economy and society and more accessible to all students.

20 Many economists believe that we are at the breach of fourth industrial revolution. Schwab (2016) believes that this one is different in scale, scope and complexity from any that have come before. In that manner, Allen (2017) offers an interesting overview of previous social and economic upheavals in the context of the current revolution.

21 Ethical issues related to robots cover a wide range of questions, and to spice things up a bit, there are even books about robot sex ("Robot Sex - Social and Ethical Implications" 2017).

22 For instance, just few months ago a niche of small, rustic hotels would be last to implement robots helping their employees in order to keep the atmosphere authentic for guests. However, a world health crisis caused changes so drastic that an UV disinfection robot and robot receptionist now might be their only chance to keep business going. Therefore, managers will need to balance between delicate business decisions while governments balance between strict health regulations and economic problems inevitable if health restrictions continue to drastically slow down economy.

23 To the author's best knowledge there are no courses in higher education related to economic implications of robotization, yet students gather knowledge on the theme if a professor finds it important to combine it with another core subject.

Chapter 10
Investigating the Effect of Diplomatic Representation on Trade:
A Case Study of Croatia

Danijel Mlinaric
University of Zagreb, Croatia

Hrvoje Josic
https://orcid.org/0000-0002-7869-3017
University of Zagreb, Croatia

Cindy Thompson
University of Belize, Belize

ABSTRACT

Economic diplomacy is an unavoidable tool for improving economic standards, and it needs to be an important instrument for policy makers in stimulating international trade and supporting domestic firms. This chapter analyses the impact of economic diplomacy on bilateral trade flows in Croatia in the period from 1992 to 2017. The authors use an applied gravity model of trade by employing fixed effects model (FE), random effects model (RE), and pseudo Poisson maximum likelihood (PPML) estimator. PPML estimator takes into count zero trade flows because estimating zero trade flows with OLS estimator could lead to several biases. The problem of dependence between diplomacy representatives was solved by constructing individual regressions using FE model and PPML estimator. The hypothesis of the chapter, which was tested, states that diplomatic representation has had positive and significant effects on bilateral trade flows (imports and exports) of Croatia. The results of the analysis have shown that the diplomatic representation via embassies and consulates is a relevant trade and trade-enhancing factor.

DOI: 10.4018/978-1-7998-4933-9.ch010

INTRODUCTION

How important economic diplomacy representatives are for promoting trade? What is the impact of embassies and consulates on trade flows? This chapter tries to answer the aforementioned questions. Economic diplomacy can be defined as the use of government relations and government influence to stimulate international trade, Bergeijk and Moons (2011:3). Economic diplomacy is hereby directed to open markets, use bilateral relations to help domestic companies, stimulate cross border activities and boosting exports. Diplomatic relationship between can take form of state visits, Nitsch (2007), trade missions, embassies and consulates which are significant determinant of bilateral trade flows and foreign direct investment (FDI) (Rose, 2008, Head and Ries, 2010, Yakop and Bergeijk, 2011). The investigations on this important topic have been scarce so far, Mlinarić, Perić and Matejaš (2019). There are many intercorrelated activities which have impact on country development, Jošić and Mlinarić (2018) but micro and macro influence of economic diplomacy cannot neglected anyone in the world, Mlinarić, Perić and Matejaš (2019). Croatia is aware of economic diplomacy importance but still needs medium and long term strategy. Missing strategy needs to be accomplished in short run horizon and it is condition sine qua non for Croatian economic development. There is no doubt that economic diplomacy represent the utilization of all economic instruments in furtherance of the state interest when dealing with other states, multinational companies, international institutions like NGOs and other, Mlinarić (2018). The aim of this chapter is to investigate the impact of economic diplomacy on bilateral trade flows in Croatia. More specifically, we wanted to see how would the establishment of an additional embassy or consulate affect bilateral trade flows between Croatia and diplomatic trade partner countries. The analysis is conducted by employing gravity model of trade using OLS, fixed effects (FE), random effects (RE) and PPML specification, which is highly recommended in the case of zero trade flows. The contribution of the chapter can be seen in constructing the complete time series of data observed in the period from the year 1992 to 2017 which was somewhat hard to obtain. This is improvement in regards to the most of other comparable studies on effects of economic diplomacy on trade where data were organised and structured in a 5-year intervals (for example Correlates of the war database, Bayer 2006) or only for one or few chosen years. Economic diplomacy is represented by foreign missions (embassies and consulates) for Croatia. The hypothesis is a positive interdependence between economic diplomacy and bilateral trade flows, which is in line with previous studies in this field. There are also cultural issues of diplomacy due to the Croatian tradition. This is because Croatia import-export evaluation is very close to political strategies, often criticized with the absence of clearly stated export policies and national economic weaknesses. Cultural effects will not be a part of this research.

Chapter is structured in six chapters. After the introduction, second chapter elaborates on and presents an overview of studies related to the impact of economic diplomacy representatives on trade. In the third chapter the facts about the historical background and establishment of bilateral diplomatic relations is explained. Also, the number of foreign missions and staff in Croatia and Croatia' diplomatic missions abroad is displayed and explained. In the fourth chapter data and methodology are presented while the most important results of the analysis are shown in the fifth chapter. Final chapter explains limitations of the analysis, proposes policy recommendations and gives suggestions for future research.

LITERATURE REVIEW

In this chapter an overview of studies on effect of economic diplomacy representatives on trade will be presented and elaborated. In Table A1 in Appendix is displayed the overview according to author/s, time period, trade flows, explanatory variables, sample, econometric specification and the effect of economic diplomacy representatives on trade flows. Bergeijk and Moons delivered a meta-analysis of empirical studies on contribution of economic diplomacy on trade and FDI combining 23 studies and 873 parameters. The contribution is on average significant and positive with embassies have an above average contribution to bilateral trade flows. Gil-Pareja et al (2007) estimated the effects of embassies and consulates on tourist flows from the G-7 countries. They obtained significant and positive effect on tourism ranging between 15% and 30% with impact relatively larger for developing countries. Interestingly, the effect of first foreign mission in a country is clearly larger than additional missions. Nitsch (2007) investigate the impact of state visits on international trade for France, Germany and United States for the period from 1948 to 2003. State and official visits seem to be positive correlated with exports. A visit is typically associated with higher exports by 8 to 10 percent. Rose (2007) found that creation of an embassy has a substantially larger impact on exports than additional consulate. It amounted about 120% for creation o fan embassy and 5% to 11% for creation of an additional consulate. The analysis was made for the 22 large exporters and 200 destination countries in the 2002 and 2003. Segura-Cayuela and Vilarrubia (2008) disentangle the differential effect that embassies and consulates had on trade volumes. Using 1999 data on 21 exporter and 162 importer countries, they found that the presence of a foreign service in a country increases the probability of trade between 11% and 18%. Afman and Maurel (2010) used a Correlates of War database in order to investigate the relationship between diplomacy and trade in a context of post-transition countries. Countries were grouped in groups of transition countries, EU-15 and OECD countries while the time period observed was for the years 1995, 2000 and 2005. Results have shown that there exists a positive and significant effects of embassies and consulates on the trade flows in the range between 2-8% for fixed effects estimates and 49% for random effects specification. Head and Ries (2010) in the case of Canada found that trade missions do not cause an increase in trade and have small, negative, and mainly insignificant effects. The time period observed was from 1993 to 2003 estimating imports and exports using OLS and country fixed effects. Martincus et al (2010) found, on a sample of 26 Latin American and Carribean countries in the period from 1995 to 2004, that there is a positive and significant impact of export promoting agencies, embassies and consulates on trade, in the range between 0.5% and 27.6%.

Veenstra et al (2010) studied how the level of development influenced the interaction between the network of embassies and consulates. A trade model is used for 36 countries in the year 2006. Overall effect of export promoting agencies was insignificant while the effect of embassies and consulates is positive and significant in the range of 5% to 10%. Yakop and Bergeijk (2011) on a sample of 63 importing and exporting countries for the year 2006 found that diplomatic representation via embassies and consulates is significant in bilateral trade relationships of developing countries. Their estimates on elasticity ranged from 0.06 to 0.16. On the other side, economic diplomacy did not enhance trade within the OECD countries. Hayakawa et al (2014) examined the role of export promotion agencies (EPA) in promoting exports for Japan and Korea controlling for country-pair and time characteristics in the period from 1962 to 2009. Export promotion agencies had a positive and significant effect on exports in the range between 61% and 124%. Moons and de Boer (2014) assessed the effect of economic diplomacy on exports of homogeneous, differentiated and reference priced goods on a sample of 63 countries in

2006, covering 80% of world trade. There was largest impact on bilateral trade flows between countries with different development levels and in trade of complicated products. Afesorgbor (2016) examined the impact of regional integration and trade diplomacy on exports flows for 45 African states over the period 1980-2005. The results showed that diplomatic relations are more significant of bilateral exports compared to regional integration. Zero trade flows were controlled using Poisson Pseudo Maximum Likelihood (PPML) estimator. The results positive and significant impact of diplomatic exchange on exports in the range of 62%-68%. Bagir (2017) investigated the impact of presence of foreign missions on trade of Turkey using panel dana setting for 186 countries from 2006 to 2014. The presence of an embassy increases export value by 27% while the impact on imports is higher leading to 70% increase entirely driven by homogenous goods imports. Visser (2018) analysed the effect of diplomatic representation on trade using panel dataset covering 100 countries in a 5-year interval from 1985 to 2005. Diplomatic representation had a larger average positive and significant effect on trade in differentiated goods than exports in homogenous goods.

HISTORICAL BACKGROUND AND THE ESTABLISHMENT OF BILATERAL DIPLOMATIC RELATIONS OF CROATIA

After Croatia declared its independence in 1991 field of economic diplomacy was organised as an integral part of the activities of Croatian diplomatic and consular missions. Missions abroad were organised within the Ministry of Foreign Affairs. Since gaining the independence, Croatia recognized the importance of regional and international integration and become a part in associations such as UN, WTO, CEFTA, and EU. The institutions most responsible for shaping Croatian economic diplomacy are the President of the Republic of Croatia and the Government of the Republic of Croatia, the Ministry of Foreign and European Affairs. Besides the aforementioned institutions, on the creation of Croatian diplomatic policy significant impact have other institutions such as the Ministry of Entrepreneurship and Crafts, the Ministry of Tourism, the Croatian Bank for Reconstruction and Development, the Croatian Chamber of Commerce, the State Office for Trade Policy, etc., Institute for International Relations (2012). The establishment of bilateral diplomatic relations for Croatia started in the year 1992 when Croatia established bilateral diplomatic relations with 64 countries (Figure 1). In the first few years after the declaration of independence, Croatia established bilateral diplomatic relations with most of the countries in the world. For example, in the year 2001 Croatia already had bilateral diplomatic relations with 159 countries as seen in the Figure 1 as cumulative number of countries. As of 2019 Croatia has established bilateral diplomatic relations with 184 countries.

A closer look at a number of foreign missions (embassies and consular offices with belonging staff of Croatia and to Croatia) in the year 2019 is shown in the Figure 1. Only the top ten countries with highest values have been listed. The variables named in the Figure 2 are *EMBCONSDW* (embassies and consular offices of Croatia in a particular country in the world), *EMBCONSFC* (embassies and consular offices to Croatia from a particular country in the world), *STAFFDW* (the number of staff in embassies and consular offices of Croatia in a particular country in the world) and *STAFFC* (the number of staff in embassies and consular offices to Croatia from a particular country in the world). The most embassies and consulates in Croatia have Italy and Austria with eight, mostly located in capital city of Zagreb. Croatia has the most, ten foreign missions in United States of America from which of them an embassy in Washington D. C., three consulates-general in Chicago, Los Angeles and New York and six

Figure 1. Establishment of bilateral diplomatic relations for Croatia, cumulative number of countries, in the period from 1992 to 2019
Source: Authors' according to data available from MFEA (2019)

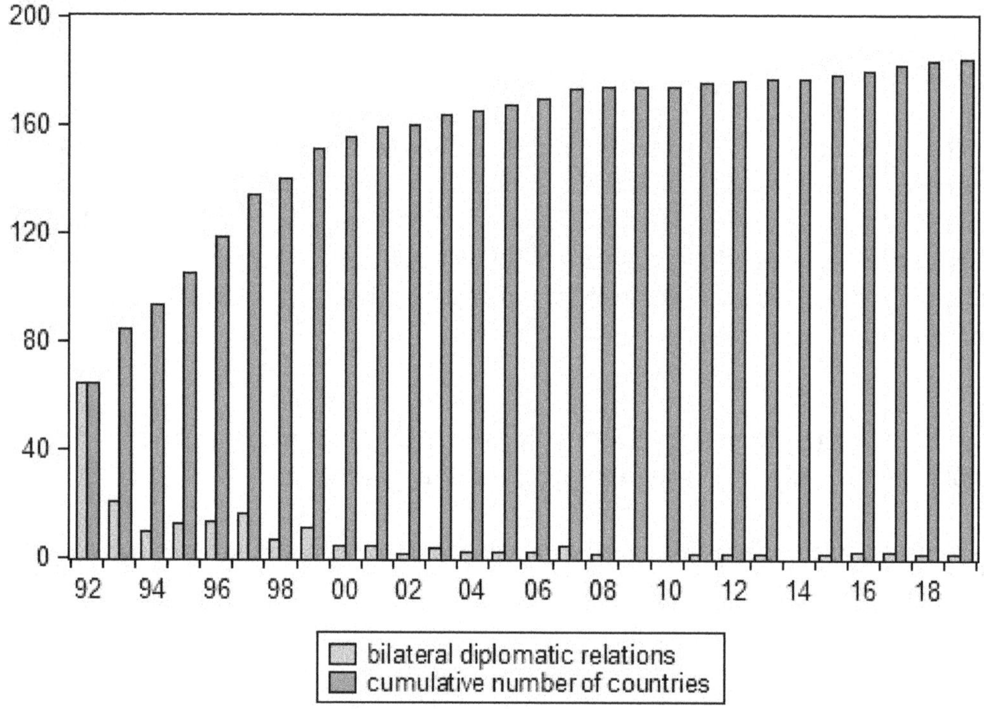

honorary consulates in Anchorage, Houston, Kansas City, New Orleans, Pittsburgh and Seattle. After United States of America, Croatia has the most foreign missions located in Italy and Germany (8) and Bosnia and Herzegovina (7).

It can be noticed that these are the countries where Croatian emigration live and where the most of Croatian citizens work abroad. More or less similar countries have the most staff working in embassies and consulates of and in Croatia. Croatia has the largest colony of diplomats situated in Bosnia and Herzegovina (27) and Germany with (26). On the other side, United States of America have the most of diplomats located in Croatia in an embassy in Zagreb.

DATA AND METHODOLOGY

Gravity model of international trade is a workhorse of international trade and economic analysis (Tinbergen, 1962). In its basic form it is similar to Newtonian law of gravity; bilateral trade flows are proportional to economic sizes of trade partner countries and reversely proportional to distance between them. In Equation 1 is presented standard gravity model.

Figure 2. Foreign missions and staff for Croatia, top ten countries, 2019
Source: Authors' according to data available from MFEA (2019)

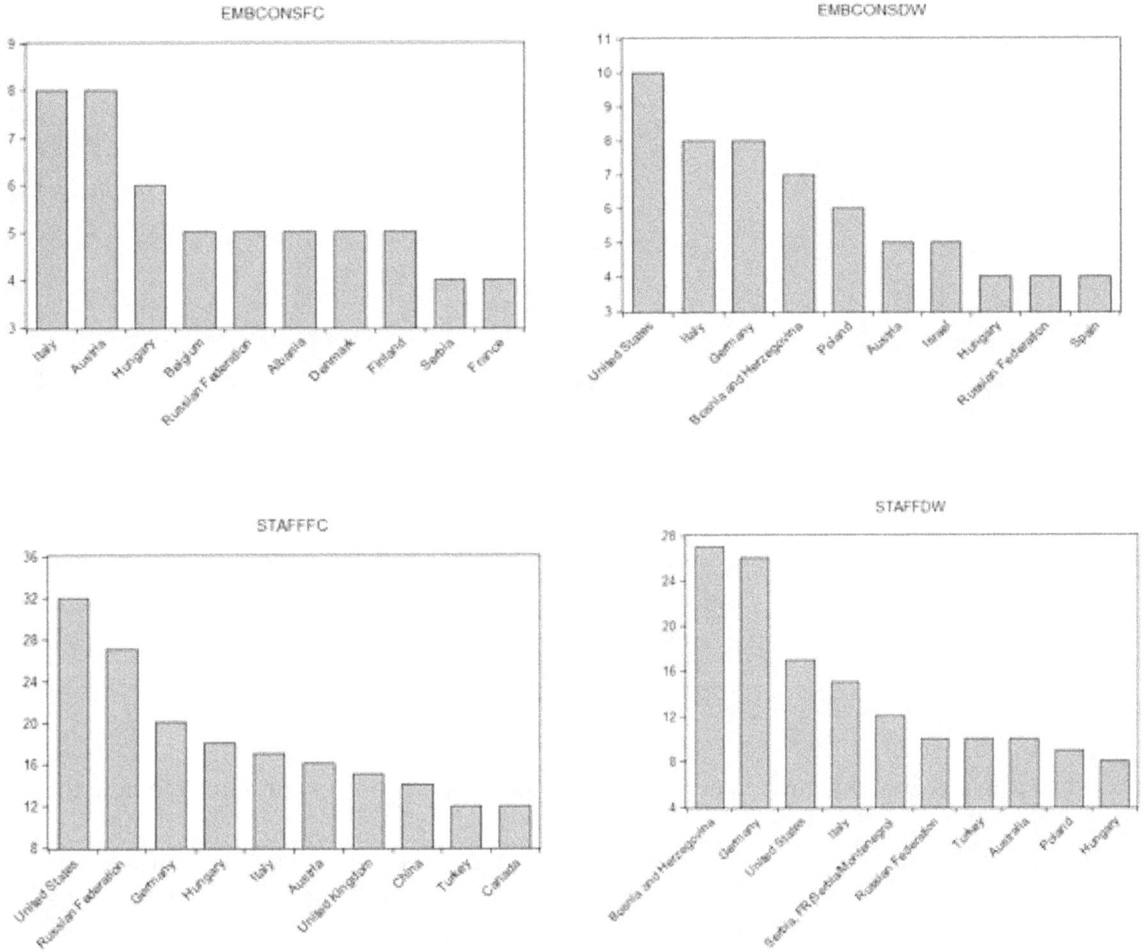

$$F_{ij} = C\frac{Y_i^{\alpha} Y_j^{\beta}}{D_{ij}^{\gamma}} \tag{1}$$

where F_{ij} are trade flows (imports, exports or total trade), C is a constant, Y_i and Y_j are national income of trading countries i and j (often represented with the GDP variable) while α, β and γ are regression coefficients. Standard gravity model is often expressed in natural logarithms, Equation 2:

$$lnF_{ij} = lnC + \alpha lnY_i + \beta lnY_j + \gamma lnD_{ij} + \varepsilon_{ij} \tag{2}$$

Augmented gravity model takes into account additional variables such as common border, common language and free trade area (FTA) dummies, remoteness, etc., Anderson and van Wincoop (2003). In the analysis the impact of economics diplomacy representatives on imports and exports of Croatia in the period from 1992 to 2017 will be investigated. Dependent variables in the regression are bilateral

Figure 3. Imports and exports for Croatia, 1992-2017, in 000 of USD
Source: Authors' according to data from WITS

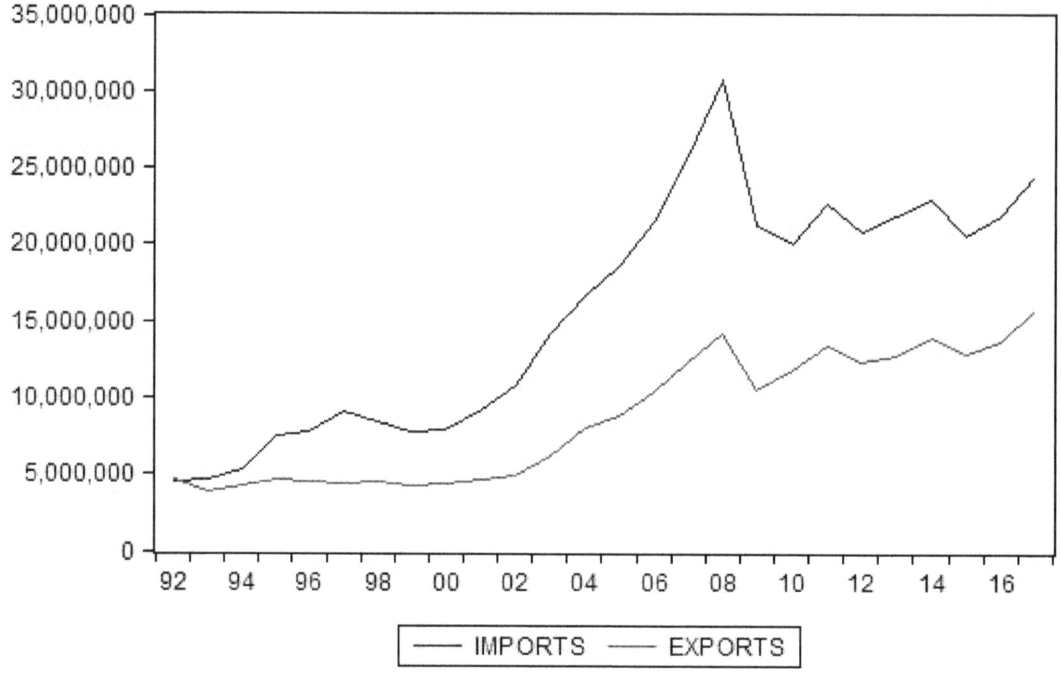

exports and imports. In the Figure 3 are presented overall imports and exports in Croatia in the period from 1992 to 2017.

It can be noticed steady growth of both trade flows in the observed period with structural break in the year 2009 as a consequence of 2008 global financial crisis. In figures 4 and 5 top ten countries for Croatian bilateral imports and exports in the year 2017 are presented.

Croatia's main trading partners are Germany and Italy and neighbouring countries Slovenia, Austria, Bosnia and Herzegovina, Serbia, Hungary and large countries such as United States and China and others.

On the other side, explanatory variables which are subject of investigation in the regression analysis are the number of embassies and consulates of Croatia in a particular country in the world $EMBCONSDW_{ij}$, the number of embassies and consulates to Croatia from a particular country in the world $EMBCONSFC_{ji}$, the number of diplomatic staff of Croatia in the particular country $STAFFDW_{ij}$, and the number of diplomatic staff to Croatia from a particular country $STAFFC_{ji}$. The presentation and description of this variables was made in Figure 2, in the third section of the chapter. Data are extracted from the Ministry of Foreign and European Affairs, MFEA (2019a) and MFEA (2019b). Additional explanatory variables included in the analysis are the part of a standard gravity model of trade. They are gross domestic product of domestic country *i*, Croatia, GDP_i, gross domestic product of Croatia's trade and diplomatic partner country *j*, GDP_j, distance between countries $DIST_{ij}$, free trade area dummy variable FTA_{ij}, common border dummy variable between Croatia and neighbouring countries $COMB_{ij}$ and common Slavic language dummy $COML_{ij}$. GDP_i and GDP_j are expressed in current US dollars and available from the World Bank database, World Bank (2019). The list of countries in the analysis is displayed in the Appendix. There are 238 countries in the full sample. Data for GDP_i of Croatia are available only

Figure 4. Imports in Croatia, top ten countries, 2017, in 000 of USD
Source: Authors' according to data from WITS

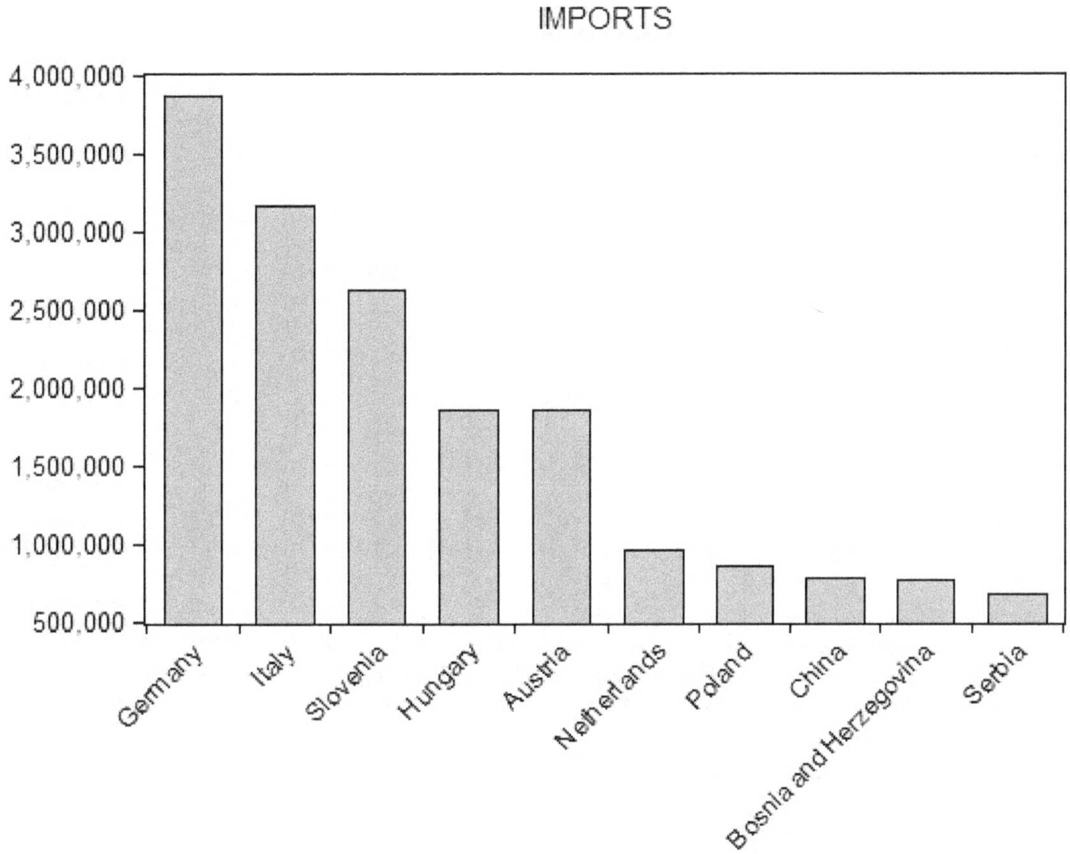

from the year 1995. Moreover, data for trade partner countries GDP_j were available for 175 countries because full time-series of data in the period from 1992 to 2017 could not be constructed for many of small and island countries. Countries for which data on GDP could not be constructed are marked with an italic in the List of countries in the Appendix. Distance between countries is expressed in kilometres and denotes an aerial distance between capital city of Croatia, Zagreb, and trade and diplomatic partner country *j*. Data are retrieved from the DistanceFromTo webpage, DistanceFromTo (2019). Free trade area dummy variable FTA_{ij} gets the value 1 if Croatia and trade partner country are the members of Central European Free Trade Area (CEFTA) or European Union (EU) in the same year in the observed period. Croatia has membership in CEFTA from 2006 to 2013 when it accessed European Union, Cefta Secretariat and European Commission (2020). Croatia borders with Bosnia and Herzegovina, Slovenia, Hungary, Montenegro and Serbia. Croatia shares common Slavic language with 12 countries. These are Russian, Ukrainian, and Belorussian to the east; Polish, Czech and Slovak to the west; and Slovenian, Bosnian, Croatian, Serbian, Montenegrian, Macedonian and Bulgarian to the south, Harvard University (2020). Cross-country panel regression analysis for Croatian bilateral exports and imports using OLS estimator will be conducted using equations 3 and 4. Due to zero trade flows for exports and imports

Figure 5. Exports from Croatia, top ten countries, 2017, in 000 of USD
Source: Authors' according to data from WITS

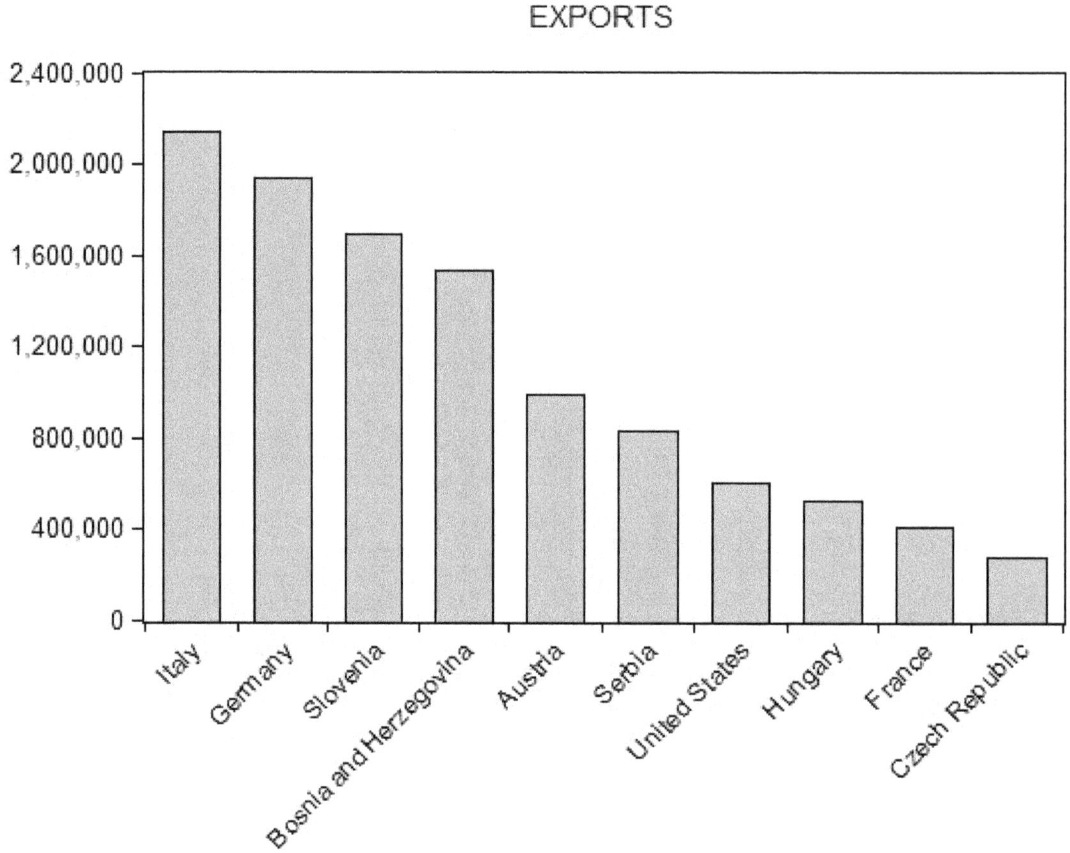

in some data the log-log model could not be estimated. Zero trade flows could be left from the analysis but in that case it can lead to significant estimation biases.

$$Exports_{ijt} = \beta_0 + \beta_1 EMBCONSDW_{ijt} + \beta_2 EMBCONSFC_{jit} + \beta_3 STAFFDW_{ijt} + \beta_4 STAFFFC_{jit} + \beta_5 GDP_{it} + \beta_6 GDP_{jt} + \beta_7 DIST_{ijt} + \beta_8 FTA_{ijt} + \beta_9 COMB_{ijt} + \beta_{10} COML_{ijt} + \varepsilon_i \tag{3}$$

$$Imports_{ijt} = \beta_0 + \beta_1 EMBCONSDW_{ijt} + \beta_2 EMBCONSFC_{jit} + \beta_3 STAFFDW_{ijt} + \beta_4 STAFFFC_{jit} + \beta_5 GDP_{it} + \beta_6 GDP_{jt} + \beta_7 DIST_{ijt} + \beta_8 FTA_{ijt} + \beta_9 COMB_{ijt} + \beta_{10} COML_{ijt} + \varepsilon_i \tag{4}$$

Firstly, pooled OLS (POLS) will be estimated. After that fixed effects (FE) model which accounts for observed heterogeneity in data will be estimated. Some variables are time invariant, so the random effects (RE) should also been estimated. Between random effects and fixed effects models, Hausman test will be used. In order to take into account zero trade flows, Poisson Pseudo Maximum Likelihood (PPML) model will be estimated because estimating zero trade flows with OLS estimator can lead to significant biases. In Figures 5 and 6 is presented PPML model for exports and imports.

$$E(Exports_{ijt}) = exp\{\beta_0 + \beta_1 logEMBCONSDW_{ijt} + \beta_2 logEMBCONSFC_{jit} \\ +\beta_3 logSTAFFDW_{ijt} + \beta_4 logSTAFFFC_{jit} + \beta_5 logGDP_{it} + \beta_6 logGDP_{jt} \\ +\beta_7 logDIST_{ijt} + \beta_8 logFTA_{ijt} + \beta_9 logCOMB_{ijt} + \beta_{10} logCOML_{ijt} + \varepsilon_i\} \tag{5}$$

$$E(Imports_{ijt}) = exp\{\beta_0 + \beta_1 logEMBCONSDW_{ijt} + \beta_2 logEMBCONSFC_{jit} \\ +\beta_3 logSTAFFDW_{ijt} + \beta_4 logSTAFFFC_{jit} + \beta_5 logGDP_{it} + \beta_6 logGDP_{jt} \\ +\beta_7 logDIST_{ijt} + \beta_8 logFTA_{ijt} + \beta_9 logCOMB_{ijt} + \beta_{10} logCOML_{ijt} + \varepsilon_i\} \tag{6}$$

Santos Silva and Tenreyro (2006) suggested the model should be estimated in the multiplicative form. With the PPML the expected trade is modelled using exponential function and exports and imports are now measured in levels, Afesorgbor (2016). Although Martin and Pham (2008) argued that using PPML on gravity model severely biases estimates when zero trade flows are frequent, Santos Silva and Tenreyro (2011) showed that PPML model could perform well even when proportions of zeroes in trade data is large.

Table 1. Descriptive statistics

Variable	Mean	Median	Max.	Min.	Std. Dev.	Sum	Sum Sq. Dev.	Obs.
Imports	65,139.06	85.05350	5,258,688.	0	300,341.4	4.03E+08	5.58E+14	6,188
EXPORTS	36,348.84	71.13300	2,694,137.	0	173,266.7	2.25E+08	1.86E+14	6,188
EMBCONSDW	1.14512	1	10	0	1.44550	7,086.	12,927.68	6,188
EMBCONSFC	1.00597	0	8	0	1.45393	6,225.	13,078.78	6,188
STAFFDW	1.86037	1	27	0	3.37182	11,512.	70,341.36	6,188
STAFFFC	2.80898	0	32	0	4.56404	17,382.	128,878.2	6,188
GDPi	4.38E+10	4.95E+10	7.05E+10	2.18E+10	1.62E+10	2.40E+14	1.44E+24	5,474
GDPj	2.60E+11	1.33E+10	1.95E+13	9,630,763.	1.15E+12	1.29E+15	6.57E+27	4,950
DIST	6,762.364	6,768.	18,304.	118	4,511.695	41,845,510.	1.26E+11	6,188
FTA	0.02908	0	1	0	0.16806	180	174.7641	6,188
COMB	0.02521	0	1	0	0.15677	156	152.0672	6,188
COML	0.05042	0	1	0	0.21882	312	296.2689	6,188

Source: Authors' calculations

RESULTS AND DISCUSSION

In this section the most important results of the analysis and discussion will be presented and elaborated. In Table 1 the descriptive statistics of variables is displayed. There are 6,188 observations on the individual sample for observed variables except in the case of GDP_i and GDP_j variables where there are 5,474 and 4,950 observations respectively.

The highest value of imports for Croatia was achieved from Italy in the year 2008 with the value of 5,258,688.6 thousands of USD. Croatia also had the highest value of exports to Italy also in the year 2008 with the value of 2,694,136.8 thousands of USD. If the Distance variable is detailed observed, the closest trade partner country of Croatia is Slovenia with the distance between capital Zagreb-Ljubljana of 118 kilometres. On the other side, New Zealand is the most distant foreign trade partner of Croatia with the distance between capitals Zagreb-Wellington of 18,304 kilometres.

Before conducting the panel cross-country regression analysis, correlation matrix of independent variables is shown. This is important in order to check correlations between pairs of independent variables because results of the analysis could be influenced and therefore biased due to that dependence.

Table 2. Correlation matrix

Variable	EMBCONS DW	EMBCON FC	STAFFDW	STAFFFC	GDPi	GDPj	DIST	FTA	COMB	COML
EMBCONSDW	1	0.61369	0.87014	0.74905	0.04215	0.50986	-0.30178	0.17340	0.36294	0.24173
EMBCONSFC	0.61369	1	0.55969	0.70651	0.00973	0.15729	-0.47857	0.28602	0.33151	0.27007
STAFFDW	0.87014	0.55969	1	0.71174	0.01666	0.45343	-0.31001	0.20736	0.48134	0.36009
STAFFFC	0.74905	0.70651	0.71174	1	0.00945	0.57965	-0.33530	0.16998	0.29259	0.29616
GDPi	0.04215	0.00973	0.01666	0.00945	1	0.06681	0.00534	0.14822	0.00512	0.00137
GDPj	0.50986	0.15729	0.45343	0.57965	0.06681	1	0.00496	0.03697	0.00877	-0.02490
DIST	-0.30178	-0.47857	-0.31001	-0.33530	0.00534	0.00496	1	-0.25250	-0.24317	-0.30647
FTA	0.17340	0.28602	0.20736	0.16998	0.14822	0.03697	-0.25250	1	0.18482	0.20499
COMB	0.36294	0.33151	0.48134	0.29259	0.00512	0.00877	-0.24317	0.18482	1	0.43525
COML	0.24173	0.27007	0.36009	0.29616	0.00137	-0.02490	-0.30647	0.20499	0.43525	1

Source: Authors' calculations

The results have shown that there exists positive and strong correlation between pairs-wise of independent variables *EMBCONSDW*, *EMBCONSFC*, *STAFFDW* and *STAFFFC*, which are representatives of economic diplomacy. In order to account for this strong correlation between aforementioned variables, each of the mentioned variables will be observed separately. In Tables 3 and 4 are presented the results of a cross-country panel regression analysis for imports and exports in the period from the year 1992 to 2017. There are four regression models estimated in the analysis. The first model is pooled OLS (POLS), the second model is fixed effects (FE) model, the third model is random effects (RE) model while the fourth model is Pseudo Poisson Maximum Likelihood (PPML) model. First three models include the GDP_i and GDP_j variables while that could not be made for PPML model. Therefore, the number of observations is 4,420 for the first three models and 6,188 for the PPML which is the full sample of observations. In the fixed effects model variables *DIST*, *FTA*, *COMB* and *COML* could not be included due to time invariant characteristics of data. Hausman test statistics have shown that the fixed effects model

Table 3. Cross-country panel regression analysis, Imports, 1992-2017

Depend. variab.	Imports			
Indep. variable/ Model	POLS	FE	RE	PPML
Constant	-150,457.5*** (14,491.24)	16,750.32 (16,976.35)	-11,384.36 (34,460.90)	9.92140*** (0.00017)
EMBCONSDW	-14,598.18*** (5,982.057)	-69,464.21*** (18,210.72)	-68,358.49*** (13,048.78)	-0.01090*** (4.72E-05)
EMBCONSFC	21,198.79*** (4,366.089)	9,900.617 (25,477.42)	23,282.34* (13,147,56)	0.017763*** (3.45E-05)
STAFFDW	40,527.96*** (2,394.471)	29,185.89** (13,437.94)	41,494.4*** (7,360.434)	0.05777*** (1.45E-05)
STAFFFC	15,129.82*** (1,660.397)	-4,746.608 (6,622.210)	1,335.876 (4,072.29)	0.13200*** (1.12E-05)
GDPi	1.57E-06*** (2.40E-07)	2.06E-06*** (1.46E-07)	1.58E-06*** (1.42E-07)	
GDPj	-1.20E-09 (4.72E-09)	6.45E-08*** (5.46E-09)	6.41E-08*** (5.07E-09)	
DIST	0.97674 (1.08853)		-6.24428 (4.01691)	-0.00021*** (3.08E-08)
FTA	180,290.6*** (20,897.97)		183,597.*** (12,311.26)	0.65334*** (0.00012)
COMB	393,331.1*** (27,637.90)		548,130.3*** (105,924.7)	0.12184*** (0.00013)
COML	-172,165.6*** (19,038.19)		-108,140.9 (74,352.89)	0.32326*** (0.00013)
Adjusted R-sq.	0.47590	0.82944	0.15913	
S.E. of regress.	253,675.7	144,691.4	141,817.2	
Prob. (F-stat.)	0.0	0.0	0.0	
Mean dep. var.	87,915.77	87,915.77	12,106.51	65,139.06
S.D. dep. var.	350,407.1	350,407.1	154,654.5	300,341.4
Restr. quasi-logl				4.06E+09
Quasi-log likelih.				4.85E+09
Durbin-Watson	0.09799	0.294527	0.29717	
Observations	4,420	4,420	4,420	6,188
Hausman test	Chi Square Stat. 64.61538, Prob. 0.00000			
Likelihood ratio test	Cross-section F Stat. 51.413423, Prob. 0.00000 Cross-section Chi-square Stat. 5461.6876, Prob. 0.00000			

*Standard errors in parentheness, * denotes significance under 10%, ** significance under 5% and *** significance under 1%, Swamy and Arora estimator of component variances, GML (Newton-Raphson/Marquardt steps), Poissson Quasi likelihood, Link log, dispersion fixed at 1, convergence achieved after 5 iterations, coeff. covar. computed using observed Hessian.*

Source: Authors' calculations

is more appropriate to data than random effects model. Furthermore, likelihood ratio test statistics have shown that fixed effects model is more appropriate than the POLS model.

Fixed effects model also have the highest adjusted R-squared meaning that the model is very well explained with the explanatory variables.

Table 4. Cross-country panel regression analysis, Exports, 1992-2017

Depend. variab.	Exports			
Indep. variable/ Model	**POLS**	**FE**	**RE**	**PPML**
Constant	-67,007.13*** (6,931.069)	-18,052.87** (8,909.979)	-25,079.44 (16,203.55)	9.62678*** (0.00023)
EMBCONSDW	-2,561.047 (2,861.18)	-70,238.47*** (9,557.836)	-45,788.9*** (6,448.803)	0.12708*** (6.54E-05)
EMBCONSFC	8,459.321*** (2,088.278)	4,739.697 (13,371.74)	14,833.18** (6,279.59)	0.06358*** (4.99E-05)
STAFFDW	31,073.63*** (1,145.261)	44,012.89** (7,052.856)	36,001.56*** (3,533.531)	0.04262*** (1.80E-05)
STAFFFC	-3,467.862*** (794.1572)	-69.66355 (3,475.645)	-3,687.876* (1,978.212)	0.09653*** (1.50E-05)
GDPi	8.06E-07*** (1.15E-07)	1.14E-06*** (7.66E-08)	8.38E-07*** (7.26E-08)	
GDPj	-1.52E-09 (2.26E-09)	3.15E-08*** (2.87E-09)	2.94E-08*** (2.59E-09)	
DIST	-0.39092 (0.52063)		-1.80545 (1.86768)	-0.00027*** (4,53E-08)
FTA	119,605.2*** (9,995.368)		127,154.3*** (6,334.662)	0.65630*** (0.00015)
COMB	453,073.4*** (13,219.03)		489,552.3*** (49,191.89)	0.70387*** (0.00018)
COML	-87,447.47*** (9,105.849)		-83,596.72** (34,435.95)	0.48178*** (0.00018)
Adjusted R-sq.	0.63108	0.85547	0.23161	
S.E. of regress.	121,331.5	75,940.81	72,851.99	
Prob. (F-stat.)	0.0	0.0	0.0	
Mean dep. var.	47,421.47	47,421.47	7,275.303	36,348.84
S.D. dep. var.	199,760.8	19,760.8	83,098.47	173,266.7
Restr. quasi-logl				2,14E+09
Quasi-log likelih.				2.61E+09
Durbin-Watson	0.10841	0.267455	0.29148	
Observations	4,420	4,420	4,420	6,188
Hausman test	Chi Square Stat. 43.85038, Prob. 0.00000			
Likelihood ratio test	Cross-section F Stat. 52.498316, Prob. 0.00000 Cross-section Chi-square Stat. 5527.35840, Prob. 0.00000			

*Standard errors in parentheness, * denotes significance under 10%, ** significance under 5% and *** significance under 1%, Swamy and Arora estimator of component variances, GML (Newton-Raphson/Marquardt steps), Poissson Quasi likelihood, Link log, dispersion fixed at 1, convergence achieved after 5 iterations, coeff. covar. computed using observed Hessian.*

Source: Authors' calculations

The results from the Tables 3 and 4 point to the following conclusions: there is positive and significant effect of gross domestic product of trade partner countries on trade flows, distance between countries negatively impacts bilateral trade which were highly accepted results according to economic theory, common membership in CEFTA or EU has positive effect on trade as well as common border. On the other side common Slavic language has not shown as the important factor for bilateral trade except in the case of PPML model, so the results are not conclusive in this case. Same can be said for results obtained for variables representing the impact of economic diplomacy on trade. There is positive and significant effect of EMBCONSFC and STAFFDW on trade flows while for the EMBCONSDW and STAFFFC variables results are mixed. However, the problem of strong dependence between economic diplomacy's representatives should be tackled with caution.

Therefore, the regressions over individual independent variables are made using fixed effect and PPML models. The results are shown in the Table 5. It can be seen that there is positive and significant effect of the chosen variables on trade. It can be concluded that economic diplomacy, represented with the embassies and consulates with its diplomatic staff, had positive impact on bilateral imports and exports of Croatia in the period from 1992 to 2017. The results of this investigation have strong implications on the importance of economic diplomacy on the economy of Croatia. The establishment of the new embassy or consulate of Croatia in the particular country in the world, or by diplomatic and trade partner country in Croatia, would have positive effects on trade flows. The same can be said about the increase in number of diplomatic staff in embassies and consulates. It means that the hypothesis

Table 5. Regressions on individual independent variable, FE and PPML models

Model/Dependent variable	Fixed effects		Imports		
Independent variable/Stat.	**Coefficient**	**Std. Error**	**t-Statistic**	**Prob.**	**R-squared**
EMBCONSDW	7,649.872	5,351.292	1.429537	0.1529	0.778274
EMBCONSFC	15,439.20	7,190.042	2.147303	0.0318	0.778369
STAFFDW	9,316.664	3,564.395	2.613813	0.0090	0.778452
STAFFFC	3,759.297	2,200.378	1.708478	0.0876	0.778306
Model/Dependent variable	**Fixed effects**		**Exports**		
Independent variable/Stat.	**Coefficient**	**Std. Error**	**t-Statistic**	**Prob.**	**R-squared**
EMBCONSDW	9,583.081	2,749.808	3.485000	0.0005	0.824084
EMBCONSFC	20,524.87	3,689.649	5.562825	0.0000	0.824637
STAFFDW	13,953.64	1,825.258	7.644752	0.0000	0.825440
STAFFFC	5,373.414	1,129.774	4.756184	0.0000	0.824393
Model/Dependent variable	**PPML**		**Imports**		
Independent variable/Stat.	**Coefficient**	**Std. Error**	**z-Statistic**	**Prob.**	**R-squared**
EMBCONSDW	0.515672	1.34E-05	38,341.45	0.0000	
EMBCONSFC	0.617068	1.72E-05	35,921.37	0.0000	
STAFFDW	0.169990	4.37E-06	38,914.03	0.0000	
STAFFFC	0.156860	4.04E-06	38,802.93	0.0000	
Model/Dependent variable	**PPML**		**Exports**		
Independent variable/Stat.	**Coefficient**	**Std. Error**	**z-Statistic**	**Prob.**	**R-squared**
EMBCONSDW	0.534889	1.79E-05	29,866.43	0.0000	
EMBCONSFC	0.598713	2.31E-05	25,971.04	0.0000	
STAFFDW	0.180850	5.74E-06	31,518.71	0.0000	
STAFFFC	0.146697	5.56E-06	26,382.57	0.0000	

Source: Authors' calculations

of the chapter which states that economic diplomacy, represented by the foreign missions (embassies and consulates) in Croatia and abroad, has positive effect on bilateral trade flows can be accepted. Our findings confirmed earlier empirical studies in this field on the importance of economic diplomacy as a strong generator of bilateral trade flows.

FUTURE RESEARCH DIRECTIONS

Future research directions could go in the way of further analysis of micro aspects of diplomatic representation on trade in Croatia by taking into account government and private enterprises. In addition, the impact of diplomatic representation on attraction of foreign direct investments (FDI) in Croatia and abroad could be observed as well.

CONCLUSION

In this chapter, the impact of economic diplomacy's representatives on the bilateral trade of Croatia is investigated. Using the gravity model of trade it was found that the establishment of an additional embassy or consulate in Croatia and abroad would have positive and significant effects on bilateral trade flows. The results obtained in the analysis are in line with economic theory. For example, the gross domestic product of trade partner countries has a positive and significant effect on trade flows, the distance between countries has a negative effect, common membership in CEFTA and EU has a positive effect on trade as well as a common border. What is also interesting is that a similar language between neighboring countries has not shown as an important factor in enhancing bilateral trade flows. The problem of zero trade flows was solved by employing a PPML estimator and the dependence between diplomacy representatives was controlled by regressing the individual independent variables and using the fixed-effects model and PPML estimator. There is a correlation between the number of foreign missions and staff with the Croatian trade output. After all, we can deliver the conclusion that diplomacy effectiveness can be related to a trading output. The results of this research have significant implications for economic diplomacy importance in Croatia and countries with similar macroeconomic and microeconomic determinants. All stakeholders in the system of economic diplomacy should take into account showed results, especially those who are deeply into trade-enhancing factors. Future investigations in this field should be conducted by investigating the impact of economic diplomacy for example, on different trade flows, levels of business interconnectedness, state hierarchy, and to explore various samples of countries in extended periods.

REFERENCES

Afesorgbor, S. K. (2016). *Economic Diplomacy in Africa: The Impact of Regional Integration versus Bilateral Diplomacy on Bilateral Trade*. Economics Working Papers 2016-9.

Afman, E., & Maurel, M. (2010). Diplomatic Relations and Trade Reorientation in Transition Countries. In P. A. G. Van Bergeijk & S. Brakman (Eds.), *The Gravity Model in International Trade: Advances and Applications* (pp. 278–295). Cambridge University Press. doi:10.1017/CBO9780511762109.010

Anderson, J. E., & van Wincoop, E. (2003). Gravity with Gravitas: A Solution to the Border Puzzle. *The American Economic Review*, *93*(1), 170–192. doi:10.1257/000282803321455214

Bagir, Y. E. (2017). Impact of the Presence of Foreign Missions on Trade: Evidence from Turkey. MPRA Paper 80845, University Library of Munich.

Bayer, R. (2006). *Diplomatic Exchange Data set, v2006.1*. Available at: http://correlatesofwar.org

Bergeijk, P. A. G., & Moons, S. J. V. (2011). *Does Economic Diplomacy Work? A Meta Analysis on the Effect of Economic Diplomacy on International Economic Flows*. Available at SSRN: https://ssrn.com/abstract=1908699

CEFTA Secretariat. (2020). *CEFTA parties*. Available at: https://cefta.int/cefta-parties-2/

DistanceFromTo. (2019). *Distance between countries' capital cities*. Available at: https://www.distance-fromto.net/

European Comission. (2020). *European Union member countries*. Available at: https://ec.europa.eu/

Gil-Pareja, S., Llorca-Vivero, R., & Martínez-Serrano, J. A. (2007). The impact of embassies and consulates on tourism'. *Tourism Management*, *28*(1), 355–360. doi:10.1016/j.tourman.2006.04.016

Harvard University. (2020). *What are the Slavic languages?* Available at: https://slavic.fas.harvard.edu/pages/what-are-slavic-languages

Hayakawa, K., Lee, H.-H., & Park, D. (2014). Do export promotion agencies increase exports? *The Developing Economies*, *52*(3), 241–261. doi:10.1111/deve.12048

Head, K., & Ries, J. (2010). Do Trade Missions Increase Trade? *The Canadian Journal of Economics. Revue Canadienne d'Economique*, *43*(3), 754–775. doi:10.1111/j.1540-5982.2010.01593.x

Institute for International Relations. (2012). *Commercial diplomacy of the Republic of Croatia or why Croatia today desperately needs a strong and systematic commercial policy*. Adris Foundation, Programme "Knowledge and discoveries". Available at: http://www.irmo.hr/wp-content/uploads/2013/10/godip-web-en.pdf

Jošić, H., & Mlinarić, D. (2018). Determinants of Sovereign Credit Ratings: Evidence from CEE Countries. *EconViews*, *31*(2), 319–335.

Martin, W., & Pham, C. S. (2008). *Estimating the Gravity Model When Zero Trade Flows are Frequent*. Working Paper. Available at: https://www.deakin.edu.au/__data/assets/pdf_file/0011/405011/2008_03eco.pdf

Martincus, C., Estevadeordal, A., Gallo, A., & Luna, J. (2010). *Information barriers, export promotion institutions, and the extensive margin of trade.* IDB Working Paper Series, No. IDB-WP-200, Inter-American Development Bank (IDB).

MFEA. (2019). *Diplomatic Missions and Consular Offices of Croatia.* Available at: http://www.mvep.hr/en/diplomatic-directory/diplomatic-missions-and-consular-offices-of-croatia/

Mlinarić, D. (2018). Theoretical Background of Economic Diplomacy. *International Conference Proceedings BSSHE-18*, 22-28.

Mlinarić, D., Perić, T. & Matejaš, J. (2019). Multi-objective programming methodology for solving economic diplomacy resource allocation problem. *Croatian Operational Research Review, 10*(1), 165-174.

Moons, S. J. V., & de Boer, R. (2014). *Economic diplomacy, product characteristics and the level of development.* ETSG 2014 Conference. Available at: https://www.etsg.org/ETSG2014/Papers/105.pdf

Nitsch, V. (2007). State Visits and International Trade. *World Economy, 30*(12), 1797–1816. doi:10.1111/j.1467-9701.2007.01062.x

Rose, A. K. (2007). The Foreign Service and Foreign Trade: Embassies as Export Promotion. *World Economy, 30*(1), 22–38. doi:10.1111/j.1467-9701.2007.00870.x

Santos Silva, J. M. C., & Tenreyro, S. (2011). The Log of Gravity. *The Review of Economics and Statistics, 88*(4), 641–658. doi:10.1162/rest.88.4.641

Santos Silva, J. M. C., & Tenreyro, S. (2011). Further simulation evidence on the performance of the Poisson pseudo-maximum likelihood estimator. *Economics Letters, 112*(2), 220–222. doi:10.1016/j.econlet.2011.05.008

Segura-Cayuela, R., & Villarubia, J. M. (2008). *The effect of foreign service on trade volumes and trade partners.* Banco de España Working Paper No. 0808. Available at: https://papers.ssrn.com/sol3/papers.cfm?abstract_id=1126598

Tinbergen, J. (1962). *Shaping the world economy; suggestions for an international economic policy.* Twentieth Century Fund.

Van Veestra, M. E. H., Yakop, M., & Bergeijk, P. A. G. (2010). *Economic diplomacy, the Level of Development and Trade.* Discussion papers in economy. Available at: https://www.clingendael.org/sites/default/files/pdfs/20101000_cdsp_artikel_%20van%20Veenstra,%20Yakop%20and%20van%20Bergeijk.pdf

Visser, R. (2018). The effect of diplomatic representation on trade: A panel data analysis. *World Economy, 42*(1), 197–225. doi:10.1111/twec.12676

WITS. (2019a). *Croatia Exports in thousand of US$, 1992-2017.* Available at: https://wits.worldbank.org/CountryProfile/en/Country/HRV/StartYear/1992/EndYear/2017/TradeFlow/Export/Partner/BY-COUNTRY/Indicator/XPRT-TRD-VL

WITS. (2019b). *Croatia Imports in thousand of US$, 1992-2017.* Available at: https://wits.worldbank.org/CountryProfile/en/Country/HRV/StartYear/1992/EndYear/2017/TradeFlow/Import/Partner/BY-COUNTRY/Indicator/MPRT-TRD-VL

World Bank. (2019). *GDP (current US$)*. Available at: https://data.worldbank.org/indicator/ny.gdp.mktp.cd

Yakop, M., & van Bergeijk, P. A. G. (2011). Economic diplomacy, trade and developing countries. *Cambridge Journal of Regions, Economy and Society*, *4*(2), 253–267. doi:10.1093/cjres/rsr002

ADDITIONAL READING

Gangi, Y. A., & Ahmed, M. H. (2017). The impact of international relations on inflow of foreign direct investment: A case study of Sudan. *Journal of Applied Economics and Business*, *5*(1), 46–66.

Nunnenkamp, P. (2002). *Determinants of FDI in Developing Countries: Has Globalization Changed the Rules of the Game?* Kiel Working Paper No. 1122.

Zhang, J., Jiang, J., & Zhou, C. (2014). Diplomacy and investment – the case of China. *International Journal of Emerging Markets*, *9*(2), 216–235. doi:10.1108/IJoEM-09-2012-0104

KEY TERMS AND DEFINITIONS

Bilateral Trade Flows: The exchange of goods between two nations promoting trade and investment.

Diplomatic Representatives: Embassies and consulates which are relevant trade and trade-enhancing factor.

Economic Diplomacy: Consists of instruments and activities which are focused on attracting foreign direct investments, boosting export, and building an efficient business environment.

Embassy: One country's main diplomatic office in another host country.

Gravity Model of Trade: The model in international economics that predicts bilateral trade flows based on economic sizes and distance between two countries.

APPENDIX

Table A1. Overview of studies on effect of economic diplomacy representatives on trade

Author/s	Period	Trade flow/s	Explanatory variables	Sample	Econometric specification	Effect of economic diplomacy representatives on trade flow/s
Gil-Pareja *et al* (2007)	2001-2003	export of services from tourism	embassies, consulates	G-7 countries	OLS	Positive and significant, in the range between 15% and 30%.
Nitsch (2007)	1948-2003	imports and exports	trade missions	France, Germany and United States	POLS, FE, RE	State and official visit have a positive effect on exports of about 8% to 10%.
Rose (2007)	2002-2003	exports	embassies, consulates	22 large exporters and 200 destination countries	OLS	Positive and significant, in the range of 120% for creation of an embassy and 5-11% for creation of an additional consulate.
Segura-Cayuela and Vilarrubia (2008)	1999	total trade	embassies, consulates	21 exporter and 162 importer countries	OLS	Positive and significant, in the range between 11% and 18%.
Afman and Maurel (2010)	1995-2005	imports and exports	embassies, consulates	transition economies, EU-15 and OECD countries	OLS	Positive and significant, in the range between 2-8% for fixed effects estimates and 49% for random effects specification.
Head and Ries (2010)	1993-2003	imports and exports	trade missions	Canada	OLS, country FE	Trade missions do not cause an increase in trade and have small, negative, and mainly insignificant effects
Martincus *et al* (2010)	1995-2004	total trade	export promoting agencies, embassies and consulates	26 Latin American and Carribean countries	OLS	Positive and significant, in the range between 0.5% and 27.6%
Veenstra *et al* (2010)	2006	exports	export promoting agencies, embassies and consulates	36 countries	OLS	Overall effect of export promoting agencies is insignificant whereas the overall effect of embassies and consulates is positive and significant in the range of 5% to 10%.
Yakop and Bergeijk (2011)	2006	imports and exports	embassies, consulates	63 importing and exporting countries	OLS	Positive and significant, in the range between 6% and 16%.
Hayakawa *et al* (2014)	1962-2009	exports	export promoting agencies	Japan and Korea	OLS	Positive and significant, in the range between 61% and 124%.
Moons and de Boer (2014)	2006	exports and total trade	embassies, consulates	63 countries	OLS	Largest impact on bilateral trade flows between countries with different development levels and in trade of complicated products.
Afesorgbor (2016)	1980-2005	exports	diplomatic exchange	45 African states	PPML	Positive and significant, in the range of 62%-68%.
Bagir (2017)	2006-2014	imports and exports	embassies	Turkey	OLS	Positive and significant, the presences of a embassy increases exports by 27% and imports by 70%.
Visser (2018)	1985-2005	exports in homogeneous and differentiated goods	diplomatic representation	100 countries	OLS, PPML	Positive and significant effect on export in differentiated goods and to a lesser extent on exports in homogeneous exports.

Source: Authors' calculations

List of Countries in The Full Sample (238)

Afghanistan, Albania, Algeria, American Samoa, Andorra, Angola, Anguilla, Antarctica, Antigua and Barbuda, Argentina, Armenia, Aruba, Australia, Austria, Azerbaijan, Bahamas, The Bahrain, Bangladesh, Barbados, Belarus, Belgium, Belize, Benin, Bermuda, Bhutan, Bolivia, Bosnia and Herzegovina, Botswana, Bouvet Island, British Antarctic Territory, Brazil, British Indian Ocean Territory, British Virgin Islands, Brunei, Bulgaria, Burkina Faso, Burundi, Cambodia, Cameroon, Canada, Cape Verde, Cayman Islands, Central African Republic, Chad, Chile, China, Christmas Island, Cocos (Keeling) Islands, Colombia, Comoros, Congo, Democratic Republic, Congo, Republic, Cook Islands, Costa Rica, Cote d'Ivoire, Cuba, Curaçao, Cyprus, Czech Rep., Denmark, Djibouti, Dominica, Dominican Republic, East Timor, Ecuador, Egypt, Arab Republic, El Salvador, Equatorial Guinea, Eritrea, Estonia, Ethiopia, Faeroe Islands, Falkland Island, Fiji, Finland, Fm Sudan, French Southern and Antarctic Lands, France, French Polynesia, Gabon, Gambia, The Georgia, Germany, Ghana, Gibraltar, Greece, Greenland, Grenada, Guadeloupe, Guam, Guatemala, Guinea, Guinea-Bissau, Guyana, Haiti, Heard Island and McDonald Islands, Holy See, Honduras, Hong Kong, China, Hungary, Iceland, India, Indonesia, Iran, Islamic Republic, Iraq, Ireland, Israel, Italy, Jamaica, Japan, Jordan, Kazakhstan, Kenya, Kiribati, Korea, Democratic Republic, Korea, Republic, Kuwait, Kyrgyz Republic, Lao PDR, Latvia, Lebanon, Lesotho, Liberia, Libya, Lithuania, Luxembourg, Macao, Macedonia, FYR, Madagascar, Malawi, Malaysia, Maldives, Mali, Malta, Marshall Islands, Mauritania, Mauritius, Mayotte, Mexico, Micronesia, Federal States, Moldova, Mongolia, Montenegro, Montserrat, Morocco, Mozambique, Myanmar, Namibia, Nauru, Nepal, Netherlands, Netherlands Antilles, New Caledonia, New Zealand, Nicaragua, Niger, Nigeria, Niue, Norfolk Island, Northern Mariana Islands, Norway, Occupied Palestinian Territory, Oman, Pakistan, Palau, Panama, Papua New Guinea, Paraguay, Peru, Philippines, Pitcairn, Poland, Portugal, Qatar, Reunion, Romania, Russian Federation, Rwanda, Saint Barthélemy, Saint Helena, Saint Maarten (Dutch part), Saint Pierre and Miquelon, Samoa, San Marino, Sao Tome and Principe, Saudi Arabia, Senegal, Serbia, FR(Serbia/Montenegro), Seychelles, Sierra Leone, Singapore, Slovak Republic, Slovenia, Solomon Islands, Somalia, South Africa, South Georgia and the South Sa, South Sudan, Spain, Sri Lanka, St. Kitts and Nevis, St. Lucia, St. Vincent and the Grenadines, Sudan, Suriname, Swaziland, Sweden, Switzerland, Syrian Arab Republic, Tajikistan, Tanzania, Thailand, Togo, Tokelau, Tonga, Trinidad and Tobago, Tunisia, Turkey, Turkmenistan, Turks and Caicos Islands, Tuvalu, Uganda, Ukraine, United Arab Emirates, United Kingdom, United States, United States Minor Outlying Islands, Uruguay, United States Miscellaneous Pacific Islands, Uzbekistan, Vanuatu, Venezuela, Vietnam, Wallis and Futuna Islands, Western Sahara, Yemen, Zambia, Zimbabwe.

Chapter 11
Mega Events and Their Effect on Mesoeconomics:
The Case of Plovdiv as Holding the Title European Capital of Culture 2019

Teodora Kiryakova-Dineva
https://orcid.org/0000-0002-1374-9999
South-West University "Neofit Rilski", Bulgaria

Vyara Kyurova
South-West University "Neofit Rilski", Bulgaria

Yana Chankova
South-West University "Neofit Rilski", Bulgaria

ABSTRACT

The chapter proposes an analysis that claims the importance of phenomena successfully revealed only in view of mesoeconomics. The authors argue that the economic processes in the field of organizing events should not be conceived merely as resulting from macro- and micro-level relationships but rather as resulting from relationships on mesoeconomic level (where a large number of unresolved and unexplored issues still exist), discussed by the authors in terms of the black box relationships on the mesoeconomic level. The main aim of this study is to investigate a specific mega event so as to trace and analyze the roles of the operators at the three levels of social-economic activity, and finally to identify the specific roles of the operators functioning at the mesoeconomic level. Making up a small part of scientific investigation in interdisciplinary research, the chapter proposes further perspectives for a proper application of mesoeconomics when discussing issues bridging micro-economics and macro-economics.

DOI: 10.4018/978-1-7998-4933-9.ch011

INTRODUCTION

Nowadays, most of the socio-economic phenomena depend on both phenomena, closely connected to the macro environment and micro-business characteristics (micro environment), and the well-established connections between them. The present research discusses the organization of mega events, while focusing on the scope of their relevance to the mesoeconomic level. The study deals with a Europe-wide initiative - the case of the European Capital of Culture, and in particular the 2019 choice of the Bulgarian city of Plovdiv as being awarded this title. As the essence of such a large-scale event might suggest, much effort is needed in order to organize and run the initiatives in the most effective way on the part of institutions and organizations, both formal and informal, at the European, national and municipal level (macro economy). On the one hand, a more dynamic interaction between the organizations is needed as well, and hence more reliable socio-cultural service providers have to be involved, so as to meet the expectations of the visitors to the various cultural events, making part of Plovdiv, ECoC 2019.

Moreover, the role of the visitors to the city has not to be neglected because they, in fact, make the greatest contribution to economic growth. We assume that a large number of interactions are required when conducting mega events of such a scale, and also that the interactions between the persons engaged lie in the sphere of mesoeconomics and are of paramount importance. Therefore, any border-type phenomenon could also be of particular interest for the present study, even more so when a culture phenomenon lies in its milieu.

The present study is devoted to the European Capital of Culture (ECoC) initiative which awards cities for their cultural environment, historical heritage and contribution to European diversity and gives them the opportunity to strengthen their image and to be located constantly on the world eventmap, to attract more tourists and to magnify their development through the lens of cultural events and program occasions. The title ECoC has a long-term impact not only in terms of cultural development but also in view of a large scale of socially and economically motivated processes whose role and function we are going to investigate herein.

Most of the activities carried out in relation to the European Capital of Culture initiative have a direct and medium-term effect for the development of the socio-cultural sector and the tourism industry and this brings about huge consequences for the city's economy. A regrettable fact that we have found out is the failure of many Plovdiv hotels to provide information on the cultural events and activities on their official websites, i.e. we have identified a gap that lies within the scope of mesoeconomics.

This chapter is structured as follows: part two outlines the reviews of the relevant literature on mesoeconomics and our conceptual framework for subsuming and discussing mega events under this level of economics. Part three presents the initiative European Capital of Culture and the nomination of Plovdiv for holding the title for the year 2019. The following part presents the nature of mesoeconomics, while the next one outlines the research setting and the methods uses. It describes the four main clusters of the one year' events in Plovdiv and proposes content analysis of these events. Drawing upon this analysis, a discussion of the economic meso-level is proposed. Part five contains some concluding remarks that recapture the concept view of mesoeconomics, its practical implication on the grounds of the events held in the city of Plovdiv as holding the title European Capital of Culture, and it also suggests some areas of future research with respect to the black box of the zone between macro and microeconomy.

BACKGROUND OF MESOECONOMICS

A survey of the academic research literature shows that the term mesoeconomics is used by Karl A. Wittfogel (1962) to describe the regional level of governance. According to Y. K. Ng (1986; 1982) mesoeconomics should be considered as a synthesis of macro- and micro-analysis. Cole (1968, 12ff) has a particular understanding of mesoeconomics. He claims that mesoeconomy is the space between micro and macro economics, manufacturing companies and economic aggregates, such as the industrial sectors, in which the "phenomenon of business system" is formed. At the same time, some authors emphasize that the macrosystem is the aggregate of mesoobjects, and that it reflects changes in the mesostructure, based on the tripartite concept of "micro-meso-macro" (Kruglova, 2017). Moreover, the economic development is formed with the emergence, adaptation, dissemination and institutionalization of mesorules at micro and macro levels (Dopfer, 2004).

The main concept of mesoeconomics in the research works of V. G. Gusakov (2018:490) is that it is currently an economy of the regions and sectors where the territorial and sectoral interests of the living and employed population dominate. Mesoeconomics, in his view, most fully characterizes the activities of enterprises operating in a given locality or industry and their competitive advantages, arising from the influence of entrepreneurial abilities (Gusakov, 2018:490). An essential feature of mesoeconomics is, then, to create the most favorable conditions for the realization of local and sectoral resources, and in particular of applied, technological and human resources (ibdm).

Discussing the essence of mesoeconomics, Kirdina-Chandler (2018:12) indicates that mesoeconomics studies the structural processes through which the coordination of participants in economic activity is carried out in order to obtain the results - the phenomena themselves discovered at the macro level. In addition, some authors believe that mesoeconomics is a "natural field of formation and action of economic institutions" (Kleyner, 2003:40-41).

In this connection, the question of clarifying the nature of the meso-level becomes crucial. It is a multidimensional construct and different approaches are used to define it. For the first time, the concept of "meso-level" was introduced by Stewart (1992) in her research work "Can Adjustment Programs Incorporate the Interests of Women?", wherein the author raises the idea of meso-leveling as the level of analysis between a country's overall economy and the level of individuals, companies and households (Stewart 1992:37). Furthermore, according to the same author and in compliance with the views of Rodgers and Cooley (1999), the mesoscale helps to determine the depth of impact of macrolevel structures, determining, for example, which property, gender groups, and industries bear the brunt of macro-level reforms (Stewart 1992:37; Rodgers and Cooly, 1999:1401).

The development of mesoeconomics theory has been accompanied by the promotion of diverse proposals on the nature and content of the meso-level. For example, the essence of the meso-level is considered by R. Matkovskyy as a set of ways to achieve the objectives of the functioning of the macroeconomic system (Matkovskyy, 2012:4). Most importantly, Kirdina-Chandler (2018:10) claims that it is on a meso-level that the mechanisms for economic growth or the main obstacles to its achievement arise as a result of cooperating the actions of micro-level economic operators. Moreover, the initiation of some events leads to a chain of others interconnected with them (Kirdina-Chandler,2018:12).

When pondering on the issue of meso-level, some authors look at it from a behavioral perspective. Much in this vein, Kolesnik (2015:6-7) points out that the meso-level takes into account, on one hand, the individual characteristics of economic operators and, on the other, the pattern of their group behavior.

The basic idea of meso-level in the theoretical proposals by some authors is that it represents a way of describing the institutions' establishment and the institutional environment processes. In this regard, Dopfer and Potts (2008:102-103) consider the meso-level as a space for the creation of common rules and the actions of their bearers. In their studies, Elsner and Heinrich (2009) elaborate on this definition. In their view, the meso-level can be defined as a space of institutionalization of rules, where collective attempts are made to overcome the conditions of uncertainty and minimize transaction costs (Elsner & Heinrich, 2009; Elsner, 2007; Elsner, 2009). Another noteworthy mention is that of Kruglova (2017:33), according to whom the meso-level is a field of interaction of micro-level operators and when certain common rules of interaction are formed, designed to minimize the possible costs in a situation of uncertainty. At the same time, in their treatment of the meso-level, some authors proceed from J. Schumpeter's concept of entrepreneurs generating innovation and claim that it should be seen as a space in which the rule developed by the individual / the entrepreneur is supported by the group and initially becomes a collective rule, later on an institutionalized one (Schumpeter, 1954; Dopfer, Foster & Potts, 2004; Dopfer and Potts, 2010). Gareev has a particular understanding of meso-level. He believes that the objective of investigation at this level is to "identify the area in which ascending processes of new rules are formed and downward processes of stabilizing constitutive rules collide" (Garev, 2010:45). In the opinion of Cole (1968:11ff) the meso level can be conceived as a space between micro- and macroeconomics, manufacturing companies and economic aggregates, such as the industrial sectors, in which the phenomenon of the "business system" is formed.

Along the same lines, M. A. Deryabina's (2018:18) view is also of importance for interpreting the essence of the meso-level. According to her, in the substantive aspect, the meso-level is the totality of its constituent complex systems with their structure, internal hierarchy and interactions. It should be borne in mind that the scope of the meso-level includes "not only the aggregate socio-economic subsystems of the middle level of the economic hierarchy, but also the aggregate subsystems that lie at lower levels, in particular, the enterprises and their groups" (Mesoeconomics, 2001:10). Kruglova, Volynskii & Kirilyuk (2019) also draw attention to the systematic approach in determining the meso-level. In their view, the meso-level refers to the process of intra-industry interactions between economic agents with the goal of harmonizing the economic system (ibidem, 2019:45). It is important to bear in mind that micro-level systems, which are controlled by the actions of informal institutions, help to expand the implementation of innovative solutions and, as a result, contribute to the achievement of high economic efficiency of joint activities (Heinrich et. al, 2004). Such solutions can be achieved by the means of communication and digitalization as a managerial tool (Trencheva & Zdravkova, 2019; Kyurova, 2017).

Furthermore, in the relevant literature, the meso-level is also considered to be composed of the following four components: sectoral mesoeconomics; interindustry mesoeconomics (interindustry vertical complexes and sub-sectoral complexes of the type of agroindustrial complexes and military industrial complexes); regional mesoeconomics (regions, territorial groups of enterprises); interregional mesoeconomics (territorial socio-economic entities) (Mesoeconomica razvitiya, 2011:9).

It needs to be noted that in topical research literature, the meso-level is regarded primarily as a formation of institutions' space. This view gains support from Mayevskiy's (2018:20) assumption that the meso-level should be seen as a generator of institutions that optimize and organize the interaction of micro- and macro-level entities in the growth process. At the same time, Elsner (2007) draws the important conclusion that the meso-level is the level of economic hierarchy in which the observed processes of social and economic evolution occur, resulting in the emergence of new institutions. In this context, need arises to discuss the content of mesoinstitutions. In this regard, Kruglova (2018:50) reveals that mesoinstitutions are intermediate organizational structures whose task is to implement macro-level (mainly government and international organizations) reform projects. At the same time, she argues that their availability depends to a large extent on the implementation of strategies and the introduction of formal standards of behavior in a historically formed institutional environment, filled with a set of institutionalized informal standards of behavior (ibd.). In a former work Kruglova (2017:30) examines the ability of mesoinstitutions to create effective guiding principles and the adoption of game rules by participants as an important condition for the successful fulfillment of the intermediary functions of such institutions. In turn, Menard (2014) draws attention to the fact that mesoinstitutions should be regarded as intermediaries responsible for implementing the common rules by formulating specific recommendations and providing feedback from operators who are affected by the rule implementation process. Mesoinstitutions also refer to the intermediate relationship between the level at which the common rules and rights are determined and the conditions for their distribution are fixed, and the level of organizational mechanisms (markets, firms, hybrids) through which economic transactions are actually accomplished (Menard, 2018:8). The position, held by some authors is that the conceptualization of the meso-level as a socio-economic hierarchical level becomes necessary due to the development of formal and informal individual institutions which are not usually found within the "micro-macro" paradigm (Hodgson, 2000; Ayres & Martinas, 2005).

The City of Plovdiv as Holding the Title European Capital of Culture

The initiation and exploitation of the European Capital of Culture (ECoC) is a relatively new mega event type in the tradition created by the European Union and is one of the most successful and prestigious cultural events world-wide at the present time. The ECoC was initiated in 1983 by Melina Mercury, who was then Greek Minister of Culture and it was established by the Council of Ministers of the European Union. The first ECoC was Athens, and now, in 2020 the implementation of the initiative ECoC is marked by its 35th anniversary.

ECoC is one of the most prominent and prestigious European international cultural events of a considerable impact not only for social life and the sharing of culture values but also for the economic growth of local economies, including tourism entertainment industry. As a concept the title ECoC builds on the strategic goal to bring the European countries together through culture, social and art events, inclusion. Since 1983 more than 40 cities have been awarded the title „European Capital of Culture". Initially, the aim of the event was to promote the culture of the major European cities which, at the same time, made part of the EU measure concerning social and cultural integration. This overarching goal continues to this day, and through their uniqueness, historical and cultural heritage and identity, the nominated European cities add value to the event.

In this chapter, we focus on the above initiative because it has the character of a mega event and also because it specifically reflects the interaction between the macro and micro economies. As some authors rightly point out (Ugreanu, 2001; Palmer, 2004; Richards and Rotariu, 2013), the motive of any city wishing to become an ECoC is by promoting its cultural heritage to achieve economic growth through popularity, sustainable partnerships and cooperation networks. In this sense, the ECoC can be considered as a market-based instrument for regional development, involving both national and international players and small and medium-sized business stakeholders. Last but not least, the ECoC initiative has made a significant contribution to social inclusion and intercultural dialogue, a fact recognized by the Council of the European Union and the Council of Europe.

The title is awarded on the grounds of a varied and unadulterated cultural program that must also attest to a strong pan-European dimension, stimulate participation and active involvement of the residents of the city and contribute to the long-term development of the city and the region [1]. The title European Capital of Culture also gives an excellent opportunity to the nominated cities to change their image, be featured on the world map, attract more tourists and rethink their development through the lens of culture. This title has a long-term impact not only culturally speaking but also socially and economically, both for the city nominated and for the region in which it is located.

Plovdiv is the first Bulgarian city being awarded for holding the title European Capital of Culture. The nomination of Plovdiv for the award was made in 2015 by an international jury selection. All nominated cities are given a 4-year period to plan in detail and organize an event of such a mega rank. The preparatory stage is concentrated on popularizing the event, on opening calls for different national and international projects. The assessment of projects to be included in the event happens in accordance with a set of established criteria during the pre-selection phase. All submitted project proposals are evaluated by independent cultural experts. The major responsible institution is the relevant Ministry of Culture and its offices on the regional level. Notably, the first stage of the mega event starts on the macro level. This stage takes place 'behind the curtains' and remains invisible for the general public until the very start of the mega event European Capital of Culture.

The official launch of the mega event Plovdiv – the European Capital of Culture took place between January 11th and January 13th, with more than 30 events held on both indoor and outdoor stages. The highlight of the opening ceremony was the unique show, combining music, light and dance "We are all colors", held on 12th of January 2019. "We are all colors" featured over 1500 spectacular performances of artists from Bulgaria and abroad, recreating the main themes of the Plovdiv - European Capital of Culture programme, e.g. the exhibition "Smoke. Tobacco Stories", as well as the exhibition "The Art of Freedom - from the Berlin Wall to Street Art", dedicated to the 30th anniversary of the Fall of the Berlin Wall, the play "Eurydice in the Underworld" by the Plovdiv Drama Theater, the opera "Maria of Buenos Aires" by the Plovdiv State Opera, to mention just a few. For the children there was intended a special children's programme, part of which was the presentation of the travelling exhibition "Eureka".

The magnificent opening was watched by hundreds of thousands of in-person audiences on site as well as on television and online. The opening of the mega event attested a large number of delegations' representatives, including representatives from more than 20 cities that previously held the title European Capital of Culture. Special guests were the members of the team from Matera - the twin European city that also held the title European Capital of Culture for 2019.

The overall programme for Plovdiv – the European Capital of Culture 2019 was organized under the motto "Together" and was subdivided into 4 thematic platforms, related to the typical features of the city, its cultural heritage, history, pace of life, as well as challenges and stereotypes that need to be overcome. The respective platforms were named: FUSE, REVIVE, TRANSFORM, RELAX.

The FUSE platform brings together 3 clusters - Mahala, Regionale and Beauty and the (B)East. The projects under the FUSE platform envisage topics for the integration of ethnicities and minorities and aim to strengthen the relations between generations and social groups, as well as to eliminate the borders between isolated territories and areas.

The Mahala cluster was focused mainly on the Stolipinovo neighborhood and in particular on the children being raised there. The projects and events comprising this cluster aimed to improve children's social, educational and health integration and to stimulate their creativity and communication skills. Some of the more important and interesting projects here are: "Together for Better Education and Health";

"Plovdiv Together: Elimination of the Ghetto Boundaries"; "Crafts enter the Mahala"; "Building Together: Learning from Stolipinovo"; "From Toledo to Plovdiv: The Journey of the Jewish Sephardic Song"; "Kaj Dzias Performance about Roma Culture and Integrative Workshops" and others.

The Regionale cluster brings together cultural, social and tourist projects aimed at presenting traditions, customs and crafts in the everyday life of small and large towns and villages from the Plovdiv region. It also aims to assist in the process of intergenerational continuity and the transfer of experience, heritage and traditions from small settlements to big cities. Among the more significant projects are: "Meeting Thrace's Folklore"; "Baba's Show-How"; "Staro Zhelezare Street Art Village Festival"; "Vazduharia, a Festival of Free Flying"; "Electric Orpheus" and others. The events and festivals of this cluster attracted not only native tourists but also visitors from the EU – fans of folklore music and dancing. The Beauty and the (B)East cluster targets foreign audiences. It aims to present the culture and traditions of the Balkans to the European counties and the world. The projects carried out under this cluster are implemented thanks to the kind cooperation not only of Matera – the twin city bearing the title of European Capital of Culture for 2019 – but also of cities all around the world. Remarkably, Plovdiv is the first European capital of culture to use the Cyrillic alphabet and many of the cluster's projects are aimed at presenting Cyrillic to the world, the key project being called "Cyrillization".

The TRANSFORM Platform embraces the following clusters: Urban Dreams, River of Imagination and edYOUcate. It is mainly aimed at preserving our environment and rethinking the way we perceive it. The Urban Dreams cluster includes projects through which forgotten and abandoned urban spaces, buildings and venues can be revitalized and renovated creatively, such as: old tobacco warehouses, Kosmos Cinema, Kapana, the Maritsa river and Adata Island, etc.

The River of Imagination cluster focuses on one of the most important natural resources of Plovdiv – the Maritsa River. The purpose of this cluster is to launch, through various activities and initiatives, the process of revitalizing the river and the island of Adata, the key transforming tools being culture, arts and green innovation. By turning the riparian zones into small oases, the events and festivals of this cluster attracted many Bulgarian and foreign tourists who love water adventures and water sports. Some of the most significant projects internationally include: "Adata Air", "Adata Open Air", "The River" and "International Youth Festival of Watercolour". The third cluster from this platform - edYOUcate is aimed at children and young people. The projects making part of it provide an excellent opportunity for young persons to develop their creative potential and accumulate soft skills and for cultural and educational institutions to foster contacts and partnerships in the field of cultural management.

The REVIVE platform also consists of 3 clusters: Culture Meets People, Art for a Forgotten Future, and Time Machine. The platform brings together projects focused on new ways of protecting and presenting cultural legacy and cultural diversity in a contemporary context. The aim is to improve the access of citizens to the Arts and culture as well as to build a stronger connection between audience and performers. Many projects here relate to the ways in which modern art can inspire new life or breathe artistic flavour into the city's rich past, as well as restore interest in outdated or forgotten landmarks and tourist attractions.

The RELAX platform includes the clusters EUrhythmica, Animate the City and Ayliak City. The projects comprising these clusters are focused on enhancing happiness, harmony and relaxation and leading more peaceful, sustainable and slow life. Emphasis is also laid on the connection between sport and art as a way of bringing people together and a tool of achieving harmony between body, mind and spirit. The events and festivals included here promote the values of culture, family and community as well as the non-consumerist outlook and way of life.

Benefits of the Mega Event Plovdiv European Capital of Culture

In recent years, the number of cities applying for European Capitals of Culture has increased five-fold. This is due both to the proven benefits to the cities awarded the title and to the successful achievement of the goals they have set for themselves through the project. Studies in cities that have been European Capitals of Culture show that the initiative has the following benefits:

- Benefits for the Culture
    - Stimulates creativity
    - Creates new audiences for culture
    - Stimulates the construction of new infrastructure for culture
    - Encourages international cooperation
    - Creates new career opportunities for artists
    - Contributes to a more dynamic cultural life in the city
    - Professionalizes the local cultural sector
- Benefits for the Economics
    - Contributes to urban renewal and development
    - Stimulates tourism
    - Creates drive in other sectors
    - Creates new jobs Improves the image of the city
- Benefits for the Social life
    - Contributes to social life in the city through public events
    - Helps for the social inclusion of vulnerable groups through cultural events accessible to everyone
    - Encourages civic participation through voluntary programs
    - Encourages audience involvement in the creation of art.

RESEARCH METHOD

To begin with, we would like to draw your attention to Stöbe's analysis of historic key events and the media in "The concise encyclopedia of communication" (Stöbe, 2015: 246). We have chosen to adopt his approach and apply it to our data analysis for several reasons. First of all, it is the fact that Stöbe's approach is designed in order to describe and analyze large-scale events, in particular historic key events whose status he defines in the following way: „The status of an event as 'historic'and 'key'depends on its importance, which is relative, not absolute. For instance, many historic key events are only important for a particular nation." The same author discusses different methodologies that have been applied in analyzing historic key events in terms of their coverage and argues that the content analysis methodology is fundamental to such studies. However, Stöbe also claims that: „Future research should take into account a combination of content analysis, reception research, media structure analysis, and historical criticism" (2015: 246).

Much in the same vein, in her study Image, Logo, Brand and Nation: Destination Marketing, Nationalism and the 2007 Cricket World Cup Leanne White (2011:160) applies a combined methodologies approach (semiotic analysis and content analysis, to be quite precise) for deconstructing mediated representations of national imagery and branding which results in a combination of primary and secondary research. What is of special interest for us in White's analysis is the dual framework exploration of nationalism and destination marketing.

The mentioned above methodologies provide us with some guiding principles in our study of the mega event Plovdiv - European Capital of Culture 2019. We, however, believe that mega events could hardly be analyzed exclusively by the application of a combined methodology. We are convinced that content analysis makes the most essential part of the methodology that should be used in doing research on mega events since: „content analysis is effectively a counting strategy and is put forward as an objective method for counting content. It is a useful research tool for identifying, categorizing and describing trends." (White, ibid).

On the other hand, we do not intend to sweep under the rug an important fact that emerges from the survey of literature, namely the fact that at least one more research approach is needed for the purposes of investigating event management, hence our choice fell on the Business Analysis Techniques, proposed by Cadle et. al. (2014). The authors identify and discuss a large number of analysis techniques but, specifically, we have decided to adopt and apply to our data the so-called business event analysis technique which combines system event analysis and business process triggers. Cadle et. al. arguethat: „business event analysis is concerned with examining a business system or an area of activity in order to identify the events the organization needs to handle" (Cadle et.al., 2014:99). The authors' account of this analysis technique is based on three types of events: external events, internal events and time-based events. Cadle at al. state that the first step is the identification of the business event, the second step is the monitoring of costs as the event proceeds, whereas the third step is the model and analysis of the business processes that will be triggered by the event and will deliver the outcome.

The scope of the present study does not include steps two and three mentioned above, but it well accommodates step one which is aimed at a detailed identification and exhaustive presentation of the event. Notably, in order to achieve the objectives of this research, we have chosen to apply a combined analysis approach, namely, one based on qualitative content analysis and business event analysis. The content analysis of the operators involved in the organization of the mega event Plovdiv - European Capital of Culture 2019 is carried out in three stages, i.e. classification of the main operators, functional principle and the horizontal principle. The combined content analysis methodology is motivated by the heterogeneous nature of the organization of the mega event in question and the fact that taking a direct approach to our data is unfeasible.

Taking into account the variety of small-scale events that make up the Plovdiv ECoC 2019 mega event profile and in order to analyze the role of the meso-level operators, the present authors propose the following algorithm of analysis:

- Step one: Main operators are classified first

For the purpose of a proper categorization, macro-level operators have been classified at stage one, including national institutions, international institutions, cultural institutions, national galleries, national museums, international foundations and international associations. Their function in the projects is justified by the prestige of the respective event. Artists, performers, creators or celebrities also take part in many of these events. The involvement of world-wide recognized operators enhances the importance of each event and adds value to each project. Artists and celebrities often play an additional testimonial function and increase the visitors' interest to the event.

- Step two: The functional principle as a rule for operators on the micro- and meso-level

The differentiation between meso-level operators and micro-level operators is essential to both the analysis to be carried out and the ensuing results since the assignment to one or the other type of operators reveals the importance of mesoeconomics or microeconomics, respectively, in organizing a given mega event.

We assume that the guiding principle in the classification of operators should be the functional principle, which, in our view, is tantamount to the specific function of the organization, enterprise, training institution or another body in each specific project. In this way, a distinction is to be drawn between the types of functions which the operators implement in their main activity and the activity which the operator implements under a given project. For instance, it is possible for a micro-level publishing house to operate on a meso-level since such is the role of the latter operator in a specific project (e.g. consider the bkvAR project). Or vice versa, it is possible for an operator to implement an activity linking the micro and macro economies, e.g. an association may have a support activity under a project and hence fall within the group of micro-level operators.

- Step three: The horizontal principle has to be applied applies a rule for operators in one event

The horizontal principle is applied when more than one operator participates in a certain event. When the roles of operators make up a hierarchy, we apply the horizontal principle and thus we differentiate between a lead operator and a support operator, or operators in an equal partnership.

ANALYSIS OF THE OPERATORS ON THE MESOECONOMIC LEVEL

The mega event Plovdiv - European Capital of Culture 2019 involves the organization of over 320 events, arranged in four thematic platforms. Our investigation on the four platforms mentioned and on the opening event as well reveal that operators from all three levels take part in each specific event.

Thematic-Functional Presentation of the Mega Event Plovdiv ECoC 2019

Thematically speaking, events should be considered in terms of their character, to begin with. In this respect, it is important to establish the distribution of events and the participation of operators in them. Figure 1 illustrates the distribution of events and the participation of operators:

The illustration shows that from a thematic-functional perspective certain major event groups have been attested and included in the model of the events. Due to its nature the official Opening of ECoC 2019 has been classified separately. These major event groups can be classified as follows: open air performances, festivals, communitybased projects, exhibitions, theater and music and dance, educational workshops.

A characteristic feature of the ECoC 2019 mega event is the fact that a huge number of operators are involved in implementing the projects under each platform. Remarkably, operators from all three levels take part in the organization of events under three of the platforms and it is only in the RIVIVE platform events that primarily meso-level operators are engaged. The distribution of operators at the micro-, meso- and macro-levels is analyzed and illustrated below. Additionally, some prospective reasons that are assumed to underlie this distribution will be suggested, based on the proposed qualitative

Figure 1. Thematic-functional presentation of the mega event Plovdiv ECoC 2019
Source: the authors

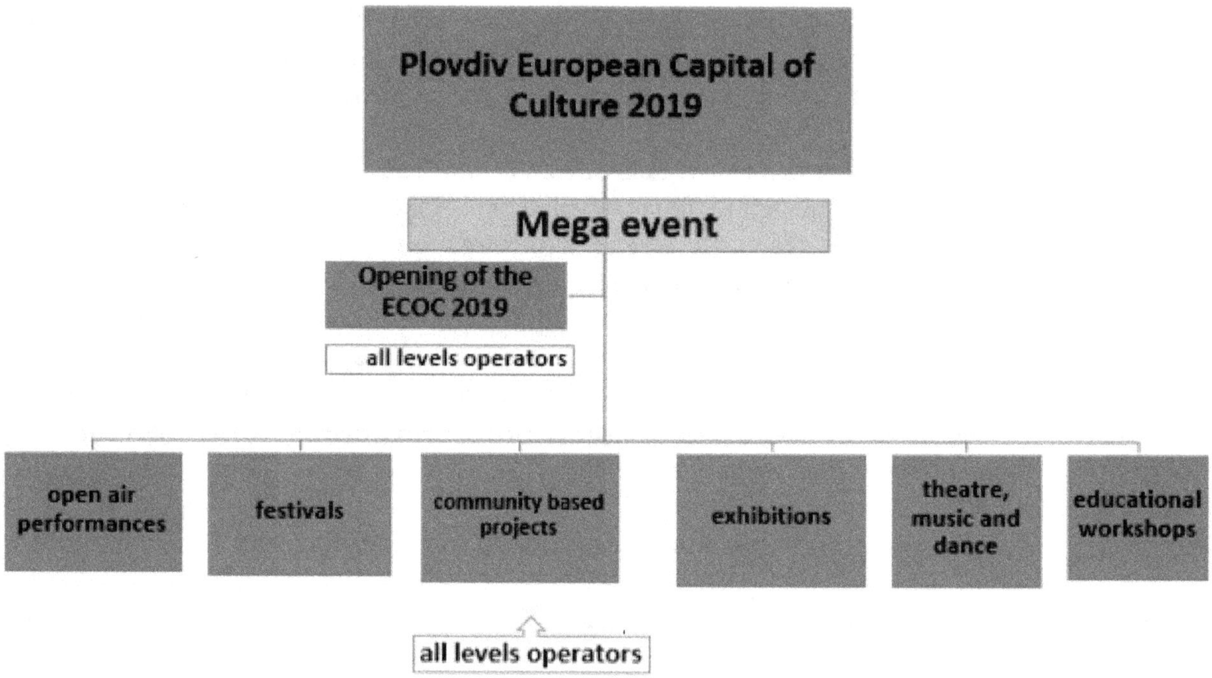

content analysis. The distribution of operators in charge of organizing the Opening event of ECoC 2019 will be presented first.

The Opening of ECoC 2019 Event and the Meso-Level Operators

The Opening of the ECoC Plovdiv 2019 will be presented first. Based on the proposed technique for combined qualitative content analysis and business event analysis of mega events, the following specific

Table 1 Distribution of the operators taking part in the organization of the Opening event of the Plovdiv ECoC 2019

Type of operators	Macro level operators	Meso level operators	Micro level operators
main operator		Plovdiv 2019 Foundation	
support operators	Plovdiv minicipality		Individual artists
	Cultural institutions in Plovdiv		Citizens
	Several international organizations		Sponsors
	The Ministry of Culture		
	Broadcasting companies		
	The French Institute in Bulgaria		

Source: the authors

distribution can be put forward in view of the operators at the different levels engaged in organizing the Opening of Plovdiv the ECoC 2019

The presented results show that the main responsibility for organizing the Opening event lies with the Plovdiv 2019 Foundation. Since organizing and holding the official Opening of the mega event Plovdiv - European Capital of Culture 2019 is a culminating moment one main operator assumes responsibility for it. The Plovdiv 2019 Foundation is an organization whose activities are carried out at the level of the mesoeconomy of cultural and social activities. With more than 1,500 participants, the Opening is large-scale event, hence, a large number of different institutions and organizations are also involved in the organization, whereby the more important ones are macro-level operators, e.g. Plovdiv minicipality, Cultural Institutions in Plovdiv, the Ministry of Culture, International organizations, Broadcasting companies, The French Institute in Bulgaria. A number of other macro-level operators also take part in this event, namely, partnering organizations and institutions representing former European Capitals of Culture. The group of micro-level operators includes a great number of micro-units, e.g. artists, performers, as well as a large number of citizens.

The Platform FUSE and the Meso-Level Operators

The FUSE Platform comprises three clusters: Regionale, Mahala and Beauty and the (B)East. The underlying concept of the FUSE platform is the integration of ethnic and minority groups, since Plovdiv is a city famous for its multicultural diversity, where multiple cultural traditions have been forever present. The main initiatives here range from festivals to various cultural, tourist and social projects. We have attempted a detailed study of the operators, responsible for the organization of the events under FUSE, categorizing them in Table 2 in accordance with the three main levels.

Table 2. Distribution of the operators taking part in the organization of events under the FUSE Platform

Type of operators	Macro level operators	Meso level operators	Micro level operators
	17	43	32

Source: the authors

The distribution in the three main type of operators demonstrates that there is a huge number of diverse operators participating in all events under the FUSE platform - 92 operators, to be quite precise. The proposed methodology reveals that the macro-level operators are 17, the meso-level operators are 43, and the micro-level operators are 32.

The Platform TRANSFORM and the Meso-Level Operators

The TRANSFORM platform comprises 45 different events which are run by numerous Bulgarian and foreign operators. The platform is aimed at transforming abandoned urban spaces and changing the way they are perceived. The transformation is based on activities related to children's and youth audiences, artistic performances, educational and creative projects as well as environmental projects. The transformed spaces are the Tobacco City, Kapana, Kosmos Cinema, the Maritsa River area and Adata Island. The distribution of operators at the three levels of economy is based on the proposed methodology. Table 3 presents the results as follows:

Table 3. Distribution of the operators taking part in the organization of events under the TRANSFORM Platform

Type of operators	Macro level operators	Meso level operators	Micro level operators
	6	33	23

Source: the authors

The above table reveals that among the operators involved six can be identified as main operators and that they all function at the macro-level, namely, the Plovdiv 2019 Foundation, French Cultural Institute, Bulgarian-American Fulbright Commission, Goethe-Institute Bulgaria, Polish Institute and British Council Bulgaria. Based on the functional principle, we have attested 23 operators functioning at the micro-level and 33 operators functioning at the meso-level, whereby the majority of meso-level operators are associations and foundations.

Among the events organized under this platform, there are several that stand out in terms of their scale and significance, e.g. the Kapana Creative District, the Tobacco City Programme, the Street Arts Festival - Night of Stories, Street Masters 2019, Maritsa Nature Trail, International Youth Festival of Watercolor Plovdiv 2019, the River Feast, etc.

It has been found out that many of events have one key operator and several partner operators which are also listed as key operators, regardless of their organizational structure. For example, the Adata Programme event which runs from July to December and covers topics related to nature and culture, as well as to the Maritsa River and Adata Island is a project involving 14 different smaller events. This project is implemented by the main operator Plovdiv 2019 Foundation in partnership with Goethe-Institut Bulgaria and the Polish Institute in Sofia. Due to the fact that the Adata Programme event is of a larger scale as compared to the rest, the lead partner and the two partnering institutes are assigned to the macro-level operators.

With regard to the horizontal principle, it can be pointed out that there are cases when a main operator, such as the Plovdiv Regional History Museum performs a supporting function in a given event. A case in point is the exhibition Smoke. Tobacco Stories. which is managed by one key operator and many participating operators acting on the micro level, in particular over 20 major national and regional museums, archives, galleries, as well as a great number of individual artists. Based on the chosen methodology and the horizontal principle, the mentioned 20 units are assigned to one micro-level operator, as they collaborate in running a single event. In this platform like in the previous one, most of the operators act on the meso level.

The Platform REVIVE and the Meso-Level Operators

The REVIVE Platform includes 3 clusters, comprising 87 events, such as performing arts, music, theatre and open air events and it presents the artists to the public. The REVIVE platform differs from the rest in terms of its participants. What is special about this platform is that it tries to devise a way to present cultural heritage in its contemporary form without introducing elements of tourist attraction in it. Therefore, the participants in this platform are representatives of smaller and larger cultural centers and institutes, as presented in Table 4:

Table 4. Distribution of the operators taking part in the organization of events under the REVIVE Platform

Operators	Macro level operators	Meso level operators	micro level operators
	-	87	-

Source: the authors

Due to the specifics of the events under the REVIVE Platform, each particular event is organized by one unit or association of units in partnership which always have the same function in organizing a specific event - the presentation of a particular culture, cultural practice, art or performance.

The functional principle can be applied only to the extent that the types of meso-operators are identified. For the same purpose, the horizontal principle is also applied, whereby the results are the illustrated by Figure 2.

Figure 2. Types of the meso-level operators
Source: the authors

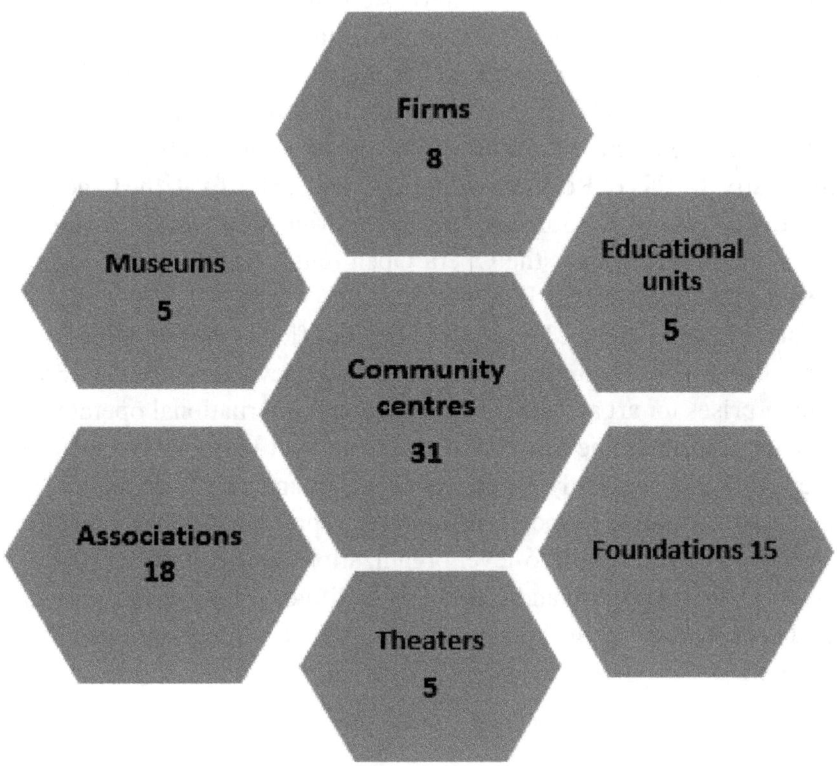

As Figure 2 reveals, the largest number of meso-level operators belongs to the libraries, second come the associations. A number of organizations and foundations are also involved. The museums, theaters and training organizations operating under this platform are also classified as meso-level operators because of the function they perform, being sole organizers of a given event.

The Platform RELAX and the Meso-Level Operators

The RELAX platform comes closest to the traditional concept of events because it is the platform of the major music festivals and performances. The number of events under this platform is 59 and they are organized in 3 clusters, promoting a sustainable, slow, green lifestyle and degrowth. Because of the profile of this platform, it is interesting to identify and outline the roles of operators here as well as the predominant level of their activity. Table 5 gives a detailed account of the distribution of the operators involved with respect to their level of economic activity:

Table 5. Distribution of the operators taking part in the organization of events under the RELAX Platform

Operators	Macro level operators	Meso level operators	Micro level operators
	9	21	18

Source: the authors

In this platform, the distribution of operators is relatively even and quite similar to their distribution in the FUSE and TRANSFORM platforms. Based on step one of the analysis, 9 macroeconomic operators can be identified, and these are major international, intergovernmental or national organizations and important public bodies, such as the European Parliament in Bulgaria, the European Commission in Bulgaria, the Bulgarian National Television. Their participation is mainly justified by the organization of events of international importance, e.g. Europe Day Festival of Lights - Explore Bulgaria: Plovdiv, Opera Open Music Festival, Hills of Rock, Plovdiv Fresh Music Festival, the Cinema Festival: "Against Forgetting" and "Plovdiv Jazz Fest". Some of the above events are held by a single operator, e.g. the Plovdiv State Opera organizes and runs the Opera Open music festival on its own and National Geographic runs the event Explore Bulgaria: Plovdiv.

Regarding the functional principle, 21 operators are identified at the meso-level, including 4 associations, 4 foundations, 1 Initiative Committee, three radio and television stations, a Symphony Orchestra, Choirs and some enterprises for art and cinema productions. International operators of arts and culture are also present. With respect to the horizontal principle, the majority of operators function at the meso-level and they work independently. In some rare cases, an event is organized by several operators at different levels, irrespective of the type of institutions, represented by the operators. This is the case when a smaller operator is a leading meso-level organization, such as the Cal y Canto Teatro in which case the Embassy of Spain in Bulgaria and Cervantes Institute-Sofia operators are classified as micro-level operators, and hence, based on the horizontal principle, the aforementioned institute and embassy are assigned to one unit.

The Meso-Level Operator as a Main Contributor to the Event

The analysis of the operators involved in organizing the Plovdiv ECoC 2019 mega event revealed the complex nature and diversity of the event organizers and it also confirmed the role of mesoeconomics. The mega event comprises 320 smaller events, out of which 31 are organized by macro-level operators, micro-level operators take part in 76 events, whereas 200 meso-level operators participate as lead or partnership operators. The attested high number of meso-operators shows that they play an important role in the organization of various events. At the same time, their role in the development of a country's economy, and in particular in the territorial and regional development is also very significant.

The meso-level operators are the missing link between the micro- and macro- level and they contribute not only to the sustainable development but also to the all-round satisfaction of the socio-cultural needs of the population of a territory or region, moreover, they play an important role not only in the organization of events but in general. The analysis above demonstrates that the meso-level operators are most active in contributing to the activities of cultural organizations and institutions. They are an important tool of shaping the institutional event environment. Based on the analysis, we can point out that the meso-level is indeed the generator of operators which are in charge of the interaction between micro- and macro- level organizations in the process of achieving economic growth.

FUTURE RESEARCH DIRECTIONS

The discussion on the specifics of the mega event European Capital of Culture confirms the role of mesoeconomics in the creation of the necessary institutional environment, and it also paves the way for future research opportunities investigating similar event phenomena. The establishment of the leading function of mesoeconomics in the development of a country's economy can be sought against the background of specific territorially and regionally significant processes of socio-economic nature. The validity of the proposed role of the operators in the initiation, creation, development, launching, and management of various mass events can be studied in greater detail by applying methodologies using analysis such as PESTLE, C-PEST or other innovative models.

The view that the operators at the mesoeconomic level can develop their potential for bridging macroeconomics and microeconomics has been discussed in terms of a mega-event, but the research scope can be applied to diverse large-scale events, occasions and local celebrations.

Further topics for discussion can be found in the direction of the possibility for post-events, events of long-term character or concurrent events. Additionally, their contribution to the sustainable development of the host region can be investigated. An interesting issue would be to search for a model measuring the economic effect of the events. In this sense, a possible line of inquiry can be proposed concerning the relation between various macroeconomic agents, microeconomic units and the operators at the meso-economic level. Another issue within the scope of future research can be formulated in terms of the socio-cultural needs and promotion of culture within a given territory or region. In a similar way, other phenomena with event-like character can be studied, i.e. organized activities in various fields such as sports, ecology, community life, etc.

In cases of mass events, it is relevant to seek for more exhaustive answers to questions on economic growth, but other aspects concerning the safety of visitors are also relevant, including the protection of visitors' health.

CONCLUSION

The European Capital of Culture mega event can be described as a branding tool on a European scale and, what is more, it is a powerful tool for preserving, promoting and sharing of European culture and contemporary art. This mega initiative is characterized by sustainability in terms of placement, time duration, experience uniqueness, gathering of target audiences and attractiveness of potential public. Along with the cultural, artistic and educational benefits, the initiative has a positive impact in terms of benefits to social globalization, the development of urban cultural spaces, and last but not least it makes numerous contributions to local economies.

The above chapter was meant to propose a specific interpretation of mega events, while focusing on the relationship between different types of institutions and organizers, identified here as operators, and the levels of economic activity, hence the operators were classified and assigned to the macro-, meso- and micro-levels. Since the meso-level of economy is a natural field in which different organizations (in their own peculiar way and within a specific territorial unit) perform a predominantly social function, they become the relevant operators at the meso-level of economy as well as the eligible operators for organizing events, including mega events. The main objective of our study was to identify the meso-level operators taking part in the Plovdiv ECoC 2019 event. To achieve this objective, we have taken account of the specific features of meso-economy and, from a theoretical perspective, we have traced out some of the functions of the operators in view of their contribution to the delivery of services in organizing cultural events. Based on the theoretical analysis and on the nature of the event itself, we suggested a combined technique for describing and analyzing the meso-level operators. The study revealed that mega events are organized by diverse types of organizations which play a main, supportive or partnering role in any specific small-scale event.

It was confirmed that the meso-level operators are of most significant importance in implementing the projects under the four platforms of the mega event. For the most part, these are associations, foundations, cultural centers, galleries and museums. In the mixed type of projects, i.e. where training workshops or open air performances are planned, operators of a more specific character are also involved. They cooperate in partnership, and very often such partnership is based on preliminary contracts and joint projects. The highest number of meso-level operators is attested when the event is of purely cultural character and when the operators implement their main activity, e.g. in the presentation of a cultural practice, an exhibition or a performance, as is the case with the REVIVE platform aimed at sharing cultural practices. On the other hand, as in the case of the culminating moment of the Opening event of Plovdiv ECoC 2019, when greater efforts and involvement of institutions at national and international level, of partners and co-organizers are required, the macro-level operators play a leading role. The proposed analysis was not intended as an exhaustive study of all the characteristics of the operators involved in organizing a mega event but it gives a good idea of what happens behind the scenes of such an event and succeeds in revealing at least to some extent what is hidden in the black box of meso-economy.

REFERENCES

Ayres, R. U., & Martinas, K. (2005). *On the Reappraisal of Microeconomics*. E. Elgar. doi:10.4337/9781845427948

Cadle, J., Paul, D., & Turner, P. (2014). *Business analysis techniques. BCS*. Chartered Institute for IT.

Cole, A. H. (1968). Meso-economics: a contribution from entrepreneurial history. *Explorations in Entrepreneurial History, 6*(1), 3-33.

Deryabina, M. A. (2018). Methodological foundations of the study of the meso-economics as a complex system. *Journal of Institutional Studies, 10*(3), 30-32.

Dopfer, K., Foster, J., & Potts, J. (2004). Micro-meso-macro. *Journal of Evolutionary Economics, 14*(3), 263–279. doi:10.100700191-004-0193-0

Dopfer, K., & Potts, J. (2008). *The General Theory of Economic Evolution*. Routledge.

Dopfer, K., & Potts, J. (2010). Why evolutionary realism underpins evolutionary economic analysis and theory: A reply to Runde's critique. *Journal of Institutional Economics, 6*(3), 401–413. doi:10.1017/S1744137410000093

Elsner, W. (2007). Why Meso? On "Aggregation" and "Emergence", and Why and How the Meso Level is Essential in Social Economics. *The Forum for Social Economics, 36*(1), 1–16. doi:10.100712143-007-0001-3

Elsner, W. (2009). The process and a simple logic of 'meso'. Emergence and the coevolutionof institutions and group size. *Journal of Evolutionary Economics, 20*(3), 445–477. doi:10.100700191-009-0158-4

Elsner, W., & Heinrich, T. (2009). A simple theory of 'meso'. On the co-evolution of institutions and platform size - With an application to varieties of capitalism and 'mediumsized'countries. *Journal of Socio-Economics, 38*(5), 843–858. doi:10.1016/j.socec.2009.05.001

Gareev, T. R. (2010). Institutions and economic development at the subregional (meso-) level. *Social Sciences and Modernity, 5*, 45.

Gusakov, V. G. (2018). Grounds of Systemic Economics. *Proceedings from the National Academy of Sciences in Belarus, 62*(44), 488–494.

Henrich, J., Boyd, R., Bowles, S., Camerer, C., Fehr, E., & Gintis, H. (2004). *Foundations of Human Sociality. Economic Experiments and Ethnographic Evidence from Fifteen Small-Scale Societies*. Oxford University Press. doi:10.1093/0199262055.001.0001

Hodgson, G. M. (2000). From micro to macro: the concept of emergence and the role of institutions. In *Institutions and the Role of the State* (pp. 103–126). Edward Elgar.

Kirdina-Chandler, S.G. (2018). Meso-economics and economics and complexity economics: actual departure from orthodoxity. *Journal of Institutional Studies, 10*(3), 6-17.

Kleyner, G.B. (2003). Meso-economic problems of Russian economy. *Economic Bulletin of Rostov State University, 1*(2), 11-18.

Kleyner, G. B. (2011). *Mesoeconomics of the transition period: markets, industries, enterprises*. Science.

Kleyner, G. B. (2011). *Mesoeconomics of development*. Science.

Kolesnik, G. V. (2015). *Modeling competition in hierarchical socio-economic systems*. Lenand.

Kruglova, M. S. (2017). Mesoeconomic Theory in English-scientific Literature. *Journal of Institutional Research*, *9*(3), 25–35.

Kruglova, M. S. (2018). Claude Menard's Meso-Institution Theory and It's Application in the Institutional Design. *Institutional Studies Journal*, *10*(3), 49–57. doi:10.17835/2076-6297.2018.10.3.049-057

Kruglova, M. S., Volynsky, A. I., & Kirilyuk, I. L. (2019). *Meso-Level of Economy: Theoretical Approaches and Math Modeling. Institutional Studies Journal.*

Kyurova, A. (2017). Communication as a managerial tool for the processes in organizations. *Entrepreneurship*, *V*(2), 61–69.

Maevskiy, V. I. (2018). Meso-level and hierarchical structure of the economy. *Journal of Institutional Research*, *10*(3), 17–30.

Matkovskyy, R. (2012). *A Meso-level Representation of Economic Systems: a Theoretical Approach*. School of Economics, North-West University, MPRA Paper No. 44093.

Menard, C. (2014). Embedding organizational arrangements: Towards a general model. *Journal of Institutional Economics*, *10*(4), 567–589. doi:10.1017/S1744137414000228

Menard, C. (2018). Research Frontiers in New Institutional Economics. Revista de Administração. *Management Journal*, *53*(1), 8.

Ng, Y. K. (1982). A Micro-Macroeconomic Analysis Based on a Representative Firm. *Economica*, *49*(194), 121–139.

Ng, Y. K. (1986). *Mesoeconomics: A Micro-Macro Analysis*. St. Martin's Press.

Rodgers, Y., & Cooley, J. (1999). Outstanding Female Economists in the Analysis and Practice of Development Economics. *World Development*, *27*(8), 1397–1411. doi:10.1016/S0305-750X(99)00063-7

Schumpeter, J. A. (1954). *History of economic analysis*. Oxford University Press.

Stewart, F. (1992). Can Adjustment Programmes Incorporate the Interests of Women? In H. Afshar & C. Dennis (Eds.), *Women and Adjustment Policies in the Third World* (pp. 13–45). Women's Studies at York/Macmillan Series. Palgrave Macmillan. doi:10.1007/978-1-349-11961-5_2

Stöbe, R. (2015). Historic Key Events. In *The concise encyclopedia of communication* (pp. 245–246). J. Wiley & Sons.

Trencheva, T., & Zdravkova, E. (2019). Intellectual Property Management In Digitization And Digital Preservation Of Cultural Heritage. *EDULEARN19 Proceedings*. 10.21125/edulearn.2019.1468

White, L. (2011). Image, Logo, Brand and Nation: Destination Marketing, Nationalism and the 2007 Cricket World Cup. In Sports event management: the Caribbean experience. New directions in tourism analysis. Ashgate.

Wittfogel, K. A. (1962). Agrarian Problems and the Moscow-Peking Axis. *Association for Slavic, East European, and Eurasian Studies.*, *21*(4), 678–698.

ADDITIONAL READING

Borisova, L. (2018). Hospitality As An Industry. *Knowledge International Journal*, *28*(5), 1661–1667. doi:10.35120/kij28051661L

Bowdin, G. A. J., McDonnell, I., Allen, J. and O'Toole, W. (2012). Events Management. Amsterdam: BH.

Dimitrov, P., Todorov, I., Tanchev, S., & Yurukov, P. (2019). Monetary Discretion By Fiscal Means: *The Case Of Bulgaria. CBU International Conference Proceedings*, 7.

Ferdinand, N., & Kitching, A. (2012). *Events management: An international approach.* SAGE.

Gruneau, R., & Compton, J. (2017). Media Events, Mega-Events and Social Theory. Sport, Media and Mega-Events, 33-47.

Harding, D., & Pagan, A. (2016). The Econometric Analysis of Recurrent Events in Macroeconomics and Finance.

Kolev, V. (2019). Plovdiv – The Cultural Capital Of Bulgaria. CBU International Conference Proceedings, 7.

Lukanova, G. (2019). Restaurant Chains: Opportunities and Prospects for Bulgarian Foodservice Operators. Izvestia Journal of the Union of Scientists - Varna. *Economic Sciences Series*, *8*(3), 91–100.

Naumov, N., & Green, D. (2016). Mass tourism. Encyclopedia of Tourism, 594-595. doi:10.1007/978-3-319-01384-8_378

Quinn, B. (2009). The European Capital Culture Initiative And Cultural Legacy: An Analysis of the Cultural Sector in the Aftermath of Cork 2005. *Event Management*, *13*(4), 249–264. doi:10.3727/152599510X12621081189077

Roche, M. (2017). *Mega-events and macro-social change*. Mega-Events and Social Change.

KEY TERMS AND DEFINITIONS

Event: We use event with reference to various occasions of public, official, or private character, which may be spontaneous or organized, and which differ in their impact and size.

Macro-Level Operator: The applied notion here refers to representatives of state institutions, international organizations, service providers and entrepreneurs who take part in the mega-event organizing process. As opposed to the term economic agent, through the term macro-level operator we emphasize its nature (intangible goods producers) and function (mega-event managers). This type of operators include state institutions, public bodies, state-public organizations, cultural institutes, national televisions, museums, municipalities, and other public goods providers, playing the role of image makers and know-how providers.

Mega-Event: We use it to refer to well-known and large-scale organized occasions with fixed time, place, and duration. They often emerge in a certain context, according to a planned schedule, or are dedicated to a certain celebration. Mega-events are part of the social and cultural landscape and are developed within the umbrella of social welfare. Among their obligatory requirements can be mentioned: constructed environment, established event's brand, ancillary management, marketing and logistics, national and international media coverage and high number of event visitors. Long-term effects upon the social and cultural life of the host community, urban development and economic growth are also achieved.

Meso-Level Operator: The applied notion here refers to representatives of state institutions, international organizations, service providers and entrepreneurs, which are mediators between the macro-level and micro-level operators. In order for an organization, enterprise, training institution, company or other body to be classified as operator at the mesoeconomic level, it is not of paramount importance whether it is a profit or a non-profit agent. The most important characteristic feature of a meso-level operator is its key role throughout the whole event, for which reason it cannot be replaced by another similar operator (organization, service provider, public goods provider, public body, non-profit organization, etc.).

Micro-Level Operator: The applied notion here refers to individual business units involved in the mega-event organization. These can also be representatives of households who play a micro role in the mega event. The services of the micro-level operators comprise non-profit activities and are characterized by their uniqueness and importance for the mega-event structure. Such operators can also be individuals, small or medium-sized firms who are associated with a certain activity in the programm of the mega event, etc.

APPENDIX

Table A1. List of operators of the Platform FUSE

Macro level operators	Meso level operators	Micro level operators
Plovdiv municipality	Plovdiv 2019 Foundation	Panayot Volov Secondary school
The Ministry of Culture	The City Art Gallery	Pencho Slaveykov Secondary school
Bulgarian-Swiss cooperation programme	Ivan Vazov National Library	Yordan Yovkov secondary school
Iztok primary centre	State Opera	Bee bop café
Italian theatre company 'GOMMALACCA Teatro'	Regional Ethnographic Museum	Centre for Work with Children on the Street
Plovdiv Cultural Institute	Association 'Independent Theatre Company– Empty Space'	Theatre students
Goethe-Institute (Bulgaria)	Association 'Our World'	The Children's Architectural Workshop
Wilo Foundation	Complexfor Social Services for Children and Families (KSUDS) – Plovdiv	Nikola Vaptsarov Secondary School
Paisii Hilendarski University Plovdiv	Youth ClubRoma – Stolipinovo 1996 Association	Trakart centre
New Bulgarian University	IAC (Integrated Centre of Arts) Matera	Knyaginya Maria Luiza children's care home
Arax Foundation	DiscoveredSpaces Association	Ongal Association
Shalom Organization of the Jews (Bulgaria)	Metaart Foundation	Children´s Architecture Workshop
Yiddish Waves Foundation	POANTA Association	Atelier 3
Ivan Vazov National Library	Boris Hristov House of Culture	Plovdiv City Council Gallery
National and University Library of North Macedonia	Regional Development Foundation 'Roma-Plovdiv'	Deya Sto Ltd.
Tommaso Stigliani Library Matera	Alliance for Equal Rights and Sustainability Association	Kiril Nektariev Secondary School
National Art Academy	Stolipinovo – Evropa 21 Association	Living Space Theatre
	EASYART Foundation	Open Space Ltd
	Association 'Youth Club Roma – Stolipinovo 1996'	Lucky House of Cinema
	Petko R. Slaveykov – 2008 Cultural centre chitalishte	Pencho Slaveykov school
	Galeria Theatre	Studio PUNKT
	National Alliance for Work with Volunteers Foundation	The network of Bulgarian schools abroad
	Arete Youth Foundation	Kuklen Association
	Chitalishte 'Aleko Konstantinov	Studio OTAIKA
	Aleko Konstantinov – 1945 community centre	Typedepot
	Pen & Quill Association	Plakat Kombinat Ltd
	International Council for Cultural Centres	Letter Collective
	Multi Kulti Kolektiv Association	ATOM Theatre and Fools on the Hill Association
	Ideas Factory Association	AV Group Bulgaria
	Pamet Foundation	Pro Rodopi Art Centre
	Lettera Publishing House	
	NIKE Publishing	
	Bulgarian Institute of Culture at Bratislava	
	Association of Bulgarian Schools Abroad (ABSA)	
	LodzHouse of Literature	
	Creative Ray	
	GLAS Foundation	
	Common Future Association	
	Théâtre des Chemins	
	Bulgarian Association for Alternative Tourism (BAAT)	
	Ideas Factory Association	

(Data Source: https://plovdiv2019.eu/data/fms/Plovdiv2019_ProgramBook_website.pdf)

Table A2. List of operators of the Platform RELAX

Macro level operators	Meso level operators	Micro level operators
Plovdiv 2019 Foundation	Melformator Collective	Dr Petar Beron School
Slow Food Plovdiv Fest	Localfood.bg Foundation	Confesercenti Bulgaria and Frase Contemporary Art
Bulgarian National Television	Professional Education Forum Association	Komplekt Studio
European Parliament in Bulgaria, the European Commission in Bulgaria	CESCOT VENETO	Generali Insurance AD
Festival Hello Health	Bozhura Art	Nescafé Dolce Gusto
MOVE Week Plovdiv		Bulgarian MP-Studio
FARA – Bulgarian Association of Communications Agencies Festival	Metaart Foundation	5 community Centres:
National Geographic	FIRE theatre-art-culture Foundation	Eliahshai Music Productions Ltd
State Opera Plovdiv	Vidya Project Association	AGITPROP production company
	BG Be Active Association	Beehive Co-Working Space
	Cal y Canto Teatro	Embassy of Spain in Bulgaria and Cervantes Institute-Sofia
	BG Radio	VIVACOM,
	Bulgarian Association of Communications Agencies (BACA).	B2B
	Trimontium Female Choir	Art Voice Center
	Sofia Music Enterprises	Eeyore Centre for Work with Children
	Bremen Youth Symphony Orchestra	ARENA CINEMA
	MusicArtissimo Foundation for Culture and Art	Shirting Slovenia
	Creative Ray production	Initiative Committee Plovdiv – Sofia
	All Channels Communication	Blue M.
	Classic Stage Entertainment	
	Initiative Committee Plovdiv – Sofia	
	Lindy Hop Bulgaria	

(Data Source: https://plovdiv2019.eu/data/fms/Plovdiv2019_ProgramBook_website.pdf)

Chapter 12
What Drives Euro Area Labour Productivity Growth?
An International Production-Frontier Examination

Marcelo Sanchez
European Central Bank, Germany

ABSTRACT

This chapter uses a nonparametric, international production-frontier approach with a focus on euro area growth accounting. The authors uncover two robust findings for the period since 1980. First, estimated euro area efficiency scores lie much below the world production frontier (gap mostly in the range of 10% to 20%), suggesting the need for structural reform efforts to enhance resource use. Second, the use of human capital series points to a significant effect on euro area labour productivity—highlighting the positive macroeconomic return to education—while entailing a considerable reduction in the estimates of technological progress. Third, they fail to detect significant changes in cross-country distributions of labour productivity both before and after 1995. The only exception concerns the shift in the labour productivity distribution between 1980 and 1995—attributable to the role of physical capital deepening—when they employ the Barro and Lee human capital measure together with World Penn Tables data for the full set of countries, and this only at the 10% significance level.

INTRODUCTION

There is a broad empirical literature that studies economic growth, with two basic branches standing out. One attempts to determine whether there is a tendency for the world's economies to converge over time, drawing from Baumol's (1986) cross-sectional regressions. The other, building on Solow's (1957) decomposition of US growth into two components attributable to capital deepening and technological progress, investigates what are the sources of economic growth. Most of the literature is heavily model-

DOI: 10.4018/978-1-7998-4933-9.ch012

driven, relying on particular assumptions about the technology, market structure, technological change, and other aspects of the growth process.

The standard approach to growth accounting makes strong assumptions about technology at the country level (often postulating country-specific Cobb-Douglas production functions) in order to decompose labour productivity growth into the contributions of production factor accumulation and total factor productivity growth. In contrast with the traditional growth accounting approach, Kumar and Russell (2002) (henceforth KR), and more recently Henderson and Russell (2005) (henceforth HR), have employed nonparametric production-frontier methods to carry out a growth accounting exercise and analyse international macroeconomic convergence. This approach decomposes labour productivity growth into components attributable to (1) technological change (shifts in the world production frontier), (2) technological catch-up or "efficiency change" (movements toward or away from the frontier), and (3) capital accumulation (movement along the frontier) – in HR case further splitting capital deepening into its physical and human components.

The present paper employs nonparametric production-frontier methods to obtain growth accounting results for the euro area. Given the international scope of the study, we also report results for a wider number of countries. We extend the literature by undertaking extensive robustness checks of growth accounting results with the aim to identify consistent patterns. Robustness is assessed in two main ways. First, by using two different databases for labour productivity and physical capital deepening, namely, Penn World Tables (PWT) and Groningen Growth & Development Centre (GGDC). Second, by employing two series for human capital, namely, one based on Barro and Lee (2001) data on years of schooling and Alvarez and Ayuso's (2002) measure based on public spending on education.

Another paper addressing the role of human capital as control in a production-frontier context is HR, who significantly modify KR result that productivity growth is driven solely by physical capital accumulation over 1965-1990. HR attribute about one-third of physical capital accumulation's productivity growth contribution to human capital accumulation instead. Moreover, Salinas et al. (2006) report an rise in estimated efficiency levels when introducing public and human capital among EU-15 countries over 1980-1997.1 Using PWT and Barro-Lee data for OECD countries over 1975-1990, Maudos et al. (1999) find a significant effect of human capital on productivity, while highlighting its relevance for an accurate measurement of TFP (especially in Japan).

This article is structured as follows. We start by describing all the data used. We then present the growth accounting results in the absence of human capital. A later section examines the role of introducing each of our two measures of human capital. A final section concludes.

Data

We employ two main datasets for deriving measures of labour productivity growth and capital deepening.2 First, we use information from PWT version 6.2. This update (like its predecessor version 6.1) lacks data on capital stocks, so the latter are obtained by applying the perpetual inventory method (PIM) to gross capital formation.3

PWT measures labour as the number of workers, with which we compute real GDP and capital per worker for 95 countries over 1980-2003. Among these countries, we distinguish between EU-15 plus the US, other advanced countries and developing economies; due to space constraints, this paper only reports results – when available – for the first group of countries.4 Second, we use GGDC data from the Total Economy and Total Economy Growth Accounting Databases. These data cover 16 countries

(EU-15 plus the US) over 1980-2004 and refer to labour productivity per hour worked (using the Geary-Kheamis approach), real GDP and the real capital stock. No attempt is made at amending PWT data for their mishandling of the net foreign balance (see Feenstra et al., 2007).5

This paper uses two human capital measures. First, we extend HR measures up to 2000 with the latest Barro and Lee (2001) data and updated returns to education in Psacharopoulos and Patrinos (2004). Second, we use a human capital measure derived from applying the PIM to real government spending on education, as computed by Alvarez and Delgado (2002). The use of Barro and Lee (2001) data, alongside the update for returns to education in Psacharopoulos and Patrinos (2004), can more concretely be described as follows. Let $\varepsilon_{it}(t=1,\ldots,T;\ i=1,\ldots,N)$, represent the average number of years of education of the adult population in country i at time t, and define labour in efficiency units in country i at time t by $H_{it}L_{it}$. We assume that $H_{it} = h(\varepsilon_{it}) = \exp\left\{\phi(\varepsilon_{it})\right\}$, where φ is a piecewise linear function, with a zero intercept and a slope of 0.117 through the fourth year of education, 0.097 for the next four years, and 0.075 for education beyond the eighth year.6 Clearly, the rate of return to education (where φ is differentiable) is $d\ln h(\varepsilon_{it}) / d\varepsilon_{it} = \phi'(\varepsilon_{it})$ and h(0)=1.7

Concerning the PIM methodology à la Alvarez and Delgado (2002), our point of departure are EU KLEMS data on real education output (see van Ark et al., 2007), which is transformed into a stock series using the PIM.8 A related approach has been put forward by Salinas-Jiménez et al. (2006), but considering only the public component of spending on education (see also Alvarez-Ayuso and Delgado-Rodríguez, 2002). We estimate the initial value of the 1970 human capital stock as $I_{HK,1970} / (g_{HK} + \delta_{HK})$, where $I_{HK,1970}$ denotes education output in 1970, g_{HK} is the average geometric growth rate from 1970 and 1980 of education output and δ_{HK} is human capital's depreciation rate. The value used for human capital's depreciation rate is 0.04, which lies somewhere between the international range of values (from 0.03 and 0.04) reported by Romer (1989) and the figure (0.05) used by Salinas-Jiménez et al. (2006).

Throughout, we consider two basic periods, namely, the one between 1980 and 1995 and that between 1995 and the most recent possible year. The choice of 1995 as a benchmark has become customary in growth accounting studies for the US, which experienced a productivity surge in the mid-1990s. The same benchmark is used for Europe as analysts are interested in potential technological spillovers from the US (see e.g. the references in Inklaar et al., 2007).

Euro area labour productivity growth is measured differently in GGDC and PWT. In the former case, it is estimated to be higher in 1980-1995 than since 1995, while the opposite is true for PWT. The difference arises both if GGDC labour productivity is measured per hour worked and per worker (PWT data for hours worked are not available). The reason is that, while measured differences in euro area output growth are marginal ever since 1980, PWT computes larger labour input growth in the earlier period and GGDC reports faster labour input growth since 1995.9

Results Obtained Abstracting from Human Capital

This section reports results for growth accounting exercises and associated density distributions obtained without consideration of human capital, which is left for next section.10 We follow KR method very closely in calculating the world production frontier and efficiency levels for individual economies (distances from the frontier). Our technology contains three aggregate variables: output and two inputs:

Figure 1. World production frontiers for 1980, 1995 and 2003
Note: Computations are based on data from the Penn World Tables version 6.2. They are expressed in thousands of international US dollars (in 2000 constant prices) per worker. The euro area data exclude Cyprus, Luxembourg, Malta, the Slovak Republic and Slovenia.

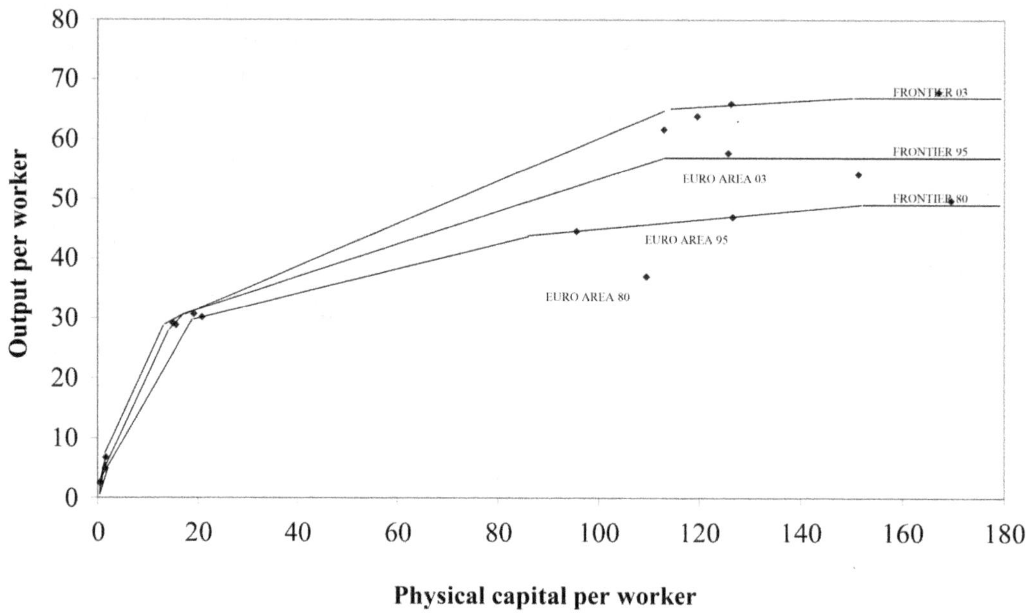

labour and physical capital. The production frontier is constructed using dynamic panel data, which precludes implosion of the frontier over time.

Results Using PWT Data

PWT data are available for 95 countries, which is our broadest representation of the world economy. The international production frontier, which underlies efficiency computations, is illustrated in Figure 1 with data for 1980, 1995 and 2003 alongside the scatter-plot of euro area points. The Figure is depicted in y−k space, where y=Y/L and k=K/L are the ratios of output and capital, respectively, to labour. The maximum or best-practice score is 1. Technological progress is found to be non-neutral, mostly taking place for high levels of capital deepening with developing countries benefiting little from it. This is in line with KR and HR findings for a period (1965-1990) starting before those used here (1980-1995 and 1995-2003).

Efficiency is estimated in terms of countries' distance from the production frontier.11 At the world average level, over 1980-2003 efficiency did not change much, falling slightly over time (Table 1). Euro area efficiency remained rather stable, decreasing only marginally over the years. Its level was lower than in the US, owing to a poor performance in Italy, the Netherlands and Spain. Over the whole period considered, efficiency remained relatively stable in France and Germany (at around 0.85 and 0.8, respectively), while improving considerably over time in Ireland.

Figure 2. Counterfactual labour productivity distributions

Note: The solid curve shown in each panel is the actual (mean preserving) 1995 distribution of real GDP per worker. The dashed curve in panel (a) is the actual 1980 distribution of real GDP per worker. The dashed curves in panels (b) and (c) are counterfactual distributions isolating, sequentially, the effects of physical capital deepening, human capital accumulation and technological progress on the 1980 distribution of real GDP per worker.

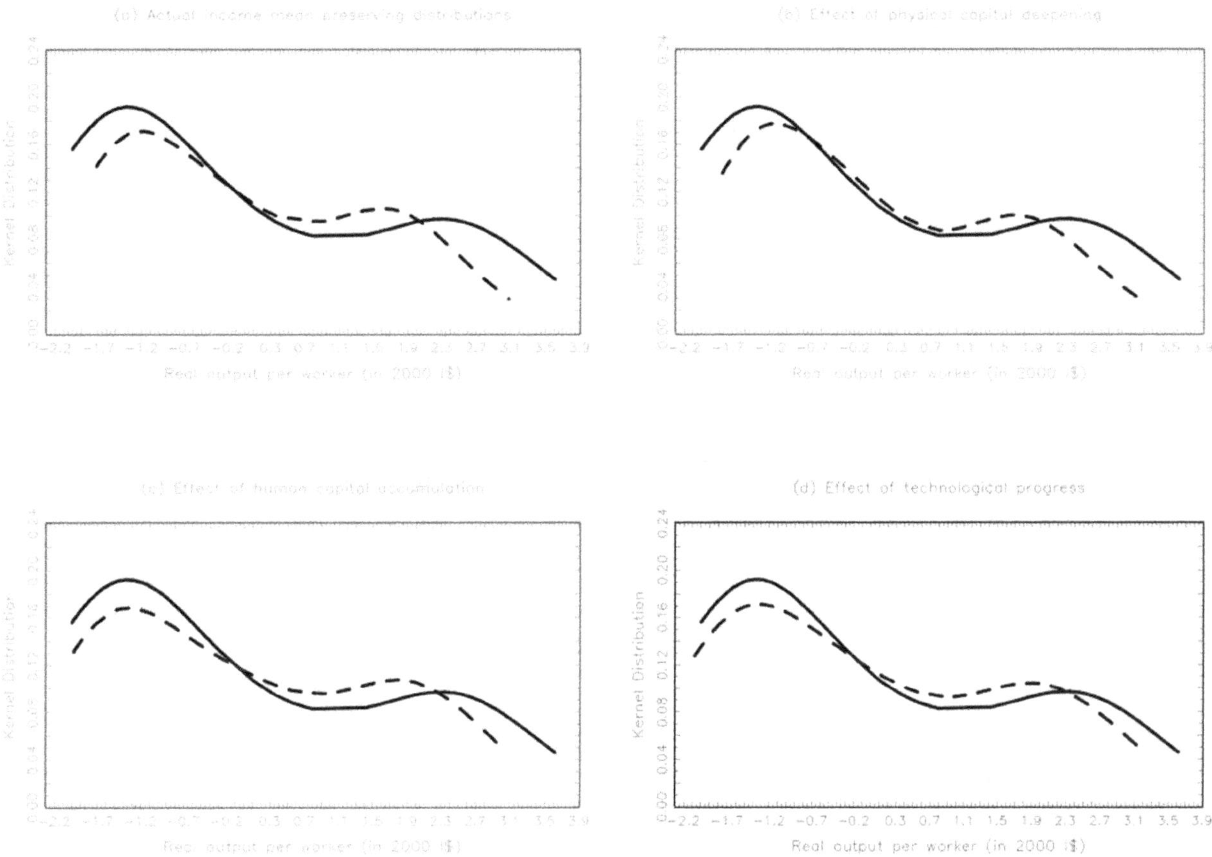

Decompositions and Cross-Country Distributions of Labour Productivity

We decompose labour productivity growth into components due to efficiency change (EFF), technological progress (TECH), and capital deepening (KACC). Letting b and c be the base period and the current period, respectively, we obtain two alternative decompositions:12

$$\frac{y_c}{y_b} = \frac{e_c}{e_b}\frac{\overline{y}_c(k_c)}{\overline{y}_b(k_c)}\frac{\overline{y}_b(k_c)}{\overline{y}_b(k_b)} = EFF \times TECH^c \times KACC^b;$$

and

Table 1.

Efficiency scores using Penn World Tables data

Economies	1980 No human capital	1980 Barro-Lee	1980 PIM	1995 No human capital	1995 Barro-Lee	1995 PIM	Latest year No human capital 2003	Latest year Barro-Lee 2000	Latest year PIM 2001
Euro area[1]	0.81	0.85	0.72	0.79	0.89	0.70	0.77	0.87	0.66
Germany	0.80	0.75	0.67	0.80	0.84	0.68	0.76	0.80	0.64
France	0.86	0.92	0.75	0.86	0.94	0.68	0.84	0.95	0.66
Italy	0.86	1.00	1.00	0.81	0.99	0.83	0.78	0.99	0.67
Spain	0.74	0.90	0.73	0.75	0.90	0.73	0.71	0.86	0.75
Netherlands	0.95	0.90	na	0.84	0.91	na	0.85	0.93	na
Belgium	0.93	0.92	0.79	0.93	0.99	0.74	0.91	1.00	0.65
Austria	0.87	0.83	0.73	0.88	0.93	0.67	0.88	0.97	0.62
Ireland	0.72	0.72	0.85	0.88	0.90	0.92	1.00	1.00	0.98
Finland	0.68	0.66	0.57	0.62	0.64	0.52	0.73	0.70	0.62
Portugal	0.61	0.84	0.77	0.69	0.90	0.72	0.61	0.83	0.66
Greece	0.68	0.75	0.74	0.65	0.68	0.70	0.67	0.64	0.67
United Kingdom	0.81	0.79	0.65	0.89	0.91	0.75	0.85	0.83	0.74
United States	1.00	0.82	na	1.00	0.93	na	1.00	0.88	na
Denmark	0.79	0.74	0.70	0.83	0.84	0.78	0.77	0.78	0.69
Sweden	0.80	0.74	0.96	0.77	0.72	0.92	0.77	0.70	0.84
Mean[2]	0.60	0.66	0.76	0.56	0.62	0.74	0.54	0.61	0.71
Standard deviation[2]	0.21	0.21	0.12	0.22	0.22	0.11	0.23	0.22	0.10

Note: Two human capital measures are considered, namely, a Barro-Lee measure and that applying the perpetual inventory method (PIM) to government spending on education. For no human capital and the Barro-Lee case, results are based on overall samples of 95 and 80 economies, respectively.
1) Excluding Cyprus, Luxembourg, Malta, the Slovak Republic and Slovenia. PIM results also exclude the Netherlands.
2) The mean and standard deviation do not include the euro area as a whole. They refer to the full set of countries used, which is larger than that reported here for no human capital and the Barro-Lee case.

$$\frac{y_c}{y_b} = \frac{e_c}{e_b}\frac{\bar{y}_c(k_b)}{\bar{y}_b(k_b)}\frac{\bar{y}_c(k_c)}{\bar{y}_c(k_b)} = \text{EFF} \times \text{TECH}^b \times \text{KACC}^c \quad (1)$$

where e stands for efficiency. As in KR, the two labour productivity decompositions in (1) measure the effects of technological change and capital accumulation in different ways, with the ambiguity being resolved by adopting a geometric average of the two measures (the so-called "Fisher Ideal" decomposition), as follows:

$$\frac{y_c}{y_b} = \text{EFF} \times \left(\text{TECH}^b \cdot \text{TECH}^c\right)^{1/2} \left(\text{KACC}^b \cdot \text{KACC}^c\right)^{1/2} = \text{EFF} \times \text{TECH} \times \text{KACC} \quad (2)$$

Table 2 reports decompositions of labour productivity growth for 1980-1995 and 1995-2003. In the former period, world labour productivity growth was 0.7%. The fraction owing to technological progress was 1.1%, far exceeding that due to capital accumulation (0.1%). The overall loss in efficiency was 0.5%. Technological progress contributed with 1.2% to euro area labour productivity growth of 1.3%, well above the fractions due to capital accumulation (0.2%) and efficiency change (-0.2%). Within the euro area, higher efficiency greatly supported Ireland and Portugal, in sharp contrast with the experience of

Table 2.

Tripartite decomposition of labour productivity growth (in annual average percentage growth rates)

Economies	labour productivity (real GDP per worker) 1980-1995	1995-2003	efficiency 1980-1995	1995-2003	technology 1980-1995	1995-2003	capital deepening 1980-1995	1995-2003
Euro area[1]	1.30	1.76	-0.15	-0.34	1.21	1.74	0.24	0.37
Germany	1.50	1.36	-0.02	-0.53	1.32	1.79	0.19	0.11
France	1.51	1.79	-0.06	-0.18	1.22	1.87	0.35	0.10
Italy	1.13	1.34	-0.40	-0.49	1.30	1.74	0.24	0.10
Spain	1.18	2.43	0.06	-0.78	0.81	1.58	0.30	1.63
Netherlands	0.38	2.06	-0.78	0.03	1.31	1.77	-0.13	0.26
Belgium	1.51	1.75	-0.02	-0.29	1.26	1.91	0.26	0.14
Austria	1.64	2.05	0.12	0.00	1.25	1.94	0.26	0.11
Ireland	2.51	5.99	1.37	1.65	0.68	1.47	0.45	2.75
Finland	0.85	3.74	-0.65	2.00	1.31	1.71	0.20	0.00
Portugal	2.19	1.91	0.81	-1.55	0.53	1.22	0.84	2.28
Greece	-0.41	2.89	-0.29	0.43	0.75	1.21	-0.87	1.23
United Kingdom	1.88	2.51	0.66	-0.62	0.68	1.42	0.53	1.70
United States	1.73	2.05	0.00	0.00	1.10	1.85	0.63	0.20
Denmark	1.33	2.12	0.35	-0.85	1.03	1.64	-0.05	1.33
Sweden	0.74	2.29	-0.23	0.01	0.97	1.53	0.00	0.73
Mean[2]	*0.65*	*1.32*	*-0.52*	*-0.62*	*1.07*	*1.44*	*0.13*	*0.52*
Standard deviation[2]	*2.01*	*2.24*	*2.00*	*2.09*	*0.48*	*0.95*	*2.07*	*1.88*

1) Excluding Cyprus, Luxembourg, Malta, the Slovak Republic and Slovenia.
2) The mean and standard deviation do not include the euro area as a whole. They correspond to the full set of 95 economies used to obtain the results reported here for a smaller sample.

Finland and the Netherlands. In the US the contribution of technological progress was somewhat larger than that of capital accumulation.

For the period 1995-2003, world labour productivity growth was 1.3%. The fraction owing to technological progress (1.4%) was higher than that due to capital accumulation (0.5%), but to a smaller degree than prior to 1995. The overall loss in efficiency was around 0.6%. For the euro area as a whole, labour productivity growth of 1.8% was mostly driven by technological progress (1.7%), well above contributions of efficiency change and capital accumulation (at -0.3% and 0.4%, respectively). Capital accumulation did play a key role in euro area countries Greece, Ireland and Spain. Efficiency gains contributed greatly in Finland and Ireland.

Turning to labour productivity distributions,13 we compare the impact of each individual source of growth and jointly with any other source. We use kernel density estimates and Li-Fan-Ullah tests for the identity of distributions (Fan and Ullah, 1999; Li, 1996).14 For both 1980-1995 and 1995-2003, there is no evidence to reject the equality of distributions.15 This includes the comparison between initial and end-of-period distributions, as well as that between any type of counterfactual and actual end-of-period distributions. The different factors driving labour productivity growth thus affected the mean rather than the spread of the distributions of real GDP per worker.

Results Using GGDC Data

Using GGDC data, euro area efficiency was below that of the average of the advanced economies included here over 1980-2004 (Table 3). The euro area experienced a slight decline in efficiency over both of the periods 1980-1995 and 1995-2004. This notwithstanding, compared with the US euro area's gap narrowed (due to a larger drop in efficiency in the US) over the former period. Instead, that gap widened considerably between 1995 and 2004 as the US reached the world production frontier in 2004.

Table 3.

Efficiency scores using Groningen Growth & Development Centre data

	1980			1995			Latest year		
	No human capital	Barro-Lee	PIM	No human capital	Barro-Lee	PIM	No human capital	Barro-Lee	PIM
Economies							2004	2000	2001
Euro area[1]	0.86	0.82	0.83	0.83	0.82	0.71	0.82	0.84	0.65
Germany	0.80	0.72	0.72	0.81	0.77	0.70	0.82	0.78	0.65
France	0.96	0.91	0.90	0.96	0.93	0.68	1.00	0.99	0.63
Italy	1.00	1.00	0.98	0.92	1.00	0.84	0.83	1.00	0.73
Spain	0.91	0.90	0.92	0.74	0.80	0.66	0.64	0.76	0.60
Netherlands	0.93	0.81	na	0.91	0.81	na	0.91	0.86	na
Belgium	0.95	0.84	0.65	0.97	0.89	0.64	0.97	0.95	0.62
Austria	0.85	0.81	0.83	0.82	0.80	0.70	0.90	0.85	0.62
Ireland	0.84	0.80	0.85	0.94	0.92	0.93	1.00	1.00	0.99
Finland	0.70	0.66	0.67	0.74	0.65	0.57	0.80	0.73	0.62
Luxembourg	0.93	na	0.83	0.98	na	0.87	1.00	na	0.78
Portugal	1.00	1.00	na	0.93	0.96	na	0.74	0.85	na
Greece	0.82	0.79	0.82	0.63	0.55	0.62	0.57	0.57	0.58
United Kingdom	1.00	0.95	1.00	0.94	0.92	0.91	0.85	0.86	0.83
United States	1.00	0.81	na	0.92	0.85	na	1.00	0.81	na
Denmark	0.90	0.84	0.86	0.89	0.84	0.77	0.86	0.81	0.66
Sweden	0.88	0.77	0.77	0.78	0.71	0.68	0.85	0.72	0.70
Mean[2]	*0.90*	*0.84*	*0.83*	*0.87*	*0.83*	*0.74*	*0.86*	*0.84*	*0.69*
Standard deviation[2]	*0.09*	*0.10*	*0.11*	*0.10*	*0.12*	*0.12*	*0.13*	*0.12*	*0.12*

Note: Two human capital measures are considered, namely, a Barro-Lee measure and that applying the perpetual inventory method (PIM) to government spending on education.

1) Excluding Cyprus, Malta, the Slovak Republic and Slovenia. When incorporating human capital measures, Luxembourg is missing for the Barro-Lee measure, and the Netherlands and Portugal in the PIM case.

2) The mean and standard deviation do not include the euro area as a whole.

Decompositions and Cross-Country Distributions of Labour Productivity

Labour productivity decompositions are reported for the periods 1980-1995 and 1995-2004 in Table 4. Between 1980 and 1995, for the average of the advanced economies, labour productivity growth (at 2.3%) was led by capital accumulation (1.4%), followed closely by technological progress (1.2%). Efficiency change contributed negatively (-0.3%). Euro area labour productivity growth, was driven by fast-converging countries – such as Finland, Ireland and Spain – showing rapid capital accumulation, and partly marred by efficiency losses exceeding those of the US.

For 1995-2004, world labour productivity growth (at 2.0%) was dominated by technological progress, whose contribution (1.5%) exceeded that of capital deepening (0.7%) and efficiency change (-0.2%). Efficiency losses were broad based, including in some euro area countries (-0.2 for the grouping as a whole, dragged down by Italy and especially Spain). Ireland instead ranks among those that gained in efficiency, even reaching the world production frontier in 2004. Efficiency losses drove the result that,

Table 4.

Tripartite decomposition of labour productivity growth (in annual average percentage growth rates)

	labour productivity (real GDP per hour worked)		efficiency		technology		capital deepening	
Economies	1980-1995	1995-2004	1980-1995	1995-2004	1980-1995	1995-2004	1980-1995	1995-2004
Euro area[1]	2.37	1.32	-0.20	-0.21	1.19	1.50	1.37	0.03
Germany	2.40	1.69	0.05	0.16	1.33	1.50	1.01	0.03
France	2.61	1.98	0.05	0.40	1.20	1.56	1.35	0.01
Italy	2.12	0.48	-0.55	-1.08	1.07	1.51	1.60	0.06
Spain	3.09	-0.17	-1.41	-1.61	1.18	1.46	3.34	0.01
Netherlands	1.75	1.58	-0.13	0.02	1.88	1.56	0.00	0.00
Belgium	1.99	1.60	0.11	0.04	1.88	1.56	0.00	0.00
Austria	2.45	2.56	-0.24	0.98	1.12	1.52	1.56	0.04
Ireland	3.68	4.97	0.77	0.65	0.61	1.60	2.27	2.65
Finland	3.02	2.42	0.36	0.90	1.15	1.51	1.48	0.00
Luxembourg	2.65	1.78	0.33	0.22	1.34	1.50	0.96	0.05
Portugal	2.16	1.97	-0.48	-2.45	0.63	0.89	2.01	3.61
Greece	0.90	2.54	-1.69	-1.21	0.57	1.53	2.05	2.24
United Kingdom	2.61	2.21	-0.43	-1.01	0.74	1.64	2.29	1.59
United States	1.31	2.46	-0.55	0.92	1.57	1.49	0.29	0.04
Denmark	2.49	1.08	-0.07	-0.47	1.20	1.51	1.36	0.04
Sweden	1.34	2.51	-0.86	0.98	1.40	1.49	0.80	0.03
Mean[2]	*2.29*	*1.98*	*-0.30*	*-0.16*	*1.18*	*1.49*	*1.40*	*0.65*
Standard deviation[2]	*0.72*	*1.11*	*0.64*	*1.04*	*0.40*	*0.17*	*0.90*	*1.18*

1) Excluding Cyprus, Malta, the Slovak Republic and Slovenia.
2) The mean and standard deviation do not include the euro area as a whole.

between 1995 and 2004, euro area labour productivity growth lagged that in the US, which managed to regain the production frontier in 2004. Both the euro area and the US benefited more from technological progress than capital accumulation.

Finally, density estimates and Li-Fan-Ullah tests (not reported) do not suggest that actual 1980 and 1995 distributions are significantly different from each other. Moreover, by introducing one or two of the three components of labour productivity growth at a time, the tests for identity of the counterfactual and actual 1995 distributions indicate that any of the sources of labour productivity growth played only a minor role in affecting the distribution between 1980 and 1995. Similar conclusions are found for the period 1995-2004.

Summarising results from this section (i.e. without human capital), technological progress was consistently found to be a key source of euro area labour productivity growth ever since 1980. It was even dominant since 1995, and also – using PWT data – over 1980-1995. Two other robust results are that, ever since 1980, euro area efficiency remained some 15% to 20% below best practice, and that it tended to drop in both periods considered. A final robust result is that we fail to detect significant changes in international labour productivity distributions ever since 1980.

Results Obtained Using Human Capital Measures

This section introduces into the analysis the two human capital measures described above. We start by using the Barro-Lee human capital measure, then turning to employ the measure applying the PIM to public education spending.

Results From Employing The Barro-Lee Human Capital Measure

If our previous production-frontier setup followed KR, the present one draws heavily on HR. More specifically, the worldwide production frontier is constructed by explicitly modelling labour-enhancing technological progress. Our technology now contains four macroeconomic variables: aggregate output, two aggregate inputs: labour and physical capital, and a technology index capturing labour-enhancing technological progress. Let $\langle Y_{it}, H_{it}, L_{it}, K_{it} \rangle$; t=1,…,T; i=1,…,N, where $H_{it}L_{it}$ denotes labour in efficiency units, represent T observations on these four variables for each of the N countries for a total of NT observations.

The constant-returns-to-scale, period-t technology using all data up to that point in time becomes:

$$\Psi_t = \left\{ \langle Y, HL, K \rangle \in \Re^3_+ \mid Y \leq \sum_{s \leq t} \sum_i z_{is} Y_{is},\ HL \leq \sum_{s \leq t} \sum_i z_{is} H_{it} L_{is}, K \leq \sum_{s \leq t} \sum_i z_{is} K_{is}, z_{is} \geq 0, \forall i, s \right\}$$

where Z_{is} represents the level of operation of country i's production process at time s.

The output-based efficiency index λ_{it} for country i at time t is defined by

$$E(Y_{it}, H_{it} L_{it}, K_{it}) = \min\{\lambda_{it} \mid \langle Y_{it} / \lambda, H_{it} L_{it}, K_{it} \rangle \in \Psi_t\}$$

This index is the inverse of the maximal proportional amount that output Yit can be expanded while remaining technologically feasible, given the technology Ψ_t and the input quantities $H_{it}L_{it}$ and Kit, it is less than or equal to 1 and takes the value of 1 if and only if the it observation is on the period-t production frontier. In this case of a scalar output, the output-based efficiency index is simply the ratio of actual to potential output evaluated at the actual input quantities.

We split productivity growth into components attributable to (i) the change in efficiency, (ii) technological change, (iii) physical capital deepening (increases in the capital–labour ratio), and (iv) human capital accumulation. In order to do so, we first decompose the growth of output per unit of labour into these three components. By definition, potential (that is, production-frontier) outputs per efficiency unit of labour in periods b and c are given by $\overline{y}_b(\hat{k}_b) = \hat{y}_b / e_b$ and $\overline{y}_c(\hat{k}_c) = \hat{y}_c / e_c$, where $\hat{y} = Y / (HL)$ and $\hat{k} = K / (HL)$ are the ratios of output and capital, respectively, to effective labour, and b and c are meant to stand for the base period and the current period, respectively. We can therefore write

$$\frac{\hat{y}_c}{\hat{y}_b} = \frac{e_c}{e_b} \frac{\overline{y}_c(\hat{k}_c)}{\overline{y}_b(\hat{k}_b)}$$

Let $\overline{y}_b(\hat{k}_c)$ denote potential output per unit of labour at current-period capital intensity using the base-period technology. Moreover, let $\overline{y}_c(\hat{k}_b)$ denote potential output per unit of labour at base-period capital intensity using the current-period technology. Define $\tilde{k}_c = K_c / (L_c H_b)$ as the ratio of capital to labour measured in efficiency units under the counterfactual assumption that human capital had not changed from its base period level, and $\tilde{k}_b = K_b / (L_b H_c)$ as the counterfactual capital to efficiency–labour ratio in the base period if human capital were equal to its current-period level. Denote potential output per efficiency unit of labour at $\tilde{k}_c$ and $\tilde{k}_b$ using the base-period and current-period technologies by $\bar{y}_b(\tilde{k}_c)$ and $\bar{y}_c(\tilde{k}_b)$, respectively. Next, we multiply the numerator of the last equation by $\bar{y}_b(\hat{k}_c)\bar{y}_b(\tilde{k}_c)$ and its denominator by $\bar{y}_c(\hat{k}_b)\bar{y}_c(\tilde{k}_b)$; as a result, we obtain two alternative decompositions of labour productivity growth as follows:

$$\frac{y_c}{y_b} = \frac{e_c}{e_b}\frac{\bar{y}_c(\hat{k}_c)}{\bar{y}_b(\hat{k}_c)}\frac{\bar{y}_b(\tilde{k}_c)}{\bar{y}_b(\hat{k}_b)}\left[\frac{\bar{y}_b(\hat{k}_c)}{\bar{y}_b(\tilde{k}_c)}\frac{H_c}{H_b}\right] = EFF \times TECH^c \times KACC^b \times HACC^b$$

and

$$\frac{y_c}{y_b} = \frac{e_c}{e_b}\frac{\bar{y}_c(\hat{k}_b)}{\bar{y}_b(\hat{k}_b)}\frac{\bar{y}_c(\hat{k}_c)}{\bar{y}_c(\tilde{k}_b)}\left[\frac{\bar{y}_c(\tilde{k}_b)}{\bar{y}_c(\hat{k}_b)}\frac{H_c}{H_b}\right] = EFF \times TECH^b \times KACC^c \times HACC^c$$

The former of the last two equations allows for a decomposition of technological progress by shifting the frontier in the output direction at the current-period capital-labour ratio and measures the effects of physical capital accumulation along the base-period frontier. In contrast, the decomposition in the latter equation measures technological change at the base-period capital-labour ratio and physical capital accumulation by movements along the current-period frontier. In light of path dependency, the decompositions in the last two equations do not yield the same results. In line with KR and HR, we thus use a "Fisher Ideal" decomposition to reconcile the two approaches, which amounts to taking geometric averages of the two measures of the effects of technological change and physical capital accumulation. This can be achieved by multiplying both the numerator and denominator of the equation

$$\frac{\hat{y}_c}{\hat{y}_b} = \frac{e_c}{e_b}\frac{\bar{y}_c(\hat{k}_c)}{\bar{y}_b(\hat{k}_b)} \text{ by } \left[\bar{y}_b(\hat{k}_c)\bar{y}_b(\tilde{k}_c)\right]^{1/2}\left[\bar{y}_c(\hat{k}_b)\bar{y}_c(\tilde{k}_b)\right]^{1/2},$$

which produces:

$$\begin{aligned}\frac{y_c}{y_b} &= EFF \times \left(TECH^b \cdot TECH^c\right)^{1/2} \times \left(KACC^b \cdot KACC^c\right)^{1/2} \times \left(HACC^b \cdot HACC^c\right)^{1/2} \\ &= EFF \times TECH \times KACC \times HACC\end{aligned} \quad (3)$$

Use of (3) amounts to a modified growth accounting methodology that allows us to analyse labour productivity growth of each country, decomposing it into three sources: (i) efficiency change (or catching-up towards the best-practice frontier), (ii) technical change (shift of the technological frontier itself), (iii) physical capital deepening, and (iv) human capital accumulation. We now turn to the description of the empirical decompositions of labour productivity growth, followed by results from the kernel density estimation for the international distribution of labour productivity.

Decompositions of Labour Productivity

Results Using PWT Data

We report two sets of quadripartite labour productivity decompositions, here using PWT data for 80 countries, then turning to GGDC data. At the world average level, there were not very large efficiency changes over 1980-2000, with efficiency decreasing only marginally over time (Table 1). In the euro area, the efficiency levels have remained rather stable, remaining some 15% to 20% below the world frontier. Euro area efficiency has been broadly comparable to that registered by the UK and US economies over the sample period. There has been some variability across euro area countries, with a pattern that is not much in line with that described earlier in the absence of human capital. Among Nordic countries outside the euro area, Norway has exhibited marginally higher efficiency levels than Denmark and Sweden. Finally, Japan's efficiency levels have been slightly above the world average over the entire period.

Table 5 presents decompositions of labour productivity growth for 1980-1995 and 1995-2000. Over the former period, world average annual labour productivity growth was 0.7%. The fraction owing to human capital accumulation was 0.9%, compared to technological progress at 0.4% and -0.2% due to physical capital deepening. The overall loss in efficiency was about 0.1%, with the total fraction attributable to technological progress plus efficiency (the equivalent to standard TFP) amounting to some 0.8%. Focusing on the group of EU-15 plus US, technological progress has been on average more important than physical capital deepening and, albeit less so, than human capital accumulation. There has been considerable variability in the cross-country distribution of physical capital deepening contributions, from negative values of up to -1.0 (Greece) to positive values as large as 0.5 to 0.7 (Austria, Japan, Portugal and the US). Efficiency gains contributed by 0.3% in the euro area as a whole, led by Austria, Germany and Ireland. Overall, in the case of the euro area labour productivity growth of 1.3% over the period received the largest contributions from human capital accumulation (0.6%), followed by technological progress (0.4%) and efficiency change (0.3%), whereas physical capital deepening played a negligible role. Among extra-euro area Nordic countries, labour productivity growth was driven by efficiency gains in Denmark and by human capital accumulation in Norway and Sweden.

Over 1995-2000, world labour productivity growth was 1.8%, led by technological progress (1.5%). Human capital accumulation contributed with 0.6% and physical capital deepening with 0.2% – smaller figures than in the earlier period. The overall efficiency loss was around 0.5%. In the euro area as a whole, technological progress' contribution (1.8%) outpaced those of human capital accumulation (0.6%), physical capital deepening (0.4%) and efficiency change (-0.4%). In the US technological progress contributed with much more than overall capital accumulation. The role of efficiency was very negative in euro area countries Germany, Greece, Portugal and Spain, and very positive in the US and euro area countries Austria, Finland and Ireland.

Table 5.

Quadripartite decomposition of labour productivity growth (in annual average percentage growth rates)

Economies	labour productivity (real GDP per worker)		efficiency		technology		physical capital deepening		human capital deepening	
	1980-1995	1995-2000	1980-1995	1995-2000	1980-1995	1995-2000	1980-1995	1995-2000	1980-1995	1995-2000
Euro area[1]	1.30	2.34	0.31	-0.43	0.35	1.77	0.03	0.43	0.61	0.58
Germany	1.50	2.07	0.72	-0.85	0.33	2.15	0.07	0.52	0.37	0.27
France	1.51	2.29	0.13	0.30	0.38	0.99	0.24	0.32	0.76	0.67
Italy	1.13	1.66	-0.05	-0.02	0.39	0.83	-0.05	0.08	0.83	0.78
Spain	1.18	2.89	-0.05	-0.91	0.34	2.02	-0.07	0.54	0.96	1.23
Netherlands	0.38	3.29	0.13	0.26	0.37	1.98	-0.60	0.59	0.49	0.42
Belgium	1.51	2.26	0.49	0.14	0.36	1.20	0.28	0.62	0.37	0.27
Austria	1.64	2.84	0.75	0.87	0.36	1.03	0.51	0.37	0.01	0.54
Ireland	2.51	7.38	1.48	2.06	0.22	3.06	0.13	1.72	0.66	0.35
Finland	0.85	4.78	-0.21	1.75	0.33	2.56	-0.02	-0.08	0.75	0.48
Portugal	2.19	3.03	0.50	-1.65	0.24	2.73	0.50	1.26	0.92	0.72
Greece	-0.41	2.31	-0.64	-1.11	0.27	2.50	-0.98	0.24	0.96	0.69
United Kingdom	1.88	2.94	0.97	-1.73	0.22	3.00	0.25	1.22	0.43	0.48
United States	1.73	3.06	0.85	-1.01	0.24	2.90	0.50	1.09	0.14	0.11
Denmark	1.33	2.98	0.85	-1.32	0.28	2.97	-0.17	1.00	0.35	0.35
Sweden	0.74	3.00	-0.14	-0.76	0.26	2.95	-0.27	0.63	0.88	0.20
Mean[2]	*0.71*	*1.75*	*-0.37*	*-0.52*	*0.44*	*1.49*	*-0.20*	*0.20*	*0.87*	*0.59*
Standard deviation[2]	*2.10*	*2.32*	*1.87*	*1.82*	*0.35*	*0.85*	*1.81*	*1.91*	*0.57*	*0.39*

1) Excluding Cyprus, Luxembourg, Malta, the Slovak Republic and Slovenia.

2) The mean and standard deviation do not include the euro area as a whole. They correspond to the full set of 80 economies used to obtain the results reported here for a smaller sample.

Table 6.

Quadripartite decomposition of labour productivity growth (in annual average percentage growth rates)

Economies	labour productivity (real GDP per hour worked)		efficiency		technology		physical capital deepening		human capital deepening	
	1980-1995	1995-2000	1980-1995	1995-2000	1980-1995	1995-2000	1980-1995	1995-2000	1980-1995	1995-2000
Euro area[1]	2.37	1.64	0.07	0.51	0.56	0.25	1.12	0.31	0.61	0.58
Germany	2.40	2.01	0.48	0.26	0.33	0.84	1.20	0.64	0.37	0.27
France	2.61	2.13	0.11	1.26	0.67	0.19	1.04	0.00	0.76	0.67
Italy	2.12	0.97	0.00	0.00	0.64	0.09	0.64	0.09	0.83	0.78
Spain	3.09	-0.12	-0.76	-1.04	0.77	0.17	2.11	-0.46	0.96	1.23
Netherlands	1.75	1.75	-0.03	1.14	1.12	0.19	0.16	0.00	0.49	0.42
Belgium	1.99	1.77	0.32	1.32	1.14	0.19	0.14	0.00	0.37	0.27
Austria	2.45	3.01	-0.09	1.22	0.58	0.29	1.94	0.93	0.01	0.54
Ireland	3.68	6.27	0.94	1.64	0.36	2.39	1.67	1.77	0.66	0.35
Finland	3.02	2.75	-0.12	2.38	0.57	0.75	1.79	-0.85	0.75	0.48
Portugal	2.16	3.39	-0.27	-2.40	0.43	1.97	1.07	3.16	0.92	0.72
Greece	0.90	2.04	-2.37	0.57	0.27	2.43	1.24	0.64	0.96	0.69
United Kingdom	2.61	2.22	-0.17	-1.38	0.31	2.42	2.03	0.72	0.43	0.48
United States	1.31	2.28	0.35	-1.03	0.17	2.45	0.64	0.79	0.14	0.11
Denmark	2.49	1.11	0.02	-0.75	0.36	0.93	1.74	0.58	0.35	0.35
Sweden	1.34	2.46	-0.54	0.17	0.09	1.73	0.91	0.35	0.88	0.20
Mean[2]	*2.26*	*2.27*	*-0.14*	*0.22*	*0.52*	*1.14*	*1.22*	*0.56*	*0.59*	*0.50*
Standard deviation[2]	*0.74*	*1.40*	*0.74*	*1.32*	*0.31*	*0.98*	*0.65*	*0.95*	*0.31*	*0.28*

1) Excluding Cyprus, Luxembourg, Malta, the Slovak Republic and Slovenia.

2) The mean and standard deviation do not include the euro area as a whole.

Let us add a brief overview of the results obtained using PWT data beyond the set of developed countries just reviewed. For a number of countries we observe that some of the findings reported by KR and HR (for the period 1965-1990) find confirmation here the more recent period 1980-1995, depending on the specific case in question. First, concerning Asian economies labour productivity growth has tended to outpace the world average. In particular, in some of the region's countries such as China, Indonesia and Pakistan, real output growth per worker has been supported by the strong pace of physical capital deepening, even if other sources of growth may have also played a role. As was also the case for the results we obtained in the absence of human capital, in comparison with the afore-mentioned earlier studies, the role of physical capital deepening in Japan appears to have much diminished in the more recent period analysed here. Other Asian countries showed a large contribution to the growth spurt from human capital accumulation (Malaysia and Singapore) or from efficiency gains (South Korea and Thailand). Second, once more Latin American economies tended to under-perform in terms of productivity growth, with efficiency losses being a rather common phenomenon. Argentina's stagnation appears to have been driven by efficiency losses. However, in contrast to KR and HR earlier period under analysis, there is evidence that this country also suffered from a negative contribution of physical capital deepening, partly offset by positive contributions from human capital accumulation and, to a lesser extent, technological progress. Finally, African countries exhibited below-average productivity growth, marred by lack of technological change and/or physical capital deepening. Human capital accumulation appears to have made a positive contribution in the region, helping to partly alleviate the great difficulties faced in enhancing labour productivity. As found before, the substantial drop in Zambian labour productivity growth can be attributed to reasons other than those advanced in KR and HR: it was not the outcome of an exceptionally large drop in efficiency but it stemmed from a substantial fall in physical capital deepening.

Finally, we confirm the result highlighted by KR and HR that technological progress is non-neutral, with virtually all progress being evident at high values for physical capital intensity. We find evidence of this for a sample corresponding to periods (both 1980-1995 and 1995-2000) that occur later in time than that considered by KR and HR (1965-1990).Turning to an analysis of the distribution dynamics of labour productivity, the Li–Fan–Ullah test results for identity of the counterfactual distributions and the actual end-of-period distribution (not reported here) indicate that, both for the periods 1980-1995 and 1995-2000, we fail to reject the hypothesis of equality of distributions in any case. This is confirmed by visual comparison of graphical counterfactual exercises, which now include the contribution of human capital accumulation, and actual end-of-period distributions (not shown). That is, the various sources of labour productivity growth considered here had a bigger effect on changing the mean compared to their impact on the spread of the distributions of real GDP per worker.

Results Using GGDC Data

Our second set of results concerns GGDC data for up to 15 countries (EU-15 excluding Luxembourg, plus the US). Overall, efficiency levels remained rather stable over the entire period 1980-2000 (Table 3). Euro area efficiency increased slightly over time, ranging from 15% to 20% below the world frontier. Turning to growth accounting results, over 1980-1995 world labour productivity growth (at 2.3%) appears to have been dominated by physical capital deepening, which contributed with 1.2%, above the contributions of human capital accumulation (0.6%) and technological progress (0.5%). At the overall level, efficiency seems to have had a relatively small negative contribution (-0.1%). Efficiency increased slightly in the euro area, below the faster improvement seen in the US (0.4%) and in contrast with the drop observed in the UK (-0.2%). Concerning the latter two countries, as was also found in the absence of human capital, the UK appears to have overperformed the US mainly as a result of faster physical capital accumulation. With regard to the remaining countries, labour productivity growth exceeded the overall mean in Denmark and lay below the mean in Sweden. In the former country, the good performance can be traced to high physical capital deepening (1.7%), coupled with moderate rises in both technological change and human capital accumulation. The slower pace labour productivity growth in Sweden was mainly due to an efficiency loss (-0.5%) and poor technological progress (0.1%).

In the period 1995-2000, for the average of the advanced economies considered here, labour productivity growth (at 2.3%) appears to have been dominated by technological progress which contributed with 1.1%, which lay above the contributions of physical capital deepening (0.6%) and human capital accumulation (0.5%). The dominance of technological progress over physical capital accumulation in the most recent period stands in contrast with what was observed over the period 1980-1995. At the overall level, efficiency exhibited a relatively small positive contribution (0.2%), with an above-average performance being evident in the case of the euro area (0.5%). In contrast, large falls in efficiency were detected for Denmark, the US and the UK. Moreover, over the same period euro area labour productivity growth has lagged that in the US mostly owing to a large deficit in technological change, coupled with a smaller gap in physical capital deepening. These two differences have also characterised the underperformance of the euro area vis-à-vis the UK. Unlike what was observed in the period 1980-1995, Sweden's labour productivity growth exceeded that in Denmark, mainly as a result of a faster pace of technological progress (1.7% versus 0.9%) and a different development in efficiency (gain in the former country compared with a loss in the latter).

Discussion of Euro Area Growth Accounting Results Using The Barro-Lee Human Capital Measure

For the euro area as a whole, we can sum up on the robustness check concerning the growth accounting results obtained thus far. As was concluded above, the key robust result from the previous section is that technological progress was an important determinant of labour productivity growth ever since 1980. The various results reported in the present subsection have in common that they extend the basic analysis by introducing a Barro and Lee measure of human capital in the case of the production-frontier approach. For the period 1980-1995, this extension allows us to conclude that the critical importance of technological progress is not a robust finding, with its contribution to labour productivity growth being approximately halved (to some 0.6%) in the cases of both GGDC data and the full set of PWT data, being reduced even further (to 0.3%) when utilising PWT data for advanced countries only. With regard to the period since 1995, the high contribution of technological progress is confirmed by the use of PWT data (be it for the full sample of countries or for the advanced-economy subsample) in conjunction with a Barro and Lee human capital measure, but it is not robust to the use of the latter measure alongside GGDC data.

More specifically, for the period 1980-1995, in contrast with the previous section's result about the dominance of technological progress, here (that is, in the present subsection) we instead report that euro area labour productivity growth was instead driven by both human capital accumulation and technological progress – the latter registering a much lower pace than in the previous section. As with Maudos et al. (1999), from a statistical point of view this can be seen as a modification of the results that improves the measurement of technological advance in the context of production-frontier calculations. From an economic perspective, the result that the introduction of human capital into the framework reduces the role of technological progress over the period 1980-1995 is consistent with inappropriateness of technology. According to this view, the introduction of better technologies would require additional human capital aiming at adapting innovations undertaken abroad (say, by the technologically most advanced nation/s). In light of the evidence also reported here about non-neutral technological progress, technological adaptations associated with larger human capital needs (and thus, ceteris paribus, a lower capital to efficient labour ratio) imply a diminished scope for shifting the production frontier for such input mix.

Concerning euro area efficiency, the previous section produced two robust production-frontier results in the absence of human capital: (i) efficiency change was calculated to be negative since 1980 for all data used (GGDC data and PWT data for either the full set of countries or developed economies only); and (ii) euro area efficiency levels were seen some 15% to 20% below the world production frontier ever since 1980. Item (i) is not confirmed when we introduce in the present subsection the Barro and Lee measure of human capital into our production-frontier setup. While efficiency change does appear to be negative in the period since 1995 also using PWT data, in all other cases (that is, all models using GGDC data and in the period 1980-1995 using PWT data) there is evidence of efficiency gains. In contrast, item (ii) is largely confirmed by the use of the Barro and Lee measure of human capital, although the range of efficiency scores should be somewhat enlarged to also account for a possibly smaller degree of euro area inefficiency, leaving us with an range of some 10% to 20% for the overall set of results presented thus far.

Cross-Country Labour Productivity Distributions

Here, we analyse the distribution dynamics of labour productivity employing kernel density estimates to visualise and compare the impact of each of the sources of growth alone and jointly with another source. Our analysis is based on both visual inspection and the computation of Li–Fan–Ullah tests for the statistical significance of differences between (actual and counterfactual) distributions. Such test allows us to assess the statistical significance of the relative contributions of the three sources of productivity changes three sources (efficiency, technological progress and capital accumulation).

We report the implications from the kernel density estimation for the international distribution of labour productivity for our three sets of results obtained using a Barro and Lee human capital measure. These three types of results depend on the other data used in deriving growth accounting decompositions, namely, (a) GGDC data for 15 countries (EU-15 excluding Luxembourg, plus the US); (b) PWT data for the full set of 80 countries; and (c) PWT data for 26 developed economies. When we calculate the Li–Fan–Ullah tests on the basis of GGDC data, the null hypothesis of identity of the counterfactual and actual initial distributions is not rejected for both the period 1980-1995 and the one starting in 1995. Neither can we reject the identity between any pair of initial and final distributions. This finding is confirmed by visual inspection of the corresponding labour productivity density functions, including beginning- and end-of-period distributions as well as counterfactual exercises. (As with previous similar cases, neither tests nor densities are shown here.) For case (a) involving GGDC data, we can then conclude that all four sources of labour productivity growth are found to have exerted only minor consequences on the overall change in labour productivity over time.

Turning to results using PWT data, we reach broadly similar conclusions. Graphical counterfactuals exercises that combine any two or three out of the four sources of labour productivity growth are reported here only for the period 1980-1995 (not reported here). For the period 1980-1995, these tests indicate that none of the sources of labour productivity growth played a role in explaining the overall change in the distribution between 1980 and 1995 at the 5% significance level. At the 10% level, however, a statistically significant change is detectable for the labour productivity distribution when we use PWT data for all countries, which can be traced to the role of physical capital deepening. Indeed, the test implies values of 1.37 and 1.38 – compared with a critical value of 1.28 – for the identity of the final distribution vis-à-vis the initial and the physical-capital-deepening-related counterfactual distributions, respectively (see also Figure 2). This is the only case reported in this paper about a statistically significant shift in cross-country labour productivity distributions. For the period since 1995, regardless of whether we use PWT data for the full sample of countries or the developed-economy subsample, Li–Fan–Ullah tests show that the null hypothesis of identity of distributions is not rejected in any case (not shown). This is confirmed by looking at the Figures (not reported here) presenting distributions and various counterfactuals that combine any two or three out of the four sources of labour productivity growth.

Results Using the Permanent Inventory Method (PIM) Human Capital Measure

The growth accounting relation used here is: y_c/y_b= EFF×TECH×ACC, where labour productivity growth, y_c/y_b, is split into efficiency change, technological progress, and overall capital accumulation (ACC). The decomposition of total factor productivity into efficiency change and technological progress is done by means of Malmquist productivity indices. PIM human capital series are available for the EU-15 except the Netherlands. One other country is excluded owing to its outlier status (showing too high efficiency if included), namely, Portugal or Luxembourg when using GGDC and PWT data, respectively. Two datasets are used alongside the PIM human capital measure: (a) GGDC data for the EU-15 excluding the Netherlands and Portugal; and (b) PWT data available for the EU-15 excluding the Netherlands and Luxembourg.

Results Using PWT Data

Using PWT data, world efficiency dropped somewhat over 1980-2003 (Table 1). Table 7 reports labour productivity decompositions for 1980-1995 and 1995-2003. In the former period, world labour productivity growth was 1.4%. The part due to overall capital accumulation was 1.1%, above those of technological progress (0.4%) and efficiency change (-0.2%). Euro area labour productivity growth received a larger contribution from all-encompassing capital accumulation (1.0%) than from technological change (0.6%) or efficiency change (-0.2%). Turning to 1995-2001, world labour productivity growth was 2.9%. The fraction owing to all-inclusive capital accumulation (3.2%) exceeded that of technological progress (0.5%) by more than in 1980-1995. The pace of world efficiency losses was 0.8%. Euro area labour productivity growth of 2.2% was more than fully explained by overall capital accumulation; efficiency losses (-0.9%) more than offset technological progress (0.5%). Overall capital accumulation was very fast in euro area countries Belgium, Ireland, Portugal and Spain. Efficiency gains contributed greatly in Finland.

Results Using GGDC Data

With regard to efficiency using GGDC data, for the average of the developed economies in our sample, scores tended to be lower in 1995 than in 1980, with the exception of Ireland which got closer to the production frontier (Table 3). Between 1995 and 2001, we observe a further but smaller drop in overall efficiency, with Ireland once more being an exception as it eventually reached the production frontier. Concerning growth accounting results, over the period 1980-1995 world labour productivity growth (at

Table 7.

Tripartite decomposition of labour productivity growth (in annual average percentage growth rates)

	labour productivity (real GDP per worker)		efficiency		technology		human + physical capital deepening	
Economies	1980-1995	1995-2003	1980-1995	1995-2003	1980-1995	1995-2003	1980-1995	1995-2003
Euro area[1]	1.35	2.16	-0.24	-0.94	0.56	0.49	1.02	2.63
Germany	1.50	1.90	0.12	-1.10	0.62	0.38	0.76	2.63
France	1.51	2.20	-0.65	-0.59	0.53	0.49	1.63	2.30
Italy	1.13	1.66	-0.33	-0.73	0.42	0.58	1.04	1.83
Spain	1.18	2.80	-0.40	-1.40	0.42	0.36	1.16	3.87
Belgium	1.51	2.01	-0.41	-2.28	0.64	0.66	1.28	3.72
Austria	1.64	2.49	-0.48	-1.45	0.61	0.59	1.51	3.39
Ireland	2.51	6.85	0.56	0.91	0.50	0.72	1.44	5.14
Finland	0.85	4.19	-0.63	3.03	0.48	0.56	1.02	0.56
Portugal	2.19	2.75	-1.25	-3.41	0.40	0.43	3.07	5.93
Greece	-0.41	2.61	0.96	-0.17	-1.03	0.49	-0.33	2.27
United Kingdom	1.88	2.76	-0.26	-1.61	0.54	0.70	1.60	3.73
Denmark	1.33	2.59	0.67	-1.87	0.58	0.80	0.07	3.73
Sweden	0.74	2.60	0.01	0.41	0.43	0.13	0.30	2.05
Mean[2]	*1.35*	*2.88*	*-0.16*	*-0.79*	*0.40*	*0.53*	*1.12*	*3.17*
Standard deviation[2]	*0.72*	*1.34*	*0.61*	*1.61*	*0.44*	*0.18*	*0.85*	*1.43*

1) Excluding Cyprus, Luxembourg, Malta, the Netherlands, the Slovak Republic and Slovenia.
2) The mean and standard deviation do not include the euro area as a whole.

Table 8.

Tripartite decomposition of labour productivity growth (in annual average percentage growth rates)

	labour productivity (real GDP per hour worked)		efficiency		technology		human + physical capital deepening	
Economies	1980-1995	1995-2001	1980-1995	1995-2001	1980-1995	1995-2001	1980-1995	1995-2001
Euro area[1]	2.40	1.51	-0.98	-1.58	0.21	1.17	3.20	1.94
Germany	2.40	1.98	-0.21	-1.29	0.21	1.10	2.40	2.18
France	2.61	1.94	-1.85	-1.34	0.21	1.06	4.32	2.25
Italy	2.12	0.90	-1.05	-2.37	0.05	1.37	3.16	1.94
Spain	3.09	-0.14	-2.16	-1.74	-0.01	0.82	5.36	0.80
Belgium	1.99	1.39	-0.13	-0.52	0.21	1.23	1.91	0.68
Austria	2.45	2.45	-1.12	-1.94	0.21	1.42	3.41	3.00
Ireland	2.65	1.68	0.33	-1.83	0.21	1.29	2.11	2.25
Finland	3.02	2.64	-1.12	1.57	0.21	1.20	3.98	-0.14
Luxembourg	0.90	2.47	-1.83	-1.29	-0.55	1.01	3.35	2.78
Greece	2.61	2.05	-0.65	-1.38	0.21	1.45	3.07	2.00
United Kingdom	2.49	0.83	-0.74	-2.52	0.21	1.63	3.03	1.77
Denmark	1.34	2.14	-0.88	0.43	0.21	0.33	2.02	1.36
Sweden	3.68	5.81	0.59	1.17	0.21	1.46	2.86	3.08
Mean[2]	*2.41*	*2.01*	*-0.83*	*-1.01*	*0.12*	*1.18*	*3.15*	*1.84*
Standard deviation[2]	*0.72*	*1.39*	*0.83*	*1.30*	*0.21*	*0.34*	*0.98*	*0.95*

1) Excluding Cyprus, Malta, the Netherlands, Portugal, the Slovak Republic and Slovenia.
2) The mean and standard deviation do not include the euro area as a whole.

2.4%) was dominated by overall capital accumulation (3.2%), well above the contribution of technological progress (0.1%) (Table 8). A similar pattern applied to the euro area as a whole. Concerning efficiency change, at the overall level it made a large negative contribution (-0.8%). The drop in efficiency computed for the euro area (-1.0%) was widespread, except for Ireland (0.3%).

Over 1995-2001, world labour productivity growth (at 2.0%) was driven by overall capital accumulation (1.8%), above the contribution of technological progress (1.2%) (Table 8). Capital accumulation's dominance marks a continuation – even if at a much slower pace – from the period 1980-1995. At the overall level, efficiency dropped markedly (-1.0%). Euro area labour productivity growth (1.5%) was driven by the large contributions of technological progress and especially overall capital accumulation, which more than offset the effect of efficiency losses.

Discussion of Euro Area Growth Accounting Results Using The PIM Human Capital Measure

As we have seen above, the previous section's result that technological progress was a key determinant of euro area labour productivity growth ever since 1980 is not robust to the introduction of a Barro-Lee human capital measure. This lack of robustness is further documented when we employ the alternative, PIM measure of human capital, which tends to substantially reduce the estimated role of technological progress in driving euro area labour productivity growth. Admittedly, when the PIM human capital series is used in combination with GGDC data we still find a considerably high contribution of technological progress (1.2%) for the period since 1995. However, the remaining cases when the PIM human capital measure is used would indicate otherwise. Indeed, when we also employ PWT data since 1995, technological change's contribution to euro area labour productivity growth drops to 0.5%. Even more, for the period 1980-1995 the contribution of technological progress is found to be substantially reduced (to only 0.4% otherwise employing PWT data, and to 0.1% utilising GGDC data).

Finally, the previous section, which proceeded in the absence of human capital, uncovered two robust results ever since 1980: (i) efficiency change was negative; and (ii) euro area efficiency scores ranged from 15% to 20% below best practice worldwide. Item (i) was found not to be robust when allowing in the last subsection for the Barro-Lee measure of human capital. The results we now obtain utilising the PIM human capital measure are consistent with the notion of euro area efficiency losses over time, as found in the previous section. With regard to item (ii), our results using the PIM human capital measure further confirm the robust finding that the euro area suffers from inefficiency. While the inefficiency range proposed on the basis of joint consideration of the previous section and the present subsection – namely, 10% to 20% – is broadly in line with some estimates reported in the present subsection, the combined use of GGDC data and the PIM human capital measure since 1995 would point to a higher degree of inefficiency (reaching even some 35%).

Cross-Country Labour Productivity Distributions

Li-Fan-Ullah tests fail to reject the identity of the initial and final distributions over 1980-1995 and since 1995, as well as both for GGDC and PWT data. Neither can we reject, for any of these two periods, the null hypothesis of identity between counterfactual and actual initial distributions. The latter conclusion holds for all possible counterfactual experiments concerning each two of the three sources of labour productivity growth in question. These findings are broadly consistent with visual inspection of the corresponding density functions. (Neither tests nor densities are reported here.) In sum, all sources of labour productivity growth appear to play only a minor role in modifying the distribution between 1980 and 1995, and also for the period since the latter year.

FUTURE RESEARCH DIRECTIONS

Future research may rethink how to use international production-frontier methods to deal with the dramatic worldwide upheaval of the growth process implied by the financial and economic crisis of the late 2000s – a challenge now compounded by the recent coronavirus pandemic. While the approach used here could be extended beyond the present focus on the euro area economy, let us – for the sake of clarity – explore what future research avenues might look exclusively for the euro area case. (For other economies one might have to add the need to start by undertaking corresponding analyses also for "normal" pre-crisis times.) The most promising starting point would be to first try to identify the new growth patterns emerging from data that are very noisy due to high-frequency, crisis-driven macroeconomic fluctuations. Once new key stylised features start to emerge from such challenging expert analyses, the production-frontier approach could be used to test for informed hypotheses about how the growth process might have been driven by its various relevant sources, not least changes in how efficiently resources are utilised.

CONCLUSION

This paper studies the contribution of the different sources of labour productivity growth (derived within a growth accounting approach) onto the change in the distribution of real GDP per unit of labour across countries. In so doing, it focuses on a nonparametric production-frontier approach that permits to decompose labour productivity developments into changes in efficiency, technology and capital deepening. The production-frontier approach used here follows HR in amending KR methodology in two ways: (a) by using a dynamic panel of countries, thus precluding implosion of the international production frontier over time; and (b) by separating the analysis of changes in the productivity distribution to analyses of changes in the mean and mean preserving shifts in the distribution of productivity.

This paper undertakes extensive robustness checks and manages to identify the following (robust) growth accounting results. First, euro area efficiency is estimated to be much below the world production frontier. In most cases, euro area technology level is found to exhibit a gap of some 10% to 20% from best practice worldwide. This helps sharpen policy discussions about how to increase labour productivity, pointing to the need for structural reform efforts to improve resource use. Broadly speaking, these policy measures tend to overlap with those proposed to encourage technological advance, including through higher R&D spending, less regulated product and labour markets, enhanced education, etc. Judging from our results, these reforms appear to be most productive when focused on raising efficiency, with technologies available globally counting among the resources that are currently underutilised in the euro area.

Second, the introduction of human capital measures into the analysis reveals their significant effect on euro area labour productivity growth, attesting to the positive macroeconomic return to human capital investment and the favourable role of education policies. Consideration of human capital helps refine the measurement of technological change's contribution to euro area labour productivity growth, cutting it by no less than half ever since 1980. This finding can be interpreted, on a statistical basis, as capturing a more refined measurement of technological advance. From an economic perspective, it can be regarded in connection with the inappropriateness of technology, also in light of the evidence also reported here about non-neutral technological progress.

Third, we find no compelling evidence that any source of growth affected the spread of the distribution of real GDP per unit of labour. The only exception concerns the shift in the labour productivity distribution between 1980 and 1995 – attributable to the role of physical capital deepening – when we employ the Barro and Lee human capital measure together with World Penn Tables data for the full set of countries, and this only at the 10% significance level. Our quite general result that distribution shifts were statistically insignificant over 1980-1995 contrasts with previous studies (KR and HR), which detected a transition from unimodalism to bimodalism for a period (1965-1990) both starting and ending earlier than ours. This apparent contrast can be reconciled by noticing that a bimodal distribution is already embedded in the data at the time our analysis starts in 1980. Our results indicate that poorer countries have neither dropped further down the international distribution of labour productivity, nor moved to close the existing gap. Much is thus left for many poorer nations to adopt better governance and democracy as well as implementing structural policies aimed at fostering convergence towards more affluent countries – a process that would also benefit from the latter's enhanced external aid and technology transfer.

The present analysis is based on a unique dataset which is very detailed for a meaningful period of time. From the second half of the 2000s the analytical challenge posed by a major global financial and economic crisis has to be taken into account, not least after most economies (including those that had shown signs of superseding some of the depression symptoms) have all but collapsed in the face of the coronavirus pandemic outbreak. The general methodology advocated here, by allowing for efficiency changes, offers in the present crisis environment a better chance of disentangling the distinct role played by the different contributors to economic growth, namely factor accumulation, technological progress and efficiency itself. No method will be free of problems during such protracted and anomalous crisis period, in particular owing to the difficulty in distinguishing between macroeconomic fluctuations and growth patterns. The present methodology is likely to prove better prepared for this task; even if macroeconomic noise is expected to contaminate efficiency measures – depriving the latter from a purely technical connotation – modern micro-founded macroeconomic theory is in line with the notion that macroeconomic uncertainty is damaging to economic performance, e.g. by reducing the efficiency of relative price signals.

Another line of defence concerns our focus on the euro area economy. Motivating this are existing narratives that, based on different methodologies, have agreed on some basic features about reality and policy consequences. This includes the performance gap vis-à-vis the US that emerged in some sectors, and which has been traced to matters concerning the adoption of new technologies in the mid-1990s. Over the more recent crisis period there is not a comparable clarity on the main issues. Arguably, the availability of various growth accounting methodologies to tackle ongoing structural change – a situation aggravated by noisy data dominated by high-frequency macroeconomic fluctuations – has prevented the profession from detecting key stylised features. In the face of this confusing situation, our proposal is twofold. First, one may look back at the widest possible array of data for a relatively normal pre-crisis period – the present paper being offered as an example of that. Second, one may evolve views by carefully looking through the noise of macroeconomic fluctuations in crisis times; as more robust views emerge these could prove useful in fine-tuning the methodologies and data sources used. Overall, it is our belief that the analysis contained here could prove useful, given that it resorts to sound unique data from more normal times and it employs a promising methodology that can be extended in follow-up studies.

ACKNOWLEDGMENT

I thank comments received from Neale Kennedy, Helena Marques, Julian Morgan and Battista Severgnini. This paper has also benefited from discussions at a presentation at the European Central Bank and the 10th International Network for Economic Research (INFER) Annual Conference. All errors are the author's responsibility.

REFERENCES

Alvarez-Ayuso, I., & Delgado-Rodríguez, M. (2002). *Estimación del Capital Público, Capital Privado y Capital Humano para la UE-15*. Instituto de Estudios Fiscales Working Paper 12/02.

Barro, R., & Lee, J.-W. (2001). International Data on Educational Attainment: Updates and Implications. *Oxford Economic Papers*, *53*(3), 41–63. doi:10.1093/oep/53.3.541

Fan, Y., & Ullah, A. (1999). On Goodness-of-Fit Tests for Weekly Dependent Processes Using Kernel Method. *Journal of Nonparametric Statistics*, *11*(1-3), 337–360. doi:10.1080/10485259908832788

Feenstra, R., Heston, A., Timmer, M., & Deng, H. (2007). *Estimating Real Production and Expenditures across Nations: A Proposal for Improving the Penn World Tables*. Policy Research Working Paper No. 4166. Washington, DC: The World Bank.

Hall, R., & Jones, C. (1999). Why Do Some Countries Produce so Much More Output per Worker than Others? *The Quarterly Journal of Economics*, *114*(1), 83–116. doi:10.1162/003355399555954

Henderson, D., & Russell, R. (2005). Human Capital and Convergence: A Production-Frontier Approach. *International Economic Review*, *46*(4), 1167–1205. doi:10.1111/j.1468-2354.2005.00364.x

Hulton, C., & Wykoff, F. (1981). The Measurement of Economic Depreciation. In C. Hulton (Ed.), *Depreciation, Inflation, and the Taxation of Income from Capital*. The Urban Institute Press.

Inklaar, R., Timmer, M., & van Ark, B. (2007). Mind the Gap! International Comparisons of Productivity in Services and Goods Production. *German Economic Review*, *8*(2), 281–307. doi:10.1111/j.1468-0475.2007.00408.x

Jerzmanowski, M. (2007). Total Factor Productivity Differences: Appropriate Technology vs. Efficiency. *European Economic Review*, *51*(8), 2080–2110. doi:10.1016/j.euroecorev.2006.12.005

Kumar, S., & Russell, R. (2002). Technological Change, Technological Catch-up, and Capital Deepening: Relative Contributions to Growth and Convergence. *The American Economic Review*, *92*(3), 527–548. doi:10.1257/00028280260136381

Li, Q. (1996). Nonparametric Testing of Closeness between Two Unknown Distribution Functions. *Econometric Reviews*, *15*(3), 261–274. doi:10.1080/07474939608800355

Maudos, J., Pastor, J., & Serrano, L. (1999). Total Factor Productivity Measurement and Human Capital in OECD Countries. *Economics Letters*, *63*(1), 39–44. doi:10.1016/S0165-1765(98)00252-3

Psacharopoulos, G., & Patrinos, H. (2004). Returns to Investment in Education: A Further Update. *Education Economics*, *12*(2), 111–134. doi:10.1080/0964529042000239140

Romer, C. (1989). The Prewar Business Cycle Reconsidered: New Estimates of Gross National Product, 1869-1908. *Journal of Political Economy*, *97*(1), 1–37. doi:10.1086/261592

Salinas, M., Alvarez, I., & Delgado, M. (2006). Capital Accumulation and TFP Growth in the EU: A Production Frontier Approach. *Journal of Policy Modeling*, *28*(2), 195–205. doi:10.1016/j.jpolmod.2005.07.008

Sánchez, M. (2010). Euro Area Growth Accounting: Comparing Standard and Production-Frontier Approaches. In *Challenges for Economic Policy Design: Lessons from the Financial Crisis*. Lambertz Academic Publishers, INFER Research Perspectives.

Sheather, S., & Jones, M. (1991). A Reliable Data-Based Bandwidth Selection Method for Kernel Density Estimation. *Journal of the Royal Statistical Society. Series B. Methodological*, *53*(3), 683–690. doi:10.1111/j.2517-6161.1991.tb01857.x

Simar, L. (2003). Detecting Outliers in Frontier Models: A Simple Approach. *Journal of Productivity Analysis*, *20*(3), 391–424. doi:10.1023/A:1027308001925

van Ark, B., O'Mahony, M. & Ypma, G. (2007). *The EU KLEMS Productivity Report*. Groningen Growth and Development Centre, University of Groningen, and University of Birmingham, Issue No. 1.

ADDITIONAL READING

Bartelsman, E., Lopez-Garcia, P. & Presidente, G. (2019). Labour reallocation in recession and recovery: evidence for Europe, *National Institute Economic Review* No. 247, "Productivity: Past, present and future", February.

Filippetti, A., & Peyrache, A. (2017). Productivity growth and catching up: A technology gap explanation. *International Review of Applied Economics*, *31*(3), 283–303. doi:10.1080/02692171.2016.1249831

McAdam, P., & Willman, A. (2018). Unraveling the Skill Premium. *Macroeconomic Dynamics*, *22*(1), 33–62. doi:10.1017/S1365100516000547

Sickles, R., & Zelenyuk, V. (2019). *Measurement of Productivity and Efficiency*. Cambridge University Press. doi:10.1017/9781139565981

van Ark, B. (2016). The Productivity Paradox of the New Digital Economy. *International Productivity Monitor*, *31*, 3–18.

van Ark, B., Erumban, A., & de Vries, K. (2019). Fellowship Initiative 2018-2019 "Productivity and Innovation Competencies in the Midst of the Digital Transformation Age: An EU-US Comparison". *European Economy Discussion Paper* No. 119, European Commission's Directorate-General for Economic and Financial Affairs, Brussels.

KEY TERMS AND DEFINITIONS

Barro-Lee Human Capital Measure: Human capital series based on the methodology originally developed Barro and Lee (2001), which relies on data on years of schooling and returns to education.

Efficiency: Extent to which resource use allows the economy to get close to the optimum performance attainable, as given by available technology.

Growth Accounting: Method used to decompose some measure of output growth into its relevant sources (such as changes in input use, technology, and efficiency).

International Production Frontier: It indicates the optimum performance in production attainable, as given by existing technology, for any given combination of efficiently used production inputs.

Labour Productivity Growth: Change in output relative to the labour input.

Nonparametric Estimation: Statistical method that allows the functional form of a fit to data to be obtained without the estimation of meaningful parameters.

Perpetual Inventory Method: Method of constructing estimates of capital stock from time series of gross fixed capital formation.

PIM Human Capital Measure: Human capital series obtained by applying the perpetual inventory method (PIM) to real spending on education.

ENDNOTES

1. Among other robustness checks, Jerzmanowski (2007) finds that the fraction of income differences due to physical plus human capital in 1960-1995 greatly increases when moving from a Cobb-Douglas environment to a production-frontier approach. Sánchez (2010) compares the latter with a standard setup in the absence of human capital.
2. In what follows, the expression "capital" (e.g. in "capital deepening") – wherever used without being qualified – is meant to refer to the physical component of overall capital accumulation (also involving human capital).
3. The method used here has previously been employed by Adalmir Marquetti (see http://homepage.newschool.edu/~foleyd/epwt/DataDoc2.1.html). This procedure, which in turn draws on Hulton and Wycoff (1981), assumes that the depreciation takes a geometric form. Hulton and Wycoff (1981) calculated the rate of depreciation (d) with the expression (d = R/T) where R is the factor that defines the degree of declining balance due to depreciation, and T is the average asset life. The average value found by Hulton and Wycoff (1981) for R is 1.65 for equipment categories, and 0.91 for structure categories. The R employed for us is 1.05. It was calculated considering that equipment categories represent 20% and structure categories 80% percent of the gross capital formation. The asset life considered was 14 years, hence the depreciation rate was 0.075. For the country of

interest, the net capital stock was computed using the expression $K_t = \sum_j^T (1-0.075)^{T-j} I_{T-j}, (j = 1,\ldots,T; T = 14)$, where I denotes the investment series. In the application conducted here using PWT series for an international panel of countries, we limit our sample to countries with investment data going back at least to 1960 and use all available investment data.

4 Full results are available from the author upon request. Luxembourg is excluded from the PWT sample due to its outlier status (too high efficiency for the last fifteen years or so). This was confirmed using the test described in Simar (2003).

5 There are differences between the PWT and GGDC measures of labour productivity growth that are not entirely attributable to the way the labour input is computed (in terms of hours worked in GGDC data and number of workers in the PWT). This is the case of euro area labour productivity growth over the last ten years, which appear to be considerably lower according to PWT data partly owing to a different measurement of real GDP growth.

6 The same piecewise linear functional form has been used by e.g. HR and Hall and Jones (1999).

7 Maudos et al. (1999) use a nonparametric production-frontier approach and PWT data for their study of OECD countries over 1975-1990, also accounting for human capital (on the basis of the Barro and Lee measure only).

8 A more extensive use of the EU KLEMS database (which is still at a preliminary stage) is left for further research. This database consists of time series covering the period since 1970 which measure output growth, employment, capital formation and total factor productivity (TFP) at a disaggregated industry level across 25 EU countries as well as in the United States and Japan.

9 Part of this statistical discrepancy relates to changes in the unemployment rate, given that PWT defines the number of workers on an economically active population basis, while GGDC defines them in terms of actual employment. Still, a significant part of the discrepancies involved relate to measurement problems that are difficult to pin down.

10 In this paper, results are discussed only for the broadest country average (i.e. the "world"), the euro area (as a whole and with country detail) and the US.

11 See Appendix 1 for the methodology.

12 See Appendix 2 for the methodology.

13 See Appendix 3 for the methodology.

14 See Appendix 4 for the methodology used for density estimation.

15 For lack of space, this result is not reported here. In all cases where this is so, results are available from the author upon request. The only distributional results actually reported in this paper feature in the subsubsection labelled "Cross-country labour productivity distributions". We thank Daniel J. Henderson for graciously sharing his code.

16 The expression "potential output" utilised here is not to be confused with the one frequently used in macroeconomics; in the present case, by definition it is not possible for output to lie above potential output.

17 Note that these two formulations would be identical if the technology were Hicks neutral.

18 In what follows, the expression "capital deepening" has to be understood as referring to the physical component of overall capital accumulation (which also involves the human capital input).

19 We use a Gaussian kernel and estimate *h* to minimise the cross-validation function. The results reported in the text are robust to using the method proposed by Sheather and Jones (1991) instead.

APPENDIX 1

The KR approach to constructing the worldwide production frontier and associated efficiency levels of individual economies (distances from the frontier) is based on the pioneering work of Farrell (1956) and others. The basic idea of this so-called data envelopment analysis is to envelop the data in the "smallest," or "tightest fitting," convex cone, and the (upper) boundary of this set then represents the "best practice" production frontier (the graph of the production function). Although this data-driven approach, implemented with standard mathematical programming algorithms, requires no specification of functional form, it does require an assumption about returns to scale of the technology (as well as free input and output disposability). Our technology contains three macroeconomic variables: aggregate output and two aggregate inputs: labour and physical capital. Let $\langle Y_{it}, L_{it}, K_{it} \rangle$, t=1,...,T, i=1,...,N, represent T observations on these four variables for each of the N countries for a total of NT observations.

Our approach to constructing the frontier uses a dynamic panel data set to preclude implosion of the frontier over time (see Diewert, 1980). In particular, we construct the constant-returns-to-scale, period-t technology using all data up to that point in time,

$$\Psi_t = \left\{ \langle Y, L, K \rangle \in \Re_+^3 \mid Y \le \sum_{s \le t} \sum_i z_{is} Y_{is}, L \le \sum_{s \le t} \sum_i z_{is} L_{is}, K \le \sum_{s \le t} \sum_i z_{is} K_{is}, z_{is} \ge 0, \forall i, s \right\} \quad \text{(A.1)}$$

where Z_{is} represents the level of operation of country i's production process at time s.
The output-based efficiency index λ_{it} for country i at time t is defined by

$$E(Y_{it}, L_{it}, K_{it}) = \min\{\lambda_{it} \mid \langle Y_{it} / \lambda, L_{it}, K_{it} \rangle \in \Psi_t\} \quad \text{(A.2)}$$

This index is the inverse of the maximal proportional amount that output Yit can be expanded while remaining technologically feasible, given the technology Ψ_t and the input quantities Lit and Kit, it is less than or equal to 1 and takes the value of 1 if and only if the it observation is on the period-t production frontier. In this case of a scalar output, the output-based efficiency index is simply the ratio of actual to potential output evaluated at the actual input quantities.16

APPENDIX 2

We decompose the growth of output per unit of labour into three components attributable to (i) the change in efficiency, (ii) technological change, and (iii) capital deepening (increases in the capital–labour ratio). Letting b and c stand for the base period and the current period, respectively, potential (production frontier) outputs per efficiency unit of labour in the two periods are, by definition, given by $\overline{y}_b(k_b) = y_b / e_b$ and $\overline{y}_c(k_c) = y_c / e_c$, where eb and ec are the values of the efficiency indexes in the respective periods. Thus,

$$\frac{y_c}{y_b} = \frac{e_c}{e_b}\frac{\bar{y}_c(k_c)}{\bar{y}_b(k_b)} \tag{A.3}$$

Denote potential output per unit of labour at current-period capital intensity using the base-period technology by $\bar{y}_b(k_c)$. Similarly, potential output per unit of labour at base-period capital intensity using the current-period technology is denoted $\bar{y}_c(k_b)$. Multiplying the top and bottom of (A.3) alternatively by $\bar{y}_b(k_c)/\bar{y}_b(k_c)$ and $\bar{y}_c(k_b) /_c (k_b)$ yields two alternative decompositions of labour productivity growth, as follows:

$$\frac{y_c}{y_b} = \frac{e_c}{e_b}\frac{\bar{y}_c(k_c)}{\bar{y}_b(k_c)}\frac{\bar{y}_b(k_c)}{\bar{y}_b(k_b)} = EFF \times TECH^c \times KACC^b \tag{A.4}$$

and

$$\frac{y_c}{y_b} = \frac{e_c}{e_b}\frac{\bar{y}_c(k_b)}{\bar{y}_b(k_b)}\frac{\bar{y}_c(k_c)}{\bar{y}_c(k_b)} = EFF \times TECH^b \times KACC^c \tag{A.5}$$

The decomposition in (A.4) measures technological change by the shift in the frontier in the output direction at the current-period capital-labour ratio and measures the effects of physical capital accumulation along the base-period frontier. The decomposition in (A.5) measures technological change at the base-period capital-labour ratio and physical capital accumulation by movements along the current-period frontier.17 The two decompositions in (A.4) and (A.5) do not yield the same results; that is, the decomposition is path dependent. In fact, in the absence of neutrality of technological change, this ambiguity is endemic to growth accounting exercises. In line with KR and HR, we resolve this ambiguity by adopting the "Fisher Ideal" decomposition, based on geometric averages of the two measures of the effects of technological change and physical capital accumulation and obtained mechanically by multiplying top and bottom of (A.3) by $\left[\bar{y}_b(k_c)\right]^{1/2}\left[\bar{y}_c(k_b)\right]^{1/2}$, which yields:

$$\frac{y_c}{y_b} = EFF \times \left(TECH^b \cdot TECH^c\right)^{1/2}\left(KACC^b \cdot KACC^c\right)^{1/2} = EFF \times TECH \times KACC \tag{A6}$$

Use of (A.6) amounts to a modified growth accounting methodology that allows us to analyse labour productivity growth of each country, decomposing it into three sources: (i) efficiency change (or catching-up towards the best-practice frontier), (ii) technical change (shift of the technological frontier itself) and (iii) capital deepening (increase in the capital-labour ratio).

APPENDIX 3

The tripartite decomposition of labour productivity changes can be written as follows:

$y_c = (EFF \times TECH \times KACC)y_b$

Thus, the labour productivity distribution in – say – 1990 can be constructed by successively multiplying labour productivity in – say – 1965 by each of the four factors. This in turn allows us to construct counterfactual distributions by sequential introduction of each of these factors (where b = 1965 and c = 1990). For example, the counterfactual 1990 labour-productivity distribution of the variable,

$y_E = EFF \times y_b$

with its mean extracted, isolates the (mean-preserving) effect on the distribution of changes in efficiency only, assuming a stationary world production frontier, no capital deepening, and the counterfactual 1990 labour productivity distribution of the variable,

$y_{ET} = (EFF \times TECH)y_b$

with its mean extracted, isolates the (mean-preserving) effect on the distribution of changes in efficiency and the technology, assuming no capital deepening.18

APPENDIX 4

To briefly outline the kernel density estimation method, let f be the probability density function of a univariate random variable u (labour productivity, in our case) and let $\{u^i: i=1,\ldots,N\}$ be a random sample from this distribution. The histogram or 'naïve' estimator for the density of u gives a simple and way of estimating and visualising the distribution. A generalisation of the histogram is the kernel density estimator

$$\hat{f}_h(u) \equiv \frac{1}{nh}\sum_{i=1}^{N} K\left(\frac{u-u^i}{h}\right), \qquad \text{(A.7)}$$

where h=h(N) is the band- or interval-width ($h \to 0$, $Nh \to \infty$ whenever $N \to \infty$)19 while K is an appropriate kernel function, and u is a point at which we aim to estimate the density f. The estimator (A.7) is consistent for the true f and asymptotically normally distributed under quite weak regularity conditions on the data generating process.

Using (A.7) for samples of original and fitted estimates of labour productivity would give us estimates of the corresponding true, but unknown densities at any points of their supports. These estimates will then be plotted against the corresponding points of the support to obtain visual representation of the changes in the distribution. To make formal statement, we use the statistical test on equality of densities proposed by Fan and Ullah (1999), building on earlier work by Li (1996).

Chapter 13
Attempting an Assessment of the MoUs' Role in Confronting the Greek Crisis

Charalampos K. Arachovas
Panteion University of Social and Political Sciences, Greece & Institute of Commerce and Entrepreneurship (IN.EM.Y. of ESEE), Greece

Manolis M. Manioudis
University of Crete, Greece & Institute of Commerce and Entrepreneurship (IN.EM.Y. of ESEE), Greece

ABSTRACT

This chapter wishes to analyze the full impact of the three (3) Memoranda of Understanding signed between the Greek corresponding governments and the European Commission, ECB, and IMF representations. The first Memorandum was considered as necessary due to Greece's inability to access international financial capital, while the other two (2), which followed, tried to correct "implementation errors," control for "ownership" of the programs, and confront the prolonged and severe economic crisis and unemployment derailment. This chapter will present a series of key macroeconomic and microeconomic figures and will argue that despite the fiscal consolidation, which came at an extremely high social and economic cost, Greek economy still has a lot challenges to tackle and serious impediments to overcome. It will also shed some new light on whether Memoranda actually helped Greece to recover or used a whole country as a "guinea pig" and as an example of compliance, allowing the final reader to decide.

INTRODUCTION

Greek economy faced an unprecedented economic depression during the period between 2008 and 2018. The economy, in the peak of the crisis, lost more than the ¼ of its GDP; unemployment rates exceeded 27%; households faced material deprivation; many enterprises closed while both productivity and Foreign Direct Investments (FDI), core tenets of Economic Adjustment Programmes (Memoranda), achieved

DOI: 10.4018/978-1-7998-4933-9.ch013

disappointing low rates. It is indicative that productivity was decreased by 15.5% (EL.STAT.) between 2008 and 2016 while FDIs were reduced by 52.7% between 2013 and 2015 (OECD). These facts elevate the failure of economic policy, connected with memoranda, which in many cases highlights the fact of mistaking the beauty of theoretical models for truth.

This chapter wishes to analyse the full impact of the three (3) Memoranda of Understanding signed between the Greek corresponding governments and the EU, ECB and IMF representations. The first Memorandum was considered as necessary due to Greece's inability to access international financial capital, while the other two (2), which followed, tried to correct «implementation errors», control for «ownership» of the programs and confront the prolonged and severe economic crisis and unemployment derailment. This chapter will present a series of key macroeconomic and microeconomic figures and will argue that despite the extreme fiscal consolidation, which came at an extremely high social and economic cost, Greek economy still has a lot challenges to tackle and serious impediments to overcome. It will also shed some new light on whether Memoranda actually helped Greece to recover or used a whole country as a «guinea-pig» and as an example of compliance, allowing the reader to decide.

ECONOMIC CONVERGENCE PROJECT: THE ERA OF ALCYONIDES DAYS[1]

The period before crisis (1994-2008) was crucial regarding the Greek economy's performance. It is the period through which Greece attained high convergence rates being connected, in real terms, with other European economies. The privatization of state assets (such as communications), the liberalization of capital markets and the enlargement of the stock market are signs of modernization and economic development. It is indicative that between 1994 and 2008 the Greek GDP had been increasing with a mean annual rate of 3.5% (Varoufakis and Tserkezis 2014). In addition, the monetary policy of 'hard drachma' confronted inflation and improved the balance of payments. However, in accordance to all these positive facts, the Greek economy was transformed into a typical economy of services. The 'new paradigm', emerged during the Euro era, was associated with the sectoral specialization of Greece's 'comparative advantages': tourism, shipping, real-estate, banking and telecommunications.

However, some of these sectors were (despite extensive privatizations) tightly connected with the state. Initially, this hermaphroditic intermixture is one of the chief reasons behind Greece's fragile and problematical economic structure. Furthermore, Greece's participation in the Eurozone in 2001 was associated with the absence of state's intervention which was crucial for enterprises' protection through tariffs and economic policy (Hadjimichalis 2011). Unavoidably, this elimination accelerated the course of de-industrialization which was evident already by late 1980s. Some cases such as Kastoria's beaver industry, Lavrion's mining and textile and fruit in Naoussa are illustrative of the path of de- industrialization (Liddle 2009). Historically (and theoretically) speaking, the immediate result of de-industrialization is manufacturing decline and productivity loss. Thus, Greece's productivity was much lower to other European Union's nations, thus affecting the hard core of country's competiveness (Mitsopoulos and Pelagidis 2011). Additionally, the second 'development' law (Law 3229/2004), which was voted by the Conservative Party and aimed to provide initiatives to potential national (or international) investors, brought sparse economic outcomes.

On the other side, the mega-project of the 2004 Olympic Games exemplified a (typical) economic disaster, as Whitson and Horn (2006) put it, due to huge economic costs (20 billion euros). In addition, Olympic Games sharpened inter-regional contrasts, which brought about, as in other countries organizing Olympic Games, public finance (Andranovitch et al. 2001). Ad addendum, a peculiar feature of the Greek social formation, «clientelism», was diffused within political parties and became prevalent across all governance levels influencing the effectiveness of public policy and the progress of public revenues (Mavrogordatos 1998). Essentially, clientilism is one of the main factors determining the size of the Greek shadow economy.

Apart from all these, Greece acceptance into the Eurozone implied the cancellation of its exchange rate policy and its monetary policy due to the emancipation of capitals' mobility and the institutionalization of fixed exchange rates (Bryan and Rafferty 2006; Milios and Sotiropoulos 2010). As such, the Greek economy was plagued by several problems (exempli gratia high inflation rates, fiscal and trade deficits, low growth rates and frequent exchange rate crises), which were transformed into productive and macroeconomic instability. Series of stability programs (1985-1987, 1990-1993, 1996-2000 and 2005-2007) decreased deficit but augmented debt as a percentage of GDP. In microeconomic terms, the chief cause of economy's poor performance was its low profitability which led to low investments and fostered high (in comparison to other European nations) unemployment (Tsoulfidis and Tsaliki, 2014).

Greek Crisis: The Era Of Thunderstorm

Thus the strong development performance of Greece in the period 1994-2008 was seated on unsustainable growth drivers, namely (private and state) consumption and residential investment. As such, "high real wages increases, rapid credit growth – supported by financial sector liberalization and low interest rates associated with euro adoption- and loose fiscal policy contributed to buoyant growth" (European Commission 2010: 7). Naturally therefore, this fragile economic performance affected Greece's macroeconomic performance and accelerated the downfall of its economy during the crisis. This downfall was the chief cause of the fact that the global financial crisis of 2008 was transformed in Greece into an unprecedented debt crisis. This crisis is crystallized into two indicators: the public debt accounting in 2008 for the 120% of GDP while the fiscal deficit amounted 13.6% of the product. These facts elevate economy's imbalance which was connected with spreads' ejection, unstable debt and confidence's collapse (Christodoulakis 2010).

Naturally, creditors feared the diffusion of crisis from Greece to Eurozone. Bailout loans from 'troika' (namely International Monetary Fund, European Commission and European Central Bank) were followed by Economic Adjustment Programs (EAPs) between Greek governments and its creditors. The IMF, the EC and the ECB believed that EAPs would be crucial in facing crisis being an opportunity of launching a new model of economic growth (Valaskakis 2012; Tsakloglou et al. 2016). The great importance of consumption (over 70% of GDP) was regarded as one of the most astonishing weaknesses of the Greek economy. As such EAPs attempted to facilitate the growth of Foreign Direct Investments (FDI) and exports at the expense of both individual consumption and imports of goods. The key word in this new developmental paradigm was competitiveness.

For creditors, as well as for many economists, competitiveness should be seated on three pivotal pillars: productivity, Foreign Direct Investments (FDI) and large firms. The reduction of the cost of production was regarded as instrumental in augmenting competitiveness, through low prices, being a motive of attracting mega-investments. Moreover, small and medium enterprises (SMEs) were considered as an obstacle of economic development. According to this view large firms cause productivity increases (through economies of scale, internalization of knowledge, learning etc.) (Pitelis and Antonakis 2003). The direct effects of all these was the elimination of wages, in both private and state sectors and the creation of incentives to large enterprises through the formation of the Hellenic Republic Asset Development Fund (henceforth HRADF). According to creditors these reforms would pave the post-crisis way of improved business practices and mega-investments (MoU 2012).

Memoranda of Understanding (MoU): A Short Tale Of Devasting Reforms?

As it is already been noted, bailout loans, either from the European Financial Stability Facility (EFSF) or from European Stability Mechanism (ESM), were tightly connected with Economic Adjustment Programmes (EAPs) or Memoranda of Understanding (MoUs). The drama inaugurates in April 2010 when the Greek authorities requested bilateral financial assistance from Euro area member states and from the IMF (European Commission 2010: 12). Assistance's precondition was a sweeping policy package to restore fiscal and macroeconomic stability. On May 2nd of 2010 the government and creditors agreed for the first MoU "on a comprehensive policy package for the period 2010-2013 supported by official financing for a total amount of EUR 110 billion" (p. 12).

The first MoU (2010) forecasted objectives in both short-term, medium-term and long-term terms. More specifically, short-term programme objectives implied the restoring of confidence and the maintenance of financial stability while medium-term objective was to improve competitiveness and transform economy's structure towards a more investment and export-led growth model (p. 15). According to the joint statement of Commissioner Oli Rehn and IMF Managing Director Dominique Strauss-Kahn (3rd May 2010), "[...] the program will lead to a more dynamic economy that will deliver the growth, jobs and prosperity that Greece needs in the future" (emphasis added).

On the 14th of March 2012, Eurogroup, due to the failure of the first Economic Adjustment Programme, approved the second EAP for Greece which forecasted an additional 130 billion euros for the period 2012-2014. The second MoU (2012) was financed by EFSF and was connected with the Private Sector Involvement (PSI) to improve the sustainability of the Greek debt. However, the implementation of PSI implied, among others, the hair cut of the Greek social insurance funds' reserves. In addition, on 26-27 November, Eurogroup and IMF agreed the extension of the fiscal adjustment path by two years. More specifically, this involved a "reduction of the primary surplus target for 2014 from 4.5% of GDP to 1.5% of GDP and an even annual adjustment of 1.5% of GDP until a primary surplus of 4,5% of GDP is achieved in 2016".2 The second MoU implied a variety of reforms. More specifically, privatizations receipts approximated 2.6 billion euros in 2013 (European Commission 2014: 28). In addition a major reform of the tax system has been introduced to broaden the tax base, simplify tax legislation and face tax evasion (p. 30). The milestone of these reforms was the introduction of the «ENFIA» Property Tax as a unified property tax to replace existing taxes with a single real estate tax on both properties and land. President Jean-Claude Juncker (14th March 2012) noted in passing "[...] This second programme constitutes a unique opportunity for Greece that should not be missed" (emphasis added).

The third MoU was enacted in 2015 and provided financial assistance of up to 86 billion euros. The third EAP was seated on four pillars: a) restoring fiscal sustainability, b) safeguarding financial stability, c) implementing reforms conducive to economic growth and jobs creation and d) modernizing the government sector.3 Fiscal sustainability was tightly associated with an in extremis medium-term primary surplus of 3.5% of GDP. More specifically, according to the 'agreement' between the (left & social democratic) government and 'institutions' (former 'troika') fiscal sustainability was to be generated through fiscal reforms and fighting tax evasion which is, as said well before, a structural weakness of the Greek tax system. On the other hand, financial stability planned to be achieved through a threefold way: i) the (direct) addressing of Non-Performing Loans (NPLs) in the banking sector, ii) the third recapitalizing of banks and iii) the strengthening of the governance of the Hellenic Stability Fund. As such, ESM disbursed 5.4 billion euros to complement the required recapitalization.

Furthermore, according to the third EAP, a wide range of reforms was necessary to promote growth, competitiveness and mega-investments. These reforms include labour markets, product markets and the energy market. Again, the role of privatizations was regarded as a key element in promoting economic growth. The formation of the independent fund Hellenic Corporation of Assets and Participations (HCAP) constitutes a milestone in the Greek tragedy as the fund acquired all assets (such as ports) to privatize them in the future. Privatizations expected to contribute into the threefold framework: i) the repayment of recapitalization of banks (and other assets), ii) the reduction of Greece's debt to GDP ratio and iii) Foreign Direct Investments (FDI) (Eurosummit 2015). The statement on Greece by the European Commission in liaison with the European Central Bank (13th August 2015) is indicative "The structural reform package to be enacted is significant, particularly in the area of business environment and competition policies, which are key for unlocking the growth potential of the economy" (emphasis added).

MoUs Simply Failed To Deliver What They Had Promised To

According to key facts and figures, memoranda have not achieved their predictions. Of course, there have been some worth noting improvements on some aspects of the economy but as official data concerning economic performance show, memoranda have nothing but very few to brag about. The basic economic index, GDP, provides a more than clear view of the mistakes and misinterpretations during the programmes implementations. Greek GDP in 2013 had lost more than 25% from its 2007 value in real terms. On top of that, even four and a half years after the last MoU the domestic growth still doesn't seem to had finally found a solid rhythm to catch up with the rest of the Eurozone, since the corresponding rate have not even reached 2%. The theory that after the implementation of the MoUs the Greek economy would just take off is not verified in real life (figure 1).

The unemployment rates went sky high due to the downsizing of the demand, the major reductions in salaries, the shrinkage of liquidity, the increased tax burdens, the evaporation of trust and so on. Greece suffers from by far the highest unemployment rate in Euro-Area, not only during the implementation of the MoUs but also years after it (Figure 2), losing more than 625 thousands jobs since 2008 and despite the upward trend during the last years. Of course, Greece has also the «privilege» of the highest long-term unemployment, which implies that there are still many structural challenges which have not been confronted yet. But it is not just that. According to the official data provided by the «ERGANI» (Ministry of Labour and Social Affairs database), more than half of the new jobs for employees provided by the private sector over the last years are characterized by extended flexibility, i.e. they refer to either part-time or temporal employment. In 2019 the «flexible» jobs for wage-earners in the private sector rose to 54.9%. Furthermore, according to the same source, 20.5% of all private sector employees earn less than 500 euros per month and almost half of them (48.0%) receive less than 800 euros.

However, this discouraging performance should not have come as a surprise. The financial condition of Social Insurance Funds, especially after the bond haircut which they hold in 2012, as well as the structure of the domestic Social Insurance System (Pay as You Go, early retirements' schemes, height of pensions etc) increased the pressure for more revenues. This necessary policy actually cancelled the benefits of the salaries reductions for the competitiveness since the non-wage cost remained extremely high (Table 1), thus pushing up the total labour cost. Lower net wages resulted in decrease in consumption

Figure 1. Real Greek GDP developments and according to average EA-19 growth rates since 2008 (Eurostat, in millions of euros)
Source: Eurostat.

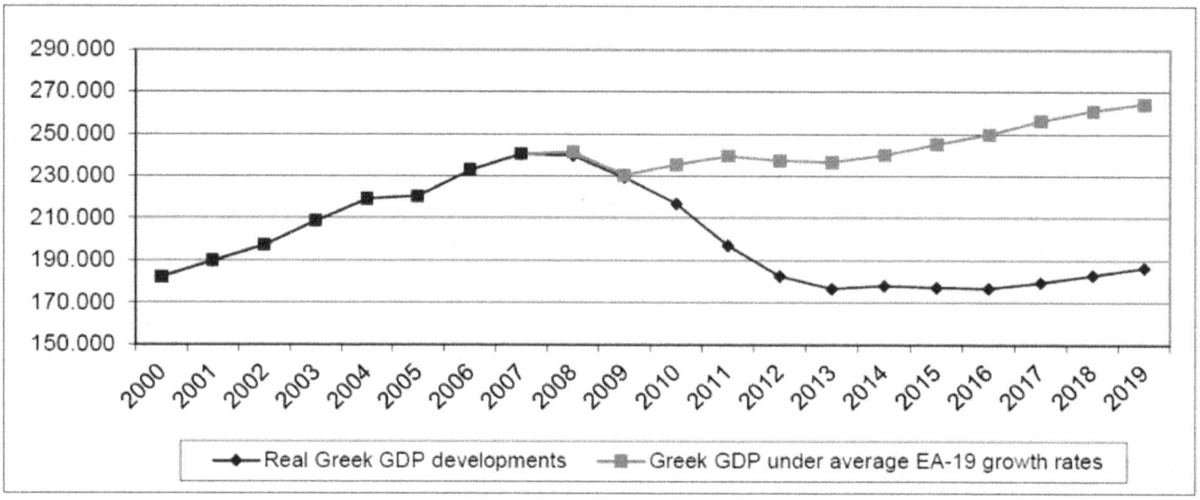

Figure 2. Unemployment rates in Euro Area-19 and in Greece, 2007-2019 for both sexes, aged 15-74 (in %)
Source: Eurostat

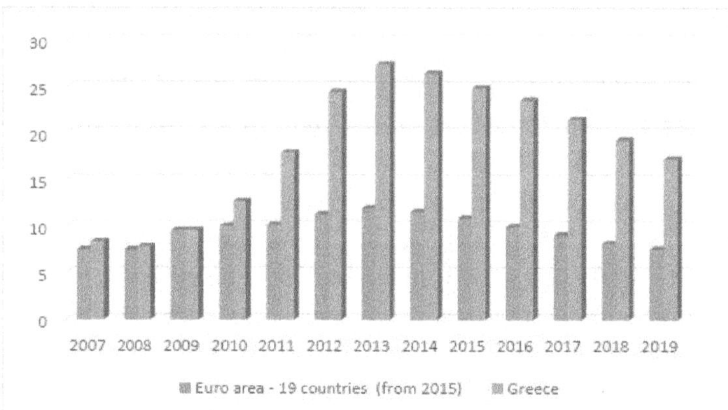

which in turn triggered new downtrend pressure on wages, forcing economy and salaries into an endless loop of turnover shrinkage, unemployment and Social Insurance Funds deficits, while discouraging investment at the same time. This puzzle remains even today, despite the recent decrease in Employers social contribution rate.

Unfortunately, the so necessary fiscal consolidation for the Greek economy was achieved mainly through increased tax revenues, reductions to public sector salaries and shrinkage of Public Investment Programme. To make this more clear, the Ministry of Finance estimates tax revenues to sum up to 51.4 billion euros in 2019 while in 2006 tax revenues amounted to 45.0 billion euros, despite the fact that the Greek GDP in 2019 is 19.9% lower than in was 13 years ago (Ministry of Finance). The new tax reforms were mainly translated into new tax burdens such as abolition of tax free threshold for freelancers/ indi-

Table 1. Total Labour Cost in Greece (examples in euros)

Net monthly wage (1)	EFKA (Social Insurance) Contribution (2)	Tax paid directly to the Tax Authorities (3)	Non-regular Solidarity Contribution (4)	Gross monthly wage (5)	Employers Contributions (6)	Total cost for employer (7)
(5)-(2)-(3)-(4)	(5)*15.75%			(1)+(2)+ (3)+(4)	(5) * 24,81%	(5)+(6)
548	102	0	0	650	161	811
750	145	21	0	916	227	1.143
850	169	50	1	1.070	211	1.281
1.000	207	98	6	1.311	325	1.636
1.200	257	165	12	1.634	405	2.039
1.500	341	298	33	2.172	539	2.711
1.800	433	457	61	2.751	683	3.434
2.000	502	594	83	3.179	789	3.968
2.500	695	1.058	159	4.412	1.095	5.507
3.000	889	1.513	238	5.640	1.399	7.039

Source: "After tax Database" and authors' estimations

vidual enterprises from a € 10.500 threshold in 2009, imposing a 15% tax rate on distributed dividends, increasing the next year's down payment (in advance) for enterprises of all legal forms including individual enterprises to 100%, imposing non-regular or temporary fees like the Solidarity Contribution, New Property Tax (ENFIA) and Business Fee which are still in effect, raising the regular VAT rate to 24%, from 19% in 2009, while the EU average is much lower, to mention but a few.

In addition to this, the Public Investment Programme in 2019 is estimated to reach 6.8 billion of euros while in 2006 it had reached 8.2 billion of euros, in a period were the economy is in deep need for investment boost. Another Memoranda structural failure is the fact that tax revenues are originated by indirect taxation. Greece (and Portugal) has the lowest direct/indirect tax revenue ratio among other EA-19 countries. This paradox is a characteristic of developing rather of developed economies.

But poor Memoranda performance is also noticed on the field which MoUs had actually reassured to cure: The Greek Economy Competitiveness. The low Competitiveness argument was used extensively throughout the negotiations between the Greek Governments and the troika (institutions). The latter insisted that by severely reducing wages would be just enough to make the Greek economy much more competitive and capable to enter new markets, consistently and strongly opposing to different approaches. Of course, this proposal was neither enough nor took into considerations the special characteristics and rigidities of the domestic economy but it was part of the «this is how we do things around here» approach, which the institutions felt safe to implement for economies facing severe challenges. Ten years later, this narrow minded policy led the economy to achieve mixed results, which compared to the size of the sacrifices and the duration of the crisis can justifiably be seen rather as a bold failure (Table 2).

To be fair, the Europeans never saw the crisis coming, since there was no monitoring and control over macroeconomic imbalances. So, when the Greek crisis burst out, the EMU had actually no tools to constrain the crisis (Katsimi and Moutos, 2010). Furthermore, the European institutions relied, probably excessively on the EU fiscal rules (Stability and Growth Pact – SGP), which had already been outdated by the economic developments. It is worth noting that the hesitation of the Europeans to decisively intervene was based to a great extent on moral hazard concerns.

Table 2. Assessing Memorandums' Outcomes on competitiveness, Ease of Doing Business and Economic Freedom

Index	Period/ Ranking*	
Global Competitiveness Index, World Economic Forum	2008/2009	2019
	67 →	**59**
IMD World Competitiveness Rank	2008	2019
	42 →	**58**
Ease of Doing Business Report, World Bank Group	2009	2020
	96 →	**79**
Fraser Index of Economic Freedom, Fraser Institute	2009	2019
	52 →	**102**

*: According to the reference title of the report.
Source: World Economic Forum, IMD, World Bank, Fraser Institute

Of course, the entry, during the last decade, of new countries into the group of the economies analysed each year could influence the rankings. However, the performance of the Greek economy is not what a benevolent policy maker would expect after the implementation of three Memoranda and a series of reforms. Even the argument that the effects of Memoranda need time to be realised does not hold because the most recent Memorandum was decided in July 2015, which allows for enough time in order to bring the impact of Memoranda to the surface.

At least one could think that Memoranda had a positive and «cooling» effect on public debt since Greece was actually excluded from the international capital markets. In other words, since no state or private fund trusted the Greek economy after the collapse of the Lehman Brothers bank and the following crisis, the intervention of the European Governments and that of the institutions European Commission, IMF and ECB would smooth the rough edges in two ways: i), it would provide the Greek government the necessary liquidity in order to keep afloat the vital state functions and ii) it could provide the necessary time to implement the reforms needed to achieve fiscal consolidation and viable public finance. Things did not turn out as planned. The public debt rose from 109.4% of Greek GDP in 2008 to 176.6% in 2019 or from just above 260 billion euros to 356 billion euros (Trading Economics).

The so much anticipated PSI haircut did actually lowered public debt to GDP ratio to less than 160% in 2012 but this had only a temporary effect. In fact, more light should be shed on the PSI public debt reduction process: The ECB refused to participate in the haircut in 2012 since it characterized the approximately 43.3 billon euro (in market and not in nominal value) Greek bonds it had bought back in 2010 through the Securities Markets Programme (SMP) as monetary policy. Along with the above bonds another 13.3 billion euro bonds bought by European Central Banks (ANFAs). However, these exceptions are at least questionable since the haircut is not supposed to be implemented by discriminating the holder of the bonds. To be fair, the profits of the SMPs and ANFAs was decided to be returned to the Greek Government but the latter lost time and opportunities due to political games and «short sighting».

In any case, the international investments still do not trust the Greek economy, despite the so far efforts. Greek 10-year bonds are still characterized as «junks» in the financial circles (Table 3). The fact that the returns of the 10-year bond fall lower than 1% in the mid-February of 2020 was attributed to the negative returns of other, lower risk assets like the German bind. The fact that Greek bonds have not yet reached the investment grade is without any doubt a solid proof that the Memoranda were too slow to enhance trust to the international investors.

During the negotiations with the Greek government, the institutions constantly neglected the arguments of the Greek side. For example, the fact that the households consumption to GDP ratio had been for many years extremely high in Greece was rightly highlighted by the troika from the very start. Thus, the latter insisted on salaries reduction and tax rises in order to release assets for other purposes like investment with the Greeks to underline the contradiction: The shrinkage of consumption with such a huge share on GDP will inevitably lead to strong product downsizing and in this way will self-cancel the whole effort. Statistical data show that the ratio shrunk from 68.1% in 2009 to 68.0% in 2019 (OECD).

Table 3. Greek debt and Credit Rating Agencies (evaluation at the end of each year)

<table>
<tr><th></th><th>Moody's</th><th>Fitch</th><th>S&P</th><th></th></tr>
<tr><td>2008</td><td>-</td><td>"A" stab.</td><td>-</td><td rowspan="2">Upper medium or Lower Medium grade</td></tr>
<tr><td>2009</td><td>"A2" neg.</td><td>"BBB+" neg.</td><td>"BBB+" neg.</td></tr>
<tr><td>2010</td><td>"Ba1" neg.</td><td>"BBB-" neg.</td><td>"BB+" neg.</td><td rowspan="10">"Junk Bonds"</td></tr>
<tr><td>2011</td><td>"Ca" neg.</td><td>"CCC" n/a</td><td>"CC" neg.</td></tr>
<tr><td>2012</td><td>"C" neg.</td><td>"CCC" n/a</td><td>"B-" stab.</td></tr>
<tr><td>2013</td><td>"Caa3" stab.</td><td>"B-" stab.</td><td>-</td></tr>
<tr><td>2014</td><td>"Caa1" stab.</td><td>"B" stab.</td><td>"B" stab.</td></tr>
<tr><td>2015</td><td>"Caa3" stab.</td><td>"CCC" n/a</td><td>"CCC+" stab.</td></tr>
<tr><td>2016</td><td>-</td><td>-</td><td>"B-" stab.</td></tr>
<tr><td>2017</td><td>"Caa2" pos.</td><td>"B-" pos.</td><td>"B-" pos.</td></tr>
<tr><td>2018</td><td>"B3" pos.</td><td>"BB-" stab.</td><td>"B+" pos.</td></tr>
<tr><td>2019</td><td>"B1" stab.</td><td>-</td><td>"BB-" pos.</td></tr>
</table>

Source: Moody's, Fitch, S&P

This behaviour probably arose partly because they considered the Greek political system as responsible and partly due to the fact that they felt sure for the success of their program. It is true that there have been many cases were rude and provocative behaviours from the troika side had been reported. This behaviour actually evaporated the arguments of the Greek side, which besides a series and bold mistakes in the past, had better knowledge of the country's unique characteristics. The final impact resulted in mutual luck of trust and the feeling that the institutions were deciding by their own for a country's future based not on Greece's interests but on those opposed by their employees (Varvitsioti and Dendrinou 2015). In addition, MoUs ignored the Greek economic culture and reality, since their assumptions were too theoretical and could not accept what their models had not predicted, e.g. some empirical studies suggested that the level of shadow economy has increased during the period of economic crisis (Vlachos and Bitzenis 2015).

This disastrous policy was more than obvious in the banking sector. The improvident credit expansion was replaced by severe liquidity scarcity in times which was more necessary than ever. The Greek Banking System on the one hand refused to continue lending the private sector, thus deepening the crisis, and on the other had to face collapse of Bank Sector stocks, which among others led to three recapitalizations of the banking system, as well as exploding Non-Performing Exposures. The latter peaked to 49.1% of all loans (or 101.8 billion of euros) in June of 2017 before they cooled off to 42.1% (or 71.2 billion of euros) in September of 2019 (Bank of Greece). This development was probably not expected by the troika's policy makers, although it was more than obvious. Of course the Covid-19 pandemic is more likely to boost these figures again.

This negative development, combined with the unfriendly and uncertain economic and entrepreneurial environment forced the domestic banking system to refrain from its main purpose: To lend money to the economy, businesses and individuals. There was and still is a pile of paper work to be filled in when applying for a loan, while the collaterals can reach the size of the amount requested. On top of that, interest rates were so high that they actually constituted a disincentive for borrowing or re-financing (Table 4).

Table 4. Credit to Domestic private sector by the Greek banking sector and interest rates of outstanding amounts (mil. euros and %)

	Credit to Non-financial Corporations	Interest rates to Sole proprietors		Interest rates to non-financial business loans	
	Outstanding Amounts	Up to 1 year	From 1 to 5 years	Up to 1 year	From 1 to 5 years
2012	100.758	10.12%	7.09%	7.33%	5.34%
2013	96.610	9.51%	7.34%	7.00%	5.45%
2014	95.198	8.47%	7.07%	6.52%	5.45%
2015	89.141	7.55%	6.02%	5.89%	4.97%
2016	87.502	7.32%	6.19%	5.62%	4.89%
2017	82.114	7.10%	6.24%	5.25%	4.69%
2018	76.379	6.92%	6.36%	4.99%	4.24%
2019	67.349	6.79%	6.19%	4.63%	3.96%

Source: Bank of Greece

Why Did the MoUs Actually Fail?

They are a series of explanations for what went wrong and the crisis in Greece had the longest duration and the strongest negative impact on the economy compared to other countries under Memoranda regimes. In this chapter, the authors chose not to refer to Greek governments' mistakes. Not that they were not any, but because they were numerous, bold and in enough cases absolutely short-sighted. Karamouzis and Anastasatos (2019) charge the domestic part low ownership of reforms, delays in realizing the problem and its size, resistance to reforms by vested interests, unsuccessful confrontational negotiation stance, especially that during H1 2015, absence of a national reform plan etc, to mention but a few. But the problems of the economy that caused the crisis had come a long way. Kaplanoglou and Rapanos (2013) underlined the rather consistent preference of the Greek governments to accumulate public deficits while fiscal institutions were too weak to react properly and in time.

Therefore, the negative role that the Greek political system played during the crisis is well-acknowledged. Tsebelis (2015) focused on the incomplete information of the domestic government on how the European institutions work as well as on the use, on its behalf, of the elections proclamation as a threat to vote for the reforms. Even at the very crucial steps on the burst of the crisis the Greek political system was divided and characterized by populism (Vasilopoulou et.al. 2013). This polarization and introversion did not allow a clear view and a decisive stance that would shorten the duration and narrow the impact of the economic depression. However, since the troika did assess the reforms' progress and controlled for the payments releases, it is rather fair to put some blame on their shoulders too.

Leaving behind the flaws and weaknesses of the Greek political system and shedding some light to those of the troika, it has to be noted that the Greek economy was requested to achieve right from the start two contradictory and self-cancelled targets: i) The internal devaluation in order to enhance competitiveness and ii) The achievement of demanding primary surpluses goals. This has to do with the philosophy and the design of the programmes (Argeitis et.al. 2018). Put differently, this effort was condemned to failure since each target opposed to the other. The first (internal devaluation) is achieved through salaries reductions, decrease of public spending and price deflation. All these result to the shrinkage of the tax base and the tax revenues, thus seriously threatening the target of fiscal consolidation. This was actually the reason why the Greek state was forced to impose far more taxes that it was necessary with harsh economic and social consequences (Lekkos 2019). This question was noticed but without any further discussion in report by the European Commission in March 2012.

The governor of the Greek Central Bank (Bank of Greece) Yiannis Stournaras, a person who cannot be blamed for Euroscepticism, attributed the reasons for the duration and depth of the Greek crisis into seven major failures. Although all set impediments during Greece's effort to exit the crisis, the first four underline the negative role of the troika/ institutions (emphasis added):

- *«The fiscal multipliers turned out to be higher than initially anticipated (see Blanchard and Leigh, 2013, 2014). Furthermore, the focus of fiscal policy on higher taxes led to an increase in the informal sector of the economy, a loss of tax revenue due to tax evasion and additional measures in order to meet the fiscal targets (Dellas et al., 2017). As a result, the economy was soon caught in a vicious circle of austerity and recession».*
- *«There were certain flaws in the design of the economic adjustment programmes. Given the size of the initial fiscal imbalances, more emphasis was placed on fiscal consolidation, streamlining budgetary procedures and increasing fiscal transparency, at the expense of growth-enhancing reforms, tackling tax evasion and reorganising the public sector».*
- *«Political economy deliberations in the euro area also played their part in delaying the recovery of the Greek economy. The Eurogroup decision of November 2012 to grant further debt relief was put off for several years and was implemented only in June 2018. This undermined the growth prospects of the Greek economy and prolonged the duration of the crisis».*
- *«The idiosyncratic sequencing of structural reforms led to real wages declining more than initially planned, deepening the recession. The reform effort focused more on the labour market than on goods and services markets (see Berti and Meyerman, 2017, on the 'sequencing' and 'packaging' of reforms). Hence, nominal wages declined faster and more strongly than prices. Households ex-*

perienced a massive drop in purchasing power, which, in turn, constrained personal consumption and deepened the recession».

- The unprecedented size and speed of fiscal consolidation since the initial macroeconomic imbalances were much higher in Greece than in other countries
- The non-performing loans (NPLs) proved a bigger challenge than initially estimated, while the hesitation on confronting them deepened the problem.
- Delays in implementing certain reforms for various reasons.

But the wrong approach is, up to some extent, acknowledged by very high ranked European officials and bold European institutions. For instance the former Eurogroup head Jeroen Dijsselbloem stated at a session at the European Parliament's Employment and Social Affairs Committee on November 9th, 2017 (emphasis added): "*We had a banking crisis, a fiscal crisis and we spent lot of the tax-payers' money – in the wrong way, in my opinion – to save the banks" outgoing Eurogroup head Jeroen Dijsselbloem said adding "so that the people criticizing us and saying that everything was being done for the benefit of the banks were to some extent right.*"

On a study conducted on behalf of the European Parliament, the bad performance of the Memoranda programmes in Greece was attributed to various reasons, one of which was: «*European policy indecision can be indicated as a more significant aggravating factor in the performance of the programme. The unclear European stance on debt restructuring in general, and on its application in Greece in particular, left many investors in a state of high uncertainty, which weighed on sentiment and on investment decisions*». In other words, the hesitation of the European organizations actually was one of the reasons for the deepening of the crisis and the increase of the funds needed.

In the same framework, the European Court of Auditors (2017) mentioned that: "*Some key measures were not sufficiently justified or adapted to specific sector weaknesses. For others, the Commission did not comprehensively consider Greece's implementation capacity in the design process and thus did not adapt the scope and timing accordingly. We also found cases of conditions with too narrow a scope to address key 10 sector imbalances and late inclusion of measures addressing key imbalances in the programme*".

FUTURE RESEARCH DIRECTIONS

Future Research may focus on the full impact of MoUs on the Greek economy examining the effectiveness of the programs adopted to confront the Greek dept-crisis. In addition to this, future research should highlight the role of (historical) imbalances of the Greek economy to confront internal and external (such as COVID-19 pandemic) shocks.

CONCLUSION

In the above text, we have made no reference to the Greek governments' mistakes, weaknesses and implementation errors. This is a long discussion and of course the Greek governments are mostly responsible for the chaos that emerged and threatened the whole Euro-area. But this chapter actually focused on the confrontation of the crisis on behalf of the European Union's institutions and the IMF.

From all the above figures, it is easy for one to understand that the MoUs were not properly designed. There were certainly time constraints, lack of adequate knowledge for the real problems of the Greek economy, different agendas and targets for each institution, low capacity of the Greek government to implement a series of measures, hesitation on behalf of the Europeans to take generous measures on time, insisting on errors etc.

It is not far from truth to say that the Europeans followed the norm «Too little, too late» since some analysts support the view that if there had been a debt restructuring in the beginning of the crisis, its impact would have been 50% smoother (Gourinchas et.al. 2016). On the other hand, the IMF intervention is better described as «one size fits all», since they tried to implement their experience from less developed or developing countries to a country which faced different type of challenges. The disaster came when every component of the troika (ECB, European Commission and IMF) requested various not self-consistent actions from the Greek governments, putting the burden on the Greek side. On top of that, the benefits from structural reforms were not, or were only partial realised, thus boosting scepticism, resistance and awkwardness. These developments made even the most necessary reforms to been seen suspiciously

REFERENCES

"Aftertax" database, Estimating net and gross wages. (n.d.). Available at: https://aftertax.gr/

Andranovitch, G., Burbank, M., & Heying, C. (2001). Olympic cities: Lessons learned from mega event politics. *Journal of Urban Affairs, 1*(2), 113–131. doi:10.1111/0735-2166.00079

Argeitis, G., Koratzanis, N., Paitarides, D., Passas, K., & Pierros, C. (2018). *The delution of the economic adjustment programme*. Papazisis editions. (in Greek)

Bank of Greece. (n.d.). *Data Statistics, Developments on Loans and Non Performing Exposures*. Available at: https://www.bankofgreece.gr/statistika/ekseliksh-daneiwn-kai-kathysterhsewn

Bank of Greece. (n.d.). *Publications and Research, Publications, Browse Publications, Bulletin of Conjunctural Indicators*. Available at: https://www.bankofgreece.gr/ekdoseis-ereyna/ekdoseis/anazhthsh-ekdosewn?types=9e8736f4-8146-4dbb-8c07-d73d3f49cdf0&years=2020

Berti, K., & Meyermans, E. (2017). *Maximising the impact of labour and product market reforms in the euro area - sequencing and packaging*. Quarterly Report on the Euro Area (QREA), Directorate General Economic and Financial Affairs (DG ECFIN), European Commission, vol. 16(2), pp. 7-19, October. Available at: https://ideas.repec.org/a/euf/qreuro/0162-01.html

Blanchard, O., & Leigh, D. (2013). Growth forecast errors and fiscal multipliers. *The American Economic Review, 103*(3), 117–120. doi:10.1257/aer.103.3.117

Blanchard, O., & Leigh, D. (2014). Learning about fiscal multipliers from growth forecast errors. *IMF Economic Review, 62*(2), 179–212. doi:10.1057/imfer.2014.17

Christodoulakis, N. (2010). Crisis, Threats and Ways out for the Greek economy. *Cyprus Economic Policy Review, 4*(1), 89–96.

Dellas, H., Malliaropulos, D., Papageorgiou, D., & Vourvachaki, E. (2017). *Fiscal policy with an informal sector.* Bank of Greece Working Paper, No. 235.

Euro Summit. (2015, July 12). *Euro Summit Statement.* Author.

European Commission. (2010). *European Economy: The Economic Adjustment Programme for Greece.* Occasional Papers 61.

European Commission. (2012). *Occasional Papers 94, "The Second Economic Adjustment Programme for Greece."* Available at: https://ec.europa.eu/economy_finance/publications/occasional_paper/2012/pdf/ocp94_en.pdf

European Commission. (2014). *European Economy: The Second Economic Adjustment Programme for Greece Fourth Review.* Occasional Papers 192.

European Commission. (2020). *Eurostat, Data, Database, various variables examined.* Available at: https://ec.europa.eu/eurostat/data/database

European Court of Auditors. (2017). *The Commission's Intervention in the Greek Financial crisis, Special Report, No 17.* Available at: https://www.eca.europa.eu/Lists/ECADocuments/SR17_17/SR_GREECE_EN.pdf

European Parliament. (2014). *Committee Study on the Troika and Financial Assistance in the euro area: Successes and Failures.* Study on the request of the Economic and Monetary Affairs Committee, Directorate General for Internal Policies, Economic Governance Support Unit (EGOV). Available at: https://www.bruegel.org/wp-content/uploads/imported/publications/20140219ATT79633EN_01.pdf

Fraser Institute. (n.d.). *Economic freedom of the World: 2019 Annual Report.* Available at: https://www.fraserinstitute.org/studies/economic-freedom-of-the-world-2019-annual-report

Georgia, K., & Vassilis, R. (2013). Fiscal Deficits and the Role of Fiscal Governance: The case of Greece. *Economic Analysis and Policy, 43*(1), 5–27. doi:10.1016/S0313-5926(13)50001-4

Gourinchas, P.-O., Philippon, T., & Vayanos, D. (2016). *The Analytics of the Greek Crisis.* VOX CEPR's Policy Portal. Available at: https://berkeley.app.box.com/s/fkjjefyar69wt31oqnsuy0khzm0xel64

Hellenic Republic, Ministry of Finance. (n.d.). *Economic data, Greek Budget various years.* Available at: https://www.minfin.gr/web/guest/proupologismos

Hellenic Republic, Ministry of Labour and Social Affairs. (n.d.). *ERGANI Database, various editions.* Available at: https://www.ypakp.gr/

Hellenic Statistical Authority (ELSTAT). (n.d.). *Labour Force Quarterly Surveys, various years.* Available at: https://www.statistics.gr/el/statistics/-/publication/SJO01/-

IMD World Competitiveness Center. (n.d.). *IMD World Competitiveness Rankings 2019.* Available at: https://www.imd.org/wcc/world-competitiveness-center-rankings/world-competitiveness-ranking-2019/

Karamouzis, N., & Anastasatos, T. (2019). Lessons from the Greek Crisis. *Economy & Markets, Eurobank Research, 14*(1). Available at: https://www.eurobank.gr/en/group/economic-research/economic-bulletin/lessons-from-the-greek-crisis

Katsimi, M., & Moutos, Th. (2010). EMU and the Greek Crisis: Are There Lessons to Be Learnt? *European Journal of Political Economy*, *26*(4). https://papers.ssrn.com/sol3/papers.cfm?abstract_id=1981034#%23

Lekkos E., (2019). *A critical assessment of the Memoranda era*. Kathimerini. (in Greek)

Liddle, J. (2009). Regeneration and Economic Development in Greece: De-industrialisation and Uneven Development. *Local Government Studies*, *35*(3), 335–354. doi:10.1080/03003930902999472

Mavrogordatos, G. (1998). *Between Pitiokampti and Prokrousti: Pressure Groups in Modern Greece* (2nd ed.). Odysseas. (in Greek)

OECD. (n.d.). *OECD Database, Household spending*. Available at: https://data.oecd.org/hha/household-spending.htm

Pitelis, C., & Antonakis, N. (2003). Manufacturing and competitiveness: The case of Greece. *Journal of Economic Studies (Glasgow, Scotland)*, *30*(5), 535–547. doi:10.1108/01443580310492826

Stournaras, Y. (2019). *87th International Atlantic Economic Conference "Lessons from the Greek Crisis: Past, present, future*. Speech by the Governor of Bank of Greece. Available at: https://www.bankofgreece.gr/en/news-and-media/press-office/news-list/news?announcement=eb7533db-172f-4a65-a2a7-7d350bcbcb0b

TE Database. (n.d.). *Greek Public Debt*. Available at: https://tradingeconomics.com/greece/government-debt-to-gdp

Tsebelis, G. (2015). Lessons from the Greek crisis. *Journal of European Public Policy, 23*(1), 25-41. Available at: https://sites.lsa.umich.edu/tsebelis/wp-content/uploads/sites/246/2015/03/Lessons-from-the-Greek-crisis.pdf

Tsoulfidis, L., & Tsaliki, P. (2014). Unproductive labour, capital accumulation and profitability crisis in Greek economy. *International Review of Applied Economics*, *28*(5), 562–585. doi:10.1080/02692171.2014.918939

Varoufakis, Y., & Tserkezis, L. (2014). Financialisation and the Financial and Economic Crises: The Case of Greece. *FESSUD, Studies in Financial Systems*, 1-68.

Varvitsioti, H., & Dendrinou, V. (2019). *The last bluff*. Papadopoulos editions. (in Greek)

Vasilopoulou, S., Halikiopoulou, D., & Exadaktylos, T. (2013). Greece in crisis: Austerity, Populism and the Politics of Blame. *Journal of Common Market Studies*, *52*(2), 388–402. doi:10.1111/jcms.12093

Vlachos, V., & Bitzenis, Ar. (2015). *Entrepreneurship and Tax Compliance Games: Evidence regarding enterprise behavioral dynamics in Greece* (Vol. 2). Global Business and Economics Anthology.

Whitson, D., & Horn, J. (2006). The global politics of sports mega-events. *The Sociological Review*, *54*(2), 73–89. doi:10.1111/j.1467-954X.2006.00654.x

World Bank Group. (n.d.). *Ease of Doing Business Report 2020*. Available at: https://www.doingbusiness.org/en/reports/global-reports/doing-business-2020

World Economic Forum. (n.d.). *The World Competitiveness Report 2019*. Available at: http://www3.weforum.org/docs/WEF_TheGlobalCompetitivenessReport2019.pdf

ADDITIONAL READING

Doxiadis, E., & Placas, A. (Eds.). (2018), Living Under Austerity: Greek Society in Crisis, Berghahn Books editions.

Ignatiou M. (2015). Troika, the Road to Disaster, Livanis editions (In Greek).

Karyotis, G., & Gerodimos, R. (Eds.). (2015). The Politics of Extreme Austerity: Greece in the Eurozone Crisis, Palgrave Mcmillan editions.

Kostis, P. (2019). Are IMF Stabilization Programs in the European Union Disastrous? From the Maastricht Treaty up to Recent Bailouts. In Y. Bayar (Ed.), *Handbook of Research on Social and Economic Development in the European Union* (pp. 1–21). IGI Global.

Milonakis, D., Drakaki, E., Manioudis, M., & Tzotzes, S. (2020). (forthcoming). Accumulation by dispossession and hegemony in place: The Greek experience. *Capital and Class*.

KEY TERMS AND DEFINITIONS

European Stability Mechanism (ESM): The ESM manages €80.15 billion of capital paid in by the euro area Member States. The paid-in capital contributes to ensuring the institution's creditworthiness, an essential factor supporting the ESM's capacity to borrow on financial markets at favourable rates.

Hellenic Corporation of Assets and Participations (HCAP): Includes public enterprises that operate in key sectors of the national economy (energy, water supply and sewerage, infrastructures, transport, services, etc.) and thus have a great impact on investment and consumption decisions of the private sector as well as affect critical economic factors.

Memoranda of Understanding (MoUs): Economic programmes to supervise the Greek economy in order to reduce consumption, increase competitiveness and improve the national economy.

Troika: Decision group formed by the European Commission, the European Central Bank and the International Monetary Fund whose usage arose in the context of the "bailouts" of Cyprus, Greece, Ireland, and Portugal necessitated by their prospective insolvency caused by the recent global financial crisis of 2008.

ENDNOTES

1. Alcyone (or halcyon/kingfisher bird) is a bird which lays its eggs between January 16-31 when temperature in Greece reaches even 20°C during the peak of winter. These phrase has a literal meaning in Greece meaning peaceful days.

2 https://ec.europa.eu/info/business-economy-euro/economic-and-fiscal-policy-coordination/eu-financial-assistance/which-eu-countries-have-received-assistance/financial-assistance-greece_en

3 https://www.consilium.europa.eu/en/policies/financial-assistance-eurozone-members/greece-programme/

Chapter 14
Diversity of Monetary Regimes and Reactions to the Pandemic Crisis:
Bulgaria, Romania, and Serbia Compared

Cornelia Sahling
Independent Researcher, Germany

Nikolay Nenovsky
University of Picardie Jules Verne, France

Petar Pandushev Chobanov
University of National and World Economy, Bulgaria

ABSTRACT

This chapter analyses to what extent the type of monetary regime in three Balkans countries (Bulgaria, Romania, and Serbia) determines the scope and nature of reactions to the pandemic crisis in the short run (providing liquidity to different sectors) and considers the possibilities for a long-term recovery. A comparative perspective is particularly suitable for the Balkan countries with great institutional diversity of the monetary regimes. In particular, the two members of the EU, Bulgaria and Romania, have been following different principles of monetary regimes for decades (Currency Board versus discretionary Monetary Policy). Both Bulgaria and Romania follow closely the ECB monetary policy. Serbia, which is outside the EU, is not affected by the constraints of European integration and actually has its independent monetary policy (although the Euro is also an important external anchor).

DOI: 10.4018/978-1-7998-4933-9.ch014

INTRODUCTION AND POLICY MOTIVATIONS

In the middle of April 2020, the Government of the Republic of Bulgaria unexpectedly announced that it will submit the application for membership in the ERM II and the Banking Union as a first step to enter the Eurozone and soon after that requested a swap line with the ECB. That occurred at the height of the Pandemic Crisis whereas the governments' actions aimed at overcoming the health crisis and trying to safeguard economic activity, so all long-term strategies were forgotten. At first glance, the rationality of the Bulgarian government's step can hardly be explained by taking into account the tension in the Eurozone related to the difficulties of finding a solution for financing the recovery, the gigantic increase of the debts after the crisis and certainly the level of incomes and standard of life in Bulgaria. That event provided the occasion for this chapter.

The aim of this chapter is to demonstrate to what extent the type of monetary regime determines the scope and nature of reactions in the event of a new type of shock and crisis associated with systemic uncertainty and the possibilities for a long-term recovery. On the example of the influenza pandemic in 2009 some contagion effects on the financial system could have been observed over that crisis (see, e.g., Peckham, 2013). The pandemic of 2019/20 seems to provide an uneven distribution of the economic consequences. Recent evidence suggests that the pandemic crisis shocked both demand and supply; the challenge for the policymakers becomes the trade-off between mitigating the effects of the short-term economic recession and managing the long-term economic performance (Eichenbaum et al., 2020; Boissay et al., 2020). The shutdown prevents households and firms from spending and investing; rising the questing of the appropriate fiscal and monetary policies and their coordination.

A comparative perspective is particularly suitable for the Balkan countries1 with great institutional diversity of the monetary regimes2 although they are marked by the characteristics of "dependent monetary regimes". In particular, the two members of the EU, Bulgaria and Romania, have been following different principles of monetary regimes for decades. While Currency Board (Bulgarian National Bank/BNB) has been operating in Bulgaria since 1997 and actually there is no monetary policy, in Romania (at least officially) an inflationary targeting regime has been imposed since 2005 and an active interest rate policy (Nenovsky et al., 2013). And while Bulgaria and Romania follow closely the ECB monetary policy, Serbia which is outside the EU is not affected by the restrictions of European integration and actually has its own monetary policy. The Euro is also important for Serbia, and one of the main tasks of the National Bank of Serbia (NBS) is the expansion of the sphere of national currency (so-called "dinarization"). In general, monetary regimes are part of a wider institutional configuration; they define the guiding rules in other economic policy areas (Magnin and Nenovsky, 2020). The authors are interested above all in the restrictions that the monetary regime imposes on public finances and the fiscal policy. As a rule, the more restrictive the monetary regime is, the more conservative public finances should be (low levels of the deficit and of the public debt).

Below the authors first explained some basic theoretical ideas that support our argumentation. Then the authors reviewed briefly the monetary regimes and macroeconomic effects of the Pandemic Crisis in the three countries (third part). In the fourth part, the authors have dwelt on the short-term measures (aimed at preserving liquidity in the economy) undertaken by governments and the Central banks in a comparative perspective. This is namely about fiscal, monetary and banking policy. In the last part, the authors have set forth some feasible trends determined by the extent to which the monetary regime provides opportunities for long-term recovery and growth.

THEORETICAL MOTIVATIONS

A pandemic crisis is a systemic crisis of a new type. First, it appeared completely unexpectedly, second, it covers both supply and demand sides, and third, it affects all, without exception, business agents (household, enterprises and banks). The initial "microeconomic" shock, expressed in the cessation of economic activity and a total lack of liquidity – in a second stage was transferred to macroeconomic dynamics. The economy as a whole comes to a sudden halt, recovery is in question, and opportunities for growth and long-term development are changing for the worse. In this system configuration, the state and the central bank have a leading role. In order to preserve economic networks and relations, they are financiers, creditors and guarantors of last resort.

In the short term, this is clear and events have shown it. In the long run, it remains to see how, to what extent and in what forms the state and monetary policy will provide the basis for the restoration of growth and for a transition to a qualitatively new phase of development. Here, the controversy between economists has not yet been enriched with new theoretical and empirical arguments, and in general the ideas (and interests) formed since the pre-pandemic period still dominate. This contribution here is more modest, to enrich with new information two theoretical debates, that of "the optimal exchange rate choice" and that of "the systemic crisis policy reactions". This is our contribution to the coming theoretical debate about the monetary regimes and the monetary policy in the post-covid world.

Concerning the first debate is on the "costs and benefits" of choosing the optimal monetary and exchange rate regime for small, open and peripheral, and in this case Balkan economies. In general, external exchange rate regimes are dominated by external sources of money creation and capital inflows. Monetary sovereignty in this case is delegated to a big core Central bank. These regimes also impose tight budgetary constraints on public finances. For example, according to the theory of the monetary approach to the balance of payments and the first generation of currency crises (e.g. Krugman, 1979), the internal creation of money is limited to a certain limit, after which the fixed exchange rate is attacked and collapses. This is even more pronounced in the Currency Boards, where the requirement to cover the monetary base is added to the fixed exchange rate. In the Currency Board, in a systemic crisis, the exchange rate can be attacked for purely speculative reasons (regardless of large foreign exchange reserves and budget surpluses).

The second debate, intertwined with the first, concerns the possibilities for economic policy response to a new type of systemic risk. Pandemic Crisis is testing fixed exchange rate regimes, not only in the short term (sudden and massive lack of liquidity) but also in the long term (bank credit and funding sources). Here this chapter can give additional information about the response to such crisis of new types – whether and under what conditions it is appropriate to be part of a common currency area and part of an integration zone. In the common currency area, there is a powerful central bank, ready to buy public and probate debts (in different QE programmes) and serve as a creditor and guarantor of First instance. In our particular case, it is a matter of the eurozone, to which the Balkan countries seek to integrate.

The theoretical frameworks of our reasoning can be presented through the following scheme (fig. 1). This scheme illustrates the interrelation of the micro and macrolevel in the context of the pandemic crisis. In the short run, the central bank (through the monetary policy) and the government (through fiscal packages) provide liquidity on the microlevel (for households, enterprises and banks). If the authors consider the long-run perspective, the macroeconomic effects on economic growth, employment, inflation and related consequences of rising indebtedness and budget deficits are of particular importance.

Figure 1. Theoretical framework of the interrelation between micro and macrolevel
Source: Authors

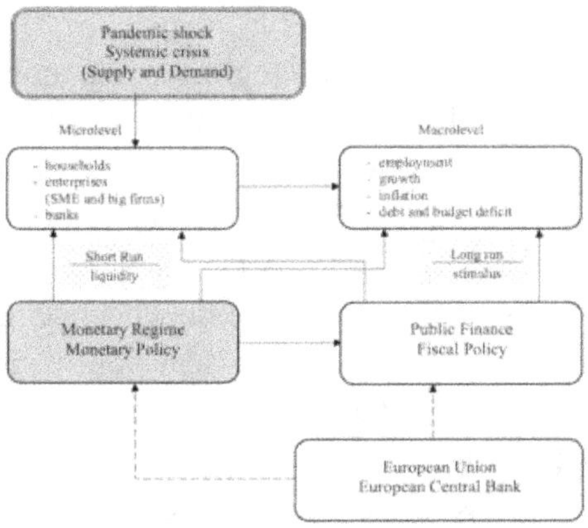

In addition, an EU level should be considered, especially for Bulgaria and Romania (as members of the EU); the ECB and its monetary policy also affects non-Eurozone countries.

PANDEMIC CRISIS AND MONETARY REGIMES IN THE BALKANS

The authors have reviewed briefly the monetary regimes of the chosen countries, explained their differences and linked their capacity to react to a sudden liquidity and structural crisis. Then, the authors have provided brief information about the coronavirus pandemic and how it affects the macroeconomic performance of the three countries (table 2).

Bulgaria, Romania and Serbia, the Diversity of Monetary Regimes

As the authors have already mentioned, the monetary regimes in the former communist countries and in those in the Balkans in particular can be considered as a manifestation of "a dependent monetary regime" (limited monetary sovereignty) which fits into the institutional matrix of dependent capitalism (Magnin and Nenovsky, 2020). (Being dependent does not certainly mean to be unsuccessful). The degree of the dependence (or independence) of the country's monetary regime is based on several factors. According to Magnin/ Nenovsky (2020), the more independent a central bank can perform the following functions, the more its monetary regime can be considered independent:

- to serve fully the main functions of money (unit of account, means of payment, medium of exchange and store of value);
- to raise monetary income (seigniorage[3]);
- to make monetary policy decisions and use related monetary policy instruments (especially interest rates, open market operations (OMO) and quantitative easing (QE)) according to national economic conditions;
- to act as a Lender and Insurer of Last Resort; to have control over the national banking system;

- to maintain the political independence of the central bank and to develop a national identity of the monetary system.

In general terms, the more dependent a monetary regime is, the more the money supply is determined externally and this happens automatically. In this case, the exchange rate is closer to a fixed regime (fixed to the currency of the monetary center) and the interest rates are determined in the interbank market (without the intervention of the Central Bank). Further on, the more dependent a regime is, the more limited the functions of the Lender of Last Resort (LOLR) are, i.e. the less the sources of liquidity (primarily national) should be. And yet, the greater the dependence and the static status are, the more limited the opportunities for implementing an active fiscal policy and for increasing the public debt should be. Within the above dependencies, the three countries under review may be ranked (from a greater to a lesser dependence) – (i) Bulgaria (Currency Board, legally fixed exchange rate, 100% coverage of monetary base, no OMO), (ii) Romania (de jure inflation targeting, but de facto exchange rate control, closely following ECB interest rate policy, recently some QE measures) and (iii) Serbia (not EU member, inflation targeting, but facto control of exchange rate, more freedom of interest rate policy).

Moreover, a new external institutional anchor is added as regards the three countries – that of the EU and the Eurozone. In this respect, Bulgaria and Romania have less opportunities for independent maneuvers than Serbia, they are more strongly integrated in the common EU rules. However, it is possible to suppose, and there is certain empirical evidence to that effect that countries applying for EU membership follow more restrictive rules in order to meet the membership criteria. Once members of the EU, constraints are decreased for those countries (they start to receive European funds which slacken the discipline, see Nenovsky and Mihailova-Borisova, 2015).

Two characteristics of the monetary regime are important for us from the standpoint of the objectives of this paper. First, providing liquidity for the economic agents in the short term as far as it is possible to do it directly or indirectly (via the fiscal policy). Second, its capacity to provide recovery mechanisms and sustainable post-crisis growth in the long run. The recovery must be related both to aggregate demand (internal and external) and the aggregate supply (production chains). Against the background of the openness of the three Balkan countries' economies (Bulgaria, 124%, Romania 85%, and Serbia 113%)4, the key issue is the dynamics of the balance of payments (positive trade balance, capital inflow, etc.). The issue about the scope of the countries' reaction (fiscal and monetary space) as regards their recovery becomes even more important. That refers also to the key problem within the frameworks of Europe – the dangers of divergence as a result of the different options for reaction.

The most restrictive is the Bulgarian monetary regime where the BNB has no monetary policy instruments (Open Market Operations), cannot refinance the banks and indirectly monetize the debt of the government. The Currency Board is a conservative institution that creates clear rules and rigid budgetary restrictions. Most often the Currency Board is accused of not being able to react to a liquidity crisis, i.e. it cannot create money on the basis of internal sources. Another accusation is that the fixed exchange rate limits the options for maneuvers in the balance of payments. This is true mostly for the orthodox case, while second generation Currency Boards have some flexibility.[5]

According to this binary logic, Romania has more opportunities for reactions, not only as regards the monetary regime but also in fiscal terms. As the authors have already mentioned, Romania has a "normal" Central Bank (the National Bank of Romania/ NBR), which has been working in inflationary targeting regime since 2009 and as a whole follows the ECB's rules and instruments. It can fully implement its monetary policy be it through interest rates or even through the new methods of quantitative alleviations (whether it does so is a different matter).

Logically, Serbia for its part, being outside the EU (and far away from the Eurozone), has even greater opportunities for discretion in a liquidity crisis. Serbia, however, which aims at integration into the EU6 and must observe certain pre-accession rules, formally copies the type and instruments of the ECB. Since 2008 the NBS has been announcing that it is in an inflation targeting regime (Martin, 2015). A specific task of the National Bank of Serbia is to increase the share of the use of assets and transactions denominated in dinars.

Pandemic Crisis's Effects in Bulgaria, Romania and Serbia

As regards the purely health terms (number of sick and deceased), the three countries have not been hit so hard by the pandemic crisis (unlike other leading European countries). This is not so as regards economic losses which will be probably huge. Although the Balkan countries didn't report a high level of positive cases or deaths as in the USA, Brazil, Russia and other countries (see table 1), strict limitations were implemented. For example, the Government of the Republic of Serbia has taken several measures to limit the spread of the COVID-19 virus. Among them it is worth to mention the closing of shopping malls (with some exceptions), suspension of public transport, limitations for movements (between 5pm and 5am and at the weekends) and closed borders (IMF, 2020a). As the number of new cases declines, a gradual easing of the restrictive measures was approved. As regards the immediate measures to combat the spread of the coronavirus, similar measures (closed shopping malls, limitations for movements and others) were also implemented in Bulgaria and Romania.

Table 1. COVID-19 by selected countries (data of the 12th of June 2020)

Country	Confirmed cases of COVID-19	Total deaths	Deaths per 100.000 inhabitants
USA	2.023.347	113.820	34,8
Brazil	802.828	40.919	19,5
Russia	501.800	6.522	4,5
UK	292.860	41.364	62,1
...			
Romania	21.182	1.369	7,0
Serbia	12.102	252	3,6
Bulgaria	3.086	168	2,4
Worldwide	7.563.929	422.981	

Source: (John Hopkins Coronavirus Resource Center, 2020)

Over the last years, the three chosen Balkan countries demonstrated a positive development of the main macroeconomic indicators (the dynamics of the main indicators are summarized in table 2).

Given the extent of the crisis and the limitations of the public life after the spread of the virus, the Vienna Institute for International Economic Studies estimates a sharp decrease in GDP growth for all

Table 2. Overview of macroeconomic performance in the sample countries

	Bulgaria				Romania				Serbia			
	2018	2019	2020 (f)	2021 (f)	2018	2019	2020 (f)	2021 (f)	2018	2019	2020 (f)	2021 (f)
Real GDP Growth (%)	3,1	3,4	-6,3	1,7	4,4	4,1	-7,0	3,0	4,4	4,2	-4,0	4,0
Inflation (%)	2,6	2,5	1,5	2,0	4,1	3,9	3,0	4,0	2,0	1,7	1,1	1,6
Budget Deficit (% of GDP)	2,0	2,1	-2,8	-1,8	-2,9	-4,3	-9,2	-11,4	0,6	-0,2	-7,7	-2,1
Public Debt (% of GDP)	22,3	20,4	25,5	25,4	34,7	35,2	46,2	54,7	54,5	52,8	62,2	59,5
Unemployment (%)	5,2	4,2	10,0	9,0	4,2	3,9	10,0	7,0	12,7	10,4	13,4	12,7
Current Account (% of GDP)	1,4	4,0	1,9	1,7	-4,4	-4,6	5,0	-4,5	-4,8	-6,9	-7,5	-7,0

(Source: Vienna Institute for International Economic Studies (2020), 6 May 2020, and Eurostat for deficit and debt figures)

three countries (-6,3% in Bulgaria; -7,0% in Romania and -4,0% in Serbia for 2020) and, according to Eurostat, the budget balance also gets worse (-2,8%, -9,2%, and -7,7% correspondingly). Without knowing the real long-term macroeconomic consequences of the pandemic crisis 2020, the history of pandemics suggests quiet far-reaching economic consequences (for a historical comprehension with historical pandemic events see Jordà et al., 2020). The related fiscal and monetary responses to the current crisis in the short term will be overviewed in the next part.

BULGARIA, ROMANIA AND SERBIA: SHORT-TERM MONETARY AND FISCAL RESPONSES

Bulgaria

In response to the COVID-19 pandemic, the Government imposed a State of Emergency in the country on the 13 of March 2020. Some urgent measures and administrative restrictions were imposed. Let's consider the BNB measures and fiscal packages.

Monetary Policy

These measures are not exactly of monetary policy nature because of the Currency Board arrangement.7 The authors could call them macroprudential and supervisory policy (mainly inspired by ECB measures), and some of them have substantial impact on overall liquidity in the economy during a stressful period.

On the 19th of March the BNB announced a package of measures worth BGN 9,3 billion (approximately 4,76 billion euro)8 in reaction to the COVID 19 pandemic (Bulgarian National Bank, 2020a). These measures are aimed at ensuring banking system stability and flexibility. The BNB ordered banks to capitalize the entire profits amounting to BGN 1,6 billion (app. 0,82 billion euro) by non-distributing dividends. The increases in countercyclical capital buffer scheduled for 2020 and 2021 should be cancelled amounting to BGN 0,7 billion (app. 0,36 billion euro). The liquidity in the banking system should be increased by BGN 7 billion (app. 3,58 billion euro) by reducing commercial banks' foreign exposures.

On the 10th of April the BNB approved the draft Procedure for Deferral and Settlement of Liabilities Payable to Banks and their Subsidiaries (Bulgarian National Bank, 2020b) – Financial Institutions in relation to the State of Emergency and in accordance with the Guidelines of the European Banking Authority (EBA/GL/2020/02). Private moratorium could be agreed between a commercial bank and its clients, which provides opportunities for changes in the principal and/or interest payment schedule of liabilities, without changing any key parameters of the loan agreement (already agreed interest). These payments could be deferred for a term of up to 6 months, but ending on the 31st of December 2020.

Fiscal Policy

The State budget for 2020 was amended in the beginning of April9. These amendments envisage an increase in expenditures by BGN 1,07 billion (app. 0,55 billion euro) and a decrease in tax and social security revenues by BGN 2,44 billion (app. 0,36 billion euro); so instead of a balanced budget a cash deficit amounting to BGN 3,5 billion (app. 1,79 billion euro) would be accumulated. The deficit on consolidated basis would be equal to 3,1% of GDP. The Government decided to increase capital of the state-owned Bulgarian Development Bank by BGN 0,7 billion (app. 0,36 billion euro), and to provide additional possibility of issuing government guarantees for the bank amounting to BGN 0,7 billion (app. 0,36 billion euro). The ceiling for the newly issued government debt in 2020 was increased from BGN 2,2 billion (app. 1,12 billion euro) to BGN 10 billion (app. 5,11 billion euro) in order to provide additional fiscal flexibility in case of more severe deterioration of the economic situation. This means that the interest expenditures under the state budget are increased by BGN 70 million (app. 35,79 million euro).

The first part of additional expenditures is connected with preventive and anti-pandemic actions. The budget of the Ministry of Health is increased by BGN 7 million (app. 3,58 million euro) for the provision of personal protective medical equipment. To increase the anti-pandemic protection of borders and to provide disinfectants, medical devices and thermal cameras of additional BGN 7,6 million (app. 3,89 million euro) were provided to the Ministry of Health. EU funds financing amounting to BGN 40,4 million (app. 20,66 million euro) will be used to buy modern laboratory equipment and diagnostics units.

The second part of measures is intended to support medical and non-medical personnel by an additional wage bonus amounting up to BGN 1000 (app. 511 euro). The financing would be taken from EU funds and amounts to BGN 60 million (app. 30,68 million euro). Regional health inspectorates will have additional financing of BGN 10,7 million to control the compliance with the mandatory isolation of patients, contact persons and persons entering the territory of the country from abroad.

The third part of measures is consisted of additional remunerations for the police and fire safety authorities which should provide restricting movement, blocking and isolating measures for some cities, towns and settlements if needed. This type of measures will cost BGN 161 million (app. 82,32 million euro). Social measures for vulnerable groups include providing hot lunch for the low-income persons and elderly in 172 municipalities amounting to BGN 5,2 million (app. 2,66 million euro).

Business and employment measures are also envisaged.10 Measure 60/40 is designed to be the most powerful in terms of maintaining employment and incomes. The state covers 60% of the individual insurance income and the related social security contributions due by employers in the sectors which business is mostly affected by the emergency quarantine measures imposed by the government. The main precondition to be met is that the drop in sales compared to the same period of previous year should be at least 20%. This measure will apply for the whole or a part of the period of State Emergency, so additional financing at BGN 1 billion is provided to the Unemployment Fund to cover the expenditures for this measure, as well as for newly granted benefits for the unemployed persons.

Another measure is to increase the capital of the Bulgarian Development Bank (BDB) by BGN 0,7 billion (app. 0,36 billion euro). BGN 500 million (app. 255,65 million euro) will be available for the BDB to provide guarantees to other commercial banks credit portfolios which consist of credits to SMEs. BGN 200 million (app. 102,26 million euro) will be the guarantee to commercial banks to provide consumer interest-free loans for the period of three months up to BGN 1500 monthly (app. 767 euro).

Tax policy measures are more of administrative nature and give the opportunity to postpone and pay some taxes for 2019; the new deadline is 30 June instead of 30 April. The deadline for publishing annual financial statements under the Accountancy act is extended from 30 June to 30 September.

Looking for EU and ECB Help

Of particular interest are the political steps taken by the Bulgarian government to join the ERM II and the Banking Union, as well as the numerous declarations (by the Prime Minister, government representatives and leading experts) that the monetary regime limits the ability to react. Despite good fiscal performance and extremely low public debt (see table 2), the Bulgarian government has begun to seek sources of financing and raised the domestic debt ceiling through a change in the budget. Various options were discussed: (i) a domestic loan, (ii) borrowing from financial markets, (iii) an IMF loan, (iv) EU initiatives, and, finally, a swap line with the ECB. Thus, ECB and BNB set up swap line at Euro 2 billion on the 22nd of April, which is precautionary and will remain in place until the 31st of December 2020, unless it is extended. The BNB will be able to borrow up euro in exchange for Bulgarian lev (BGN). This measure is quite strange in case of currency board arrangement; such an operation is not envisaged in the Law on the BNB and the signals stemming from this act are ambiguous.

Obviously, there were other options that were not discussed, due to the extreme sensitivity of the population and economic agents to any change in the functioning of the Currency Board (legally fixed 100% coverage of the Currency Board liabilities and the level of the exchange rate).

Romania

Monetary Policy

The main measures of the NBR to maintain financial stability during the spread of the COVID-19 cover three directions: the country's monetary policy, the banking sector and operational measures. If we consider the monetary policy, then we can see some similarities between Romania and other European countries. One important decision of the NBR was the cut of the monetary policy rate from 2,5% to 2,0% and later to 1,75%. The interest rate corridor consisting of the credit and deposit facility rate also changed. This corridor was narrowed from +/-1,0% to +/-0,5% (in table 3 the related interest rates and their changing values are shown). Furthermore, the central bank provided liquidity to credit institutions by repurchasing government securities (repo transactions); the real and the public sector were supported by purchases of government securities on the secondary market (denominated in the national currency) (National Bank of Romania, 2020a).

The NBR is, among other tasks, responsible for the authorization, regulation and prudential supervision of credit institutions.11 The banking resolution in Romania is conducted by the NBR along with

Table 3. NBR's interest rates decisions (entry into force date values)

Date	Policy Rate *% p.a.*	Credit facility rate *% p.a.*	Deposit facility rate *% p.a.*
02/Jun/2020	1,75	2,25	1,25
23/Mar/2020	2,00	2,50	1,50
08/May/2018	2,50	3,50	1,50
08/Feb/2018	2,25	3,25	1,25
09/Jan/2018	2,00	3,00	1,00
08/Nov/2017	1,75	2,75	0,75
04/Oct/2017	1,75	3,00	0,50
07/May/2015	1,75	3,25	0,25
01/Apr/2015	2,00	3,75	0,25
05/Feb/2015	2,25	4,25	0,25
08/Jan/2015	2,50	4,75	0,25
05/Nov/2014	2,75	5,25	0,25
01/Oct/2014	3,00	5,75	0,25
05/Aug/2014	3,25	6,25	0,25
05/Feb/2014	3,50	6,50	0,50
09/Jan/2014	3,75	6,75	0,75

Source: (National Bank of Romania, 2020e).

the Bank Resolution Fund. In order to help credit institutions in the context of the current crisis, the NBR postponed the initial deadline for the annual contributions in 2020 to the Bank Resolution Fund by three months (extension possible) and the reporting deadline of information on resolution planning (in accordance with the recommendations of the European Banking Authority) (National Bank of Romania, 2020b).

Another measure regulates the relationship between lender and borrower in the case of payment delays. As the moratorium in Bulgaria, it is allowed to delay payments (applicable to individuals and companies affected by the pandemic and its economic consequences) without loan reclassification or restructuring (National Bank of Romania, 2020c). To improve the financial situation of the banks they may, on a temporary base, use their own capital buffers (National Bank of Romania, 2020c). In addition, the NBR supports the smooth functioning of the payment system by cashflows in national currency (National Bank of Romania, 2020d).

As the NBR adopted inflation targeting as the monetary policy strategy the main propose of the provided policy is to influence the inflation rate and to keep it on a stable level.12 Even if the anticipated policy framework seems to be quite simple the practical experience of many countries shows many difficulties. Considering the empirical data of the last years in Romania, the CPI rarely fell within the target bounds (see figure 2). The unexpected shock due to corona could serve as a downward pressure on inflation.

Figure 2. Consumer prices in Romania, 2014-2019
Source: (National Bank of Romania, 2020f)

Fiscal Policy

The Romanian tax and spending measures include additional assistance for the healthcare system, for the labour market and tax measures.13 Special attention is given to the healthcare system. Some related measures are the reimbursement of local government's expenditure (395 million RON or app. 81,57 million euro)14 in the context of quarantine, additional 0,35 million euro for the budget of the Ministry of Health and a monthly 500€-bonus for medical workers who treat infected persons (European Commission 2020a, pp. 43-44).

To avoid tensions on the labour market some measures have been adapted for the period of emergency. First, employees receive a compensation of 75% of their salary in the case of temporary termination of the employment contract (if this termination is initiated by the company). The company should be affected by the current epidemic crisis with lower business activity and lower incomes. These donations will be covered by the unemployment insurance budget.15 In addition, a compensation of 75% of the salary is intended for parents who are temporary unable to work due to home childcare (for children under 12 years). The Romanian authorities also approved the payment of the national minimum wage for people who are unable to apply for unemployment benefits (e.g. family enterprises or self-employed) (European Commission 2020a, p. 44).

The Romanian package of tax measures provides different benefits to their taxpayers. The authorities implemented faster VAT reimbursements and the cancellation of VAT for medical and sanitary equipment related to the coronavirus. Furthermore, the tax measures allow for postponed deadlines for property taxes (until 30 June 2020), a postponement of healthcare insurance payments and social contributions for companies with financial losses related to the epidemic crisis and a discount for the corporate income tax if it is paid by the 25th of April (5% or 10% discount) (European Commission 2020a, p. 45).

To help small and little enterprises in times of the COVID-19 spread in Romania the European Commission approved a support scheme at the amount of 3,3 billion euro. Under this scheme companies can apply for direct grants (up to 800000 euro per enterprise) and for state guarantees. The main goal of these measures under the Temporary Framework is to provide the necessary amount of immediate working capital and needed investments and to make sure the continuation of their business activities (European Commission, 2020b).

Serbia

Monetary Policy

The current pandemic crisis motivated governments and central banks all over the world to exceptional policy responses. In the case of Serbia, the years prior to the pandemic crisis demonstrated a quite positive performance. According to the report of the NBS, the pre-crisis period could be characterized by a low inflation (see fig. 3), a stable economic growth, strong FDI inflow, reinforced banking sector stability and a lowering unemployment rate (National Bank of Serbia, 2020h). But the situation changed with the COVID-19 pandemic and consequent fall in domestic demand, lower investments and a decline in demand for Serbian exports. The World bank expects an economic recession in 2020 but a return of economic growth to its previous trajectory is possible over the medium term (2021-2023) (World Bank, 2020).

Figure 3. Consumer prices in Serbia, 2014-2019[16]
Source: (NBS, 2020a)

The main policy measures of the NBS to maintain financial stability may be categorized using three groups of measures: interest rate cuts, liquidity providing and suspension of debt payment. Let's evaluate every of these measures.

The key policy rate was cut several times during the period March-June 2020 by the NBS. The Executive Board voted for a cut by 0,5 pp (to 1,75%) in March, by additional 0,25 pp (to 1,5%) in April and by additional 0,25 pp (to 1,25%) in June. The current key rate is the lowest since the introduction of the inflation targeting regime (for the development of the key rate in Serbia during the last five years see table 4). Accordingly, related interest rates were also lowered.17 This measure aims to provide more favourable lending conditions for the domestic economy. The NBS expects that the inflation will remain within the bounds of the target in the medium terms; inflationary pressures were evaluated as to remain low (National Bank of Serbia, 2020i).

To support the banking sector the NBS supplied additional liquidity (dinar and foreign). The central bank used FX swaps (regular and additional) and repo securities purchase auctions. The first additional FX swap auction in times of the spread of COVID-19 was held at the end of March. The NBS fixed a favourable interest rate at 0,85% (for dinar) and 0% (for euro) for the three-month swaps (National Bank of Serbia, 2020e); after the cut of the key rate in April the interest rate is calculated as the deposit facility rate plus 10 bp (National Bank of Serbia, 2020j). Later the NBS changed the realization principle and

Table 4. NBS key policy rate decisions (decision date)

Date	Policy Rate *% p.a.*	Credit facility rate *% p.a.*	Deposit facility rate *% p.a.*
11/Jun/2020	1,25	2,25	0,25
08/Apr/2020	1,50	2,50	0,50
11/Mar/2020	1,75	2,75	0,75
07/Nov/2019	2,25	3,50	1,00
08/Aug/2019	2,50	3,75	1,25
11/Jul/2019	2,75	4,00	1,50
12/Apr/2018	3,00	4,25	1,75
14/Mar/2018	3,25	4,75	1,75
09/Oct/2017	3,50	5,00	2,00
07/Sep/2017	3,75	5,25	2,25
07/Jul/2016	4,00	5,50	2,50
11/Feb/2016	4,25	6,00	2,50
14/Oct/2015	4,50	6,50	2,50
10/Sep/2015	5,00	7,00	3,00
13/Aug/2015	5,50	7,50	3,50
11/Jun/2015	6,00	8,00	4,00
11/May/2015	6,50	8,50	4,50
09/Apr/2015	7,00	9,50	4,50
12/Mar/2015	7,50	10,00	5,00
13/Nov/2014	8,00	10,50	5,50
12/Jun/2014	8,50	11,00	6,00
08/May/2014	9,00	11,50	6,50

Source: (NBS, 2020d)

the realized purchase volume of the swap could differ from the sale volume (National Bank of Serbia, 2020g). In addition, the NBS provided repo auctions at 0,75% with a maturity of seven days or three months (National Bank of Serbia, 2020f). By purchasing additional dinar government securities, the NBS supports the banking sector with liquidity. On the whole, the central bank provided additional FX liquidity at the amount of 106 million euro and dinar liquidity at the amount of 41,1 billion dinar (app. 349,5 million euro)18 (National Bank of Serbia, 2020b).

To mitigate the negative consequences for borrowers who got into payment difficulties due to the current crisis the NBS decided to introduce suspension of debt payment as a temporary measure. No compensations at the expense of the borrowers are intended for the banks (paragraph 5 NBS decision, (National Bank of Serbia, 2020c)). This measure aims to support the private sector and is coordinated with the Serbian Government. The moratorium on loan repayments should be offered to every borrower (it is applicable to natural persons, farmers, entrepreneurs and corporates) by the bank. The Duration of the moratorium should be not shorter than 90 days.

Fiscal Policy

At the end of March, the Government of the Republic of Serbia presented an Economic Measures Programme with the aim to respond to the possible economic consequences of the COVID-19. The cost of this programme is estimated at 5,1 billion euro. The programme covers different directions: fiscal policy measures, direct assistance to the private sector, liquidity preserving, moratorium and fiscal stimulus (The Government of the Republic of Serbia, 2020a). Therefore, to ensure confidence among the ordinary people, the Government ordered a payment of 100 euro for Serbian citizen of legal age (an amount of RSD 70 billion or app. 595,3 million euro is intended for that aim in the state budget).

The Serbian business is also supported with liquidity. For example, entrepreneurs, micro, small and medium-sized enterprises can apply for subsidized loans (with an interest rate of 1%) from a development fund (with an estimated total amount of 200 million euro). Furthermore, the Serbian Government is working on a guarantee scheme (loans backed by the state) worth 2 billion euro (The Government of the Republic of Serbia, 2020b). In addition, the Tax Administration web portal offers the possibility to apply online for the deferral of tax payments and for payments in the value of a minimum monthly salary for their employees. These donations are intended only for companies that preserve the jobs of their employees (only up to 10% can be laid off) to keep a high level of employment during the pandemic crisis (The Government of the Republic of Serbia, 2020c).

CONCLUDING REMARKS AND LONG-TERM PERSPECTIVES

In general, this study does not reject the main hypotheses that the authors had at the beginning and which can be reduced to the following statements.

First, the monetary regimes of the Balkan countries (here concretely Bulgaria, Romania and Serbia) are dependent and are a core institution in the model of European peripheral dependent capitalism. The monetary policy of the three countries closely follows that of the ECB (determined by the leading European countries, especially Germany, France and Italy). The external goals of monetary policy command the internal goals because the external sources of money supply dominate the internal ones.

Second, the dependent monetary regime places severe restrictions on public finances. Deficits and debts in all three countries are among the lowest in Europe (see table 2).

Third, the assumption is generally confirmed that the more dependent the monetary regime is and the stricter the restrictions on public finances are, the more hesitant and weaker the measures taken in the short term by governments and the Central Bank (see table 5), the more it also relies on external assistance. (We note that all three countries were weakly affected by the pandemic – infected and sick, see table 1.) Of course, the sanitation strategy also plays a role in solving the crisis (testing, organizing additional capacities in hospitals, restriction measures) but the authors consider the opportunities of the budget and the central bank to be the most important. In a country with a dependent monetary regime there are less opportunities to react to the crisis (no possibilities to make deficit and to raise debt, because of the hard budget constraints); e.g. the central bank could not finance government debt, because there is no space for domestic monetary policy.

For example, in Bulgaria (the country with a Currency Board) the measures are the weakest. This is followed by Romania and Serbia, which, despite the pre-accession requirements for EU membership, have the greatest opportunities to pursue an independent monetary and fiscal policy. Specifically, this is shown by the data for fiscal measures (% of GDP): (i) for Serbia: 6,5% (IMF; as of 21 May) and 7,0% (WIIW; as of 16 April) (ii) for Romania: 2,0% (IMF); 4,0% (WIIW) and the lowest level in Bulgaria – approx. 2,1% (IMF) and 2,4% (WIIW) (Vienna Institute for International Economic Studies, 2020a and IMF, 2020a). These are indicators well below the double-digit figures in other EU countries. It should be noted that due to the restrictions of the Currency Board, no monetary policy measures have been taken in Bulgaria. And the primary budget surplus at the end of April speaks for the "restrictiveness" of the Bulgarian government! The scheme to compensate those who have stopped working is also indicative – in Bulgaria the state/ employer ratio is 60/40, while in Romania it is 80/20.

Table 5. Summary of key policy measures (short-term)

	Central Bank	Government
Bulgaria (Currency Board, fixed exchange rate regime, EU member)	- requirement for banks to capitalize the entire profits by non-distributing dividends - increasing liquidity in the banking system by reducing commercial banks' foreign exposures - bank lending charges moratorium	- additional capital for the BDB - wage bonus for medical personnel and for police and fire safety authorities - wage coverage 60/40 (government/employer) - postponed deadlines for some taxes and for publishing annual financial statements
Romania (Central Bank, Inflation Targeting, EU member)	- lower monetary key policy rate (1,75%) - liquidity providing through FX swaps and repo securities purchase auctions - postponed deadlines for reporting to the Bank Resolution Fund - debt moratorium	- a monthly 500€-bonus for medical workers - a compensation of 75% of the salary in the case of temporary termination of work - faster VAT reimbursements and cancellation of VAT for medical and sanitary equipment - postponed deadlines for property taxes
Serbia (Central Bank, Inflation Targeting, non-EU member)	- lower key interest rate policy (1,25%) - liquidity providing through FX swaps and repo securities purchase auctions - suspension of debt payment	- a one-time payment of 100 euro for Serbian citizen - subsidised loans for SME (at 1%) - a guarantee scheme for loans - deferral of tax payments

Source: Authors' collection

Fourth, in the medium and long term, the role of dependent monetary regimes is not entirely clear. A number of factors can have an impact. What matters is how far it recovers and what the potential growth of the EU will be. Here things are not very optimistic, not only in terms of growth, but also due to the accumulation of large public debts (far above the levels in the Balkan periphery). It is important to what extent the Balkan countries will continue to comply with the restrictions of the dependent monetary regimes, or will switch to discretionary forms of monetary policy oriented towards stimulating domestic sources of money supply. All three countries in question have relatively wide fiscal spaces for public projects and investments.

This is especially true in Bulgaria, where much depends on whether the country will be accepted into ERM II and the European Banking Union. This is expected to happen; and then the country will have to follow even more passively the trajectory of a dependent monetary regime, as well as the development of the EU, without realizing all the accompanying risks. In the non-entry scenario, the opportunities for monetary and fiscal policy management in Bulgaria are significantly greater. In this respect, Romania and Serbia seem to have more possibilities to react and pursue active policies but they are also characterized by a higher level of public debt.

REFERENCES

Begall, K., & van Doorne-Huiskes, A. (2019). The institutional context of a sustainable workforce. In T. van der Lippe & Z. Lippényi (Eds.), *Investments in a Sustainable Workforce in Europe* (pp. 17–36)., doi:10.4324/9781351105323-2.

Boissay, F., Rees, D., & Rungcharoenkitkul, P. (2020). *Dealing with Covid-19: Understanding the policy choices. BIS Bulletins, 19.* Bank for International Settlements.

Bulgarian National Bank. (2020a). The BNB implements, within its mandate, a package of measures worth BGN 9.3 billion in relation to the COVID 19 pandemic. Press release on 19 March.

Bulgarian National Bank (2020b), The Governing Council of the Bulgarian National Bank approved the draft Procedure for Deferral and Settlement of Liabilities Payable to Banks and their Subsidiaries – Financial Institutions. Press release on 10 April.

Eichenbaum, M. S., Rebelo, S., & Trabandt, M. (2020). The Macroeconomics of Epidemics. NBER Working Paper No. 26882.

European Commission. (2019c). European Neighbourhood Policy and Enlargement Negotiations. Retrieved from https://ec.europa.eu/neighbourhood-enlargement/countries/detailed-country-information/serbia_en

European Commission. (2020a). Policy measures taken against the spread and impact of the coronavirus – 14 April 2020. Retrieved from https://ec.europa.eu/info/sites/info/files/policy_measures_taken_against_the_spread_and_impact_of_the_coronavirus_14042020.pdf

European Commission. (2020b). State aid: Commission approves €3.3 billion Romanian scheme to support SMEs in coronavirus outbreak. Retrieved from https://ec.europa.eu/commission/presscorner/detail/en/IP_20_649

Hanke, S. H. (2002). On dollarization and currency boards: Error and deception. *Journal of Policy Reform*, *5*(4), 203–222. doi:10.1080/1384128032000096814

ICCV. (2020). Pandemia şi standardul de viaţă. Poltici de protecţie social. Institutul de Cercetare a Calităţii Vieţii.

IMF. (2020a). Policy Responses to COVID-19. Policy Tracker. Retrieved from https://www.imf.org/en/Topics/imf-and-covid19/Policy-Responses-to-COVID-19#S

IMF. (2020b). Special Data Dissemination Standard Plus. Retrieved from https://dsbb.imf.org/sdds-plus/dqaf-base/country/BGR/category/INR00

John Hopkins Coronavirus Resource Center. (2020). Mortality Analyses. Retrieved from https://coronavirus.jhu.edu/data/mortality

Jordà, Ò., Singh, S. R., & Taylor, A. M. (2020). Longer-Run Economic Consequences of Pandemics. Federal Reserve Bank of San Francisco Working Paper, 2020-09. Doi:10.24148/wp2020-09

Krugman, P. (1979). A Model of Balance of Payments Crisis. *Journal of Money, Credit and Banking*, *11*(3), 311–325. doi:10.2307/1991793

Lampe, J. R. (2014). *Balkans into Southeastern Europe, 1914-2014. A century of war and transition* (2nd ed.). Palgrave Macmillan., doi:10.1007/978-1-137-05777-8.

Magnin, E., & Nenovsky, N. (2020). Dependent Monetary Regimes in the Balkans: Enlarging the "Varieties of Capitalism" Hypothesis. International Journal of Public Administration, 1–15. Advance online publication. doi:10.1080/01900692.2020.1742157

Martin, V. (2015). Monetary Policy Analysis in Serbia. *Journal of Central Banking Theory and Practice*, *3*(3), 147–180. doi:10.1515/jcbtp-2015-0016

Mazower, M. (2003). *Der Balkan. Deutsche Erstausgabe* (2nd ed.). Berliner Taschenbuch-Verlag.

Ministry of Finance of Bulgaria. (2020). *2020-2023 Convergence Programme*. Author.

National Bank of Romania. (2020a). NBR Board decisions on monetary policy. Retrieved from https://www.bnr.ro/page.aspx?prid=17617

National Bank of Romania. (2020b). Press release on the decisions of the National Bank of Romania Board. Retrieved from https://www.bnr.ro/page.aspx?prid=17677

National Bank of Romania. (2020c). Press release on the decisions of the National Bank of Romania's Supervisory Committee. Retrieved from https://www.bnr.ro/page.aspx?prid=17656

National Bank of Romania. (2020d). NBR measures in the context of the COVID-19 epidemic. Retrieved from https://www.bnr.ro/NBR-measures-in-the-context-of-the-COVID-19-epidemic--21313.aspx

National Bank of Romania. (2020e). NBR's interest rates – entry into force date values. Retrieved from https://www.bnr.ro/StatisticsReportHTML.aspx?icid=801&table=605&column=2566,4267,4268,3800,3801,3802&startDate=01-01-2014&stopDate=29-04-2020

National Bank of Romania. (2020f). Inflation Reports. Charts' Data Series. Retrieved from https://www.bnr.ro/Inflation-Reports-3343.aspx

National Bank of Serbia. (2020a). Inflation Report. Retrieved from https://www.nbs.rs/internet/english/90/ioi.html

National Bank of Serbia. (2020b). Monetary Policy Measures. Retrieved from https://www.nbs.rs/internet/english/15/Covid19/Covid19_1.html

National Bank of Serbia (2020c). Decision on temporary measures for preserving financial system stability. RS Official Gazette, 33.

National Bank of Serbia. (2020d). Interest Rates of the National Bank of Serbia. Retrieved from https://www.nbs.rs/internet/english/30/30_4/30_4_5/index.html

National Bank of Serbia. (2020e). Additional FX Swap Auction – Support to Financial System Dinar Liquidity. Retrieved from https://www.nbs.rs/internet/english/scripts/showContent.html?id=15331&konverzija=no

National Bank of Serbia. (2020f). Securities Repo Purchase Auctions – NBS Provides to Banks Additional Liquidity Worth RSD 25.2 Billion. Retrieved from https://www.nbs.rs/internet/english/scripts/showContent.html?id=15345&konverzija=no

National Bank of Serbia. (2020g). FX Swaps and Repo Purchase of Securities – NBS Provides Additional Dinar and FX Liquidity to Banks. Retrieved from https://www.nbs.rs/internet/english/scripts/showContent.html?id=15372&konverzija=no

National Bank of Serbia. (2020h). Macroeconomic developments in Serbia. Retrieved from https://www.nbs.rs/internet/english/18/18_3/presentation_invest.pdf

National Bank of Serbia. (2020i). Key policy rate cut to 1,5%. Retrieved from https://www.nbs.rs/internet/english/scripts/showContent.html?id=15392&konverzija=no

National Bank of Serbia. (2020j). Even More Favourable Supply of Liquidity to the Banking Sector – NBS Cuts Dinar Interest Rate in FX Swap Auctions. Retrieved from https://www.nbs.rs/internet/english/scripts/showContent.html?id=15407&konverzija=no

Nenovsky, N., & Mihaylova-Borisova, G. (2015). Debts, Ideas and Interests in the Balkans. Chronology of the post-Communist Transformation, 1990-2013. Économie et Institutions, 23(2), 121-145.

Nenovsky, N., Tochkov, K., & Turcu, K. (2013). Monetary regimes, economic stability and EU accession: Comparing Bulgaria and Romania. *Communist and Post-Communist Studies*, *46*(1), 13–23. doi:10.1016/j.postcomstud.2012.12.002

Peckham, R. (2013). Economies of contagion: Financial crisis and pandemic. *Economy and Society*, *42*(2), 226–248. doi:10.1080/03085147.2012.718626

The Government of the Republic of Serbia. (2020a). State sets aside €5,1b to mitigate coronavirus economic blow. Retrieved from https://www.srbija.gov.rs/vest/en/152964/state-sets-aside-51b-to-mitigate-coronavirus-economic-blow.php

The Government of the Republic of Serbia. (2020b). Measures for aid to companies as of Monday. Retrieved from https://www.srbija.gov.rs/vest/en/153899/measures-for-aid-to-companies-as-of-monday.php

The Government of the Republic of Serbia. (2020c). Call on businessmen to apply for Economic measures Programme. Retrieved from https://www.srbija.gov.rs/vest/en/154133/call-on-businessmen-to-apply-for-economic-measures-programme.php

The National Bank of Romania Act, Law No. 312/ June 2004.

Vienna Institute for International Economic Studies. (2020a). Summary of CESEE key measures regarding COVID-19 as of 16th April, 2020. Retrieved from https://wiiw.ac.at/files/news/summary-of-measures-cesee-16-04-2020-n-439.pdf

Vienna Institute for International Economic Studies. (2020b). wiiw further cuts its forecast for economic growth in Eastern Europe to below 2009 level and sees weaker recovery. Press Release, 6 May 2020. Retrieved from https://wiiw.ac.at/press-release-wiiw-further-cuts-its-forecast-for-economic-growth-in-eastern-europe-wiping-out-at-least-two-years-of-gdp-growth-english-pnd-79.pdf

World Bank. (2020). The World Bank in Serbia. Recent economic developments. Retrieved from https://www.worldbank.org/en/country/serbia/overview#3

ADDITIONAL READING

Čizmović, M., Redzepagic, S., & Bazin, D. (2019). Heterogeneous common factor approach to examination of real effective exchange rate determinants. *International Journal of Economic Policy in Emerging Economies*, *12*(4), 348–361. doi:10.1504/IJEPEE.2019.104634

Dąbrowski, M. A., Papież, M., & Śmiech, S. (2019). Monetary Independence of Central and Eastern European Economies with Flexible Exchange Rate Regimes. *Eastern European Economics*, *57*(4), 295–316. doi:10.1080/00128775.2019.1610897

Daianu, D., Kallai, E., Mihailovici, G., & Socol, A. (2017). Romania's Euro Area Accession: The Question Is Under What Terms! *Romanian Journal of European Affairs*, *17*(2), 5–29.

Eller, M., Martin, R., Schuberth, H., Vashold, L. (2020). Macroprudential policies in CESEE – an intensity-adjusted approach. Focus on European Economic Integration Q2/20, OeNB, 65-81.

Fidrmuc, J., & Kapounek, S. (2020). The Risks and Financial Vulnerability of Foreign Bank Ownership in CEECs: Evidence from Exchange Rate Depreciation after the Financial Crisis. *Eastern European Economics*, *58*(1), 34–48. doi:10.1080/00128775.2019.1666412

Frömmel, M., Garabedian, G., & Schobert, F. (2011). Monetary policy rules in central and Eastern European countries: Does the exchange rate matter? *Journal of Macroeconomics*, *33*(4), 807–818. doi:10.1016/j.jmacro.2011.05.003

Săvoiu, G., Jasko, O., & Ţaicu, M. (2014). The Evolution of the Public Debt in Romania and Serbia, During and After the Global Recession. Management. *Journal Of Sustainable Business And Management Solutions In Emerging Economies*, *19*(72), 5–13. doi:10.7595/management.fon.2014.0021

Stoica, O., Roman, A., & Diaconaşu, D.-L. (2019). Real Convergence and European Integration with Focus on the New Member States. Scientific Annals of Economics and Business; 66 (Special issue - dedicated to the International Conference on "20 Years of the Euro: Achievements and Challenges"), 215-228. DOI: 10.2478aeb-2019-0035

Żuk, P., Polgar, E.K., Savelin, L., Diaz del Hoyo, J.L., & König, P. (2018). Real Convergence in central, eastern and south-eastern Europe. ECB Economic Bulletin, Issue 3.

KEY TERMS AND DEFINITIONS

European Exchange Rate Mechanism II (ERM II): A framework that narrows the fluctuations between the single European currency and other EU country currencies as a preparation for these countries to join the Eurozone. This mechanism was established in 1999 and currently only Denmark has pegged its currency to the euro within the ERM II (and maybe soon Bulgaria will introduce the same).

Inflation Targeting: A monetary policy framework with a project (or target) inflation rate. In this framework the main goal of the central bank is to control the price level (to be close to the defined target).

Monetary Base: The total amount of currency in circulation and commercial banks' reserves hold in central banks (narrow definition).

Monetary Sovereignty: The ability to independently control the sources of money supply, interest rates and exchange rates.

Open Market Operations (OMO): A monetary policy instrument that regulates the money supply and banking sector's liquidity and affects short-term interest rates. The central bank buys or sells government securities on the open market.

Quantitative Easing (QE): An unconventional monetary policy when the central bank creates money to buy securities (government bonds or bonds from financial institutions) from commercial banks with the aim to boost the economy. As a consequence of QE, the monetary base increases in the country (higher commercial banks' reserves).

ENDNOTES

1 The economic performance of the Balkan states and their political integration into the European landscape can be regarded as an important part of the EU development and of the determination of the directions of the European Neighbourhood Policy. The peculiarities of the historical development of these countries in the South-eastern part of Europe (conflicts of various nature, unstable economic development and foreign interventions) are explained in Mazower (2003).

2 For some aspects how the history of the Balkan states shaped the monetary regimes over the time see Lampe (2014).

3 In this context the authors understand seigniorage as the ability of the central bank to generate a seigniorage income from issuing money.

4 The trade openness is calculated as the sum of exports and imports of goods and services as a share of GDP. The data is for 2019 and is taken from Eurostat.

5 According to Hanke (2002), the main characteristics of orthodox currency boards can be summarized as following: the CB supplies notes and coins only, the full convertibility of the national currency, non-fulfillment of the mandate as the Lender as a Last Resort, the lack of commercial bank regulation, the inability to finance government spending and 100% foreign reserve backing of national currency. More "modern" currency board arrangements deviate from these features and are closer to typical central banks.

6 After the adoption of the European partnership for Serbia in 2008, the country was granted candidate status in March 2012. In January 2014 the official opening of accession negotiation took place. For more details see European Commission (2019c).

7 The policy framework of the Currency Board Arrangement could be characterized as a monetary system that guarantees the coverage of liabilities by a foreign currency. According to the Law on the BNB, Art. 28 (1):
„The aggregate amount of monetary liabilities of the Bulgarian National Bank shall not exceed the lev equivalent of the gross international reserves, and the lev equivalent shall be determined on the basis of the official exchange rate of the lev against the Deutschemark pursuant to Article 29."
So the national currency was fixed to the Deutschemark (1 BGN = 1 DM as an official exchange rate, Art. 28-29(1)) and later pegged to the euro as it became the legal tender in Germany (Art. 19 (2)). As a consequence, instead of using usual monetary policy instruments the central bank conducts its policy based on simple rules (a rule-based monetary system). In Bulgaria there is also no key rate; after the introduction of the Currency Board in 1997 the base interest rate is only a refence rate and no longer used as a policy instrument. Currently, the base rate is computed as the average overnight deposit transaction rates in the national currency on the interbank market/ LEONIA Plus (for further details see IMF, 2020b).

8 Since 1999 the Bulgarian currency has been pegged to the single European currency at a fixed rate (1 euro = BGN 1,95583) under the Currency Board regime.

9 For a more detailed description of measures and figures used in this part see Ministry of Finance (2020), "2020-2023 Convergence Programme", April 2020.

10 We should consider the importance of the labor protection measures in Bulgaria where, as in many other post-soviet countries, the institutional context of the workforce is less favorable (weak unions, autocratic management structures and a high risk of poverty) then in Western European countries (see Begall and van Doorne-Huiskes, 2019).

11 The National Bank of Romania Act, Law No. 312/ June 2004.

12 The inflation target in Romania is defined as 2,5% since 2013; it is set within a target band (+/-1,0%) that is shown on fig. 2 (dotted lines).

13 For a deeper overview of economic and social policy issues in Romania see ICCV (2020) *Pandemia şi standardul de viaţă. Poltici de protecţie social.*

14 The value is based on the exchange rate of the Romanian leu from the 29th of May 2020 (1 euro = RON 4,8426).

15 Official Gazette of Romania (2020).

16 The inflation target is defined as 3+/-1,5% since 2017; before that a target of 3+/-1,5% was anticipated. The NBS sets the inflation target within a tolerance band (+/-1,5%) that is shown on fig. 3 (dotted lines).

17 In Serbia the deposit facility rate is calculated as key rate – 1,0 pp and the lending facility is computed as key rate + 1,0 pp. For a deeper insight in the interest policy of the NBS see National Bank of Serbia (2020d).

18 The rate is calculated as the base of the exchange rate of the Dinar from the 29th of May 2020 (1 euro = RSD 117,5878).

Compilation of References

"Aftertax" database, Estimating net and gross wages. (n.d.). Available at: https://aftertax.gr/

Abdullah, H. (2020). Fiscal policy, institutions, and economic growth in Asian countries: Evidence from Pedroni's Cointegration approach. *Malaysian Management Journal, 12*(1-2), 117–135.

Acemoglu, D., & Robinson, J. A. (2012). Why Nations Fail: The Origins of Power, Prosperity and Poverty. New York: Crown.

Acemoglu, D., Johnson, S. H., Robinson, J. A., & Yared, P. (2004). *Income and De- mocracy.* Working paper, Massachusetts Institute of technology.

Acemoglu, D., Johnson, S. H., & Robinson, J. A. (2001). The Colonial Origins of Comparative Development: An Empirical Investigation. *The American Economic Review, 91*(5), 1369–1401. doi:10.1257/aer.91.5.1369

Acemoglu, D., Johnson, S., & Robinson, J. A. (2002). Reversal of Fortune: Geography and Institutions in the Making of the Modern World Income Distribution. *The Quarterly Journal of Economics, 117*(4), 1231–1294. doi:10.1162/003355302320935025

Acemoglu, D., & Robinson, J. (2012). *Why Nations Fail: The Origins of Power, Prosperity, and Poverty.* Crown Publishers.

Adamov, V., Dimitrova, T., Nenkov, V. & Petev, M. (2013). *Tehnika na danachnoto oblagane.* Svishtov: SA "Tsenov".

Afesorgbor, S. K. (2016). *Economic Diplomacy in Africa: The Impact of Regional Integration versus Bilateral Diplomacy on Bilateral Trade.* Economics Working Papers 2016-9.

Afman, E., & Maurel, M. (2010). Diplomatic Relations and Trade Reorientation in Transition Countries. In P. A. G. Van Bergeijk & S. Brakman (Eds.), *The Gravity Model in International Trade: Advances and Applications* (pp. 278–295). Cambridge University Press. doi:10.1017/CBO9780511762109.010

Agrawal, G. (2015). Foreign direct investment and economic growth in BRICS economies: A panel data analysis. *Journal of Economics. Business and Management, 3*(4), 421–424. doi:10.7763/JOEBM.2015.V3.221

Ahsan, A., & Pagés, C. (2009). Are all labor regulations equal? Evidence from Indian manufacturing. *Journal of Comparative Economics, 37*(1), 62–75. doi:10.1016/j.jce.2008.09.001

Alacevich, M. (2016). Albert O. Hirschman and the Rise and Decline of Development Economics. Research in the History of Economic Thought and Methodology, 34, 13-39. doi:10.1108/S0743-41542016000034B001

Alam, K. J., & Sumon, K. K. (2020). Causal Relationship between Trade Openness and Economic Growth: A Panel Data Analysis of Asian Countries. *International Journal of Economics and Financial Issues, 10*(1), 118–126. doi:10.32479/ijefi.8657

Alam, S., Sultana, A., & Butt, M. S. (2010). Does social expenditures promote economic growth? A multivariate panel cointegration analysis for Asian Countries. *European Journal of Soil Science*, *14*(1), 44–54.

Albrecht, J., Navarro, L., & Vroman, S. (2009). The effects of labour market policies in an economy with an informal sector. *Economic Journal (London)*, *119*(539), 1105–1129. doi:10.1111/j.1468-0297.2009.02268.x

Alchian, A., & Demsetz, H. (1972). Production, Information Costs and Economic Organization. *The American Economic Review*, *62*(5), 777–795.

Alchian, A., & Demsetz, H. (1973). The Property Right Paradigm. *The Journal of Economic History*, *33*(1), 16–27. doi:10.1017/S0022050700076403

Aleksieva, N. (2016). Danachnoto oblagane v stranite-chlenki na ES – spetsifichni harakteristiki, dinamika i tendentsii. *Godishen almanah "Nauchni izsledvania na doktoranti"*, *9*(11), 134-153.

Alesina, A., & Ardagna, S. (2010). Large changes in fiscal policy: taxes versus spending. *Tax Policy and the Economy*, *24*(1), 1-37. Doi:10.3386/w15438

Alesina, A., & Giuliano, P. (2015). Culture and Institutions. *Journal of Economic Literature*, *53*(4), 898–944. doi:10.1257/jel.53.4.898

Al-Iriani, M. (2007). Foreign direct investment and economic growth in the GCC countries: A causality investigation using heterogeneous panel analysis. *Topics in Middle Eastern and North African Economies*, 9.

Allen, P. M. (1990). Why the Future is Not what it was. *Futures*, *22*(6), 554–570. doi:10.1016/0016-3287(90)90127-4

Allen, R. C. (2017). Lessons from history for the future of work. *Nature*, *550*(7676), 321–324. doi:10.1038/550321a PMID:29052648

Alvarez-Ayuso, I., & Delgado-Rodríguez, M. (2002). *Estimación del Capital Público, Capital Privado y Capital Humano para la UE-15*. Instituto de Estudios Fiscales Working Paper 12/02.

Anand, R., & Khera, P. (2016). *Macroeconomic impact of product and labor market reform on informality and unemployment in India*. IMF Working Paper. Washington, DC: International Monetary Fund, WP/16/47.

Anderson, J. E., & van Wincoop, E. (2003). Gravity with Gravitas: A Solution to the Border Puzzle. *The American Economic Review*, *93*(1), 170–192. doi:10.1257/000282803321455214

Andranovitch, G., Burbank, M., & Heying, C. (2001). Olympic cities: Lessons learned from mega event politics. *Journal of Urban Affairs*, *1*(2), 113–131. doi:10.1111/0735-2166.00079

Andrews, E. L. (2008). Greenspan Concedes Error on Regulation. *The New York Times*. https://www.nytimes.com/2008/10/24/business/economy/24panel.html

Angelov, G. (2016). Ploskiyat danak – kulminatsia na pragmatichni danachni reformi. In K. Hadzhinedelcheva (Ed.), *Plosak danak v Bulgaria. Predistoria, vavezhdane, rezultati* (pp. 37–48). I.P.I.

Apergis, N., Katrakilidis, C. P., & Tabakis, N. M. (2006). Dynamic linkages between FDI inflows and domestic investment: A panel cointegration approach. *Atlantic Economic Journal*, *34*(4), 385–394. doi:10.100711293-006-9026-x

Area, N. T. (2015). The Validity of Walras' Law in a Monetary Exchange Economy: Money, Prices and the Integration of Monetary and Value Theory. *Iberian Journal of the History of Economic Thought*, *2*(2), 101–114.

Argeitis, G., Koratzanis, N., Paitarides, D., Passas, K., & Pierros, C. (2018). *The delution of the economic adjustment programme*. Papazisis editions. (in Greek)

Argitis, G. (2019). Evolutionary Financial Macroeconomics. Routledge.

Aristotle. (350 BC). *Nicomachean Ethics* (W. D. Ross, Trans.). https://www.constitution.org/ari/ethic_00.htm

Armantier, O., Ghysels, E., Sarkar, A. & Shrader, J. (2011, Aug. 31). *Is there Stigma to Discount Window Borrowing.* Federal Reserve Bank of New York, Liberty Street Economics.

Arrow, K. J., Block, H. D., & Hurwicz, L. (1959). On the Stability of the Competitive Equilibrium. Econometrica, 27.

Arrow, K. J., & Hahn, F. H. (1972). *General Competitive Analysis*. Holden-Day.

Arthur, W. B. (2013). *Complexity and the economy: a different framework for economic thought.* SFI Working Paper: 2013-04-012, 2013-04-012.

Asghar, N., Nasreen, S., & Rehman, H. (2011). Relationship between FDI and economic growth in selected Asian countries: A panel data analysis. *Review of Economics & Finance*, *2*, 84–96.

Asteriou, D., & Price, S. (2005). Uncertainty, investment and economic growth: Evidence from a dynamic panel. *Review of Development Economics*, *9*(2), 277–288. doi:10.1111/j.1467-9361.2005.00276.x

Autor, D. (2015). Why Are There Still So Many Jobs? The History and Future of Workplace Automation. *The Journal of Economic Perspectives*, *29*(3), 3–30. doi:10.1257/jep.29.3.3

Ayres, R. U., & Martinas, K. (2005). *On the Reappraisal of Microeconomics*. E. Elgar. doi:10.4337/9781845427948

Bagir, Y. E. (2017). Impact of the Presence of Foreign Missions on Trade: Evidence from Turkey. MPRA Paper 80845, University Library of Munich.

Bahmani-Oskooee, M., & Miteza, I. (2006). Are devaluations contractionary? Evidence from panel cointegration. *Economic Issues*, *11*(1), 49–64.

Bai, J., & Ng, S. (2004). A PANIC attack on unit roots and cointegration. *Econometrica*, *72*(4), 1127–1177. doi:10.1111/j.1468-0262.2004.00528.x

Baker, D., Rawlins, S., & Stein, D. (2017). *The Full Employment Mandate of the Federal Reserve: Its Origins and Importance*. CEPR, Fed Up and CPD. https://cepr.net/images/stories/reports/full-employment-mandate-2017-07.pdf

Baltagi, B. (2008). *Econometric analysis of panel data*. John Wiley & Sons.

Bandura, A. (1963). Behavior theory and indemnificatory learning. *The American Journal of Orthopsychiatry*, *33*, 591–601. doi:10.1111/j.1939-0025.1963.tb01007.x PMID:13966305

Bandura, A. (1971). Behavior therapy from a social learning perspective. *Proceedings of the XIXth International Congress of Psychology.*

Banerjee, A., Marcellino, M., & Osbat, C. (2004). Some cautions on the use of panel methods for integrated series of macroeconomic data. *The Econometrics Journal*, *7*(2), 322–340. doi:10.1111/j.1368-423X.2004.00133.x

Banerjee, A., & Zanghieri, P. (2003). *A new look at the Feldstein-Horioka puzzle using an integrated panel* (Vol. 22). CEPII.

Bangake, C., & Eggoh, J. C. (2011). The Feldstein–Horioka puzzle in African countries: A panel cointegration analysis. *Economic Modelling*, *28*(3), 939–947. doi:10.1016/j.econmod.2010.11.011

Bank of Greece. (n.d.). *Data Statistics, Developments on Loans and Non Performing Exposures*. Available at: https://www.bankofgreece.gr/statistika/ekseliksh-daneiwn-kai-kathysterhsewn

Bank of Greece. (n.d.). *Publications and Research, Publications, Browse Publications, Bulletin of Conjunctural Indicators*. Available at: https://www.bankofgreece.gr/ekdoseis-ereyna/ekdoseis/anazhthsh-ekdosewn?types=9e8736f4-8146-4dbb-8c07-d73d3f49cdf0&years=2020

Barbier, E., & Burgess, J. (2017). *The Sustainable Development Goals and the systems approach to sustainability*. Discussion Paper. Economics. No. 2017-28.

Barro, R., & Lee, J.-W. (2001). International Data on Educational Attainment: Updates and Implications. *Oxford Economic Papers, 53*(3), 41–63. doi:10.1093/oep/53.3.541

Bartneck, C., Nomura, T., Kanda, T., Suzuki, T., & Kennsuke, K. (2005). Cultural Differences in Attitudes Towards Robots. In *Proceedings of the AISB Symposium on Robot Companions: Hard Problems And Open Challenges In Human-Robot Interaction* (pp. 1-4). Hatfield: Academic Press.

Barwell, R., Chadha, J. S., & Greely, M. (2020). *Monetary Policy in Troubled Times: New Governor, New Agenda.* National Institute of Economic and Social Research Occasional Paper LIX.

Barzel, Y. (1997). *Economic Analysis of Property Rights*. Cambridge University Press. doi:10.1017/CBO9780511609398

Basher, S. A., & Mohsin, M. (2004). PPP tests in cointegrated panels: Evidence from Asian developing countries. *Applied Economics Letters, 11*(3), 163–166. doi:10.1080/1350485042000203788

Basher, S. A., & Westerlund, J. (2009). Panel cointegration and the monetary exchange rate model. *Economic Modelling, 26*(2), 506–513. doi:10.1016/j.econmod.2008.10.006

Basu, S. S., Chamon, M., & Crowe, C. (2017). *IMF, A Model to Assess the Probabilities of Growth, Fiscal, and Financial Crises*. WP/17/282.

Bayar, Y., & Gavriletea, M. D. (2018). Foreign direct investment inflows and financial development in Central and Eastern European Union countries: A panel cointegration and causality. *International Journal of Financial Studies, 6*(2), 55. doi:10.3390/ijfs6020055

Bayer, R. (2006). *Diplomatic Exchange Data set, v2006.1*. Available at: http://correlatesofwar.org

Beckmann, J., Endrich, M., & Schweickert, R. (2014). *Government activity and economic growth: One size fits all?* Kiel Working Papers 1903, Kiel Institute for the World Economy (IfW).

Begall, K., & van Doorne-Huiskes, A. (2019). The institutional context of a sustainable workforce. In T. van der Lippe & Z. Lippényi (Eds.), *Investments in a Sustainable Workforce in Europe* (pp. 17–36)., doi:10.4324/9781351105323-2.

Beinhocker, E. D. (2006). *The Origin of Wealth: Evolution, Complexity, and the Radical Remaking of Economics*. Harvard Business School Press.

Beinhocker, E. D. (2007). *The Origin of Wealth: The Radical Remaking of Economics and What It Means for Business and Society*. Harvard Business Review Press.

Bellofiore, R. (2020). Hyman Minsky at 100: Was Minsky a Communist? *Monthly Review (New York, N.Y.), 71*(10).

Bénassy-Quéré, A., Béreau, S., & Mignon, V. (2009). Robust estimations of equilibrium exchange rates within the G20: A panel BEER approach. *Scottish Journal of Political Economy, 56*(5), 608–633. doi:10.1111/j.1467-9485.2009.00500.x

Béreau, S., Villavicencio, A. L., & Mignon, V. (2012). Currency misalignments and growth: A new look using nonlinear panel data methods. *Applied Economics, 44*(27), 3503–3511. doi:10.1080/00036846.2011.577022

Bergeijk, P. A. G., & Moons, S. J. V. (2011). *Does Economic Diplomacy Work? A Meta Analysis on the Effect of Economic Diplomacy on International Economic Flows*. Available at SSRN: https://ssrn.com/abstract=1908699

Berger, H., & Danninger, S. (2007). The employment effects of labor and product markets deregulation and their implications for structural reform. *IMF Staff Papers*, *54*(3), 591–619. doi:10.1057/palgrave.imfsp.9450014

Bergh, J., & van den Gowdy, J. (2003). The microfoundations of macroeconomics: An evolutionary perspective. *Cambridge Journal of Economics*, *27*(1), 65–84. doi:10.1093/cje/27.1.65

Berti, K., & Meyermans, E. (2017). *Maximising the impact of labour and product market reforms in the euro area - sequencing and packaging*. Quarterly Report on the Euro Area (QREA), Directorate General Economic and Financial Affairs (DG ECFIN), European Commission, vol. 16(2), pp. 7-19, October. Available at: https://ideas.repec.org/a/euf/qreuro/0162-01.html

Bertola, G., Boeri, T., & Cazes, S. (1999). Employment protection and labor market adjustment in OECD countries: evolving institutions and variable enforcement. Employment and Training Papers International Labor Organization, Geneva, No. 48.

Bird, R. M. (2004, Feb.). Managing tax reform. *International Bureau of Fiscal Documentation Bulletin*.

Blanchard, O., & Leigh, D. (2013). Growth forecast errors and fiscal multipliers. *The American Economic Review*, *103*(3), 117–120. doi:10.1257/aer.103.3.117

Blanchard, O., & Leigh, D. (2014). Learning about fiscal multipliers from growth forecast errors. *IMF Economic Review*, *62*(2), 179–212. doi:10.1057/imfer.2014.17

Bloom, E. D., Sachs, J. D., Collier, P., & Udry, C. (1998). Geography, Demography, and Economic Growth in Africa. *Brookings Papers on Economic Activity*, *2*(2), 207–273. doi:10.2307/2534695 PMID:12295931

Bluszcz, A., & Manowska, A. (2019). Panel Analysis to Investigate the Relationship Between Economic Growth, Import, Consumption of Materials and Energy. In *IOP Conference Series: Earth and Environmental Science* (Vol. 362, No. 1, p. 012153). IOP Publishing. 10.1088/1755-1315/362/1/012153

Boissay, F., Rees, D., & Rungcharoenkitkul, P. (2020). *Dealing with Covid-19: Understanding the policy choices. BIS Bulletins, 19*. Bank for International Settlements.

Bonoli, G. (2010). The political economy of active labour market policy. *Politics & Society*, *38*(4), 435–457. doi:10.1177/0032329210381235

Bordo, M. D., Dittmar, R., & Gavin, T. W. (2007). *Gold, Fiat Money and Price Stability*. Federal Reserve Bank of St. Louis, Working Paper Series, Working Paper 2003-014D.

Bossmann, J. (2016). *Top 9 ethical issues in artificial intelligence*. World Economic Forum. Retrieved from https://www.weforum.org/agenda/2016/10/top-10-ethical-issues-in-artificial-intelligence/

Boulding, K. E. (1961). *The image: Knowledge in life and society*. University of Michigan.

Boyd, R., & Richerson, P. J. (1985). *Culture and the Evolutionary Process*. University of Chicago Press.

Boyd, R., & Richerson, P. J. (2005). *The Origin and Evolution of Cultures*. Oxford University Press.

Boylan & O'Gorman. (2018). Philosophy of Mathematics and Economics Image, Context and Perspective. Routledge.

Breitung, J., & Candelon, B. (2005). Purchasing power parity during currency crises: A panel unit root test under structural breaks. *Review of World Economics*, *141*(1), 124–140. doi:10.100710290-005-0018-8

Bresser-Pereira, L. C. (2020). Financing Covid-19, the inflation and the fiscal constraint. *The Forum for Social Economics, 49*(3).

Bromley, D. W. (1989). *Economic interests and institutions: The conceptual foundations of public policy*. Blackwell.

Brunet, G. (2005). A Brief Introduction to Hamilton Cycles in Random Graphs. Department of Computer Science University of Toronto.

Bujang, I., Hakim, T. A., & Ahmad, I. (2013). Tax structure and economic indicators in developing and high-income OECD countries: Panel cointegration analysis. *Procedia Economics and Finance, 7*(13), 164–173. doi:10.1016/S2212-5671(13)00231-1

Bulgarian National Bank (2020b), The Governing Council of the Bulgarian National Bank approved the draft Procedure for Deferral and Settlement of Liabilities Payable to Banks and their Subsidiaries – Financial Institutions. Press release on 10 April.

Bulgarian National Bank. (2020a). The BNB implements, within its mandate, a package of measures worth BGN 9.3 billion in relation to the COVID 19 pandemic. Press release on 19 March.

Cadle, J., Paul, D., & Turner, P. (2014). *Business analysis techniques. BCS*. Chartered Institute for IT.

Cagan, P. (1984). The Report of the Gold Commission (1982). *Carnegie Conference Series on Public Policy, 20*, 247–268. doi:10.1016/0167-2231(84)90050-2

Cantelmo, A., & Melina, G. (2017). *Monetary Policy and the Relative Price of Durable Goods*. IMF, WP/17/290.

Canzoneri, M. B., Cumby, R. E., & Diba, B. (1999). Relative labor productivity and the real exchange rate in the long run: Evidence for a panel of OECD countries. *Journal of International Economics, 47*(2), 245–266. doi:10.1016/S0022-1996(98)00021-X

Carabelli, A. M. (1988). *On Keynes's Method.* St. Martin's Press. doi:10.1007/978-1-349-19414-8

Carabelli, A. M., & Cedrini, M. A. (2015). From Theory to Policy? Keynes's Distinction between Apparatus of Thought and Apparatus of Action, with an Eye to the European Debt Crisis. *Challenge, 58*(6), 509–531. doi:10.1080/05775132.2015.1105666

Carey, H. (1868). *The Harmony of Interests: Agricultural, Manufacturing and Commercial*. Industrial Publisher.

Cassel, G. (1918). Abnormal Deviations in International Exchanges. *Economic Journal (London), 28*(112), 413–415. doi:10.2307/2223329

Cavalcanti, T. V. D. V., Mohaddes, K., & Raissi, M. (2011). Growth, development and natural resources: New evidence using a heterogeneous panel analysis. *The Quarterly Review of Economics and Finance, 51*(4), 305–318. doi:10.1016/j.qref.2011.07.007

CEFTA Secretariat. (2020). *CEFTA parties*. Available at: https://cefta.int/cefta-parties-2/

Cencini, A. (2017). Introduction. In J.-L. Bailly, A. Cencini, & S. Rossi (Eds.), *Quantum Macroeconomics: The legacy of Bernard Schmitt* (pp. 1–20). Routledge.

Charfeddine, L. (2017). The impact of energy consumption and economic development on Ecological Footprint and CO2 emissions: Evidence from a Markov Switching Equilibrium Correction Model. *Energy Economics, 65*, 355–374. doi:10.1016/j.eneco.2017.05.009

Charfeddine, L., & Mrabet, Z. (2017). The impact of economic development and social-political factors on ecological footprint: A panel data analysis for 15 MENA countries. *Renewable & Sustainable Energy Reviews*, *76*, 138–154. doi:10.1016/j.rser.2017.03.031

Chen, C. F., Shen, C. H., & Wang, C. A. A. (2007). Does PPP hold for Big Mac price or consumer price index? Evidence from panel cointegration. *Economic Bulletin*, *6*(16), 1–15.

Chick, V. (2017). On Open Systems. In L.-P. Rochon & S. Rossi (Eds.), Post-Keynesian Economics. Volume 1. Issues in Methodology (pp. 124–137). Edward Elgar.

Chick, V. (1995). "Order out of Chaos" in Economics? In S. Dow & J. Hillard (Eds.), *Keynes, knowledge and uncertainty* (pp. 25–42). Edward Elgar.

Chick, V., & Dow, S. (2005). The meaning of open systems. *Journal of Economic Methodology*, *12*(3), 363–381. doi:10.1080/13501780500223585

Chick, V., & Dow, S. C. (2001). Formalism, logic and reality: A Keynesian analysis. *Cambridge Journal of Economics*, *25*(6), 705–721. doi:10.1093/cje/25.6.705

Chintrakarn, P., Herzer, D., & Nunnenkamp, P. (2012). FDI and income inequality: Evidence from a panel of US states. *Economic Inquiry*, *50*(3), 788–801. doi:10.1111/j.1465-7295.2011.00384.x

Chiu, C.-y., & Hong, Y-y. (2007). Social psychology of culture. New York: Psychology Press.

Choi, I. (2013). *Panel Cointegration*. Working Papers 1208, Research Institute for Market Economy, Sogang University.

Choi, I. (2001). Unit root tests for panel data. *Journal of International Money and Finance*, *20*(2), 249–272. doi:10.1016/S0261-5606(00)00048-6

Chowdhury, M., & Das, A. (2011). Aid-growth nexus in south Asia: Evidence from time series and panel cointegration. *Research in Applied Economics*, *3*(1), 1. doi:10.5296/rae.v3i1.601

Christodoulakis, N. (2010). Crisis, Threats and Ways out for the Greek economy. *Cyprus Economic Policy Review*, *4*(1), 89–96.

Christopoulos, D. K., & Tsionas, E. G. (2003). Testing the Buchanan-Wagner hypothesis: European evidence from panel unit root and cointegration tests. *Public Choice*, *115*(3-4), 439–453. doi:10.1023/A:1024213614689

Claeys, P. (2007). Sustainability of EU fiscal policies: A panel test. *Journal of Economic Integration*, 112-127.

Clower, R. W. (1967). A Reconsideration of the Micro foundations of the Monetary Theory, Western. *Economic Journal (London)*, *6*(4), 1–8.

Clower, R. W., & Howitt, P. W. (1978, June). The Transaction Theory of the Demand for Money: A Reconsideration. *Journal of Political Economy*, *86*(3), 449–466. doi:10.1086/260681

Coakley, J., Fuertes, A. M., & Spagnolo, F. (2001). *The Feldstein-Horioka puzzle is not as bad as you think*. Birkbeck College, Department of Economics.

Coakley, J., Kulasi, F., & Smith, R. (1998). The Feldstein–Horioka puzzle and capital mobility: A review. *International Journal of Finance & Economics*, *3*(2), 169–188. doi:10.1002/(SICI)1099-1158(199804)3:2<169::AID-IJFE74>3.0.CO;2-H

Coase, R. H. (1988a). The Nature of the Firm. Academic Press.

Coase, R. H. (1988b). The Problem of Social Cost. Academic Press.

Coase, R. (1937). The Nature of the Firm. *Economica*, *4*(4), 86–405.

Coase, R. (1988). *The Firm, the Market and the Law*. University of Chicago Press.

Coase, R. H. (1988). *The firm, the market, and the law*. The University of Chicago Press.

Colander, D. (2000). The Death of Neoclassical Economics. *Journal of the History of Economic Thought*, *22*(2), 127–143. doi:10.1080/10427710050025330

Cole, A. H. (1968). Meso-economics: a contribution from entrepreneurial history. *Explorations in Entrepreneurial History, 6*(1), 3-33.

Companies already replacing humans with robots. (2019). Retrieved from https://www.lovemoney.com/gallerylist/61607/companies-already-replacing-humans-with-robots

Copeland, M. A. (1952). The Quantitative Functions of Money. In *A Study of Money flows in The United States*. NBER. https://www.nber.org/books/cope52-1

Corneo, G. (2000). *The efficient side of progressive income taxation*. CESifo Working Paper No 364.

Crouch, C. (2011). The strange non-death of neoliberalism. *Polity.*

Crowe, S. (2019). *Top 5 countries using industrial robots in 2018*. Retrieved from https://www.therobotreport.com/top-5-countries-using-industrial-robots-2018/

Cullen, J., & Gordon, R. (2002). *Taxes and entrepreneurial activity: Theory and evidence for the U.S.* NBER Working Paper No. 9015.

Cunha, D. (2016). *The educational strategy that's turning students into unimaginative robots*. Retrieved from https://qz.com/605452/the-educational-strategy-thats-turning-students-into-unimaginative-robots/

Danaher, J., & McArthur, N. (Eds.). (2017). *Robot Sex: Social and Ethical Implications*. The MIT Press. doi:10.7551/mitpress/9780262036689.001.0001

Danish, U., Ulucak, R., & Khan, S. U.-D. (2020). Determinants of the ecological footprint: Role of renewable energy, natural resources, and urbanization. *Sustainable Cities and Society*, *54*, 101996. doi:10.1016/j.scs.2019.101996

Davidson, P. (1972, March). Money and the Real World. *Economic Journal (London)*, *82*(325), 101–115. doi:10.2307/2230209

Davidson, P. (2004). A post Keynesian view of the Washington consensus and how to improve it. *Journal of Post Keynesian Economics*, *27*(2), 207–230.

Davis, J. B. (2009). Identity and Individual Economic Agents: A Narrative Approach. *Review of Social Economy*, *67*(1), 71–94. doi:10.1080/00346760802431009

Davis, J. B. (2011). *Individuals and identity in economics*. Cambridge university press.

Davis, J. B. (2015). Stratification economics and identity economics. *Cambridge Journal of Economics*, *39*(5), 1215–1229. doi:10.1093/cje/beu071

De Jong, E. (2011). Culture, institutions and economic growth. *Journal of Institutional Economics*, *7*(4), 523–527. doi:10.1017/S1744137411000117

De Vita, G., & Kyaw, K. S. (2008). Determinants of FDI and portfolio flows to developing countries: A panel cointegration analysis. *European Journal of Economics. Finance and Administrative Sciences*, *13*(13), 161–168.

DeCanio, S. J. (2016). Robots and humans–complements or substitutes? *Journal of Macroeconomics*, *49*, 280–291. doi:10.1016/j.jmacro.2016.08.003

Decker, M., Fischer, M., & Ott, I. (2017). Service Robotics and Human Labor: A first technology assessment of substitution and cooperation. *Robotics and Autonomous Systems*, *87*, 348–354. doi:10.1016/j.robot.2016.09.017

Dellas, H., Malliaropulos, D., Papageorgiou, D., & Vourvachaki, E. (2017). *Fiscal policy with an informal sector.* Bank of Greece Working Paper, No. 235.

Demetriades, P. O., & James, G. A. (2011). Finance and growth in Africa: The broken link. *Economics Letters*, *113*(3), 263–265. doi:10.1016/j.econlet.2011.08.007

Demsetz, H. (1967). Toward a Theory of Property Rights. *The American Economic Review*, *57*(2), 347–359.

DeNederlandschebank. (2020). *Central Bank Digital Currency* (Vol. 20-01). DeNederlandschebank Occasional Studies.

Deryabina, M. A. (2018). Methodological foundations of the study of the meso-economics as a complex system. *Journal of Institutional Studies, 10*(3), 30-32.

Destek, M. A., & Sarkodie, S. A. (2019). Investigation of environmental Kuznets curve for ecological footprint: The role of energy and financial development. *The Science of the Total Environment*, *650*, 2483–2489. doi:10.1016/j.scitotenv.2018.10.017 PMID:30293003

Di Iorio, F., & Fachin, S. (2010). *Savings and Investments in the OECD, 1970-2007: a Panel Cointegration test with breaks.* Academic Press.

Dias, M. B., Mills-Tettey, G. A., & Nanayakkara, T. (2005). Robotics, Education, and Sustainable Development. In *Proceedings of the 2005 IEEE International Conference on Robotics and Automation* (pp. 4248 – 4253). Barcelona, Spain: IEEE. 10.1109/ROBOT.2005.1570773

Dinda, S., & Coondoo, D. (2006). Income and emission: A panel data-based cointegration analysis. *Ecological Economics*, *57*(2), 167–181. doi:10.1016/j.ecolecon.2005.03.028

Dirican, C. (2015). The Impacts of Robotics, Artificial Intelligence On Business and Economics. *Procedia: Social and Behavioral Sciences*, *195*, 564–573. doi:10.1016/j.sbspro.2015.06.134

DistanceFromTo. (2019). *Distance between countries' capital cities.* Available at: https://www.distancefromto.net/

Dixon, R. (2017). *Walras' Law.* https://www.online.fbe.unimelb.edu.au/WalrasLaw.pdf

Djankov, S., Lieberman, I., Mukherjee, J., & Nenova, T. (2002). *Going informal: benefits and costs", mimeo.* The World Bank.

Donaubauer, J. (2014). Does foreign aid really attract foreign investors? New evidence from panel cointegration. *Applied Economics Letters*, *21*(15), 1094–1098. doi:10.1080/13504851.2014.909570

Dopfer, K. (2013). *Evolutionary Economics.* Papers on Economics and Evolution, Max Planck Institute of Economics, No. 1308.

Dopfer, K. (2012). The origins of meso economics. *Journal of Evolutionary Economics*, *22*(1), 133–160. doi:10.100700191-011-0218-4

Dopfer, K., Foster, J., & Potts, J. (2004). Micro-meso-macro. *Journal of Evolutionary Economics*, *14*(3), 263–279. doi:10.100700191-004-0193-0

Dopfer, K., & Potts, J. (2008). *The General Theory of Economic Evolution.* Routledge.

Dopfer, K., & Potts, J. (2010). Why evolutionary realism underpins evolutionary economic analysis and theory: A reply to Runde's critique. *Journal of Institutional Economics*, *6*(3), 401–413. doi:10.1017/S1744137410000093

Douglas, M. (1987). *How institutions think*. Routledge & Kegan Paul.

Dow, S. C. (1985). *Macroeconomic thought: A methodological approach*. Basil Blackwell.

Dow, S. C. (2005). Axioms and Babylonian thought: A reply. *Journal of Post Keynesian Economics*, *27*(3), 385–391.

Drine, I., & Rault, C. (2004). Does the Balassa-Samuelson hypothesis hold for Asian countries? An empirical analysis using panel data and cointegration tests. *Applied Econometrics and International Development, 4*(4).

Dubey, P., Geanacoplos, J., & Shubik, M. (2003). Is Gold an Efficient Store of Value? *Economic Theory*, *21*(4), 767–782. doi:10.100700199-002-0266-y

Dugger, W. M., & Sherman, H. J. (2000). *Reclaiming evolution: A dialogue between marxism and institutionalism on social change*. Routledge. doi:10.4324/9780203160589

Duval, R., & Elmeskov, J. (2006). *The effects of EMU structural reforms in labour and product markets*. ECB Working Paper Series, No. 596.

Easterlin. (1974). *Nations and Households in Economic Growth: Essays in Honor of Moses Abramovitz*. New York: Academic Press, Inc.

Ee, C. Y. (2016). Export-led growth hypothesis: Empirical evidence from selected Sub-Saharan African countries. *Procedia Economics and Finance*, *35*(2), 232–240. doi:10.1016/S2212-5671(16)00029-0

Égert, B. (2002). Investigating the Balassa-Samuelson hypothesis in the transition: Do we understand what we see? A panel study. *Economics of Transition*, *10*(2), 273–309. doi:10.1111/1468-0351.00112

Égert, B., Drine, I., Lommatzsch, K., & Rault, C. (2003). The Balassa–Samuelson effect in Central and Eastern Europe: Myth or reality? *Journal of Comparative Economics*, *31*(3), 552–572. doi:10.1016/S0147-5967(03)00051-9

Eggertsson, T. (1990). *Economic Behaviour and Institutions*. Cambridge University Press. doi:10.1017/CBO9780511609404

Eichenbaum, M. S., Rebelo, S., & Trabandt, M. (2020). The Macroeconomics of Epidemics. NBER Working Paper No. 26882.

Eichengreen, B. (1991). *Is Europe an optimum currency area?* NBER Working Paper Series, no. 3579.

Eichengreen, B. (2009, May). The Last Temptation of Risk. *The National Interest*.

Eliasson, L., & Turnovsky, S. J. (2004). Renewable Resources in an Endogenously Growing Economy: Balanced Growth and Transitional Dynamics. *Journal of Environmental Economics and Management*, *48*(3), 1018–1049. doi:10.1016/j.jeem.2003.12.004

Elmeskov, J., Martin, J., & Scarpetta, S. (1998). Key lessons for labour market reforms: Evidence from OECD countries' experiences. *Swedish Economic Policy Review*, *5*, 2.

Elsner, W. (2007). Why Meso? On "Aggregation" and "Emergence", and Why and How the Meso Level is Essential in Social Economics. *The Forum for Social Economics*, *36*(1), 1–16. doi:10.100712143-007-0001-3

Elsner, W. (2009). The process and a simple logic of 'meso'. Emergence and the coevolutionof institutions and group size. *Journal of Evolutionary Economics*, *20*(3), 445–477. doi:10.100700191-009-0158-4

Elsner, W., & Heinrich, T. (2009). A simple theory of 'meso'. On the co-evolution of institutions and platform size - With an application to varieties of capitalism and 'mediumsized' countries. *Journal of Socio-Economics, 38*(5), 843–858. doi:10.1016/j.socec.2009.05.001

Elsner, W., Heinrich, T., & Schwardt, H. (2015). *The microeconomics of complex economies: Evolutionary, institutional, neoclassical, and complexity perspectives*. Academic Press. doi:10.1016/B978-0-12-411585-9.00001-4

Engerman, S. L., & Sokoloff, K. L. (1997). Factor Endowments, Institu-tions, and Differential Paths of Growth AmongNew World Economies: A View from Economic Historians of the United States. In How Latin America Fell Behind. Stanford University Press.

Erdal, L., & Göçer, İ. (2015). The effects of foreign direct investment on R&D and innovations: Panel data analysis for developing Asian countries. *Procedia: Social and Behavioral Sciences, 195*(3), 749–758. doi:10.1016/j.sbspro.2015.06.469

Erdem, E., Nazlioglu, S., & Erdem, C. (2010). Exchange rate uncertainty and agricultural trade: Panel cointegration analysis for Turkey. *Agricultural Economics, 41*(6), 537–543. doi:10.1111/j.1574-0862.2010.00469.x

Eregha, P. B. (2012). The dynamic linkages between foreign direct investment and domestic investment in ECOWAS countries: A panel cointegration analysis. *African Development Review, 24*(3), 208–220. doi:10.1111/j.1467-8268.2012.00317.x

Espinoza, R. A., Segoviano, M. A., & Yan, J. (2020). *Systemic Risk Modeling: How Theory Can Meet Statistics*. IMF, WP/20/54.

Euro Summit. (2015, July 12). *Euro Summit Statement*. Author.

European Comission. (2020). *European Union member countries*. Available at: https://ec.europa.eu/

European Commission. (2010). *European Economy: The Economic Adjustment Programme for Greece*. Occasional Papers 61.

European Commission. (2012). *Occasional Papers 94, "The Second Economic Adjustment Programme for Greece."* Available at: https://ec.europa.eu/economy_finance/publications/occasional_paper/2012/pdf/ocp94_en.pdf

European Commission. (2014). *European Economy: The Second Economic Adjustment Programme for Greece Fourth Review*. Occasional Papers 192.

European Commission. (2017a). *Evropeyski semestar: Tematichen informatsionen document. Danachno oblagane*. European Commission.

European Commission. (2017b). *Evropeyski semestar: Tematichen informatsionen dokument. Preodolyavane na neravenstvata*. European Commission.

European Commission. (2019). *Taxation trends in Europe 2019*. European Commission.

European Commission. (2019c). European Neighbourhood Policy and Enlargement Negotiations. Retrieved from https://ec.europa.eu/neighbourhood-enlargement/countries/detailed-country-information/serbia_en

European Commission. (2020). *Eurostat, Data, Database, various variables examined*. Available at: https://ec.europa.eu/eurostat/data/database

European Commission. (2020a). Policy measures taken against the spread and impact of the coronavirus – 14 April 2020. Retrieved from https://ec.europa.eu/info/sites/info/files/policy_measures_taken_against_the_spread_and_impact_of_the_coronavirus_14042020.pdf

European Commission. (2020b). State aid: Commission approves €3.3 billion Romanian scheme to support SMEs in coronavirus outbreak. Retrieved from https://ec.europa.eu/commission/presscorner/detail/en/IP_20_649

European Court of Auditors. (2017). *The Commission's Intervention in the Greek Financial crisis, Special Report, No 17*. Available at: https://www.eca.europa.eu/Lists/ECADocuments/SR17_17/SR_GREECE_EN.pdf

European Parliament. (2014). *Committee Study on the Troika and Financial Assistance in the euro area: Successes and Failures*. Study on the request of the Economic and Monetary Affairs Committee, Directorate General for Internal Policies, Economic Governance Support Unit (EGOV). Available at: https://www.bruegel.org/wp-content/uploads/imported/publications/20140219ATT79633EN_01.pdf

European Union. (2019). *Evropeyski zelen pakt: stimuli za ikonomikata, podobryavane na zdraveto i kachestvoto na zhivot na horata*. Brussels, Belgium: European Union.

Fan, Y., & Ullah, A. (1999). On Goodness-of-Fit Tests for Weekly Dependent Processes Using Kernel Method. *Journal of Nonparametric Statistics*, *11*(1-3), 337–360. doi:10.1080/10485259908832788

Farrell, D. (2004). The hidden dangers of the informal economy. *The McKinsey Quarterly*, 3.

Fayerabend, K. P. (1975). *Against Method: Outline of an Anarchistic Theory of Knowledge*. New Left Books.

Feenstra, R., Heston, A., Timmer, M., & Deng, H. (2007). *Estimating Real Production and Expenditures across Nations: A Proposal for Improving the Penn World Tables*. Policy Research Working Paper No. 4166. Washington, DC: The World Bank.

Fegatelli, P. (2019). *Central Bank Digital Currencies: The Case of Universal Central Bank Reserves*. Banque Centrale Du Luxembourg Working Paper No 130.

Feldstein, M. S., & Horioka, C. Y. (1979). *Domestic savings and international capital flows*. NBER Working paper nr. 310.

Feldstein, M., & Horioka, C. (1980). Domestic Saving and International Capital Flows. *Economic Journal (London)*, *90*(358), 314–329. doi:10.2307/2231790

Fiorentini, R. (2015). Neoliberal Policies, Income Distribution Inequality and the Financial Crisis. *The Forum for Social Economics*, *44*(2), 115–132. doi:10.1080/07360932.2014.951376

Fiori, G., Nicoletti, G., Scarpetta, S., & Schiantarelli, F. (2012). Employment effects of product and labor market reforms; are there synergies? *Economic Journal (London)*, *122*(558), 79–104. doi:10.1111/j.1468-0297.2011.02494.x

Fisher, I. (1963). *The Purchasing Power of Money* (rev. ed.). Kelley.

Fisher, S. R. A. (1932). *Statistical Methods for Research Workers*. Oliver and Boyd.

Foks, N., & Bergherm, D. (1998). *Metodi i tehniki za provezhdane na danachni revizii: Rabotna sreshta s instruktori ot Ministerstvo na finansite na SASht*. MF GUDA.

Forsyth, P. (1992). A perspective on microeconomic reform. In P. Forsyth (Ed.), *Microeconomic Reform in Australia*. Allen and Unwin.

Foster, J. (2011). Evolutionary Macroeconomics: A Research Agenda. In Catching Up, Spillovers and Innovation Networks in a Schumpeterian Perspective. DOI doi:10.1007/978-3-642-15886-5_2

Foster, J., & Pyka, A. (2014). *Introduction: co-evolution and complex adaptive systems in evolutionary economics*. Jour -014-0339-7.

Foster, J. (Ed.). (2004). *Applied Evolutionary Economics and Complex Systems*. Edward Elgar Publishing. doi:10.4337/9781845421564

Foucault, M. (2008). *The birth of biopolitics: Lectures at the Collège de France, 1978-79. Palgrave Macmillan* (M. Senellart, Ed.).

Frank, T. (2005). *What's the matter with Kansas? How conservatives won the heart of America*. Henry Holt.

Fraser Institute. (n.d.). *Economic freedom of the World: 2019 Annual Report*. Available at: https://www.fraserinstitute.org/studies/economic-freedom-of-the-world-2019-annual-report

Freeman, J. (2018). *Behemoth: A history of the factory and the making of the modern world*. Norton.

Fride. (2006). *The Individual as an agent of change: The Empowerment Process*. Development "In Perspective".

Friedman, D. (1979). Money-Mediated Disequilibrium in a Pure Exchange Economy. *Journal of Mathematical Economics*, *6*(2), 149–167. doi:10.1016/0304-4068(79)90004-1

Furubotn, E., & Richter, R. (1998). *Institutions and Economic Theory: The Contribution of the New Institutional Economics*. The University of Michigan Press.

Galabov, N. (2009). Ploskiyat danak - teoria i praktika. *Ikonomicheska misal*, (2), 3-18.

Gallois, F., & Hédoin, C. (2017). From Identity to Agency in Positive and Normative Economics. *The Forum for Social Economics*, 1–17. doi:10.1080/07360932.2017.1394897

Ganchev, G. T. (2015). Towards Holistic Theory of Money: Overcoming Twentieth Century Neoclassical Monetary Paradigm. Economic Studies, 4, 3-24.

Ganchev, G.T. (2013). *The Theory of Monetary Circuit*. Economic Thought No. 1/2013.

Ganev, P. (2016). Plosak danak i tezhest varhu truda. In K. Hadzhinedelcheva (Ed.), *Plosak danak v Bulgaria. Predistoria, vavezhdane, rezultati* (pp. 73–83). I.P.I.

Gareev, T. R. (2010). Institutions and economic development at the subregional (meso-) level. *Social Sciences and Modernity*, *5*, 45.

Garganas, N. C. (2007). Does one size fit all? Monetary policy and integration in the euro area. Address by Mr Nicholas C Garganas, Governor of the Bank of Greece, at a visit to the Central Bank of Chile, Santiago, Chile.

Gengenbach, C., Palm, F. C., & Urbain, J. P. (2006). Cointegration testing in panels with common factors. *Oxford Bulletin of Economics and Statistics*, *68*, 683–719. doi:10.1111/j.1468-0084.2006.00452.x

George, S. (1999, March 24). *A Short History of Neoliberalism*. Transnational Institute. https://www.tni.org/en/article/short-history-neoliberalism

Georgia, K., & Vassilis, R. (2013). Fiscal Deficits and the Role of Fiscal Governance: The case of Greece. *Economic Analysis and Policy*, *43*(1), 5–27. doi:10.1016/S0313-5926(13)50001-4

Gerschenkron, A. (1962). *Economic backwardness in historical perspective*. The Belknap Press of Harvard University Press.

Gerxhani, K. (2003). *The Informal Sector in Developed and Less Developed Countries. Amsterdam Institute for Advanced Labour Studies*. University of Amsterdam.

Gil-Pareja, S., Llorca-Vivero, R., & Martínez-Serrano, J. A. (2007). The impact of embassies and consulates on tourism'. *Tourism Management*, *28*(1), 355–360. doi:10.1016/j.tourman.2006.04.016

Gladwell, M. (1997, March 17). The Coolhunt. *The New Yorker*. https://www.newyorker.com/magazine/1997/03/17/the-coolhunt

Godley, W., & Lavoie, M. (2007). *Monetary Economics*. Basingstoke, Hampshire: Palgrave Macmillan.

Goodhart, C.A.E. (2018). *Central Bank policies in recent years*. LSE Research Online.

Gore, C. (2000). The Rise and fall of the washington consensus as a paradigma for developing countries. *World Development*, *28*(5), 789–804. doi:10.1016/S0305-750X(99)00160-6

Gourinchas, P.-O., Philippon, T., & Vayanos, D. (2016). *The Analytics of the Greek Crisis*. VOX CEPR's Policy Portal. Available at: https://berkeley.app.box.com/s/fkjjefyar69wt31oqnsuy0khzm0xel64

Graetz, G., & Michaels, G. (2018). Robots at Work. *The Review of Economics and Statistics*, *100*(5), 753–768. doi:10.1162/rest_a_00754

Grandmont, J. M. (1985). *Money and Value: A Reconsideration of Classical and Neoclassical Monetary Theories*. Cambridge University Press.

Graziani, A. (2003). *The Monetary Theory of Production*. Cambridge University Press. doi:10.1017/CBO9780511493546

Gregory, R. G. (1992). An ovetview ofmicroeconomic reform. In P. J. Forsyth (Ed.), *Microeconomic Reform in Australia*. Allen and Unwin.

Griffith, R., Harrison, R., & Macartney, G. (2007). Product market reforms, labor market institutions and unemployment. *Economic Journal (London)*, *117*(519), 142–166. doi:10.1111/j.1468-0297.2007.02039.x

Gurley, J. G., & Shaw, E. S. (1960). *Banking in a Theory of Finance*. The Brookings Institution.

Gusakov, V. G. (2018). Grounds of Systemic Economics. *Proceedings from the National Academy of Sciences in Belarus*, *62*(44), 488–494.

Haakonssen, K. (1981). *The Science of a Legislator: The Natural Jurisprudence of David Hume and Adam Smith*. Cambridge University Press. doi:10.1017/CBO9780511628276

Haakonssen, K. (1982). What might properly be called natural jurisprudence? In R. Campbell & A. Skinner (Eds.), *The Origin and Nature of the Scottish Enlightment* (pp. 205–225). John Donald.

Haberler, G. (1946). *Prosperity and Depression: A Theoretical Analysis of Cyclical Movements* (3rd ed.). United Nations.

Hadri, K. (2000). Testing for stationarity in heterogeneous panel data. *The Econometrics Journal*, *3*(2), 148–161. doi:10.1111/1368-423X.00043

Hall, R., & Jones, C. (1999). Why Do Some Countries Produce so Much More Output per Worker than Others? *The Quarterly Journal of Economics*, *114*(1), 83–116. doi:10.1162/003355399555954

Hamit-Haggar, M. (2012). Greenhouse gas emissions, energy consumption and economic growth: A panel cointegration analysis from Canadian industrial sector perspective. *Energy Economics*, *34*(1), 358–364. doi:10.1016/j.eneco.2011.06.005

Hanke, S. H. (2002). On dollarization and currency boards: Error and deception. *Journal of Policy Reform*, *5*(4), 203–222. doi:10.1080/1384128032000096814

Harari, Y. N. (2017). Reboot for the AI revolution. *Nature*, *550*(7676), 324–327. doi:10.1038/550324a PMID:29052637

Harris & Lewis. (Eds.). (1995). The New Institutional Economics and Third World Development. London: Routledge.

Harris, D. J. (2003). *Joan Robinson on History versus Equilibrium.* J. *Robinson Centennial Conference*, Burlington, VT.

Harrison, A. E. (1994). Productivity, imperfect competition and trade reform. Theory and evidence. *Journal of International Economics*, *36*(1-2), 53–73. doi:10.1016/0022-1996(94)90057-4

Harvard University. (2020). *What are the Slavic languages?* Available at: https://slavic.fas.harvard.edu/pages/what-are-slavic-languages

Harvey, D. (2005). *A brief history of neoliberalism.* Oxford University Press.

Hassan, G. M., & Holmes, M. J. (2013). Remittances and the real effective exchange rate. *Applied Economics*, *45*(35), 4959–4970. doi:10.1080/00036846.2013.808311

Hausman, M. D. (1981). *Capital, Profits and Prices: An Essay in the Philosophy of Economics.* Columbia University Press. doi:10.7312/haus90554

Hausman, M. D. (1989). Economic Methodology in a Nutshell. *The Journal of Economic Perspectives*, *3*(2), 115–127. doi:10.1257/jep.3.2.115

Hausmann, R., Rodrik, D., & Velasco, A. (2008). Growth Diagnostics. In J. Stiglitz & N. Serra (Eds.), The Washington Consensus Reconsidered: Towards a New Global Governance. New York: Oxford University Press.

Hayakawa, K., Lee, H.-H., & Park, D. (2014). Do export promotion agencies increase exports? *The Developing Economies*, *52*(3), 241–261. doi:10.1111/deve.12048

Hayden, F. G. (2018). Using the Social Fabric Matrix to Establish Corporate Accounting Consistent with Normative Criteria Regarding Climate Change. *The Forum for Social Economics*, *47*(1), 64–86. doi:10.1080/07360932.2014.1002517

Hayek, F. A. von. (1937). Economics and knowledge. *Economica, 4*, 33–54.

Hayek, F. (1931). *Prices and Production.* Routledge.

Hayek, F. (1945). The use of knowledge in society. *The American Economic Review*, *35*(4), 519–530.

Hayek, F. A. (1937). Economics and knowledge. *Economica*, ▪▪▪, 4.

Hazans, M. (2011). *What explains prevalence of informal employment in European countries: The role of labor institutions, governance, immigrants and growth.* WB Working Paper No 5917.

Head, K., & Ries, J. (2010). Do Trade Missions Increase Trade? *The Canadian Journal of Economics. Revue Canadienne d'Economique*, *43*(3), 754–775. doi:10.1111/j.1540-5982.2010.01593.x

Heise, A. (2017). Walras' Law in the Context of Pre-Analytic Visions. *Economic Thought*, *6*(1), 83–96.

Hellenic Republic, Ministry of Finance. (n.d.). *Economic data, Greek Budget various years.* Available at: https://www.minfin.gr/web/guest/proupologismos

Hellenic Republic, Ministry of Labour and Social Affairs. (n.d.). *ERGANI Database, various editions.* Available at: https://www.ypakp.gr/

Hellenic Statistical Authority (ELSTAT). (n.d.). *Labour Force Quarterly Surveys, various years.* Available at: https://www.statistics.gr/el/statistics/-/publication/SJO01/-

Henderson, D., & Russell, R. (2005). Human Capital and Convergence: A Production-Frontier Approach. *International Economic Review*, *46*(4), 1167–1205. doi:10.1111/j.1468-2354.2005.00364.x

Henrich, J., Boyd, R., Bowles, S., Camerer, C., Fehr, E., & Gintis, H. (2004). *Foundations of Human Sociality. Economic Experiments and Ethnographic Evidence from Fifteen Small-Scale Societies*. Oxford University Press. doi:10.1093/0199262055.001.0001

Herwartz, H., & Xu, F. (2009). Panel data model comparison for empirical saving-investment relations. *Applied Economics Letters*, *16*(8), 803–807. doi:10.1080/13504850701221949

Herzer, D. (2008). The long-run relationship between outward FDI and domestic output: Evidence from panel data. *Economics Letters*, *100*(1), 146–149. doi:10.1016/j.econlet.2007.12.004

Herzer, D., & Donaubauer, J. (2018). The long-run effect of foreign direct investment on total factor productivity in developing countries: A panel cointegration analysis. *Empirical Economics*, *54*(2), 309–342. doi:10.100700181-016-1206-1

Herzer, D., Hühne, P., & Nunnenkamp, P. (2014). FDI and Income Inequality—Evidence from Latin American Economies. *Review of Development Economics*, *18*(4), 778–793. doi:10.1111/rode.12118

Herzer, D., & Nunnenkamp, P. (2012). The effect of foreign aid on income inequality: Evidence from panel cointegration. *Structural Change and Economic Dynamics*, *23*(3), 245–255. doi:10.1016/j.strueco.2012.04.002

Hiç, Ö. (2019). Evolution of New Keynesian Economics. *Procedia Computer Science, 158*(1), 1025-1032. Doi:10.1016/j.procs.2019.09.144

Hirschman, A. O. (1963). *Journeys toward Progress*. Twentieth Century Fund.

Hirschman, A. O. (1967). *Development projects observed*. The Brookings Institution Press.

Hlouskova, J., & Osbat, C. (2009). *Panel cointegration approaches to estimating equilibrium real exchange rates-separating the wheat from the chaff*. European Central Bank.

Hlouskova, J., & Wagner, M. (2006). The performance of panel unit root and stationarity tests: Results from a large scale simulation study. *Econometric Reviews*, *25*(1), 85–116. doi:10.1080/07474930500545504

Hodgson, G. M. (1988). *Economics and institutions, A manifesto for a modern institutional economics*. Polity Press. doi:10.9783/9781512816952

Hodgson, G. M. (2000). From micro to macro: the concept of emergence and the role of institutions. In *Institutions and the Role of the State* (pp. 103–126). Edward Elgar.

Hodgson, G. M. (2001). *How Economics Forgot History: The Problem of Historical Specificity in Social Science*. Routledge. doi:10.4324/9780203519813

Hodgson, G. M. (2002). Reconstitutive Downward Causation: Social Structure and the Development of Individual Agency. In E. Fullbrook (Ed.), *Intersubjectivity in economics: Agents and structures* (pp. 159–180). Routledge.

Hodgson, G. M. (2006). What Are Institutions? *Journal of Economic Issues*, *40*(1), 1–25. doi:10.1080/00213624.2006.11506879

Hogg, M. A., Terry, D., & White, K. M. (1995). A Tale of Two Theories: A Critical Comparison of Identity Theory with Social Identity Theory. *Social Psychology Quarterly*, ▪▪▪, 58.

Hong, Y. (2009). A dynamic constructivist approach to culture: Moving from describing culture to explaining culture. In *Understanding Culture: Theory, research and application*. Psychology Press.

hooks, b. (1992). Selling Hot Pussy: Representations of Black Female Sexuality in the Cultural Marketplace. In Writing on the Body. Female Embodiment and Feminist Theory. South End Press.

Hossain, M. S., & Mitra, R. (2013). The determinants of economic growth in Africa: A dynamic causality and panel cointegration analysis. *Economic Analysis and Policy*, *43*(2), 217–226. doi:10.1016/S0313-5926(13)50019-1

Ho, T. W. (2002). The Feldstein–Horioka puzzle revisited. *Journal of International Money and Finance*, *21*(4), 555–564. doi:10.1016/S0261-5606(02)00005-0

Houkes, W. (2012). Population thinking and natural selection in dual-inheritance theory. *Biology & Philosophy*, *27*(3), 401–417. doi:10.100710539-012-9307-5 PMID:22523438

Hristoskov, Y. (2010). Ploskiyat danak (mitove i realnosti). *Ikonomicheski alternativi*, (5), 55-56.

Hristov, S. (2013). *Neravenstvoto v Bulgaria - dinamika, sravnitelen analiz i prichini*. Sofia: I.P.I.

Hristov, V. (2014). Danachna politika i danachni tendentsii v ES. *Nauchni trudove*, (14), 22-33.

Hudea, O. S., & Stancu, S. (2012). Foreign direct investments, technology transfer and economic growth. A panel approach. *Romanian Journal of Economic Forecasting*, *15*(2), 85–102.

Hulton, C., & Wykoff, F. (1981). The Measurement of Economic Depreciation. In C. Hulton (Ed.), *Depreciation, Inflation, and the Taxation of Income from Capital*. The Urban Institute Press.

Hunt, T. (2014). Evolutionary thinking. "A conversation with Carter Phipps about the role of evolutionary thinking in modern culture. *Commun Integr Biol.*, *7*(6). doi:10.4161/19420889.2014.993267

Hurlin, C., & Mignon, V. (2007). *Second generation panel unit root tests*. Academic Press.

ICCV. (2020). Pandemia şi standardul de viaţă. Poltici de protecţie social. Institutul de Cercetare a Calităţii Vieţii.

Iliev, K. (2013). Danachno-osiguritelnata tezhest varhu truda i neformalnata zaetost v Bulgaria. In H. Blagoycheva (Ed.), Finansi i ustoychivo razvitie (pp. 62-70). Varna: Nauka i ikonomika.

Im, K. S., Pesaran, M. H., & Shin, Y. (1995). *Testing for unit roots in dynamic heterogeneous panels*. Department of Applied Economics working paper, 9526.

Imbens, G. (2019). *Potential outcome and Directed Acyclic Graph Approaches to Causality: Relevance for empirical practice in economics*. NBER Working Paper 26104.

IMD World Competitiveness Center. (n.d.). *IMD World Competitiveness Rankings 2019*. Available at: https://www.imd.org/wcc/world-competitiveness-center-rankings/world-competitiveness-ranking-2019/

IMF. (2020a). Policy Responses to COVID-19. Policy Tracker. Retrieved from https://www.imf.org/en/Topics/imf-and-covid19/Policy-Responses-to-COVID-19#S

IMF. (2020b). Special Data Dissemination Standard Plus. Retrieved from https://dsbb.imf.org/sdds-plus/dqaf-base/country/BGR/category/INR00

Im, K. S., Pesaran, M. H., & Shin, Y. (2003). Testing for unit roots in heterogeneous panels. *Journal of Econometrics*, *115*(1), 53–74. doi:10.1016/S0304-4076(03)00092-7

Inklaar, R., Timmer, M., & van Ark, B. (2007). Mind the Gap! International Comparisons of Productivity in Services and Goods Production. *German Economic Review*, *8*(2), 281–307. doi:10.1111/j.1468-0475.2007.00408.x

Institute for International Relations. (2012). *Commercial diplomacy of the Republic of Croatia or why Croatia today desperately needs a strong and systematic commercial policy*. Adris Foundation, Programme "Knowledge and discoveries". Available at: http://www.irmo.hr/wp-content/uploads/2013/10/godip-web-en.pdf

IPCC. (2014). *Climate Change 2014: Impacts, Adaptation, and Vulnerability. Contribution of Working Group II to the Fifth Assessment Report of the Intergovernmental Panel on Climate Change*. Cambridge University Press.

Ivanov, S. H., & Webster, C. (2017). *Adoption of robots, artificial intelligence and service automation by travel, tourism*. Paper presented at International Scientific Conference Contemporary tourism – traditions and innovations, Sofia University, Sofia, Bulgaria.

Jack, W., & Lewis, M. (2009). Health investments and economic growth: Macroeconomic evidence and microeconomic foundations. In M. Spence & M. Lewis (Eds.), *Health and Growth*. Commission on Growth and Development.

Jacobson, T., Lyhagen, J., Larsson, R., & Nessén, M. (2002). *Inflation, exchange rates and PPP in a multivariate panel cointegration model* (No. 145). Sveriges Riksbank Working Paper Series.

Jacobson, T., Lyhagen, J., Larsson, R., & Nessén, M. (2007). Inflation, exchange rates and PPP in a multivariate panel cointegration model. *The Econometrics Journal*, *10*, 1–21.

Jäger, P., & Schmidt, T. (2016). The political economy of public investment when population is aging: A panel cointegration analysis. *European Journal of Political Economy*, *43*, 145–158. doi:10.1016/j.ejpoleco.2016.04.004

James, S., & Nobes, C. (2015). *The economics of taxation: Principles, policy, and practice*. Fiscal Publications.

Janssen, M. (2008). Microfoundations. In The New Palgrave Dictionary of Economics (2nd ed.). Academic Press.

Jaunky, V. C. (2013). Democracy and economic growth in Sub-Saharan Africa: A panel data approach. *Empirical Economics*, *45*(2), 987–1008. doi:10.100700181-012-0633-x

Jaynes, E. T. (1957). Information Theory and Statistical Mechanics. *Physical Review*, *106*(4), 620–630. doi:10.1103/PhysRev.106.620

JEC. (2004). *Price Stability and Inflation Targets, a Joint Economic Committee Study*. United States Congress.

Jerzmanowski, M. (2007). Total Factor Productivity Differences: Appropriate Technology vs. Efficiency. *European Economic Review*, *51*(8), 2080–2110. doi:10.1016/j.euroecorev.2006.12.005

Jessop, B. (2002). Liberalism, neoliberalism, and urban governance: A state–theoretical perspective. *Antipode*, *34*(3), 452–472. doi:10.1111/1467-8330.00250

Jevons, W. S. (1875). *Money and the Mechanism of Exchange*. London: Macmillan.

Jimeno, J. F. (2019). Fewer babies and more robots: Economic growth in a new era of demographic and technological changes. *SERIEs*, *10*(2), 93–114. doi:10.100713209-019-0190-z

John Hopkins Coronavirus Resource Center. (2020). Mortality Analyses. Retrieved from https://coronavirus.jhu.edu/data/mortality

Jones, C. I. (2019). Paul Romer: Ideas, Nonrivalry, and Endogenous Growth. *The Scandinavian Journal of Economics*, *121*(3), 859–883. doi:10.1111joe.12370

Jones, R. (1994). *Australian Microeconomic Policies*. Prentice Hall.

Jordà, Ò., Singh, S. R., & Taylor, A. M. (2020). Longer-Run Economic Consequences of Pandemics. Federal Reserve Bank of San Francisco Working Paper, 2020-09. Doi:10.24148/wp2020-09

Jošić, H., & Mlinarić, D. (2018). Determinants of Sovereign Credit Ratings: Evidence from CEE Countries. *EconViews*, *31*(2), 319–335.

Juškaitė, A., Sigitas, Š., & Reichenbachas, T. (2019). *CBDC – in a whirlpool of discussion.* Lietuvos Bankas Occasional Paper No 29/2019.

Kafka, K. I. (2013). *Competitiveness and success index of the economies in the Eurozone* (Master's dissertation). Department of Economics, National and Kapodistrian University of Athens.

Kafka, K. I., Kostis, P. C., & Petrakis, P. E. (2020). Why Coevolution of Culture and Institutions Matters for Economic Development and Growth? In Perspectives on Economic Development - Public Policy, Culture, and Economic Development. Intech Open Publications.

Kaldor, N. (1964). The problem of international liquidity. In Further Essays on Applied Economics. London: Duckworth.

Kalecki, M. (1990). Political Aspects of Full Employment. In M. Kalecki (Ed.), Collected works of Michal Kalecki. Volume 1. Capitalism: Business cycles and full employment (pp. 347–356). Oxford University Press.

Kamarck, M. A. (1976). *The Tropics and Economic Development*. Johns Hopkins University Press.

Kao, C. (1999). Spurious regression and residual-based tests for cointegration in panel data. *Journal of Econometrics*, *90*(1), 1–44. doi:10.1016/S0304-4076(98)00023-2

Kapetanios, G., Pesaran, M. H., & Yamagata, T. (2011). Panels with non-stationary multifactor error structures. *Journal of Econometrics*, *160*(2), 326–348. doi:10.1016/j.jeconom.2010.10.001

Kapp, K. W. (2000). *The social costs of business enterprise*. Spokesman.

Karamouzis, N., & Anastasatos, T. (2019). Lessons from the Greek Crisis. *Economy & Markets, Eurobank Research*, *14*(1). Available at: https://www.eurobank.gr/en/group/economic-research/economic-bulletin/lessons-from-the-greek-crisis

Katagiri, M. (2018). *Equilibrium Yield Curve, the Phillips Curve, and Monetary Policy*. IMF, WP/18/242.

Katsimi, M., & Moutos, Th. (2010). EMU and the Greek Crisis: Are There Lessons to Be Learnt? *European Journal of Political Economy*, *26*(4). https://papers.ssrn.com/sol3/papers.cfm?abstract_id=1981034#%23

Katz, J. E., & Halpern, D. (2014). Attitudes towards robots suitability for various jobs as affected robot appearance. *Behaviour & Information Technology*, *33*(9), 941–953. doi:10.1080/0144929X.2013.783115

Keen, S. (1995). Finance and economic breakdown: Modeling Minsky's financial instability hypothesis. *Journal of Post Keynesian Economics*, *17*(4), 607–635. doi:10.1080/01603477.1995.11490053

Keiffer, C. (1984). Citizen empowerment: A developmental perspective. *Prevention in Human Services*, *3*(16), 9–35. doi:10.1300/J293v03n02_03 PMID:10266759

Keynes, J. M. (1964). *The general theory of employment interest and money*. Macmillan & Co.

Keynes, J. M. (1936). *The General Theory of Employment, Interest and Money*. Macmillan.

Kim, H. (2004). *The Measurement of International Capital Mobility Using Panel Cointegration Estimators*. Academic Press.

Kim, K. (2009). Adam Smith's theory of economic history and economic development. *European Journal of the History of Economic Thought*, *16*(1), 41–64. doi:10.1080/09672560802707407

Kim, K. (2012). Adam Smith's 'History of Astronomy' and view of science. *Cambridge Journal of Economics*, *36*(1), 799–820. doi:10.1093/cje/bes001

Kim, K. H. (2011). The Creativity Crisis: The Decrease in Creative Thinking Scores on the Torrance Tests of Creative Thinking. *Creativity Research Journal*, *23*(4), 285–295. doi:10.1080/10400419.2011.627805

Kim, S. (2019). CO2 Emissions, Foreign Direct Investments, Energy Consumption, and GDP in Developing Countries: A More Comprehensive Study using Panel Vector Error Correction Model. *Korean Economic Review*, *35*, 5–24.

Kirdina-Chandler, S.G. (2018). Meso-economics and economics and complexity economics: actual departure from orthodoxity. *Journal of Institutional Studies, 10*(3), 6-17.

Kirman, A. (2016). Complexity and Economic Policy: A Paradigm Shift or a Change in Perspective? A Review Essay on David Colander and Roland Kupers's Complexity and the Art of Public Policy. *Journal of Economic Literature, 54*(2), 534–572.

Kirman, A., & Teschl, M. (2006). Searching for identity in the capability space. *Journal of Economic Methodology, 13*(3), 299–325. doi:10.1080/13501780600908200

Kizilkaya, O., Ay, A., & Akar, G. (2016). Dynamic relationship among foreign direct investments, human capital, economic freedom and economic growth: Evidence from panel cointegration and panel causality analysis. *Theoretical & Applied Economics, 23*(3).

Kleyner, G.B. (2003). Meso-economic problems of Russian economy. *Economic Bulletin of Rostov State University, 1*(2), 11-18.

Kleyner, G. B. (2011). *Mesoeconomics of development*. Science.

Kleyner, G. B. (2011). *Mesoeconomics of the transition period: markets, industries, enterprises*. Science.

Kluckhohn, C. (1954). Culture and behaviour. In G. Lindzey (Ed.), *Handbook of social psychology* (Vol. 2, pp. 821–876). Addison-Wesley.

Knight, J. (1997). Social institutions and human cognition: Thinking about old questions in new ways. *Journal of Institutional and Theoretical Economics*, *153*(4), 693–699.

Kolesnik, G. V. (2015). *Modeling competition in hierarchical socio-economic systems*. Lenand.

Komlos, J. (2019). Foundations of real-world economics: What every economics student needs to know (2nd ed.). Routledge.

Koslowski, P. (Ed.). (1998). *The social market economy: Theory and ethics of the economic order*. Springer. doi:10.1007/978-3-642-72129-8

Kostis, P. C., & Kafka, K. I. (2020). *Economic Success in Eurozone: The Widening Imbalances During the Crisis.* 4th International Conference of Development and Economy ICODECON, Kalamata, Greece.

Kotsev, T. (2008). Lichno podohodno oblagane. In T. Vladimirova (Ed.), *Publichni finansi* (pp. 181–200). Steno.

Kruglova, M. S. (2017). Mesoeconomic Theory in English-scientific Literature. *Journal of Institutional Research, 9*(3), 25–35.

Kruglova, M. S. (2018). Claude Menard's Meso-Institution Theory and It's Application in the Institutional Design. *Institutional Studies Journal, 10*(3), 49–57. doi:10.17835/2076-6297.2018.10.3.049-057

Kruglova, M. S., Volynsky, A. I., & Kirilyuk, I. L. (2019). *Meso-Level of Economy: Theoretical Approaches and Math Modeling*. *Institutional Studies Journal.*

Krugman, P. (2008, November 14). Depression Economics Returns. *New York Times*. Retrieved from www.nytimes.com/2008/11/14/opinion/14krugman.html

Krugman, P. (2009, Sept. 2). How Did Economists Get It So Wrong? *The New York Times Magazine.*

Krugman, P. (2013). How Did Economists Get It So Wrong? *New York Times.*

Krugman, P. (1979). A Model of Balance of Payments Crisis. *Journal of Money, Credit and Banking, 11*(3), 311–325. doi:10.2307/1991793

Kuhn, S. T. (1977). *The Essential Tension: Selected Studies in Scientific Tradition and Change.* University of Chicago Press. doi:10.7208/chicago/9780226217239.001.0001

Kumar, S., & Russell, R. (2002). Technological Change, Technological Catch-up, and Capital Deepening: Relative Contributions to Growth and Convergence. *The American Economic Review, 92*(3), 527–548. doi:10.1257/00028280260136381

Kwiatkowski, D., Phillips, P. C., Schmidt, P., & Shin, Y. (1992). Testing the null hypothesis of stationarity against the alternative of a unit root. *Journal of Econometrics, 54*(1-3), 159–178. doi:10.1016/0304-4076(92)90104-Y

Kyiotaki, N., & Wright, R. (1989). On Money as Medium of Exchange. *Journal of Political Economy, 97*(4), 927–954. doi:10.1086/261634

Kyurova, A. (2017). Communication as a managerial tool for the processes in organizations. *Entrepreneurship, V*(2), 61–69.

Lakatos, I. (1970). Falsification and the methodology of scientific research programmes. In Criticism and the Growth of Knowledge. Cambridge: Cambridge University Press.

Lamartina, S., & Zaghini, A. (2011). Increasing public expenditure: Wagner's Law in OECD countries. *German Economic Review, 12*(2), 149–164. doi:10.1111/j.1468-0475.2010.00517.x

Lampe, J. R. (2014). *Balkans into Southeastern Europe, 1914-2014. A century of war and transition* (2nd ed.). Palgrave Macmillan., doi:10.1007/978-1-137-05777-8.

Lange, O. (1942). Say's Law: a Restatement and criticism. In Studies in Mathematical Economics and Econometrics. Academic Press.

Larsson, R., Lyhagen, J., & Löthgren, M. (2001). Likelihood-based cointegration tests in heterogeneous panels. *The Econometrics Journal, 4*(1), 109–142. doi:10.1111/1368-423X.00059

Laudan, L. (1984). *Science and Values: The Aims of Science and Their Role in Scientific Debate.* University of California Press.

Lawson, T. (1997). *Economics and reality.* Routledge. doi:10.4324/9780203195390

Lawson, T. (2006). The Nature of Heterodox Economics. *Cambridge Journal of Economics, 30*(4), 483–505. doi:10.1093/cje/bei093

Lawson, T. (2019). *The nature of social reality: Issues in social ontology.* Routledge. doi:10.4324/9780429199035

Lee, C. C., & Chang, C. P. (2009). FDI, financial development, and economic growth: International evidence. *Journal of Applied Econometrics, 12*(2), 249–271.

Lee, C. C., & Lee, J. D. (2009). Income and CO2 emissions: Evidence from panel unit root and cointegration tests. *Energy Policy, 37*(2), 413–423. doi:10.1016/j.enpol.2008.09.053

Lekkos E., (2019). *A critical assessment of the Memoranda era.* Kathimerini. (in Greek)

Lemke, T. (2001). "The birth of bio-politics": Michel Foucault's lecture at the Collège de France on neo-liberal governmentality. *Economy and Society, 30*(2), 190–207. doi:10.1080/03085140120042271

Levin, A., & Lin, C. F. (1993). *Unit root tests in panel data: new results.* University of California at San Diego, Economics Working Paper Series.

Levin, A., Lin, C. F., & Chu, C. S. J. (2002). Unit root tests in panel data: Asymptotic and finite-sample properties. *Journal of Econometrics, 108*(1), 1–24. doi:10.1016/S0304-4076(01)00098-7

Liddle, J. (2009). Regeneration and Economic Development in Greece: De-industrialisation and Uneven Development. *Local Government Studies, 35*(3), 335–354. doi:10.1080/03003930902999472

Lin, S. X., & Kueh, J. (2019). Twin Deficits and Debts in 6 ASEAN Countries: A Panel Approach. *International Journal of Academic Research in Business and Social Sciences, 9*(7), 550–559. doi:10.6007/IJARBSS/v9-i7/6147

Lipsey, R. G., & Lancaster, K. (1956-1957). The General Theory of Second Best. *The Review of Economic Studies, 24*(1), 11–32. doi:10.2307/2296233

Li, Q. (1996). Nonparametric Testing of Closeness between Two Unknown Distribution Functions. *Econometric Reviews, 15*(3), 261–274. doi:10.1080/07474939608800355

Loasby, B. (1991). *Equilibrium and evolution: an exploration of connecting principles in economics.* Manchester University Press.

Loasby, B. (1999). *Knowledge, institutions and evolution in economics.* Routledge.

Loasby, B. J. (2001). Cognition, Imagination and Institutions in Demand Creation. *Journal of Evolutionary Economics, 11*(1), 7–21. doi:10.1007/PL00003857

Luban, D. (2012). Adam Smith on Vanity, Domination, and History. *Modern Intellectual History, 9*(2), 275–302. doi:10.1017/S1479244312000042

Lucas, R. E. Jr. (1995). *Monetary Neutrality.* Prize Lecture, December 7, 1995, Economic Sciences.

Lucas, R. E. Jr. (1973, June). Some International Evidence on Output-Inflation Tradeoffs. *The American Economic Review, 63*, 326–344.

MacDonald, R., & Vieira, F. V. (2010). *A panel data investigation of real exchange rate misalignment and growth,* CESifo Working paper no. 3061.

Maddala, G. S., & Wu, S. (1999). A comparative study of unit root tests with panel data and a new simple test. *Oxford Bulletin of Economics and Statistics, 61*(S1), 631–652. doi:10.1111/1468-0084.0610s1631

Madrick, J. (2014). *Seven Bad Ideas: How Mainstream Economists Have Damaged America and the World.* Vintage.

Maeso-Fernandez, F., Osbat, C., & Schnatz, B. (2006). Towards the estimation of equilibrium exchange rates for transition economies: Methodological issues and a panel cointegration perspective. *Journal of Comparative Economics, 34*(3), 499–517. doi:10.1016/j.jce.2006.05.003

Maevskiy, V. I. (2018). Meso-level and hierarchical structure of the economy. *Journal of Institutional Research, 10*(3), 17–30.

Magnin, E., & Nenovsky, N. (2020). Dependent Monetary Regimes in the Balkans: Enlarging the "Varieties of Capitalism" Hypothesis. International Journal of Public Administration, 1–15. Advance online publication. doi:10.1080/01900692.2020.1742157

Mallorquin, C. (2019). *How economics forgot power.* Universidad Autónoma de Cuidad Juárez.

Mankiw, G. N. (2010). Macroeconomics. New York: Worth Publishers.

Manuel, P., & Carol, W. (1999). The politics of second-generation reform. *Journal of Democracy*, *10*(3), 34–48. doi:10.1353/jod.1999.0052

Manyika, J., Chui, M., Miremadi, M., Bughin, J., George, K., Willmott, P., & Dewhurst, M. (2017). *A future that works: Automation, employment, and productivity*. McKinsey Global Institute. Retrieved from https://www.mckinsey.com/~/media/mckinsey/featured%20insights/Digital%20Disruption/Harnessing%20automation%20for%20a%20future%20that%20works/MGI-A-future-that-works-Executive-summary.ashx

Mark, N. C., & Sul, D. (2001). Nominal exchange rates and monetary fundamentals: Evidence from a small post-Bretton Woods panel. *Journal of International Economics*, *53*(1), 29–52. doi:10.1016/S0022-1996(00)00052-0

Marshall, A. (1886). Answers to Questions on the Subject of Currency and Prices, circulated by the Royal Commission on the Depression of Trade and Industry, Third Report. In J. M. Keynes (Ed.), *Official Papers by Alfred Marshall*. Macmillan.

Martin, W., & Pham, C. S. (2008). *Estimating the Gravity Model When Zero Trade Flows are Frequent*. Working Paper. Available at: https://www.deakin.edu.au/__data/assets/pdf_file/0011/405011/2008_03eco.pdf

Martincus, C., Estevadeordal, A., Gallo, A., & Luna, J. (2010). *Information barriers, export promotion institutions, and the extensive margin of trade*. IDB Working Paper Series, No. IDB-WP-200, Inter-American Development Bank (IDB).

Martins, P. M. (2011). Aid absorption and spending in Africa: A panel cointegration approach. *The Journal of Development Studies*, *47*(12), 1925–1953. doi:10.1080/00220388.2011.579115

Martin, V. (2015). Monetary Policy Analysis in Serbia. *Journal of Central Banking Theory and Practice*, *3*(3), 147–180. doi:10.1515/jcbtp-2015-0016

Marx, K. (1887). Capital. Progress Publishers.

Marx, K. (1951). *Theories of Surplus Value*. Lawrence and Wishart. (Original work published 1863)

Marx, K. (1990). *Capital* (Vol. I). Penguin. (Original work published 1867)

Masters, W. A., & McMillan, M. S. (2001). Climate and Scale in Economic Growth. *Journal of Economic Growth*, *6*(3), 167–186. doi:10.1023/A:1011398431524

Matkovskyy, R. (2012). *A Meso-level Representation of Economic Systems: a Theoretical Approach*. School of Economics, North-West University, MPRA Paper No. 44093.

Maudos, J., Pastor, J., & Serrano, L. (1999). Total Factor Productivity Measurement and Human Capital in OECD Countries. *Economics Letters*, *63*(1), 39–44. doi:10.1016/S0165-1765(98)00252-3

Mavrogordatos, G. (1998). *Between Pitiokampti and Prokrousti: Pressure Groups in Modern Greece* (2nd ed.). Odysseas. (in Greek)

Mavrov, H. (2017). Dohodnoto neravenstvo, choveshki kapital i ikonomicheskia rastezh. In IPS: Sbornik s dokladi ot VIII mezhdunarodna nauchna konferentsia (pp. 269-274). Varna: Nauka i ikonomika.

Mazower, M. (2003). *Der Balkan. Deutsche Erstausgabe* (2nd ed.). Berliner Taschenbuch-Verlag.

McKenzie, L. W. (1959, January). On the Existence of General Equilibrium for a Competitive Market. *Econometrica*, *27*(1), 1–41. doi:10.2307/1907777

Meaning, J., Dyson, B., Barker, J., & Clayton, E. (2018). *Broadening narrow money; monetary policy with a central bank digital currency*. Bank of England Staff Working Paper No 724.

Mehmood, R., & Younas, Z. (2019). Purchasing Power Parity Hold in Major SAARC Countries? Panel Cointegration Analysis. *Quarterly Journal of Econometrics Research, 5*(1), 1–16. doi:10.18488/journal.88.2019.51.1.16

Mehrara, M., & Musai, M. (2013). The causality between capital formation and economic growth in MENA region. *International Letters of Social and Humanistic Sciences, 8*, 1–7. doi:10.18052/www.scipress.com/ILSHS.8.1

Mehrara, M., Pahlavani, M., & Elyasi, Y. (2011). Government revenue and government expenditure nexus in Asian countries: Panel cointegration and causality. *International Journal of Business and Social Science, 2*(7), 199–207.

Menard, C. (2014). Embedding organizational arrangements: Towards a general model. *Journal of Institutional Economics, 10*(4), 567–589. doi:10.1017/S1744137414000228

Menard, C. (2018). Research Frontiers in New Institutional Economics. Revista de Administração. *Management Journal, 53*(1), 8.

Mendick, H., Berge, M., & Danielsson, A. (2017). A Critique of the Stem Pipeline: Young People's Identities in Sweden and Science Education Policy. *British Journal of Educational Studies, 65*(4), 481–497. doi:10.1080/00071005.2017.1300232

Meramveliotakis, G. (2020). The Issue of Efficiency and the Role of State in New Institutional Economics: A Critical Perspective. *New Political Economy.*

MFEA. (2019). *Diplomatic Missions and Consular Offices of Croatia.* Available at: http://www.mvep.hr/en/diplomatic-directory/diplomatic-missions-and-consular-offices-of-croatia/

Mill, J. S. (1888). Principles of Political Economy with Some of their Applications to Social Philosophy (6th ed.). London: Longmans, Green, Reader & Dyer.

Milonakis, D., & Fine, B. (2009). *From Political Economy to Economics: Method, the Social and the Historical in the Evolution of Economic Theory*. Routledge. doi:10.4324/9780203887110

Ministry of Finance of Bulgaria. (2020). *2020-2023 Convergence Programme*. Author.

Minsky, H. P. (1992). *The Financial Instability Hypothesis*. The Jerome Economics Institute of Bard College, Working Paper No. 74.

Minsky, H. (1986). *Stabilizing an Unstable Economy*. Yale University Press.

Minsky, H. P. (1973). The Strategy of Economic Policy and Income Distribution. *The Annals of the American Academy of Political and Social Science, 409*(1), 92–101. doi:10.1177/000271627340900110

Minsky, H. P. (1984). *Can "it" happen again? Essays on instability and finance*. Sharpe.

Minsky, H. P. (1986). *Stabilizing an unstable economy*. Yale University Press.

Mirowki, P. (2013). *Never Let a Serious Crisis Go to Waste: How Neoliberalism Survived the Financial Meltdown*. Dean Baker, Central for Economic and Policy Research.

Mirowski, P., & Plehwe, D. (Eds.). (2009). *The Road from Mont Pelerin: The Making of the Neoliberal Thought Collective*. Harvard University Press. doi:10.4159/9780674054264

Mishkin, F. (2009). Is Monetary Policy Effective during Financial Crises? *The American Economic Review, 99*(2), 573–577. doi:10.1257/aer.99.2.573

Mitra, R., Hossain, M. S., & Hossain, M. I. (2015). Aid and per-capita economic growth in Asia: A panel cointegration tests. *Economic Bulletin, 35*(3), 1693–1699.

Mitrović, R. D., Glavaški, O., & Pucar, E. B. (2019). Fiscal Sustainability in Flow Model: Panel Cointegration Approach for the EU-28. *Ovidius University Annals, Series Economic Sciences, 19*(1).

Mlinarić, D., Perić, T. & Matejaš, J. (2019). Multi-objective programming methodology for solving economic diplomacy resource allocation problem. *Croatian Operational Research Review, 10*(1), 165-174.

Mlinarić, D. (2018). Theoretical Background of Economic Diplomacy. *International Conference Proceedings BSSHE-18*, 22-28.

Modigliani, F. (1944). Liquidity Preference and the Theory of Interest and Money. *Econometrica, 12*(1), 45–88. doi:10.2307/1905567

Moffatt, I. (2000). Ecological footprints and sustainable development. *Ecological Economics, 32*(1) 359-362.

Mohammadi Khyareh, M. (2019). A cointegration analysis of tax evasion, corruption and entrepreneurship in OECD countries. *Economic research-. Ekonomska Istrazivanja, 32*(1), 3627–3646. doi:10.1080/1331677X.2019.1674175

Mondello, G., Sinelnikova, E., & Trunin, P. (2020). *Taking on Board the Long-Term Horizon in Financial and Accounting Literature.* GREDEG Working Paper No 2020-02, Université Côte D'Azur.

Moniz, A. B., & Krings, B.-A. (2016). Robots Working with Humans or Humans Working with Robots? Searching for Social Dimensions in New Human-Robot Interaction in Industry. *Societies (Basel, Switzerland), 6*(3), 1–23. doi:10.3390oc6030023

Moolio, P., & Kong, S. (2016). Foreign aid and economic growth: Panel cointegration analysis for Cambodia, Lao PDR, Myanmar, and Vietnam. *Athens Journal of Business and Economics*, *2*(4), 417–428. doi:10.30958/ajbe.2.4.6

Moons, S. J. V., & de Boer, R. (2014). *Economic diplomacy, product characteristics and the level of development.* ETSG 2014 Conference. Available at: https://www.etsg.org/ETSG2014/Papers/105.pdf

Mucuk, M., & Demirsel, M. T. (2013). The effect of foreign direct investments on unemployment: Evidence from panel data for seven developing countries. *Journal of Business Economics and Finance*, *2*(3), 53–66.

Mudge, S. L. (2008). What is neo-liberalism? *Socio-economic Review*, *6*(4), 703–731. doi:10.1093er/mwn016

Muro, M., & Andes, S. (2015). Robots Seem to Be Improving Productivity, Not Costing Jobs. *Harvard Business Review*. Retrieved from https://hbr.org/2015/06/robots-seem-to-be-improving-productivity-not-costing-jobs

Murthy, N. V. (2007). Feldstein Horioka puzzle in Latin American and Caribbean countries: Evidence from likelihood-based cointegration tests in heterogeneous panels. *International Research Journal of Finance and Economics*, *11*, 112–122.

Murthy, N. V. (2009). The Feldstein–Horioka puzzle in Latin American and Caribbean countries: A panel cointegration analysis. *Journal of Economics and Finance*, *33*(2), 176–188. doi:10.100712197-008-9051-5

Musgrave, R. A. (2008). Merit goods. In The new Palgrave dictionary of economics. Academic Press.

Nachane, D. (2018). *Critique of the New Consensus Macroeconomics and Implications for India*. Springer. doi:10.1007/978-81-322-3920-8

Naim, M. (1995). Latin America: The second stage of reform. In Economic Reform and Democracy. Baltimore, MD: Johns Hopkins University Press.

Nathaniel, S., Anyanwu, O., & Shah, M. (2020). Renewable energy, urbanization, and ecological footprint in the Middle East and North Africa region. *Environmental Science and Pollution Research International*, *27*(13), 1–13. doi:10.100711356-020-08017-7 PMID:32043254

National Bank of Romania. (2020a). NBR Board decisions on monetary policy. Retrieved from https://www.bnr.ro/page.aspx?prid=17617

National Bank of Romania. (2020b). Press release on the decisions of the National Bank of Romania Board. Retrieved from https://www.bnr.ro/page.aspx?prid=17677

National Bank of Romania. (2020c). Press release on the decisions of the National Bank of Romania's Supervisory Committee. Retrieved from https://www.bnr.ro/page.aspx?prid=17656

National Bank of Romania. (2020d). NBR measures in the context of the COVID-19 epidemic. Retrieved from https://www.bnr.ro/NBR-measures-in-the-context-of-the-COVID-19-epidemic--21313.aspx

National Bank of Romania. (2020e). NBR's interest rates – entry into force date values. Retrieved from https://www.bnr.ro/StatisticsReportHTML.aspx?icid=801&table=605&column=2566,4267,4268,3800,3801,3802&startDate=01-01-2014&stopDate=29-04-2020

National Bank of Romania. (2020f). Inflation Reports. Charts' Data Series. Retrieved from https://www.bnr.ro/Inflation-Reports-3343.aspx

National Bank of Serbia (2020c). Decision on temporary measures for preserving financial system stability. RS Official Gazette, 33.

National Bank of Serbia. (2020a). Inflation Report. Retrieved from https://www.nbs.rs/internet/english/90/ioi.html

National Bank of Serbia. (2020b). Monetary Policy Measures. Retrieved from https://www.nbs.rs/internet/english/15/Covid19/Covid19_1.html

National Bank of Serbia. (2020d). Interest Rates of the National Bank of Serbia. Retrieved from https://www.nbs.rs/internet/english/30/30_4/30_4_5/index.html

National Bank of Serbia. (2020e). Additional FX Swap Auction – Support to Financial System Dinar Liquidity. Retrieved from https://www.nbs.rs/internet/english/scripts/showContent.html?id=15331&konverzija=no

National Bank of Serbia. (2020f). Securities Repo Purchase Auctions – NBS Provides to Banks Additional Liquidity Worth RSD 25.2 Billion. Retrieved from https://www.nbs.rs/internet/english/scripts/showContent.html?id=15345&konverzija=no

National Bank of Serbia. (2020g). FX Swaps and Repo Purchase of Securities – NBS Provides Additional Dinar and FX Liquidity to Banks. Retrieved from https://www.nbs.rs/internet/english/scripts/showContent.html?id=15372&konverzija=no

National Bank of Serbia. (2020h). Macroeconomic developments in Serbia. Retrieved from https://www.nbs.rs/internet/english/18/18_3/presentation_invest.pdf

National Bank of Serbia. (2020i). Key policy rate cut to 1,5%. Retrieved from https://www.nbs.rs/internet/english/scripts/showContent.html?id=15392&konverzija=no

National Bank of Serbia. (2020j). Even More Favourable Supply of Liquidity to the Banking Sector – NBS Cuts Dinar Interest Rate in FX Swap Auctions. Retrieved from https://www.nbs.rs/internet/english/scripts/showContent.html?id=15407&konverzija=no

Neelankavil, J. P., Stevans, L. K., & Roman, F. L. Jr. (2012). Correlates of economic growth in developing countries: A panel cointegration approach. *International Review of Applied Economics*, *26*(1), 83–96. doi:10.1080/02692171.2011.557048

Nelson, R.R., & Winter, S.G. (1974). Neoclassical vs. Evolutionary Theories of Economic Growth: Critique and Prospectus. *Economic Journal, 84*(336), 886 –905.

Nelson, R. R., & Winter, S. G. (1982). *An Evolutionary Theory of Economic Change*. Harvard University Press.

Nenovsky, N. (2002). *Improving Monetary Theory in Post-communist Countries- Looking Back to Cantillon*. BNB, Discussion Papers.

Nenovsky, N., & Mihaylova-Borisova, G. (2015). Debts, Ideas and Interests in the Balkans. Chronology of the post-Communist Transformation, 1990-2013. Économie et Institutions, 23(2), 121-145.

Nenovsky, N., Tochkov, K., & Turcu, K. (2013). Monetary regimes, economic stability and EU accession: Comparing Bulgaria and Romania. *Communist and Post-Communist Studies*, *46*(1), 13–23. doi:10.1016/j.postcomstud.2012.12.002

Ng, Y. K. (1982). A Micro-Macroeconomic Analysis Based on a Representative Firm. *Economica, 49*(194), 121–139.

Ng, Y. K. (1986). *Mesoeconomics: A Micro-Macro Analysis*. St. Martin's Press.

Nicoletti, G., & Scarpetta, S. (2005). *Product market reforms and employment in the OECD countries*. OECD Economics Department Working Papers, No. 472.

Niehans, J. (1969). Money in a Static Theory of Optimal Payments Arrangements. *Journal of Money, Credit and Banking*, *1*, 706–726. doi:10.2307/1991447

Nieh, C. C., & Ho, T. W. (2006). Does the expansionary government spending crowd out the private consumption?: Cointegration analysis in panel data. *The Quarterly Review of Economics and Finance*, *46*(1), 133–148. doi:10.1016/j.qref.2004.11.004

Nikolova, D. (2016). Plosak danak varhu dohodite i danachni prihodi. In K. Hadzhinedelcheva (Ed.), *Plosak danak v Bulgaria. Predistoria, vavezhdane, rezultati* (pp. 63–72). I.P.I.

Ninov, D. (2014). Kakav e i kakav tryabva da bade razmerat na minimalnata rabotna zaplata (MRZ) u nas sled vavezhdaneto na ploskia danak i premahvaneto na neoblagaemia minimum. *Sotsiologia i ikonomika*, (1), 43-54.

Nitsch, V. (2007). State Visits and International Trade. *World Economy*, *30*(12), 1797–1816. doi:10.1111/j.1467-9701.2007.01062.x

Nitto, H., Taniyama, D., & Inagaki, H. (2017). *Social Acceptance and Impact of Robots and Artificial Intelligence – Findings of Survey in Japan, the U.S. and Germany*. NRI Papers No. 211, Nomura Research Institute. Retrieved from https://www.nri.com/-/media/Corporate/en/Files/PDF/knowledge/report/cc/papers/2017/np2017211.pdf?la=en&hash=A730998FD55F6D58DF95F3479E3B709FC8EF83F4

North, D. (1981). *Structure and Change in Economic History*. W. W. Norton & Company, Inc.; doi:10.1080/13563467.2020.1721450

North, D. (1990). *Institutions, Institutional Change and Economic Performance*. Cambridge University Press. doi:10.1017/CBO9780511808678

North, D. (1994). Economic Performance Through Time. *The American Economic Review*, *84*(3), 359–368.

North, D. (1995). *The New Institutional Economics and Third World Development*. doi:10.4324/9780203444290.pt1

North, D. (2005). *Understanding the Process of Economic Change*. Princeton University Press. doi:10.1515/9781400829484

North, D., & Thomas, R. (1971). The Rise and Fall of the Manorial System: A Theoretical Model. *The Journal of Economic History*, *31*(4), 777–803. doi:10.1017/S0022050700074623

North, D., & Thomas, R. (1973). *The Rise of the Western World-A New Economic History*. Cambridge University Press. doi:10.1017/CBO9780511819438

OECD. (n.d.). *OECD Database, Household spending*. Available at: https://data.oecd.org/hha/household-spending.htm

Ojo, A. T., & Alege, P. O. (2014). Exchange rate fluctuations and macroeconomic performance in sub-Saharan Africa: A dynamic panel cointegration analysis. *Asian Economic and Financial Review*, *4*(11), 1573.

Okun, A. M. (1975). *Equality and efficiency, the big tradeoff*. The Brookings Institution.

Over 80% of Japanese positive about robotic nursing care. (2018). Retrieved from https://www.japantimes.co.jp/news/2018/11/15/national/80-japanese-positive-robotic-nursing-care/#article_history

Oviedo, A. M., Thomas, M. R., & Ozdemir, K. (2008). *Economic informality: causes, costs, and policies – a literature survey*. The World Bank.

Oyserman, D., & Sorensen, N. (2009). Understanding cultural syndrome effects on what and how we think: A situated cognition model. In Understanding Culture: Theory, research and application. Psychology Press.

Packard, V. (1957). *The hidden persuaders*. McKay.

Papadogiannis, G. (2012). *The rise and fall of Homo Economicus. The myth of the rational man and the chaotic reality*. Papadopoulos Publications.

Pardee, G., & Pardee, H. (2020). Keynesian economics: Can it return if it never died? *Review of Keynesian Economics, Edward Elgar Publishing*, *8*(1), 23–35. doi:10.4337/roke.2020.01.03

Pashev, K. (2006). *Danachna politika i administratsia: Teoria i praktika*. Sofia: Univ. izd. "Sv. Kliment Ohridski".

Patinkin, D. (1947). *On the Consistency of Economic Models: A Theory of Involuntary Unemployment* (Doctoral dissertation). University of Chicago.

Patinkin, D. (1949). Involuntary Unemployment and the Keynesian Supply Function. *Economic Journal (London)*, *59*(235), 361–383. doi:10.2307/2226869

Patinkin, D. (1965). *Money, Interest and Prices* (2nd ed.). Harper and Row.

Peckham, R. (2013). Economies of contagion: Financial crisis and pandemic. *Economy and Society*, *42*(2), 226–248. doi:10.1080/03085147.2012.718626

Pedersen, P., & Smith, N. (2001). *Unemployment traps: Do financial dis-incentives matter?* IZA Discussion Paper No. 274.

Pedroni, P. (2019). Panel Cointegration Techniques and Open Challenges. In Panel Data Econometrics (pp. 251-287). Academic Press. doi:10.1016/B978-0-12-814367-4.00010-1

Pedroni, P. (1999). Critical values for cointegration tests in heterogeneous panels with multiple regressors. *Oxford Bulletin of Economics and Statistics*, *61*(s1, S1), 653–670. doi:10.1111/1468-0084.61.s1.14

Pedroni, P. (2000). Fully modified OLS for heterogeneous cointegrated panels. *Advances in Econometrics*, *15*, 93–130. doi:10.1016/S0731-9053(00)15004-2

Pedroni, P. (2004). Panel cointegration: Asymptotic and finite sample properties of pooled time series tests with an application to the PPP hypothesis. *Econometric Theory*, *20*(3), 597–625. doi:10.1017/S0266466604203073

Pelgrin, F., & Schich, S. (2004). *National saving-investment dynamics and international capital mobility*. Working Paper 2004-14, Bank of Canada.

Perret, S., Brys, B., Alastair, T., & Pierce, O. (2016). *Tax design for Inclusive Economic Growth*. OECD Taxation Working Paper, No. 24.

Perry, G., Arias, O., Fajnzylber, P., Maloney, W., Mason, A., & Saavedra, J. (2007). *Informality: Exit and exclusion*. The World Bank. doi:10.1596/978-0-8213-7092-6

Pesaran, M. H. (2007). A pair-wise approach to testing for output and growth convergence. *Journal of Econometrics*, *138*(1), 312–355. doi:10.1016/j.jeconom.2006.05.024

Petrakis, P. E., & Kafka, K. I. (2018). Sustainable Entrepreneurial Activity Within Complex Economic Systems. In Entrepreneurial Complexity. Taylor & Francis Group.

Petrakis, P. E., Kostis, P.C., Kafka, K.I., & Valsamis, D.G. (2018). General Economic Growth and Development. Ropi Publications.

Petrakis, P. E. (2017). *Economic Development and Growth. General and Integrated Approach*. Quaestor Publications.

Petrakis, P. E., & Kostis, P. C. (2013). Economic Growth and Cultural Change. *Journal of Socio-Economics*, *47*(C), 147–157. doi:10.1016/j.socec.2013.02.011

Petrakis, P. E., & Kostis, P. C. (2014). Medium Term Effects of Culture, Transactions and Institutions on Opportunity Entrepreneurship. *Journal of Innovation and Entrepreneurship*, *3*(1), 11. doi:10.118613731-014-0011-3

Petrakis, P. E., Kostis, P. C., & Valsamis, D. G. (2013). *European Economics and Politics in the Midst of the Crisis, From the Outbreak of the Crisis to the Fragmented European Federation*. Springer.

Pfister, C. (2019). *Central Bank Digital Currency: One, Two or None?* Banque de France Working Paper #72.

Pigou, A. C. (1917). The Value of Money. *The Quarterly Journal of Economics*, *32*(1), 38–65. doi:10.2307/1885078

Pigou, A. C. (1923). The Foreign Exchanges. *The Quarterly Journal of Economics*, *37*(1), 52–74. doi:10.2307/1885909

Pigou, A. C. (1943, December). The Classical Stationary State. *Economic Journal (London)*, *53*(212), 343–351. doi:10.2307/2226394

Piketty, T. (2013). *Le capital au XXIème siècle*. Edition du Seuil, Paris XIV.

Pissarides, C. (1997). The need for labour market flexibility in a European economic and monetary union. *Swedish Economic Policy Review*, *4*, 513–546.

Pitelis, C., & Antonakis, N. (2003). Manufacturing and competitiveness: The case of Greece. *Journal of Economic Studies (Glasgow, Scotland)*, *30*(5), 535–547. doi:10.1108/01443580310492826

Polanyi, K. (1944). *The Great Transformation*. Rinehart & Company, Inc.

Polanyi, K. (1944). *The great transformation*. Rinehart & Company.

Polanyi, K. (1957). The Economy as an Instituted Process. In *Trade and market in the early empires: Economies in history and theory*. Free Press.

Poloz, S. S. (2019). *Technological Progress and Monetary Policy: Managing the Fourth Industrial Revolution*. Bank of Canada Staff Discussion Paper 2019-11.

Ponce, P., & Alvarado, R. (2019). Air pollution, output, FDI, trade openness, and urbanization: Evidence using DOLS and PDOLS cointegration techniques and causality. *Environmental Science and Pollution Research International*, *26*(19), 19843–19858. doi:10.100711356-019-05405-6 PMID:31090009

Popper, K. (1945). *The open society and its enemies* (Vol. 1). Routledge.

Posner, R. A. (2009). *A failure of capitalism: The crisis of '08 and the descent into depression.* Harvard University Press.

Pradhan, R. P. (2009). The FDI-led-growth hypothesis in ASEAN-5 countries: Evidence from cointegrated panel analysis. *International Journal of Business and Management, 4*(12), 153–164. doi:10.5539/ijbm.v4n12p153

Profeta, P. (2003). Political support and tax reforms with an application to Italy. *Public Choice, 131*(1-2), 141–155. doi:10.100711127-006-9110-4

Psacharopoulos, G., & Patrinos, H. (2004). Returns to Investment in Education: A Further Update. *Education Economics, 12*(2), 111–134. doi:10.1080/0964529042000239140

Purica, I. (2015). Evolution of Financial Crises. *Nonlinear Dynamics of Financial Crises.*

Quah, D. (1994). Exploiting cross-section variation for unit root inference in dynamic data. *Economics Letters, 44*(1-2), 9–19. doi:10.1016/0165-1765(93)00302-5

Ramazzotti, P. (2018). Public Goods beyond Markets. *Review of Political Economy, 30*(4), 573-573–594.

Ramazzotti, P. (2020a). Economic Policy, Social Identity and Social Consensus. *American Review of Political Economy, 49*(2).

Ramazzotti, P. (2020b). Economic Policy. Social Identity and Social Consensus. *International Journal of Political Economy, 14*(1).

Ramazzotti, P., Frigato, P., & Elsner, W. (Eds.). (2012). *Social costs today: Institutional analyses of the present crises.* Routledge.

Rauf, A., Liu, X., Amin, W., Ozturk, I., Rehman, O. U., & Sarwar, S. (2018). Energy and ecological sustainability: Challenges and panoramas in belt and road initiative countries. *Sustainability, 10*(8), 2743. doi:10.3390u10082743

Rawls, J. (2005). *A Theory of Justice.* Harvard University Press.

Richter, R. (2005). The New Institutional Economics: Its Start, its Meaning, its Prospects. *European Business Organization Law Review, 6*(2), 161–200. doi:10.1017/S1566752905001618

Rizvi, S. Z. A., & Nishat, M. (2009). The impact of foreign direct investment on employment opportunities: Panel data analysis: Empirical evidence from Pakistan, India and China. *Pakistan Development Review, 48*(4II), 841–851. doi:10.30541/v48i4IIpp.841-851

Rochon, L. P., & Rossi, S. (2006). *Endogenous money: the evolutionary versus revolutionary views.* Centro di studi bancari Villa Negroni-RME LAB Research Laboratory of Monetary Economics.

Rodgers, Y., & Cooley, J. (1999). Outstanding Female Economists in the Analysis and Practice of Development Economics. *World Development, 27*(8), 1397–1411. doi:10.1016/S0305-750X(99)00063-7

Rodrik, D. (2001). *The Global Governance of Trade- As if Development Really Mattered.* http://www.giszpenc.com/globalciv/rodrik1.pdf

Rodrik, D. (2007a). World Too Complex For One-Size-Fits-All Models. *Post-Autistic Economics Review, 44.*

Rodrik, D. (2006). Goodbye Washington consensus, hello Washington confusion? A review of the world bank's economic growth in the 1990s: Learning from a decade of reform. *Journal of Economic Literature, 44*(4), 973–987. doi:10.1257/jel.44.4.973

Rodrik, D. (2007b). *One Economics, Many Recipes.* Princeton University Press. doi:10.1515/9781400829354

Romer, M. P. (1989). *Endogenous Technological Change*. NBER Working Paper #3210.

Romer, M. P. (2016). *The Trouble with Macroeconomics*. Delivered January 5, 2016 as the Commons Memorial Lecture of the Omicron Delta Epsilon Society. https://www.law.yale.edu/system/files/area/.../leo16_romer.pdf

Romer, C. (1989). The Prewar Business Cycle Reconsidered: New Estimates of Gross National Product, 1869-1908. *Journal of Political Economy*, *97*(1), 1–37. doi:10.1086/261592

Röpke, W. (1960). *A humane economy: The social framework of the free market. H.* Regnery.

Rose, A. K. (2007). The Foreign Service and Foreign Trade: Embassies as Export Promotion. *World Economy*, *30*(1), 22–38. doi:10.1111/j.1467-9701.2007.00870.x

Rothschild, K. W. (2009). Neoliberalism, EU and the Evaluation of Policies. *Review of Political Economy*, *21*(2), 213–225. doi:10.1080/09538250902834038

Šabanović, S. (2010). Robots in society, society in robots: Mutual Shaping of Society and Technology as a Framework for Social Robot Design. *International Journal of Social Robotics*, *2*(4), 439–450. doi:10.100712369-010-0066-7

Sachs, J., & Kotlikoff, L. (2012). *Smart Machines and Long-Term Misery*. Working Paper No. 18629, National Bureau of Economic Research.

Sachs, J. (2005). *The End of Poverty: Economic Possibilities for Our Time*. Penguin.

Sachs, J. D., & Warner, A. M. (2001). The Curse of Natural Resources. *European Economic Review*, *45*(4–6), 827–838. doi:10.1016/S0014-2921(01)00125-8

Salinas, M., Alvarez, I., & Delgado, M. (2006). Capital Accumulation and TFP Growth in the EU: A Production Frontier Approach. *Journal of Policy Modeling*, *28*(2), 195–205. doi:10.1016/j.jpolmod.2005.07.008

Samuels, W., & Schmid, A. A. (n.d.). The Concept of Cost in Economics. In The economy as a process of valuation. Edward Elgar.

Samuelson, P. A. (1939). Interaction between the Multiplier Analysis and the Principle of Acceleration. *The Review of Economics and Statistics*, *21*(2), 75–78. doi:10.2307/1927758

Samuelson, P. A. (1954). The pure theory of public expenditure. *The Review of Economics and Statistics*, *36*(4), 387–389. doi:10.2307/1925895

Samuelson, P. A., & Nordhaus, W. D. (1992). *Economics*. McGraw-Hill.

Sánchez, M. (2010). Euro Area Growth Accounting: Comparing Standard and Production-Frontier Approaches. In *Challenges for Economic Policy Design: Lessons from the Financial Crisis*. Lambertz Academic Publishers, INFER Research Perspectives.

Santos Silva, J. M. C., & Tenreyro, S. (2011). Further simulation evidence on the performance of the Poisson pseudo-maximum likelihood estimator. *Economics Letters*, *112*(2), 220–222. doi:10.1016/j.econlet.2011.05.008

Santos Silva, J. M. C., & Tenreyro, S. (2011). The Log of Gravity. *The Review of Economics and Statistics*, *88*(4), 641–658. doi:10.1162/rest.88.4.641

Scarth, W. M. (1988). *Macroeconomics*. Harcourt Brace Jovanovich.

Schofield N. (1996). Introduction: Research Programs in Preferences and Beliefs Aggregation. In *Collective Decision-Making: Social Choice and Political Economy*. Springer Science+Business LLC.

Schumacher, E. F. (1973). Small is beautiful. *Abacus*.

Schumpeter, J. A. (1954). *History of economic analysis*. Oxford University Press.

Schumpeter, J. A. (1954). *History of Economic Analysis*. Routledge.

Schwab, K. (2019). *The Fourth Industrial Revolution*. World Economic Forum. Retrieved from https://www.weforum.org/about/the-fourth-industrial-revolution-by-klaus-schwab

Scitovsky, T. (1941, February). Capital Accumulation, Employment and Price Rigidity. *The Review of Economic Studies*, *8*(2), 69–88. doi:10.2307/2967464

Sedlarski, T. (2016). The 'Keynesian Revolution' in the History of Economic Thought. *Yearbook of St Kliment Ohridski University of Sofia*, *14*(1), 217–234.

Segura-Cayuela, R., & Villarubia, J. M. (2008). *The effect of foreign service on trade volumes and trade partners*. Banco de España Working Paper No. 0808. Available at: https://papers.ssrn.com/sol3/papers.cfm?abstract_id=1126598

Sen, A. (1977, October). On Weights and Measures: Informational Constraints in Social Welfare Analysis. *Econometrics*, *45*(7), 1539–1572. doi:10.2307/1913949

Sen, A. (1985). *Commodities and capabilities*. North-Holland.

Sen, A. (1986). Rationality, Interest, and Identity. In A. Foxley, M. S. McPherson, & G. O'Donnell (Eds.), *Development, Democracy, and the Art of Trespassing: Essays in Honor of Albert O. Hirschman* (pp. 355–373). University of Notre Dame Press.

Sen, A. (1999). The Possibility of Social Choice. *The American Economic Review*, *89*(3), 349–378. doi:10.1257/aer.89.3.349

Sen, A. (2000). *Development as freedom*. Anchor books.

Sheather, S., & Jones, M. (1991). A Reliable Data-Based Bandwidth Selection Method for Kernel Density Estimation. *Journal of the Royal Statistical Society. Series B. Methodological*, *53*(3), 683–690. doi:10.1111/j.2517-6161.1991.tb01857.x

Sheng, A., & Geng, X. (2012). *The new economics: Meso and Meta*. World Economic Forum.

Shiller, R. J. (2000). *Irrational Exuberance*. Princeton University Press.

Sigitas, Š. (2019). *Digital Currencies and Central Banking: A Sense of Déjà Vu*. Bank of Lithuania Occasional Paper No 26/2019.

Simar, L. (2003). Detecting Outliers in Frontier Models: A Simple Approach. *Journal of Productivity Analysis*, *20*(3), 391–424. doi:10.1023/A:1027308001925

Simon, H. (1961). Administrative Behaviour. New York: Macmillan.

Simon, H. A. (2004). From Substantive to Procedural Rationality. In M. Egidi & S. Rizzello (Eds.), Cognitive economics. Volume 1 (pp. 304–323). Elgar Reference Collection.

Simon, H. (1991). Organizations and Markets. *The Journal of Economic Perspectives*, *5*(2), 25–44. doi:10.1257/jep.5.2.25

Simon, H. A. (1947). *Administrative Behavior: A Study of Decision-Making Processes in Administrative Organizations*. Simon and Schuster, Free Press.

Simon, H. A. (1969). *The Sciences of the Artificial*. MIT Press.

Simon, H. A. (1978). Rationality as Process and as Product of Thought. *The American Economic Review*, *68*(2), 1–16.

Sissoko, C. (2019). *The Monetary Foundations of Britain's Early 19th Century Ascendancy*. Economics Working Paper 1906, University of West England, Bristol.

Sitrin, M., & Sembrar, C. (Eds.). (2020). *Pandemic Solidarity*. Pluto Books.

Smith, A. (1976). *An Inquiry into the Nature and Causes of the Wealth of Nations* (R. H. Campbell & A. S. Skinner, Eds.). Clarendon Press. (Original work published 1776)

Smith, A. (1978a). *Lectures on Jurisprudence (A)* (R. L. Meek, D. D. Raphael, & P. G. Stein, Eds.). Oxford University Press. (Original work published 1762-1763)

Smith, A. (1978b). *Lectures on Jurisprudence (B)* (R. L. Meek, D. D. Raphael, & P. G. Stein, Eds.). Oxford University Press. (Original work published 1766)

Smith, A. (1981). *An Inquiry into the Nature and Causes of the Wealth of Nations, Liberty Fund* (R. H. Campbell & A. S. Skinner, Eds.). (Original work published 1776)

Smith, A. (1985). *Lectures on Rhetoric and Belles Lettres* (J. C. Bryce, Ed.). Liberty Fund.

Smolin, L. (2009, Feb.). Time and Symmetry in Models of Economic Markets. Mss.

Smolin, L. (2013). *Time Reborn*. Houghton, Mifflin, Harcourt.

Soldatos, G. (2016). The Laffer Curve, Efficiency, and Tax Policy: A Note. *Review of Economics*, *67*(3), 255–262. doi:10.1515/roe-2016-0006

Solow, R. (1957). Technical change and the aggregate production function. *Review of Economics and Statistics, 39*(3), 312–320. doi:10.2307/1926047

Solow, R. (2010, July 20). *Building a Science of Economics for the Real World*. House Committee on Science and Technology.

Sothan, S. (2016). Foreign direct investment, exports, and long-run economic growth in Asia: Panel cointegration and causality analysis. *International Journal of Economics and Finance*, *8*(1), 26–37. doi:10.5539/ijef.v8n1p26

Spahn, P. (2019). *Keynesian capital theory: Declining interest rates and persisting profits*. Hohenheim Discussion Paper in Business, Economics and Social Sciences No 10-2019.

Spolaore, E., & Wacziarg, R. (2013). How Deep Are the Roots of Economic Development? *Journal of Economic Literature*, *51*(2), 325–369. doi:10.1257/jel.51.2.325

Staykov, K. (2016). Plosak danak i korporativno oblagane. In K. Hadzhinedelcheva (Ed.), *Plosak danak v Bulgaria. Predistoria, vavezhdane, rezultati* (pp. 49–62). I.P.I.

Stewart, F. (1992). Can Adjustment Programmes Incorporate the Interests of Women? In H. Afshar & C. Dennis (Eds.), *Women and Adjustment Policies in the Third World* (pp. 13–45). Women's Studies at York/Macmillan Series. Palgrave Macmillan. doi:10.1007/978-1-349-11961-5_2

Stiglitz, J. E. (1997). *An agenda for development for the twenty-first century*. https://documents.worldbank.org/curated/en/503521538245109923/pdf/An-agenda-for-development-for-the-twenty-first-century.pdf

Stiglitz, J. E. (2014). *Unemployment And Innovation*. Working Paper No. 20670, National Bureau Of Economic Research. Retrieved from https://www.nber.org/papers/w20670

Stiglitz, J. (2012). *The price of inequality: How today's divided society endangers our future*. W.W. Norton & Company.

Stiglitz, J. E. (2013). *The Price of Inequality*. Penguin. doi:10.1111/npqu.11358

Stöbe, R. (2015). Historic Key Events. In *The concise encyclopedia of communication* (pp. 245–246). J. Wiley & Sons.

Stournaras, Y. (2019). *87th International Atlantic Economic Conference "Lessons from the Greek Crisis: Past, present, future*. Speech by the Governor of Bank of Greece. Available at: https://www.bankofgreece.gr/en/news-and-media/press-office/news-list/news?announcement=eb7533db-172f-4a65-a2a7-7d350bcbcb0b

Streit, M., Mummert, U., & Kiwit, D. (1997). Views and comments on cognition, rationality, and institutions. Editorial preface. *Journal of Institutional and Theoretical Economics*, *153*(4), 688–692.

Tabellini, G. (2010). Culture and Institutions: Economic Development in the Regions of Europe. *Journal of the European Economic Association*, *8*(4), 677–716. doi:10.1111/j.1542-4774.2010.tb00537.x

Tajfel, H. (1981). *Human groups and social categories: Studies in social psychology*. Cambridge university press.

Takayama, A. (1990). *Mathematical Economics* (2nd ed.). Cambridge University Press.

Taleb, N. N. (2007). *The Black Swan: the impact of the highly improbable*. Penguin.

Taylor, L. (2019). Central Bankers, Inflation, and the Next Recession. Institute for New Economic Thinking.

Tcherneva, P. R. (2012). *Beyond Full Employment: The Employer of Last Resort as an Institution for Change*. Levy Economics Institute of Bard College Working Paper No. 732.

TE Database. (n.d.). *Greek Public Debt*. Available at: https://tradingeconomics.com/greece/government-debt-to-gdp

The Government of the Republic of Serbia. (2020a). State sets aside €5,1b to mitigate coronavirus economic blow. Retrieved from https://www.srbija.gov.rs/vest/en/152964/state-sets-aside-51b-to-mitigate-coronavirus-economic-blow.php

The Government of the Republic of Serbia. (2020b). Measures for aid to companies as of Monday. Retrieved from https://www.srbija.gov.rs/vest/en/153899/measures-for-aid-to-companies-as-of-monday.php

The Government of the Republic of Serbia. (2020c). Call on businessmen to apply for Economic measures Programme. Retrieved from https://www.srbija.gov.rs/vest/en/154133/call-on-businessmen-to-apply-for-economic-measures-programme.php

The International Federation of Robotics. (2017). *The Impact of Robots on Productivity, Employment and Jobs*. Retrieved from https://ifr.org/img/office/IFR_The_Impact_of_Robots_on_Employment.pdf

The National Bank of Romania Act, Law No. 312/ June 2004.

Thomasberger, C. (2015). Europe at a Crossroads: Failed Ideas, Fictional Facts, and Fatal Consequences. *The Forum for Social Economics*, *44*(2), 179–200. doi:10.1080/07360932.2014.951379

Tinbergen, J. (1962). *Shaping the world economy; suggestions for an international economic policy*. Twentieth Century Fund.

Tinbergen, J. (1967). *Economic policy: Principles and design (4. revised printing)*. North-Holland.

Tobin, J. (1958, February). Liquidity Preference as Behavior towards. *Risk (Concord, NH)*, *25*(2), 65–86.

Trencheva, T., & Zdravkova, E. (2019). Intellectual Property Management In Digitization And Digital Preservation Of Cultural Heritage. *EDULEARN19 Proceedings*. 10.21125/edulearn.2019.1468

Trepte, S., & Loy, L. S. (2017). Social Identity Theory and Self-Categorization Theory. In P. Rössler, C. A. Hoffner, & L. van Zoonen (Eds.), *The International Encyclopedia of Media Effects* (pp. 1–13). John Wiley & Sons, Inc. doi:10.1002/9781118783764.wbieme0088

Triandis, H. C. (2009). Ecological determinants of cultural variation. In Understanding Culture: Theory, research, and application. Psychology Press.

Triandis, H. C. (1996). The psychological measurement of cultural syndromes. *The American Psychologist, 51*(4), 407–415. doi:10.1037/0003-066X.51.4.407

Tsebelis, G. (2015). Lessons from the Greek crisis. *Journal of European Public Policy, 23*(1), 25-41. Available at: https://sites.lsa.umich.edu/tsebelis/wp-content/uploads/sites/246/2015/03/Lessons-from-the-Greek-crisis.pdf

Tsenova, L. (2020, February 20). *Kakvo predstavlyava sistemata na ploskia danak.* IK "Trud i pravo". Retrieved from http://trudipravo.bg/component/content/article?id=117

Tsoulfidis, L., & Tsaliki, P. (2014). Unproductive labour, capital accumulation and profitability crisis in Greek economy. *International Review of Applied Economics, 28*(5), 562–585. doi:10.1080/02692171.2014.918939

Uddin, G. A., Salahuddin, M., Alam, K., & Gow, J. (2017). Ecological footprint and real income: Panel data evidence from the 27 highest emitting countries. *Ecological Indicators, 77*, 166–175. doi:10.1016/j.ecolind.2017.01.003

United Cities and Local Governments. (2015). *Culture In The Sustainable Development Goals: A Guide For Local Action*. Academic Press.

Ussher, L. J. (2009, July). Global Imbalances and the Key Currency Regime: The Case for a Commodity Reserve Currency. *Review of Political Economy, 21*(3), 403–421. doi:10.1080/09538250903073461

Vahabi, M. (2019). *A Review of Péter Mihályi and Iván Szelényi, 2019, Rent-Seeking, Profits, Wages and Inequality, the Top 20%.* Palgrave Macmillan.

van Ark, B., O'Mahony, M. & Ypma, G. (2007). *The EU KLEMS Productivity Report.* Groningen Growth and Development Centre, University of Groningen, and University of Birmingham, Issue No. 1.

van den Bergh Jeroen, C. J. M., & Gowdy, J. M. (2003). The microfoundations of macroeconomics: an evolutionary perspective. Cambridge Journal of Economics, 27(1), 65-84.

Van Veestra, M. E. H., Yakop, M., & Bergeijk, P. A. G. (2010). *Economic diplomacy, the Level of Development and Trade.* Discussion papers in economy. Available at: https://www.clingendael.org/sites/default/files/pdfs/20101000_cdsp_artikel_%20van%20Veenstra,%20Yakop%20and%20van%20Bergeijk.pdf

Vanberg, V. J. (2001). *The constitution of markets: Essays in political economy.* Routledge. doi:10.4324/9780203443415

Varoufakis, Y., & Tserkezis, L. (2014). Financialisation and the Financial and Economic Crises: The Case of Greece. *FESSUD, Studies in Financial Systems*, 1-68.

Varvitsioti, H., & Dendrinou, V. (2019). *The last bluff.* Papadopoulos editions. (in Greek)

Vasilopoulou, S., Halikiopoulou, D., & Exadaktylos, T. (2013). Greece in crisis: Austerity, Populism and the Politics of Blame. *Journal of Common Market Studies, 52*(2), 388–402. doi:10.1111/jcms.12093

Veblen, T. (1899). *The Theory of the Leisure Class: An Economic Study of Institutions, Penguin twentieth-century classics*. Penguin Books.

Veblen, T. (1994). *The theory of the leisure class.* Cofide.

Vienna Institute for International Economic Studies. (2020a). Summary of CESEE key measures regarding COVID-19 as of 16th April, 2020. Retrieved from https://wiiw.ac.at/files/news/summary-of-measures-cesee-16-04-2020-n-439.pdf

Vienna Institute for International Economic Studies. (2020b). wiiw further cuts its forecast for economic growth in Eastern Europe to below 2009 level and sees weaker recovery. Press Release, 6 May 2020. Retrieved from https://wiiw.ac.at/press-release-wiiw-further-cuts-its-forecast-for-economic-growth-in-eastern-europe-wiping-out-at-least-two-years-of-gdp-growth-english-pnd-79.pdf

Visser, R. (2018). The effect of diplomatic representation on trade: A panel data analysis. *World Economy*, *42*(1), 197–225. doi:10.1111/twec.12676

Vitek, F. (2017). *Policy, Risk and Spillover Analysis in the World Economy: A Panel Dynamic Stochastic General Equilibrium Approach*. IMF, WP/17/89.

Vlachos, V., & Bitzenis, Ar. (2015). *Entrepreneurship and Tax Compliance Games: Evidence regarding enterprise behavioral dynamics in Greece* (Vol. 2). Global Business and Economics Anthology.

Vladimirov, V. (2015). Alternativna politika za rastezh na ikonomikata. In IPS: Sbornik s dokladi ot mezhdunarodna nauchna konferentsia (pp. 29-35). Varna: Nauka i ikonomika.

Vladimirov, V. (2011). *Fiskalna politika i makroikonomicheska stabilizatsia*. Steno.

Vlahov, I. (2007). Narachnik za izvarshvane na proverki i revizii na fizicheski litsa. Sofia: NAP.

Vlandas, T. (2013). Mixing apples with oranges? Partisanship and active labour market policies in Europe. *Journal of European Social Policy*, *23*(1), 3–20. doi:10.1177/0958928712463161

Vogel, S. K. (2019). Japan's Ambivalent Pursuit of Shareholder Capitalism. *Politics & Society*, *47*(1), 114–117. doi:10.1177/0032329218825160

Wagner, I. (n.d.). *Global robotics market revenue 2017/2025*. Retrieved from https://www.statista.com/statistics/760190/worldwide-robotics-market-revenue/

Wagner, M., & Hlouskova, J. (2009). The performance of panel cointegration methods: Results from a large scale simulation study. *Econometric Reviews*, *29*(2), 182–223. doi:10.1080/07474930903382182

Walras, L. (1886). Theorie de la monnaie. Academic Press.

Walras, L. (1874). *Elements of Pure Economics* (1926 ed.). Allen & Unwin.

Wang, S. (2015). One size does not fit all: The need for flexibility in policy responses to slow growth. *China Finance and Economic Review*, *3*(1), 5. doi:10.118640589-015-0020-9

Watter, T. (2019). The Janus face of Inflation Targeting: how governing through standardized expectations decouples monetary policy implementation from the future. *Futures past: Economic Forecasting in the 20th and 21st century.*

Watter, T., & Wansleben, L. (2018). How Central Bankers Learned to Love Financialization: The Fed, the Bank, and the Enlisting of Unfettered Markets in the Conduct of Monetary Policy. *Socio- Economic Review.*

Weber, M. (1922). Economy and Society. University of California Press.

Westerlund, J. (2005). A panel CUSUM test of the null of cointegration. *Oxford Bulletin of Economics and Statistics*, *67*(2), 231–262. doi:10.1111/j.1468-0084.2004.00118.x

Westerlund, J., Mahdavi, S., & Firoozi, F. (2011). The tax-spending nexus: Evidence from a panel of US state–local governments. *Economic Modelling*, *28*(3), 885–890. doi:10.1016/j.econmod.2010.10.016

White, L. (2011). Image, Logo, Brand and Nation: Destination Marketing, Nationalism and the 2007 Cricket World Cup. In Sports event management: the Caribbean experience. New directions in tourism analysis. Ashgate.

White, L. H. (2008). *Is the Gold Standard Still the Gold Standard Among Monetary Systems?* Cato Institute Briefing Papers, No 100.

Whitson, D., & Horn, J. (2006). The global politics of sports mega-events. *The Sociological Review*, *54*(2), 73–89. doi:10.1111/j.1467-954X.2006.00654.x

Wicksell, K. (1898). Interest and prices (R. F. Khan, Trans.). London: Macmillan.

Wicksell, K. (1931). *Lectures on Political Economy*. Routledge. (Original work published 1901)

Williamson, J. (1990). What Washington means by policy reform. In Latin American Adjustment: How Much Has Happened? Institute for International Economics.

Williamson, J. (2000). What should the world bank think about the Washington consensus? *The World Bank Research Observer*, *15*(2), 251–264. doi:10.1093/wbro/15.2.251

Williamson, J. (2003). The Washington Consensus and beyond. *Economic and Political Weekly*, *38*(15), 1475–1481.

Williamson, J. (2005). The strange history of the Washington consensus. *Journal of Post Keynesian Economics*, *27*(2), 195–206.

Williamson, O. (1975). *Markets and Hierarchies: Analysis and Antitrust Implications*. Free Press.

Williamson, O. (1985). *The Economic Institutions of Capitalism*. Free Press.

Williamson, O. E. (1985). *The economic institutions of capitalism: Firms, markets, relational contracting*. Collier Macmillan.

Williamson, O. E. (1993). Contested Exchange versus the Governance of Contractual Relations. *The Journal of Economic Perspectives*, *7*(1), 103–108. doi:10.1257/jep.7.1.103

Williamson, O. E. (1998). Transaction Cost Economics: How It Works: Where It Is Headed. *De Economist*, *146*(1), 23–58. doi:10.1023/A:1003263908567

Williamson, O. E. (2000). The New Institutional Economics: Taking Stock, Looking Ahead. *Journal of Economic Literature*, *38*(3), 595–613. doi:10.1257/jel.38.3.595

WITS. (2019a). *Croatia Exports in thousand of US$, 1992-2017*. Available at: https://wits.worldbank.org/CountryProfile/en/Country/HRV/StartYear/1992/EndYear/2017/TradeFlow/Export/Partner/BY-COUNTRY/Indicator/XPRT-TRD-VL

WITS. (2019b). *Croatia Imports in thousand of US$, 1992-2017*. Available at: https://wits.worldbank.org/CountryProfile/en/Country/HRV/StartYear/1992/EndYear/2017/TradeFlow/Import/Partner/BY-COUNTRY/Indicator/MPRT-TRD-VL

Wittfogel, K. A. (1962). Agrarian Problems and the Moscow-Peking Axis. *Association for Slavic, East European, and Eurasian Studies.*, *21*(4), 678–698.

Woodruff, D. M. (2019). To democratize finance, democratize central banking. *Politics & Society*, *47*(4), 539–610. doi:10.1177/0032329219879275

World Bank Group. (n.d.). *Ease of Doing Business Report 2020*. Available at: https://www.doingbusiness.org/en/reports/global-reports/doing-business-2020

World Bank. (2019). *GDP (current US$)*. Available at: https://data.worldbank.org/indicator/ny.gdp.mktp.cd

World Bank. (2020). The World Bank in Serbia. Recent economic developments. Retrieved from https://www.worldbank.org/en/country/serbia/overview#3

World Economic Forum. (n.d.). *The World Competitiveness Report 2019*. Available at: http://www3.weforum.org/docs/WEF_TheGlobalCompetitivenessReport2019.pdf

Wray, L. R. (2018). *Functional Finance: A Comparison of the Evolution of the Positions of Hyman Minsky and Abba Lerner*. Levy Economics Institute of Bard College Working Paper 900.

Wren-Lewis, S. (2012, Aug. 30). Arguments for ending the microfoundations hegemony. *Mainly Macro*.

Wu, H. (2017). One Size Does Not Fit All: The Rise of Tailor-Made Economic Policies, Kennedy. *The School Review*.

Wynne, M.A., & Koech, J. (2012). One-Size-Fits-All Monetary Policy: Europe and the U.S. *Economc Lette*.

Yakop, M., & van Bergeijk, P. A. G. (2011). Economic diplomacy, trade and developing countries. *Cambridge Journal of Regions, Economy and Society*, *4*(2), 253–267. doi:10.1093/cjres/rsr002

Yasser, M., & Toyoaki, N. (2015). Cultural Difference in Back-Imitation's Effect on the Perception of Robot's Imitative Performance. *LNAI, 9549*, 17-32.

Yeager, L. (1986, Fall). The Significance of Monetary Disequilibrium. *The Cato Journal*, *6*(2), 369–420.

Zdravković, A., Đukić, M., & Bradić-Martinović, A. (2017). Impact of FDI on unemployment in transition countries: Panel cointegration approach. *Industrija*, *45*(1), 161–174. doi:10.5937/industrija45-13548

About the Contributors

Pantelis Kostis is Adjunct Lecturer of Economics at National and Kapodistrian University of Athens and the Hellenic Open University, Greece. His research has been published in distinguished international academic journals including Journal of Business Research, Economic Modelling and the Journal of Socio-Economics. He is also the co-author of several books regarding the European and the Greek economy, and economic development and growth.

* * *

Charalampos Arachovas is an economist and the Coordinator of the Institute for Comerce and Services (IN.EM.Y.) of the Hellenic Confederation for Commerce and Entrepreneurship (ESEE). He has taught Microeconomics in Panteion University and International Economics and Development in the Athens Metropolitan College. His research interests include Regional Growth, Labour Economics and Greek economy.

Yana Chankova is an Associate Professor at the Department of Foreign languages at the South-West University "Neofit Rilski" of Blagoevgrad. Her major line of inquiry is based on multilingualism, cultural studies, strategies of intercultural communication and historical linguistics. She is a co-author of the Bulgarian translations of three poems from the The Poetic Edda.

Gancho Ganchev is full professor in South-West University, Bulgaria, Department of Finance and Accounting. He is former Minister of Economic Development and President of the Agency of Economic Co-ordination and Development, as well as Advisor the Prime Minister.

Hrvoje Jošić, Assistant Professor, works at the International Economics Department in the Faculty of Economics and Business in Zagreb. He teaches the International Economics course. His main research interests are theories of international trade and international finance. He is an author of one book and many scientific papers in international journals and conferences. Currently he is involved in studying the effects of COVID-19 infection on global economics.

Kyriaki I. Kafka holds a PhD in Economics from the Department of Economics at the National and Kapodistrian University of Athens, Greece. She is the co-author of two books and has published articles in academic journals such as Journal of Business Research and Journal of Innovation and Knowledge.

Her research interests include economic theory and methodological issues, economic development and growth, economic policy, cultural economics, institutional economics, entrepreneurship, and innovation.

Mikail Kar is a Research Assistant at Bursa Uludag University Faculty of Economics and Administrative Sciences, Department of Economics.

Teodora Kiryakova-Dineva is a researcher with an interdisciplinary profile. Her research interests lie in tourism studies, intercultural studies and all types of intangible assets, including cultural management and theoretical and practical approaches to contemporary phenomena. She is an academic member of the South-West University "Neofit Rilski".

Vyara Kyurova is Vice-Dean at the Faculty of Economics at the South-West University "Neofit Rilski" of Blagoevgrad. Her research interests include statistical approaches to entrepreneurship, marketing, management, and tourism.

Manolis Manioudis is a post-doc researcher and adjunct lecturer at the Department of Economics at the University of Crete where he teaches courses on the History of Economic Thought and Economic History. He is an economic analyst at the Institute of Institute of Commerce and Services (INEMY-ESEE). His research interests include history of economic thought, economic history, Greek economy, political economy and methodology of economics.

Georgi Marinov received his MA in Economics from the University of National and World Economy in Sofia, Bulgaria in 1994. His PhD in Economics he received in 2003, from the Higher Attestation Commission, Sofia, Bulgaria. In 1996 he was hired by the University of Economics - Varna, Bulgaria where he continues to be part of the faculty. Currently he teaches international economics and finance and writes on issues of panel econometrics, sustainable economy and economic integration.

Giorgos Meramveliotakis is a Lecturer in Economic Theory and Policy at the University of Neapolis, Paphos and at the same time, teaches as a visiting professor at the University of Crete. He has, also, taught at the Hellenic Mediterranean University, the University of Liverpool and the University of Roehampton. He has published in high-profile scientific journals (New Political Economy, Journal of Economic Issues, Science and Society, Review of Radical Political Economy, etc.), in collective volumes and has numerous presentations at international conferences. His research interests include the political economy of institutions, Marxist political economy, history of economic thought, and economic methodology.

Danijel Mlinarić is an Assistant Professor at the Faculty of Economics and Business, the University of Zagreb, and the founder and president of the Center for Economic Diplomacy. He teaches both Degree Progam as well as Postgraduate Program. His research focuses broadly on the economic diplomacy, financial and banking markets, and a correlation between economic theory and practice. He is an official juridical expert appointed from the Ministry of Justice Croatia for fields: finance, accounting, banking, financial analysis, and firm valuation. Mlinarić is a leader of a scientific research project for the University of Zagreb "Multi-objective programming methodology for economic diplomacy system" and he has been a visiting professor at the Tecnologico de Monterrey in Mexico. The Ph.D. degree he received from the University of Zagreb in 2015 in the banking field. In 2020 he graduated at Diplomatic Academy from Ministry of Foreign and European Affairs, Croatia.

Nikolay Nenovsky is Professor of monetary and international economics at the University of Picardie, France, and associated researcher at the National Research University Higher School of Economics in Moscow. He has published widely in the areas of Currency Boards and Central banking, especially of post-communist countries. He has broad, practical experience as a researcher and adviser in different financial and political institutions and currently as a member of the Governing Council of the Bulgarian Central Bank.

Bistra Svetlozarova Nikolova received her Ph.D in accounting, control and analysis of economic activity in 2012 at the University of Economics - Varna, Bulgaria. In 2013 she started working as an assistant at the University of Economics - Varna. She is currently a Chief Assistant and has a lecture course "Income Control and Insurance" at the same university. She is an expert in the tax court and a certified mediator. Her research is mainly in the field of financial control and audit. She has research interests related to sustainable development, ethical standards and anti-discrimination measures in higher education.

Paolo Ramazzotti is professor of Economic Policy at the University of Macerata, Italy. He is the managing editor of the Forum for Social Economics. He coordinates the research area on "Institutional Change" of the European Association for Evolutionary Political Economy and is associate editor of the Review of Evolutionary Political Economy.

Cornelia Sahling graduated from the Technical University of Dresden, Germany, and with a PhD in Economics from the Peoples' Friendship University of Russia in Moscow. She is currently working and publishing on monetary policy, financial stability, European integration and Russian Economy.

Cindy Thompson has been in the teaching profession for the past eleven years, seven of which were at the University of Belize. She also worked at two reputable accounting firms in Belize and in the banking sector. Her research interest is in finance and accounting related topics. As part of her job at The University of Belize, she coordinates Accounting and Finance courses and organ-izes lecturer series on business-related topics. Thompson earned an MBA with a concentration in Finance from Galen University and a bachelor's degree in Accounting from the University of Be-lize. She completed seven courses in the DBA Advanced Accounting program at North Central University and is currently pursuing a DBA for business professionals at the University of South Florida.

Josipa Višić has joined Faculty of Economics, Business and Tourism (FEBT), University of Split team in 2006. She is an associate professor and Deputy Head of Department for Economics at FEBT. Besides teaching various courses on undergraduate and graduate level, over the years she has been enrolled in scientific and professional projects related to her fields of interest (microeconomics, corporate restructuring, and economics of robotization process).

Index

H

I

L

M

N

O

P

Q

R

S

T

U

V

W

www.ingramcontent.com/pod-product-compliance
Lightning Source LLC
LaVergne TN
LVHW060415300926
849162LV00006B/1429